CHRISTIAN DOGMATICS.

THEOLOGICAL AND PHILOSOPHICAL

LIBRARY:

A SERIES OF TEXT-BOOKS, ORIGINAL AND TRANSLATED,

FOR

Colleges and Theological Seminaries.

EDITED BY

HENRY B. SMITH, D.D., AND PHILIP SCHAFF, D.D.,

PROFESSORS IN THE UNION THEOLOGICAL SEMINARY, NEW YORK.

VOLS. I. AND II. OF THE THEOLOGICAL DIVISION:

VAN OOSTERZEE'S CHRISTIAN DOGMATICS.

NEW YORK:

SCRIBNER, ARMSTRONG & CO.,

654 BROADWAY.

1874.

CHRISTIAN DOGMATICS:

A TEXT-BOOK

FOR

Academical Instruction and Private Study.

BY

J. J. VAN OOSTERZEE, D.D.,

PROFESSOR OF THEOLOGY IN THE UNIVERSITY OF UTRECHT.

Translated from the Dutch

BY

JOHN WATSON WATSON, B.A.,

VICAR OF NEWBURGH, LANCASHIRE;

AND

MAURICE J. EVANS, B.A.,

STRATFORD-UPON-AVON.

VOLUME I.

NEW YORK:

SCRIBNER, ARMSTRONG & CO.

1874.

Christianus Evangelicus mihi nomen, Reformatus cognomen.

JOHN F. TROW & SON,
PRINTERS AND BOOKBINDERS,
205-213 *East 12th St.*,
NEW YORK.

PREFACE

OF THE GENERAL EDITORS.

FROM the numerous foreign systems of Theology the Editors of the *Philosophical and Theological Library* have selected Professor VAN OOSTERZEE'S *Christian Dogmatics*, recently published in Holland, as being upon the whole the work best adapted to the wants of English and American students. It is a book of marked ability and learning, full of matter skillfully condensed, lucid in arrangement and method, fresh in style, evangelical in sentiment, showing a familiar acquaintance with German, French, and Dutch literature, sufficiently large for a text-book, and nearer, perhaps, to the prevailing type of Anglo-American Theology than any similar work produced of late years on the continent of Europe.

Dr. Van Oosterzee is already favorably known to English readers by his Commentaries on Luke and the Pastoral Epistles in Lange's *Biblework*, and by his *Theology of the New Testament*, which have been translated and published in England and the United States. He is regarded as the first pulpit-orator and divine of the evangelical school in Holland. He was born in Rotterdam, 1807, studied at Utrecht, labored for 18 years as pastor of the principal Reformed Church in Rotterdam, and since 1862 as Professor of Systematic and Practical Theology in the University of Utrecht. Besides several volumes of Sermons, some of which have been translated into German, he wrote in Dutch a large work on the *Life of Christ* (1846–'51, 2d ed. 1863–'65, in 3 vols.), and a *Christology*, or *Manual for Christians*, 1855–'61, in 3 vols. When the chair of Systematic Theology in the Seminary of the Reformed Dutch Church at New Brunswick, N. J. became vacant a few years ago, there was a strong desire to give him a call to this country, but he declined being a candidate, and felt that it was his duty to remain in his native land. In 1873 he was invited as the chief representative from Holland to the General Conference of the Evangelical Alliance in New York, and had fully made up his mind to visit America, but was prevented at the last moment, and sent his contribution, an able essay on *The Gospel History and Modern Criticism*, through his friend, Dr. Cohen Stuart.

The *Christian Dogmatics* is the most important work of this distinguished scholar. It gives the mature results of long-continued, earnest, and devout study of the articles of our Christian faith. It will, we trust, prove a safe and useful guide to students in our institutions of sacred learning.

HENRY B. SMITH AND PHILIP SCHAFF.

NEW YORK, July 6, 1874.

PREFACE TO THE FIRST PART OF THE ORIGINAL WORK.

IN accordance with the promise, perhaps somewhat rashly made, on the publication of my *Theology of the New Testament*, I now send forth a similar Handbook for the study of *Christian Dogmatics.*

That I do so not without hesitation I need hardly say; I feel I am like the sailor who is rowing against wind and current. The science which I seek in this way to advance has, in the opinion of many, no longer any right to exist, and becomes, in the hands of others, but too easily a dangerous weapon, especially against its own priests. Yet I deemed I ought not to be restrained by considerations in great part of a personal character. I look upon the publication of this work to some extent as a duty, the discharge of which I owe first of all to my Academical hearers, perhaps also to myself. In addition to this, I cannot dispute the right of those who desire to know what doctrine is taught at this critical period of transition for Church and Theology in the University of Utrecht; and willingly furnish, in this way, amongst others, testimony concerning principles of faith and life, which are dear to my heart, and are, in my opinion, however bitterly opposed and contradicted, as yet by no means refuted. I must, however, emphatically request that the great difference—especially in our day in Holland—between that which is to be required and looked for in a perfectly elaborate treatise on Christian Dogmatics, and that which is to be reasonably expected in an Academical *Manual* of this science, be not overlooked. The aim of the latter must especially be to serve as a textbook for further instruction and private study. It presents itself not in the character of a Lawgiver, but of a Guide; and the Author may at once congratulate himself, if his work has called forth a love for the science, and guided the study of it in the right direction.

As regards this Handbook itself, I have but little to say. It represents, I may hope, clearly enough the *Evangelic-churchly* standpoint, from which I seek with a free and good conscience to serve science and the Church of our Lord. The arrangement is exactly similar to that of the previous *Compendium;* because this appears to me, on the ground of my own experience, most conducive to the end in view. In this case also, in the citation of the Literature, I have attached less importance to absolute neutrality and completeness than to diversity and suitability; and I have endeavoured to place those who avail themselves of my guidance in a position to arrive at the present height of the question at issue. Ordinarily I have preferred to deal with the subject thetically and apologetically rather than polemically, and have sought not to lose sight of the claims of impartiality and courtesy towards those who think differently from me. Especially have I aimed at clearness and a strict and well-ordered presentation; since I have always been of opinion that a genuinely scientific work without clearness and regular coherence, is altogether inconceivable. For the copious use of foreign words and technical terms I have to apologise; they were nevertheless not always avoidable; many of them have been naturalised within the most recent times, and a *Manual* does not as a rule present a model of style or eloquence. If I have been at times rather lavish in the citation of the words of others, for the elucidation or confirmation of my own ideas, this was because my confidence in the expression of these ideas was not a little enhanced by the consciousness of standing in select society, and especially because I desired thus to direct my readers to honoured contemporaries or predecessors of kindred spirit, to whom I willingly confess my no small obligation.

Glancing at the little which in our land, at least, has been done within the last few years for Christian Dogmatics as a whole, and the many hindrances to its study presenting themselves on so many sides, the Author would perhaps at another time expect some appreciation, if not of the result, at least of the courage of his attempt. Now, however, he will thankfully content himself if his book is received not altogether unfavourably, and especially if by his labour something better is soon called forth. For it is his most cherished conviction, that the Church and science, in the midst of unparalleled confusion of tongue and loosing of ties in the moral-religious domain, will be the gainers, not by superficial neglect and slighting, but only by continued development and extension of Christian study, and particularly that of Christian doctrine. If my Handbook may serve in some measure to recover Dogmatics from the bath of slime and mud which has been so plenteously administered to it in our country within the past few years, and help to preserve it on the other hand from the bath of vapour and mist which seems designed for it on other sides, I shall not complain of the labour bestowed upon this work. And if it is afterwards granted me to serve my cherished *Practical Theology* in like manner, I hope to have completed my task in this domain, and, so far as my circumstances have permitted it, to have fulfilled to the best of my ability the promise of my devotion to Theological Science, made in silence some thirty years ago, when the degree of Doctor was conferred upon me.

UTRECHT, *March* 31, 1870.

PREFACE TO THE SECOND PART OF THE ORIGINAL WORK.

To that which I gave by way of Preface to the First Part, two years ago, I have now but little to add. Those for whose use this work was especially designed, know to what end, and in what spirit, it is now offered to them. As regards others who may also make use of it, I can only wish that they will here look for nothing else than what the title promises: *A Textbook for Academic Instruction and Private Study*. Such a Textbook *cannot*, it will be felt, supply all that might be reasonably expected in an elaborate Treatise on Christian Doctrine. It must rather serve as a guiding-line for further continued instruction; and far from rendering other aids entirely superfluous, must rather lead to their being consulted with augmented interest. The somewhat ample, although far from complete, *Literature* at the close of each Section, will afford abundant occasion for doing so; while the *Points for Inquiry* at the end do not as a rule call attention to matters already presented with sufficient prominence, but precisely to those particulars which by further treatment must be yet more fully elucidated. He who might too hastily suppose that, after the study of the text, he has now attained to the full height of Christian Dogmatics, may by a glance at these *Points for Inquiry* receive a preliminary lesson in modesty. For myself they might perhaps hereafter afford abundant material for a greatly enlarged edition, provided the necessity for this were to arise, the Author were ten years younger, and the book had not already grown to a sufficient size. As regards this last, I should myself have wished it otherwise, but the material as I went on gained upon me, and now that at any rate it *has* become so, I cannot do better than wholly adopt the words of Augustine at the close of his Treatise *De Doctrinâ Christianâ:* "Longior evasit liber, quam volebam, quamque putaveram. Sed legenti vel audienti, cui gratus est, longus non erit; cui autem longus est, per partes eum legat; quem vero cognitionis ejus piget, de longitudine non queratur."

Above all I lay stress upon the fact that this work must be regarded and accepted as a Manual for *Christian* Dogmatics, in the old and well-known, but also broad and kindly sense of the word. No other Dogmatics can I admit to be Christian, than that which sees in Christ the King of Truth; in the Gospel, the fruit of a Divine Revelation of Salvation; and in the Word of the Lord and His Apostles, rightly comprehended and maintained, the trustworthy standard of the Church's confession. I can thus—with all fairness in the estimate of the persons and talents of those who espouse and maintain other principles—speak of no other mode of view as Christian, than that which recognises the supra-natural character of the Doctrine of Salvation, and has inscribed upon its banners the maxim: "per fidem ad intellectum." "Le Christianisme"—I endorse without reserve the words of an eloquent Swiss Preacher of the present day*—"le Christianisme, moins l'élément surnaturel, c'est le Christianisme moins la Bible, qui n'est plus que la simple parole d'un homme; c'est le Christianisme moins Jésus Christ, qui n'est plus un Sauveur, même un Révélateur, mais simplement un sage; c'est le Christianisme moins le Dieu personnel, qui disparait dans le Fatalisme des lois de la nature; c'est le Christianisme moins tout l'extraordinare et toute l'originalité de sa morale; moins le péché, qui n'est plus qu'une imperfection naturelle et comme qui dirait la naïve et débile enfance du bien; moins la conversion, qui devient un nonsens; moins la prière, qui ne comporte plus de réponse; c'est le Christianisme ramené à la religion naturelle enfin, et la religion naturelle ramenée à sa moins religieuse formule: crois à ta raison, et fais ce qui te semble bien." In truth, such a Christianity, in which none of the Apostles, the Reformers, the Martyrs of an earlier age, would recognise his own, can hardly, even upon scientific grounds, continue to bear this name, and, unless we are entirely mistaken,

---

* F. COULIN, in the *Semaine Religieuse de Genève* of 1870.

it will within a few years be spoken of as amongst the most remarkable hallucinations of the present day, that, while advocating such a series of denials, any should still think of retaining, with any legitimate claim, the title of Christians, yea, of Ministers of the Gospel in any Christian Church. What remains in the long run of that which is Christian, where almost all that is essentially Christian is relegated to the cabinet of antiquities? To protest with all earnestness against *such* a Christianity is a duty also for the servant of the science of faith, a duty prescribed not only by honour and good faith, but also by the desire of self-preservation. If Modernism is right, not only Christian Dogmatics, but also the whole of Theological Science, loses, with the Christian Church, its right of independent existence.

But if, for these reasons, I wished to give nothing less than truly *Christian* Dogmatics, I also wished to give nothing more; Christian, not so much *Churchly* Dogmatics, at least not in the sense which is ordinarily attached to this term. Wherefore? Because I perhaps overlook the importance and the value of the last mentioned, or possibly because in the region of Dogmatics I affect a Christianity raised above diversities of belief? The Handbook itself is there to prove the opposite; it is written not merely from a universally Christian, but from a definitely Churchly point of view, and the writer rejoices that, in connection with the convictions as to the faith here expressed, he can with a good conscience remain in the fellowship of that Church, which he has in his heart never ceased to serve. But he would be afraid of not serving it in accordance with the demands and needs of the present time, if he had in his outlines of the Doctrine of Salvation conceded too large a place to the Churchly, at the expense of the Christian, element. Rather than a strictly denominational, my Dogmatics seeks to bear a strongly apologetic character; and I believe it must bear this, if it is in any measure to correspond to the most pressing wants of those for whom it was first intended. The great opposition, however, which dominates everything else, is not now that between Reformed and non-Reformed; not even that between Evangelical Protestant and Roman Catholic; but that between the Christian belief in Revelation of past ages and the Naturalism of the present day. I can on this account explain it only from the short-sightedness of incurable sectarianism, that so many in our time aim at being in a high degree Churchly and strictly orthodox, without having first scientifically acquired for themselves the right before all things still to be called Christian, in the positive, historic sense of the word. The effort, connected therewith, to raise the confessional (denominational) walls of separation as high as possible, I must for my part regard as a melancholy Anachronism, which can by no means prove a blessing to the Church, and is moreover a source of great injury to our fiercely assailed Christianity. The first question, at least for him who looks more deeply and beyond the moment, is in truth not whether the gold of your highly-lauded orthodoxy is defective to the extent of a few carats or more; but whether (in presence of a denial and assailing, which is indeed without example in history) one can still with a good conscience remain a Christian, Protestant Christian, Reformed Christian, by all means; but above all an Evangelical-Catholic Christian, who still need not hesitate to repeat Paul's glorying in the faith, to make his own the confession of Thomas, and to follow the eagle-flight of John. He who overlooks that, and at the same time, in the treatment of the doctrine of Salvation, is much more zealous for a Church system than for the defence of Christianity, may possibly serve a sect which spasmodically clings to the past, but certainly not the cause of the Lord, who is manifestly engaged in the midst of all the agitations of this age, in giving to His flock in all communities, in place of the old, something new. If there is one cause to which at the present time all are called, who are really concerned for nothing else than the triumph of the Kingdom of God, it is the advancing, in the domain of Dogmatics also, of a true, hearty, genuine *Evangelical Alliance* of all who in reality build upon the same foundation, as against an enemy whose whole aim is against not merely a particular Church life, but against the Christian life, the Religious life, the whole Spiritual life of ourselves and our children. A temperate maintenance of our own peculiar Church-life is in perfect harmony with this endeavour; but not the unhesitating swearing by what is old, because it has now obtained the sanction of time, and just as little the real suspecting of the new, because one has hitherto been wont to teach and understand something different. If my Dogmatics may contribute, in its modest degree, to serve the sacred cause of such a *Union* of all truly believing Evangelical Christians, I shall esteem it an exceeding great cause of thanksgiving, even though I must in return endure the suspicion or reproach of some, who have no trifling conception of the conflict of principles in the province of this science, and in whose estimate I am naturally not quite "sound." Just as much do I desire to be an Apologete of Christian *liberty*, as of Christian *truth*, but most of all of Christian *love*.

Should my work, at any rate, be made the means of refreshing or strengthening to others, and bear in itself a seed for eternity, to the Lord of the vineyard, who is also Lord of the harvest, alone be the praise and the glory!

J. J. v. O.

UTRECHT, *June* 30, 1872.

PREFACE TO THE ENGLISH TRANSLATION.

I CANNOT let the English translation of my Christian Dogmatics appear without, in accordance with the desire of the Translators and Publishers, prefacing it with some words by way of Introduction.

These words may, however, be few, since I need not repeat what I have already stated concerning the character and intention of the work, in the Preface to the original publication. First of all, then, a word of thanks for the very favourable manner in which several of my theological writings, and specially my *Theology of the New Testament*, translated in England by the skilful hand of the Rev. M. J. Evans, in America by that of Professor G. E. Day, have been received and reviewed both in England and America. Feeling deeply as I do the imperfection of my work, I have found in this a great cause of thankfulness to God, as well as a powerful encouragement to further labour.

The task, which my friends the Rev. M. J. Evans and Rev. J. W. Watson voluntarily undertook in translating my Christian Dogmatics, was by no means an easy one. As far as I am able to judge, they have accomplished their task not only with zeal and love, but also with conscientious skill. If their labour has succeeded, a portion of their thanks and mine is due to the energy and care of the unwearied Secretary of the Netherlands branch of the Evangelical Alliance, the Rev. M. Cohen Stuart, (now D.D. of Rutgers College N. J.,) Emeritus Predikant at Rotterdam, who has carefully compared the translation with the original work, and thus has done his best to further the scientific alliance of his and my fatherland with the lands beyond the Atlantic.

For all the defects which, notwithstanding, may be found in

our common work, I ask in my own name, and in that of my fellow-labourers, the kind indulgence of my readers.

With the prayer that this, my Theology of the Kingdom, may contribute something towards the coming and flourishing of that Kingdom, which must yet embrace all the nations of the earth, I take this opportunity of offering my Christian brotherly greeting to all my companions, both in faith and conflict, far and near, on this and the other side of the ocean, among whom are so many towards whom my heart beats with love and admiration. May He, who is the Truth, lead us by each prayerful investigation more into His truth, and sanctify us through that truth; and may He bring us together one day where we shall no more prophesy in part, but shall know, even as also we are known, in and through Him who has loved us. (1 Cor. xiii. 12.)

J. J. v. O.

UTRECHT, *December*, 1873.

CONTENTS OF VOLUME FIRST.

PART I.

PART II.

PAGE

FIRST DIVISION.

THE NATURE OF GOD.

SECOND DIVISION.

THE WORKS OF GOD.

CHAPTER II.

FIRST DIVISION.

MAN'S ORIGINAL NATURE.

INTRODUCTION.

CHAPTER I.

CHARACTER OF CHRISTIAN DOGMATICS.

SECTION I.—IDEA.

CHRISTIAN Dogmatics is that part of theological science which occupies itself with the investigation and systematic development of the contents and ground of the religious truth which is believed and confessed by the Christian Church as a whole, or by one of its sections in particular. It must thus, as an historical-philosophical science, be distinguished from the Biblical Theology of the Old and New Testaments, as well as from the so-called speculative philosophy.

1. Christian Dogmatics treats of dogma as such, and thus has, at the outset, to define the idea contained in this word. In doing this, we must carefully distinguish between the classical, biblical, and ecclesiastical use of the word. This latter use, too, is variable, but yet dogma always denotes something more than a merely individual and temporary opinion. The ecclesiastical dogma is the expression, formulated as accurately as possible, of the avowed *belief*, not merely of the individual, but of the community. We might also call it the ripened fruit of Christian experience, in so far as the doctrine is the product of the inner life, and the theory is preceded by practice. We must not, however, forget that other factors contribute to the formation and determination of dogma, and that every dogma, as the human expression of divine truth, is always susceptible of reformation and development.

2. Christian Dogmatics (*Dogmatica sc. scientia*) makes the subject-matter and origin of dogma the object of special investigation. It was formerly

called *Theologia positiva*, *systematica*, *thetica*, and even *theoretica*. The last appellation, derived from Doederlein, († 1792,) was accepted in Holland by Muntinghe and others. The name of *Theologia dogmatica* has been in use since the time of Buddeus († 1729), and has now and then been replaced by the names of *Theologia didactica*, *didascalica*, and *scientifica*, in contrast with *popularis*. In the present century, more than in previous times, distinction has been made—though, in our opinion, without sufficient reason—between Doctrine of Faith and Dogmatics (Schleiermacher, Rothe, Schweitzer). In this work both names will be used indiscriminately.

3. The object of Dogmatics is the moral religious truth (ἀλήθεια) confessed by the Christian Church as a whole, or by any Christian community in particular. It will thus exhibit either a general Christian or a special ecclesiastical character. In both cases it investigates what is to be held as truth within its sphere, and the reasons for this avowal. Not content with an atomic examination, it seeks to know and present truth in its entirety, *i.e.*, in the mutual coherence of all its parts. Its design is not merely to collect and arrange the various stones, but to combine them into one architectural whole.

4. There is no necessary opposition between Christian and Ecclesiastical Dogmatics. The general Christian dissolves into the individual ecclesiastical, as light into different colours. On the contrary, the latter must proceed from, and return to, the former, else it becomes confined and sectarian. The manner in which we must treat of Christian Dogmatics is of itself determined by the particular relation in which the student stands to the confession of faith of his own Church; while a sincere attachment to his Church leaves, at least in the realm of Protestantism, room for independent representation and development of doctrine.

5. Christian Dogmatics and Biblical Theology, though so closely allied, are yet definitely distinguished the one from the other. The latter supplies the materials which the former is to employ. The Biblical Theology of the Old and New Testaments asks, in a purely historical manner, What does Holy Scripture teach? Christian Dogmatics, on the contrary, investigates philosophically the question, What must I hold as truth? The former presents objectively what Holy Scripture tells with regard to the highest life-questions; whilst the latter develops the subject-matter of the confession as it has become subjectively truth and life. It is "a living reproduction or belief from the soul of the believer" (Twesten).—Dogmatics, again, is distinguished from speculative philosophy in this, that while the latter takes the pure human consciousness as its starting-point; Dogmatics, on the contrary, must above all take account with an historical fact, with the belief of the community in a Divine revelation. It makes the subject and ground of this belief the material for its investigation, in order to purify the idea, to develop it, and, where necessary, to defend it. It is "une philosophie, dont la base est donnée" (Vinet), and thus as a science sustains a twofold character. It proceeds from that which is given, not in order to leave it as it is given; it reasons and philosophizes, but not in the abstract. Its material is an historic product, but it must treat this in a Christian philosophical (really critical) method.

Compare, besides the well-known handbooks and encyclopædias of Theology, the article *Dogmatik*, by J. MÜLLER, in *Herzog's Real. Enc.* iii., and the books quoted in it; F. LICHTENBERGER, *Des Eléments Constitutifs de la Science Dogmatique* (1860); R. ROTHE, *Zur Dogmatik* (1863), pp. 2—55; and OOSTERZEE, *Theology of New Test.* Eng. trans., 2 ed. 1873, p. 4.

POINTS FOR INQUIRY.

Gradual change in the meaning of the word dogma.—Different import and value of this idea from the Romanist and Protestant standpoint.—Further elucidation of the idea of Dogmatics.—Is there sufficient reason for distinguishing between Dogmatics and Doctrine of Faith?—Can Dogmatics be both Christian and ecclesiastical?—The relation of Dogmatics and Symbolism.—Is it right to define Dogmatics as the description of the life of the Christian community?—Criticism of some other definitions of the idea.

SECTION II.—ITS POSSIBILITY.

The possibility of carrying on with satisfactory results such an investigation as Christian Dogmatics purposes, though it has often been disputed, is placed beyond all reasonable doubt. It has its ground, objectively, in the fact that a spiritual world exists, and in its domain an eternal truth; subjectively, in the disposition and ability of man to rise from the visible to the invisible, and to recognise and accept as such that which within him manifests itself to him as divine. From a Christian, and especially from a Reformed Christian standpoint, this possibility has throughout all time been either presupposed or directly stated, with the highest right.

1. The investigation to which Dogmatics devotes itself would never have required to be set on foot, if there were *no* spiritual world whatever, or if at least there were no possibility of rising to its domain. This indeed has been, and is still, actually asserted in various ways; and on this ground Theology, as the "science of nescience," has been rejected by the systematic supporters of Materialism, Scepticism, Empiricism, Positivism, etc. The whole history of religion and philosophy may be called a constant struggle between Pyrrhonism on the one hand, and Dogmatism on the other. It is, then, the continuing duty of Dogmatics to maintain against all these attacks its right to existence and to action.

2. A thorough defence of that right would require an express criticism of the above-named tendencies of thought, accompanied by the presentation of an elaborate theory of the human capacity for knowledge. These subjects, however, do not come within the scope of the prolegomena of Dogmatics. The one is the vocation of the Christian dogmatist; the other, of the teacher of Metaphysics and Psychology. The first, keeping strictly within the limits of his science, must rest content with a short defence of

his principles, of which his further investigation is alike the natural result and the best justification.

3. The folly of all dogmatical investigation would be unquestioned, if those who are in principle opposed to it succeeded in maintaining their own standpoint against the opposition which has been encountered by them in every age. Hitherto, however, they have had so little success, that, on the contrary, the greatest difficulties have shown themselves, not on the dogmatical, but on the anti-dogmatical side. Materialism, indeed, can explain neither the origin of organic life as a whole, nor the unity and continuity of the human self-consciousness, nor the moral power of conscience. Scepticism destroys itself in principle as soon as it formulates and proves; indeed, the absolute certainty of uncertainty is a purely dogmatic expression. "Le Scepticisme, quand il commence à raisonner, se mord dans la queue" (Vinet). If the empirical philosophy from its standpoint only knows that which comes within the reach of experience, yet until now the proof has never been given us that in the domain of the spiritual sciences the same method exclusively and unconditionally applies as in the domain of natural science. If the supra-sensuous lies beyond the reach of our experience, it does not yet, for this reason, lie beyond the limits of our knowledge. Positivism, lastly, notwithstanding the arrogance with which it puts forth its claims, is psychologically so superficial, and has taken so little notice of the deepest aspirations of humanity, that it is oppressed with no less difficulties than Materialism itself, in which it inevitably ends.

4. In opposition to these morbid phenomena in the domain of thought, Dogmatics proceeds with a good conscience, from the supposition of the reality of a world higher than this visible one. True, the existence of metaphysical thought cannot be demonstrated by like evidence, as a mathematical proposition. "Geometrica pingi atque oculis subjici possunt; hæc autem, de quibus hîc dicimus non ita, sed attentâ consideratione paulatim magis intelliguntur" (Melancthon). And yet closer consideration shows this is sufficient, partly from the original and indestructible consciousness of mankind (*testimonum animi*); partly from nature, whose mysteries and questions find their satisfactory solution only in a realm higher than her own; partly, in fine, from history and experience, which always point further than to merely natural results of final causes. He who here speaks of hypothesis must at least allow that without it an infinity of questions would remain unexplained, whilst, on the other hand, by its help the greatest enigma is solved to a remarkable degree. He, on the other hand, who regards the entire idea of God, and everything connected with this idea, as a fantastical illusion, and considers the proper secret of Theology to lie in Anthropology (Feuerbach), declares, in other words, all mankind to be mad, and arbitrarily puts aside all the other questions, which he is rendered utterly unable to answer.

5. God and truth are one. Can truth in this sphere, though not completely, yet in some degree, be known? Certainly not, if man is destitute of all power of rising from the visible to the invisible. We cannot, however, possibly in seriousness dispute this power in a rational and moral being. "War nicht das Auge sonnenhaft, wie könnten wir das Licht

erblicken? Lebt' nicht in uns des Gottes eig'ne Kraft, wie könnt'uns Göttliches entzücken?" (Göthe). The divine cannot be entirely comprehended, but, notwithstanding, it can be apprehended; it cannot be completely known, but yet can be spiritually seen; it cannot be perfectly attained, but yet it can be approached, in consequence of the law of affinity, which makes *like seek like.* The ceaseless feeling of man after God[1] may lead to an endless failing, but yet it testifies to a compulsion of nature, which is one with its inner being. Mind, intellect, and conscience cannot rest so long as they find no rest in God. Independent of all reasoning and observation, man seeks his God as the sunflower the sun, the hart the waterbrooks, and the infant its mother's breast. The organ by which man satisfies as much as possible this impulse of nature is reason, as distinguished from intellect, the faculty of ideas, not separate from, but most closely united with, the heart and conscience. A denial of this faculty must inevitably lead in philosophy to nominalism and scepticism; in theology, to a blind belief in authority. If man is utterly unable to rise to the invisible, he must mechanically bow to that which from without is enforced on him as revelation, unless he has an inner criterion, by means of which he can properly distinguish truth and falsehood in this domain.

6. It is evident that this recognition of the existence and relative right of a natural knowledge of God, hereafter to be more closely defined and proved, is really biblical and Christian; for not only do Israel's sacred singers and seers,[2] but Jesus Himself,[3] and His apostles, and Paul specially,[4] presuppose and justify it. The entire existence of *Theologia Naturalis*, as distinguished from *Acquisita* or *Revelata*, is founded on this supposition, and even in these days we must of necessity be on our guard, so that we neither slight it nor exaggerate it. But we must never forget that the knowledge of God, which for these reasons we deem to be possible, possesses one *peculiarity*, which we at once proceed to discuss at greater length.

Comp. J. T. BECK, *Einleitung in das System der Christl. Lehre* (1838), i. p. 2; K. SEDERHOLM, *Die Ewigen Thatsachen* (1845); ULRICI, *Gott und die Natur* (1862), vol. i. ch. iv.; E. NAVILLE, *La Vie eternelle* (1862), p. 45, etc. A. CONTE, *Le Camposante de Pise, ou le Scepticisme* (1863); F. FABRI, *Briefe gegen den Materialismus* (1864); P. JANET, *Du Materialisme contemporain*, Dutch translation (1865); E. DE PRESSENSE, *Jésus Christ, son Temps, etc.*, English translation (1866), pp. 1—68; GUIZOT, *Meditations* (1866), ii., p. 145. Compare, concerning the rights of a natural knowledge of God, in connection with the principles of doctrine developed at the Reformation, J. H. SCHOLTEN, *Léer. der H. K.*, 4th ed. (1861), i., p. 270, etc.; J. J. VAN TOORENENBERGEN, *Bydragen tot verklaring enz. van de leer d. H. K.* (1852), i., p. 6, etc. Special notice must be taken of *Calv. Inst. Rel. Chr.* i., cap. iii., etc.

POINTS FOR INQUIRY.

Importance of this investigation. — Distinction between the work of Christian Dogmatics and that of the general philosophy of religion.— By whom, in earlier and later times, has the possibility of all Dogmatics been denied or doubted?—On wha

---

[1] Acts xvii. 27.
[2] Ps. xix. 2—4; Isa. xl. 26.
[3] Matt. vi. 22, etc.
[4] Rom. i. 19, 20; ii. 14, 15.

ground, and with what justice, has this been done?—Closer estimation of Materialism, Scepticism, Empiricism, Positivism, of the present century.—The decree and conditions under which the reality of invisible things is sustained against all these.—Cause and consequence of the representation that the Divine, as such, lies *wholly* beyond the limits of man's intellectual capacity.—The ignoring of the claims of a natural knowledge of God conflicts with Holy Scripture and the principles of the Reformation.—Over-estimation of those claims possible and dangerous.

SECTION III.—ITS PECULIARITY.

The truth, to the investigation of which "Christian Dogmatics" devotes itself, belongs to the domain of a world which is only beheld by the eye of faith. Though we may therefore speak with a very proper meaning of a science concerning God and Divine things, this science is, and always remains, a science of faith, *i.e.*, a science which is born of faith, and strives to attain to a clear insight into its subject-matter and ground, and possesses that definite decree of certainty which is the only possible one in this sphere of thought, but is also perfectly sufficient. The ignoring of this its peculiarity can only be fraught with fatal effects; the recognition of it, on the other hand, with the most beneficial results.

1. Religious truth (ἀλήθεια) as little falls within the reach of perception by the senses, as it can be produced by reason out of itself. The invisible world only reveals itself to the spiritual eye, and on this ground the peculiar character of our science can scarcely be denoted by a better name than that of the science of faith. This faith, considered as a whole, is firmly convinced of the reality of "things not seen."[5] "It is not indefinitely opposed to knowledge; but to sight, as well as to doubt. In its inmost essence it is confidence, fixed in the heart, yet in such a manner that by it is determined, not merely the conviction of the intellect, but also the bent of the will. It embraces, therefore, nothing less than the whole inner life, and from this as a centre exercises a most powerful influence on the character and conduct of man.

2. We see already in what degree we may speak of a science concerning God and Divine things. Were the word *wetenschap* (knowledge) used in the sense of "exact science," in order to denote that which is so positively proved that no sound mind can entertain any doubt about it, it would be here surely out of place. It is different when by science we mean

---

[5] Heb. xi. 1.

accurate, well-founded, and well-ordered knowledge, in whatever manner that knowledge be acquired. In this case, indeed, the knowledge which is gained as a result of faith may certainly bear, with no less right, though in a wider sense, the name of *science*, than that which is the result of reasoning and observation. The eye of faith sees the truth, and the believer knows what he has seen.

3. In the most extended use of the word it is true of our science that it is the child of faith, and without a principle of personal faith it is utterly inconceivable. Faith, first of all in ourselves, and the original, unchangeable utterances of our self-consciousness; a confidence, in other words, that the inner voice of the heart and conscience of humanity does not deceive it. But then it is also faith in that God of whom our inner consciousness testifies, and of whose Being and Will we shall never know anything until we have begun to believe in His existence. Above all, belief in Him in whom truth was personally revealed and manifested, and who grants to His own, first to behold the mysteries of the kingdom of God, and afterwards, as far as is possible and necessary, to *know* them.[6]

4. Religious and Christian faith, once originated, cannot rest until it attains to a clear insight of its subject-matter and ground; faith seeks understanding (*Fides quærit intellectum*). The believing one (πιστικός) will of necessity, as such, become the knowing one (γνωστικός). "Faith will not *remain* without knowledge; for it is in the very nature of freeing, living faith to generate of itself both action and knowledge" (Wieseler). This intimate coherence of faith and knowledge is constantly and expressly referred to in the Gospel itself.[7] The Alexandrine school did special justice to this truth, though on the other hand it too often confused Theology and Philosophy. The grand declaration of Tertullian (*cum credimus, nil desideramus ultra credere*), that the believer requires nothing but his faith, proclaims a great truth, which cannot, however, lastingly hinder the pressure of faith towards knowledge. In opposition to this the principle of Anselm, through faith to understanding (*per fidem ad intellectum*) maintains its unconditional claims; though we must never forget that it is not belief in a traditional infallible dogma, but only belief in God, and His revelation in Christ, which is the principle of Christian dogmatic science. With this last limitation we may accept the maxim that the most perfect faith leads to the most certain knowledge.

5. Dogmatics, as the science of faith, has its own peculiar degree of certainty. Its subject-matter cannot be demonstrated as a palpable fact or a mathematical proposition. In our domain we must be contented with internal evidence, obtained, not by the method of demonstration, but by that of proof and assertion (*vindicatie*). We have not here, however, certainty in a less degree than elsewhere, but rather certainty of a different kind. I may be as firmly convinced of what I believe as of what I know, but I am so in a different manner, and generally on different grounds. It is therefore not correct to contrast the certainty of knowledge with the probability of faith,

---

6 Matt. xiii. 11.

7 Luke x. 21; 1 Cor. xiii. 12, 13; xiv. 20; 1 John ii. 20; v. 13.

as if we were contrasting a higher with a lower. The believer, too, has more than probability;[8] he is as certain of that which he truly believes, as of his own existence. "Faith is by no means a lower degree of certainty; and the believer, as such, is not more certain of anything than the object of his faith. The expression *Ich glaube es nur* must seem strange to the really believing" (Erdmann). And yet this certainty cannot always show itself, much less impart itself to others, for this very reason, that it is nothing less, but also nothing more, than a certainty of faith. Exact science is a knowledge of the intellect, which may be imparted to every man of sound mind. Faith is a confidence of the heart, which we can only affirm and justify for those in whom the moral condition for the recognition of the truth is to be found.[9] Here, if anywhere, we see the deep meaning of the requirement that we must will to be able to believe. (*Nemo credit, nisi volens.*) The representation and recommendation of the science of faith serves only to lead all those who have the capacity thereto, in like manner to faith, and by this means to knowledge. Divine truth cannot be brought to any one by external demonstrations; it proves and justifies itself by itself to the spirit capable of receiving it. We must have it, to know it; we must experience it, to recognise it. Through faith we understand, and without it we understand nothing here.[10]

6. The exact estimation of Christian Dogmatics as a science of faith is of great importance. A misconception of this truth must necessarily lead to misunderstanding and disappointment. Many a one in this matter desires the same clearness and certainty as he obtains, *e.g.*, in natural science, while he forgets that he is here moving in quite another sphere; just as if the metaphysical must be measured by the same rule as the physical; and Dogmatics would stand so much higher, if it were able to demonstrate its propositions to every one, without caring what his moral condition may be. On the other hand, the recognition of this peculiar character of the science will lead to its just estimate and fitting study. It is, as a science of faith, as indispensable and as venerable as this faith itself; but it also makes upon its student comprehensive and suitable demands. The more it is considered from the standpoint we have denoted, the less will faith and knowledge be separated or confounded; the more, on the other hand, will they be reconciled and united. Thus Dogmatics fulfils its task by justifying as reasonable what faith has already recognised as real; and the ideal is attained, which a father of the Church has before conceived, "Ut ea, quæ fidei firmitate jam tenes, etiam rationis luce conspicias."

Comp. J. MÜLLER, *Ueber Glauben und Wissen. Deutsche Zeitschrift* (1853) No. 20—22; JÄGER, *Ueber die Natur der theologischen Erkenntniss*, a critical and historical Essay in the *Jahrbuch für wissensch. Theol.*, 1857, 1; I. KÖSTLIN, *Der Glaube, sein Wesen, Grund, und Gegenstand*, 1856; S. HOEKSTRA, *Bronnen en Grondslagen van het Godsdienst Geloof* (1864), p. 26, etc.; R. GRAU, *Der Glaube, als die höchste Vernunft*, and PEIP, *Ueber die Grenzen, die Mitte, und die Spitze des Beweises*,—two treatises of the greatest value, which appeared in the *Apologetisch Zeitschrift der Beweis des Glaubens*, 1865—1867.

---

[8] Cf. Job xix. 25; 2 Tim. i. 12; Rom. viii. 38.
[9] 1 John iv. 6.
[10] Heb. xi. 3.

POINTS FOR INQUIRY.

Nature, object, ground for, and reality of religious belief in general.—Explanation of Heb. xi. 1, comp. with 2 Cor. v. 7.—Can we speak of a science concerning God and Divine things, or only of a science of religion?—The conclusion to be drawn with regard to the *nil desideramus ultra credere* of Tertullian.—Historical elucidation and necessary limitation of the principle of Anselm.—To what extent, and under what conditions, is certainty in the sphere of faith possible?—Theoretical and practical importance of the result thus obtained.

SECTION IV.—ITS PLACE.

Christian Dogmatics, as a science of faith, possessing its own principles and method, lays claim to an independent and honourable place in the domain of human thought. It stands as an historical-philosophical science in the Encyclopædia of Theology, at the head of Systematic Theology, and, in conjunction with Christian Ethics, furnishes its principal subject-matter. Distinguished, though hardly to be separated, from Christian ethics, it receives the most important services from exegetical and Historical Theology, and on its rt applies these to every part of Practical Theology.

1. He who acknowledges that faith, as well as reasoning and observation, can lead the way to exact, well-grounded, and well-ordered knowledge, must also grant to the science of faith the right to an independent place in the boundless circle of human science. That place may at the same time be a most honourable, since the answer to the final questions of every investigation, whether directly or indirectly, cannot be found elsewhere than in the theological domain. Try the experiment with the science of law, history, natural philosophy, and psychology, and see what it is without, and what with, a belief in a living and self-revealing God. That which is the condition for all knowledge cannot possibly be excluded from the domain of knowledge. We might with the same fairness relegate all philosophy to the sphere of illusion; but we know that the key of physics, too, is to be found in the domain of metaphysics. The path of denial must here lead inevitably to Materialism.

2. He who, in general, regards Theology as a science, will not dispute the right of Dogmatics to existence. The continual cry, "No more Dogmatics," is the utterance of the veriest superficiality. It is as if we said to the natural philosopher, No more physics; to the mathematician, No more mathematics! The repugnance of many to Dogmatics is merely the consequence of a tacit despair of the existence or recognisability of

objective truth. Yet this repugnance cannot be kept up where the systematic denial of all Dogmatics becomes at last itself a dogma. Dogmatics is a psychological necessity; faith cannot cease to reflect upon its object; the intellect cannot rest before it has found, and as best it can expressed, the unity of this conception. It is not easy to see how Theology as a science could exist without Dogmatics (Hagenbach).

3. Some (Schleiermacher and others) incorrectly place Dogmatics at the head of Historical Theology. It is true that it not only investigates what *is* held as truth, but what *must be* held as such. And thus the exegete and the historian must have already accomplished their work before the dogmatist can think of his. It only remains a question whether, in regard to Systematics, dogmatical science must be separated from ethical or not.

4. The separation of Dogmatics and Ethics, after a previous union of long duration, prepared by Dannæus and M. Amyraldus in the seventeenth century, completed by G. Calixtus (1634), and since almost universally recognised and maintained, has been of greater service to the latter than to the former. We cannot be surprised that distinguished divines of the present century have opposed by word and deed this separation. (Schleiermacher, to a certain extent; specially C. J. Nitzsch, Sartorius, and others.) True spiritual knowledge springs indeed from the womb of life; and 'αλήθεια is not a merely metaphysical, but ethical and practical thing. And yet we acquiesce more readily in the actually existing separation, since along with unmistakable difficulties we meet with real advantages. The two sciences are so rich as to render a separate treatment not only possible, but desirable. And so the separation of the two is important enough to lead to a division of labour. Dogmatics has to do with the doctrine of salvation, Ethics with that of life; the first with the works of God, the second with the vocation of men; the one with the theoretical, the other with the practical side of truth. "Dogmatics and Ethics are as certainly independent sciences as God and man are really distinct. It is only a standpoint, such as that of Spinoza, which can dispute the independence of Ethics by the side of Dogmatics." (Dorner.)

5. Dogmatics must not dominate over Exegetical and Historical investigation, but it must respect the complete independence of both. On the other hand, it has a preponderating influence on Ethics (as Ethics has on it), and so upon every part of Practical Theology—that is, Homiletical, Liturgical, Catechetical, and Pastoral. This is almost self-evident, but at the same time proves the value of Dogmatics.

Compare the best known Handbooks of Theol. Encycl.; the article "Ethik," of DORNER in *Herzog. R. E.*, iv., p. 188, etc., and NITZSCH, *Syst. der Chr. Lehr.*, 6 Aufl., 1851, p. 4, etc.

POINTS FOR INQUIRY.

By whom, and with what right, has the scientific character of Theology, and specially of Dogmatics, been denied or doubted?—Is it possible and desirable to remove Dogmatics from the Theological Encyclopædia?—History of the separation of Dogmatics and Ethics. —Lights and shadows of the division; criticism of the later attempts at a renewed union.—What service does Dogmatics gain from Exegetical and Historical Theology?—What are the mutual services of Dogmatics and Ethics, and of all Practical Theology?

SECTION V.—ITS VALUE.

From the nature of the case, Christian Dogmatics can only have a relative value, since we cannot call any development of the subject-matter and grounds for the doctrines of salvation an entirely accurate and complete expression of Christian truth. And yet our science is of weighty importance for every thinking member of the Church, still more for a genuine theologian, most of all for a future minister of the Church; and, far from this value being diminished or done away with in these times, many a sign of the times calls for its progressive study.

1. Just as faith here is always imperfect, so the science of faith must always be partial too.[11] This consciousness is in a certain degree the cross of theology, but this cross becomes alike its crown, since that recognition of its limits tells of self-knowledge, promotes humility, and inclines to greater caution. This is specially evident when we compare the confessions of the most celebrated theologians with those of the heroes of absolute knowledge. Least of all in our times will Dogmatics spring at once full-grown from the head and heart of its priest, as Minerva from the skull of Jupiter.

2. The relative value of Dogmatics is nevertheless indisputable and essential. No one can do without it, since every one seeks for a more or less formulated expression of his holiest convictions. For the theologian, specially, no other branch of investigation exceeds this in value. It stands in relation to the others, as the queen to her retinue, the Sabbath to the other days of the week. In proportion as Dogmatism may be dangerous, is a thorough Dogmatics indispensable. The pastor and teacher, who will teach his flock with blessing, cannot do without it. It is necessary for him and for it that he should have a clear consciousness of the relation in which his personal convictions stand to the consciousness of the Church's belief.

3. From various causes we may say that the present time is as unfavourable as possible for Christian dogmatic studies. And yet these studies will be among the means by which many a suspicious phenomenon in the domain of Church and science will be combated with good success. Moreover, there is not an entire absence of more favourable signs. The powerlessness of negation to satisfy the deepest wants of man is more evident than ever; a renewed thirst after truth exhibits itself in varied ways; the striving after Church Reformation, at the same time, excites interest in the investigation of her creeds, and excellent guides appear to

---

[11] 1 Cor. xiii. 9—12.

give us light for the prosecution of our investigation. Under these circumstances, "Excelsior" is for the student of science more than an idle cry.

Comp. H. PLITT, *Evang. Glaubensl.* (1863), i., pp. 101—114; A. SCHWEITZER, *Ueber die Entwerthung der Dogm.*, *Theol. Stud. u. Kritik.* (1865), iv. See also the complaint of LUTHARDT, at the end of the preface to his *Compendium der Dogm.* (1865), to which we might add the voices of many others.

POINTS FOR INQUIRY.

Christian Dogmatics has a *real* value, even because it announces it as *relative*.—Knowledge in part, confessed by St. Paul, Augustine, Anselm, Pascal, and many others.—In what special manner is the indispensability of Christian Dogmatics shown?—By what is its study most hindered and limited in these days?—What signs of the times, on the other hand, call more strongly for this study?

CHAPTER II.

SOURCES OF CHRISTIAN DOGMATICS.

SECTION VI.—GENERAL SURVEY.

THE question as to the sources of Christian Dogmatics is of preponderating importance, and has at divers times been answered in divers ways. From the standpoint of the Christian Reformer, an immediate distinction between the primary and subsidiary source (*fons primarius et secundarius*) is at once required. The estimate of Christ Himself, as the Fountain-head, properly so called, must precede the consideration of these two, and must also be joined with the investigation, whether, and how far, the Christian consciousness must be accepted as one of the sources of our science.

1. The subject-matter of this chapter is naturally closely connected with that of the preceding. He who knows the *character* of a science, sees himself naturally led to inquire after its *sources*. Even where "*credendo scire*" is our motto, the value of the investigation into the condition of its sources is an independent one. We do not, however, here speak of the sources of religious faith in general, but specially of those from which the knowledge of Christian doctrine is derived. The first-named inquiry belongs to General Religious Philosophy and Anthropology, the last to an Introduction to the Christian system of doctrine.

2. In the investigation of the doctrine of salvation men have not always drawn from the same sources. In the first century we may say that the Spirit of Christ was the pure fount of the knowledge of truth for His Church.[1] Since, however, that Spirit was not given in like measure to all, and was, besides, soon intermixed with the spirit of the world, man soon required a source of knowledge external to himself. This was found at

---

[1] 1 John ii. 20, 27.

first in tradition (§ xl.); in after days, when the canon was finally closed, in Holy Scripture, specially in the New Testament. Scripture and tradition were now regarded as two streams, flowing side by side, and sprung from the same source. In controversy with heretics an appeal was made to both, but the increasing influence of the hierarchy soon gave occasion to the elevation of the authority of the constantly living above that of the once for all written, word. Scholasticism supported tradition with all its powers, and asserted the right of the Church to pronounce from time to time new dogmas. A Raymond of Sabunde (1436), who placed the book of nature on a par with the Bible, was an extraordinary exception. Mysticism, on the other hand, while it did not completely neglect Scripture, yet placed a misty feeling, or an immediate intuition of the truth, either on a par with or above it. The Reformation, while avoiding the one-sidedness of both schools, returned to the Scriptural principle, which the Reformed Churches preferred and maintained even more strongly than the Lutherans. Even by the latter this was held, (Artic. Smalc. ii. 2,) "verbum Dei condit articulos fidei, et præterea nemo, ne angelus quidem." The mystical principles, however, soon showed their presence again (Anabaptists, Labadists, Quakers, etc.), while, on the other side, a rationalistic tendency (Socinians, Deists, etc.) exhibited an increasing power. In opposition to both these parties, the orthodoxy of the seventeenth century often co-ordinated Scripture and creed, until the pressure of a more Biblical tendency led to the more definite distinction of a *fons primarius et secundarius*. Lessing († 1781) had to remind those who appealed to the Bible in defence of their system, that tradition was even older, and the Romish Church in particular clung with still greater hold to this latter, after it, in the first half of the present century, had been placed in a more attractive light by J. A. Möhler († 1838). On the part of Protestantism, the estimation of the sources of Dogmatics underwent a not unimportant change, chiefly through the influence of F. Schleiermacher († 1834).

3. This historical survey of the estimation of the sources of Dogmatics is important, since it shows, on the one side, how men have never found it possible to separate themselves entirely from Holy Scripture; and at the same time, on the other, how men again have constantly felt the need of placing something else, whether it be something individual (reason, feeling, conscience), or something collective (tradition, confession), along with it. This observation justifies the distinction between *primary* and *subordinate* source, which is further required by the nature of the case, and the spirit of Protestantism; whilst also, in estimating this latter in the present time, a closer analysis of the Christian consciousness must not be omitted. A glance at the Fountain-head must, however, precede the entire investigation.

Compare specially, in addition to the other handbooks, A. D. C. TWESTEN, *Vorlesungen über Dogm.* (1838), i., p. 265, *sqq.*; G. BOON, *Diss. Theol. de Dogm. Christ. fontibus, eorumque usu* (1860), i.

POINTS FOR INQUIRY.

The necessity, extent, and course of the investigation of the sources of Christian Dogmatics.—Whence are we to denote the change which has taken place, in the course of time, in the choice of the sources which have been consulted in preference?—Have we not enough in the *fons primarius* alone?

SECTION VII.—THE FOUNTAIN-HEAD, CHRIST.

No one can be the Fountain-head for the investigation of Christian Dogmatics, but He who is its principal subject-matter, and who is not only the faithful witness, but Himself the highest revelation of truth in the domain of religion. True Dogmatics is thus, from its nature, Christo-centric; and nothing in regard to the doctrine of salvation can be acknowledged as truth, that is in irreconcilable contradiction with the word and spirit of Christ, the King of truth.

1. The need of a higher unity furnishes the reason for considering first the Fountain-head. We have to deal with different sources of varying value; where then is the point from which all proceed? "Certum, propriumque fidei catholicæ fundamentum Christus est" (Augustine). Everything which we here presuppose concerning the person of the Lord must of course be afterwards properly attested and developed.

2. The representation of Christ as the Fountain-head is in complete agreement with the letter and spirit of the writings of the New Testament. Jesus Himself declares that He is the truth,[2] and is confessed by His apostles as its best interpreter and witness.[3] He is the ruler of the religious domain, considered in its widest sense. The reference to this source accords entirely with the historical character of revelation (§ 32), and is never disavowed without real injury.

3. The claim that Christian Dogmatics shall be Christo-centric, does not denote that the Christology must therefore be treated of first of all; on the contrary, there are preponderating difficulties in this method. But this is the idea, that everything which Dogmatics has to teach concerning God, man, the way of salvation, etc., must be viewed by the light which streams forth from Christ as centre. This proceeds from His exalted character, and is also contained in the apostolic statement in Colossians ii. 3. The most celebrated confessions of all ages are marked by this character, and the best dogmatists of our own century place it constantly more in the foreground. (Liebner, Lange, Thomasius, and many others.) Christ, as the highest revelation of God, must also be to the dogmatist the light of his science.[4] As the King of truth is the head of the Church, so is He the heart of Christian Dogmatics. The so-called Modern Theology is therefore already condemned in principle, since Christ has either no place or a very unimportant one in its system, which exhibits an anthropo-centric character.

4. That which is *Antichristian* must, as such, in the dogmatic sphere, be

---

[2] John xiv. 6; xviii. 37.
[3] John vi. 68; 1 Tim. vi. 13; Rev. i. 5.
[4] Ps. xxxvi. 9.

necessarily rejected as *untrue*. Dogmatics can indeed proclaim a truth, which does not exclusively exhibit a Christian character (*e.g.* the doctrine of the creation, or of the spirit-world). Anything, however, which is in direct contradiction with the word and spirit of Christ, bears on itself the brand of entire reprobation. To the saying of the old sophist, Πάντων μέτρον ὁ ἄνθρωπος (man is the measure of all things), the Christian dogmatist replies, Πάντων μέτρον ὁ Χριστός, or, if preferable, ὁ θεὸς ἐν Χριστῷ (Christ, or God in Christ, is the measure of all things). "To show itself as an authorised element in the connexion of Christian Dogmatics, every dogmatical proposition must prove its own connexion with the events, words, and deeds of Christ. So it is Christ upon whom every truth of dogmatical propositions finally rests. Is there still anything beside Him, which has the power to be the ground of the dogmas, and the foundation of their proof? This power must spring from Christ, and rest on its connexion with Him." (J. Müller, R. E., iii., p. 440.)

Comp. TH. A. LIEBNER, *Die Chr. Dogm. aus dem Christol. Princip. dargestellt* (1849), i., p. 4, etc. ; B. TER HAAR, *Oratio de Histor. Rel. Chr. indole, hodie nimis spretâ* (1860) ; J. J. VAN OOSTERZEE, *Het licht onzer Kennis* (1869). For many years the Groningen school in Holland has in its way set expressly in the foreground the truth which we have here stated.

POINTS FOR INQUIRY.

Is it not sufficient to descend into one's self, in order to find the highest truth ?—Christ, the highest revelation of truth, according to His own testimony, and according to that of the Church in all ages.—Closer definition and defence of the Christo-centric character of Dogmatics.—The meaning of Colossians ii. 3, comp. ver. 9.—The distinction between anti-christian, extra-christian, pro-christian, and half-christian, in the domain of truth.

SECTION VIII.—HOLY SCRIPTURE.

No certain knowledge of the doctrine of salvation without Christ; no clear knowledge of Christ without the books of the Old and New Testaments. So with the fullest right the Reformed Church in particular clings to the Holy Scriptures, especially those of the New Testament, as the principal source and touchstone of truth (*fons primarius*) in the Christian religious domain. Those of the Old Testament can therefore neither unconditionally be placed on a level with them, nor can they be separated from them much less can they be entirely overlooked. In general, the comparative value of the different parts of Holy Scripture for dogmatic investigation depends upon the more or less direct relation in which they stand to the person and work of Christ.

1. As a witness to Christ (§ 7), Holy Scripture, though not indeed the only one, is by far the most important source of our knowledge of the doctrine of salvation. As such it must hereafter maintain its right in the express investigation to which it will be submitted in the treatment of Bibliology (§§ 35—41). Here we can only point out the place which falls to its lot in the settlement and development of the Christian doctrine, in the spirit of the Reformed Confession.

2. The Lutherans and Swiss both reverenced the Scripture principle, with this distinction, however, that the former generally retained whatever was not in direct conflict with Scripture, the latter left out what could not be directly proved from Scripture. All the Confessions of the Reformed Church agree so completely in their recognition of Holy Scripture as the highest rule and arbiter of faith, that it is unnecessary to bring proofs of this fact.

3. It cannot be denied that, under the influence of the reviving Scholasticism of the seventeenth century, the Scripture principle was for a time mechanically conceived and unspiritually used. Ecclesiastical orthodoxy has often treated Scripture *en bloc* as a code, just as the jurist has made use of the Corpus Juris. The isolated letter was not unfrequently employed as a proof of some dogma, whilst the historical coherence and the spirit of the whole was disregarded. This was partly connected with a well-known theory concerning the inspiration of Holy Scripture (§ 39) which has in later years been recognised as untenable. It was reserved for our later days to regard Holy Scripture in a more historical light, as a collection of original records of very varied value. Hence arose at the same time the right and the duty of a cautious sifting and valuation of its separate parts.

4. This sifting, if it is not to become quite arbitrary, must be made on a settled principle. That principle is declared in the proposition that the value of the different parts of Scripture is fixed by their greater or less degree of relation to Christ. The right to ground this proposition arises from the nature of the case, the authority of the Lord, the words and example of the Reformers, and the expression of the Christian consciousness which even involuntarily observes this rule in its use and estimation of the Bible. On this principle the writings of the New Testament must be placed before those of the Old, and in the first, again, that part of the book must be preferred which points most expressly to Christ, and to the salvation wrought by Him. "It is to the writings of the New Testament that the dogmatic proof must return to found its dogmas securely on Christ Himself" (J. Müller).

5. From this standpoint it is not difficult to fix the value of the writings of the Old Testament for Dogmatics. Perfect equality with those of the New is at variance, not merely with the historical character of the Scriptures, but also with the spirit of the Reformation. *Novum multo melius Vetere* (Beza). In opposition to such an over-estimation of the first half of the Scripture, as is justly chargeable on the Dogmatics of the seventeenth century, and which even in our time is observable in the Romish Church and among some Protestant sects, we meet with a disavowal of their value, which we may characterise not merely as injustice, but as ingratitude

itself. Following in the wake of the old Gnosticism and the later Socinianism and Rationalism, Schleiermacher especially, and above all the modern Rationalism, has laid itself open to this charge of one-sidedness. We best avoid either extreme when we look upon the Old Testament with the eye with which it was regarded by Jesus Himself and the Apostles; and while we confess that it is indispensable, allow that it is insufficient.

6. The rules for the dogmatic use of the writings of the Old Testament are easily adduced from what has been already said. We have no right for a use of these Scriptures in which we do not alike take heed of their peculiar character, as distinguished from those of the New Testament. The Old Testament revelation must always be regarded first in relation to Israel, and has only value for our Dogmatics in so far as it is confirmed by the Gospel of the New. The letter of the Old Testament must thus be tested by the spirit of the New, and whatever therein stands in opposition to the New has as little binding force for our belief as for our life. A dogma which can be supported only by an appeal to the Old Testament can only maintain its place in Christian Dogmatics if it manifestly does not conflict with the letter and spirit of the New, and also stands in close connection with other propositions derived from the New Testament. If anything in the Old Testament had no religious or soteriological value, it would have no import for Christian Dogmatics. As a whole, the Old Testament must be regarded as a *propædeusis*, or preliminary training to the Christ which supports the New, without standing on the same level. "The question here is as to the relative value of the Old Testament, and this depends in general upon its organic relation to the New. By means of this organic relation the imperfection of the Old Testament as contrasted with the New is shown chiefly in the fact that what is present in a concealed manner in the Old, is first really revealed in the New." (Müller.)

Compare A. SCHWEITZER, *Die Glaubenslehre der Ev. Ref. Kirche* (1841), i., § 6; H. PLITT, *Evangel. Glaubensl.* (1863), i., §§ 7—9; L. DIESTEL, *Geschichte des A. T. in d. Chr. Kirche* (1869).

POINTS FOR INQUIRY.

The Scripture principle in the Lutheran and the Reformed Churches.—Testimonies of the Reformers and of the most celebrated Creeds.—The Scripture principle in Dogmatics alternately overrated and mistaken.—How to be preserved from arbitrary views in our definition of the value of the different parts of Scripture.—The different estimation and use of the Scriptures of the Old Testament in earlier and later times.—The distinction between the *usus hermeneuticus, historicus, dogmaticus et moralis* of the Scriptures of the Old Testament.—Necessity for a continuous and well-directed examination of Scripture for the study of Christian Dogmatics, especially in the present time.

SECTION IX.—THE SYMBOLICAL WRITINGS.

The Confessional Writings of the Church (*fons secundarius*) cannot possibly be placed on a line with Holy Scripture, but must, on the contrary, be tested by, and if necessary altered according to, this latter. They contain no law for, but an expression of, the belief which the Christian Church since the earliest times has constantly confessed, and the Reformed Church, in contradistinction from others, has maintained with relative purity. On these grounds Christian Dogmatics accepts the guidance of the Symbolical Writings rather in the historical than in the philosophical part of its investigation, and should in this latter by no means let its freedom be tried by the letter of the Creed, however much, on the other hand, it must be on its guard against all individualistic depreciation of the continuity of the faith in the Church which its aim is to serve.

Our sources of the second rank are, partly the so-called Œcumenical Symbols, partly the Symbolical Writings of the Churches of the Reformation. A short survey of these treasures of the Church must precede our closer estimate.

I. 1. To the first class belong (1) the Twelve Articles of the Catholic Christian faith. commonly called the Apostles' Creed, and incorrectly regarded as the work of the Apostles themselves, still now as always recognised as one of the most venerable memorials of Christian Antiquity, which gradually sprang from the extension of the baptismal command (Matt. xxviii. 19), and in their present form are derived from the Rome of the fifth or sixth century, and on this account called Symbolum Romanum: (2) the Creed of Nicæa (325), enlarged at Constantinople (381), composed in support of the orthodox belief concerning the Son of God and the Holy Ghost against Arius, Apollinaris, and Macedonius; (3) the creed "Quicunque," thus called from its commencement, and attributed for centuries, though without the least right, to Athanasius, and probably composed in the sixth century, by an unknown hand in Gaul or Spain.

2. Next to these Œcumenical Creeds, the Reformed Church has her own Creeds, though here she falls behind the Lutherans. She has no such well-known banner as the Augsburg Confession. She uses, on the contrary, the most excellent Symbolical Writings of different countries and nations. These may be divided either geographically or chronologically (Conf. Gallica, Scotica, Belgica, etc.), or more Dogmatically, having regard to their different characters, into those which exhibit a pure Zwinglian, and those which show a definite Calvinistic type. Those of the Dutch Reformed Church, though in various degrees, may still be all brought within the last-named class.

3. The creeds of the Dutch Reformed Church are (1) the Netherlands Confession, composed by Guido de Brès, assisted by Sarávia, Modet, and other theologians, published in French in 1561, and in Dutch in 1562, and accepted in the same year as a general Church confession, and sent in 1566, with a touching address, to the Emperor Maximilian at the Diet of

Augsburg, as an eloquent apology for the sorely combated faith; (2) the Heidelberg Catechism, composed at the command of the Elector Palatine Frederick III., by Zacharias Ursinus and Caspar Olevianus, published in German, and introduced in 1563, and translated by Peter Dathenus into Dutch in 1566, when it was at once eagerly received, and after long use as a lesson-book, and recommendation from various Synods, accepted in the Synod of Dordt in 1619, for the whole Church, as a recognised confessional writing; (3) the Canons of Dordt, containing the sentence of the National Synod, those in 1618-19 relating to the five Articles, concerning which a difference had arisen between Remonstrants and Counter-Remonstrants; viz., Predestination, Reconciliation through Christ, Free-Will, the Resistibility of the Holy Ghost, the Perseverance of the Saints. There is just as little reason to doubt of the binding power of these canons on the whole Dutch Church as there is to speak of a dogmatic difference in principle between the one and the other. The oldest confession of faith of the Dutch Church (1551), which, probably composed by à Lasco, has first seen the light again in the present century, has never on this account been reckoned among her Creeds. The four questions which are put to and answered by the congregation before communion, in use since 1817, might in a certain sense be counted among them.

II. 1. The value of the Symbolical Writings, viewed as a whole, is already denoted by calling them our *fons secundarius*. According to the Dutch Confession of Faith itself, they can in no way be placed on an equality with Holy Scripture, but must be tested by it. Even in 1565, the Synod under the Cross at Antwerp resolved that at the opening of every synod the Confession of Faith should be read "as much to profess our union as to consider if there be anything to change or modify."[5] It does not express what every Christian *must* believe in order to be saved, but what *is* believed and confessed by the Church itself, in distinction from other churches. As such, the Symbolical Writings define also the physiognomy of the Church, and mark out the point of departure for the further line of its historic development. But they were never intended to confine within bonds the spirit of investigation, still less to fill the hated part of "a paper pope."[6] Holy Scripture alone is the *norma normans*, the Confession the *norma normata* of the belief of the Church.

2. We must neither over-estimate nor under-estimate the value of the Symbolic Writings for Christian Dogmatics. They are of the utmost service in the investigation of the belief and confession of the Church, but of less value in individual philosophic speculation on the question, What is the truth necessary to salvation? Undoubtedly we must in these matters listen to voices such as these. No one, in fact, begins his investigation entirely unprejudiced; all stand, even unconsciously, in the footsteps of venerable forerunners, and feel the influence of the atmosphere in which their own consciousness of belief develops itself. No dogmatic investiga-

---

[5] Tant pour protester de notre union, que pour adviser s'il n'y a rien à changer ou à amender.

[6] Expression commonly used since the seventeenth century, on the Continent, by such as accused the Church of lending a character of infallibility to the Symbolic Writings.

tion, however, can claim the name of independent and scientific, which, dominated by the Symbolic Writings, sees its results prescribed even before begun. The first question always is, What is truth? the second, What does the Church teach? This latter would renounce her peculiar Christian and Protestant character if she attacked the freedom of scientific investigation. It is, however, quite another matter whether she must admit every result of that investigation in her domain, and can use it in her service. The Church permits the liberty of scientific investigation, but also retains the liberty of rejecting what injures and destroys her, and this liberty she is bound to maintain.

3. The practical question, how far the dogmatist, in his work as minister of the Church, must consider himself bound by her Confession, can here only be touched upon. Thus much however is evident, it is not with any dogmatic conviction whatever (much less with a complete want thereof), that a man has a right to place himself among the teachers and leaders of a definite church. No church summons ministers to contest her belief, and no one can possibly demand of her an act of suicide in the name of progress and toleration. On the other hand, a church which wishes to remain Christian and Protestant cannot desire any other teaching than that which bears the stamp of subjective truth and thorough sincerity. Experience shows that the attempt to distinguish to the general satisfaction between fundamental and non-fundamental dogmas has thus far been as unsuccessful as the efforts to define once for all what must really be considered as essence and substance of the Confession. The wearying struggle between the *quia* and the *quatenus* is as little decided as the sharp separation between principles and doctrines of the Reformed Dogmatics is raised above reasonable suspicion. That modern Naturalism, in its resistance in principle to Christianity and doctrine, has nowhere less right of existence than in the place which it arbitrarily occupies, can only be denied when we suffer interested calculation to prevail against sound reasoning. But even when, in opposition to all this, any one has placed himself at the juridico-confessional standpoint, the question arises, what we must do in a time when all, in a greater or less degree, have departed from the letter of the Creeds, but also against an adversary who, not without great cause, emphatically reminds us of the principle, that "he who offends in one point is guilty of all." No other way seems to remain, after all, than that we prefer to call the ethical or medial way. The conscience of the minister, if properly educated, must determine whether he can boldly stand forth in the face of his Church; the consciousness of the Church, if well guided, must declare whether, in its holiest convictions, it feels itself strengthened or oppressed by him. Whenever these be united with a tender scrupulosity on both sides, the earnest wish to heal all moral and spiritual diseases by the power of truth and love, an approach is conceivable which will lead to real peace. In every case this standpoint—which we claim as ours—has this advantage, that it does not break with the past, satisfies the reasonable requirements of the present, and prepares the way for a better future.

Compare, as to the Œcumenical Symbols, the articles relating to them in HERZOG'S *R.-E.*

Encyc., and particularly G. J. VOSSIUS, *Dissertt. tres de tribus Symbb.* (1662, Ed. 2a). Upon the creeds of the Netherlands' Reformed Church, Preface to the Edition by H. A. NIEMEYER (1840); H. E. VINKE (1846), and J. J. VAN TOORENENBERGEN (1869).

POINTS FOR INQUIRY.

Origin, history, and value of the "Apostles' Creed."—The Creed of Nicæa.—How we discover that the Athanasian Creed was not written by Athanasius.—Calvin's view concerning it.—The importance of the Augsburg Confession, even for the Reformed Churches.—The peculiarity of the Confessions of the latter.—Is the generally binding authority of the canons of Dordt raised beyond all doubt?—The importance of the study of the Symbolical Writings for Christian Dogmatics.—Formularies.—Liberty of thought and the Church.—Total submission to formularies as unscientific, as dread of formularies is unchristian.

SECTION X.—THE CHRISTIAN CONSCIOUSNESS.

To the Christian truth, in accordance with the Gospel believed and confessed by the Church, the Christian consciousness gives a witness, with reason estimated highly. Only where objective truth finds a point of contact in the subjective consciousness, does it become the spiritual property of mankind, and can it be thus properly understood and valued. So far, and so far only, does the Christian consciousness deserve a place among the sources of Dogmatics. But since the doctrine of salvation can be derived neither from reason, nor from feeling, nor from conscience, and the internal consciousness only attests and confirms the truth, after having learned it from Scripture, this last must always be valued as the principal source.

1. It was only in the present century, and chiefly through the influence of Schleiermacher (†1834), that the Christian consciousness began to be considered a source of Dogmatics. He started with his investigation from man's feeling of his unlimited dependence. Dogma is for him the development of the utterances of the pious self-consciousness, as this is found in every Christian, and is still more determined by the opposition between sin and grace. In other words, it is the scientific expression of the pious feeling which the believer, upon close self-examination, perceives in his heart. Thus this consciousness is here the gold-mine from which the dogmas must be dug out, in order to "found" them afterwards as far as possible, in Holy Scripture. In the individual it is the result of the spirit of the community as this is a revelation of the Spirit of Christ. Of this "Gemeingeist" Schleiermacher allows, it is true, that it must continually

develop and strengthen itself by the words of Scripture, but not that it must find in the latter its infallible correcting rule. For him the highest principle of Christian knowledge is thus something entirely subjective, and the autonomy of his self-consciousness is the basis of his entire system. The unceasing play which since his time has been made of this word, as in later times of the word "conscience," renders necessary a short explanation.

2. Schleiermacher, with his school, speaks of the pious self-consciousness (also called immediate consciousness) usually in the sense of feeling. Meanwhile, however, the word itself points to the domain of "knowledge," which must at once be properly distinguished from feeling and disposition. The question whether this consciousness is something thoroughly immediate (primitive, original), need the less be here determined, because there is no mention here of the universal human, but of the special Christian consciousness, which has been formed in the well-known historical psychological way. In this use of the word we think of "that knowledge which the Christian has in himself of spiritual things," and in opposition to the knowledge, imparted from without, of "that which he knows by means of self-examination and spiritual experience."

3. The value which, on this conception of the word, must be conceded to the matter itself is evident. Though the claim that men should take to themselves and assimilate the truth has been misinterpreted and misused by thousands, it yet possesses an indisputable right. So long as I do not consciously accept a truth for myself, it remains a truth, external to and above me, but is not a truth for me, and in me. And therefore the Gospel looks for a point of union in man, and finds it in the highest aspirations of his heart, intellect, and conscience. Where it is faithfully accepted, a spiritual agreement springs up, and consequently an inner consciousness of truth. This consciousness of experience not only may, but must be reckoned among the sources of our knowledge. We find proofs of such a fixed and clear consciousness in John iv. 42; ix. 25; 2 Tim. i. 12. Where it is utterly wanting, even the most accurate knowledge deserves only the name of dead knowledge. A man's own experience leads to much deeper insight of things than the best attested testimony; and with one of the most distinguished thinkers of our age, we may surely grant that the Christian consciousness is "a relatively independent source of Christianity, distinct from Scripture and Church." (Martensen.)

4. Thus far, then, along with the *fons primarius et secundarius*, we may speak also of a *fons internus*. This is quite in the spirit of the Apostles and of the Reformers, not only of Calvin, concerning the doctrine of the witness of the Holy Spirit (§ 32), but also of Luther.[7] "We might preach the law for ever to a beast, and yet it will not enter into the heart. But man, as soon as the law is proclaimed to him, at once exclaims, 'Yes, it is so; I cannot deny it.' We could not convince him of this, if it were not beforehand written in his heart. But since it is so, however dim and

---

[7] 1 Cor. ii. 12, 13; 1 John ii. 20, 27.

faded, it is again quickened with the word, so that the heart must confess that it is indeed as the commandments ordain." [8] Orthodox theologians meant nothing but this when they desired an "experimental" knowledge.

5. But if that which is true here is not wholly new, the new is not wholly true. The question is not, whether the consciousness offers a point of union with revealed truth, or even whether experience, after Scripture and the Church, gives testimony to it; but whether the Christian consciousness may be considered the fountain-head of knowledge, and thus the starting-point of the investigation, in the sense that in the end every other voice must be considered as subordinate to it. In other words, whether the knowledge of the truth of salvation can be derived from the human and Christian consciousness in its widest conception. To us, upon this point, any answer but a negative one seems inconceivable.

6. Christianity, then, proclaims itself as a positive revelation of God, given in a succession of facts; a deed of His love, which glorifies itself even herein, that it has been a free work, with respect to which no human understanding could, *à priori*, form any judgment. Just as little as any philosopher could prove that God must have made the world, could any theologian determine the mode and manner in which God must have redeemed the world. That which is revealed may be, *à posteriori*, in some degree understood and discovered, but it could never have been discovered by reason. A recognition of the supremacy of reason in this domain must inevitably end in a disavowal of the supranatural character of the whole of Christianity. Besides, our conception of God and Divine things is already partly dominated by the contents of the Gospel made known to us, and it is mere fancy to imagine that reason could evolve the doctrine of salvation from itself. "Revelation is a matter of the purest and freest will. Thus no one, who so much as knows what the question is, when he is speaking of revelation, would imagine that this was something which could be conceived *à priori*. On the contrary, the philosophy of revelation must admit that everything which it is able to declare of revelation is only declared in consequence of that which has really happened." (Schelling, *Philos. der Offen.* ii., p. 11.)

7. Still less can we acknowledge pious feeling to be an infallible source of the highest truth. Indeed, its utterances are entirely different in different persons, while even in the same individual they are ceaselessly changing. Moreover, it would never thus give testimony to the truth, if the reason and the heart had not already accepted the Gospel as truth, upon what they consider valid grounds. Feeling is neither the gold mine, nor the master of the assay, but only the guardian treasurer of the hidden treasure of belief. For the believer himself it is (as consciousness, experience) the crown of his belief, the proof of his sum, and thus a source of security and peace. But still it is always the consequence, the seal (*obsignatio*), of that *which has already been learned in another way*, and it requires besides constant testing and purifying, that it may not be lost in the maze of

---

[8] *Werke*, edited by Walch, iii., p. 1575.

Mysticism. Even, too, in this mode, we cannot grant the Autonomy to self-consciousness; but this latter must always be considered as subject to the Heteronomy or Theonomy of God's word in Holy Scripture. The test stands above that which must constantly be tested. "We must consider it an erroneous conception, that in our days it has sometimes been denoted as a possible method of Dogmatics to derive its conclusions entirely from the Christian consciousness, without any reference to Scripture, and to establish them by their coherence with the facts of Scripture. The false spiritualistic Autonomy of Christian consciousness would thus lead to the most complete corruption thereof." (J. Müller.)

8. Many a one in our days expects to gain from the conscience that which he feels sure reason and feeling cannot give. A consistent Dogmatics has been formed in Germany from the standpoint of the conscience (Schenkel), and already, by this method, and by its character of prolixity, has been stigmatised as a proof of want of conscience (Strauss). In France, too, and in Holland, when the question is as to the source of truth, the conscience has been pointed out with an emphasis formerly unknown; sometimes in a manner to justify the complaint, "Avec ce mot de conscience on explique tout, on justifie tout de nos jours, et la conscience sert à cacher la faiblesse des convictions comme la fausseté des situations"[9] (Matter). Hence we see the extreme importance of defining our conception of conscience. We consider it unnecessary to say much concerning the etymology of the word (conscientia, συνείδησις). It is well known that it has been differently explained, but no sufficient proof has been given that an unanimity as to the derivation of the word would for ever put an end to every quarrel about the matter. We make a step in advance as we regard the different functions which are ascribed to conscience, and attend to the special cases where appeal is made to the conscience. It is evident, then, that we stand here in a moral domain, and over against a higher power which demands unlimited obedience. It was a striking definition of conscience, once made by a child, when it said, "it is that with which we cannot do what we like." Conscience is thus moral consciousness, a knowledge in and by one's self with regard to some definite duty. It contains the consciousness of personal vocation, obligation, responsibility, not only towards ourselves and others, but towards an inviolable law, and, since this is the expression of a personal will, towards a holy lawgiver. Thus far we may say, that in the conscience an original consciousness of God reveals itself; it is the cypher, the monogram of the Creator in the rational and moral creature.

Conscience is thus necessarily Witness, Lawgiver, Judge. Witness of the existence and right of a holy supreme authority over us; witness of a personal God, since from the pantheistic point of view conscience becomes a chimera. A Lawgiver, who maintains the unconditional right of the moral law, and yet does not express the universal good and bad, since the ideas of good and bad under divers influences widely differs among different

---

[9] "By this word *conscience* everything is now-a-days explained and justified, and conscience is used to conceal the weakness of convictions, as well as the falseness of positions."

nations, nevertheless inexorably requires that man, according to the light given to him, should cease to do evil, and learn to do well. A Judge, finally, who acquits or condemns, just as duty is considered or neglected. As an accuser, conscience made itself first known after the first sin had been committed, but it does not yet necessarily follow that it was first aroused in consequence of the sin. As a consciousness of moral duty it belongs to man's original nature as much as the reason, the feeling, and the will. Without unconditionally excluding one of these three, when we come to the question of the seat of conscience, we look for this latter rather in the domain of the heart—in the very central point of personality. And thus we follow in the steps of Scriptural usage, which recommends itself by its deep psychological truth.[10]

The question, whether and how far conscience (conceived as far as possible collectively and beyond the influence of the Gospel) can be a source of religious truth, after what has been said, is answered without difficulty. Conscience proclaims a holy God, an inviolable moral law, where this is broken, a righteous retribution, and consequently also a need of redemption, which man cannot procure for himself. But conscience, as such, does not know whether redemption is really obtainable, or in what mode it is to be gained; it will even, when thoroughly quickened, scarcely admit this idea. It knows, indeed, of law, but not of grace, which must be first revealed in deeds, and can as little be postulated *à priori* by conscience, as it can be excogitated by reason. Now that the Gospel has been revealed, conscience may bear its testimony to it, but it by no means follows that the conscience could have deduced the contents of this revelation. Such phrases as, "Christ is the subject-matter of conscience," or, "Christ, the conscience of humanity," give us hardly any clearness of conception. Christ, an historic person, is the centre of a revelation, which gives satisfaction to the conscience, and that which He demands is assented to by the conscience. But this does not yet prove that this revelation should be merely a development of that which is already present in principle in every conscience, still less that this last must be either the highest source or the supreme judge in this domain. He who seriously asserts this, forgets entirely the historic supernatural character of Christianity, and reverences a consciencialism which, properly regarded, must be called only another form of the Rationalism which, from that very side, has been so much despised.

"Consciencialism" in the domain of Dogmatics is that tendency which recognises the conscience not merely as the guide, but as the highest arbiter, in the kingdom of truth, and which will not recognise as truth anything which is not witnessed and approved by the conscience. [As a type of this conception Schenkel may be quoted, who (*l. c.* i., p. 213) permits conscience to decide what is Holy Scripture, and again, what in Scripture is to be regarded as the word of God.] Dogmatics, from this standpoint, may not properly proclaim anything which is not already slumbering in the conscience; conscience, on the other hand, will determine whether a dogmatic proposition shall be granted or not. Is much required to

---

[10] Comp. Prov. iv. 23; Rom. ii. 14, 15; Heb. x. 22.

prove the arbitrariness and untenability of this whole view? It is evident, nothing can be developed from the conscience, which is not present as subject-matter in the conscience. Conscience can bear testimony to a moral precept, but never to an historical fact, as such; it may be a test of our acts, but cannot possibly be a source of a particular revelation; it can recognise the internal value of the Gospel, but by this its truth is by no means determined. Besides, experience shows that conscience does not always speak with the same voice in different persons, and equally as the feeling and the will is under the influence of an intellect obscured by sin.[11] "When conscience ceases to read, and begins to write, then will Scripture be as diverse as the handwriting of men. Tell me of one sin, which is called a sin by all" (Cl. Harms). The same may be said of truth, specially of Christian truth, which (we must here by no means pass it by) exhibits not only an ethical, but also a metaphysical side. How many propositions are there in the domain of Theology, Christology, Pneumatology, Eschatology, concerning which conscience tells us nothing at all, because they lie entirely outside the sphere of conscience. In truth, "to derive dogmas from conscience, is to bring down the greatness of the Divine thoughts to the diminutiveness of the human, and thus revealed truth will in a greater or less degree be excluded from Dogmatics" (Auberlen). We must not shut our eyes to this inevitable consequence. If conscience is the highest source of truth, we must then put on one side as indifferent, or reject as undemonstrable, everything which cannot maintain its right before this tribunal. When the utterances of Scripture and of conscience conflict, the consistent consciencialist must not only suspend his judgment, but sooner or later must openly contradict Scripture. And even if Scripture and conscience speak with the same voice, what security have I, that what conscience testifies as a revelation is the expression of eternal truth? We cannot look for that guarantee in conscience itself; it must be sought for *ab extra* and from above; and on every side I find myself at last turned back again to the Word, which bears testimony of Christ. Can we be surprised that Holy Scripture itself says much less about conscience than would be expected from the consciencialistic point of view? Careful consideration shows the conscience to stand in much closer relation to the teaching of the Old Testament than to that of the New, and it has not unfairly been asserted by Peip, that the Gospel finds its support, less in conscience in general, than in the evil conscience, to which it comes with consolation, but from which it could not possibly have been derived.

What, then, is our result? It is not the Christian consciousness itself, in any of its forms, but Christ Himself, which is the highest source of truth; and Christ is best seen in Holy Scripture. Conscience is, indeed, a connecting link for, but still no source of, the doctrine of salvation. In exacting the autonomy of conscience at the cost of the word of Holy Scripture, the keenly listening ear hears something of the note which was heard in the first, "Ye shall be as gods."[12] In the investigation of the Christian doctrine, the services which conscience renders are much more formal than

---

[11] Tit. i. 15.

[12] Gen. iii. 5.

material; it must be carried out conscientiously, but not consciencialistically. Conscience works here less normatively than prohibitively. Just as little as it is advisable to do anything contrary to conscience, is it advisable to teach anything contrary to it. For us nothing can be truth which is loudly contradicted by our conscience; but neither is everything which is necessary to salvation required or confirmed by conscience; for revelation has a supernatural historic character, and not only refers to the conscience, but to the whole inner man. From him it demands *obedience* to the faith,[18] and that demand, when properly vindicated, must be approved by conscience.

Comp. G. H. LAMERS, *Diss. Theol. de Conscientia* (1858), and his treatise on the same subject in the "*Bydragen op het gebied van Godgeleerd en Wijsbeg.* i. (1867); F. FABRI, *Het algemeene waarheidsgevoel, het orgaan der openb. Gods in alle menschen* (1863); AUBERLEN, *Die göttl. Offenb.* ii. 1, pp. 25—61 (1864); R. HOFFMANN, *Die Lehre von dem Gewissen* (1866), and the literature quoted there; W. GASZ, *Die Lehre vom Gewissen, in Beitrag zur Ethik*; A. E. W. WERNER, *Das Gewissen*, an ethical study; HILGENFELD, *Zeitsch. für wissensch. Theol.* (1870), p. 129; CH. WADDINGTON, *Dieu et la Conscience* (1870); F. BOUILLIER, *De la Conscience en Psychologie et en Morale* (1872).

POINTS FOR INQUIRY.

Further elucidation of the standpoint of Schleiermacher.—The peculiar point in dispute.—Ignoring and over-estimation of the right of conscience in the Christian Dogmatic domain.—Further analysis of its operation, in the light of experience and Holy Scripture.—Necessity of a constant corrective, such as is found in the written word, claimed and recognised by conscience itself.

---

[18] Rom. i. 5.

CHAPTER III.

HISTORY OF CHRISTIAN DOGMATICS.

SECTION XI.—IN THE BUD.

CHRISTIAN Dogmatics, like every science, has a history of its own, and a knowledge of this history is absolutely necessary for a thorough study of this science. It is plain from the nature of the case, that the systematic investigation of the truth which belongs to salvation has never completely ceased since the birth of the Church of our Lord. Not a little has been already done, specially for the Apologetics of Christianity, and for the development of single and most important dogmas, by the ancient Church. But for Dogmatics as a whole, taken as an independent science, the first seven centuries of our era scarcely deserve a better name than that of a period of preparation. The earliest period of its history, if we denote it by a single word, has been a period of slow and gradual budding.

1. The history of the science, whilst it makes us acquainted with its past, and explains its present state, also directs our way for the future, by pointing out to us on the one side its most distinguished leaders, and on the other its threatening dangers. This history occupies a place in our introduction, not merely for completeness' sake, but because a knowledge of it, at any rate to a certain degree, is indispensable.

2. From the nature of the truth of salvation, its revelation has in every century given rise to speculation and investigation. For these it offers boundless material and a powerful stimulus; for rational faith cannot remain indifferent to that "which the angels desire to look into."[1] For

---

[1] 1 Peter i. 12.

years before the "*fides quærit intellectum*" was uttered, it had been silently practised. Discursive thinking cannot possibly satisfy the mind; the spirit seeks unity in its ideas, even in the highest domain of thought. "If man is to become entirely blessed, his reason must share in the blessing." (Lange.)

3. The working of the different stones usually precedes the erecting of the doctrinal building as a whole. The history of the first centuries fully explains why the so-called formal part of Christian Dogmatics was developed earlier than the material. The violent opposition to Christianity called forth vigorous apologists, whilst those separate dogmas were chosen for discussion, which had elicited most contradiction. Thus the development of Dogmatics, on the whole, showed a more theological character in the East, whilst in the West it was more anthropological. Christology and Hamartology were more discussed than Soteriological and Eschatological questions.

4. In general, in this first period we can still speak only of a beginning which promised much. Among the apostles, Paul, the most vigorous apologist, may also be called in a certain sense the first dogmatist. The Epistle to the Romans presents the entire truth of salvation in a regular connection, from its theoretical and practical sides. We do not find, either in the writings of the other Apostles, or in those of the Apostolic Fathers, anything which can be compared with that epistle. After their time also much more was done in the way of explication, defence, and practical application, than in the systematic combination of the doctrines of salvation. The cause of this dogmatic sobriety lies partly in the nature of the Gospel, which does not proclaim a philosophical system, but a life truth, which must be practically laid hold on before it can be theoretically conceived; partly in the unfavourable state of the times; partly in the richness of the Gospel doctrines, whose various sides were to be duly represented before a thorough representation of the whole could be thought of; partly, lastly, in the kind of satisfaction which thoughtful faith found in the gradual development of the Symbols, and in the oral rule of faith.

5. That, however, which is particularly memorable at this period, scanty as it may be, deserves even the more our attention. To these, then, exceptional phenomena belong, in the first place, the Alexandrine school, and specially the treatise of Origen Περὶ Ἀρχῶν, the *Catechesis Magna* of Gregory of Nyssa, as also the four treatises of Athanasius against the Arians, his tractate *De Incarnatione* and the catecheses of Cyril of Jerusalem, *Ad Baptizandos et Baptizatos*. In the West, Augustine furnishes his contribution to Christian Dogmatics in his *Enchiridion ad Laurentium*, which contains a short representation of the Gospel doctrine in the compass of faith, hope, and love; whilst his treatise, *De civitate Dei*, exhibits an apologetic rather than a dogmatic character. Among the dogmatists of the fifth century, Vincentius Lerinensis († 450) deserves honourable mention for his *Commonitorium*. Among those of the sixth, Fulgentius, Junilius, and Leontius Cyprius. Here specially we observe the Compilatores or Sententiarii, who carefully gathered together the dogmatic propositions of the fathers of the Church, as, *e.g.*, Gennadius Massiliensis, in his *De Fide s. de Dogmatibus Ecclesiasticis*, a treatise in

which dogmatical and ethical ideas are peacefully united, and Isidorus Hispalensis in his *III Libri Sententiarum.* But still this was merely a time for gathering materials; here, too, as in the building of the Jewish temple, the treasure-collectors go before the proper builders of the temple.

For this whole chapter compare A. IPEY, *Letterk. Geschied der System. Godgeleerdh.*, 3 vols. (1797); J. CLARISSE, *Encycl. Theol.*, 2nd edition (1835), pp. 444—447; TWESTEN, *Dogm.*, 3 Aufl., i. §§ 96—272; J. H. A. EBRARD, *Christl. Dogm.* (1851), i. § 17—51; H. E. VINKE, *Theol. Dogm.*, i. (1853), p. 116, *sqq.*; HASE, *Hutterus Rediv*, 10 Aufl. (1862), §§ 19—27; LUTHARDT, *Comp. des Dogm.* (1865), § 17—23. In connection with these sections see the different monographs on the chief persons named in them.

POINTS FOR INQUIRY.

The date from which men began more expressly to treat of the history of Christian Dogmatics.—Why has the doctrinal investigation of the truths of salvation never been able to entirely rest in any age?—What is the reason of so little systematisation in the first centuries?—Survey and estimation of the labours of the earliest apologists.—St. Paul, Origen, Augustine, as dogmatists.—Smaller treatises.—The Compilers.—General characteristics of the dogmatic efforts of the first seven centuries.

SECTION XII.—DEVELOPMENT.

During and after the eighth century, Christian Dogmatics, as a whole, was cultivated systematically, and developed dialectically, in a greater degree than before, under the varying influence of the Platonic and the Aristotelian philosophy. The noblest representatives of the Scholasticism and Mysticism of the middle ages tried their strength on the materials handed down to them, partly in collecting, defining, and proving them; partly in refining, supplementing, and defending them. If we compare this period with the preceding, the second period of this history may be called, on this account, a period of development; though it cannot by any means be denied that this development was more and more continued in a direction which rendered a reformation of the Church, as well as also of this part of the science, of continually increasing need.

1. The relative poverty of the history of this science in the first seven centuries was succeeded by a relative abundance in the following seven. Johannes Damascenus († 754) appears with his Ἔκδοσις ἀκριβὴς τῆς ορθοδόξου Πίστεως, and by this work gains for himself the honourable name

of the Father of Systematic Theology. In it he collected the dogmatical sentences of the two Gregories, Basil the Great, and other Greek fathers, and united them in one well-combined whole. His work, a portion only of his Πηγὴ γνώσεως, divided by himself into a hundred chapters, and afterwards into four books, is of special importance for Christology and the doctrine of the Trinity. In the last he, however, had but few, and those less important, followers. He who in this era wishes to observe the development of Dogmatics must turn his eye to the West, where John Scotus Erigena († after 877), not unfairly called the Origen of the West, and specially famous for his five books, *De Divisione Naturæ*, prepared the way for a new state of things. Along with him we must place Alcuin, the zealous ally of Charlemagne, who is worthy of notice, as far as Dogmatics is concerned, for his three books, *De fide sanctæ et individuæ Trinitatis.*

2. Scholasticism now devotes itself expressly to systematizing the traditional Church doctrine, by the aid of the philosophy of Aristotle, looked upon as the John the Baptist of Heathenism (*præcursor Christi in naturalibus*). Conspicuous at the head of its representatives is Anselm, Archbishop of Canterbury († 1109), the Augustine of the middle ages, of great influence, not only for his *Monologium* and *Proslogium*, but even more for his essay, *Cur Deus homo*, and most of all for his theological principle, *Non quæro intelligere ut credam sed credo ut intelligam.* "*Volo me perducas huc.*"—'Tis thus he explains his chap. xxv. of his *Cur Deus homo*—"*ut rationabili necessitate intelligam esse oportere omnia illa, quæ nobis fides Catholica de Christo credere præcepit.*" In him, too, we see the Realism which defends the reality of general ideas against Roscellin and Peter Abelard († 1142). In this last, who maintained the principle, *nil credi posse, nisi prius intellectum sit*, dogma meets with an acute antagonist, and Nominalism a powerful ally. Along with his *Theologia Christiana*, we must here make special mention of the work of another congenial spirit, the renowned Peter Lombard, the well-known Magister Sententiarum, who clung much closer, however, than Abelard to the standpoint of ecclesiastical orthodoxy. His *IV Libri Sententiarum*, prepared, according to his own words, "in multo labore et sudore," made him the forerunner of the later *Sententiarii*, who collected the doctrines of the Church into single *Sententiæ*, derived from the writings of the Fathers, and arranged systematically.

3. The golden age of Scholasticism, which was of paramount importance for Christian Dogmatics, begins in the thirteenth century. Contemporary with, and subsequent to, the *Sententiarii*, the *Summistæ* are seen, so called after the *Summa universæ Theologiæ* of the Franciscan Alexander Hales († 1245). His renown is eclipsed by that of the Dominican Albertus Magnus († 1280), who, in addition to Commentaries on Aristotle and Peter Lombard, published his own *Summa Theologiæ*. The *Partes* were divided into *Tractatus*, these into *Quæstiones*, these into *membra*, and the *membra* into *articulæ*, *particulæ*, and *sub-particulæ*, an architectural building of severely symmetrical beauty. He, however, was surpassed in his turn by his disciple, Thomas, Count of Aquino († 1274), whose *Summa totius Theologiæ*, divided into three parts (God, Man, the person and work of Christ), within half a century after his death, procured him the honour of canonisation, and remained of decisive influence on the development of

the doctrine of the Romish Church. His force, as well as that of other scholastics, lay not so much in the material as in the formal, more in the classification than the exposition of truth. Science is entirely, in the service of that Church, deemed infallible. Its special occupation is to make the most subtle definitions, acute distinctions, and logical arrangement of the subjects. The categories of Aristotle, suspected sometimes in their physical, but never in their dialectical value, direct the investigation of which generally the conclusion was already fixed *à priori*. The identity of the doctrine of the Church with that of Holy Scripture and the most renowned Fathers was generally taken for granted, but seldom proved. When men cannot descend into the depths, they proportionately busy themselves in the breadth, and betake themselves to subtilties which later on in the history of dogma obtain a sad renown. Dogmatics becomes ever more and more a merely dialectical development of traditional ideas. A blind belief in authority is the danger which threatens Realism, an unbridled scepticism that which threatens Nominalism. Matters by no means improved when the Quodlibetarii arose against the Summistæ (the Dominicans). They were followers of the Franciscan John Duns Scotus, the doctor subtilis († 1308), the defender of the immaculate conception, the glory of his age, and by his barbarisms the corrupter of its language; a pupil of Aristotle, of such a degree, that, as was said, the philosopher, if he had lived in later times, would have desired to be taught by him. His *Quæstiones in IV Libr. Sentt.*, and *Quæstiones Quodlibeticæ*, entertain their readers with the investigation of the Quidditas, the Hæcceitas, the Incircumscriptibilitas, etc., of the subjects on which he treated, through which the dignity of science too often perished in a sea of subtilties. No one condemned this sophistry more keenly than one of the Franciscans, Roger Bacon, the doctor mirabilis († 1294), who again and again expressed the ardent wish to see all the books of Aristotle committed to the flames.

4. As a consequence of this we see Scholasticism decay. The supremacy of Nominalism increases, and along with it the wide separation of philosophy and theology. This was specially effected by the influence of William Durandus (Dr. resolutissimus, † 1334), and of William Occam (Dr. invincibilis, † 1334), who sought in the authority of the Church a counterpoise to the results of free criticism. Occam may deservedly be called a pure type of Nominalism. "Science has only to do with phenomena which it observes; that which lies beyond this is the object of belief alone." Thus true philosophy of the Divine is inconceivable, and that which theology declares of God rests solely on the authority of the Church. The whole system resolves itself into a *probabilism*, which even undermines to its very depth the principles of moral life. This Nominalism, represented by Peter d'Ailly and John Gerson, was victorious at Paris; but at Oxford, Realism was defended by Wycliffe; in Germany, by Huss. The very last of the so-called *scholastici*, G. Biel († 1495), the commentator on Occam, was an out and out Nominalist.

5. For Apologetics less was done in this second period than in the first; and this is natural, for Christianity had been established, heathenism partially conquered, partially the object of practical missionary zeal. Against the Jews wrote Agobert, Archbishop of Lyons, Abelard, and

Rupert of Deutz; against the Mohammedans, Euthymius Zigabenus, Peter of Clugny, and afterwards Æneas Sylvius. On the other hand, we now see individual dogmas, (*e.g.*, the dogma of the sacraments,) which formerly had been neglected, developed in a much higher degree. In general, the theology of Scholasticism, in after times so often and so very unfairly treated, (*e.g.*, by Semler and others,) merits the eulogy of Ullmann, that "it has been at its beginning a real scientific advance; in its entire course a great dialectical training school for western humanity; in its completion a stately monument of the human spirit, artistically worked out like a Gothic dome."

6. Mysticism meanwhile presents a more satisfactory scene to our view. At the head of this movement stands Bernard of Clairvaux (Dr. mellifluus, † 1153), the renowned opponent of Abelard, advocate of the Pauline doctrine of justification, and himself a living evidence of the force of his theological principle, "Tantum Deus cognoscitur, quantum diligitur." Though he left no dogmatic work properly so called, by letters, sermons, and essays he has had salutary influence on the development of Dogmatics. In a certain sense we might call him the Pascal of his time. Even before his time, a better way had been attempted in the convent school of St. Victor, at Paris. His friend, Hugo of St. Victor, called by his contemporaries a second Augustine, who wrote *De Sacramentis fidei Christianæ*, had enunciated the great axiom, "De veritate quisque potest videre, quantum est." Still more inclined than he to the principles of Mysticism was Richard († 1173) the prior of the convent; who attempted the development of Mysticism in a philosophical manner. His successor, Walther (1180), shows himself a passionate enemy of Scholasticism, and wrote against its four most celebrated representatives at the University in Paris, in his treatise, *Contra quatuor labyrinthos*. The renowned Francis Bonaventura must not be forgotten here (Dr. seraphicus, † 1274), whose *Breviloquium* the pious Gerson wished to introduce generally; an "Israelite indeed," as his contemporaries called him, "in whom Adam seemed not to have sinned," and who also favoured a more mystic tendency. Not to mention again the wonder of Oxford, Roger Bacon, who lashed with severity the profound ignorance hidden under the appearance of science, and sought to prepare the way for a better method than that of Scholasticism.

7. Mysticism, under the support of these influences, begins to lead the way to a better Dogmatics, that of the Reformation. Among these forerunners we dare scarcely give a place to Eckart († 1329), whose speculative tendency was lost in a misty Pantheism, and in this respect has not unjustly been condemned by Rome. We would rather mention here, along with Ruysbroeck and H. Suso, John Tauler (Dr. sublimis et illuminatus, † 1361), the mighty preacher, of whom Luther bore witness that he had nowhere found a sounder and more evangelical theology. Besides, the writer of the golden little book upon "German Theology," and the author of the *Imitatio Christi*, in every respect the obedient son of his Church, but not the less, by his practico-my tic tendency, the herald of a brighter day. More powerfully, too, is this better era predicted by the properly so-called forerunners of the Reformation, by Wycliffe († 1384), in his *Trialogus;* by

Gerson († 1429, doctor Christianissimus), in his *Considerationes de Theol. Myst.*; by I. van Goch (†1475), in his *Dialogus de quatuor erroribus*, and in his essay *De libertate Christianâ;* by I. van Wesel († 1481), *adv. indulgentias de jejunio, de potestate Eccl.;* and specially John Wessel (lux mundi, magister controversiarum, † 1489), and the brothers of the common life with him. All do not go as far as Wycliffe, when he declared "Si essent centum papæ et omnes fratres versi essent in cardinales, non deberet concedi sententiæ suæ in materiâ fidei, nisi de quanto se fundaverit in Scripturâ." But all are at one in founding Dogmatics on firmer ground than that of a varying tradition; and in putting an end to the ever sharper Dualism between belief and knowledge which brought both Church and theology to the very verge of destruction.

Compare, beside the best monographs of the persons already named (HASSE on Anselm, NEANDER on Bernard of Clairvaux, MARTENSEN on Dr. Eckart, etc.), the articles *Scholastische Theol. und Mystik* in Herzog, R.E. Also, A. PIERSON, *Diss. Theol. de Realismo et Nominalismo* (1854); C. ULLMANN, *Reformers before the Reformation*, Eng. Trans. On Wycliffe, DE RUEVER GRONEMAN, *Diss. Theol.* (1837); *and further*, R. VAUGHAN, *Life of Wycliffe*, 2 vols. (1831); and especially G. V. LECHLER, *Joh. v. Wiclif und die Vorgeschichte der Reformation*, 2 vols. (1873). On Bonaventura as a Dogmatist, an essay of HOLLENBERG in *Theol. Stud. u. Kritik* (1868).

POINTS FOR INQUIRY.

What was the cause of the increasing decay in Dogmatics in the East after John of Damascus?—Plato and Aristotle in their relation to the treatment of dogma.—Importance of Anselm in this sphere.—The conflict between Realism and Nominalism—Mysticism in its various evolutions.—The attempts to reconcile Scholasticism and Mysticism—The relative gains and losses of Dogmatics at the end of this period, in comparison with the former.—Necessity of Reform, even in this respect, ever more clearly recognised.

SECTION XIII.—REFORMATION.

Prepared by the better tendencies and the courageous witnesses (to the faith) of earlier times, the reformation of doctrine by and in consequence of the Reformation of the Church in the sixteenth century has been both many-sided and salutary. The founders of the Reformed, as well as of the Lutheran Church, were at the same time their first dogmatists, often in this domain also imitated, but never surpassed, by their fellow-believers and followers. Even the opposition, which the Reformation excited has had a partially favourable influence on the development of Dogmatics. The gain would have been still greater, had not this development been only too quickly hindered by the mutual divisions of the Protestants and the degeneration of the spirit of the Reformation.

1. The Reformation has purified, not only the Christian faith itself, but also its doctrine. It gave to Dogmatics a freedom, stability, simplicity, and fertility, such as it had never known under the iron sceptre of Scholasticism. We meet with countless traces of this fourfold blessing, whether we cast our glance on the Lutheran, Reformed, or even on the Romish Church.

2. The services which Luther has rendered to the doctrine of faith are beyond value, both by means of his opposition to Scholasticism and by his advocacy of the utterly neglected truth of justification by faith. Attempts have been made to construct out of his numerous writings of different periods a kind of dogmatic edifice, by arranging in certain order his utterances concerning God, man, Christ, etc., and we may also learn his own belief from his two catechisms, as well as from the articles of Torgau and Smalkald which he has written; but still Luther was never the man to shine as a dogmatist properly so called. The father of the Dogmatics of his Church was Melancthon, whose *Loci Communes*, composed originally for his own use, first published in 1521, and then from time to time altered and enlarged, were published for the last time under his inspection in 1543. This is a book which, even before the death of its author, had been reprinted nearly eighty times in various editions, which Luther had declared to be deserving, not merely of immortality, but almost of a place in the canon; and which, in the subsequent alterations of its contents, may be called the very mirror of the dogmatic progress experienced by the author himself. Like the Heidelberg Catechism afterwards, it proceeded, not from theological, but from anthropological principles, and in various ways exhibited an eminently practical character. Its contents are at the same time dogmatic and ethical; its demonstration biblical; its type of doctrine in some degree a middle link between the purely Lutheran and the strict Calvinistic teaching. For almost an entire century these *Loci* served as the basis and model of the dogmatic teaching of the Lutheran Church. They were commented upon by Victorinus Strigil († 1569); Nic. Seilnecker († 1592), who first added the so-called Prolegomena to the Dogmatics of the Lutheran Church; and specially by the most renowned dogmatist of this circle, Martin Chemnitz, whose lectures on the *Loci* were published by his pupil and successor, P. Leyser, after the death of his master († 1586).

3. On the field of the Swiss Reformation a fresh dogmatic life is quickly seen. The essay of Zwingle, *De verâ et falsâ Religione* (1525), may be pointed out as a first revelation of this, the more because it, when compared with the *Loci*, makes the peculiarity of the Reformed conception and study of doctrine already evident. In this respect also his *Christ. fidei brevis et clara expositio* (1536) is of importance. His renown was, however, far overshadowed by Calvin's *Institutio Rel. Chr.*, a work of like influence on contemporaries and posterity with the *Loci* of Melancthon, but formally and materially of much higher literary and theological value. The first edition (1536), called by the writer himself a "breve dumtaxat Enchiridion," consisted of only six chapters, the second of seventeen, while the last, which was revised by the Reformer himself (1559), had mounted to eighty chapters. The three principles of the Apostolic Confession are treated in

the first three books, while in the fourth the doctrine of the Church and the sacraments is discussed. No dry analysis is able to give a worthy idea of this book, now much more praised than read. Prefaced by the renowned letter of apology to Francis I., "a vestibule worthy its stately edifice," it points to the knowledge of God as the key to the sanctuary of eternal truth. While strictly systematic in its plan, it is thoroughly practical in spirit, the expression of the author's personal belief, and entirely founded on Holy Scripture, explained most strikingly by the exegete Calvin. The idea of an independent and unchangeable decree of God rules over every theory, accompanied by the deep feeling of the complete damnability of sin, whilst the writer quails not for a moment before the consequence of any of these tenets. And this leading idea is developed, not in a scholastic, but in a thoroughly practical manner, in a style captivating, scientific, thoroughly theological, and in every way human. No wonder that under such influences the Dogmatics of the Reformed Church obtained a preponderating Calvinistic character. With a single exception,—Peter Martyr Vermilius of Florence, originally a Roman Catholic, who died as Professor of Theology at Zurich, whose *Loci Comm. Theol.* bear evidence of a Zwinglian tendency,—this character appears in the dogmatical writings of Bullinger, Wolfg. Musculus Benj., Aretius († 1574), W. Bucer, G. Hyperius († 1564), P. Ramus († 1572), specially, too, in Beza († 1605), in his *Brevis Explicatio totius Christianismi*, which gives a thoroughly abstract and almost mathematical tabulated representation of Calvin's doctrine of predestination, and not last in the Heidelberg Catechism, though here it has a thoroughly practical tendency. Its co-redactor, Olevianus, published afterwards a short epitome of Calvin's *Institutio*, and J. Piscator collected its chief doctrines into short propositions.

4. Both the Lutheran and Reformed Dogmatics of this time, though in a varying degree, deserve the eulogy, "The subtleties of Scholasticism fade before the seriousness of life and the simplicity of the Scripture" (Hase). In learning the first Reformed Dogmatics unmistakably excels the Lutheran; the latter, on the contrary, has more freshness and biblical simplicity. Both take their stand on Holy Scripture, but the Reformed is still more independent of tradition than the Lutheran. Both wage war against anti-Christian principles, the Lutheran against Judaistic hypocrisy, the Reformed against pagan deification of the creature. Both glorify the grace of God; but at Wittenberg the question, How are we saved? at Geneva, Who is the Saviour? stands in the foreground of investigation. In the Lutheran there speaks the joy, in the Reformed the earnestness of belief; the former is more a matter of the Church, the latter of the school. Both within their circle excite sympathy, without it they call forth reaction.

5. The Reformation has had a good effect on the dogmatic life even in the Romish Church. We can here, after the declarations of the Council of Trent (1545—1563), scarcely speak of a proper development of doctrine, yet even here we see something more than a dead uniformity. "The Reformation has gradually delivered the Romish Church from the dominion of the Romish Curia, and the contact with the Evangelic Church has furthered scientific investigations; it has destroyed much which would have remained without the Reformation, and called into life much which (without

it) would never have existed" (Ellendorf). It may be enough to mention the Dominican Melchior Canus († 1660), who in *XII Libri Loc. Theol.*, combated the scholastic method of the Jesuits. Among the dogmatists of this latter order we must specially mention Peter Canisius, Alphonse Salmeron, J. Maldonatus, Frans. Suarez, Gabriel Vasquez, Martin Becan, and others, and specially Cardinal Bellarmine († 1621), "la meilleure plume de son temps en matière de controverse" (Bayle), who defended the Romish dogma with so much acuteness, and at the same time with so much moderation, that he was opposed, not only by Protestants, but even by Romanists. But above all, while anticipating a later period, we mention here the eagle of Meaux, the brilliant J. B. Bossuet († 1704), whose renown throws all others into the shade, just as his influence surpassed that of others, as much by the talent with which he idealised Catholicism in his *Exposition de la Doctrine de l'Egl. Cath.* (1672), as by the tact with which he, in his *Histoire des variations de l'Egl. Protest.*, brought to light the weak points of his opponents.

6. The sects and heresies which appear during this century have been of as little benefit to the normal development of dogmatic science as to the progress of the Evangelical Church. Among the Anabaptists and their supporters we cannot speak of scientific life; and even for Servetus we can hardly claim a place among dogmatists, properly so called. The anti-trinitarian tendency of this epoch appears first in its full extent in the works of the Socinian theologians, collected in the *Bibliotheca fratrum Polonorum* (1656). Besides this, the catechism of Racov (1609), and the *Summa Rel. Chr.* (1611) of F. Socinus, is the best known source of a tendency which has afterwards, without injustice, been called the common cradle of the later Rationalism and Supranaturalism. It represents the reaction, not so much of the conscience as of the so-called sound reason against Rome, but also against the mystery of Christianity itself. The praise which the Socinian dogmatists and their allies claimed for themselves, that they had been true sons of the Reformers, and continuers of their work, cannot possibly be granted to them by an impartial criticism. But even those who can agree neither with their principles nor with their results, must acknowledge that they resisted Scholasticism with all their might, furthered the independence of Christian dogmatic investigation, and led theologians of the Church to a by no means superfluous criticism of their tenets, as well as of the proofs thereof.

7. When we thus, at the end of the period of the Reformation, draw our comparison with the preceding time, we observe unmistakable progress. Dogmatics is studied with a restless energy, not only more, but better than before. In the Reformed Church especially the influence of a better exegesis is felt; and even where the strife gradually becomes more violent, irenical endeavours are not wanting. We call to mind here, among others, our renowned countryman, Francis Junius († 1602) who not only published *Theses* of importance, but also an essay, *De verâ Theologiâ*, and an *Irenicon;* and the German Theologian of Peace, Rupert Melden, to whom we owe the well-known proverb, "*In necessariis unitas*," etc.;[2] and specially

[2] Compare as to him, Lücke's Monograph.

the ornament of the University of Helmstadt, G. Calixtus (1634), who, inspired by a spirit of real Christian moderation, did not even dread the reproach of syncretism, if he might only prepare the way for a union of the divided churches. A century after the first publication of the *Loci* of Melancthon, J. Gerhard († 1637) brought to an end his complete elaboration of the legacy of the Reformer, in a manner which showed great acuteness joined with comparative moderation. Yet this spirit became constantly more rare, in opposition to the increasing hatred of religion which was dividing the sons of the Reformation. The age of confessions was followed by that of compendiums; the energy and freshness of belief by a renewed Scholasticism; and in place of the former over-rating of works, the over-rating of knowledge begins now most powerfully to make its influence felt.

Compare W. GASZ, *Gesch. der Protest. Dogm.*, i. (1854), ii. (1857), iii. (1862), iv. (1867); J. A. DORNER, *Gesch. der Protest. Theol.* (1867); I. KÖSTLIN, *Luth. Theol. in ihrer Geschichtl. Entwick.* ii. vol. (1863); S. CRAMER, *Zwingli's leer van het Godsd. gel.* (1864). For CALVIN'S *Institutio*, the compact edition of A. THOLUCK, and the Eng. Ed. of Calvin Translation Society, 3 vols., (Edin. 1845, 1846); and also an important essay of J. KÖSTLIN in the *Theol. Stud. u. Krit.*, 1868, i.; on the Romanist Dogmatics of this and the preceding age, F. A. STAUDENMAIER, *Die Christl. Dogmatik*, i. (1844), p. 201, *sqq.*; A. HERRLINGER, *Studien über die Theologie Melancthon's* in the *Jahrbuch für Deutsch. Theol.* (1870), iii., 303, *sqq.*

POINTS FOR INQUIRY.

Further elucidation of the influence of the Reformation on Dogmatics.—The reason why Melancthon, and not Luther, is the dogmatist of the Church; and the differences which are generally discovered between the earlier and later editions of the *Loci.*—The Institutes of Calvin; their history and import.—The influence of the Reformation on the study of Dogmatics in the Romish Church.—History and criticism of Socinian Dogmatics.—Reaction of newly awakened dogmatism.

SECTION XIV.—DEGENERATION.

The development of Dogmatics in the seventeenth and eighteenth centuries has, on the whole, only imperfectly corresponded to that which the heroic age of the Reformation had given reasonable ground to expect. Under the varying influences, first of Scholasticism, then of Rationalism, and occasionally of Mysticism in its various forms, that development can neither proceed prosperously nor lead to satisfactory results. The Christian-philosophic investigation of truth at the commencement of this epoch is hindered by theological dogmatism; at its close is led away into many an erroneous path by philosophic criticism. In the study of Christian Dogmatics, too, within and without the Reformed Churches, in the Netherlands as well as everywhere else, the continually increasing degeneration of the original spirit of Christianity and of the Reformation is clearly seen; not without the counterbalancing influence of some eminent men of a true reforming spirit, who, coming out as healers of a period of disease, prove themselves at the same time the prophets of a better epoch.

1. The history of Dogmatics is like a stream, becoming ever wider. It is not possible, nor is it absolutely necessary, to mention all the names and tendencies. It is sufficient to observe the most important phenomena which occur between the Reformation and the commencement of the present century. And then it can be scarcely doubted that "Degeneration" is the best name for a period which answered but too little to that which the sixteenth century had promised, degeneration, of course, in the relative, and not in the absolute, sense of the word, accompanied with not a little which is good and gladdening, and not without the intermittent appearance of phenomena which in many respects may be called "signs of life." And yet only too often there is a state of things which reminds one of a cloudy noon after a bright morning, and which strikes us again and again, as we look on the varying influence of Scholasticism, Rationalism, and Mysticism.

2. Scholasticism took its rise in the Lutheran Church from the one-sided attempts to preserve untainted and to hand over to posterity the entrusted pledge of a "pure doctrine." Gradually Melancthon is suspected, and Luther left behind. Ecclesiastical system is tightened into a logico-formalistic corset, and every new dispute elicits more subtle definitions. The subject-matter of doctrine, formerly synthetically presented, is now analytically deduced by the definitive and causal method, and an increasing schematism promotes dogmatic clearness, but also—sophistry. Three names may here suffice,—Leonard Hutter, professor at Heidelberg, and a pillar of Lutheran orthodoxy, who, at the command of Christian II. of Saxony, wrote a dogmatic compendium (1610), defended the *Formula Concordiæ* in its entirety, and reproached Melancthon with his "defectio a puritate doctrinæ cœlestis;" A. Calovius († 1686), the opponent of Calixtus, whose morning prayer was, "Domine imple me odio hæreticorum;" and J. A. Quenstadt († 1688), whose *Theologia Polemica* has exercised so important an influence on the dogmatical life of his own and succeeding times, that he has not incorrectly been called "Buchhalter und Schriftführer seiner Genossen." (Tholuck.)

3. In the Reformed Church, too, we see, partly even prior to, but specially after, the triumph of orthodoxy at the Synod of Dordt (1618), Scholasticism find its representatives in dogmatists such as Keckerman at Heidelberg († 1609); Wolleb at Basle († 1629); H. Alting († 1644), and Maresius

at Groningen († 1673); Maccovius at Franeker († 1644); but particularly Gilbert Voetius, chosen Professor at Utrecht in 1634 († 1676), whose influence on the Dogmatics of the Netherlandish Reformed Church was akin to that of Quenstadt on the Lutheran, a violent opponent of Des Cartes and Coccejus, but not less opposed to the Labadists and corrupt Mystics; a man of piety, acuteness, and learning, of restless activity, and great influence,—both loved and hated as few men have been. In his *Selectæ Disputt.*, v. vols. (1648), especially, he has handed down the results of his own investigation, and, among others, has left in William a Brakel, the renowned author of *Reasonable Theology* († 1711), a distinguished disciple and fellow-thinker. In this school exegesis served merely for Dogmatics, as this in its turn was made serviceable to a closer definition and stricter defence of orthodoxy even in the most unimportant particulars. On the opposite side, in John Coccejus, professor at Leyden († 1669), we observe a powerful effort to set Dogmatics free from the yoke of Scholasticism, and to establish it upon a pure biblical basis. His Federal method sought to combine the whole doctrine of faith within the compass of God's covenant with man, in which we find the key to all His words and works. A firm supporter of the mechanical theory of inspiration, he nevertheless, in the domain of typical and prophetical Theology, was only too often involved in ingenious subtleties, and too much lost sight of the distinction between the Old and New Testaments; but still he gave a powerful impulse to a movement which in many respects might be called one of progress. His *Summa Doctrinæ* (1648), for which no publisher could at first be found, soon became the text-book of a school, which not only in the Netherlands, but in Germany too, found distinguished supporters and imitators (Puffendorf, Jäger, and others), and which for some time divided the Netherlands Church into two violently conflicting parties. Cocceianism was partly developed, partly simplified and amended, by A. Heidanus, at Leyden († 1678), F. Burman († 1679), and M. Leidecker († 1721), at Utrecht, who made the doctrine of the Trinity the basis of his dogmatic investigation, and some others. Among the most distinguished and at the same time thoroughly independent theologians of this period must be specially enumerated F. A. Lampe († 1729). As little Cocceian as Voetian, he forms, as it were, the connecting link with that catalogue of properly biblical theologians, at whose head is so justly placed the name of Hermann Witsius († 1708), named in the same breath with those of the two Vitringas and Venema.

4. A completely different path was trodden by the Reformed theologians of the University of Saumur. They were distinguished by an attempt towards a more moderate conception of the churchly idea of predestination, towards a more exegetical method, and towards a closer union of Dogmatics and Ethics. In the footsteps of Cameron († 1629) we see the so-called hypothetic universalism defended by his pupil and fellow-thinker, Moses Amyraut († 1646), with the not unnatural consequence that Determinism lost not only somewhat of its harshness, but also of its rigid consistency. No wonder that the systematic Calvinists first suspected and then opposed him and his pupils, Ludov. Capellus and J. de la Place. This opposition was made by Rivet († 1651) and Fr. Spanheim († 1701), and particularly by the learned and acute J. H. Heidecker at Zurich († 1698), the compiler of

the *Formula Consensus*, directed specially against the professors at Saumur, but only accepted by a few Swiss cantons for a short time. The teaching of Amyraut was independently continued by his pupil, Claude Payon († 1665), while P. Durieu († 1713) resisted it with powerful effect. The Swiss orthodoxy, on the other hand, after it had spoken its last word in acknowledging the inspiration even of the Hebrew vowel points, was followed by the prevalence of a more moderate tendency, specially represented in a fitting manner by Bened. Pictet († 1724), J. A. Turretine († 1737) [a son of the ultra-orthodox Franc. Turret.], and Sam. Werenfels († 1740).

5. We find at this period the study of Dogmatics carried on by the Arminians from their standpoint with much zeal and skill. Among the dogmatists of this school stand out in particular Episcopius († 1643), Curcellaeus († 1659), and Philip of Limborch († 1714), whose Theology has not incorrectly gained the renown of being biblical, irenical, and practical. We see these men, while relatively free from Scholasticism, tread a more exegetical path, guided by the light of Hugo Grotius, their most distinguished apologist and commentator. Even where we cannot admit their premises, we can hardly deny that their method is far superior to that of many of their contemporaries. We must at least call it unjust to name them, as has often been done, in the same breath with the Socinians, though we cannot deny that at least their later representatives have been also the forerunners of Rationalism.

6. There is but little to call for remark in the history of Dogmatics in England during this period. The Scotchman, R. Barclay († 1676), gave to the doctrines of the Quakers, as far as that could be done, scientific form and symbolic expression.—The dogmatic life in the Romish Church felt constantly the influence of Scholasticism and Jesuitism, opposed by Jansenists rather in a practico-ascetic, than in a strictly philosophic form.—In the Greek Church, attempts to sow there the seed of the Reformation proved ineffectual. We see a more free and crypto-Calvinistic teaching reverenced by the patriarch Cyril Lucaris († 1638), but at the cost of his life, and that afterwards (1642) prepared as a confession of faith for the Russians by the Metropolitan Peter Mogilas, and sanctioned in 1672 by the Synod of Jerusalem, favoured far more the principle of stability than the striving after progress.

7. A powerful reaction against Scholasticism was specially urged on in Germany by the Pietistic School. Even before this, Joh. Val. Andreæ († 1654) had with deep earnestness waged war against a dead orthodoxy, while Spener († 1705) with increasing force had proclaimed the absolute necessity of a *theologia regenitorum*. Against the dead objectivity of ecclesiastical doctrine he asserted and maintained the right of a Christian subjectivity, and exalted above the so-called official theology the prayerful study of Holy Scripture. Though his care was infinitely less about the doctrine than about the life, he yet attempted, specially in the domain of Eschatology, partially to fill in that which in his view was wanting in the Dogmatics of Luther. His views on the Millennium were afterwards systematically worked out by two of his followers, Petersen and Dippel. In this respect his work was specially continued by A. H. Francke († 1727), who pointed out to his disciples the energetic and practical way as the most excellent. In the violent contest between Pietism and Scholasticism, self-defence soon

became for the latter an object of duty and importance. This contest was principally carried on by Bened. Carpzov (†1699), and the reaction which was thus elicited made the Pietists even still more one-sided in many of their views. Many of the accusations on both sides rested without doubt on misunderstandings; but that Pietism had both aroused and strengthened in many minds the repugnance to Scholasticism is evident from the writings of D. Hollaz (†1713), who was not incorrectly called "the last orthodox dogmatist of the Lutheran Church of his time," and who had accepted not a little which was good from his opponents. Pietism has exercised great influence, just because it has been externally subdued.

8. The dogmatic development of this epoch was not less unfavourably influenced by Rationalism than by Scholasticism; of course not without many a bright light showing itself amid the increasing darkness. In Würtemberg in the eighteenth century a biblical theosophic tendency appears in men such as J. A. Bengel (†1752) and his fellow-thinker, J. C. Oetinger (†1782), who considered life as not only the fruit, but also as the starting-point and basis of doctrine. A more independent historical direction was broached at Jena by J. F. Buddeus (†1729), who grants to the history of dogma more influence than had ever before been allowed to it. J. A. Ernesti (†1781) works at Leipzig in a certain degree favourably, since he insists on an accurate exegetical investigation of the so-called *dicta probantia*, and submits some ecclesiastical dogmas to exegetic criticism with a good result. His fellow-thinker in the domain of the Old Testament at Göttingen, J. D. Michaelis (†1760), deserves even as a dogmatist the name of being relatively conservative. Yet in him especially we see newer ideas coming forth, jointly with the old, which preluded important revolutions in the world of doctrine.

9. In this period, more than in former years, Dogmatics begins to feel the varying influence of the different philosophic schools. Like the school of Des Cartes in Holland (B. Bekker, † 1695), so did that of Wolf and Leibnitz, in Germany, make its powerful influence felt on the students of Christian doctrine. Among the theologians of the school of Wolf, Bernsau (†1763), Stapfer (†1775), Dan. Wyttenbach (†1779), J. C. Beck (†1785), and S. Endemann (†1789), deserve particular mention. In its origin certainly this school was not hostile to Christianity; its first followers were orthodox; the renowned S. J. Baumgarten (†1757) saw 300 or 400 listeners standing round his chair, and was a rigid conservative. The new method seemed even to be able to demonstrate the truth of dogma so clearly, that nothing more could be offered in opposition to it. But the very striving after accuracy of idea and definition forced in an intellectualism, by which truth was more and more separated from life. Natural theology is first placed as an independent science alongside of revealed, at whose expense it is soon exalted and developed. Philosophy, formerly regarded as the humble handmaid of Theology, is now honoured and obeyed as a queen; reason is recognised as the supreme judge in the realm of truth, and independence as to doctrine is succeeded by indifference, and by-and-by by repugnance. It is here as impossible to give an outline of the gradual development of Rationalism as of the earlier Deism, but when we require a representative name to which we can best

join a review of this period, not one strikes us more than that of J. S. Semler († 1791), the man who, "though he did not found a school, yet brought with him the fire, from which the sparks were to rise which might fall upon the powder lying everywhere ready at hand." A theologian of conscientious mind and of astounding reading, but at the same time of a restless spirit, seizing with a revolutionary hand on almost every field of thought, and with an eye rather for ever-varying forms, than a heart for the spirit and essence of Christianity. Among the "little Judaic local ideas" of the New Testament, above which he considers he must raise himself, he brings, *e.g.*, the idea of the kingdom of God, and hesitates not to assert that Jesus and His apostles, though they knew better, constantly accommodated themselves to the mistaken ideas of their contemporaries. Owing to the influence of Semler, the distinction between Church and Bible doctrine became constantly more an irreconcilable opposition; while from the last everything was rejected which was not sufficiently enlightened for the heroes of "Enlightenment." The ecclesiastical system, of which even a Lessing († 1781) had spoken with undisguised respect, is treated with increasing disrespect, as "a confused work of blockheads and semi-philosophers," and under the influence of the last-named thinker a sharp distinction is made between purely historical and so-called religious truth, which could but work in a most thoroughly injurious manner for the development of doctrine so much desired. The historical basis of the entire doctrinal system is soon audaciously attacked (*Wolfenb. Fragm.*); periodical literature for years together is given up to the systematic service of unbelief (*Allgem. Deutsche National Biblioth. of Nicolai*); and the frivolous spirit of the times, which spread from Paris to the Court at Berlin, as well as to other places, declares with ever-increasing force war against the severity of the Gospel. In place of the earlier yearning for system, we see now Indifferentism and Utilitarianism. Steinbart († 1809), from his standpoint of the happiness of mankind, praises Christianity as the best teaching in this respect for the needs of his enlightened fellow-countrymen, but at the same time teaches "that Augustine, on account of his ignorance in religion, was not worthy of a place in the Church or in its history." The whole science of Dogmatics is reduced to a popular philosophy of religion, in which the substance of the Gospel was utterly lost. A Christian ought, above all, to be "a rational worshipper of God;" his motto was, "Culture for time and eternity by the aid of religion," and the really sound reason was the supreme authority in the most subtle questions respecting life. As heroes, and partly as victims of this teaching, we may mention A. S. Reimarus († 1761), K. F. Bahrdt († 1792), J. A. Eberhard († 1809). In opposition to these bold attacks, the modest resistance of the "chilled orthodoxy" offered by Zachariä († 1777), Stosch († 1781), Mursinna († 1795), and others, had no preponderating weight, however much we may admire the attempts at more biblical simplicity. Apologetics was now more carefully and zealously studied than Dogmatics; in England, by Lardner, Addison, Newton, Berkeley, and others; in Germany, by Haller, Leo, Nösselt, Lilienthal, and others.

10. Rationalism begins to exhibit a more fitting and scientific character in the treatment of Dogmatics through the labours of Kant († 1804) and

his followers. By means of a strict criticism of man's capacity for knowledge, he showed the impossibility of such an accurate demonstration of God and divine things as the school of Wolf had arrived at. But he attempted to restore by another method that which he had thus lost and demolished; for practical reason continued to postulate virtue, and its reward by a righteous God in a better life than this. Thus, finally, the whole of theology was reduced to the well-known trilogy of God, virtue, and immortality. The Gospel now became the highest moral law; Christ the spotless ideal, and thus far the Son of God; and the Church the efficient means of maintaining moral order. Not many Dogmatists, however, have been pure Kantians. The most distinguished were Tieftrunk († 1837) Von Ammon († 1849), and for a time Stäudlin († 1826). These are the most worthy representatives of a school which recognised the individual reason as the highest authority in the realm of truth, and therefore submitted to its supremacy the subject-matter of Christian revelation.—Very quickly, however, we see this standpoint succeeded by the so-called "Common Rationalism," which found its supreme arbiter in the (unreasonable) reason, denied the necessity of higher revelation and redemption, and reduced the entire doctrine of revelation to that of mere providence. At first its interpreters addicted themselves to the method and results of critical philosophy, but they did not always retain the severely moral fervour of their Master. Here we must note the names and writings of Henke († 1809), Eckerman († 1836), and Schmid († 1812), but more particularly the still better known J. F. Röhr († 1848), the influential writer of Letters concerning Rationalism (1813), and H. E. G. Paulus († 1851), of Heidelberg, the supporter of the (un)natural explanation of sacred history, and J. A. L. Wegscheider († 1849), who had dedicated "*Piis manibus Lutheri*," his *Institutiones Theol. Dogm.*, in which every principle of the Gospel and of the Reformation was systematically denied. Notwithstanding differences in principles or accessories, all these men agreed in regarding Christianity only as the historical introduction or the providential confirmation of mere reasonable truth. Along with the idea of special revelation, that of miracle was now naturally given up; sin was henceforth called imperfection; redemption, enlightenment; faith, the conviction of reason: conversion became amendment, Christ a teacher of morality, the Church a school of discipline and development, baptism a form, the Lord's Supper a feast of brethren; whilst the hope of eternal life,—above all, that of individual immortality and a happy meeting again,—was not seldom depicted with sentimental pathos.

11. Against this Rationalism arose a Supranaturalism, which we must properly distinguish from the old orthodox Church faith. It recognised the necessity and reality of a particular revelation, given in the teaching of Christ, and specially confirmed by miracles and portents on the part of God. With this primal belief in revelation there was joined, however, the evident attempt to rub off as much as could be done from the sharp corners of revealed truth, and to recommend it specially on account of its tendency to practical value. The path for this teaching had been already opened by the *Institutiones* of Doederlein (1780), the *Epitome* of Morus (1787), and other essays; but it derived its importance from the names of

Storr († 1805), F. V. Reinhard († 1812), and the venerable Professor T. C. F. Steudel († 1837), at Tübingen. The *Vorlesungen* of the pious G. C. Knapp, published in 1827, may be partially brought under this section. Between it and its antipodes some, as may be expected, were not wanting, who wished to unite both, and who, on this account, received the name of rationalistic supranaturalists. To them belonged (with others) H. A. Schott († 1835), H. G. Tzschirner († 1828), and K. G. Bretschneider († 1848), author of a *Systematische Entwicklung*, etc., and of several other more popular dogmatic works, which have been translated and used in Holland, where also this school has been for many years represented by the *Godgeleerde Bydragen.*

12. When Rationalism was exhibiting such activity, it was impossible that Mysticism should be silent. In fact, it was felt during this period, as well in the bosom of the Romish Church as in that of the various divisions of the Evangelical. With regard to the Dogmatics of the Church of Rome, the Spanish priest, M. Molinos († 1690) must not be left unmentioned here, who set himself in opposition to the Jesuits, and caused the outbreak of the Quietistic disputes in France, where Fénélon († 1715), whose doctrine of pure love found a bitter antagonist in Bossuet, is the representative of Dogmatic mysticism in its noblest form. In Germany the mystic Angelus Silesius (properly Scheffler, † 1677) expressed similar thoughts in his *Cherubinischen Wandersmann*, in a manner which, in poetical forms, reminds us but too much of Pantheism.—In the Lutheran Church Mysticism was united with Theosopy and Asceticism, and not always held very closely to the doctrine of the Church. As in the former period Theophr. Paracelsus († 1541) and V. Weigel († 1588) had been influential, so in the present epoch did J. Böhme († 1620) exercise a powerful effect in this line of thought.—For some reasons, and failing a better place, we might mention here Count Zinzendorf († 1760), the ardent advocate of the mystic "theology of blood and wounds;" and E. Swedenborg († 1772), the founder of the Church of the New Jerusalem, in whom the hidden rationalistic character of the Theosophy is seen in a surprising degree. In the Reformed Church we see the principle of Mysticism brought over from the Romish, in the Netherlands, by Jean de la Badie († 1674) and his followers; in France, by P. Poiret († 1719), the disciple of Ant. Bourignon († 1680). It does not, however, exercise any preponderating influence on the course of Dogmatics, and the whole contest between Rationalism and Supranaturalism had had much more effect in the Lutheran than in the Reformed Church.

13. With particular regard to the Netherlands, we see the perceptible decline of orthodoxy during the course of the eighteenth century; whilst, though heresy on single points (H. A. Roell, † 1718) was felt, Dogmatics preserves its strong supranatural character. As a type of this teaching we may point to the *Institutiones* of B. Broes (1788), of Leyden, and specially to the *Pars. Theol. Chr. Theoretica* of H. Muntinghe of Groningen, first published in 1801, which, orthodox in principle, biblical in colouring, was not free from concessions which subjected its author to the suspicion of heresy. Stricter was the teaching which was represented at Utrecht by Gilb. Bonnet and Herm. Royaards, the former in a more philo-

sophical, the latter in a more exegetical manner; these were both for a while strongly opposed by their colleague, J. Heringa El. z. († 1840), who, at first declared heretical, and afterwards suspected as too narrow-minded, has all his life claimed the honour of being a biblical theologian. The only theologian of the Reformed Church of this period, by whom an actually rationalistic Dogmatics was taught in the schools and from the pulpit, is J. H. Regenbogen, author of the somewhat superficial *Christelijke Godgeleerdheid* published in 1811. This school of thought has found its most powerful support among the Baptist, Lutheran, and Remonstrant Theologians, as well as in the influence of political Liberalism and the spirit of revolution.

14. When we combine our survey into one general view, the result of our glance at this period cannot be as satisfactory as that of the former time. We must notwithstanding, in conclusion, not omit the few names which, hitherto unmentioned, have not only appeared with honour in their circle in this domain of thought, but have also been the prelude of a better future. Bl. Pascal († 1669), in France, obtained among the apologists of Christianity a place not merely honourable, but unique. In England, in the midst of all the methodistical onesidedness, we find the doctrine of free grace popularly but powerfully defended, specially by Whitefield († 1770). In Switzerland, J. C. Lavater († 1801), both from the pulpit and his writings, maintained the Christo-centrical character of doctrine with all the warth of a loving heart. In Germany, too—not to speak of the increasing influence exercised in part at least on our subject by men like Gellert, Klopstock, and Hamann—a man like J. G. Herder (†1803) has not lived and worked without effect on dogmatical study. The most special dogmatic ideas in his writings were collected by one of his friends in 1805. Neither rationalist nor supranaturalist, in the common sense of the word, he was, particularly in his first period, Christian humanitarian *par excellence*, who, on the one side, called out the spirit of free inquiry, but on the other, by means of his deeply religious spirit, offered to many of his contemporaries a beneficial antidote to the unbelief of some and the indifference of others. Although in many ways he is no longer at one with us, with him we may fittingly close this portion of our survey, since, while the light of his age, he at the same time is the herald of a new and in many respects better time.

Compare, beside the very important works of GASZ and DORNER, mentioned in section xiii., specially THOLUCK, *Vorgeschichte des Ration.* i. ii. (1853, 1861); *Geschichte des Ration.*, *Vermischte Schriften* (1839), pp. 1—147; on Voetius, J. J. VAN OOSTERZEE, article in Herzog, R. E. xviii.; on Coccejus, the *Theol. Diss.* of G. VAN GORKOM (1856), and A. VAN DER FLIER (1859); on Witsius, HERINGA (1861); on Vitringa, VAN HEEL, 1865; on Roell, VAN HOORN (1856); on A. Limborch, A. DES AM. V. D. HOEVEN, Jr. (1845); on Herder, VAN DIBBITS (1852), and the important monograph of A. WERNER, *Herder als Theolog. Ein Beitrag zur Geschichte der Protest. Theologie* (1871); on Pascal, WIJNMALEN (1865); on Lampe, the monograph of THELEMANN (1868); on Bengel, a *Vorlesung* of C. SEPP (1848); on the Netherlands Theology of the conclusion of this period, SEPP's prize essay (1863); H. BOUMAN, *De Godgeleerdheid en hare beoefenaars in Nederlandenz* (1862), p. 344, *sqq.*, and the literature so copiously quoted there.

POINTS FOR INQUIRY.

How best to explain the resurrection of Scholasticism in the Protestant Church?—The contest between Voetius and Coccejus.—Closer survey of the Theology of Saumur.—The collision between Orthodoxism and Pietism.—The reason why Rationalism has had so much more influence in the Lutheran than in the Reformed Church.—The degree of independent development in the Dogmatics of the Netherlands Reformed Church of the period.—Further elucidation of some special errors and morbid appearances.

SECTION XV.—REVIVAL.

A new era, even for Dogmatics, has dawned in our century, which has not incorrectly been called the century of the regeneration of Christian Theology. Instead of the earlier Rationalism and Supranaturalism, both of which were in their standpoint equally one-sided, a more exact and fruitful conception of the truth arose as life from God, historically revealed in Christ, and only learnt through the light of Scripture by individual spiritual experience. This school of thought in Dogmatics, starting from Germany, has made its influence felt in the various Churches of other countries, and has held its own with increasing clearness and firmness against the attacks of an unbelief becoming every day more devoid of shame. Enriched by the wisdom of the past, and purified by the ordeal of the present, science strives restlessly—although in countless windings and not without a strong reaction—towards a fairer future, in which, in even a greater degree than before, she can fulfil her undeniable requirements.

1. The title prefixed to this section is not meant to imply an unconditional eulogy, but simply to give evidence of the aroused scientific life of the present as definitely contrasted with the repose and decay of the preceding century. We do not, of course, in any way deny that this revival has not been accompanied by new retrogression and dangerous disease.

2. The name of F. Schleiermacher († 1834), the German Plato, is closely connected with the history of the revival of Dogmatics in Germany. In estimating this theologian, who is much more eulogised than read, men have not always kept within due bounds, and have ofttimes but too quickly conceded an eternal import to that which possesses great historical value. At any rate, the claim that every thorough dogmatic investigation must always take its beginning from Schleiermacher, is entirely one-sided, and will not readily be granted by him who has studied his *Christl. Glaubenslehre* (1st ed. 1821), carefully, and with the Gospel in his hand. Yet, on the other, it is impossible to deny that he has given to the scientific movements of his time "the impulse to an eternal motion," and, as another John the Baptist, may

be called a new forerunner of Christ. He has inspired with a fresh reverence for religion (*Reden über die Rel.*, 1st ed., 1799) a century numbed with the chill breath of Rationalism, and has recommended Christianity as a personal union of life with Christ, in whom he saw the highest ideal of humanity, the deliverer from the power of sin. Originally not free from Pantheism, he has gradually come nigher to a Christian Theism, and has secured for religion its immovable place in the inmost sanctuary of the human consciousness. The so often misunderstood, besides the so often disowned, cardinal principle of Reformed Dogmatics, man's unlimited dependence upon God in the work of salvation, has been again brought by him into reverence, though he has developed it in a peculiar manner; and the ethical character of revealed truth, though accompanied with a lamentable misconception of its historic side, has by him been emphatically brought to the front. We cannot be at all surprised that with the wealth of his spirit, and the many-sidedness of his influence, even his pupils and fellow-thinkers, who started from his principles, have constantly struck off into their own paths. This is true, especially of the (incomplete) *Dogmatik* of A. D. C. Twesten (i. ii., 1. 1 Ausg., 1826), who inclined more to an ecclesiastical orthodoxy; and of C. I. Nitszch († 1868), whose *System der Christl. Lehre* (1 Ausg., 1829) might be called a vigorous attempt to reunite Dogmatics and Ethics.

3. While Schleiermacher attempted generally to secure for Theology an independent place by the side of Philosophy, there were many others whose activity was inspired by the preponderating influence of a definite philosophic school. In connexion with the principles of Jacobi, as developed by Fries, we see Dogmatics studied by W. M. L. de Wette (†1849), a pious mind, of a critical spirit, with a tendency to Scepticism and Idealism (*Lehrb. d. Chr. Dogmat.*, 1 Ausg., 1816; *Wesen des Chr. Glaubens*, 1846); while it was treated by L. J. Rückert (*Christl. Philosophie*, 1825) in the spirit of the elder Fichte. We must call C. Daub († 1836), when we look at his *Theologumena* (1806) and other dogmatic writings, an independent thinker of the school of Schelling in his first period. Marheinecke (†1846), particularly in his *Dogmat. Vorlesungen* (1847), was the chief representative of Hegelianism in the field of Dogmatics. Many a follower of the speculative school of thought was misled, though in all good faith, with the idea that peace had now been concluded for good between belief and knowledge. It was asserted that Theology confessed the same truth in a formal presentment which Philosophy acknowledges in the higher sense of a philosophic conception. This self-deceit, however, could not last long, and soon the school of Hegel split up into two parties, of which the first clung to the faith, but daily lost in influence, whilst the other very soon preached an absolute separation between faith and knowledge as the highest wisdom; whilst both most arbitrarily mistook the history and the doctrine of Christianity. The names of D. F. Strauss (*Christl. Glaubensl.*, 1840, 1841., ii. Th.), Bruno Bauer, Feuerbach (†1872), and others, have acquired a sad celebrity, which renders further mention unnecessary. According to the blasphemy of the latter, we must seek the secret of Theology exclusively in the domain of Anthropology—in other words, religion becomes conjecture, self-worship a duty, and the emancipation of the flesh is equal to the highest

triumph of the spirit. It is no wonder, when such was the fruit of the tree, that the school of Hegel was the last speculative-philosophic school, which has exercised such preponderating influence on the Dogmatics of later times. T. A. Dorner, however, in his Christology, has shown in the most striking manner that even from the speculative standpoint it was possible to dedicate the most excellent gifts to the science of faith.

4. Without any definite accord with a philosophic school, Dogmatics in this period was studied in a free independent spirit by Theologians whose names must not be passed over in a survey such as this. We place them here together, though the teaching of the one shows a more eclectic, and that of the other a more conciliatory character. To these belong Carl Hase, professor at Jena, a theological character which could not easily be interchanged with any other. Genial, vigorous, æsthetic, full of sympathy for the historic side of Christianity, though in no ways emancipated from Rationalism, he has even in this domain sought and found his way independently of others. He enriched science with an *Evang. Dogmatik* (1 ed., 1826), a more popular *Gnosis* (1 ed., 1827), and a reproduction of the church system according to the necessities of our time in the *Hutterus Redivivus* (1 ed., 1833); in contrast to which we must place *Melancthon Redivivus*, an anonymous work in praise of the ideal spirit of Christianity, which could not, however, gain so much sympathy. In addition, though not as excelling his, must here be mentioned the dogmatic writings of Cramer (1829), Baungarten Crusius (1830), and F. F. Fleck (1846, I.), as well as the *Philosophische Dogmatik* (1855) of C. H. Weisse, composed in order to "harmonise" these different schools of thought. A less speculative, more rationalistic, and historico-critical character is exhibited in the *Institutio Theol. Dogm.* of Dr. C. W. D. Grimm (1848).—Among the Apologists of this period the place of honour is deserved by C. Ullmann († 1865), a Christian humanist and historian, to whom few are equal, for his excellent treatises on *Die Sündlosigkeit Jesu* (1 ed., 1828), and *Das Wesen des Christenth.* (1845, 1 ed.); and by A. Tholuck, more conservative in his teaching than Ullmann, but also still more many-sided, witty, and edifying, specially for his excellent works, *Die wahre Weihe des Zweiflers* (1 Aufl., 1823), and *Die Glaubwürdigk. d. Evang. Gesch.* (1 Aufl., 1836); while his friend and kindred thinker, J. Müller, has rendered excellent service to Dogmatics in his masterly treatise on the Christian Doctrine of Sin (1839).

5. A still more definite biblical character is seen in the Dogmatists whom we can regard as the continuers of the former supranaturalistic line, as A. Hahn (*Dogm.*, 1828), D. Böhmer (*Christl. Glaubenswissensch.*, 1840-43, ii. Th.). The second volume has special reference to the *Glaubenslehre* of Strauss. In Switzerland we see this school of thought worthily represented by J. L. S. Lutz (*Bibl. Dogm.*, 1847); in Würtemberg, by J. T. Beck, who develops the dogmatic subject-matter of Scripture from Scripture, whilst he tries to keep as far as possible free from philosophic and modern ideas, and allies himself with the earlier Biblical Realism of Bengel and Oetinger (*Christl. Lehrwissensch.*, i., ii., 1838, 1841). The more popular *Calwer Dogmatik* (iv. Th., 1854—1858) may also be brought into this class, as also to a certain extent the *Schriftbeweis* of J. C. K. von Hoffman (ii. Th.,

1857—1859); in any case a very remarkable attempt to justify the results of his own gnosis by an appeal to Holy Scripture.

6. In other countries also there was little want of a new treatment of Dogmatics from the ecclesiastical standpoint. On the side of the Lutheran this was done, in a strictly conservative tone, chiefly by F. A. Philippi (*Kirchl. Glaubensl.*, iv. Th., 1853, 1861), and G. Thomasius (*Christi Person und Werk*, iii. Th., 1853, 1861, Eng. Trans. T. and T. Clark), and more independently by C. F. A. Kahnis (*Luth. Dogm.* 3 vols., 1861, 1868); and specially in a brilliant and ingenious manner in Denmark by H. L. Martensen (*Christian Dogmatics*, Eng. Tr., 1866). Th. A. Liebner († 1871) wrote the first vol. of a *Christl. Dogmatik*, developed from the Christological principle (1849), as well as two *Programmata* as *Introductio in Dogm. Chr.* (1854-55). As a treatise of Dogmatics from the standpoint of the Moravians, the *Evang. Glaubenslehre nach Schrift und Erfahrung* of Herm. Plitt. (ii. Th., 1863-64) deserves the highest appreciation. The Reformed Dogmatics was extensively worked from its original sources, and reproduced by H. Heppe, Elberfeld (1861), after this had been before done more subjectively by A. Ebrard (1 Ausg., 1851-52), in violent opposition to the principles and results of Al. Schweitzer (*Die Glaubenslehre der Evangel. Reform. Kirche*, ii. Th., 1844-47, *Protestant. Centraldogmen*, ii. Th., 1854-56). Even the elaborate and original dogmatic work of J. P. Lange (iii. Th., 1849, 1852) started from the Reformed principles, whose subject-matter he attempts in an ingenious and clever manner to bring into unison with the results of later thought.

7. This last-mentioned name has unquestionably brought us back again to a freer Christian speculative region. The striving after a deeper conception of doctrine than seemed to be expressed in the letter of Scripture or of the Confessions, attempted as it was by some, could not fail to find an echo among others. The witty J. F. von Meyer († 1848) author, with other works, of the *Blätter für Höhere Wahrheit* (1830, 1832), found a distinguished pupil in Rud. Stier († 1867), "the Theologian of the believing conception of Scripture" (Hase), who, though he himself wrote no Dogmatics, has yet in more than one instance had an important influence upon its study. We may say the same, but with more right, of the amiable and profound theosoph, R. Rothe († 1868), who by his *Ethics*, as well as by his *Zur Dogmatik* (edn. pub. 1863), and by his *Dogmatik* (i. ii. edited by Schenkel, 1869, 1870), has deserved the eulogium formerly bestowed by Cajetan on Luther, " Habet profundos oculos et mirabiles speculationes in capite suo." The (still unfinished) essay of Ph. F. Keerl, *Der Mensch das Ebenbild Gottes* (Basel, ii. Th., 1861, 1866) cannot be better placed than in this class. The theosophical school of thought, viewed generally, finds a powerful supporter in the philosophical principles of Fr. von Baader († 1841), whose *Vorlesungen über speculative Dogmatik* were published much earlier, in 1828, but whose ideas first began to work with influence after his death. Among the theosophistic apologists, the name of the too early dead C. A. Auberlen († 1864) deserves to be remembered with respect, specially for his excellent but unfinished apologetical essay, *Die Göttl. Offenbarung.*

8. If the theosophistic Dogmatics cannot always escape the reproach

that it wishes to be wise beyond that which is written, the philosophic Dogmatics has been studied by the representatives of modern consciousness in a spirit more or less directly opposed to biblical. The most complete essay on this side was written by Dr. Schenkel, who formerly inclined to a conservative and believing school of thought, afterwards composed *Die Christl. Dogm. vom Standpunkt des Gewissens aus* (ii. Th. 1858, 1859), and, in opposition to Schleiermacher, sought to recommend conscience in place of feeling as the religious organ. In German Switzerland, H. Lang published in 1858 (2nd ed. 1863) a *Christl. Dogmatik,* in which Christology had ceased to occupy a separate place. Even the *Christl. Glaubenslehre* of A. Schweitzer (i. 1863, ii. 1, 2, 1869, 1872) appeared as the scientific expression of theological Modernism, and the *Chr. Dogmatik* of his colleague, A. E. Biedermann (1869), offered a scientific elaboration of the Church Dogma, which contradicted in a striking manner the impetuous cry of many of his own school of thought, "No more Dogmatics."

9. If we turn our eyes for a moment from Germany to Switzerland and France, we are met by some important analogies, but also by more than one unusual phenomenon. We must not here speak of any other before we mention the name of the man who has been not incorrectly called the Schleiermacher of his time, though his lucidity far surpasses Schleiermacher's profoundness,—A. Vinet (†1847), a personality of the highest import, particularly for Ethics, but also for Apologetics and Dogmatics. As little a Rationalist as a Mysticist, he was Individualist and Spiritualist in the noblest sense of the word. His peculiarity consists in this, that with a full recognition of the supranatural origin of revealed truth, and of the historical character of Christianity, he has laid a too long forgotten stress on its ethical as well as its metaphysical side. In opposition to the Theology of the former moderate supranaturalism on the one side (Chenevière and others), and that of the so-called "Réveil" on the other (Bost, Malan, Gaussen, and others), he supported not exactly a different conviction, but another method. While setting aside the mechanical conception of the authority of Scripture, for so many "le dogme des dogmes," he chose conscience for his starting-point, and attempted by a specially psychological method to bring down to and into men that which so many had considered as truth external to and above them. Such a man, a refined critic, and of a most elegant style, may be both an inestimable ally to the conservative school of thought, and also a forerunner of further freedom of thought, reverenced by the liberal-minded. This is now often the case, and the name of Vinet is not seldom inscribed on colours from which, if he could now lift his head, he would probably turn with aversion. The exaggeration of the principle of Scripture in his own immediate circle led the talented Edm. Scherer (*La Critique et la Foi, deux Lettres,* 1850) on a path which was constantly declining, and on which the name of Alex. Vinet was still only one of the first milestones. Even the new Strasburg school (whose organ is the *Revue de Théologie*), with T. Colani at its head, very quickly passed that mark; while in that of Montauban, where the formerly moderate Supranaturalism still found defenders most worthy of respect, among others, in P. Jalaguyer (*Le Principe Chrétien,* 1853, and other essays), the spirit of Vinet was effective for the development and maintenance

of Christian truth. As the organ of the most influential pupils and co-thinkers of Vinet, the *Revue Chrétienne* of Edm. de Pressensé, and its *Bulletin Théologique*, may be pointed out. In the meantime the modern supranaturalism pursues in France and Switzerland its severe contest with the naturalistic negation (Rénan, Réville, Cocquerel) which, as far as we can here still speak of Dogmatics, aims at its thorough reconstruction. But the names of Bersier, Godet, Astié, Naville, and others, justify the hope that even there the contest will not terminate without producing real fruit. Among the Apologists of Christianity against the modern Naturalism, as a soldier of the old guard, N. Poulain († 1868) has left an irreproachable and honourable remembrance.

10. In England and America the spirit of the older time wrestles still, with ever varying chances, against the spirit of the later period, under the undeniable influence of what is done in Germany and elsewhere. Among the literature of the latter country, Ch. Hodge, *Systematic Theology*, 3 vols. [reprinted, London, 1871–1873], is specially deserving of attention. In opposition to the apologetic tendency of former years a modern critical school of thought (*Essays and Reviews*, Colenso) has been developed; and eloquent interpreters of Unitarianism and Naturalism (Channing, Parker, and others) boldly raised their voices at the same time with the undaunted defenders of the old orthodoxy. As the organ of a free, believing, and at the same time scientific school, more than one magazine, but specially the *Contemporary Review*, 1866, gives a promise of much good in the future. Even the still waters of Denmark and Sweden were agitated, and—not to speak of J. P. Mynster—the name of Grundtvig, as well as the discussion between Martensen and Nielsen, proves that in Denmark at least no dead stability can be said to prevail.

11. In the Romish Church also during the present century the study of Dogmatics has not been suffered to rest. At times, under the influence of renowned philosophers (Hermes, Günther, v. Baader, and others), it found deserving students in Dobmeyer (1807), Brenner (1815), Klee († 1840), and Staudenmaier (*Christl. Dogmat.* iii. Th., 1844), and J. von Kuhn (*Kathol. Dogm.* i. ii., 1869). Among the best Apologists of our own time J. F. von Deey (*Apologetik* iii., BB. 1838—1847) specially deserves mention, whilst the "*Symbolik*" was treated by J. A. Möhler († 1838) in a manner which most justly gained for him the epitaph "Ecclesiæ Solamen." The reaction against the superficial German Catholicism has been, in its result, of advantage for the scientific life of this Church.—Far fewer signs of life in this respect are seen in the Greek (Russian) Church, which defended its Confession against the attacks of the Jesuits by the mouth of the Imperial Councillor, Alex. de Stourze, in 1816. Yet it possesses, among others, a more complete than attractive handbook of this science, written by the renowned Bishop Macarius, to which an extensive introduction is added, containing hints worth knowing concerning the theological literature of his country. (*Théologie Dogmat. Orthodoxe, par Macaire, etc., traduit par un Russe*, iii. vol., Paris, 1857—1861. Cf. W. Gass, *Symbolik der Gr. Kirche*, 1872.)

12. In the Netherlands, too, the later history of Dogmatics, while it by no means speaks of stagnation, cannot boast of quiet progress. In the first third of this century, the supranaturalistic biblical school, of which we have already spoken (§ xiv. 13), continued quietly to maintain its position

in a more scientific manner in the school of Heringa and J. van Voorst (*Comp. Theol. Chr.* 1st ed., 1808), and in a more popular form under the lead of L. Egeling (*De weg der Zaligheid*, 2 vol., 1 ed., 1820). The orthodox side was also scientifically advocated by the learned follower of Kant, J. J. le Roy (*De Godd. Openbar., d. B.* 2 DD. 1829, 1830). On the other hand, traces of more rationalistic sympathies appeared, *e.g.*, in the well-known essay of P. W. Brouwer (*Bybelleer aangaande den person van Christus*, 1826), and in that of P. van der Willigen concerning *Het wezen des Christendoms* (1 ed. 1836). The *Godgel. Bydragen* continued also, in the conflict about the binding authority of the Confessions, which was meanwhile becoming more vehement, to support the defenders of free thought. Whilst thus among many persons we find "indefiniteness and half-heartedness," a new phase was opened by the appearance of the Groningen school, which began in 1837 (and employs the magazine *Waarheid in Liefde* as its organ), and first published its *Compendium Dogmatices et Apologetices Christianæ* in 1845. In contradistinction from the previous one-sided estimation of Christian doctrine, the person of Christ was made by them the centre of their system, and increased stress was laid upon life in his communion. No wonder that this school found on one side eager supporters, and on the other frequent contradiction. In its conception of God it was Unitarian, in its Hamartology almost semi-Pelagian, in its Christology Arian-Apollinarian; its entire estimation of the Gospel had a more pædagogic than soteriological colouring, whilst its Demonology was wanting, and its Eschatology was concluded by the doctrine of the restitution of all things. It thus appeared to one to offer too little, to another to yield too much; but this must be said in its honour, that it only rejected that which it conceived could nowhere be learned from the Gospel of the Bible. It continued, not merely in its time of success, but even in after times, unchangeably firm in its historico-supranatural conception of the Gospel. And so little does it deserve the reproach of having been the forerunner of the modern Naturalism, that, on the contrary, it exhibits against it a developed and strongly apologetic character. The schools of Utrecht and Leyden, as well as that of Groningen, published each its dogmatic handbook; the first in the *Compendium Theol. Chr. Dogm.*, 1853, of H. E. Vinke († 1862), a pupil of Heringa, as well as of Van Heusde, a biblical, pacific, and practical theologian, *par excellence;* the other in the "*Initia Dogmatices Christianæ*" of J. H. Scholten (1 ed., 1854). Moreover, already in 1848 had the last-named theologian appeared with a work of much greater importance, "*De leer der Hervormde kerk in hare grondbeginselen uit de bronnen voorgesteld en beoordeeld,*" (ii. vols., 4 ed., 1861), which he afterwards partly supplemented in a monograph over "*De vrije Wil*" (1858). Seldom has the *habent sua fata libelli* been so fulfilled in any essay as in this; and it is perhaps not yet the time to point out its peculiar place in the history of science; its objective denotation may be sufficient here. While the Groningen school had shown a manifest inclination to Evangelical Catholicism, that of Leyden, on the contrary, sought to bring again into honour the Reformed Confession, after it had been purified and developed. According to the writer's own testimony, his book was "a criterion of the doctrine of the Church according to its own principles, which, without an absolute declaration of hostility, contained an attack upon existing theology in all its systems." Making a sharp distinction between principle and dogma, he represented this latter in a light which seemed to many utterly irreconcilable with the subject-matter and essence of their Evangelical and Ecclesiastical Confession. Hence it came to pass that he of necessity met with much resistance, even from the Theologians of other Churches. He himself, however, stood as little unmovable as the stream of time. He gradually drew nearer to the principles of the Empiric school, until at last he openly declared war with all Supranaturalism (1867). That it was not impossible, while treating Dogmatics in a scientific spirit, to arrive at different results, was meanwhile shown by the "*Bijdragen tot de verklaring, toetsing en ontwikkeling van de leer der Herv. Kerk*" of J. J. van Toorenenbergen (1865).—The "*Inleiding*" and "*Schets*" published by F. J. Domela Nieuwenhuis († 1869), gives evidence of the manner in which Dogmatics was studied in the Lutheran Church. The Dogmatics of the Teleio-Baptists were brought to light again in the "*Beginselen en leer der oude Doopsgezinden*," by S. Hoekstra Bz. (1863), who also came out as an independent student of Dogmatics, from an indeterministic standpoint, in the spirit of Modernism, but on idealistic principles, as we see in his *Bronnen en Grondslagen van het Godsdgeloof* (1864). It is plain, from the nature of the case, that the empirical tendency of philosophic investigation must in many respects operate with injurious effect on the study of Dogmatics. The dogma, that there certainly neither can nor ought to be any more Dogmatics, has become an axiom with many; yet not without men being even in this way compelled to admit a minimum of absolutely indispensable dogmas. A. Pierson, in his *Bespiegeling, Gezag, en Ervaring* (1855), has expressed what finally must remain as dogmatic principle and result according to this method; after Opzoomer had earlier given a sketch of Dogmatics, in the *Kunst en Letterb.* (1854, p. 295). The rupture of Empiricism with Church and Theology has, besides, after manifold misunderstandings, been so clearly manifested that the illusion of the modern school is confessed and lamented by almost everybody. Among others the Ethical school entered the lists against its naturalistic principles, specially by the mouth of its talented leader, D. Chantepie de la Saussaye. While it conceived of Dogmatics as "the description of the Christian life of the community which is necessarily one with the highest truth," it was most specially guided by its striving "to transfer Christianity from the purely religious into the moral sphere, or rather, to bring into prominence the moral side of the supranatural doctrine, and thus to make the doctrine become truth and life." Thus it attempted, though not in a manner clear enough to be well understood by all, to become for the Church and Theology of the Netherlands, what Vinet was for that of France and Switzerland.

Whilst the Ethical school does not without much hesitation accept the qualification of being supranaturalistic, the modern Supranaturalism on the other hand comes boldly forward, with the assurance that by the firm maintenance and application of its principles the salvation for Church and Science may be expected. From this standpoint, which is also that occupied by the writer of this book, Christianity is conceived as the fount of a supranatural revelation; Dogmatics consequently as the Doctrine of Salvation (not to be confounded with Ethics, as the Doctrine of Life), while the historical character of the Christian Religion is emphatically urged. This school calls itself *Supranaturalistic*, because it starts from the belief in a God, who is Lord over His own creation, and has revealed Himself in Jesus Christ in a mode which cannot possibly be explained as the merely natural result of merely material causes: and *Modern* Supranaturalistic, because it will not continue to stand immovably by the old, but strives to advance, in such wise that it (as distinguished from an earlier Supranaturalism) does not start from a deistic, but from a theistic conception of God; and places, not the doctrine, but the person of the Lord in the foreground, and wishes to do full justice to the ethical as well as the metaphysical and historical character of revealed truth. It wishes to be the science of belief, but specially one derived from God's revelation in Christ, as this is made known to us in the Gospel, and is confessed by the light of spiritual experience. It displays, while historico-philosophic in its nature, at the same time an apologetical and irenic character. With its roots in the past, it struggles with the present, and has its eye specially directed to the future. Whether it has itself a future in store, and what that future is to be, time alone can show.

Compare specially, in addition to the before-named writings of Gasz and Dorner, A. MUECKE, *Die Dogm. des 19. Jahrh.* (1867); C. SCHWARTZ, *Zur Gesch. der Neuesten Theol.* (1 ed.), 1856; PHIL. SCHAFF, *Germany, its Universities*, etc. (1858.)—As regards more special views, on Schleiermacher, Vinet, and other distinguished theologians, the articles in Herzog, R.E., and the literature quoted in them, as well as J. J. VAN OOSTERZEE, Essays on the *Glaubenslehre von Strauss*, in the *Godgel. Bijdr.* 1842, 1843; on that of Schweitzer, in the *Jahrbb.* of 1848; on De Wette and Scholten, in those of 1850; and on Martensen, in those of 1851.—On the Groningen school, P. HOFSTEDE DE GROOT, *De Gr. Godgeleerden in hunne eigenaardigheid*, 1855. On the Leyden school, the discussions of D. Chantepie de la Saussaye, Gorter, Douwes, and others. On Ethical Theology, J. F. ASTIÉ, *Les deux Theologies nouvelles* (1862), and the principal writings of La Saussaye. On the aim and efforts of the Modern Supranaturalism, J. J. VAN OOSTERZEE, *Oratio de Scepticismo, etc.* (1863). J. J. Doedes has furnished an important contribution to popular Dogmatics from this standpoint in *De leer der Zaligheid enz.* (1870), while J. H. Gunning, jun., has very cleverly done the same, from the principles of the Ethical school, in his *Blikken in de Openbaring* (1866, *sqq.*).

POINTS FOR INQUIRY.

Closer defining and criticism of Schleiermacher and his school.—Orthodoxy and Speculative Philosophy in apparent peace and increasing conflict.—The standpoint of the Eclectic and the Mediary Theologians.—The latest labours of Ecclesiastical Dogmatics.—The peculiarity exhibited by the Theology of the present time.—Modernism and Christian Dogmatics.—The tendency and influence of Vinet.—Lights and shadows of the Groningen school.—The Ethical Theology of the Netherlands.—Influence exercised by foreign Dogmatics on the Dogmatics of the Netherlands.

CHAPTER IV.

CLAIMS OF DOGMATICS.

SECTION XVI.—THE STARTING-POINT.

WHILE the history of Dogmatics attests the necessity of further investigation, that investigation itself wholly depends on its starting-point. No starting-point can, however, be the true one, which directly conflicts with the character and design of the science. Neither an unbridled Scepticism nor an inflexible Dogmatism offers it a trustworthy point of departure, but only the personal Christian belief in revelation, founded on Scripture and experience, and protected against every attack by a vigorous Apologetics. The determination of this principle defines at the same time the relation of Dogmatics to other non-theological sciences, and by that means marks off the boundaries of its own territory.

1. We reach the end of our historical researches with the conviction that Dogmatics has not yet by any means spoken its last utterance. But then comes the question, in what direction must it further move forth? Everything depends now upon our starting-point. The Δός μοι που στῶ thus becomes for us a question of the utmost importance. All research is guided by its premisses, and the stateliest building, if founded upon the sand, sinks into ruin.

2. It is hardly necessary to call to mind that the starting-point of any scientific investigation must not conflict with the nature of the science itself. He who considers all philosophy as a chimera can hardly study its history with a satisfactory result; he who thinks that there are no laws of beauty, cannot possibly compose a treatise on Æsthetics. And yet in the study of Christian Dogmatics this rule is so often forgotten, that it is imperatively necessary, when its claims are discussed, never to lose sight of what has been said in Chapter I. concerning its character.

3. If Dogmatics is a science of faith (§ 3), then can its starting not possibly be placed in an unbridled Scepticism. The dogmatist, as such, may and must have doubts concerning many things,—specially concerning the infallibility of himself, and others along with him,—and he who doubts honestly, and is seeking with diligence, may hope to attain to certainty; but the systematic doubt, whether it be of the existence, or of the possibility of knowing unseen and eternal things, can never be the *point de départ*, properly so called, of dogmatic investigation. Who will ever raise himself to the heights of spiritual contemplation when he has doubts either of the reality of the highest sphere or in the power of his own wings? No, "Dogmatics does not take its starting-point in doubt, which is often propounded as the requirement for philosophy. It is not developed from the emptiness of doubt, but from the fulness of belief. A consciousness starved by doubt has never yet been able to produce a Dogmatics." (Martensen.)

4. As little profit, on the other hand, can be expected from an inflexible Dogmatism, which clings spasmodically to that which has been handed down, and sets on one side the distinction between subjective conviction and objective truth. Such a Dogmatism as that which guided the Scholasticism of the middle ages and of the seventeenth century, renders renewed dogmatic investigation partly impossible and partly superfluous. In the form in which it is seen here and there in our own days, and scents the taint of heresy wherever the mere word "purification of doctrine" is uttered, it takes the part of confessional orthodoxy, but forsakes the Protestant character of science. When the only permissible reply on every point is fixed beforehand, the renewed question, "what is truth?" is deprived of all further serious meaning.

5. It is only from the force, constantly renewing itself, of personal faith and life that Dogmatics can develop in ever new forms. Where that principle is wanting, the ground for its study not only fails, but even the first element of the possibility of obtaining a successful result is missing. "They who are void of faith either interchange their varying conviction with historic faith, and unconsciously present their personal views, while they think they are giving a scientific expression to Christian doctrine, or they are thoroughly conscious themselves of this distinction, and their interest in the Christian Religion is thus merely historical." (J. Müller.)

6. The personal Christian belief in revelation, which we claim as the starting-point for Dogmatics, is by no means an unconditional assent of the reason, which has accepted the whole mass of Church doctrine at once, without understanding it; but a trust of the heart, as well in the existence and recognisability of an eternal truth, as in Him, in and through whom it has been made known by revelation. It recognises in that which with the greatest plainness and force is expressed as the immediate utterance of human consciousness, a fundamental truth, and builds upon it with caution. As such a fundamental truth it reckons, too, that which is the basis of all Religion and its philosophy; the existence, namely, of a higher world, a kingdom of light and of life, for which the heart yearns with its deepest aspirations. He who likens such a representation to a childish belief in spectres, may perhaps be rescued by more thorough psychological study,

but is meanwhile thoroughly unfitted for the study of Dogmatics, since he denies its *primum verum*.

7. In a still more definite sense must the personal life of the believer be the starting-point of Dogmatic investigation, and the *credo ut intelligam* has a deep significance. In the Christian domain the highest knowledge is born of spiritual life, as it, on its part again, must lead to real life. "He who loveth not hath not known God."[8] Without internal sympathy, real intelligence, especially in this domain of thought, is inconceivable; because the sphere of thought is that of life also. "Che ben ama, ben sa" (A. Conti). Of course this belief, on which we ground our inquiries, ought thoroughly to justify itself; but with the well-founded confidence that it will be able to do so, the undeniable right of the starting-point we mentioned may be most earnestly insisted on. Yes, the depth and clearness of knowledge will always rise or fall with that of the life of faith. "Just because Christian science is not merely a knowledge about Religion, but religious science; not merely a science of belief, but a believing science; just for that very reason faith and knowledge make up an organic unity, that is, science springs living from faith, as a confession, partial indeed and relative, but still always advancing." (Martensen.)

8. Dogmatics, starting on this principle, has no hostile relation to any other science, but remains free in its relation to all sciences. As for Natural Science, neither this nor the Science of Faith has yet spoken its last word, and the latter would not deserve its name if it had not learned to wait. There may be momentary contradiction between a certain special tendency of the two; but Nature and Revelation cannot possibly contradict one another,—nor do they do so. Where contradiction appears, the fault must lie hidden, either in the reasoning or in the observation. The Bible is not a handbook of Natural Science, and Natural Science has no answer for the questions to which the Bible replies; of both the "suum cuique" is true.—As for Philosophy—if that word is used in a subjective sense (*sapientiæ amor*)—then it is easily shown that it can proffer the most useful service for the exposition and maintenance of the doctrine of Faith, so that the true philosopher will also be the best dogmatist. If, on the other hand, we speak of Philosophy in an objective sense to denote a definite speculative philosophic system, then the relation between it and Dogmatics will naturally depend upon the peculiarity of the philosophic principles. A naturalistic or pantheistic philosophy cannot possibly proffer to Dogmatics aught but a Judas kiss; while the contrary may be easily true of a theistic or spiritualistic school of philosophy. No theologian will look upon the results of thoroughly scientific thought with disdain, and a theologian of the Reformed Church especially will never for a moment hesitate to repeat the words of Calvin, "Philosophia præclarum est Dei donum, et qui omnibus sæculis exstiterunt viri docti, eos Deus ipse excitavit ut ad veri notitiam mundo prælucerent" (Ep. ad. Bucerum. Opp. Tom. ix. Epp., p. 50). But no more will he in the dogmatic contest grant the highest judgment to the allied science, because he has to do with an historical revelation, which the philosopher might consider *à posteriori*, but could

---

[8] 1 John iv. 8.

never think out *à priori*.[4] True philosophy and true theology will reverence and love one another, but will still pursue each its own path. A negative reply only can be given to the question whether anything can be philosophically true and theologically false, or *vice versâ*. Dogmatics does not in principle stand in any constrained relation even to the empirical philosophy, if it does not at least ground its arguments merely on external observation. For Dogmatics certainly takes counsel with spiritual experience, and, not less than the other, considers itself called to observation and combination.[5] The hostility commences only when the empiricist applies his own experience and that of others as the supreme test in the judgment on the well-proved facts of revelation, and, passing over from the empirical to the speculative region, utters with a bold voice the word impossible! in other words, decides arbitrarily what may or may not be historically trustworthy. The true philosopher of experience will gladly confess "the further progress we make in experience, the nearer we come to the inscrutable" (Göthe), that is, to the domain of Faith.

9. The starting-point thus fixed marks out at the same time the boundaries of the dogmatic territory. That only, but all that, does thus belong to it, which is the expression of Christian belief in revelation, or at any rate is in direct connexion with it. Belief in revelation postulates a mutual relation between God and man; questions, therefore, which have not the slightest value for the knowledge of this revelation belong to some other domain rather than to ours. The application of this simple but far-reaching principle to the many subtleties of the earlier and later Scholasticism is very easily made, but is not unnecessary even in these days.

Comp. KLING, *Ueber Gestaltung der Christl. Dogm.* in the *Tübing. Zeitschrift für Theol.* (1834), iv.; H. MARTENSEN, *Ueber Glauben und Wissen*, in the *Jahrb. für Deutsche Theol.* (1869), xiv., pp. 399, *sqq.*; O. MARPURG, *Das Wissen und der religiöse Glaube* (1869), pp. 254, *sqq.*; TH. ZOLLMANN, *Bibel und Natur in der Harmonie ihrer Offenb.* (a prize Essay), 2 ed. (1869); A. STUELER, *Schriftlehre und Naturwissenschaft: neun Vorlesungen* (1869); H. E. VINKE, *Oratio de Germano Philosopho, Optimo Theologo* (1836), *De Empirie van Jesus' Apostelen en verdere Tijdgenooten* (1860); ANASTASIO, *Christendom en Empirisme*, bl. 45, *sqq.* (1862); THE BISHOP OF PETERBOROUGH, *Scepticism* (Dutch Tr., with Preface by J. J. van Oosterzee, 1863).

POINTS FOR INQUIRY.

Connexion between this and the preceding chapter.—Necessity and requirements of an acceptable starting-point.—Is any benefit still to be expected from Scepticism, or from Dogmatism being taken as our starting-point?—Meaning and basis of the demand of belief as the first condition of all dogmatic knowledge.—The origin of the constantly recurring conflicts between Dogmatics and Natural Philosophy.—How can this be best directed?—The value of a sound philosophy acknowledged in every age by the most distinguished and orthodox theologians.—What must Dogmatics, according to our proposed principles, accept in its investigation?—What may it safely put on one side?

---

[4] 1 Cor. ii. 9.

[5] John i. 14; iv. 42.

SECTION XVII.—ITS METHOD.

We must have not only our starting-point, but our method of investigation too, in agreement with the nature and object of the science.' Each dogma ought to be derived naturally, and according to its essence, from its chief source, be critically examined and united with others by an analytical-synthetical method, so that each of its parts derives its light and right, its importance and value, from its coherence with this organic whole. On this account we can only speak of the so-called dogmatic proof, where a common principle of fundamental estimation, at least to a certain degree, exists. The character of this proof is determined by the nature of the particular propositions, yet its end is gained when it has been made evident that belief is reasonable, unbelief unreasonable. The highest evidence for the truth of any dogmatic proposition is given in its agreement at the same time with the utterance of God's word in Holy Scripture, and with the testimony of spiritual experience.

1. Though the question as to the method of an investigation may seem less attractive, it is, nevertheless, absolutely necessary, as opposed on the one hand to an indefiniteness, and on the other to the conflict, specially seen in our days. The old proverb, never entirely true, "methodus est arbitraria," deserves more than ever to be followed by the maxim, "methodus est necessaria." The very fact of the most diverse methods having been pursued in different ages, proves the importance of our problem, and advises caution. Dogmatics, too, ought to distinguish itself by the scientific accuracy of its method from the more popular forms (*e.g.* Catechism or Confession) in which the consciousness of belief expresses itself.

2. Since the method of each science must be in accord with its character, neither the purely empirical nor the absolutely speculative method can here be called the only available one, though both, when properly employed, proffer most important service to Dogmatics. For it is a science of *faith* in a special revelation, which, while partly within the reach of spiritual experience, exhibits at the same time an historical and metaphysical character. He who will choose no other way than that of daily experience, or of abstract reasoning, and then consistently persists in that way, can only distrust and reject that which is the very essence of Christianity. Experience itself forbids us to choose here exclusively the Empiric method as our guide, and sound reasoning makes us feel in this sphere the insufficiency of our reason. We can scarcely expect that a holy Theology will bind itself to a rule which in principle neglects all distinction between sacred and

profane, and leads but too early to a denial of its object and of its entire character. It is not by mere external perception, but by spiritual intuition and sanctified reflection on that which the eye of faith has contemplated, that we arrive in this domain at knowledge worthy of the name.

3. In Christian Dogmatics, a biblical, an historical, and a scientific element are most closely united. The first naturally comes first in order; the question of questions is, "What does God's word teach us in Holy Scripture?" "Non nisi Dei lumine potest Deus cognosci et coli ad salutem, prouti nec sol a nobis videri aut possideri potest nisi per proprium ipsius lumen" (Maresius). Nothing may be accepted as a part of a Christian doctrine which cannot be proved to rest really, whether κατὰ τὸ ῥητον, or at least κατὰ τὴν διάνοιαν, upon the word of revelation. Hence it is plain that the so-called *loca probantia* must not only be counted, but weighed; so that we do not prove the doctrine of the Trinity from 1 John v. 7, or that of Predestination from Acts xv. 18. Only when Biblical Theology, and that specially of the New Testament, has been duly investigated, and its well-understood authority has been maintained, does the Dogmatics of the Church begin to speak. It must not be derived from any but indisputable sources, must be developed and proposed according to its own principles, and must be tested by the word and Spirit of Christ as the supreme Judge. The philosophical criticism which the dogmatist must apply to the doctrine of Scripture and of the Church, is by no means that of the merely natural understanding, but that of the Holy Spirit, who lives in every believer, and first guides to a right judgment in spiritual things. "Spiritualis homo κριτικώτατος" (Bengel). We must, however, remember always that in the last instance the word of Christ is to be the test of, and not to be tested by, the Christian consciousness. What we do not see given, at least in principle, as the word and spirit of Christ, or as necessarily following from it, as the oak from the acorn, has no further claim to existence in the Christian dogmatic sphere.

4. If, then, in dogma, too, we first obtain one whole by uniting the several parts, on the other hand each part can only be properly known and valued by the light of the whole. We cannot too plainly state, in opposition to the atomic criticism which neglects the tree for particular branches of which it consists, and the whole body for its several limbs, that the cardinal point here is not to divide, but to unite. Dogmatic proportions are like the cross-beams of a roof, of which the separate balks could easily be loosened, but which, when all are joined together, mutually support one another, and as one vast structure defy the winds. He who attains to the mountain summit, and from it surveys with piercing eye the whole landscape, will best see and take in each part of that landscape. "Dogmatic conception is first of all an *explicative* conception, a development of that which the contemplation has already given, a development of that which belongs to the inner connection of all the essential parts of the subject" (Martensen). Many a truth or fact, in itself strange or offensive, has a very different character when it is considered as part of a well-constructed whole. [Compare, *e.g.* many prophetic miracles of the Old Testament which are apparently so inconsistent until they are placed in the light of the Theocracy as a whole.] It is therefore of the utmost importance that, in the spiritual study of

Dogmatics, analysis should never be preferred at the expense of synthesis, or *vice versâ*.

5. From what has been said, we are naturally led to the question as to the requirements of the so-called dogmatic proof in so far as we can speak of such a thing. From the nature of the case this must be the indicating of reasons, sufficient for ourselves, on which belief in the truth of dogmatic propositions rests. It offers, in other words, an account of the reasons for the conviction of faith, and this account can only then be given with success when this proposition is never forgotten; *Contra principia negantem non valet disputatio.* Who will succeed in proving the possibility of miracles to the man who starts with a pantheistic conception of God; or the necessity of reconciliation to him who hesitates to recognise sin as guilt and ruin? At the same time, the method of this proof must always vary according to the nature of the dogmatic propositions. Where these exhibit an historic character, it will specially call for an accurate examination of testimony; where this character, on the contrary, is metaphysical or ethical, preference must be given to the speculative and psychological method. Then we ought gradually to ascend as far as possible, without too great a step, from that which is known and agreed, to that which is still unknown and doubtful, and aspire to win the testimony once borne by a philosopher to another thinker: "What I understand of his doctrine is so excellent, that I can no longer doubt of the excellency of that which I do not understand."—In any case, in dogmatic demonstration, we may be considered to have reached our end where the acceptability of the standpoint and the expression of belief is so maintained as to convince him who is, as far as possible, impartial and qualified to judge, though the opponent himself will not yet acknowledge that he is defeated. Internal conviction, indeed, depends not only on intellectual, but also on moral conditions; and faith is not a necessary result of mere logical demonstration, but the ripe fruit of a psychological condition of life. Dogmatic proof has thus not to show that nothing at all can be adduced in opposition to a proposition, but that we are bound notwithstanding to accept it, because the truth is too powerful, even against not unimportant contradiction. In a word, it will arouse a confident assent, which may be invited, but never can be imposed.

6. As dogmatic testimony has various requirements, so the dogmatic evidence which is founded on it has various degrees, and moreover is at all times confined within its own limits. As to the first, the mere fact that something is found in the Bible can hardly, without anything more, be produced as a sufficient proof. We get to much firmer ground as soon as it is seen that the proposition in question necessarily follows from all that on good evidence we know of God and His revelation. What Christ, the King of truth, by word and deed announces as truth, has, when suitably elucidated and tested, already decisive authority for all His true disciples. The Protestant can, therefore, in a thoroughly proper manner, testify with Erasmus, "Non parum me movet Ecclesiæ auctoritas." That which not merely the individual but the collective Christian consciousness throughout all ages expresses concerning saving truth, throws no small weight into the trembling scale of investigation. When the utterance of God's word in Holy Scrip-

ture accords with that of spiritual experience, the highest degree of dogmatic certainty is attained which in this domain can be expected. (We add this designedly here). Certainly, the most distinguished theologian does not produce the truth ; he only reproduces it as, and in so far as, it is revealed and announced in the Bible, is taken up into his life of thought, and up to a certain extent mastered. But still the science of belief always remains devoted to things which are not seen,[6] and the empty dream that their reality can fall within the sphere of that which is properly called demonstration, must inevitably lead to disappointment. Without any hesitation, we, at any rate, subscribe to the words of a distinguished Theologian : " For the Christian Theologian I cannot recognise any higher standpoint than that of the Apostles, who held rather with the foolishness of God[7] than w th the wisdom of men; and though there is no one who would not rather walk by sight than by faith, who would not rather himself recognise the truth than receive it upon the testimony of authority; although I, too, consider it the highest aim of the theologian really to know the knowable, and am thankful to any one who helps me on in the way, yet I neither may nor will permit myself any illusions about the event. I cannot accept the will for the deed, the promise for the fulfilment. I cannot, in things of the highest moment, found my conviction on reasons by which no one would suffer himself to be guided, where he had to venture or to risk something in matters of daily life. I do not, therefore, deny that there are important dogmas, which, notwithstanding the much-vaunted (and in their way, too, honourable) attempts to represent them as true and necessary by arguments from reason, would remain thoroughly problematical if I did not admit the word of Scripture to be ultimately decisive." (Twesten.)

Comp. J. T. BECK, a. a. O. i., p. 43, *sqq.* ; REUTER, *U Aufgabe und Methode des Dogmat. Beweises*, in the *Zeitsch. für Deutsche Theol.* (1851); CH. SECRETAN, *Recherches de la méthode qui conduit à la vérité*, etc. (1857) ; HOEKSTRA *Bronnen en Grondsl. enz.*, pp. 41—44 (1864). On the connection of Dogmatics, Apologetics, and Personal Experience, the first appendix to THOLUCK's *Lehre von der Sünde*, 3rd ed. (1862) ; a treatise of Prof. V. D. GOLTZ, in Basle, *Der Weg zum System in der Dogm. Theol.*, published in the *Jahrb. für Deutsche Theol.* (1870), iv., (1871), iv.

POINTS FOR INQUIRY.

The importance of method in general, and specially in connection with this subject.—Historical survey of the most celebrated dogmatic methods.—Why cannot the sciences of nature and of spirit be treated entirely in the same method ?—Must we ascend from the parts to the whole, or from the whole comprehend the parts ?—Nature and claims of dogmatic demonstration.—Is not the simple appeal to Scripture quite sufficient to put an end to all strife and doubt ?—Is the highest criterion within or without us ?—How far is a truth shown to be such by the vigour of life which proceeds from it ?

---

[6] 1 Heb. xi. 1.

[7] 1 Cor. i. 21, 25.

SECTION XVIII.—ITS DIVISION.

The same conditions which define the starting-point and method, apply to the division, of Christian Dogmatics. If it is to be more than a fruit of mere arbitrariness, and to possess a higher than a merely logical value, then must it not be derived from elsewhere, but be in direct accordance with the central thought of the Christian Revelation, place all the parts of saving truth in their right connexion, and thus be of service in the estimation of the great whole. The division which starts from the idea of the Kingdom of Heaven, —whose mysteries the Christian Theologian must understand and explain, satisfies better than any other these requirements. The Dogmatic Theology which understands its vocation will be neither more nor less than a Theology of the Kingdom in all the force of the word.

1. The necessity of division is founded, objectively, in the abundance of the materials, which can only be managed in this way; subjectively, in the claims of the thinking mind, which seeks order and unity. The idea of this necessity became more forcible as the treatment of dogma became more scientific. This division, as far as the word can be used here, was originally thoroughly simple; it afterwards became more artistic and intricate, whilst specially in our days it shows an even greater variety.

2. The division of the dogmatic material must naturally not be arbitrary, but must be carried out according to a fixed principle—the *principium dividendi.* A thoroughly good division requires that all the parts of the whole be included in it; that each part has its own proper place; and that the collective parts be not only co-ordinated by each other, but be subordinated to one great principal thought, which they illustrate and develop. We may specially desire that the basis of the division be not sought elsewhere, but be derived from the domain of the science itself. Who would seek the clue to the treatment of some part of natural science in the domain of speculative philosophy? Who will not divide the history of the Church differently from the history of the world? and again, who will not place the history of dogma in an order different to that of the Church? A division may be logically irreproachable, and yet unsuited to its purpose, and thoroughly faulty. The cause of many failures in this method has been, that men only asked, how can the doctrine of faith be brought in a symmetrical scheme to a well-defined whole? instead of considering what was the inner unity and connexion of the revelation, and into what parts that unity spontaneously divided itself before the investigating eye.

3. Testing the various divisions by these principles, we quickly discover

their weak points. The greater portion of different *Loci*, arranged and thoroughly classed in a greater or less degree, as has been done since the time of Melancthon, certainly deserves no higher praise than that of practical utility. Even the simple division into Theology, Anthropology, Christology, etc., has little to recommend it as specially suitable to Christian Dogmatics. It is certainly better when the distribution is directed by the great antithesis of sin and grace (Schleiermacher); yet the benefit is made less when, as in this case, the doctrine of sin itself is not allowed its proper rights, and its true essence as apostacy and guilt is disavowed.—Without doubt the partition is specially Christian, in which Christ is made the starting-point (as in Holland in the Groningen school; in Germany, though in a different method, in the dogmatic works of Liebner, Lange, Thomasius); but this, too, has its dark side, since under its rule Hamartology cannot possibly have its proper rights, whilst from this standpoint injustice is easily done to the rights of the Old Testament.—It is true this mistake is avoided when (Scholten) the higher unity of dogmatic investigation is found in the idea of religion, if we can consecutively treat of God, or the object; of man, or the origin of religion, etc.: but it is evident that this scheme, with some slight changes, will serve for any non-Christian doctrine, as well as for this. It is clear, the guiding principle must here be derived, not from the universal religious, but from the specially Christian domain. We have here to do with a guiding thought, which can rule the whole system of doctrine, as the sun rules the planets. This was already felt by Coccejus, when he tried to construe the whole dogmatic subject into the biblical idea of a covenant. Even, leaving aside other considerations, this method was more suited to the Old Testament than to the New: more Biblical than Evangelical.—Much more was it certainly in the spirit of Christianity that a theologian of the Lutheran Church of the present time developed the doctrine of salvation from the principle of love (Schöberlein); a principle, however, which is perhaps more fertile in the domain of Ethics than of Dogmatics; so that, for instance, another (Sartorius) was led to seek in it a foundation for his "Doctrine of Holy Love." In the dogmatic domain we should rather give the preference to the disposition in which the baptismal formula is made our starting-point, and thus everything is connected with the doctrine of the Father, the Son, and the Holy Ghost. This, following in the footsteps of Calvin, has been accepted as the basis of their dogmatic edifice by several theologians of later times (Marheinecke, Martensen, Vinke, and others), and is certainly entirely in the spirit of the Lord and His apostles. In this method, however, Anthropology as a whole finds only a subordinate and forced position; while as to the whole the accuracy of the remark cannot be contradicted, "When the later dogmatists build their system without any more ado upon a Trinitarian presupposition, they act with a *naïveté* for which no real and adequate justification can be found in the scientific conditions of the times" (Schenkel). It is certain that many a theologian of this century, who has called the doctrine of the Trinity with much emphasis the corner-stone of his dogmatic building, has in this word thought more of an immanent movement and development in our idea of God, than of a revelation of the personal existence and life of God considered in its relation to humanity.

4. We escape, however, all these difficulties when we place another thought in the foreground, that of the kingdom of God and of heaven. With this as our starting-point we find ourselves in happy agreement with the word and spirit of Holy Scripture, and specially of the New Testament. In this direction the Theocracy under Israel already points, as well as the voice of the Prophets, and the whole religious economy. John the Baptist came forth preaching this;[8] Jesus Himself started from this point in His popular instruction, and returned to it; and even in the writings of the Apostles this idea everywhere occupies a by no means unimportant place.[9] The Gospel itself is a Gospel of the kingdom,[10] and Christianity a method of salvation, not for the individual only, but for the entire community. We cannot then be surprised that this side of the matter was, at a comparatively early date, and in after times more expressly, placed in the foreground. This in some measure had been done already by Augustine in his apologetic essay, *De civitate Dei*, and even in the present century by one of the most useful apologists in Wurtemberg, C. H. Stirm, in his *Apologie des Christenthums*, i. pp. 81—113. Different dogmatists have paid greater or less attention to this cardinal point; and yet we do not know of one scientific work on Christian doctrine in which it serves as a clue to the mode of treatment, and *commune vinculum* of all the leading parts. As we determine on this, the word of the Lord in Matt. xiii. 11, rises up to our view, and we place the great thoughts of the kingdom of God as a bright light at the entrance of the sanctuary. That light breaks of itself before our eyes into a seven-fold ray. We treat consequently of—

I.	God, or the Sovereign King of this kingdom.—	Theology.
II.	Man, or the Subject ,,	Anthropology.
III.	Christ, or the Founder ,,	Christology.
IV.	Redemption, or the Character ,,	Objective Soteriology.
V.	The way of salvation, or the Fundamental Law ,,	Subjective Soteriology.
VI.	The Church, or the Training-School.	Ecclesiology.
VII.	The Coming of the Lord, or the Completion of the kingdom of God.	Eschatology.

If the plan of the dogmatic edifice (its material parts) is thus sketched, the foundation must be laid in the so called formal portion, which exhibits a thoroughly apologetic character. Then, after answering a few preliminary questions, the foundation of all dogmatic investigation,—*Religion*, *Revelation*, *Holy Scripture*,—must be treated consecutively and in the same order. And thus "the construction of the entire dogmatic building must give proof of its truth and value, as well from the conception of the dogma in itself, and its several sides, as from the measure of its exposition." (Lange).

[8] Matthew iii. 2.

[9] 1 Cor. xv. 24—28; Eph. v. 5; Heb. x. 12, 13; James ii. 5; Rev. xii. 10; xix. 16; and many other places.

[10] Matt. xxiv. 14.

Comp. LANGE, *Chr. Dogm.* i., § 20; EBRARD, *Chr. D.* i., §§ 55, 56; C. SCHWARZ, *Grundriss der Christl. Lehre*, 1868.

POINTS FOR INQUIRY.

Necessity and requirements of a good division.—Historico-critical survey of the best divisions.—Meaning and tendency of Matt. xiii. 11.—The idea of the Kingdom of God; its prominent place in the Theology of the Scriptures of the New Testament; its import for Christian Dogmatics.—Must not Apologetics rather follow Dogmatics, than precede the discussion of this last?

SECTION XIX.—ITS PERFECTIBILITY.

The perfectibility of Christian Dogmatics, as distinguished from that of Revelation itself, is raised beyond all doubt from an Evangelical, and particularly from a Protestant Reformed standpoint. It is the natural consequence of the peculiarity of thoughtful faith, that it never thoroughly surveys or conquers its abundant materials, and the history of the science itself continually evinces this character of perfectibility. Here, however, we must by no means overlook the difference in principle between Evolution and Revolution, lest any one should welcome as progress that which necessarily leads to the undermining and destruction of the whole doctrinal building. True progress in this matter consists in this, that the building be constantly more perfectly erected on an immovable foundation; in other words, that the contents of the doctrine of Salvation be always more accurately described, more powerfully justified, more thoroughly developed, and more generally applied, whilst a constant attention is paid to the phenomena and needs of the time.

1. The belief in progress is in this domain, as well as in every other, a need, a duty, and a blessing. But it is important, in order that no one should be misled by great words, to ask as to this, in what sense, on what grounds, how far, and by what path?

2. At the very outset we must distinguish sharply between the perfectibility of the doctrine, and that of Christian revelation. The doctrine of the objective perfectibility of Christianity, which, proclaimed in early times by the Montanists, and afterwards by some of the Mystics of the middle ages, was enounced in the commencement of the preceding century by a number of Rationalists, is, properly understood, nothing else but a denial of the historical and supranatural character of saving truth. The case is, however, different when we consider the proposition that Dogmatics,

as such, is capable of perfection, and has a constant need for it. Truth is eternal, but the insight into truth may be made clearer, extended, and even in some respects changed. Thus far we can admit for Christian dogma the attribute of perfectibility both in its objective and subjective meaning.

3. The ground for this proposition lies in the nature of saving truth itself, which is not revealed in the form of an accurately defined system, but rather in that of a principle of life which is gradually showing itself more clearly. Hence we find in Holy Scripture so many exhortations to growth in the knowledge of faith.[11] In all ages there have been Christians who, in consequence of painful deception, listen with mistrust to the demand for progress and development in this domain. Their dogmatising, as far as we can speak of it, is nothing but an endless repeating and reiterating of the faith which has been once delivered. They are like the man who is always counting the coins which he has inherited, and is satisfied if only the number remains undiminished, without troubling himself about their intrinsic value. It is plain that such a conservatism is devoid of all spirit, but it is also in conflict with all Protestant principle. From the Romish standpoint men must of necessity cling to a Church doctrine which is considered infallible; but the true son of the Reformation, the advocate of freedom of investigation, must, as such, also believe in the possibility of development. The "not that I have already attained" is for him, even in a higher degree of knowledge of faith, the expression of a deep consciousness, and at the same time of a great want. At best, Dogmatics is the expression of the consciousness of belief, as it has actually and for the present moment developed itself, by the light of the Gospel and in the bosom of the Church, to a defined and clearly measurable height. We all stand on the shoulders of our predecessors; others will raise themselves on ours, and strive to see further. We are ourselves constantly correcting our conceptions, and show thus that our former ones did not completely satisfy us. It is not therefore a real eulogium, when any one says of himself that his convictions during twenty or thirty years have not changed in the slightest degree. Though our knowledge through faith is the same as before, yet a conscious faith, after such a lapse of time, will know the same continually in another and better degree. "Faith must be in every point entire and firm; never finished, but always susceptible of further development." (Schaff.)

4. Besides, the whole history of Dogmatics shows us not only a restless striving after, but a constant, though sometimes slow, approach to greater perfection. Even in the first apostles a constant increase in Christian insight cannot be denied. (The Petrine doctrine, etc.) During the first four centuries we hear the Christian consciousness as to the person of the Redeemer proclaiming truth continually with greater firmness and clearness. The sixteenth century adds to the development of Soteriology that which has not been supplied by any one before; perhaps the same may hereafter be said *e.g.*, on the subject of Eschatology of the nineteenth century. Every side of the truth, which is now better understood than before, casts at the same time

---

[11] 1 Cor. xiv. 26; Eph. iii. 14—19; Col. i. 9, 10; 1 Thess. v. 21; 2 Peter iii. 18.

a light upon other sides which are still in shadow. How could the perfectibility of Dogmatics be still disputable where the promise of the Lord (John xvi. 12—15) is understood, believed, and fulfilled? But to contemplate that fulfilment, we must look back not merely for years, but for centuries, and never forget that the *patiens quia æternus* is of constant application to the operation of the Spirit of truth in the Church.

5. The distinction between evolution and revolution must by no means be passed by, when the question is asked, How far must this progress extend? We must here look for amplification, and not for alteration. It occurs wherever that which is virtually contained in principle in the word of truth is brought gradually into light, just as it is in the growth of a child, who does not get any new limbs, but sees those which it already has slowly increase and strengthen. We see development in the opening bud, which opens according to its nature; it would be degeneration if the rose bush were to become gradually a thorn. "Ad profectum pertinet ut in semet ipsam unaquæque res amplificetur; ad permutationem vero, ut aliquid exalio in aliud transvertatur" (Vincentius Lerinus). Christianity is an historic religion; and when this is evident, it can never be welcomed as progress, when this its character is first neutralised and then denied. Progress presupposes that we remain on the path in which we have hitherto been, not that we all at once choose an opposite one (μετάβασις εἰς ἄλλο γένος.) Thus, Dogmatics as a science is conservative as to its principles, progressive as to their development. Just as it was once with the fettered Apostles, the Christian Dogmatic spirit sees its chains from time to time broken, even where the previous forms remain intact;[12] but does he therefore, any more than these Apostles, receive a command to preach an entirely different Gospel?

6. After all that has been said, it is not difficult to point out the path by which we may approach always nearer to the ideal of the progressive character of Dogmatics. We must welcome it as progress when the chief subject-matter of the doctrine of salvation is *described* with continually increasing accuracy. Dogmatics has to take account, not merely with facts of the Christian consciousness, but with the very deeds of God for saving mankind (*e.g.*, revelation, incarnation, inspiration), the true conception of which must always remain defective. Now the claim cannot be that what has thus far been only believed, should henceforth be thoroughly known—in that case we could no longer call Dogmatics a science of faith—but that we conceive something, and that as far as it is conceivable, and also that we know *why* we cannot go any further. Our business is with a Dogmatics, freed from the dust, but not from the learning, of the schools; from the thorns, but not from the sharp definitions, of the old systems; a scientific exposition of faith, according to the golden word of Da Costa, "in its essence the fruit of ages: in outward form, of these our days" (V. d. Hoeven, junr.).—And that which is thus more accurately defined, ought also to be continually better *vindicated*. The history of Apologetics has attested that the good cause has been defended more with awkward weapons than with

---

[12] Acts v. 19—23.

a faulty strategy; such lessons must not be lost on the Dogmatics of the present time. It advances when it looks more closely into the nature and strength of its so-called proofs, which it not only counts, but also weighs; while, though paying special heed to the historical, it never loses sight of the psychological mode of argument. Moreover, it must always ally itself more frankly with each element of truth which it finds even beyond its own proper bounds, and apply the "all things are yours" without any fixed limits.—Thus it acts by its own nature so that its object may be always *developed* more thoroughly and fundamentally. The command, "Launch out into the deep," is laid, too, upon Dogmatics. That which really can be understood by faith, it must not only desire, but also attempt to know, remembering that it has to do first with the *Ita*, but then also with the *Quare*, of spiritual matters. Modesty is good, but it must not become a cloak for sloth. Not merely a deeper knowledge of each of the parts, but, above all, a more accurate and thorough estimation of the whole, is the boundless task to which the science has to devote its powers.—Finally, the more science is *applied* in various ways, the better it fulfils its duty. The light which rose on her domains must also cast its beams over the surrounding country. True theology will the more approach its ideal, as it more fully contributes to the solution of the various questions of the day, and to the healing of the reigning diseases, by setting forth and maintaining the eternal truth. So far each period requires its own elaboration of the doctrine of faith, and no single method can be said to be constantly adequate to the changing wants of different centuries.

Always perfectible, it is never perfect (§ v.). To understand and express thoroughly the truth, we ought to be morally perfect, since truth and life are one. Nevertheless, the object of Dogmatics needs not remain absolutely unattainable.

Compare the *Commonitorium of* VINCENTIUS LERINUS, cap. 28; *Herzog*, R. E. x., p. 389, *sqq.*; KRUG, *Briefe über die Perfectibilität der Chr. Rel.* (1795); C. F. VON AMMON, *Fortbildung des Christenth. zur Weltreligion*, 4.Th. (1836-1840); LANGE, *Chr. Dogm.* i., § 17; SCHWEITZER, *Christl. Glaubensl.* i. (1803), §§ 20—22; J. J. VAN OOSTERZEE, *Reformatie en Revolutie*, fifty Aphorisms (1867), bl. 6.

POINTS FOR INQUIRY.

Historic progress of the conflict about the perfectibility of (1) Christianity, and (2) of Christian Dogmatics.—What is the meaning of 1 Cor. iii. 11—15?—Elucidation of 1 Cor. viii. 1—3, Col. ii. 8, etc.—Can we not see in the history of Dogmatics standing still and retrogression?—How may the distinction between reformation and revolution be recognised in this matter?—What are the hindrances, and what the greatest aids to the perfecting of Dogmatics?

SECTION XX.—ITS OBJECT.

The final object of Christian Dogmatics lies not in the science itself, still less in its students alone, but entirely and completely in the up-building of the Kingdom of God in and around them, and in the glorification of God, which inseparably accompanies it. The intellectual and moral attributes of its students must, no less than the method of its proposition and study, be in agreement with its object. That object is better attained in proportion as the student of the science is a sincere believer, who has learnt by his own experience to know the truth as life, and thus also as light.

1. This chapter, which began with the question as to the starting-point of dogmatic investigation, will be properly concluded with that as to its object,—"Whence comest thou, and whither goest thou?" It is evident that this part of the science is often studied with a very different aim, and so it is the more necessary to point out with what object it must be studied.

2. We cannot find the object of our science in itself, still less in its student. The maxim that science should only be studied for itself is as alluring, but also as deceptive, as the oft-repeated, "Art only for art's sake, and virtue only for virtue's." Here we accept much rather, "Sunt, qui scire volunt ut sciant, et magna stultitia est; sunt, qui scire volunt ut sciantur, et magna inanitas est." Dogmatics is not a pure abstract science, in the sense in which the higher mathematics or speculative Philosophy can be so called; but it is positive, and, as to its tendency, practical. Its object is in harmony with its essence; the science of the mystery of the Kingdom of God has no less a destination than to serve the cause of that Kingdom itself.

3. By the study of the science the Kingdom of God must be promoted first of all *in* its student himself. We have not to do here with a mere "scientia," but with a "sapientia," not incorrectly called by J. Gerson, a "*cognitio affectiva*." That ideal hovered over the spirit of Melancthon, as is evident from his beautiful words, "Ego mihi conscius sum me nullam aliam ob causam theologiam tractâsse, nisi ut vitam emendarem."—— But then also *by* and *around* him. Here is the main law, not "vivat scientia, et pereat cœtus," but "floreat scientia, et ædificatur Ecclesia."— It is the merest superficiality to assert that the Church, if it will really flourish, must know and hear as little as possible of Dogmatics. Men speak of "barren Dogmatics," of "Dogmatics of the school," of "the corslet of Dogmatics," and demand that religion shall be preached without Dogmatics. As if such a thoughtless wish did not ask for the utterly unattainable! As if they who resisted all Dogmatics did on that account cling less to their own dogmas! As if the in many respects weak and faulty doctrine of faith, which rules the life of the Church, could be succeeded and conquered by anything than by a better! As if the need for "more light" was not always revealing itself even here! It is evident that the systematic apathy and antipathy to Dogmatics can in its results be nothing else but fatal to all spiritual and church life, which, on the contrary, will be the more powerfully advanced in proportion to *its* prosperity. Then only, however, has this study, specially when carried out in the spirit of the Reformation, first attained its object, when He is glorified, by and through

whom all things even in the kingdom of science exist. It is with the *in majorem Dei gloriam* in his heart that man can step boldly within the sanctuary.

4. The study of the science must be organised in agreement with this object. We may lay down as our rule "Dogmatics will not suffer itself to be acquired by mere study; it must, as a spiritual possession, be striven after, and gained in earnest struggle." (Hagenbach.)

Hearing from others must continually accompany and amplify our own meditation; the study of separate dogmas must precede, before we can with a successful result try to frame our own sketch of the complete Dogmatics. Everything must begin with a thorough explanation of Scripture; to this must be added the historico-critical invesigation of Church Confessions; and then only do we come, by the increasing light of experience, on the right way to pass, with independence and decision, a Christian philosophical judgment on the principal questions of life. Throughout all this work we must never for a moment pass over the peculiar character of our science. "The science of faith contains two quite distinct elements—one, variable and and progressive, the conception always imperfect and always perfectible, of the fact of salvation and the inductions which are made therefrom; the other immovable—viz., the fact of salvation itself; externally the revelation of God in Jesus Christ; internally the testimony of the Holy Spirit in the heart: it is on this fact of history and experience that the thoughts of the theologian are exercised. To be always drawing nearer to a more perfect comprehension of that which God has given him the grace to believe, and to express scientifically that faith, is the aim of the Christian theologian" (J. Monod). The presentation, by word of mouth, of this science which will promote this end, can, from the nature of the case, only be a regularly coherent and progressive one (acroamatic not erotematistic or Socratic) uninterruptedly pursued in an unbroken line from step to step, and now and then interchanged by a freer discussion.

5. Above all, this object requires intellectual and moral qualities in the student of Dogmatics, which we must leave not unnoticed: "Decision without exclusiveness or rebuking presumptuousness; independence, without vain self-sufficiency; consistency without intolerance; firmness without obstinacy or passion: and all this, resting on the basis of a Christian mind, guided by the fulness of the Spirit and of science, is what makes the theologic character" (Ullmann). When looked at more closely, the threefold claim of *oratio*, *meditatio*, *tentatio*, obtains a higher importance. "Orando facilius Deus invenitur, quam disputando" (A. H. Francke). Further, we require, in the study of Dogmatics, that profound mind which has the courage to leave the safer course along the coast, and boldly put out to sea, and which looks for something more than mere sounds; a degree of truth which will learn not only from friend, but from foe; and, in continued investigation, asks for something more than a confirmation of our own deeply rooted thoughts; an independence of spirit, too, which is true to the *nemini cuiquam me mancipavi;*[13] a holy liberality (gentle-

---

[13] 1 Cor. vii. 23.

ness) towards those of different views, diametrically opposed to any unholy liberalism; an honesty which does not look on language as given to conceal our thoughts, and which simply speaks what it can justify before the God of truth; and, above all, a seriousness, which never touches that which is holy but with pure hands. Frivolity and would-be humorism is far from being a happy phenomenon in the ecclesiastical or dogmatic world. How sad is it to hear some play with principles, or consider that they are but logarithmic formulæ, concerning a subject external to themselves. And yet we are not treating here of a truth over which we are only to argue, but of one which is to be held by us, and from which we are to point to others the way of life. Θεολογεῖν δεῖ οὐ τεχνολογεῖν (Basilius Magnus.)

6. This object cannot possibly be gained unless the student of the science is at the same time a sincere believer. Only the πιστικός can become γνωστικός; only the disciple of Christ the genuine doctor of Theology. The nature of the case, history, and experience, all equally proclaim the same maxim, which only needs one word to prevent misunderstanding. This maxim does not at all declare that we must wait with all dogmatic studies until we are wholly fit to speak of a proper, well-founded, and full-grown spiritual life; on the contrary, the doctrine of faith, studied with diligence and success, may be the very means of increasing spiritual life. But where there is an entire want of every principle of a life of faith, there we had better not begin this study; and then only shall we enter upon it steadily and prosperously when we stand in close union with Him who is the way, the truth, and the life. Spirit alone can understand the Spirit; only life can conceive the life. Πρᾶξις ἐπίβασις θεωρίας. (Gregory Nazianzen). Where this principle of life really exists, there the object, at least to a certain degree, is attained, and—the general introduction of Christian Dogmatics can close with no fairer prospects—the words of the wise man of old are fulfilled: "The way of life is upwards to the wise."[14]

Comp. E. D. Krummacher, *Expectorationen über d. Stud. der Theol.* (1847); Schenkel (Senr.), *Die Idee der Persönlichkeit in ihrer Zeitbedeutung für die Theol. Wissensch, u.s.w.* (1850); J. J. van Oosterzee, *Toespraken tot opening der Acad. Less.* in 1865, 1866, 1868, *passim*; J. J. Doedes, *De Theol. Studiengang geschetst.* (1866).

Points for Inquiry.

The different aims with which our science has been studied in earlier and later times.—Connexion of the aim, which is here pointed out, with the spirit and tendency of Reformed Dogmatics.—The true theologian, at the same time, taught of God.—The Life the Light of men (John i. 4).

---

[14] Prov. xv. 24.

PART I.

THE APOLOGETIC FOUNDATION.

CHAPTER I.

RELIGION.

SECTION XXI.—ITS NATURE.

WE require, as the foundation for the building of Christian Dogmatics, an express examination, both as to its nature and character, of Religion, viewed generally. In order to define that nature accurately, we must not only observe the word, but specially the thing itself; since it, amidst an endless variety of forms, when properly considered, always displays the same character—of man in personal relation with God. Thus the word denotes, subjectively, a certain tendency of man's spiritual life; whilst objectively is indicated the veneration of God, which springs up in consequence of this tendency. The biblical use of the word agrees with this description, whilst a comparison with other definitions shows that this is to be preferred.

1. The investigation into the contents and foundation of religious truth, to which Dogmatics has to devote itself, necessarily rests on an accurate and exact conception of Religion itself. For what profit will the most closely dogmatic demonstration be to him who considers the whole

subject to which it belongs an idle fancy? In proportion, then, as the study of dogma obtained a more philosophic character, was the absolute necessity of such profound investigation more unanimously felt and recognised. Yet we can here only express and attest briefly, what must elsewhere—*e.g.*, in treating of Natural Theology—be examined more at length.

2. In order to understand rightly the nature of religion, we must neither lose ourselves in the etymology of the word, nor must we attend only to single, even though they be very eminent, manifestations of religious life. For the thing itself is far older than the word, and even its lower forms belong to that highest sphere of life, which exhibits to us all the nobility of religion. We must trace out the *general* truth which forms the foundation of what is more *particular*, and not until this subject has been properly elucidated are we in a position to make an intelligent choice between the different derivations of the word.

3. Our first glance at the religious life of mankind shows such an endless variety, that we have scarcely courage to speak of a higher unity. First, because religion is the highest and holiest of all things for him who seriously accepts it, its inner nature is not so easily distinguished as those which belong to the world of sense. And yet we soon discover, as well in the most savage Fetich worshipper, as in the most philosophic Theist, an inward compulsion to rise, not merely above themselves and this visible world, but to the Endless, to the Godhead, whatever their view of the Godhead may be; a longing to give something to God, and to receive something in return from Him; a striving, in a word, to enter into an immediate relation with Him. It is upon this phenomenon that we base our definition. Religion is *Life;* each revelation of the religious sense is at the same time a manifestation of life. *Of man;* for to him, as distinguished from other creatures, must we here exclusively attend. *In personal communion with God;* for with this communion, whatever may be its nature or fruit, Religion has always to do, and without self-consciousness and freedom it is utterly impossible. Since, however, every communion is, from the nature of the case, reciprocal, we can distinguish between Religion in its active and passive sense. Passive religion we might call an existence of God in man; active religion, an existence of man in God. The contrast between religion in the subjective and objective sense of the word is, however, simpler and plainer. The first denotes the inner striving, which serves as the foundation of every religious action; the other, the various forms of worship in which this desire reveals itself. It is only in the latter sense that we can speak, in the plural, of religions. In the really religious man, objective and subjective religion is united; with the hypocrite and formalist, they are often directly opposed to one another.

4. The words, by which Religio has been described in earlier and later times, denote this state of the case. According to Cicero (*D. N. D.* ii. 28), *Religio* is derived from *relegere=diligenter retractare*, a derivation certainly preferable to that given by Lactantius (Hist. Div., iv. 28), where he considers it derived from *religare*, to bind back. It denotes a disposition and dedication of spirit like that which is expressed in the German *Andacht*, the peculiar tendency of the inner life, and its self-concentration in the most exalted object. In modern languages, even as in the Dutch, we feel the

want of an accurate name. The German *Frömmigkeit* still remains the best; unfortunately the Dutch *Vroom* has acquired an unfavourable sound in the ears of many. This is the case too with *Godzaligheid* (fulness of God), which has a somewhat pietistic flavour. The words, *Godsvrucht* (*fürcht*) and *Godsdienst* (God's service), exhibit, when literally taken, a too decidedly legal character. *Godeleven* (Life for God), in the sense in which we speak of natural or spiritual life, seems more fit, provided we associate it in our thoughts, especially with the inner life; an idea which in the Greek words, θρησκεία, λατρεία, δεισιδαιμονία, is either wanting, or only obtains a part of its right.

5. The religious life and striving is set forth in Holy Scripture in a very varied, but most sententious manner. The idea of personal communion is strikingly indicated in the account of Enoch's walk with God (Gen. v. 24), of Abraham's faith and piety (Gen. xv. 1, xvii. 1, xxii. 12), and of the fear of God (Gen. xlii. 18) which adorned Joseph. Love to God is the highest demand of the law on Israel (Deut. vi. 5), and faith is the demand of the prophets (Isa. vii. 9; Hab. ii. 4). We ought also to observe the description of those persons in whom this disposition is the ruling one (Luke i. 6; ii. 25), and of the perfect servant of the Lord, "who shall be of quick understanding in the fear of the Lord" (Isa. xi. 3). In the New Testament the objective side of the matter is described as λατρεία (Rom. xii. 1) and θρησκεία (James i. 27), and the subjective as πίστις, whilst in the word εὐσεβεία (1 Tim. iv. 7, 8) the two are united.

6. It will not be difficult, after these remarks, to point out the defects which are to be found in several definitions of religion, which have been current at various times. The older dualistic definition (Reinhard), *certus modus Deum cognoscendi et colendi*, will certainly not find approval anywhere. But that of Schleiermacher also, which describes Religion as *Hinneigung Zum Weltall*, cannot be used for theistic religious forms without further explanation. In that of Kant, who understands by Religion "the acknowledgment of our duties towards the law of God," a too partial stress is laid on the ethical facts, while, not to speak of others, in that of Hegel, —Religion = God's thinking and knowing Himself in the human consciousness,—God is not only the object, but the subject of Religion; and this last is an action and reaction of God upon Himself. Enough has been already said to show that the definition which we have given deserves preference in more than one way.

Religion is nothing less than a communion of life, and in this character different from religious knowledge or philosophy. "Whilst the masters in the domains of art and science have the image of God only in the mirror of their thoughts and phantasy, the pious believer possesses it in his own being" (Martensen).

Compare as to this entire chapter the article *Religion und Offenbarung*, by J. KÖSTLIN, in *Herzog*, R. E. xii. etc., besides LUTHARDT, *Apologet. Vorträge* (1864), § 97, with notes; and particularly O. PFLEIDERER, *Die Religion, ihr Wesen und ihre Geschichte*, i. (1869). See also C. W. OPZOOMER, *De Godsdienst* (1867), and the various replies and essays. Compare especially J. MUELLER, *Ueber Bildung und Gebrauch des Wortes Religio. Stud. und Krit.* (1835), i.; REDSLOB, *Sprachliche Abhandlungen zur Theol.* (1840), pp. 1—40; LECHLER, *Bemerkungen zum Begriff der Religion mit besondern Rücksicht auf die psychol. Fragen Stud. und Kritik* (1851), iv.; J. J. DOEDES, *Leer van God* (1871), p. 241, *sqq.*

POINTS FOR INQUIRY.

Necessity of a preliminary investigation of religion in general, especially in the present day.—Determination of the idea, attempted in various ways.—The higher unity of all religious life.—Criticism of the various derivatives and designations of the word.—Does the description of Religion in the writings of the Old and New Testament exhibit quite the same character?—Critical comparison of some other definitions of the idea.—Difference between the purely æsthetic and the really ethic appreciation of Religion.

SECTION XXII.—ITS ORIGIN.

Religion, which is as old and as widespread as mankind upon the earth, is as little the product of silly fancy as of cunning calculation. It has its origin in the nature and essence of man, who cannot truly live without God; and it is thus a consequence of the original relation of mankind to God, which was thus willed by God Himself. The early awakening religious feeling is in reality nothing else but the consciousness of that relation of which we are constantly becoming more distinctly aware from every glance within and around us. Hence each man has unconditional claims on Religion, as Religion in turn has on him; and the denial of all religious belief, as far as such is possible, is nothing less than the violation of our own nature.

1. The investigation into the nature of religion leads naturally to the question as to its ground; and here it occurs to us at once that we have to do with something more than a mere sporadic phenomenon. "You may see towns without laws, or coins, or literature, but no one has ever yet seen a people without a God or prayer, without religious ceremonies or sacrifices." This phenomenon has been pointed out by numberless writers of antiquity,[1] and their testimony has been contradicted, but never confuted, by those of later inquirers. Travellers who had asserted that they had met with nations without any religion, have not seldom been seen to have been partially or imperfectly informed; and even where a belief in a Godhead was wanting, there appeared the fear of a devil. At the worst, we might ask with Rousseau, "whether we can have any doubt as to the existence of a well-organized class of beings, because a few monsters have been found among them?" and, above all, whether that which may seem to us Atheism, as, *e.g.*, the religion of the Buddhistic peoples, be such, too, from the standpoint of those who have accepted this form of religion. Even the child never hears of God or Divine things, without at once revealing his

---

[1] ARISTOT., *De cælo*, i. 3; CIC., *D. N. D.*, i. 3; *Tusc. Dispp.* 1—13; SENECA, *Epist.* 117.

natural inclination to accept at once this belief; and where it is lost, that loss has always been preceded by the violent suppression of another conviction.

2. This phenomenon, old and general as it is, can have as little been born of fear as of policy or deceit. The well-known *primus in orbe Deos fecit terror* is the veriest superficiality. Sacerdotal imposture! it is easy enough to utter the words, but whence came the priests themselves, and the universal sway of the fear? Tradition! but whence did it come, and whence its power to resist so much which contradicted and opposed it? He who speaks of a "world-wide delusion," must at least explain how it is that all mankind has been smitten with an incurable monomania, or must allow that "it is as natural to man to believe in a God, as to walk upon two feet" (Lichtenberger). With what right does he who mistrusts the utterances of the moral and religious consciousness, listen to those of the rational consciousness, since the credibility of the two is most closely and intimately connected?

3. With full confidence we call man a religious being, just as, *e.g.*, he may be called a social being. We do not therefore declare that all men are (actually) religious, but that man (potentially), as such, is originally designed and born for religion. He has a feeling of religion, just as he has a feeling of beauty or of truth. The spiritual *vis vitalis*, the central function of personal life, is religion. Religion is the deepest, or the absolute relation of man; his relation absolutely we might even say, man himself in this his fundamental relation (Lange); in other words, religion is the being of man. Everything within him cries after the living God, his reason, his heart, his conscience. The reason cannot rest until it has found the highest unity, the final cause; the heart remains void and restless when occupied with the finite only; the conscience proclaims a law, but postulates thereby the lawgiver. Certainly God Himself is the greatest mystery, but, at the same time, the only key to the mystery of man and mankind. "Take away God, and life is decapitated," is the dictum of the Christian philosopher Naville. Let us even say, Take away God, and not only is the head of humanity struck off, but its heart torn from its bosom. This, too, was the supreme reason for the destroying punishment of the flood; mankind had become atheistic, not polytheistic; had lost God, and itself too; had become inhuman, and morally impossible thereby; because man without God is no longer man, but either beast, or stone, or vegetable—nothing more. The possibility of becoming truly man, inborn in every one, is only realized by a personal communion with God, the natural element of man, as water is of the fish, and air of the bird.

4. If Religion in man may thus be called something natural and original, the last ground for this phenomenon cannot possibly exist in mankind itself. Religion is based on the essence of man, because the essence of man is based in God. "Self-consciousness, essentially and originally, is neither the firm basis nor the constant cause of Religion" (Beck). Man requires God, because God, whatever may be our conception of God, has created him for Himself.[2] The existence of the fruit could never be

---

[2] *Ad Te creasti.*—AUGUSTINE.

explained, if the seed were not cast into the fitting soil by the planter's own hand. All deeper thought confirms the proposition, "There cannot be a Religion without an active God" (Schelling). Religion is thus not merely sweet and charming poetry, but rather the defective expression of the sublimest reality. God has put Himself originally in communication with mankind; and by this act of God an indestructible consciousness has been implanted in man.[3] Little ground as there is for the hypothesis of innate ideas, we have yet much right to assume that a dim conception (Ahnung) of the Infinite slumbers in the depth of each human heart. That consciousness, sprung from this already pre-existent relation, develops itself so soon as man comes to a knowledge of himself and of the world around him. It is aroused, not in consequence of a logical conclusion (for then the deepest aspirations of the heart would not be explained), but as a remembrance (Inne werden) of something, which originally has been given; as a natural impulse of life towards a point, where we, as it were instinctively, feel that we must be. The more man develops his nature, the more he strives after God;[4] and, again, the more religious he is, the more human does he become in the real sense of the word. "Domine, *quia nos creasti ad Te*, cor nostrum inquietum in nobis, donec requiescat in Te" (Augustine).

5. This doctrine seeks not in vain for support and commendation in the words of Holy Scripture. The Old Testament has already given eloquent testimony thereto, while the New Testament, and St. Paul specially, do the same. This, too, is the profound meaning of the sacred declaration that everything was made, not only by but for the Logos, the Son of God.[5] The heart of man seeks after God, because man is made after the image of God, the Logos. On this, too, we ground, first, the right of each man to religion (in a similar sense to that in which he may, against others, lay claim to that which he absolutely requires for the realization of his life's destiny); and then, the unconditional claim of religion upon him and on the application of all his powers. We cannot demand from every man to be ingenious or talented; but we may ask that he be religious, because, and so far as, he is really man. Indifferentism on this point is both unnatural and immoral, even where it comes with the mask of toleration.

6. The question whether there are atheists is properly distinguished from that, whether peoples have been found without religion, and has always been differently answered. In any case, they are less in numbers than has often been supposed, and not without reason are we warned not to consider any one too quickly as an atheist, or even as entirely without religion. Yet, when we regard the wiles of Satan as they have been shown in this century, we cannot deny entirely the existence of Atheism, which both theoretically and practically is constantly gaining more frightful power. Least of all can we do so now, when there are those who do not hesitate to declare: "Even Atheism is still a religious system; the Atheist is not freer than the Jew who eats ham. We must not wrestle with religion, we must forget it" (Ruge). Some really have made great progress in this

---

[3] Gen. ii. 7: Ecc. iii. 11; Ps. lxxiii. 25, 26; Amos v. 6.
[4] Acts xvii. 27, 28; Rom. i. 19, 20; xi. 36.
[5] John i. 4; Col. i. 16.

forgetfulness; their religion has become a worship of genius; their worship of genius a worship of self; though even in this form their need of veneration and prayer be unmistakable. And yet, though the fool says, not merely in his heart, but with his mouth and life, "There is no God," this blasphemy proves nothing against the truth. No one has begun by being an Atheist; and he who, after a long violation of his nature, has become an Atheist, and continues to be one, ceases then to be really a man, *i.e.*, to be a rational and moral being. Atheism, not Religion, is monomania. Our relation to God is not merely the fruit, but the foundation of our entire personality; that which really forms that personality, and gives it its tone and measure. This will be more clearly seen when we have looked at the seat of religion.

Comp. J. P. ROMANG, *Natürl. Rel. Lehre* (1841), §§ 9—29; A. DES AMORIE VAN DER HOEVEN, Jr., *De Godsdienst, het Wezen van den Mensch.* (1848); E. NAVILLE, *Le Père Céleste, Sept. Discours.* (1865), pp. 35—144; DE QUATREFAGES, *Les Caractères supérieurs de la race humaine*, in the *Revue Chrétienne* for 1867, p. 519, *sqq.*; GUIZOT, *Meditations*, ii. (1866), p. 353, *sqq.*

POINTS FOR INQUIRY.

Criticism of the most noted objections which in our times have been urged against the universality of Religion.—How far is Religion properly called the essence of man?—Historical and philological evidence in support of the enunciated principle.—Why cannot Religion in man be explained entirely and solely from man himself?—The connexion between the development of the consciousness of self, of the world, and of God.—Does any degree of truth lie at the base of the doctrine of *ideæ innatæ*?—Elucidation of the scriptural proof.—How is the progress and power of Atheism in the present century to be explained?

SECTION XXIII.—ITS SEAT.

Religion, founded on the nature and essence of mankind, occupies a place quite peculiar in the inner life of man. We must not look exclusively for the seat of the religious principle either in the Reason, or in the Will, or in the Feeling, or in the Conscience. In the inmost sanctuary of the Soul, where these are still originally one and undivided, is seen the fountain-head of the spiritual, and specially of the God-life of mankind. Starting from this centre, Religion embraces, penetrates, and directs in the truly religious man his entire internal and external existence. It is in this central position which Religion occupies, that the secret of its power, the cause of its conflict, the warrant of its imperishable stability and future triumph lies.

1. It is scarcely necessary to remind that the seat of the religious principle in man is not in any case to be found in the material sphere. The phenomenon that the religious life is often most completely developed where bodily strength decays,[1] serves as a proof to the contrary. Might it then be preferable to place the seat of religion in our reason? That it was often looked for there appears, if we cast our eyes at Scholasticism, Orthodoxism, or, not to mention any other philosophic schools, Hegelianism. And yet we must reject this conception, as plainly contradicting the facts. For do we not see the religious life more completely developed just where the intellectual is most contracted, and a most extended knowledge of God accompanied with entire Godlessness?[2] Religion unites men; but is there anything which separates them more than their notions of religion? Does not experience teach us that in many the so-called sound understanding stands in the way of religious belief?[3] and does not Holy Scripture oppose most emphatically the presumption of knowledge on this subject?[4] It is in vain that some appeal to expressions, such as John viii. 32, xvii. 3, Eph. v. 17, in favour of this definition, as the knowledge and understanding here alluded to is quite another thing from the natural results of an isolated tendency of the reason.

2. With just as little right can the *will* be regarded as the birthplace and organ of religion. That the latter should consist specially in willing and acting is a thesis which is strongly supported, specially by the Romish Church, and among philosophers by Kant. In fact, religion is as much concerned with the will as with the understanding; *Nemo credit nisi volens* is a saying of deep meaning. The connexion between religion and morality is close, even in the statements of the Bible,[5] but—and this is the dark side of the said theory—the distinction between the two is liable in this way to be completely forgotten. A man may have deep religious feelings without those feelings leading to any moral activity; even further, many an act may be morally wrong and abominable, and yet the expression of a degenerate religious feeling; while, on the other hand, many an action will exhibit a moral character, though it is entirely void of a religious disposition. The moral man will do what is good; the religious man, besides, will receive something from the All-good. Religion gives rise to worship, and morality to practice. In the first the feeling of dependence is revealed; in the other the voice of free self-determination. A *separation* of religion and morality seems, after all, impossible; and the well-known expression, "It is no matter what a man's belief is, if he only lives well," is the utterance of the veriest superficiality. As long, however, as the *distinction* still exists, one must scruple to look for the seat of religion exclusively or chiefly in the will of man.

3. "Godliness, considered by itself in the abstract, is neither knowledge nor act, but a determination of the feeling, or of the immediate

---

[1] 2 Cor. iv. 16.
[2] James ii. 19.
[3] Acts xvii. 18; xxvi. 24.
[4] Luke x. 21; 1 Cor. i. 18; 2 Cor. x. 4; comp. Isa. xlvii. 7—10.
[5] Matt. vii. 21; James i. 27.

self-consciousness." It is with this thesis that Schleiermacher came out to prove that religion was something more than a "mixture of metaphysical and moral crumbs." Yet, though we praise what is commendable in this proposition, we must not overlook its one-sidedness and incompleteness. Not to speak of the obscurity of the expression, or of the important difference in the manner in which it was formulated in his earlier and later times by the renowned theologian, it is at once seen that feeling, thus sharply separated from knowledge and action, is in man the lowest, and not the highest quality, which he has in common with many animals. From this feeling of dependence, moreover, the worship of a personal God, actually distinguished from the "Universum," can by no means be explained. If man by his feeling discovered God so immediately, as those who hold this view assert, it is inconceivable that a Sceptic or Atheist could exist. In opposition to its aim, this conclusion leads inevitably, on the one hand, to a religious fanaticism and arbitrariness; on the other, to an irreconcilable separation between faith and knowledge, by which, at best, man continues "at heart a Christian, in his reason a heathen." So at last religion becomes a beautiful poetic fancy; and the denial of God, on the other hand, the formal result of science.

4. But thus, after all, we might possibly discover in conscience, regarded by itself, what we have hitherto looked for in vain in man's reason, feeling, and will! After the remarks which have already (§ 10) been made respecting Consciencialism, it will not be necessary to justify our doubts on this point by many grounds. It is evident that the first and most natural manifestations of religious life cannot possibly be explained as the revelation and operation of the conscience only. "Conscience, as such, does not give utterance to love, gratitude, prayer, and praise; and, on this account, it cannot be the organ of religion, any more than reason, which here equally fails" (Hagenbach). Hence we observe that, in fallen man, conscience is at the same time a consciousness of guilt, which will separate him much more from God than it will drive him to Him. It is just the conscience which makes the sinner tremble before Him, to whom the heart is unceasingly attracted. Besides, all religion is, from its nature, social and attractive; conscience, on the other hand, isolates us from others, just as the understanding does, because it individualizes us as much as possible. So it may tell us of an obligation towards religion, but it does not call religion itself into existence, either in the individual or in the community. Truth looks for, and finds, a point of union in the conscience;[6] but religion, *l'élan de l'âme vers Dieu*, cannot possibly be conceived as the mere product of conscience.

5. We are thus from every side driven back into the inmost sanctuary, where that which we separate in our representation lies still unseparated, and which we can only call conscience when this word is used in that more extended sense in which it was declared, *e.g.*, of Vinet, "Il désigna par ce mot de conscience, l'ensemble de sentiments, de besoins et d'idées qui constituent chez l'homme sa nature superieure" (Astié). We would rather

---

[6] 2 Cor. iv. 2; v. 11.

call that *ensemble* heart, while we accept the confession *pectus est quod religiosum facit*. That heart, by no means the same as feeling and conscience, —the heart, in which the issues of life are found, and in which conscience is written as the law of God,—is the germ and core of the entire personality; the holy hearth from which the sparks spread in all directions, as also the cradle of the religious life of mankind. This already appears from the fact that, in general, that man is the most religious in whom the secret life of the soul is most powerfully developed. The soul urges to gratitude, prayer, love,—in a word, to everything which makes and marks out religion; for not to think of God, not to will, nor to feel, but to *have* God, because man is innerly united with Him—that is the cardinal point. The greatest thoughts do not spring from the understanding, but enter into it from the heart of man; "The heart is the bud of the head"[7] (Jean Paul). So also the pressure towards God, whose name is stamped deeply and ineffaceably in the conscience, but whose face none would look for, if the heart could live without His communion. "My son, give me thine heart,"[8] is therefore the highest, and at the same time the deepest, word of supreme wisdom. With its voice in Holy Scripture our definition agrees, as we see, if we call to mind the words of Moses in Deut. xxx. 6, and specially those of Jesus, Matt. xxii. 37—40. Very remarkable, too, in this light, is the language of the Old Testament, where it speaks of the bending of the heart to the Lord, and after strange gods; the one the natural tendency, the other the sad deflection, to be explained by sin, but yet in the highest sense unnatural. It is scarcely necessary to remind the reader that that which is seated in the heart must and will work with power on the reason, feeling, and will; must and will of course penetrate the entire man, and exhibit itself in his life. But that which reveals itself in this way has only value and import in so far as it is the expression of the sincere religion of the heart.

6. The heart, the seat of religion! Therein lies the secret of its power; for that which is the most deeply seated, and from thence embraces and penetrates the whole life, of course exercises the most powerful influence. Consciously or unconsciously the religious question lies at the bottom of every question; for really "the conflict between belief and unbelief is the deepest, the sole problem of the history of the world" (Goethe).—Here, then, we find the reason for that conflict which has been caused in the heart and the world by religion, more than by any other thing. Religious hate is the bloodiest and deepest of all, and no wonder, since no other discord seizes thus directly and powerfully on the most hidden principles of life; man only struggles thus for that which is the very highest life of the soul.—Here, lastly, is the warrant for the duration of religion, and its future triumph. The religious principle cannot possibly be entirely blotted out of the heart of mankind; for if so, man would lose that which distinguishes him from other creatures. The heart is as it were the palimpsest, on which the older letters, however pale and effaced, will come to light again when it has been properly handled. The

[7] Les grandes pensées viennent du cœur.—PASCAL.

[8] Prov. xxiii. 26.

"pious sigh" of the reviving Atheism, "The world would have been happier if it had never known of God," is not merely blasphemous, but thoroughly unnatural. *Naturam expellas furcâ, tamen usque recurret.* If, in the conflict of the present century, Religion were to be finally defeated, superstition would always have at least one chance of life more than an unbridled unbelief. Take away from man his God, and he will not rest until you have given him a godhead back again—it may be in the form of an idol.

7. The result thus gained has a very varied importance. It is of importance for Pædagogics. The religious feeling cannot be instilled, but must be called out as much as possible. The want of it generally arises from this, that while the brain suffers from hypertrophy, the life of the heart is not sufficiently developed.—Of importance for Apologetics. Religion cannot be proved to demonstration, nor be recommended by mere intellectual motives. "The heart has its reasons which reason does not know" (Vinet).—Of importance for Dogmatics. It will be treated in a thoroughly different manner, just as the question as to the seat of religion is differently answered. A faulty psychology will be injurious to the whole of theology. On the contrary, the deeper we dig into the domain of the inner life, the more certainly we attain the spot where we cannot touch religion without wounding the tenderest susceptibilities. "In a certain sense the expression, consciousness, soul, etc., avails for an allowed, though only provisional, escape from the conflict" (Nitzsch). On the other hand, it is ever more and more seen that that which is the finest and deepest can never be anatomized and sounded. It is therefore doubly necessary to see that, while we continue our investigations into the essence and seat of religion, we never lose sight of its final object.

Comp. ELWERT, *Ueber das Wesen der Religion* in the *Tübing. Zeitschrift* for 1835; E. ZELLER on the same subject in the *Theol. Jahrb.*, 1845, i.; J. T. BECK, *Bibl. Seelenlehre*, 2 Aufl., p. 64 (1862); AUBERLEN, *Die Göttl. Offenb.* ii., pp. 25—61 (1864); H. O. PFLEIDERER, *Moral und Religion nach ihren gegenseitigen Verhältniss u. s. w.*; Works of the *Teyler. Godgel. Genoolsch.* (1871).

POINTS FOR INQUIRY.

Criticism of the Materialistic explanation of Religion.—Historical survey of the different theories concerning the seat of Religion.—Strength and weakness of the theories of Schleiermacher and Schenkel.—The heart, in its relation to feeling, understanding, will, conscience.—Construction of the biblical proof of our proposition.—Maintenance of its practical importance.

SECTION XXIV.—ITS FINAL OBJECT.

Every manifestation of the Religious Sense is either consciously or unconsciously founded on a striving after an object, which, however, is differently conceived according to different degrees of

development. The object at which the truly religious man of God aims can be as little to render God a service in the literal sense of the word, as merely to seek in communion with Him profit and enjoyment to himself. The final object of this communion with God is personal union with Him, whereby He is glorified, and the heart of man is completely satisfied. This object, however, is only really attainable in connection with a Theistic conception of God.

1. Although the thirst after God in man may be called natural, and in so far involuntary, yet all religious life and effort is directed to the gaining of a certain end. Each religion exhibits in its degree a teleological and elpistic character, to which it is absolutely necessary that we should pay attention if we would obtain a proper estimation of our subject. Since, however, there is so great variety of religious presentment and development, it is not possible that this object should be the same in every case.

2. Their standpoint is lowest, who consider religion as the means, of, literally, doing service to God. This view, which belongs to the rudest form of heathendom, has been combated by some excellent thinkers before the time of Moses or of Christ. It was refuted with power by the poets and prophets of Israel,[1] and was rejected with indignation in the New Testament by St. Paul, as well as others. It is in direct conflict with every better, every purer idea of God's majesty and independence,[2] and cannot maintain its position for a moment, except, perhaps, before the tribunal of a speculative philosophy, which only acknowledges a not really existing Godhead, coming into being and full consciousness only in the human soul.

3. Without doubt, their attempt is somewhat more reasonable, who try to benefit themselves by their religion. Though the selfishness which suggests this view be a principle[3] as well known as it is impure, it is yet conceivable, and more worthy of respect, since it welds itself to religion with the object of drawing from it a treasure of light and power, of comfort and hope. It is an exaggerated demand that men ought to be religious without in a certain degree giving heed to the reward both for oneself and for others attached to a sincere devotion. The doctrine of the so-called pure love (Fénélon) rests on exaggeration and misunderstanding. That which cannot be a principle may still always serve as a stimulus. Yet the final object of real worship cannot possibly be placed in anything but in God Himself. As religion, in its deepest ground, is from God, so does it reach also to God. By communion with God it aims at the closest possible union with Him, by which He is glorified, and the heart which cannot rest in any finite thing is completely satisfied. If religion, properly considered, is nothing but the impulse of life and love, the love remains unsatisfied so

---

[1] Ps. l. 10—12; li. 16, 17; Isa. i. 11—18; Job xxii. 3; Acts xvii. 24.
[2] 1 Tim. vi. 13.
[3] Job i. 9; 1 Tim. vi. 6.

long as it remains in any degree separated from the object which is loved more than aught else.

4. Meanwhile we must above all take care that while we strive towards the summit we may avoid a dangerous precipice. Every sound manifestation of religious life seeks *personal* union with God, *i.e.*, one in which our individuality is not lost in the contemplation of God, but, on the contrary, is preserved, emancipated, and purified. It sounds very poetical to talk, as is often done, of being absorbed and lost in God's communion, but taken literally, these expressions have rather an æsthetical than an ethical and philosophical value. Communion is only conceivable when the individual life of those between whom it is held is retained, and so personality ought not to be considered as a hindrance, but, on the contrary, as the *sine quâ non* of the highest of all religious life. The warmest love, even, will only lose itself in the loved object, to find itself soon again in that beloved object; the contrary would be the death of love, which (Plato) is nothing less than the striving after immortality. The religious man is in relation to God, not as the dewdrop, which is dried up by the sun, but as the sunflower, which turns towards and opens itself before its light. This, indeed, is the glory of God, that He demands the sacrifice of our heart, but not of our individuality, and only accepts the first in order to give it back again, at rest and purified. Inasmuch, however, as this object is only imperfectly attained here below, is life in communion with God (we shall return again to this point) the pledge of an eternal future in which He will be all indeed, but *in* all, *i.e.*, without destroying their personal life.

5. Although we may, whilst starting from a very different conception of God, be striving after the same object, this by no means will be attained from every standpoint. Where a deistic conception of God is professed, we cannot properly and seriously speak of a constant communion with God. God is here not only merely raised too far above the creature, but is separated too far from him. As little is real religion conceivable where pantheistic principles are professed, because there the personal distinction between Creator and creature is done away. Only where, from a theistic standpoint (which we shall hereafter advocate), we do justice alike to the immanence and transcendence of God, can the highest object of Religion be sufficiently accurately defined and properly realized. While this observation is itself true, it likewise offers a measure by which to determine the unequal value of the different forms of Religion.

Comp. VON SCHUBERT, *Gesch. d. Seele*, 3 Aufl. (1832), §§ 1 and 67; DE WETTE, *Ueber Religion, u. s. w.* (1817), p. 61, *sqq.*, and the article *Eudæmonisme* in Herzog's *R. E.*

POINTS FOR INQUIRY.

The different definitions and judgments as to the objects of religion at different times. —Is it possible to be religious from selfish motives?—Something as to the *amour pur* of Fénélon.—How does Religion work to the glory of God, and in what connexion does it stand with our personal happiness?—Peculiarity and value of the Pantheistic conception of God.—Is it then impossible on Deistic or Pantheistic principles to be sincerely religious?

SECTION XXV.—ITS DIVERSITY.

The various forms in which the religious life of mankind expresses itself, and the abundance of which renders a further division of Religions necessary, point back to one origin and one need. Even the most faulty form of Religion is so far worthy of respect, whilst on the other hand the most excellent still always remains below the ideal of perfect Religion. Yet the value of the different forms of Religion is by no means the same; and specially the distance between Monotheistic and Non-monotheistic Religions is too great to make mention only of gradual differences. Among Monotheistic religions Christianity has an excellency, which only becomes clearer when it is impartially compared with other Religions.

1. Hitherto we have spoken of Religion as a whole, without paying attention to its variety. In this domain, however, the difference is equally great with that betwen nations and between men. An endless variety of forms is displayed here, and the history of Religion has to occupy itself with pointing out their origin, peculiarity, and mutual connexion. And yet, on so extensive a field as this, Dogmatics must, in some degree at least, consider what its position is. It cannot possibly duly represent the essence of Christianity, as long as it is wholly unacquainted with the character of other religions.

2. The different forms of religion have been and are divided in more than one manner: A. With an eye upon the *subject*, which practises the religion, into general or individual, true or false, external or internal religion. B. Looking to the *object* of worship; (*a*) as to quantity, into monotheistic, dualistic, polytheistic, etc.; (*b*) as to quality, into the worship of a perfect being, or of imperfect finite things. C. With an eye on the *source*, into natural and revealed, in the stricter sense of the word. D. According to the degree of *culture* of the peoples, into religions of the childhood, youth, manhood of mankind. We might also speak of other divisions, *e.g.*, psychological and ethnographical; but completeness is here superfluous, and the difficulty in choosing a division which will not call forth a single objection, is already evident enough. The most acceptable division, which is also sufficient for our purpose, is that into Monotheistic and Non-monotheistic religions, which will separately claim our attention.

3. At once the question meets us here, which of these two is the older? In other words, does this history of religion begin from above or from below? Is Polytheism a degenerate Monotheism? or has mankind, on the contrary, raised itself slowly from the lower standpoint to the higher? This question must be discussed here, since the answer mnst greatly in-

fluence our decision on the value of religions. That answer is more difficult, because it is often even involuntarily governed by certain premises. If it is asserted, with the supporters of the development hypothesis, that man is the merely natural product of the lower kinds of animals, sprung on their part from inorganic materials, we shall probably also assume that he very slowly ascended to an obscure conception, first of many, then of one higher Being. If, on the contrary, we place God at the beginning of history, and consider man as a new link in the chain of finite beings, we shall inevitably incline to the opposite view. In fact, much more can be said in favour of the latter than of the former view. It is, indeed, much more conceivable that mankind declined from Monotheism to Polytheism, than the converse. The first is a decay, for which we can find many analogies; the other would be a development, of which we cannot find a second example. The cradle of Polytheism is not discovered; if we do not conceive of it as a decline from a former better way,—in other words, as a degeneration from Monotheism,—its fundamental basis is yet unexplained. It must also be observed that polytheism generally tends, not to the better, but to the worse; in other words, that it is continually increasing the number of its gods, not decreasing them; which ever-growing numbers constantly lead to more divisions, in which, however, something of a monotheistic background may here and there be observed. In many polytheistic forms of religion we often seem to meet with broken rays of a previously undivided and originally purer light, and we often discover among the older nations purer ideas on this subject than in a younger race. "It is indeed striking, that the most ancient nations, which in other things were quite uncultivated, had very true representations and knowledge of God, of the world, of immortality; whilst the arts, which concern the conveniences of life, are much younger. In matters of the highest import the men of the most ancient times had right ideas, while in the business of life they were children" (Joh. v. Muller). "Antiquitas, quo propius aberat ab ortu, eo melius fortasse quæ erant vera cernebat" (Cicero). The striking phenomenon, that it is in the highest sphere of thought that the earlier ideas were so much purer than the later, ceases to be quite inexplicable when we regard Monotheism—and to this conclusion, for other reasons too, we must come (as will be shown hereafter)—as the fruit of an *original revelation*. While accepting this, we must also allow that it is not the error, but the truth, which was afterwards forgotten, which has been the basis of the oldest form of religion, and that Monotheism originally revealed, disappeared almost immediately, and was afterwards raised to higher honour in consequence of a renewed revelation.

4. If from this standpoint we cast our glance over the most distinguished forms of religion, we may collect the Non-monotheistic forms under the general name of *Heathendom*, and understand this latter as a deterioration of a better principle, as a descent from a previous height. This view had been taken, not only by the prophets of Israel, but by St. Paul in Rom. i. 18; ii. 14, 15. "Heathendom is in general to be regarded as a falling away and debasing of true religion" (Lange). It has thus a basis which is decidedly immoral; it is an error, brought into existence by the power of sin, which, on its part, leads on to other sins. It is, as St. Paul has

already shown,[1] in its inmost essence a deification of nature, by which the border-line between sensual and spiritual is of itself done away, and even the most unbridled emancipation of the flesh receives the consecration of religion. It is not easy to come to a properly fair decision upon Heathendom, considered as a moral and religious phenomenon. At all times there has been a wavering in thought between a pessimistic and an optimistic tendency. As a type of the first we might mention the *Splendida Vitia* of Augustine, while the *Die Götter Griechenlands* of Schiller may be considered as the interpreter of the other. Besides, a judgment cannot easily be made without further distinction, since Heathendom, like the Corinthian copper of olden time, was made up of very different elements. In general, while we are estimating these *wildwachsende Religionen* (Schelling), we must never forget that even where God suffered the heathen to walk in their own ways, the Logos was already, before His incarnation, the light and life of men.[2] Fetichism without doubt occupies the lowest place of all these forms of religion; somewhat higher is the more organised worship of fire and light, as the fundamental force which penetrates everything (Astrolatry or Sabianism, Fire-worship). Above which, again, the Egyptian's worship of animal life (Zoölatry) is raised. The deification of man in all its forms (Anthropolatry) reaches the very summit of Apotheosis in the gods of Greece, presented as objects of regard and reverence under the most beautiful human forms. If deified men are still here the objects of veneration (hero-worship), we see this rendered elsewhere to higher spirits (Demonolatry), which, regarded from a moral standpoint, too often deserve the name of evil spirits. As in the countless grains of broken crystal the image of the higher power is reflected for us in the ever-increasing number of gods (Polytheism). Lastly, everything becomes God; Pantheism steps forth as a settled religious system, that even in these days finds an effective, though variously diversified, expression in the two chief forms of Indian Mythology. First, in the religion of the Parsees, does Dualism show itself in an actually ethical character, while in the background the belief in an Almighty God is most undoubtedly declared. Elsewhere, too, in Heathendom we meet with traces of a Monotheistic view. (The Orphic wisdom, Anaxagoras, Xenophanes, Plato, etc.), although we rise here at best to the idea of a powerful demiurge, not to the conception of an absolutely perfect Creator of the world. But even where the numerical unity of the highest Being is confessed by some, it is done in a manner far above the reach of most; and even while we observe with interest the most astonishing aspirations towards a higher light, we nowhere find Heathenism completely escape the danger of a deification of nature. Whither human wisdom, when left to itself, can attain in this domain, we see in a striking manner in Buddhism, the most tragic form of religion; but even where the precipice of misery is veiled from our gaze by countless flowers, we cannot grant to Heathendom, viewed as a whole, any higher name than that of the religion of *helpless despair*.

5. We meet with a more pleasing view when we look at the Monotheistic

---

[1] Rom. i. 24 *sqq*.

[2] Acts xiv. 17; John i. 4.

forms of religion, and first of all regard that of the Israelites. Here we see the Divine and the human, not confounded, but sharply distinguished in Hebraism, while even in Judaism they were not seldom separated from one another. In the Patriarchal period the power of God is put in the foreground; in the Mosaic, His holiness; in the Prophetic, the mercy and truth of God as contrasted with His justice. But all these periods have this in common, that not only was the unity of God confessed against the number of false gods, but God also was conceived of as the living God, in immediate and constant relation with His people. Religion and morality, in Heathenism oftentimes distinctly placed in contrast, are here most closely united; every relation of life is ruled by a higher law, and, where that law fills the sinner with consternation and fear, prophecy unfolds the view of a golden age of deliverance. The place which is occupied by the Mosaic religion, not only as contrasted with, but also as raised far above, all heathen religions, is quite unique. "Its basis is special revelation, its character monotheistic, its form theocratic, its public worship typico-symbolic, its tendency purely moral, its standpoint one of external authority, and at the same time one of conscious preparation for a higher development" (J. J. van Oosterzee). Every renewed investigation which is not guided by naturalistic principles, proves the impossibility of considering this religion as a merely natural fruit of the tree of humanity. The glancing lights of Mosaism are only explicable by the fact of a special revelation; whilst its shadows—as, *e.g.*, its sternly limited character, and the absence of very important doctrines, such as Eschatology—find their solution in the pædagogic and preparatory character of the entire dispensation. All Israel, like Daniel the prophet, is a *vir desideriorum*, and its religion is that of a growing expectation of salvation founded on the revelation of old.

6. That expectation is satisfied by Christianity, which in fact reveals, announces, and establishes a real union between God and man, which Heathenism was merely seeking, and Judaism waiting for. God and man are no longer confounded in thought, nor only distinguished; they are truly reunited. In Heathenism we see humanity deified; here, on the contrary, the Divine becomes man. In consequence of a supranatural (when we look at it from a human standpoint) act of Divine love, a moral communion is established, and the spiritual union of fallen man with his Maker is restored. Heathenism places man in a purely natural relation to God, Judaism in a strictly legal one, while Christianity represents it as a childlike spiritual relation, because God Himself fulfils His promise.[3] It is not merely as a new doctrine, more excellent than any other, but as a new revelation of the highest love, which for that very reason is a new principle of life, that it has astonished the world, and already to a certain extent reformed it. Here the Founder is at the same time the centre of his religion, which proclaims itself as the fruit of a special revelation,[4] and hence is rightly called the religion of *spiritual satisfaction.*

7. The transition from Christianity to Islamism cannot be anything but a decline, though the historic import of the religion of Mahomet is much

[3] Jer. xxxi. 31—34.

[4] 1 Cor. ii. 9; Heb. i. 1.

greater than its internal value. Later investigation confirms much more than it contradicts the saying of Luther, that "Islamism might be called a collection of scattered sentences from the law and the Gospel." In any case it is, both theoretically and practically, far inferior to Mosaism and Christianity. Its conception of God is Deistic, its revelation mechanical, its doctrine of predestination fatalistic, its religion itself fanatical, its morality eudæmonistic, and its eschatology grossly sensual. Islamism is in character oriental, but not catholic nor human, still less is it purely spiritual; it is a religion sprung from man, and therefore agreeable to man; and it is this peculiarity which has given it its wide authority and temporary success. Whatever merit it may have, it owes more than aught else to its Christian elements; but when compared with the Gospel itself, it deserves no higher name than that of a religion of "*petted sensuality.*"

8. The time for the rise of really new religions seems to have departed centuries ago; whatever has been propounded in later times, and even in ours, (as, *e.g.*, Mormonism) seems to be merely a caricature of the old. Hence the question naturally arises, whether we can indeed discover a specific, or merely a gradual diversity between the well-known forms of religious life; in other words, whether Christianity—if its Divine origin be once proved—may be called the absolutely true, or merely the relatively most excellent religion. From the Supranaturalistic standpoint the answer is easy. Even when we duly value each higher aspiration, which is not wanting in any one religion, there yet exists a difference, not merely of degree, but of kind, between that which is the consequence of special revelation, and that which is not. This is very plain when we carefully compare the Monotheistic and Non-monotheistic religions. The latter are generally in unison, the former, on the contrary, in conflict with the natural bias of the people by whom they are professed; the Greek mythology, for example, is in perfect harmony with its Hellenistic character; the Israelitic Monotheism, on the contrary, offers a constant protest to the slavish, sensual, idolatrous tendency of the nation. This distinction is specially observable when we look at Christianity. In contrast with all the Non-monotheistic religions, it exhibits a purely spiritual character; it does not bear the stamp of nationality, but of the purest humanity; and gives us an evidence of the highest unity of religion and morality. Where in other religions man is petted and flattered, he is here brought low and humbled, while God alone receives the honour of the work of redemption. The idea, moreover, of the original preventing and seeking love of God for us, His enemies, which here lies at the foundation both of doctrine and morality,[5] never sprung up in the heart of man; and the ideal of a kingdom of God, which embraces all, and overcomes everything, has nowhere been so purely conceived or at first so happily attained. Whatever value we may put on the germs of truth which are present in every religion, for all these reasons we cannot deny that we are here on a completely different ground from that which the lower Non-monotheistic religions present.

---

[5] 1 John iv. 19.

9. If we afterwards sufficiently prove what we have here stated, we hereby already and at once define the relation which, starting from a Christian standpoint, we must occupy to other forms of religion. That relation cannot be one of a so-called toleration which considers all religions equally good, in so far at least as they are honestly held; still less can it be that of a narrow Exclusiveness, which considers everything which is not directly Christian as utterly false and inadmissible, and passes by the precious iron hidden under the thick coating of rust. But it will be that of a thankful recognition of our own privileges, accompanied with the earnest endeavour to recommend and communicate them to others. The acknowledgment of the great excellence of the Christian religion above all others is, at the same time, the basis of Christian Apologetics, and of true theological Therapeutics. The ever-existing needs of this last will appear when we observe religious life in its multifold degeneration.

Comp. PARET, *Ueber die Eintheilung der Religionen, Stud. u. Krit.* (1855), ii., p. 261, *sqq.*; HOFSTEDE DE GROOT, *Instit. Theol. Nat.*, 4th ed. (1861), p. 214, *sqq.*; THOLUCK, *Der Sittliche Character des Heidenthums*; VAN OOSTERZEE, *Biblical Theology*, Eng. Trans., §§ 4—6; G. R. NIEMAN, *Inleiding tot de Kennis van den Islam* (1861); and also the chief handbooks of the *History of Religion*, in whose constantly increasing number we must not forget J. GARDNER, *The principal Religions of the World*; C. HARDWICK, *Christ and other Masters.*

POINTS FOR INQUIRY.

Which division of religions, generally considered, is the best?—Further examination of the reasons for and against the priority of Monotheism.—Agreement and differences of the Non-monotheistic religion.—Mutual relations of Mosaism, Christianity, and Islamism.—The reason why no new religions have arisen since Islamism.—The fable of the three rings in Lessing's *Nathan der Weis.*

SECTION XXVI.—ITS DEGENERATION.

As the history of mankind shows an endless variety of forms of Religion, so the history of Religion exhibits a boundless scene of deep degeneration. Where Religion, which ought to animate the whole man, is exclusively ruled by one faculty of human nature, morbid symptoms, in consequence of this one-sidedness, will inevitably appear. These symptoms produce sects, which on their side contain the seeds of new diseases. The unhindered development of these diseases may become so deadly to individual and social life, that Religion itself degenerates at last into Godlessness.

1. "Optimi corruptio pessima" is nowhere more clearly seen than in the domain of religion. As it in itself may be called the highest benefit, where the religious principle harmoniously penetrates and rules man's whole internal and external life; so what is good in itself really becomes death when the spiritual life develops itself in a one-sided manner. Morbid symptoms appear, at one time of an individual, at another of a social kind, whose destructive effects can hardly be estimated. Of the most dangerous at least we must get a general knowledge, if, as Theologians, we will fulfil our obligation to be God's pathologists. They will successively reveal themselves to our view, as we observe Religion under the preponderating influence of those powers and faculties of man, in which its seat has at different times been exclusively sought.

2. Where religion is regarded exclusively or principally as a matter of the understanding, there the tyranny of *Intellectualism* is soon felt. It is this tendency which over-rates the value of a correct *conception* of faith, even to the detriment of the spiritual life, and confounds the subjective conception of truth with truth itself. This intellectual bent easily degenerates into an unhealthy gnostic tendency, which attempts to grasp religious truth merely by the reasoning and speculating understanding, and confounds thought with knowledge, while the distinction between religion and theology is gradually lost. Since, however, this system must not only be formulated, but also defended, the Intellectualist is very easily drawn into the path of Doctrinalism, which discovers the nature of religion exclusively in dogma as such. Doctrinalism may exhibit the form of Rationalism, as well as that of Supranaturalism. The former considers reason not merely as the organ, but as the very source and supreme arbiter, of religious truth; the other accepts the existence and the contents of a supranatural revelation, but receives this rather as a *doctrine* announced by supreme authority. The adherent of the last-named view easily becomes a strict orthodoxist with regard to the traditional confession, valuing *soundness* of faith even at the expense of the *faith* itself. From this standpoint the intellect works only receptively, whilst with the rationalist it has more a critical sway. Where the sovereignty of this partial tendency of the intellect is not encountered by any other forces, it may finally lead the believer to the precipice of unbelief, the Protestant into the arms of Rome.

3. Symptoms of disease not less dangerous are seen where the religious life is too partially governed by *feeling*. No one will deny that a deep and holy Mysticism is conceivable in the religious and Christian domain, or even that it is in a certain sense inseparable from the spiritual life. Such a sound Mysticism is that of John, as contrasted with the more doctrinal spirit of Paul. Such was that of Tauler and Thomas à Kempis. "The internal life and vigour of religion is always Mysticism" (Nitzsch). But from this delicate inner disposition we must carefully distinguish that cloudy and sickly Mysticism, in which feeling and experience speak at the expense of reason and conscience. Whilst the Intellectualist maintains the letter, even against the spirit; the Mystic places the spirit, such as he conceives it, infinitely above the letter. His feeling decides what is true and untrue, what is Divine and human, and against this judgment the most close reasoning is useless. He easily slights the church for the

conventicle, and the sacrament for secret prayer. When this over-excited feeling is joined with an ardent fancy, an unbridled fanaticism is seen, not a soft, cherishing fire, but a wild destructive flame. Propagandism may be considered as one of its relatively moderate forms, types of which are pointed out in Matt. xxiii. 15. But the more audacious Zelotism is also a fruit of this soil; a disease, whose victims are pointed out in Rom. x. 2 and John xvi. 2; and at the end of this gloomy road, when it is followed to the end without interruption, in the dusky distance appear—the flames of the *auto da fés*.

4. Though we are preserved from these dangers, where the religious life is considered by preference as a matter of the *will*, we shall then the sooner suffer shipwreck on the rock of another peril. Here threatens that of that *Moralism* or *Legalism*, which looks rather at the external form than at the essential principle of life; in other words, which values the fruit of faith at the expense of the root. From this point of view, but little importance is conceded to the religious conception or feeling, but all the more to the action. It is not Paul, or still less John, but James, who, though wholly misunderstood, is by preference taken as a guide. He who, continuing in this path, does not decline into a formal Pharisaism, will very quickly find himself on the track of a narrow Pietism. This appellation, though often used unfairly, is yet the best description of the tendency which suffers itself to be guided by the spirit of a legal force, rather than by that of evangelical freedom, and confounds the means of godliness with godliness itself. It may be known, amidst other symptoms, by a methodistical uniformity, which prescribes the same way of regeneration for all, and by a timid horror of the world, which shuns even all allowed enjoyment, such as those of nature or art. "Touch not, taste not, handle not,"[1] is its motto, and at the end of this road stands the door of the cloister.

5. Closely allied to these last are the morbid symptoms exhibited under the influence of an awakened *conscience*. We think here of Asceticism, allied to Pietism, but not therefore homogeneous to it. However excellent a suitable Asceticism[2] may be, when directed by the awe of conscience, it will very soon acquire the character of arbitrariness and hypocrisy. The entire theory of "thesaurus supererogationis" has been developed under its influence. Whence, indeed, does all superstition spring, if it be not from the desire to still the restlessness of conscience by a self-chosen method? There can be no doubt that such a painful fear inevitably excludes love, and thus destroys the principle of all religion;[3] but it is moreover evident that Consciencialism, in the domain of Religion, leads more than any other school of thought to *Individualism*. What is there which is announced as truth, or condemned as sin, by the conscience of absolutely all? Thus isolation takes the place of communion, and never is man further removed than there from the ideal of a cheerful worship of God.

6. Every disease in the religious realm is infectious: thus the sect naturally springs from the morbid symptoms in the individual. Sect (derived from the Latin *sequor* or *sectari*, and not from *secare*) is the translation of the Greek

---

[1] Col. ii. 21. [2] 1 Tim. iv. 7. [3] 1 John iv. 18.

αἵρεσις, whence our *heretical* is derived, a word mostly used in the sense of heterodox, to denote one who denies the ecclesiastically accepted (orthodox) creed. In Biblical language the word has not originally this unfavourable meaning. It means there, in general, one party as distinguished from another; for instance, the yet new Christianity, as distinguished from traditional Judaism.[4] It was, however, used very early in *malam partem*,[5] to denote those who destroy the unity of the Church by producing divisions. Since this was usually the consequence of differing views, "the man that is an heretic,"[6] as well as the heterodox, was condemned as such more severely, in proportion to the degree in which unity of Church and confession was sought. So we may say that the oldest heresy was uncharitableness and faction, very soon united with disavowal or contradiction of the confessed truth, if indeed it did not spring from it. Heresies were already attributed in the earliest days to ψευδοδιδάσκαλοι,[7] and Luther, too, uses the word *Sectirer* in the sense of *Rotten und Schwärmgeister*. Since this heresy usually exhibits an aggressive character, and seeks to exert a revolutionary influence in its domain, it was from early times treated by the Church, not merely as sickly, but as hostile. While, therefore, rejecting as heretical the views of those who contradict the doctrine which is considered orthodox, the Church condemns as *Schismatics* those who, in consequence of their zeal for personal opinions, sever themselves from the body of the Church to found a separate community.

7. We have historic evidence that every religion which contains any vitality, has from that very reason been the prolific mother of many sects; but the question now arises, whether we are here entitled to speak of a *morbid* phenomenon. Our affirmative answer does not deny that the arising of sects is natural, necessary, and even relatively good,[8] and that the excessive number of sects, which chiefly divides the professors of Christianity and Religion, may be called in some degree an evidence of the manifoldness of revelation, and of the inexhaustible riches of the Gospel. But still we must for more than one reason deplore this restless eagerness in the formation of sects, as a fatal phenomenon; for it generally springs from an egotistical desire to be "something wholly independent," and thereby inevitably sins against, not only love, but also the truth; for even that which relatively is right becomes wrong, where it is maintained at the expense of equity towards a brother. Each disruption, besides, in consequence of the conflict of opinions, inevitably bears in itself the seeds of new dissensions. Finally, every tendency to separation rests (specially in the domain of Christianity) on a deplorable forgetting of the distinction between Church and spiritual community, or must at least inevitably lead to it. On this subject we shall treat more amply hereafter, when we come to speak about Ecclesiology. Saddest of all is it that this disease generally appears with the presumptuous assertion that it is the very thing which represents, or at least

4 Acts xxiv. 5, 14; xxvi. 5; xxviii. 22.
5 1 Cor. xi. 18, 19; Gal. v. 20.
6 Tit. iii. 10.
7 2 Pet. ii. 1.
8 1 Cor. xi. 18, 19; Matt. xviii. 7.

prepares the way for, the normal and healthy condition of the Church. The sect will not merely be a part of, but a surrogate for, the pure Church. In a certain sense we might call Sectarianism Individualism on a more extended scale, separating itself egotistically from others. If it be supported by powerful leaders, it may appear even as a presumptuous *Hierarchism*, with all its consequences of persecution, of heresy, and hate. If one sinner destroyeth much good,[9] how much more will a close union of sick and erring ones injure the highest and the best!

8. Fortunately, one morbid phenomenon generally neutralizes another; in many, too, nature resists the fatal influence of the wrong doctrine: otherwise, as the final result of each disease, the death of that Religion, which is the highest life of mankind, is threatened. By the exclusive supremacy of the understanding, the delicate plant of the soul's inner life is crushed, and the fierce dread of superstition may lead, under the banner of religion, to the most fearful cruelties.[10] Thus the wish of its opponents, that Religion —in their view more a plague than a blessing—may be entirely abolished and destroyed, becomes, to a certain extent, comprehensible. If this, however, be as little possible as desirable, we shall at least, after discovering so much degeneration, acknowledge the justice of the desire that the religious life, no longer left entirely to itself, may be guided by an infallible *rule*.

Compare, as regards most of the subjects discussed here, the articles relating to them in Herzog, *R. E.*, and especially the artt. *Heresy*, by JAEGER, and *Sects*, by PALMER. Consult also, as to these diseases, and their remedies and modes of treatment, J. P. LANGE, *Christl. Dogm.* iii. (1852). See also J. J. VAN OOSTERZEE, *Strijd en Verzoening* in the Jbb. of 1853, p. 194, *sqq.*; as well as E. W. KRUMMACHER, *Ueber Gewisse Krankhaftigkeiten des Pietismus*; MME. A. DE GASPARIN, *Quelques Maladies des Chrêtiens d'aujourd'hui.*

POINTS FOR INQUIRY.

How is the origin of so much degeneration generally in the religious domain to be explained and judged?—Closer analysis and criticism of the morbid phenomena sketched here.—Explanation of the ideas; orthodox and heterodox; heretical and schismatic.—Ecclesiastical separatism viewed in the light of history.—Is it possible entirely to avoid onesidedness in the domain of religion?—Is it not to be expected, and so quite satisfactory, that this evil will at last correct itself?

SECTION XXVII.—ITS RULE.

If the Religious Life is to be developed not merely without hindrance, but normally and harmoniously, and to answer to its aim, it requires another rule than that which human intelligence

---

[9] Eccles. ix. 18.

[10] 2 Kings iii. 27.

and self-will supplies. The service, which with fullest right God claims from us, must be a voluntary, but cannot in any case be a wilful, one. It belongs only to God Himself to prescribe for man how He wishes to be served and worshipped, and man from his side requires such a prescript. There is no Religion where there is no original Revelation; no pure Religion where no continuous and nearer Revelation of God.

1. The statement that Religion, to be of the right stamp, must be directed by a trustworthy rule, seems in itself hardly to admit of serious contradiction. Some think it sufficient, indeed, if God be only worshipped sincerely, and after the dictates of the individual conscience, as all religions may be equally good; yet this assertion is nothing but the veriest superficiality. From this standpoint, good intention is the only demand, insincerity the only heresy, and the subject-matter of belief is without any importance. In believing, it is said with Göthe, the cardinal point is *that* we believe; *what* we believe is a matter of perfect indifference. But what? Is there not the slightest difference whether, *e.g.*, mothers cast their children into the fire to Moloch, or bring them to Jesus, since in both cases they love their children? or, again, whether, with the early Christians, we offer our lives for the brethren, or, with the Thugs in India, we go out to murder, since both are animated by a pious zeal? whether men crucify the flesh from religious principle, or prostitute themselves in the temple of Venus vulgaris? We can hardly maintain such propositions without incurring the appearance of insanity. If every religion be good, provided it be only honestly entertained, then every kind of morality is equally holy: in other words, the difference between good and bad becomes merely traditional. This folly condemns itself, and will seek vainly in Holy Scripture for a mere semblance of support. Holy Scripture knows only one way of salvation,[1] and he who thinks that he reads the contrary in the words of the Apostle,[2] only shows that he does not understand the meaning of those words, because he loses sight of the context.

2. If, then, every religion is not equally good, the question arises, whether it is not at least enough that every one is guided on this subject as far as possible by his own intellect, feeling, and conscience. Without contradiction, this is desirable and necessary, only we must not forget that that which is indispensable cannot by any means be therefore called sufficient. Opinion here interchanges with opinion, prescript with prescript. The image worship, which the Monotheist considers folly, is, perhaps, for the Polytheist quite rational. That same feeling, which restrains us from human sacrifice, leads the Hindoo to expose his dying father to the crocodiles of the Ganges; and the conscience, which to us forbids suicide, impels the widow of the Brahmin to the funeral pyre. But even in the almost inconceivable case that all men, laying on one side their peculiar views, suc-

[1] John xiv. 6; Act iv. 12. [2] Acts x. 34, 35.

ceeded in forming a conventional religion (just in the same way as Leibnitz dreamed of a conventional language), this would not exhibit any higher character than that of a religion of will-worship,[3] which, on that very account, would cease to be religion of the true stamp. A real consecration of a man and his all to God, may and must be voluntary, but in no case arbitrary. Religion, in its deepest form, is always sacrifice, and the necessity of offering something to God is a peculiar characteristic of grateful love.[4] But that sacrifice only can be well pleasing to Him, which is not only well meant, but is, besides, presented according to His will, and in agreement with His design. Freedom of worship is as much a right as a privilege; no creature is capable of placing himself between God and our conscience. But serving God after the dictates of the conscience is something else than serving Him after the inspirations of our own self-will. Though in my worship I am bound to nothing but the voice of my conscience, that conscience itself is not unconditionally free. On the contrary, it acknowledges its duty to obey a higher will, and submits itself to that higher will. That only is true religion, which is voluntarily guided by God's will; God's will must be our sole rule in the domain of religion.

3. Or may man, perhaps, consider himself as entirely free from any obligation towards religion? In that case, certainly, there is no need of speaking of a rule, but the case itself is inconceivable. Both in the objective and subjective sense in which we can speak of religion, it is evident that man has not only a conditional but an unconditional obligation towards religion, yea, that religion must be all to us, else it is nothing in our life. The tie which unites man to God as his Creator, Benefactor, Lawgiver, and Judge,[5] may be called absolutely indissoluble. But if this is so, then is it clear as the noonday sun that God has the fullest right, not only to demand that He should be served, but also to prescribe how man shall serve Him. Religion is then objectively good, when it agrees with the will of God; yet how shall man learn to know that will, if He Himself does not, in some way or other, make Himself known? Thus the idea of Religion is closely united with that of *Revelation*, and as the result of this part of our investigation we boldly collect our conclusion in the twofold proposition: (1) *All religion has its origin in original revelation.* (2) *Pure religion requires continuous and nearer revelation.* On these two subjects we have a word of conclusion, and of transition.

4. What is involved in Revelation we naturally do not here determine. We use the word here simply in the sense of a communication of God to man, in whatever form this may be conceived; and we state in other words, religious life would never have arisen without a revelation of God to and in man. Of two things, one; either religion is something purely accidental and conventional—but in this case neither is its origin, nor its continuance, nor its universality, nor power, explicable; or religion is originally planted by the Creator in the heart of humanity; in other words, religion itself is the fruit and evidence of an original revelation of God. As, after all that has been said, this last position may be called absolutely

[3] Col. ii. 23. [4] 2 Sam. xxiv. 24. [5] Cf. § 22; 1 John iv. 19.

necessary, so it appears of itself acceptable, especially on account of the following facts :—

First. The *religious feeling* is either potentially or actually present in all men. We have already observed, "There are no innate ideas; the knowledge of a higher Being is inborn in us as little as any other knowledge. Man is born with the faculty of sight, not with the views themselves; with the feeling for art, but not with the capacity for execution. But his desire, inclination, and necessity to believe in God, when he hears of Him, is incontestable; and if that disposition is derived from none other than the Creator Himself, this in itself betrays at once, and without any ambiguity, the hand of the architect." "Only by the aid of the higher revelation can we explain the original development of the religious life." (Köstlin.)

A second proof is the *tradition*, found almost everywhere in the most varying forms, of an original communion between the Godhead and mankind, between heaven and earth; a tradition which, in its universality and relative agreement, seems utterly inexplicable if it had not the very least basis of truth.

A third proof is the origin of *language* and the first development of the *power of speech*. This gift of God, and goodliest of His gifts, who can satisfactorily explain it, who does not find with Plato and so many others something originally Divine in language, and assume that it must have been spoken in some way to man, if it were to be spoken again by him? Even Rousseau declares that he "was thoroughly convinced of the almost demonstrated impossibility that languages could have arisen and developed themselves by merely human means."

Lastly, there is *Monotheism*, whose origin remains quite unexplained if we do not believe in an original revelation. For its derivation from the peculiar instincts of the Semitic race (Renan) is merely a well-sounding phrase. All Semitics were not Monotheists; and, as regards Israel, the popular tendency was almost invariably towards idolatry and image-worship. He who asserts that the Hebrew had, by his own strength, mounted to an idea, to which the highly civilized Greek so many centuries afterwards attained scarcely or not all—from his antipathy to the Supranatural, forces upon us the Unnatural. Indeed, "if we are asked whence Abraham alone and singly had not only the first vision of God, but also *how*, whilst he forswore all other gods, he came to the knowledge of the One God, only one answer can satisfy us : by personal Divine revelation." (Max Müller.)

5. As long as all these facts remain certain, and besides can only be explained by this one hypothesis, ignorance and prejudice are not specially to be sought on the part of the supporter of a belief in Revelation. As little admits it of serious contradiction, that a pure religion has an absolute need of constant and further revelation of God, and that without this it would at least be inconceivable. That feeling is the source of the yearning of the soul which re-echoes so often and so touchingly through the pages of Holy Scripture.[6] However man may be inclined towards God, that inclination would soon be choked if we might not on reasonable

[6] Exod. xxxiii. 18; Isa. lxiv. 1; John xiv. 8.

grounds be convinced that God, on His part, continues, in some way or other, to hold communion with man. Réville has called prayer "une gymnastique spirituelle," of which a true fulfilment on God's part is out of the question. If this conviction were generally accepted and applied, the wings of prayer would be broken. The religious feeling, too, is nothing but the disposition and capacity to accept that which God reveals of Himself; and where this last is consciously and stubbornly rejected, the first too will lose its power. No wonder that all founders of religion have appealed to special revelation; without such appeal they never would have succeeded or even appeared. Men talk of a purely natural religion; but this is much less general than it seems, and in the best case is only to be met with among a few of the most highly developed. Yea, even this form of religion, as well as the positive facts of history, point back at last to revelation; for continued investigation ever attests the saying of the Christian philosopher, "To desire to know God without God is impossible; there is no knowledge without Him who is the prime source of knowledge." (Von Baader.)

Comp. H. LUEKEN, *Die Traditionen des Menschen-geschlechts, oder die Uroffenb. Gottes unter den Heiden* (1856); H. STEINTHAL, *der Ursprung der Sprache in zusammenhang mit den letzten Fragen alles Wissens* (1858); DIESTEL, *der Monotheismus des alten Heidenth. vorzüglich bei den Semiten, in de Jahrbücher für Deutsche Theol.* (1860), iv.; H. C. MILLIES, *Oratio de Monotheismo Israelitarum*, etc. (1867); and particularly MAX MUELLER, *Essays* (1867), The Essay, *Semitic Monotheism.*

POINTS FOR INQUIRY.

The soundness of the proposition, Religion everything or nothing to man.—Sources and consequences of the assertion that all religions are equally good.—Explanation of Acts x. 34, 35.—Is it possible for man to act in accordance with his conscience, and yet in direct conflict with the will of God?—The ἐθελοθρησκεία of earlier and later times.—Are the mysteries of the religious life really insoluble if we will not admit an original revelation?—Why is a pure religion not lastingly conceivable without a continued and even closer revelation?—Transition to the treatment of Apocalyptics.

CHAPTER II.

REVELATION.

SECTION XXVIII.—ITS IDEA.

By Revelation we understand that work of the living God by which He, in certain ways and for certain ends, makes known to His rational creatures the secrets of His will and nature. So far all Revelation is only one; though real distinction, together with an undeniable union, exists between External and Internal, General and Special Revelation, the Revelation of words and of facts. The one as well as the other, but the special or extraordinary Revelation above all, offers to Christian Apocalyptics a field for particular investigation, equally extensive and important.

1. The connexion between this chapter and the preceding is evident. If all religion rests upon revelation (§ 27), the consideration of the former leads of itself to that of the latter. Apocalyptics is that part of the science of Dogmatics which teaches us more expressly about the idea, the subject-matter, and the grounds for the certainty of Divine revelation. It is only in later times that it has become the custom to treat of this *Revelation* in general, and as a separate subject. In former times this doctrine was treated along with that of Holy Scripture. The Bible was regarded as a whole as a "*revelatio Dei mediata*," while by "*revelatio immediata*" men denoted that enlightening by the Holy Spirit, which was enjoyed by the sacred writers. Thus the ideas of revelation and inspiration were easily confounded. As distinguished from "*Theologia Naturalis*," "*Theologia Revelata*" was simply that which was derived from Holy Scripture; and to the question, what we must understand by "*Revelatio*," and what we must think of it, the answer was sometimes utterly defective. If we will put an end to this uncertainty and confusion, it can only be

done by a sharper distinction between the two ideas—Revelation and Holy Scripture.

2. At once the question meets us, how can we gain an accurate idea of God's revelation? It is well known how inexcusably this word has often been played with in the theological, philosophical, and even the æsthetical domain. Even the creations of a Mozart, or a Dannecker, for example, have been called a revelation from the kingdom of tones and statues, while Hegel has given the same name to his philosophy. The confusion of speech was increased by the fact, that the idea of revelation was construed in an arbitrary manner, under the influence of other religious ideas imported into it. The danger of all this is seen in various examples, and is specially evident where it is felt that even the human understanding suffers under the influence of sin.[1] It may be said to be impossible to determine anything here *à priori*, and it must be stated at the outset that a pure idea of revelation cannot in any case be obtained by a merely speculative, but only by an historico-philosophic method. It is true that this idea always presupposes the existence of a God, which we shall afterward expressly demonstrate, as far as possible, and that of certain facts to which, whether correctly or not, a character of revelation has been assigned. Here, too, we cannot of ourselves *produce* any idea out of our mind; but only *reflect*, and ponder afterwards, on that which has already been historically established. The idea of revelation can be deduced from the *facts* only of revelation, provided these be sufficiently established.

3. To a certain extent the word revelation explains itself. It may be said, etymologically considered, to denote the *becoming manifest* as well as the *making manifest*. We employ it in this latter active sense, to denote an act of the living God, who thus not only unconsciously *becomes* manifest, but *makes* Himself manifest to the reasonable creature, which, as such, has the necessary receptivity for such manifestations. Revelation is, therefore, a bringing into light, imparting, unveiling, of that which, without this act, would be and continue, unknown; a *becoming-known* of God, directly effected by Himself, an act whose consequence is that something completely new is brought to our knowledge. Thus revelation can never be something involuntary. It is always something purposed, which is free, and has been willed. However much the Gospel may give occasion to speak of a revelation of God the Father to the Son,[2] as well as to the world of spirits,[3] we expressly mean here that which is imparted to man. To the question, what does God reveal? our answer can only be, He reveals Himself, His will and being, in so far as He can and will be known by the creature; in Biblical language, He reveals the thoughts of His heart. The subject-matter and material of Revelation is thus not one abstract idea, not a chequered collection of facts of all sorts, nor even a number of truths side by side, but *the* Truth (ἡ ἀλήθεια) in the domain of morality and religion, which is the expression of God's nature, will, and counsel.

4. The Biblical form of expression agrees with this definition of our subject. God's act or deed of revelation is denoted by two nouns:

---

[1] Eph. iv. 18. [2] John v. 20. [3] Eph. iii. 10.

φανέρωσις (making plain, manifestatio),[4] and ἀποκάλυψις, (unveiling, revelatio).[5] For the elucidation of the same idea, the words, δηλοῦν (1 Pet. i. 11), γνωρίζειν (Luke ii. 15), δεικνύναι (Matt. xvi. 20), ἐμφανίζειν (John xiv. 21, 22), and a few others, are still to be noticed. As the next classical place, Hebrews i. 1 deserves to be considered, where revelation is presented as a speaking of God, at sundry times and divers manners by the prophets, afterwards followed by the word of the Son as His last and highest revelation. What God utters by the prophets must thus, according to the meaning of Holy Scripture, be distinguished from the utterance of their own merely human consciousness, as is proved by a number of instances.[6] When we try to define our conception of revelation, facts of this kind must by no means be passed over; and it is not science, but arbitrariness, when these facts are purposely denied, because they belong to that which has been arbitrarily declared to be improbable or impossible. The idea of revelation must not be deduced from some, but from all the facts of revelation combined, and compared with one another, as far as these facts admit of an historico-critical vindication. And when we do this, it soon appears that here a Divine and a human factor are working, distinct from one another, but still most closely united. In the act of revelation, God is speaking, demonstrating, proving; man is hearing, learning, receiving. In former times no doubt a mechanical representation of revelation was too easily accepted, and this revelation was too much looked upon as a mere outward imparting of ideas, which were to man, not merely new, but entirely strange. The later Theology, on the contrary, maintains, with reason, a more dynamic conception, in consequence of which we can speak of a mystic, but not of a magical, operation of God. Revelation, too, however metaphysical in its origin, is undoubtedly brought about by psychological means, and presupposes a decided receptibility on the part of him to whom it is made known and explained. But though the receptivity is here an indispensable condition, the subjectivity is never, and in no way, the source of the revelation of God. If this were the case, then the entire belief in revelation would be nothing but a fruit of self-deceit, at least of want of sufficient self knowledge, in consequence of which the so-called interpreters of Divine revelation would have regarded their subjective feelings as objective teachings of God. The truth, as appears from the facts, is found in a higher sphere, and only then receives its proper recognition when we conceive of revelation as "a self-imparting of God, an imparting of Divine truth, in which the imparting of light and life mutually condition each other" (Martensen, page 12). Revelation is always a word of God to man, which is heard and understood by him, not a word of man to himself.

5. Revelation, even where it has come in a greater or less degree within reach of the organs, can only be received and accepted, as such, by the eye and ear of the spirit. Νοῦς ὁρᾶ καὶ νοῦς ἀκούει, τἄλλα δὲ τυφλὰ καὶ κωφά.

---

[4] John ix. 3; Rom. i. 19; iii. 21; xvi. 26, etc.

. 21; Rom. xvi. 25; 1 Cor. ii. 10; Gal. i. 16, etc.

xv. 11; xvi. 6. 7; 2 Sam. vii. 3—5; 2 Kings iv. 27.

We should have less discussion concerning the peculiar character of that organ, if we kept more in mind that revelation was given "in divers ways." Why should a revelation by dream or vision be necessarily observed by the same organ, as *e.g.* that by Urim or Thummim? Even the formula "the Lord said," need not always be explained in the same manner. The distinction also between the historical and poetical books of the Bible is here to be remarked; and the nature, too, of the different subjects to which this speaking of God refers, ought to be considered. The ordinance for the single ornaments in the tabernacle, *e.g.*, was hardly made in the same manner as the unveiling of the expectation of a Messiah. Generally speaking, the utterance of God must be regarded as neither external and mechanical, nor as merely figurative. The Spirit of God reveals itself internally to the spirit of man, and this receives the voice of God, not less plainly than the bodily ear receives sounds. By its own internal clearness and force this voice makes itself known to the consciousness as Divine, well distinguished indeed from that which the mere natural insight announces, and on that very account irresistible.[7] And thus the subject-matter of the revelation is always something which man would not have known if it had not been imparted to him by God. It appears, as the sun, from behind the dark clouds.

6. We are thus naturally drawn on to the allied idea of Mystery; as to which we must at once carefully distinguish between the Biblical and the ecclesiastical use of the word. The Church has for ages used the word μυστήριον to denote things in the domain of religion, which, from their character, were beyond human insight. It was granted that, as there were solemnities in Christianity which must be concealed from the uninitiated, there were also doctrines, not only uncomprehended, but utterly incomprehensible, which could be best denoted by the name *Mystery.* In the New Testament something quite different is denoted by μυστήριον. Jesus calls the kingdom of God a μυστήριον, which "it is given to His disciples to know,"[8] and Paul speaks of the Gospel as "a mystery which is now made manifest."[9] The absolutely incomprehensible is not thus denoted by this word, but merely that which is not yet made manifest, and which, in consequence of its manifestation, has ceased to be a mystery. As such it is above the reach of the natural, but not of the spiritual man.[10] The word besides refers, in the New Testament, not to doctrines, but to facts which are partly now made known,[11] and partly to be waited for in the future.[12] Now, indeed, we see from the nature of the case that even a revealed mystery may have its dark sides: the sun come forth from behind the clouds nevertheless still dazzles our eyes. But Holy Scripture nowhere teaches that mystery as such lies, and must necessarily lie, entirely beyond the reach of all human ken; the contrary is evident from 1 Cor. xiii. 2, Eph. iii. 4. Mystery, too, though never wholly penetrated, may still be known, but only by means of Revelation.

---

[7] Amos iii. 8; Jer. xx. 7—10.
[8] Matt. xiii. 11.
[9] Rom. xvi. 25, 26.
[10] 1 Cor. ii. 14—16.
[11] 1 Tim. iii. 16.
[12] 1 Cor. xv. 51, 52.

7. We must carefully distinguish between External and Internal revelation. In the New Testament the first-named is always called φανέρωσις (manifestatio), the other ἀποκάλυψις (revelatio). The first presents the objective, the second the more subjective side of the matter. The first is that act of God by which He from His side exhibits or makes known that which before was unknown; the second, that operation by which is taken away from the eye of the spirit the veil (κάλυμμα) which prevented its seeing the truth. The purely exegetical question, whether the New Testament makes everywhere a sharp distinction between these two words, or uses them sometimes indiscriminately, need not here occupy our time, since even in the latter case the right and importance of the distinction in itself cannot possibly be doubted. What avails the brightest light, if the eye is not open for the light? The appearing of Christ was undoubtedly a revelation of the glory of God; but the Jews saw it not, because a veil was upon their face;[13] and when it was understood by Peter, it was in consequence of an internal revelation of the Father.[14] Even the sight of the external manifestation of Christ would have been without influence for the inner life of St. Paul, if God had not pleased to reveal His Son in him.[15] In this respect, too, there is a difference between objective revelation (φανέρωσις) and subjective (ἀποκάλυψις), that while the former is given in a definite fact, which has either happened, or must happen afterwards;[16] the latter, on the contrary, continues and proceeds everywhere, where a subjective view of the objectively revealed truth prevails, because in every sensuous man there is a κάλυμμα or veil which must be removed, if he is to see spiritual things. This whole distinction is of great importance when we are dealing with Socinians on one side, or Mystics on the other. The Socinian reverences the objective side of the matter at the expense of the subjective, while the Mystical view is an exact opposite. The acknowledgment of the distinction and union of these two sides is necessary to an accurate representation of the truth. Where external and internal revelation is united, there is found the properly so called science (σύνεσις) of the mystery of Christ,[17] which on its part again kindles the light for him who has received an eye from God to see.[18]

8. The distinction between General and Special revelation, too, is founded on the nature of the case and the statements of the Bible. By the first, or the ordinary, we think of that which is given to all men, without distinction of time or place; by the second, called extraordinary, that which is as yet only given to one, and of which we know from Holy Scripture. The question whether this second really deserves the name of special revelation, can of course only be answered later. We are here speaking only of the distinction in general, and there can be no doubt that from a logical standpoint this is accurate and necessary. Manifestly the knowledge of God, in which the Christian or even the Israelite rejoices, is one thing; that which man may have without the light of the Gospel another. Enough that the distinction is everywhere made in Holy

13 2 Cor. iii. 15, 16.
14 Matt. xvi. 1
15 Gal. i. 16.
16 See, *e.g.*, 1 Pet. i. 20; v. 4.
17 Eph. iii. 4.
18 1 Cor. ii. 10—12.

Scripture,[19] and also expressed in the Confession of the Reformed Churches; while, on the contrary, from the standpoint of Naturalism it is reduced to an empty sound. It is, however, less accurate to define, as is sometimes done, the first as the Natural, the second as the Supranatural revelation *par excellence*. All revelation indeed, as to its origin, has a Supranatural character; it is a revealing of the Supranatural, of the God, raised above nature.

9. A third distinction, that between revelation by Word and by Facts, only occurs where there is a question of special or extraordinary revelation. If it be granted that this last really exists, it is a question whether it is only given in the facts with which Holy Scripture makes us acquainted, or also in the doctrine proclaimed there. Whilst in former times a too partial value was attributed to the last named, others, especially the Groningen school in the Netherlands, have directed the mind to the great facts of the revelation, as the proper kernel of revelation, and recognised the doctrine (*e.g.*, of the Apostles) as an authentic explication of those facts, whilst denying to its utterances the character of a revelation, properly so called. It is, however, evident that the one can scarcely be separated from the other, and that a revelation, derived only from facts, which must speak further for themselves, would be alike obscure and aimless. St. Paul at least does not hesitate to exalt his teaching, as well as that of his fellow-witnesses,[20] as the fruit of a special revelation of God; and the Lord, too, attributes to His words a proper character of revelation.[21] We speak, then, thoroughly in the spirit of Scripture, of a special revelation of God, not only in but also by Christ, as by the Apostles and Prophets.

10. Less accurate, on the other hand, is the distinction ofttimes made between mediate (=ordinary) and immediate (=extraordinary) revelation; for this last, too, is made by *means*, and the first, too, comes immediately, or rather directly, from God. Besides, the idea of "immediate" is of course subjective; we usually denote as such that of which we do not see, or cannot indicate the means; but it does not hence necessarily follow that no means at all existed or were employed. On the contrary, as far as we can see, God works in both domains of revelation, though at least in special revelation the means and ways exhibit a very varying character. A very ancient form, which at the same time was the lowest, is undoubtedly that in dreams, above which Moses was already raised.[22] That was a higher form which took effect in visions seen in a waking exstatic condition, such as were vouchsafed to different prophets. In Jesus Christ, however, God's highest revelation, everything which was visionary or exstatic at once subsides. He speaks what He has heard with clear consciousness in His most intimate union and communion with the Father, and presents the image of the Father in His own person.[23] In Him, the Incarnate Logos, the φανέρωσις reaches its climax, without its appearing that He Himself needed ἀποκάλυψις; for even the Holy Ghost, the Paraclete,

[19] Ps. xix. cxlvii; Rom. iii. 1, 2.
[20] 1 Cor. ii. 10; xii. 7, 8; Eph. iii. 3—5.
[21] John xii. 49, 50.
[22] Num. xii. 6—8.
[23] John xii. 49, 50; xiv. 8, 9.

does not bring any entirely new revelations, but merely interprets what has been given in Him.[24]

11. Whatever distinctions may further be considered necessary in this domain, there always remains a higher unity in the different ways and forms of the Revelation. External and internal, general and special revelation, revelation by word and by fact, do not exclude one another, but supplement one another in important particulars. Even the contrast between Ordinary and Extraordinary revelation becomes unjust, if we forget that the latter, though given for a definite end, and in a special manner, is yet bestowed in the same domain in which the former is given. If a general revelation is given in Nature, History, Humanity, the special is certainly not unnatural, unhistorical, extra-human. Thus the last does not supplant the first, still less does it contradict it, but completes and crowns it. Both testify of one God, who works in divers ways, according to the pithy saying of Augustine, "Opera mutas, nec tamen mutas consilium." Apocalyptics, then, must be occupied with both, but specially with the extraordinary. The importance and difficulty of this investigation readily appears.

Compare, as to this chapter in general, the article of KÖSTLIN, named above; C. A. AUBERLEN, *Die Göttl. Offenbarung* (1861), i. ii. 1. (Eng. Trans.); R. ROTHE, *Zur Dogmatik* (1863), pp. 55—121; A. E. KRAUSS, *Die Lehre von der Offenb.* (1868); C. T. TRIP, *Die Theophanien in den Geschichts büchern des A. T.* (1868); for this section concerning the idea of Mystery, the dissertation of J. BOELES, *De Mysteriis in Rel. Chr.* (1843); as concerning Revelation by word or fact, the Prize Essay of P. V. D. WILLIGEN (Haag. Genoots. 1844); concerning the distinction between φανέρωσις and ἀποκάλυψις, the essay of Dr. F. G. VAN BELL (1849), and the treatise by Dr. J. CRAMER, in the *Nieuwe Jbb.* for 1860, pp. 1—70, as well as G. E. W. DE WIJS, *De Droomen in en buiten den Bijbel.* (1858); A. BOUVIER, Jr., *La Révélation, cinq Conférences* (1870).

POINTS FOR INQUIRY.

Nature, extent, and importance of the task of Christian Apocalyptics.—Necessity of distinguishing it from Bibliology.—Elucidation and defence of the accepted idea of Revelation drawn from the use of language in Holy Scripture and the Confession of the Church.—What is mystery?—Unity of Revelation in all its variety of forms.—Modern Naturalism as contrasted with the Christian idea of Revelation.—The antithesis between ordinary and extraordinary, as unchristian and unphilosophic as the denial of the actual difference between the two.

SECTION XXIX.—GENERAL REVELATION.

General Revelation is that which was originally given to all in nature, history, and humanity. It declares, from the morning of the creation, the certainty of God's existence, the majesty of His

[24] John xvi. 12—15; Col. ii. 3.

being, and the sanctity of His requirements, with loud and irrefragable authority. Its sublimity has been at all times recognised by the noblest of our race; its obscuration is sufficiently explained by the power of sin in the world; its defence, especially from the standpoint of the Reformed Christian Church, is of great importance; and its aim for humanity gained when it, properly employed, has aroused along with the capacity the desire for a special or extraordinary revelation.

1. That there is a general Revelation, is evident from the existence of Religion, which would be inexplicable without it (§ 27). It is true, we reason here in some way in a circle; for he who speaks of Revelation, already supposes that there is a God, and to establish this last conviction he again appeals to Revelation. This circle cannot be avoided, but presents, however, no insuperable difficulty. "Is reasoning in a circle absolutely illicit in the kingdom of truth? Is not every logical proof in a certain degree founded on a circle? If the conclusion were not contained in the premises, how could it ever be deduced therefrom? Upon what then does all demonstration depend, if not on the evidence that we already acknowledge in another form as truth that which is to be established?" (Tholuck.) Each proposition, maintained as far as possible for itself, supports and assists the other, and the existence of a general revelation can only be denied when the existence of a God, and the possibility of all well-founded knowledge of God, is denied.

2. The sphere of general revelation must, from the nature of the case, be conceived as threefold. First of all, the Invisible reveals Himself in His work; *Nature* reflects His being; the creation makes us see the Creator. But there is more: a God who not only lives, but rules, must also make Himself known by His acts; *History* is thus the second general sphere of Revelation. But we could not speak of either of these spheres if it were not that God had specially revealed Himself in *Man* himself, who surveys nature, and consults history. We speak more particularly, but not more exclusively, of man's conscience. Reason, too, with its faculty of ascending to the idea of the infinite; and the heart, with its boundless needs, cannot be conceived as aught else than an original revelation of God. We thus think here of the entire man as a rational and moral being, in other words, of humanity as a whole.—Holy Scripture points expressly to this threefold kingdom of Revelation. To Nature, in Psalm xix. 1; Isa. xl. 26; Rom. i. 19, 20. To history, Exod. ix. 16; Acts xiv. 15—17; xvii. 25, 26. To humanity, Eccles. iii. 11; Acts xvii. 27, 28; Rom. ii. 14, 15. No one among the Apostles has developed this so-called Natural Theology with so decided interest as St. Paul; but his Master had shown him the way.[1]

3. To define accurately the Subject-matter of general revelation is not

[1] Matt. vi. 22—34.

easy for us who already know, and cannot possibly entirely forget, the light of special revelation. In order to discover it as well as we can, we must expressly attend to the general fundamental ideas, which as latent presuppositions lie at the basis of every religious form, and find these in their expression more or less clearly. Considering this, we may assign as the subject-matter of General Revelation, first, the certainty of God's existence as supreme Cause of all things; secondly, the majesty of His being as the mighty Creator, the wise Governor, the tender Provider of all, whose justice and independence became apparent in the course of the world's history; while conscience in particular expressly proclaims His holiness; and, lastly, the holiness of His claims, which follows of itself from what has been said. The Almighty demands worship; the Only Wise, confidence; the Merciful, gratitude; the Just and Holy One asks for acknowledgment of His rights, and performance of His will. The notions of good and evil are infinitely various, but the claim that a man, in proportion to the light he has received, should do that which is morally good, and avoid evil, is written in every conscience. It is not proved, on the other hand, that this revelation could teach anything positive concerning a future life.

4. The Sublimity of this revelation is evident from its general intelligibility, its antiquity and unchangeableness, and has the testimony of all sides through every age. As far as concerns sacred antiquity, this is seen by a glance at the books of Job and Isaiah, and the Psalms of Nature—such as Psalms viii., xix., xxix., civ., and cxlvii. But profane antiquity had, too, an eye open to the rich meaning of the book of Nature.[2] Utterances of later days, both in the Christian and non-Christian domain, have re-echoed the very same sounds. Remember the words of Bonnet, "I have looked for the Author of nature in His smaller productions, as well as in those where He is seen in all His majesty, and everywhere I have heard these sublime words, 'It is I;'" or those of Schiller, "The history of the world is the judgment of the world;" or those of Jean Paul, "God has written His name in the stars, and sown it in the flowers of the earth." True, others, on the contrary, testify (La Place, *e.g.*) that they do not require the hypothesis of the existence of God to explain the riddles of nature. And certainly it cannot be denied, creation and history hide God from us, as well as reveal Him to us. Yet even this does not present any overpowering difficulty, if we only do not forget that the revelation of God in man himself is not only the key, but also the basis of the sanctuary of His revelation in nature and history. The books of both these are, as it were, written with consonants only, like the Hebrew Bible; man himself, listening to the voice of intellect, heart, and conscience, supplies the vowel points. Where both are united, there the name of God, plainly uttered, sounds in our ears. We must seek Him in order to find Him, and in some measure already know Him in order to seek Him; but where we *do* thus seek Him, there we must find Him, *because He is really there.* As the poet says (Rückert):

"Nature is God's own book, which, without revelation, human experience vainly strives to scan."

---

[2] *Cicero de Nat. D.* II. 2, *De divinat.* II. 72. *Xenophon, Memorabilia* I. c. 4, § 5, etc.

5. The Obscuration of general revelation for a great part of mankind is the sad effect of sin. To the question, "How could idolatry and the forsaking of God, with all its horrors, arise, if there has ever been an original revelation?" the only satisfactory and acceptable answer is that given in Rom. iv. 24—28. The power of truth is, as it were, kept under by that of unrighteousness;[3] when the vowel within was effaced, the word without became illegible. Polytheism, not less than Atheism or Pantheism, is the fruit of the fall. It is not the indistinctness of the light, but the clouding of the eye, which affords here a reasonable ground of complaint. This, however, does not afford any excuse for considering general revelation as unimportant or uncertain.

6. On the contrary, its maintenance is constantly of great importance for the cause of religion and Christianity. For general revelation is the ground in which the heavenly plant of special revelation is sown and grows; he who does not understand the voice of the former, misses at the same time that by which he can receive, understand, and judge the special revelation as such. So it is usually seen that disavowal of the first leads to denial of the second; yea, even in its consequences produces a materialistic conception. From the Christian Reformed standpoint specially it is necessary and possible to maintain general revelation on the basis of that which the Reformed Church, in accordance with Scripture and experience, teaches about the existence and the right of a natural knowledge of God. "Hoc quidem recte judicantibus semper constabit, insculptum mentibus humanis esse divinitatis sensum, qui deleri nunquam potest. Immo, et naturaliter ingenitam esse omnibus hanc persuasionem esse aliquem Deum, et penitus infixam esse quasi in ipsis medullis, locuples testis est impiorum contumacia" (Calvin, Inst. I. 3, 3). The same conviction is most decidedly expressed in the Neth. Conf., Art. II. It is with reason defended by the most celebrated Reformed Theologians, in opposition to the Socinian one-sidedness, which considered all knowledge of God as traditional, and spread in a mechanical way in consequence of a merely external communication. How far in this respect the Reformed Theology surpasses that of Luther or of Rome can only be glanced at here. The remembrance of the existence and value of general revelation still continues, even within the Reformed Churches, of great importance, as opposed by so many who at its expense too partially exalt the extraordinary, and scarcely seem to possess eye or ear for that which God speaks by the mouth of Nature, Humanity, and History.

7. The right Use of general revelation is not to remain there where it brings us, and exalt it above the special; still less to borrow from it our weapons for combating the other; it lies much more in this, that we suffer ourselves to be roused by its voice to the glorifying of God, and by its silence on many an important point are further led to ask for a nearer revelation which satisfactorily supplies its defects. This nearer revelation will be naturally valued more highly in proportion as the general revelation has

---

[3] Rom. i. 18.

given us a deeper impression of the majesty and glory of God, and agrees with it in a more surprising manner on cardinal points.

8. By such a use the Object of general revelation is at last attained. It is neither intended nor fitted to make special revelation in any degree superfluous for sinful man. Much rather was it given to make man, such as he originally *was*, acquainted with his Creator, and his moral obligation towards that Creator, and it is *now* intended to serve as a schoolmaster to man as he now is, as without it there would not be a capacity for, or a feeling of need of, an extraordinary revelation. Both in the non-Christian and in the Christian world such propædeusis, or preliminary teaching, is indispensable, but, without more, insufficient.

Comp. TERTULLIAN, *De Testimonio Animæ;* J. CALVIN, *Inst. R. C.*, I. 4. 1; A. SCHWEITZER, *Glaubensl. der Ref. K.* (1844), i., p. 241; J. H. SCHOLTEN, *H. K.*, 4th ed. (1861), i., pp. 304—326; J. J. VAN TOORENENBERGEN, *Bydr.* (1852), I. bl. 4 enz.; besides O. ZOECKLER, *Theol. Naturalis* (1860); BUNSEN, *Gott in der Geschichte* (1851); and the writings of VON HUMBOLDT, UILKENS, and TEN KATE'S *Creation.*

POINTS FOR INQUIRY.

How can we prove that there is a general revelation?—How is there so much disunion in the definition of its subject-matter?—The voice of antiquity and of later times, as well as those of the more recent natural philosophers, concerning its beauty and value.—The subject-matter and authority of revelation in the conscience.—Explanation of Rom. i. 18, *sqq.*—The importance of the acknowledgment of a general and original revelation of God for the Reformed system of doctrine.—How can we explain and how combat the over-valuing of general revelation on one side, and its misconception on the other?

SECTION XXX.—SPECIAL REVELATION—ITS NECESSITY.

Special Revelation embraces those nearer manifestations of God which are not yet communicated to all, though they are intended for all. Its necessity, which has been confessed in every age as differing from and convincingly attested by the history of Religion and Philosophy, springs from the miserable position into which the dominion of error, sin, misery, and death has brought all mankind. It cannot, therefore, be proved to any one who ignores the power of sin and the necessity for redemption. Where, however, these last are confessed, there the absolute indispensability of a special revelation, even in the form of a Revelation of Salvation, is placed beyond all doubt.

1. The question whether, and to what extent, there exists in the Divine Being Himself the desire to reveal Himself in other modes than the ordi-

nary ones to His creatures, does not belong to the domain of Christian Dogmatics, but rather to that of speculative philosophy. Here we have only to do with the necessity for a Special Revelation on the side of mankind. We maintain this on historical and empirical grounds, but not without important conditions.

2. The history of Religion, as viewed generally, has already offered more than one indubitable proof of the necessity for a special revelation. It is at once to be observed that so many founders of Religions have appealed to such a revelation, and have thus involuntarily declared that natural Religion leaves questions which could not be set aside, and yet remained unanswered. It is, indeed, more than sufficiently apparent that the general revelation originally granted was almost nowhere preserved in its purity, but has been everywhere forgotten. "Igniculos dedit nobis parvulos, quos celeriter malis moribus opinionibusque depravati, sic restinguimus, ut nusquam naturæ lumen appareat" (Cicero). Where the consciousness of God is obscured, morality has also sunk to a depth, as profane literature most sadly testifies. The people of Israel, ever raised, in respect to religion, so far above all other nations, are seen to fall back constantly into a depth from which it can only be lifted by the hardest trials. If this be the most favourable exception, how sad must the ordinary condition of the vast majority have been!

3. The history of Philosophy, too, very far from leading us to different conclusions, supports, in its own way, the conviction we have expressed; as will be seen, if we think of the folly and inconsistency of many propositions concerning God and Divine things, which have been accepted, defended, and applauded; of the conflicts of systems and schools, struggling one against the other, each with more or less of right; of the lasting uncertainty even about the best results of philosophic thought and effort, so long as the confirmation of a closer revelation was wanting; of the utter powerlessness of the schools of philosophy to satisfy the deepest needs of the individual, and specially to found a really religious communion; lastly, of the disdain and distrust with which we see that, in consequence of all this, philosophy, shortly before the appearance of Christianity, was treated on every side, whilst the despair of all firmly established truth is ever more forcibly expressed in the last pages of the older history of philosophy. In order to form a right judgment, we must not look on that philosophy which has received Christian baptism, but at the results of human reflection, utterly devoid of the light of a nearer revelation; and thus we shall be led now and then, it may be, to admiration, but much oftener to sorrow and painful astonishment, when we see in this domain the most sublime so closely connected with the most absurd.

4. No wonder, then, that we see the necessity for a Special Revelation recognised on various sides, and confessed in divers ways. According to a striking fancy of Christian antiquity, of all philosophers, Plato, it is said, was the first to hasten to meet, and to kneel before the feet of the crucified Lord, as He appeared in Hades. Certain it is that Plato has more distinctly than any one else expressed the want which has been, supplied by the revelation of the Light of the world. The journeys, too, which he and others made to the East, in order to learn the religions there

show how little they were content with their own private and national ideas of religion. We might point to many a place in his writings, which testifies to the longing after, and presentiment of, a nearer revelation; to the wants which, expressed or excited by so many of the mysteries of antiquity, were still very far from being satisfied; to the profound meaning of the fable of Prometheus, the myths of Hercules; and elsewhere to the expectations of Mithras and Sosiosch; to the remarkable ease with which the expectations of salvation, entertained by the otherwise despised Jews, were spread and embraced in the East, as well as to other phenomena. Even among the nation which had the privilege of a special revelation we meet voices which testify of the deeply felt need of higher light and life.[1] Prophecy symbolises and calls out that want, but is not able to fulfil it. Even Christian philosophy is not ashamed to confess "that we might as well try to run without feet, as to know the Divine without a revelation from on high, and that without its light we should be like beasts fattened in the dark, merely to die." (Clem. Alex.) The image may not be very choice, but the fact is not the less true. Even the opponents of Special Revelation gave now and then, involuntarily, a similar testimony, as, *e.g.*, the English Deist, Lord Herbert of Cherbury († 1648), who, after he had completed an essay to undermine this belief, wished a proof of higher approval, and, as he narrates himself, thought he heard this, in answer to his prayer, in a soft rustling of the wind. Who, after listening to the highest oracles of human wisdom, has not had something of that peculiar feeling, so naïvely interpreted by Goethe in his paraphrase of the question, "Are here all thy children?"[2] We are not surprised to hear the confession and prayers of Kepler, Leibnitz, Bacon, Newton, and so many of the most brilliant minds, which show how little the light which nature and reason supplies, satisfied them. If there were still anything wanting to the importance of all these testimonies, it would be furnished by pointing to the lamentable blindness and folly to which, in these days, so many have come, who have entirely broken with the belief in a Special Revelation; and who now, as far as they still occupy themselves in the domain of human thought, waste their strength in a wearying but vain task of Sisyphus.

5. We can fully account for the number and force of these testimonies, when we look at the miserable condition of man and mankind in this world. For centuries has been felt the power of the most fatal *errors*, even in regard to the most important questions. With regard to the being of God, as well as to the method of His worship, the restless feeling of man, left to itself, must lead to a ceaseless groping without finding. His knowledge of God is partially impure, partially uncertain; his worship, without a nearer revelation, at best arbitrary, and mostly immoral.—Along with the power of the error which obscures the intellect, comes that of *sin*, which disturbs the conscience. It calls sin a debt, which the sinner must credit to himself, but which he is utterly unable to acquit. No peace within, if there be not an absolute certainty that the debt is paid: no certainty on this point by the light of nature and reason alone.

---

[1] Ps. xiv. 7; Isa. lxiv. 1.

[2] 1 Sam. xvi. 11.

Nature speaks of the goodness of God, but is silent about grace; and the reason of the most celebrated philosophers has never risen to the notion of His redeeming love. As little do either of them know of any means by which, not merely the guilt, but the power and dominion of sin in the heart and the world can be broken. The sinner is as powerless for regeneration as for averting the righteous sentence of God.—Thus he must be always in this life a prey to increasing *misery*. Because the sinner ever remains man, he feels a deep discord within; because man is a sinner, he cannot restore the impaired balance of his moral powers. The sorrows and struggles of this earthly life daily call for comfort, but philosophy cannot supply this want; all that it can do is to rock to sleep the suffering heart, or else to petrify its feeling.—Thus we grow up for *death*, which is already dreaded and hated, and know not whether it will offer us any other prospect than that of complete annihilation. The desire of life, almost ineradicable, gives thoughts of continuance; nature makes us everywhere see life spring out of death, and now and then there arises a strong presentiment of it, but the absolute certainty is wanting. Besides, the question here is not merely as to an endless, perhaps joyless existence, but as to eternal life in the full force of the word; and with regard to this question sinful man is entirely deprived of sufficient data. Why should we say more? Even if sin and death had not come into the world—we shall afterwards hear whence they came—God would, perhaps, for the further perfection of man, have granted to him the privilege of a nearer revelation of His will and being. At least, the sacred account [3] of the first trial-command makes us think this not utterly improbable. But now, since nature and history, as well as reason and conscience, remain silent as to the most pressing questions of the restless and sinful heart, a nearer revelation of God may be called, not merely a most desirable blessing, but at the same time an undeniable need.

6. In this condition we might be naturally surprised that *all* voices do not unanimously agree to what has been already heard, if we did not at the same time remember that the acknowledgment of the necessity of a special revelation, however reasonable, always depends at least on an important condition. We call to mind here the words of a distinguished Theologian: "He only, who self-righteously denies the sinfulness of the natural man, can dispute the necessity of a supranatural revelation" (Sartorius). He alone will acknowledge it, who considers the fact of sin, and the necessity for redemption in the full light of conscience. "Revelation obtains its proper place only in the Divine plan of redemption" (Nitzsch). He, therefore, who does not see the necessity of redemption, will still less allow the indispensability of revelation. The principle of its denial was stated centuries ago in the words, "They that are whole need not a physician, but they that are sick." [4] A Pelagian Anthropology necessarily leads to a systematic contest against Christian Apocalyptics. So it is ever a folly, how often committed, to wish to prove the necessity of a special revelation to every individual without exception. We shall do

---

[3] Gen. ii. 16, 17.   [4] Matt. ix. 12.

well to learn first his notions about the great problem of sin; and for him who in his own view is healthy, to keep for a better hour the commendation of the physician, now considered unnecessary. Where, on the other hand, the power of sin is recognised as guilt and the source of all misery, it will at once be seen that any nearer revelation would be utterly without effect if it did not specially supply to the sinner that which he does not find in general revelation, thereby displaying the character of a Divine Revelation of Salvation.

7. In reality, as history attests, special revelation first appeared after the fall,[5] as a revelation of grace and life, encountering guilt and death. But from this its character it naturally follows that it is not only relatively but absolutely necessary, and that it ever is the same for every sinner. Has special revelation been often valued as quite indispensable, either to confirm that which reason had already proclaimed, or to educate man, and to raise him to such a height that he can at last even do without *its* light? this must be considered still too weak a tribute to the truth. Man, as a sinner, required not merely a confirmation of the truth taught by reason, but a higher revelation of salvation; we require not merely education, but redemption from sin and misery, and a further revelation can alone point out to us the way to this height. To whatever height he may rise in other respects, sinful man by himself will always be unable to deliver himself and his race from the combined power of error and sin, of misery and death. All Hamartology, if conceived in its real depths, is a continual proof of this thesis. In consequence of all that has been said, the question whether that which must be called indispensable, may also be considered as possible, becomes thus of still greater importance.

Comp. J. LELAND, *The Advantage and Necessity of the Christian Revelation* (1764); W. T. LANG, *Ongenoegzaamh. der natuurl. Godgeleerdh.* (*Haagsch. Gen.*, 1796); E. DE PRESSENSÉ, *Histoire de l'Eglise Chrét., etc.*; G. C. B. ACKERMANN, *Das Christliche in Plato* (1835); A. C. VAN HEUSDE, *De Consolatione apud Græcos* (1840); J. N. SEPP, *Das Heidenthum und dessen Bedeutung für das Christenth.* iii. Th. (1853); A. NICOLAS, *Etudes Philosoph. sur le Christianisme* (1851), i., pp. 197—303; C. E. LUTHARDT, *Apologet. Vorträge* (1864), pp. 116—127; F. HETTINGER, *Apologie des Christenth.* (1865), ii., pp. 47—109; H. CREMER, *Vernunft, Gewissen und Offenbarung*, being pp. 51—99, of the *Neun Apologet. Vorträge*, held in Bremen (1869); K. GEROK, *Sind das die Knaben alle.*

POINTS FOR INQUIRY.

Further elucidation of the proof derived from the history of Religion and Philosophy.—In what connexion, according to the nature of the case and history, does the denial of the necessity of a special revelation stand to theoretical and practical Pelagianism?—The difference between revelation and education. (Lessing.)—Ought not the necessity referred to, in order to be admitted by us, to be everywhere acknowledged and confessed?

SECTION XXXI.—ITS POSSIBILITY.

The possibility of a Special Revelation, however much it has been

---

[5] Gen. iii. 8—15.

denied, now in the name of Speculation and now in that of Experience, can be just as little reasonably doubted as its necessity. Its idea presents no insuperable difficulty, logically, metaphysically, or psychologically. The realisation of this idea conflicts neither with the majesty and unchangeableness, nor with the wisdom and goodness of God. Even the very great number of pretended special revelations does not give any right to reject the existence of a real and authentic one, as in itself unreasonable; and that which does not now occur may nevertheless have been communicated before. The impossibility of a Special Revelation can only be said to be for ever proved, when that of Miracle is demonstrated.

1. An express investigation into the possibility of Revelation—we use this word now and hereafter to denote the extraordinary—seems at the first glance almost superfluous. For unbelief at once calls the idea of such a revelation so foolish, that a serious weighing of its possibility might almost be called labour in vain; and belief, on the contrary, convinced on good reasons of the reality and Divinity of revelation, feels already sure that this which really exists must of course be possible too. Yet these considerations ought not to restrain the Apologist from expressly treating of the question in point. A thoughtful belief, at least in a healthy state, requires that that should be justified as reasonable, which it confesses as existing in fact; and unbelief celebrates too quickly its victory, when it simply puts on one side the idea of a special revelation, as we do that of wooden iron or of a square circle. Certainly, if the question, Can God give a nearer revelation of Himself, and can that revelation be understood and conceived by man? may henceforth be tacitly placed on a level with that as to belief in the goblins of childish fables, Naturalism has decided and won its great cause. But as long as a speaking tongue is still granted to one priest of the science of faith, he will resist such violent measures as the very pitch of arbitrariness, and never be weary of repeating Πάταξον μὲν, ἄκουσον δὲ, in opposition to the rudest assaults.

2. There is not the slightest trace of novelty in that denial of the possibility of revelation which has been renewed in our time. Already Epicurus taught "Dei humana non curant," and even among the Israelites they were not wanting who said, "The Lord does neither good nor evil." Christian Apologists have always for centuries had to resist this denial in various forms; and since the time of the English Deists, the Rationalists in Germany have specially sharpened their weapons for the destruction of the Christian idea of revelation; whilst it is scarcely necessary to remind that the pantheistic philosophy of earlier and later times cannot possibly admit this idea. The Naturalism and Positivism of our days, too, at once rejects the idea of such a revelation, as in itself utterly unworthy the consideration of any serious and independent thinker.

3. In opposition to these different voices, the possibility of Revelation

cannot naturally be maintained from *any* standpoint, but only from one which is duly determined and defined. Here, too, as in so many other questions, everything depends on our conception of God. The atheist considers the notion of revelation a mockery, whilst he, who though recognising the existence of God, considers Him as separated from the world by an impassable gulf, stands in silent despair on this side of the chasm. He, however, who places himself at a Christian-theistic standpoint—which shall be afterwards justified—must inevitably allow that there are no insuperable difficulties against the idea of a special revelation, nor against its wished-for realisation.

4. No *logical* difficulty, from any side, can be brought against the idea of a Revelation *per se.* It conflicts as little with itself, as with other sound ideas of God and Divine things. A revelation is as conceivable as a sun, which at first rises through the darkness. Yea, the idea itself, when once the need of such a benefit is acknowledged, is both attractive and worthy of God. Neither is there any *metaphysical* difficulty, which should force us to reject this idea at once as absurd. A living God must be able to reveal Himself; a God who is love must will to do so, where He considers it necessary. "Could He who is the Life be the unmoveable; He who is Love be the silent one? It would be a contradiction to His being; and even when His existence had been fully demonstrated, this contradiction would make us falter in our belief. So little is revelation a contradiction of God's nature, that the want of it would much rather contradict Him" (Luthardt). Lastly, a revelation of God would only be *psychologically* inconceivable, if it were proved that man was entirely void of capacity, either to discern it as such, or to accept duly its contents. It may, however, be plainly stated to the honour of mankind, this incapacity has never yet been proved, nor can it be proved, so long as the *humanitas divinitatis capax*, which was formerly professed by heathen lips,[1] is anything more than a well-sounding phrase. All new discoveries, combinations, snatches from the treasure-house of genius, in that domain of the world which is higher than the material, give proof of man's capacity for the higher and the highest, and so far deserve to be called "typical signs of revelation." Besides, General revelation has preceded Special, and by it has man been developed and prepared for the latter. Indeed, the poetic "child of the world" who spoke the words, "The spirit-world is not closed, thy mind is closed, thy heart is dead," has had more real and worthy thoughts of mankind than a materialistic philosophy which snatches from our race the crown, just as it wishes to dethrone God.

5. If, then, the Idea of Revelation does not present any preponderating difficulty, still less can we advance any against its Realisation. This last has been considered irreconcilable with the high *Majesty* of God, and everything has been thought to be said when the puny man who dreams of special revelations has been made to glance for a moment at the perplexing sight of the canopy of heaven glittering with the starlight of myriads of worlds. But in opposition to the discoveries of the telescope, the won-

---

[1] Acts xvii. 28.

ders of the microscope appear in their endless succession; and never certainly is the Infinite greater than when He bends down to the lowliest and the humblest.[2] For the same reason might the entire creation, sustenance, and government of so unimportant a world be classed among the catalogue of absurdities.—Nor is the fact of revelation, as here supposed, in conflict with the *Unchangeableness* of God. This unchangeableness cannot in any case be thought of as a rigid immobility; God, the rock, the Petra of ages, is not a petrifaction of Himself. The necessity of a special revelation is not a consequence of the defectiveness of the general, which had in later time seemed to require some completion; but a consequence of the new condition in which man has been brought by sin after he first had received the general revelation. Where even in human life an abnormal condition demands an extraordinary measure, why should it there be unworthy of God to expel the disease of sin by a new medicine? Even that which in His mode of operation seems an alteration in our eyes is, when viewed from God's side, without doubt, nothing but the gradual and regular realisation of His adorable plan.—Or should His *Goodness* forbid Him to confer so needful help upon only a relatively few, instead of all? Before we repeat this, let us remember that God certainly has no obligation to any man, and that even the special revelation, really intended for the race, originally was in its heads (Adam and Noah) bestowed in principle on humanity. Neither can God be reproached with the consequence of delay and neglect of duty on the part of those who were called to make His revelation known to their contemporaries; and we know that God will not reap where He has not first sowed.—Least of all have we right, with reference to His *Wisdom*, to maintain constantly that a revelation, really derived from Him, would not at any rate show any dark side, but must much rather be raised above even the possibility of doubt. Certainly it is easy here to advance various claims, which may seem quite acceptable at first; but, on the other hand, the question maintains its indisputable right, What would a revelation be which revealed nothing but what man could find out for himself? Mysteries surround us everywhere, the least in the lowest domain, why then should they be beyond measure offensive to us in the very highest domain? "Do ye not see," so said the acute Hamann (†1788), taunting the Rationalists of his time, "that God is a genius, who inquires very little about what ye call rational or irrational?" And as for proofs, can they not be in themselves sufficient, though they are constantly exposed to opposition on many sides? and would a belief which rested upon reasons of mathematical certainty exhibit a so much higher moral character, or could it even be properly called a religious belief?

6. Still less insuperable are the difficulties which have been raised against the possibility of revelation in the name of *History* and Experience. It does not decide anything to the detriment of our revelation to point out the great number of pretended revelations amongst nations and founders of religions of all kinds. In every case this phenomenon testifies of a deeply

---

[2] Ps. cxiii. 5, 6.

felt need, and rather causes us to suspect that a true coinage must exist, of which the false one is a copy. If twenty impostors were to struggle for the possession of an inheritance on insufficient reasons, will the judge then decide that there is no legal heir—perhaps that there never was a testator? —If it be said, that at any rate at present (as far as we know) there is no longer a Special Revelation, yet one must once for all establish his right to decide that, because a thing does not occur at the present instant, such a thing never happened before, nor could ever have taken place. Might not this extraordinary revelation have been of such a nature as to render its repetition in after days unnecessary for any one?—The complaint, lastly, that the notion of a Revelation is rejected by the modern scientific thought as wholly absurd, justifies on our side the objection that such a philosophy, even taken for granted that it were to be considered as a full-grown science, would only then be qualified for speaking so boldly if it had really taken all the facts into account, and among these had explained satisfactorily the general belief of mankind in the possibility of revelation. Hitherto this has not been the case, and on this account we refuse to yield to the protest of a party which we consider as neither thoroughly impartial nor properly instructed.

7. Only in one case might the impossibility of a revelation be said to be for ever made good, viz., when that of miracle is not only asserted, but proved. The question as to Revelation is properly the question as to Miracle, and will as such be soon discussed. For the present we are content if that is granted which indeed cannot be contradicted; the *Possibility* of a miracle being granted, that of revelation must also be recognised, and the only remaining question is whether there is sufficient reason to believe in its *Reality*.

Comp. F. DE ROUGEMONT, *Le Christ et ses têmoins* (1856), ii., pp. 57—146; C. H. BOSEN, *Das Christenthum und die Einsprüche seiner Gegner* (1864), pp. 542—554; TH. CHRISTLIEB, *Moderne Zweifel am Christl. Glauben* (1870), pp. 121—127; and for the astronomical difficulties, in addition to TH. CHALMERS' *Astronomical Discourses*, A. EBRARD, *Het Geloof aan de H. Schrift, enz.* (1862), bl. 1; TEN KATE, in his *Planeeten.*

POINTS FOR INQUIRY.

With what right is the whole inquiry into the possibility of revelation excluded *à priori*?—Historic declaration of the direct connexion of the question with the conception of God.—Name *any* attribute of God which is made known to you by general revelation, which would appear in greater dignity if special revelation had not been given, or had not been given as it was.—Might not the grounds for the reality of extraordinary revelation have been more indubitable, and ought they not to have been so?—In what sense can we assert that *now* there is no more extraordinary revelation? and what are we hence to conclude as to the question under discussion?—Further exposition of the close connexion between belief in revelation and in miracle.

SECTION XXXII.—ITS REALITY.

The reality of the special Revelation of Salvation, of which Jesus

Christ is the centre, is acknowledged by the Christian Church of all ages, and defended in various ways against continued opposition. Its character is manifested, not by proofs independent of this revelation, but by such as it has abundantly in itself. As the sun is known by its shining, so Revelation is recognised by its own light, and everywhere maintains its Divinity on external and internal grounds, where only the moral conditions for its recognition exist. The external grounds are to be found in the history of the Kingdom of God; specially in miracles and prophecies: the internal, in the contents of the Revelation itself. In the right connexion of the internal and external proofs lies the true force of the Apology for the Christian belief in Revelation, and upon the certainty thus indicated the testimony of the Holy Spirit imprints its infallible seal.

1. The investigation into the necessity and possibility of revelation has prepared us for the wider and more important one as to its reality. And here our starting-point is an undeniable fact. Not to speak here again of Israel as the people of revelation under the old covenant, the fact must strike us that Christianity in all ages has acknowledged the existence of a special revelation, of which the historic Christ is the living centre. It is conscious that something new has been given to it from God in Christ, which is nowhere found without Him. This regards not the belief of any single Church, still less of a party, but that of the holy Catholic Christian Church from its birth to the present day. If it be said that there are now many Christians who refuse to see in Christianity the fruit of a special revelation, it may be questioned whether such may be still called Christians at all. We do not judge here as to any one's heart and character; but the opinion of those who deny the reality of an extraordinary revelation can never be considered Christian, unless a meaning be attributed to this word, such as never before was known. Every one is not Christian who chooses to call himself by this name, but only he who shares the belief on which the Christian Church is founded. Christianity is an historical Religion, which declares itself to be the fruit of special revelations,[1] and he who denies to it this character has virtually placed himself beyond the limits of the Christian community. This is so plain, that no one can for a moment doubt about it, save he who has an interest in the denial, and has been assented to with praiseworthy impartiality by the ablest and most influential opponent of Christianity.[2]

---

[1] 1 Cor. ii. 9.

[2] See STRAUSS, *Glaubenslehre*, ii., p. 175 (1841); A. PIERSON, *De moderne Richting en de Kerk* (1866). "Is it not time, noble Réville, to put an end to this confusion of language?" The impression produced to a very wide extent by the arbitrary reply, "We remain," in answer to the above question, has not been doubtful.

2. Where Christianity confessed that faith in the midst of an unbelieving world, she saw herself continually summoned again to maintain her conviction, in obedience to the apostolic command;[3] but in every age Apologetics, in defending this vital principle, had to change its method according to the nature of the attack. At first this assumed a more *practical juridical* character, as is seen in the writings of the earliest Apologists. Afterwards it begins to assume a more *philosophic* character, as is seen in the Alexandrine school, in opposition to the Greek philosophy; soon after it exhibits a more *ecclesiastical* character and tone. The orthodox believer now defends his belief on this point[4] against heretics; in the middle ages,[5] against Jews, Heathen, and Mohammedans. The same line is still followed by the Romish Church. In the Protestant Church, on the other hand, we find a more *historico-biblical* tendency of apology showing itself,[6] whilst afterwards the more psychological and philosophic line, traced out by the master-hand of Pascal, has been followed on different sides. In our days the defence of the belief in revelation has assumed a more *Christocentric* character. The attention of friends and foes has been drawn more than ever to this much threatened centre of the circle of Divine truth; and men begin to understand better, that when this is safe, the conquest of what belongs to the circumference will not be long difficult, and both Church and science thankfully acknowledge the inestimable service which an increasing number of well-prepared Apologists have rendered to them in the great strife of the century. Still, this feeling gives her no liberty to let her hands lie idly by her side. A constant maintenance of the belief in Revelation is necessary, partly for the believer himself, who finds himself equally bound and impelled to such a testimony;[7] partly for the unbeliever, to win him, if possible, or, at any rate, to shame him; partly, lastly, for the Gospel and Christianity itself, which with reason demands that, at least, it be not condemned unheard.

3. The aim, which Christian Apologetics, as it thus continues its task, must set before it in accordance with the requirements of the age, is to show expressly that the Christian Church rightly believes in an extraordinary revelation, of which Jesus Christ is the centre. (Comp. § 17, 5.) It can never be its object to *prove*, in the strictest sense of the word, the reality of the Revelation. If this were its task, it would have to demonstrate, first, that there is a God; and this demonstration has never yet been so given, that contradiction has proved absolutely impossible. We stand here in the domain of sacred history, but the distinction between the evidence given of the most obvious historical facts, and that of mathematical propositions, is universally known. We cannot possibly convince ourselves of the accuracy of an historico-scientific reasoning quite in the same manner as we can of that of an arithmetical sum. The intelligent Apologist will not, therefore, expound a series of syllogisms, which end with a

---

[3] 1 Pet. iii. 15.
[4] Augustine.
[5] Abelard, Agobard of Lyons, etc.
[6] H. de Groot (Grotius), the English Apologists, Lilienthal, etc.
Acts iv. 20.

Q. E. D., but will rather repeat the "Come and see" of Philip; and rarely will he do this in vain, if he only meet with a Nathaniel.[8] As regards others, to evince our belief is our duty, but to convince *them* is more than a merely human work. *Faith finds its firm basis in grounds, but not its ultimate ground in demonstration.* If the apologist has placed the grounds for his belief so clearly in the light, and has answered its deniers so powerfully, that he may boldly count on the testimony of the impartial intellect, of the soul desirous of salvation, and of the awakened conscience, he may consider his task as fulfilled, and leave to a Greater One the proper work of converting opponents into friends of the truth.

4. The mode of attaining this end, which the Apologist of the Christian belief in revelation sets before himself, is *to let the revelation speak simply for itself.* Attempts have often been made to prove its reality by applying to it criteria which seemed to be completely independent of it. For instance, some characteristics were *à priori* determined, to which a revelation, in case it were given, ought to respond, if it were to be considered as really Divine. Thus, as Bretschneider says, in order to deserve confidence, it must exhibit signs of gradual development. It must be able to found a Church, in order to spread its pure doctrine. It must be suited, not merely for some, but for all nations; must work by purely moral means, and must also be contained in sacred writings. If revelation answers all these requirements, it must be accepted, and—happy coincidence!—such reasonable demands are not made upon Christian revelation in vain.—The conclusion of the reasoning is evident; but its self-deceit is too apparent. It is just as if a man had modelled the shape of a key in wax; from that impress he makes a key, and then, behold! it just fits in the lock! All these criteria were simply fixed by the light of the knowledge of the special revelation which was to be indicated by them. Suppose it had never been written, this criterion would most probably have been accepted, A real revelation cannot be propagated by means of the dead letter, but only by the living word, etc. No, the demonstration must not proceed from arbitrary criteria from without, but from the revelation itself. If ever any line of reasoning were *à priori* utterly free, it would, without doubt, be this, If there is a revelation, it will, without doubt, make itself known as such, as the sun is seen by its own light. Its credentials must be found in itself, and show a character homogeneous with it. "Real revelation has so little need of criteria, that it does not even give a place for them. Revelation springs immediately from itself, whilst it gives to the world a new idea of God, in itself resplendent with evidence. But when once such an idea exists in the world by revelation, it must then prove itself by itself" (Rothe). If it be once attested that the centre of Divine revelation has really been given in Christ, then the other at once follows, and an accurate test has been obtained for estimating the revelation given in the Scriptures of the Old Testament, and in the Apostolic testimony.

5. This only must never be forgotten, that the acknowledgment of the

---

[8] John i. 46, 47.

Divinity of the Gospel, even with and after the strongest defence, depends ultimately upon moral conditions. That which is Divine cannot, even as God Himself, be demonstrated in the strictest sense of the word. But it can be indicated, as shown to the eye which is open for the sight of God and Divine things. A holy love of truth, moral earnestness—in a word, a personal need of light and life in God—is here not only desirable, but absolutely indispensable. That requirement, placed in the forefront by the Gospel itself,[9] is founded on the nature of the case, and is justified, in many ways, by history and experience. Where this disposition is wanting, there men reason about, for, and against the truth, without understanding it, as a blind man would reason about colours. Where it is found, there men will lay hold of the truth, and then learn to spiritually understand that which they have laid hold of.

6. Only in one case would this be impossible; viz., if the doubt entertained by some as to *recognisability* of a revelation by men, as such, is entertained with sufficient right. It has actually been asserted that, even if we grant the probability of revelation, no Prophet or Apostle possessed an infallible criterion by which he could distinguish it, either from his own thought, or from demoniac inspirations. The answer to this charge is not far to seek. If God can give a revelation, He can also, without doubt, make it so plainly recognisable as such, that he who receives it will not have the slightest shadow of doubt on this point. Naturally we cannot now at once show how He did this in each particular case; and the first interpreters of revelation were called to live in faith on the word of God which they had received; much which to their consciousness was absolutely incontestable, might perhaps be communicated by them to others but imperfectly or not at all. On the other hand, however, each truth had undoubtedly its own clearness, and we hear interpreters constantly distinguish, with the utmost soberness, between the utterances of their own consciousness[10] and those of the Spirit of the Lord; and ofttimes a prophetic word is made manifest as Divine by its issue.[11] The ideas called forth by revelation, in the spirit of Apostle or Prophet, were not completely strange and unheard of to them, but they are usually connected with that which was already known and granted. As for ourselves, it is true that we cannot sharply define in this domain the limits of the merely human and the really Divine; but though we do not always know where these lie, we know, notwithstanding, that these exist, and also that there are things which lie on this side, and not on that side of these limits. As for what may in many special cases be doubtful, we meet in Holy Scripture with a number of words and deeds which rise, not only above our consciousness and faculties, but above those of all men. Besides, where the Divine really reveals itself, it there addresses itself with its own peculiar force to the spirit which is capable of receiving it. Certainly, where men obstinately deny the Supranatural, there men cut themselves off from the probability of recognising the revelation of the Supranatural as Divine. Men will then, even as to the most impressive signs, only say,

---

[9] John vii. 17; viii. 47; xviii. 37; 1 Cor. ii. 12-14; 1 John iv. 6.
[10] 1 Cor. vii. 10, 12, 25.
[11] Jer. xxviii. 15—17.

Astonishing, but never Divine; because the premises for this acknowledgment are wanting. But, then, they are like the man who has placed a handkerchief over his eyes, and is thus utterly unable to see the sun, even by its own light. We naturally do not claim any other recognisability for revelation, than one by those whose eyes are properly opened. For these its reality, *i.e.*, its Divinity, is sufficiently shown by reasons, found not without, but in itself. We treat *first* of the *external* proofs; then of the *internal;* afterwards of the *connexion* of both; and lastly we look at the *testimony of the Holy Spirit*, as the seal and crown of the whole.

I. 1. The *founding of Christianity by a crucified Nazarene* at once arouses, and to a certain extent justifies, the supposition that we are here on another domain than that of the merely natural course of things. That Jesus Christ lived and died under Pontius Pilate, is a fact, which is demonstrated by the evidence of the heathen and Jewish writers, as also is the fact that the preaching of His Gospel met with a completely unheard-of reception among Jews and heathen, and in a relatively short time has transformed the face of a great part of the moral world. This astonishing event can only be explained, if not merely His word and person made a quite unusual impression; but if, besides, there occurred something in His life which could in such eyes outweigh the disgrace of the cross. As such a fact appears the Resurrection of the Lord,—*i.e.*, the full revelation in Him of the Supranatural. Deny it, and—as will be shown hereafter—the existence of the Christian Church remains an enigma. Hitherto, at least, no attempt to explain Christianity as the merely natural product of its time has succeeded. He who cannot give a natural explanation must accept a supranatural, or rest in the confession of a not innocent ignorance. The *principium rationis sufficientis* pleads for the cause which we advocate.[12]

2. A glance at the *careful preparation of the Jews and the heathen for Christianity* strengthens the suppositions already suggested. A diligent investigation of history shows ever again how this is based entirely on a kingdom of God; so that Christ, in the fullest sense, may be called the centre of the history of the world. One of the most eminent historians of last century gave his testimony to this in a manner which is an honour to him, no less than to the Gospel: "The light which shone round Paul on his way to Damascus was not more surprising to him than what I suddenly saw, the fulfilling of all expectations, the summit of all philosophy, the explanation of all revolutions, the key to all seeming contradictions in the material and spiritual world, life and immortality" (J. v. Müller). We shall treat of this subject afterwards, when we are discussing the "fulness of the time." At present we only observe how the oft-repeated question, "Why has a revelation which seems so indispensable, appeared so late?" finds in this very phenomenon its satisfactory solution. That which is most noble in the natural and spiritual world usually is developed most slowly, and only appears after a long-continued preparation.

---

[12] Compare the essay of C. ULLMANN (which, though often ridiculed, has never yet been refuted), entitled *Was setzt die Stiftung des Christenth. durch einen Gekreuzigten voraus?* reprinted from the *Stud. u. Krit.*, in the pamphlet *Historisch oder Mythisch* (1838), pp. 1—40.

3. Of not less import is *the successful extension, careful preservation, and powerful vindication of Christianity.* The fulfilment of the parables of the mustard-seed and the leaven gives indubitable testimony to the Divinity of the Gospel, the more so if we glance at the spiritual character of that Gospel, the violent opposition made to it, the weakness of its adherents, and the greatness of the triumph which was gained. Even an unbeliever must confess that "the Gospel preached by persons of no name, no education, no eloquence, and under cruel persecution, and destitute of all human aid, nevertheless established itself in a short time all over the world. This is a fact which is undeniable, and proves it to be the work of God" (Bayle, art. Mahomet). The attempts[13] to explain this phenomenon in a natural way have utterly failed.[14] The difference between Christianity and Islamism is too great to justify an appeal to the rapid spread of Islamism. Even error may spread and obtain credence with wonderful rapidity, but it cannot possibly maintain itself under the most unfavourable circumstances, unless it bears within itself a proper element of truth. That the kingdom of God, which met with such fell opposition, has not disappeared from the earth without leaving any trace of its existence, cannot possibly be explained from human wisdom and strength.[15] Evidently God has made the cause of Jesus of Nazareth His own. The whole history of Christianity is a history of struggle, but of triumph too, which, even in the midst of the apostacy of these days, constantly causes men to tremble for the lot of its opponents.

4. In addition to these we must by no means omit the *beneficent influence* of Christianity. This testimony will first show itself in its full force when the Kingdom of God shall be completed, but even now its materials may be gathered everywhere. It is true, even atrocities have been committed in the name of Christianity. "Christianity, this is your work!" cried Voltaire, with a tragic air, as he looked on so many pages stained with blood and tears. But against these there are far more which testify of inestimable blessings, and we cannot at any rate attribute to the Founder of the Church its sins. We must think here, though only mentioning is allowed, of the blessed influence of Christianity on Family Life, Society, State, Civilisation, Art, Science, Philosophy, and the entire Life of man and mankind;[16] and besides, of all which the history of missions[17] tells as to the renewing power of the word of truth. Nor must we by any means forget how in this domain a great part of the most precious of the seed is hidden from the short-sighted eye, yet every now and then is revealed in a surprising manner, and then, after all, ask where we can find a parallel to that which, in all these respects, the history of God's kingdom proclaims.

5. All these historic evidences, when elucidated and properly combined, would undoubtedly be sufficient, if not to create, at least to justify, a well-

---

[13] Gibbon, etc.

[14] See, *inter alia*, the essay of K. F. Seltenreich on this subject, in the publications of the Hague Society (1816).

[15] Acts v. 38, 39.

[16] Comp. H. GUTH, *Die weltumgestaltende Kraft des Christenth.*, in the periodical *Der Beweis des Glaubens* (1868), p. 293, *sqq.*

[17] Comp. N. POULAIN, *L'Œuvre des Missions Evangel.* (1867).

grounded conviction of the reality of revelation, if it were not that the cry, louder than any of these voices, "Away with these miracles of the Gospel," was heard on all sides, especially in our days. It is but too true, the domain of miracles, "formerly a garden of exotic plants, but now a field of thistles" (Lange), for believers and Apologists, presents difficulties which require an express discussion. The days are gone by when a simple appeal to predictions and miracles seemed almost enough to prove the Divinity of the Gospel. And yet we hope that the days are now still far distant when Christian Apologetics shall rashly and proudly scorn the assistance which these extraordinary facts, properly looked at and used, offer to her in her good fight. It has only to take care not to sever such phenomena from their historical ground and context, in order to look at them wholly by themselves. *Miracles and predictions are no proofs for revelation, when added to it from without, but co-elements of revelation itself, which in their way testify to the Divinity of its origin and contents.*

6. As we are treating the question of miracles, (*a*) the *idea* of miracle naturally comes the very first in our discussion. Denoted by different names in the Bible (*θαύματα, θαυμάσια, παράδοξα*, etc.), miracle immediately suggests something which differs entirely from the usual course of things, and therefore excites a not unnatural surprise. This element of the unusual is, however, only a part of the notion, and the properly called wonder (*miraculum*) must be distinguished from that which seems to us very wonderful (*mirabile*, miraculous). While this latter has a mere subjective character, and directs itself purely to the senses, we have to do with the objective character of the former, which meets our consciousness at the same time as a revelation of a higher power.[18] It is certainly difficult to give here a right definition, but it is not difficult to indicate the cause of this inconvenience. A real miracle is nothing less than a direct *Divine act;* but God's mode of operation is to us as mysterious as His existence and the nature of His relation to this finite world. If there is much already in His ordinary agency which we cannot understand, how much more when we see Him act in a completely extraordinary manner! Every miracle has a side which we see, the fact in itself; but also a side which we do not see, the operating cause. Can it be otherwise but that definitions should differ, while not one is possible which does not leave room for objection? Yet every one knows what he must think of when he hears of miracles; that word offers a series of facts to his mind, which he tries to combine as far as possible under one notion. *A miracle is an entirely extraordinary phenomenon in the domain of natural or spiritual life, which cannot be explained from the course of nature as it is known to us, and must therefore have been brought about by a direct operation of God's almighty will, in order to attain a definite object.* Thus God Himself is at work in a miracle, but in a manner differing from the usual. "The character of miracles taken in the strictest sense is this, that they cannot be explained by the nature of created things" (Leibnitz). But it is this very conviction which makes the man who believes in a living, almighty, free-working God here exclaim with awe, "This is the finger of God."

---

[18] [*σημεῖον, δύναμις.*]

(*b*) Only where this belief is found, can the *possibility* of miracle be explained to a certain extent. It is lost labour to discuss this possibility with the man who holds a Deistic or Pantheistic conception of God. Hence it arises that the Naturalism and Positivism of the present time simply presupposes the impossibility of miracle, and does not consider it worth while to treat further of the subject. From this standpoint the historical criticism *may* not recognise as credible any narrative in which miracles are found; and even though the experimental proof required on that side were to be successful, how could a belief in miracles take root but upon the soil of Theism? "Historical sciences take for granted that no supernatural agent troubles the march of humanity; that there is no free being superior to man, to whom we might attribute an appreciable part in the moral guiding of things, any more than in the material government of the universe. As for me, I think that there is not in the universe any intelligence superior to that of man. Absolute justice and absolute reason only manifests itself in man; considered as outside mankind this absolute is merely an abstraction. The Infinite only exists when it is clothed in a form" (Renan). If this be not Atheism, what is it? In truth, we can only consider it as a happy inconsistency in the supporters of modern Naturalism, which does more honour to their heart than to their head, that the denial of miracle will still assume a religious character. From the opposite standpoint we shall scarcely create any difficulty in saying with Augustine, "Dandum est Deo, Eum aliquid facere posse, quod nos investigare non possumus."

The general belief in miracles among all nations in itself makes us incline to recognise their possibility. To the natural consciousness of God the idea at least seems to have nothing absurd in it. How would it be possible to grant to man a certain degree of freedom, and to deny this to God? If we state that the conceptions, Law of nature and Will of God, so completely and entirely cover one another, that an operation of God's will beyond the fixed course of these laws is utterly inconceivable, then with consistent reasoning nothing at least will be left of the personality of God. He who really recognises this is forced to confess with one of the greatest thinkers of our age, "I sincerely reverence the laws of nature, and heartily rejoice when man learns to know them better. God Himself has indeed submitted to man the powers of nature; but He never submitted to him Himself, or made Himself subject, as well as His freedom and His almighty will. When God organised the laws of nature, He could not relegate to them the operation of His causality, and so place in them a barrier to His own free working" (Rothe). Neither His wisdom nor His unchangeableness stand in the way of such an operation of His power and freedom (§ 31, 4); and least of all does an accurate conception of the laws of nature. Is that idea indeed anything else but an abstraction of the thinking spirit? We observe the usual rule by which the facts, in so far as they have been noticed till now, commonly happen, and express this rule in a certain formula; but new facts may show themselves, by which it is at once seen that the formula was too narrow in its limits. The whole idea of a law of nature is indeed elastic, and as long as we do not know all the phenomena, the word Impossible is premature. And never do we require the belief that a miracle should conflict with the whole of nature and all her laws. *Non pugnant contra naturam, sed contra nobis cognitam naturam* (Augustine), and above this stands highest the will of Him who works all things after the counsel of His will. Besides, the law of nature which is known to us is not broken or abrogated by miracle, but only superseded in a certain point by a sovereign Cause. There is no talk here of conflict, because the law in itself remains intact, but is only in a special case set on one side : the miracle takes place, not in opposition to it, but simply beyond it, perhaps by a higher law not yet known to us. When the free movement of my hand casts a stone into the air, which without it would fall to the ground, what law of nature is there contravened? "Miracles belong to a higher order of things, which is a nature also" (Nitzsch). It is indeed as if nothing could be more fatal to nature than to come into so close a connexion with her Creator and Lord. Do we not everywhere see the sphere of the higher life of nature appear in and beside a lower one, without the possibility of explaining the first by the last? Is then really the animal world already explained as the merely natural result of the plant world, man as the natural result of the animal world? and if not, is it then utterly inconceivable that One should appear among mankind. who is not to be explained by mankind only, and may be called the absolute miracle in its history? and if so, why should this One have no power to work miracles? "Unnatural," men repeat; but they forget then that nature, in her actual condition, is under the power of sin, and has a King, whose will is to renew and release her. If the human spirit can work dynamically on matter, then the sinless One, in whom dwells the fulness of the Spirit, must have been able to do so in a manner which infinitely exceeds the usual course of things. Once more; whoever boldly repeats here the word "impossible," in principle denies the belief in a living God, in a properly so called creation of the world, in providence, and the hearing of prayer. Against such a precipice of negation we have nothing to do but to warn; against such a purposed unbelief we can only protest with all seriousness in the name of science and conscience. It is both satisfactory and remarkable that so many natural philosophers are on this point more cautious than some theologians and philosophers. Even if the Empiric philosopher had proved that a real miracle had never been observed, he would not be able to proclaim the doctrine of this absolute impossibility, without stepping unlawfully into a domain which is closed to him; and the Christian is allowed to make an appeal from a narrow experience to one on a more extended scale, that of his own spiritual life not excluded.

(*c*) The *recognisability* of miracles cannot be denied, any more than their possibility, at least by him who brings to his investigation a belief in the living God (§ 31, 4). It is true that a terrible deception in this domain is conceivable, even presaged in Matt. xxiv. 24, and ofttimes effected. But the criterion of the real miracle lies not merely in the act being in itself unusual and unheard of, but, at the same time, in the moral character of the worker of miracles, and in the Godly aim of his act. No miracle of a false prophet can make a lie truth.[19] And the Scripture narrations of

[19] Deut. xiii. 1—3.

miracles on the whole obviously show such higher characteristic (the healing of the one born blind, raising of the dead, etc.). Besides, the deeds of God, as well as His words, are directed, not merely to the senses, but also to the heart and conscience of man, and furnish an internal evidence which cannot be doubted. Shall man, who is allied to God, possess *no* means at all by which he, at least by continued examination, can distinguish the Divine from the demoniacal in this domain? No omniscience indeed is needed to determine whether anything which occurred was or was not according to the fixed course of nature. True, the border-line where the natural ceases in many cases is difficult to indicate, still we know that there is a border-line. It is as with the colours of the rainbow,—they melt into one another, and yet no one will mistake one for another. It is not necessary to know the whole code of laws in order to assert that in one special case a prescript of the code has been departed from. Whoever, on the other hand, affirms that he would rather deny than assent to the evidence of his own senses, and that of a thousand spectators, that, *e.g.*, a dead man had been raised from the dead, cannot properly be placed on any other list than that which contains the victims of an irremediable "idée fixe." By such views he may certainly withhold himself and others from faith, but cannot possibly prevent God's activity or man's observation.

(*d*) When we investigate the *reality* of miracles, it is important to distinguish between that of the sacred, and specially of the evangelic narratives in general, and that of any single narrative of a miracle, regarded by itself and apart. That, so far as the former is concerned, the first century of Christianity was a century of miracles, which then gradually disappeared, is proved by a series of unsuspected and clear testimonies.[20] The expressions of St. Paul in particular, even in his epistles of undeniable authenticity, leave no doubt on this point.[21] They excite the greater confidence because they proceed from a man not naturally given to the miraculous,[22] and are only incidentally mentioned, without any apologetic intention. He who thus speaks is himself a moral miracle in history, not explained, nor explicable, unless a real appearing of the risen Christ was vouchsafed to him, as he testifies repeatedly and with the greatest certitude.[23] If we must now —as will be further shown afterwards, on the evidence of his experience too —grant that the dead Nazarene has risen in a bodily form from the grave, then is the supranatural actually revealed, and miracle thus in principle maintained. Indeed, it cannot for a moment appear incredible to us, that, with regard to Him, who is the Lord of Life and Conqueror of Death, great and matchless miracles should have been done by Him or worked in Him. He Himself appears before us as the greatest miracle in the moral and religious domain,—the Sun, of which all separate miracles are only so many, to a certain extent, natural radiations. This shining sun cannot, however, be conceived of without its morning dawn or evening splendour, proportionate to the brightness of its light. So before and after the great

[20] Cf. Tholuck, *Ueber die Wunder der Kathol. Kirche, u. s. w.*, in the first volume of his *Vermischte Schriften* (1839), p. 28, *sqq.*
[21] Rom. xv. 18, 19; 1 Cor. xii. 10, 28; Gal. iii. 5; Heb. ii.
[22] Phil. ii. 27; 2 Tim. iv. 20.
[23] 1 Cor. ix. 1; xv. 8.

miracle of Christ's appearance in the world are the miracles of the Prophetic and Apostolic period. Here, too, in order to master the whole sphere, we do our best by starting from its centre.

While in this way the reality of the Scriptural miracles in general can be proved—and we may say that the rise and first victory of Christianity would be inconceivable, if no such signs at all had been given—it is still self-evident that the credibility of each separate miracle is not yet thereby made out. This is shown only by means of an express historico-critical investigation, which, if it is to deserve the name, must be quite impartial, and entirely free from arbitrary presuppositions. If on so-called philosophic grounds the impossibility of miracle be tacitly accepted as a starting-point, the fate of many a narrative can be easily guessed, and an inevitable wrong is done to the investigation itself. It is not allowed to ask philosophy beforehand to determine what may be historical or not. First of all, then, we are invited to a criticism of the sources, the so-called subjective criticism. The question here is whether they are derived from well-instructed, truth-loving, competent witnesses? This first question, however, is not, even in the most favourable circumstances, the only one; to the subjective criticism the objective must be joined, that of the facts themselves which are related. The question whether the narrators were not only trustworthy, but whether the narratives were credible, must be put and answered. But here the experience of our days must be by no means the highest, much less the only test of our judgment; that which does not happen now, may, nevertheless, have happened in former times,[24] and the utterances of the experience of former epochs ought therefore to be consulted. The narrative, too, must be compared with all we know concerning the person, acts, and works and sufferings of the miracle-worker; the internal character of the event, in union with the aim ascribed to it, must also be tested; its result, too, must also show whether we have to think here of a natural cause or not. When considering particularly the miracles of our Lord, the objective criticism must pay special heed to their inseparable connexion with words[25] whose genuineness hardly admits of doubt; to their superiority above those of all other messengers of God, in connexion with a sublimity of self-consciousness not to be found elsewhere; and not last, to the surprising difference between the canonical and apocryphal miracles, which testify so plainly in favour of the former (J. J. van Toorenenbergen, P. H. Hugenholtz). Finally, we must most earnestly examine the question whether the denial in principle of all miracles does not lead to much greater difficulties than the method of such an impartial historico-critical investigation. The reality of miracles will on all these grounds be the more readily accepted, the better we understand that in connexion with God's counsel, and the whole personality of the Saviour, they may be called natural, and even absolutely necessary.

(*e*) We have already in principle answered the question as to the best *explanation* of the Scriptural miracles. Miracle, as the proper and personal act of the incomprehensible God, can never be fully explained, but only under-

---

[24] Cf. H. E. VINKE, *De empirie van Jezus' Apostelen en verdere Tijdgenooten, enz.* (1864).
[25] As, *e.g.*, Mark viii. 17—21.

stood and conceived to a certain degree. That end is, however, attained neither by the Natural and Mythical, nor by the Allegorical and Symbolical interpretation. We shall afterwards show (§ 91) why in particular the two first methods cannot be applied to the domain of the Evangelical history. Here we place against all arbitrariness the demand that the explanation aimed at must be a purely grammatico-historical one in all the force of that word. Thus will it be at once truly psychological and theological. But above all we must, in our treatment of miracle, maintain the Christocentric character of Dogmatics (§ vii. 3). It is by the light given to us in the person and words of the Lord that we first see the full light rise on His own miracles, as well as on those of His Prophets and Apostles. Contexts will very often explain much which, taken by itself, would be absolutely incredible.

(*f*) The *demonstrative value* of miracles has been partly misunderstood and exaggerated; and this latter particularly by the earlier Supranaturalism, which regarded miracles and predictions as the very chief evidences of the Divinity of revelation. It is clear, however, that the Lord Himself never attributed such a high import to His miracles, but always considered faith founded on His words as of higher value than that grounded on signs.[26] Notwithstanding the most astonishing signs, many of His contemporaries remained unbelieving, and in any case these signs were adapted much more to the wants of the first beholders than to those of later times. So Luther already judged rightly when he said, "Such signs, therefore, were done that the Christian Church might be founded, established, and accepted. But these are unimportant and almost childish signs when compared with the sublime wonders which Christ unceasingly works in His Church." While he says again, that God must "allure men by such external miracles, as children are tempted by apples and pears."—But still this does not give us the right to estimate the value and evidential force of miracles at so low a rate as has been done by many in our days. He who asserts that Christ Himself attached only little import to His miracles, has certainly never studied carefully such expressions as those in Matt. xi. 4, 5, 20—24; xii. 28, 39, 40; John v. 36; x. 25, 37, 38; xi. 41; xiv. 11; xv. 24. It is true, the works to which Jesus appealed were not exclusively His miracles. Still these last undoubtedly were understood by Him to belong to them. The history indeed shows that not a few were led to belief, or had their belief strengthened, by their means. How was it possible that facts of this kind should have been done without being of deep, in a certain sense eternal, import?—Against both these extremes we come on the right track merely by observing the real character of these works as signs (σημεῖα, τέρατα), Prodigium = porro digium (Hugo of St. Victor), a finger pointing to him who works the sign. It is not as an external credential added to revelation, but as itself a part of it, that a miracle proves the Divine mission of him who works it; and by legitimate consequence the Divine origin of the word which he proclaims. That even a well-established miracle cannot by itself prove the truth of a doctrine, may be safely granted, but it is nevertheless a sign that God is with him who does

[26] John iv. 48; x. 38; xiv. 11.

such signs.[27] The miracles of Jesus must be decidedly regarded as revelations of His glory,[28] and, at the same time, as striking symbols of the salvation which He proffers and promises.[29] Such revelations and symbols were of course originally adapted to the wants of the first witnesses; but when properly established and understood, they retain their high value for all after-time. We undoubtedly in our days believe rather in miracles for Christ's sake, than in Christ for the miracles' sake; but a miracle may nevertheless lead to belief in Him, and support this belief against sundry contradictions. Christianity legitimates miracles; but miracles also furnish very important evidence in regard to Christianity and its origin. But they do this only when they are not looked upon as isolated facts, but in connexion with one another, in union with the person of the miracle-worker, and by the light of His own utterances.

(*g*) The *objections* unceasingly brought against the so-called evidential force of miracles, after what we have said, are easily encountered. As for the philosophic objections, those of the speculative philosophy fall away when the theistic conception of God is satisfactorily maintained, and empiric criticism has a right to claim that so surprising a departure from the usual order of things as miracles presuppose, be not believed without sufficient grounds but in no case has it the right to say here "impossible;" rather does the saying, "The true is not always the probable," suit better here. If the experience of the present time teaches that an appeal to miracles is often a hindrance rather than a benefit to the sacred cause of faith, this indeed is a charge against the spirit of the time, but by no means against the miracles themselves. More than one who declares that he does not require these supports to his faith, neither knows true faith nor himself. The remark that the belief in miracle is in direct conflict with the modern conception of the world, and is dwindling away with the increase of civilisation, justifies without doubt a doubly accurate criticism of the old narratives of miracles, but also of the new cosmogony itself; and in no case does it give an actual right to consign with one stroke of the pen all the narratives of miracles to the domain of imagination. N thing is more inexorable than a fact," says the proverb, and the warning which the Germans give against that which they call "emptying out the child with the bath," may in our case be both timely and necessary. Finally, he who asks why there are now no longer miracles, when they are more than ever necessary, must not forget, so far as he is right in his supposition, that we cannot in any case make any claim on God; that in earlier times it was only the great turning-points of the history of revelation which were glorified by a number of miracles; and, lastly, that the Christian lives in the hope of a future, which promises new revelations of God's glory both in the natural and spiritual worlds.

The *historical* objections, to be sure, would be weightier if they had unconditional right, but they, too, to no small extent, rest on exaggeration and misunderstanding. It is said (1) that the sacred writers make no special distinction between ordinary and extraordinary operations of God, since they always attribute everything to His intervention. But though

---

[27] John iii. 2. [28] John ii. 11. [29] John vi. 35; viii. 12; xi. 25.

they do not place prominently in the front a sharply defined idea of what belongs to nature, they nevertheless recognise a fixed order of nature;[30] and, as distinguished from this, a special series of facts called into being by the direct intervention of God.[31] "While the idea of miracles is fixed, the mental presentment thereof is less closely defined" (Köstlin). It is asserted (2) that the sacred writers have suffered themselves to be carried away by their love of the miraculous, in order to adorn their own narratives. But when it is remarked that the Evangelists (only to mention these) do not tell of any miracle of the Baptist;[32] nor of the infancy and childhood of Jesus; that we never hear the disciples ask their Master to work a miracle, but, on the contrary, see Him often refuse to give a sign, and hear the desire for miracles sharply rebuked by Him, we are led to a different opinion. (3) As far as concerns the many imaginary miracles of the heathen religions, the thoughtful words of Pascal are always applicable: "Instead of concluding that there are no true miracles, because there are so many false ones, we must, on the contrary, say that there are certainly true miracles, because there are so many false ones; and there would not have been any false miracles, but for the reason that there are true miracles." Finally, if we are asked what credence must be given to those many Christian narratives of miracles, *e.g.*, of the middle ages and the Romish Church, in whose favour, as it seems, so much trustworthy evidence has been brought, we answer that a blind belief is as unsuitable as a systematic unbelief, but that careful investigation remains our duty. As yet we are waiting till such narratives are supported by proofs as clear as those which support the narratives of the New Testament. In no case will they ever prove anything against these; on the contrary, the comparison tends more to the advantage than to the injury of the narratives of the Holy Scripture.

(*h*) The *importance* of this question as to miracles must not, after all our discussion, be estimated too lightly. It is a question of principle, and also an eminently practical one. It is by no means a matter of indifference for the religious and Christian life to know whether God can work only by natural and finite causes, or whether the Spirit of the Infinite One stands really above matter, and its blind necessity, and works with unlimited power and freedom. He who denies this last, cuts away, not only the Christian belief in revelation, but also the main artery of Ethics, and cannot possibly always avoid the precipice of the Deification of Nature and Atheism. On the other hand, he who recognises a God who can work miracles, will find in the narratives of these miracles no hindrance, but a finger-post to point out the road to the Christian belief in revelation. Besides, the Christian who has him self experienced the quickening power of God in prayer, has got an experimental proof of the truth of miracles in the spiritual domain, which makes its complete denial in the system of nature utterly impossible.

Compare, on the subject of miracles, J. J. VAN OOSTERZEE, *Leben v. Jez.* D. I. bl.

[30] Gen. viii. 22; James v. 7. [31] 1 Kings xvii. 1, etc. [32] John x. 41.

209, etc.; *Het Johannes-Evangelie* (1867), p. 149, etc., and the literature quoted there; to this must be added J. HIRZEL, *Ueber das Wunder, u. s. w.* (1863); N. POULAIN, *Un Christianisme sans Dogmes et sans Miracles* (1864); CREMER, *Ueber die Wunder in Zusammenh. mit der Göttl. Offenb.* (1865); F. GODET, *De Wunderen des Heeren* (1868); M. FUCHS, *Das Wunder*, in the *Neun Apologet. Beiträge* (1869), pp. 99—139; TH. CHRISTLIEB, *a. a. O.* (1870), pp. 318—391; O. FLUEGEL, *Das Wunder und die Erkennbarkeit Gottes* (1871); W. BENDER, *Das Wunder-begriff des N. T., eine dogm. Untersuchung.* (1871); J. B. MOZLEY, *On Miracles*, Bampton Lectures for 1865.

7. The predictions which are usually mentioned along with miracles, as the principal evidences for the reality of revelation, are, on their part, miracles of Divine omniscience, joined to those of Divine omnipotence and sovereignty. These same questions, just discussed, arise again here, but, after what we have already said, can be treated more briefly.

(*a*) The *idea* of predictions has its root in that of Prophetism, which has been elucidated in our work on the *Biblical Theology of the New Testament.* By prediction we understand the positive announcement of some still future facts of revelation, which cannot be calculated beforehand by the natural understanding, and therefore are *made known to the seer by direct Divine intervention.* As we enter on this domain, we must here, too, be on our guard against two opposite extremes. On the one side, that of the older Supranaturalism, which almost exclusively limited the office of the Prophets to the foretelling of all kinds of future chiefly accidental things, unexpectedly confirmed by the event; on the other side, that of the modern Naturalism, which, just as little as the earlier Rationalism, will hear of proper foretellings, and even in this domain will admit nothing which cannot be explained from man himself. From the first standpoint, the relation of the Prophets to the present is underrated; from the other, it is so exaggerated that there cannot be any further serious thought of revelation, as given in and through them. Both these representations are in conflict with a number of facts which convincingly prove, on the one hand, that the prophetic perspective was rooted in the present and the past; on the other, that it cannot possibly be explained merely and entirely thereby. Both from the nature of the case, as well as from the utterances of the prophets themselves, we must decide that the word of revelation possessed undoubtedly an historical and psychological point of union in the sphere and character of its chosen interpreters; but that nevertheless their knowledge of the future was derived from a higher source than that of their merely natural consciousness. "We must not regard prophecy merely as a Divine spark of light, which springs from the present, shaped by God, but as a heavenly light which God lets fall in the dark paths of history, to point out whither they lead. Prophecy derives its wings, which carry it far beyond the present, not from history, but from the omniscient God, who reveals Himself each time according to His will, and man's needs. If history conceals always within its bosom the next step, God has the beginning, middle, and end of all history in His bosom, and prophecy sees just so much of this as God reveals to the eye of the spirit. So heaven opens to the prophet above earth, and he does not listen to the grass which grows in history, but is a hearer of the Divine speech, and an interpreter of the Divine thoughts" (Delitzsch).

It is generally known that the Old Testament especially contains a number of these predictions: as, *e.g.*, the prophetic announcement of the plagues of Egypt; the destruction of the house of Eli; the circumstances after the anointing of Saul as king; the prolongation of Hezekiah's life for fifteen years; the seventy years' exile; the seventy weeks of Daniel, etc. Accurate exegesis and unprejudiced criticism must determine whether these narratives really contain the historically credible account of the foretelling of these facts, in a form which, at the time of the foretelling, was beyond the power of calculation Even in that case we must still take care to regard the accidental (contingent) circumstances announced by the prophets as not morally indifferent. It is this unequivocally ethical character which distinguishes true prediction from the motley array of oracles which owes its rise to the Mantics of heathen nations. We nowhere find the prophets of Israel foretelling unimportant *curiosa;* and even the apparent accidents which they announce display, on further examination, a religious theocratic character, and generally stand in direct connexion with the development of the kingdom and counsel of God. They appear in history, not as diviners or explainers of signs, but as confidants of God, for whom He Himself has raised the veil of the future.

(*b*) The question as to the *possibility* of such predictions is most closely connected with that as to their *recognisability.* The former can, of course, only be answered affirmatively, when there is belief in a God, who surveys all the future, and can, if it pleases Him, reveal it to others, and at the same time a recognition in man of the faculty of consciously receiving as a Divine word that which God reveals to him. Such an act of revelation ought to be considered as morally impossible, if by it the freedom of man were quite annihilated, and if he were brought by it under the irresistible influence of certain fate. Against this objection we must observe that God foresees even the morally free acts of man as they are, and that an event has never happened only because it was foreseen and foretold. Clever men have, with a degree of relative certainty, foreseen, *e.g.*, the French Revolution at the end of the last, or the fall of Napoleon at the beginning of this century, and have prognosticated it to their confidants; have, then, these two events taken place in consequence of their prognostications? We meet here the as yet unsolved probl m of the connexion between the foreknowledge of God and the free action of man. He, however, who in order to preserve the latter considers any revelation of the future as unworthy of God, and even useless and injurious, may for the same reasons deny the whole doctrine of Providence.—Just as little may we say that it is morally impossible that God should now and then make use of blameable and even of bad men as the interpreters of His revelation,—as, for example, Balaam, Jonah, and Caiaphas. The ideal of morality is undoubtedly higher in the days of the New Covenant than in those of the Old, because the light of truth had then risen with so much greater clearness. A seer with great imperfections of character may nevertheless be a messenger of special revelations; the confidant of God in one instance is not on that account always His favourite.—As to the possibility of this communication on its human side, the natural faculty of divination

(Ahnung, second-sight), developed so remarkably in some persons, already shows that the human spirit has an organ for the future, as well as a remembrance of the past. Why, we ask, should not this natural disposition be so elevated and strengthened by Divine operation, that the glance of the spiritual eye is not any more limited by the confining bounds of time and space?

Every Divine revelation was certainly *recognisable for* the Prophet who received it;[33] especially when that which was revealed, as was often the case, was opposed to his own views.[34] They themselves point expressly to a moment of higher inspiration, which they attempted in vain to resist, and which often transferred them unexpectedly to a domain, not of intellectual reflection, but of an intuition of the future, which was brought about by God.—For their *contemporaries*, too, it was not impossible to distinguish the true prophets of Jehovah from the false. The former, as distinguished from the others, remained faithful to the fundamental principles of Mosaism, manfully combated cherished ideas, sins, and inclinations, and were often in a position to prove their mission by sign and wonder. Besides, from the nature of the case, the Divinity of this mission continued to be for their contemporaries a point of faith and conviction, until the issue had decided the cause between them and their opponents.—To *us*, lastly, true prophecy, as distinguished from false, is recognisable, not merely by the theocratic character and sublimity of its contents and tone, but also by the testimony of the Lord and His Apostles, who point it out as such; while, finally, in many cases the surprising character of a fulfilment, which seemed at first almost inconceivable, renders all doubt as to its Divine origin once for all impossible.

(*c*) That such prophecies as we mean *really exist*, and have been already fulfilled, or are still in course of fulfilment, hardly requires demonstration. Only when certain well-known measures are applied to the treatment of the history of revelation can it be denied that there often is a most remarkable concordance between prophecy and fulfilment. This will be seen if we think of the prophecies respecting whole nations or cities (Assyria, Babylon, Nineveh, Tyre), and specially of the definite announcements as to the person and work of the Lord. It can as little be denied that such expectations were expressed for years and centuries before they were realised, as that they were raised far above the natural reach of human intellect. The saying of Tertullian is true, "Quidquid agitur, prænuntiabatur: quidquid videtur, audiebatur." Even if, under the influence of a really sound criticism, the list of these prophecies has been in many ways lessened, still not a few remain whose existence and import can only be denied as a consequence of an inexorable preconception.

(*d*) The *evidential force* of prophecies, in the question as to the reality of Christian revelation, is, from the nature of the case, twofold. It relates partly to the prophet himself, and partly to the person or matter which he has foretold. It is evident from positive proofs that a prophet has foretold something which could most certainly not be calculated, and yet notwithstanding has been fulfilled at the appointed time; he himself then

---

[33] Compare Section xxxii. 6. [34] 2 Sam. vii. 3; 2 Kings iv. 27.

undoubtedly appears before us in the character of a messenger from God, and his word, in consequence, is evidently a really Divine word. But above all, the fulfilment of the prophecy in His person and work, constitutes for belief a clear proof that Jesus Christ is really the King of the kingdom of God, who was promised of old. This indeed is uncontradictably settled, that the expectation of a Messiah has been entertained by the Jews, and even by the heathen; that this expectation was founded on the words of prophecy; and that the agreement of this word with the event has in numberless cases excited even the astonishment of honest unbelief. Jesus and His Apostles were thus never weary of pointing to[35] fulfilled prophecy as an indisputable guarantee for the divinity of the Gospel. The assertion made by Schleiermacher, that it is impossible to prove from the prophecies that Christ is the Saviour, is contradicted by the most direct statements of the New Testament, and by a multitude of facts.[36] In the first centuries of Christianity especially this proof was of inestimable value, and it is thus designedly and emphatically adduced by the oldest Apologists, Justin Martyr, Origen, and others. As to later times, though the *impression* produced by these correspondences cannot any longer be as convincing as when they were first experienced, their *importance* continues always the same, at least when we succeed in giving a satisfactory answer to the many objections which have been alleged against this kind of external evidence. Even in this case the evidential force of prophecy—superior in this respect to that of miracles—increases as time progresses, and brings to light proofs of the truth of the prophetic words.

(*e*) The *objections* which have been alleged against this evidence from prophecy, originate alternately within and without the domain of the Bible. The former are undoubtedly the least important. Only in consequence of arbitrary or intentional misunderstanding can we attempt to make it appear from Holy Scripture itself, that the Lord or His Apostles attached no great importance to the word of prophecy and its fulfilment. This hopeless proposition cannot in any case be proved from such passages as Matt. xi. 11, 1 Cor. xiii. 2, 9, etc.; while such expressions as are found in Luke xvi. 31, xxiv. 25, Acts iii. 24, xxvi. 22, emphatically contradict it.—The biblical statement, that notwithstanding the fulfilment of prophecy many continued unbelieving and disobedient, would only cause us suspicion if we had asserted that this evidence could compel any one to believe, it being quite indifferent what his moral nature might be, or if we could forget that even this obduracy was foretold.[37]—Holy Scripture, it is true, repeatedly points to the possibility of dæmoniacal working even in this mysterious domain,[38] but it calls us, at the same time, to a discerning of spirits, and supplies a test for this judgment.[39]—If a complaint be made as to the obscurity of many prophecies, in so far as this complaint is not exaggerated, it calls forth the answer that this obscurity was partly natural, partly necessary to the fulfil-

---

[35] See, *e.g.*, Luke iv. 16—21; John xiii. 19; Acts, *passim*; Rom. i. 2, etc.
[36] See, *e.g.*, Acts viii. 30—37.
[37] Acts xxvii. 23—27.
[38] Matt. xxiv. 24; Acts xvi. 16—18; 2 Thess. ii. 9.
[39] Deut. xviii. 18—22; Jer. xxviii. 15—17.

ment, and was sufficiently counterbalanced by many a ray of greater brilliancy.—The difficulty derived from the fact that many oracles in the Old Testament, when taken literally and in their original connection, appear intended for something quite different from the persons or facts of which they are explained in the New Testament, cannot be considered unimportant, but still diminishes when we more accurately investigate the meaning of the words, "that it might be fulfilled," etc.; and besides, it is by no means applicable to all the prophecies.[40]—Lastly, if our attention be called to a number of prophecies in the Bible, which still after centuries remain unfulfilled, against this palpable fact we must not, on the one hand, overlook the distinction between form and contents, letter and spirit; nor, on the other hand, forget that the last pages of the history of the world are not yet written.

But even in the domain outside the Bible, material is found for objection and contradiction; and attention is called to the known phenomena of manticism, soothsaying, sorcery, etc., existing even among heathen nations. But then the distinction in principle between this domain and the Israelitish Prophetism, which has been already pointed out, is entirely lost. "The heathen oracle is ambiguous like Dialectics; but Jehovah is no Loxias; the prophetic words point definitely and unambiguously to one thing. The consciousness of Pythia was veiled in the dense vapours which issued from the hole in the earth; her inspiration is the unconscious inspiration of nature, as in magnetic vision; it is, on the contrary, the 'hand of the Lord' which comes upon the prophets of Israel; their vision is not that of somnambulism, but that of the spirit, the co-knowledge of the human spirit with the Holy Spirit of Providence. The heathen soothsayers divined by means of entrails and the flight of birds; the prophets of Israel looked into the mirror of history, and prophesied according to the signs of the times" (Martensen). The higher expectation, moreover, of a glorious future, found even among the more distinguished heathens, may serve also as a proof that in this domain too the supranatural is by no means the contra-natural.—And as to Israel, it is known that it explains not a few of the so-called Messianic prophecies in a completely different sense, so that they lose all their evidential force as to the divinity of the Gospel. But it is also certain that that conception sprang in no small degree from reaction against Christian belief, and that very often the most ancient and best Jewish exegetes favour the Christian interpretation.[41]—The assertion that all the passages which exhibit an admittedly prophetic character have been first conceived and composed in later times in the light of the event, is an absolute falsehood. From whence did the expectation by the Jews of a Messiah, which shortly before Jesus' coming was spread over the whole East, spring, if there were not any Messianic prophecies at all? The bold affirmation of Strauss, that we are not absolutely sure that in any prophecy we have not given us a *vaticinium ex eventu*, deserves only the reply, "Stat pro ratione voluntas." The concordance of prophecy and fulfilment is only impossible, then, when belief in an omniscient, omnipotent, and free-working Lord of the future is thought a

---

[40] Comp. J. J. VAN OOSTERZEE, *Christologie*, i. p. 52.
[41] See HENGSTENBERG'S *Christology*.

chimera; "siquidem ista sic reciprocantur, ut *si divinatio sit, et Dei sint, et si Dei sint, sit et divinatio*" (Cicero de Divin. i. 5).—Lastly, if attention be called to the fearful abuse made also of this belief in the service of fanaticism and superstition, we must consider how little that abuse can testify against the right use of it, and also what a rich treasure of light and comfort this last, on the other hand, has for centuries revealed.

(*f*) After all we have said, we cannot be surprised to see this evidence held in honour by such men as Grotius, Leibnitz, and Pascal, as well as by many others. The *reasoning*, however, founded upon fulfilled prophecy, must, with respect to the Jew, be conducted in a somewhat different manner than that with respect to the philosophic sceptic; whilst the different degree, development, knowledge of the language, etc., of the opponents of the prophetic word may not be passed over in the consideration. The proofs derived from separate oracles must naturally be not only counted, but also weighed; and the sacred utterances must be carefully explained according to the well-tested rule of the Hermeneutics of the Old Testament. It is, besides, important not to separate this argument as a whole from, but to connect it most closely with, the idea of Miracle; just as this last, again, with the entire historic proof; and to have regard not only to a number of separate passages, but specially to the great "Whole" of the Old Testament dispensation in its prophetic character. It is most important to see in the prophetic utterances, not merely credentials for, but elements of, the revelation itself, serving to unfold this last to us in its gradual development. God reveals Himself ever again, now in the announcement, then in the fulfilment, of the facts of salvation, which in their turn bear in themselves the germ of new development. Thus every prophet treads in the footsteps of venerable forerunners, and all together point to One, who with a most conscious certainty appeals to them as so many witnesses of His Divine mission.[42]

Compare, in addition to the books mentioned in J. J. VAN OOSTERZEE, *Biblical Theology of the New Testament*, Eng. trans., p. 45; A. NICOLAS, *Etud. Philosoph.* (1861), iv., pp. 158—284; K. KÖHLER, *Der Profet. der Hebr. und die Mantik der Griechen* (1860); G. BAUR, *Geschichte der Alt. Testamentlichen Weissagung* (1861); but especially the important work of KÜPER, *Das Prophetenth. des A. B. übersichtlich dargestellt* (1870). The inconsistencies into which men inevitably run, when they systematically reject this evidence, are convincingly brought out by A. MONOD, in his excellent sermon, *La Crédulité de l'Incrédule.* Sermons, T. ii. (1857), pp. 311—365.

8. We have spoken of Miracles and Predictions in general; we must now pay separate heed to two kinds, the predictions spoken by Jesus, and the miracles wrought in, for, and with Him. As to the first, according to the Evangelic narrative, our Lord spoke a number of remarkable prophecies respecting His own approaching fate;[43] the behaviour and fate of His disciples, and specially Peter and Judas;[44] the destruction of the Jewish state,[45] as well as those relating to the struggle and triumph of His Gospel;[46]

---

[42] John v. 39—47.
[43] Matt. xvi. 21; xvii. 12, 22, and parallels.
[44] Matt. xxvi. 21, *sqq.*, 31, 34; John xxi. 18, 19.
[45] Matt. xxiv. 4, *sqq.*
[46] Matt. xiii. 31—33; xxvi. 13; compare Luke xii. 49—51.

and the final end of the history of the world.[47] What we have declared with respect to the Biblical prophecies in general is true also concerning those prophecies. It must first of all be shown by an exegetical and critical process that we have here real utterances, derived from Jesus Himself, of such a character that they cannot possibly be explained as naturally foreseen from the usual course of things. No authority whatever must here be conceded to such an aprioristic criticism as starts from the tacit assumption of the impossibility of such phenomena. The facts must be considered in themselves, in their historic connexion, and by the light of that which in other ways is already known concerning the Saviour. If by this method it is evident that they justify us in attributing to Him, not merely a rare knowledge of mankind; but also a properly so called foreknowledge, clearly proved by the event, we have then the fullest right to perceive in such a series of facts the sign and guarantee, not only of a Divine mission, but also, in this case, of a Divine glory. Jesus Himself pointed out to His disciples these fulfilled prophecies, as pledges of His dignity as the Messiah, and of His heavenly origin.[48] They were the more suited for them, since the knowledge also of the hidden was considered as one of the marks by which men should recognise Messsiah as the highest Ambassador of God.[49] But they continue even for later ages, by legitimate inference, to serve as evidences of the wholly unique self-consciousness which He bore within Himself, and of the wholly unique position which He occupies in the kingdom of God.

We come to a similar conception when we glance at the *Miracles* which were wrought in, for, and with Jesus, during His stay on earth. This time we do not look at His acts, but to an important part of the events of His life, as, *e.g.*, the remarkable circumstances of His birth; the angelic appearances, and the heavenly voices at marked epochs in His history; the signs at His death and resurrection, the bodily rising again on the third day; the ascent into heaven, with its wondrous consequences; and specially the outpouring of the Holy Spirit; the conversion of St. Paul, etc. Here is naturally not the place to maintain the credibility of all these facts in themselves—with regard to the most remarkable, we shall find an opportunity hereafter—but only to point out their Apologetic importance, if their credibility be presupposed. The mechanical method in which this argument has been often applied has brought it into discredit with many. The deduction put in this manner—Christianity is Divine, *because* angels were seen thus and there, and voices heard from heaven—will certainly not be convincing for many. The importance of all these facts is by no means the same. This, however, does not prevent them, when properly elucidated, and placed in their historic connexion, from contributing not a little to prove the sublimity, and even the Divinity, of the Revelation in Christ. Not only do the rays which stream from it, but also the purple clouds which float around it, alike testify to the shining of the sun. We must only take care to regard these special facts, not merely as external and accessory proofs, but also as essential elements of the Revelation. All those works of wonder are excellently fitted to strengthen the conviction of the high dignity of the

[47] Matt. xxiv., xxv. [48] John xiii. 19; xiv. 29. [49] John iv. 25; xvi. 30.

person of the Lord, which has been already aroused, and will in this manner be serviceable, provided they be only regarded not in themselves, but in connexion with the glorious whole, and in the light of Jesus' own utterances. Certainly, all these miraculous phenomena fall back into the shade, by the side of the much greater spiritual wonders which were wrought by Christ and the Gospel; but yet it would be a onesided spiritualism to call the former, for this reason, wholly unimportant. They have had a beneficial effect on some;[50] to them the Lord Himself attached a relative value;[51] and when once sufficiently established, they contain even for later times a testimony which must not be lightly valued.[52] This is specially true of the Resurrection of the Lord, to which, as will hereafter be shown, a very high apologetic value was rightly attributed by His first witnesses. It is evident that the whole estimate of His person and work becomes completely different, according as we believe, or do not believe, that He rose the third day from the dead. It may therefore be called almost inconceivable that Schleiermacher would not even admit the Resurrection and Ascension as elements of the doctrine concerning the person of the Lord; and almost incredible that it should be considered historically demonstrable, but less dogmatically significant. "I cannot understand how any one can assert, I believe in the Resurrection of Jesus, and then explain this belief as a matter of secondary consideration" (Riggenbach). Meanwhile, it is plain that this event must not be isolated from the historical connexion in which it is, we had almost said to a certain degree comprehensible, but now, for the great question which is occupying our attention, the more significant.

9. He, who for all the above-named grounds confesses the character of revelation in the appearing of Christ, has also a firm footing for looking at the *Apostolic age* in its proper light, and for estimating according to its claims the testimony which it too offers in favour of the reality of the revelation. It is impossible to understand the age of the Apostles, when separating it from the Messianic period. By the light of the latter only can it be explained: but then not a little is proved by the fact that the Apostles are those they are, and that they do what they do. Even the history of the founding and first extension of the Christian Church is not only a proof for, but an element of, the Divine revelation in the glorified Christ. Looking at it in this light, it seems to us neither incredible nor unimportant that miracles were wrought by, and in relation to, the Apostles, which, connected with the prophecies here heard and fulfilled, legitimate their claim to be men of God,[53] and invest their preaching of the Gospel with a higher character than that of a merely human word.[54] And still more than separate miracles and prophecies, which can always be disputed, does the entire individuality of the Apostles, compared with their character at an earlier period, as we learn to know it here, throw an important weight into the scale. What do personalities as those of St. Peter and St. Paul testify in favour of, and to the honour of Jesus?

---

[50] Matt. xxvii. 54.
[51] John xii. 30.
[52] Heb. ii. 3, 4.
[53] Acts iii. and iv.; xi. 28; xxvii. 21—25.
[54] Acts iv. 29, 30.

St. Paul's life, especially, is absolutely inconceivable, if the resurrection and ascension of the Lord must be called a cunningly devised fable.[55] To the question, What does a personality, activity, and experience, such as that of St. Paul, presuppose with respect to Jesus of Nazareth? the modern negation has thus far not returned any satisfactory answer. What is more, the whole spirit of the Apostolic age and its literature, compared with the immediately preceding and following ages, exhibits a thoroughly peculiar character, which cannot certainly be better explained than by the mighty influence of a new and special revelation. When we put all these things together, the alternative forces itself on us with increased strength, "there remains nothing else but either to explain Christianity as the result of a monstrous deceit, or to admit that God has really spoken and acted, *i.e.*, has, in the proper sense of the word, revealed Himself in Christ." (Auberlen.)

10. If, after all that has been said, the reality of the Revelation in Christ cannot well be denied, a light too rises before us upon the books of the *Old Testament.* We would not willingly assert that it would be impossible to prove to a certain extent the Divine authority of Moses and the Prophets, even regarded in themselves, and without the light of the Gospel. But in the present condition of the criticism of the writings of the Old Testament, that method certainly deserves the preference, which speaks only of the revelational character of Mosaism and Prophetism, after the historical foundation for belief in Christ has been laid and established. It cannot be denied that while the first ages believed in Christ partly for the sake of Moses and the Prophets, the Church in our days continues to acknowledge the authority of Moses and the Prophets, principally for the sake of Christ, and on the testimony of His word. That He and His Apostles have acknowledged the words of these men as Divine testimony, and have continued to build on it, cannot seriously be denied.[56] As little, however, can it be denied, that these men of God, according to the sacred narratives, have proved their higher mission by real prophetic words and wondrous works. The whole system of the old Covenant appears in the character of a *preliminary* revelation. Here, too, the miracles have a higher importance as they stand in a more direct connexion with the chief aim and centre of this revelation. All have not, considered in themselves, the same evidence; all indeed have not the same historical and religious import. Careful examination will here have to remove many a stumbling-stone from before the feet of the Apologist. But this may be asserted against many an unanswered question, in so far as separate facts are concerned, stands here the convincing power of the whole, which can neither be reasoned away, nor explained in a natural manner. As Christ Himself is the greatest miracle of the New Testament, so is Israel itself, from whence salvation was to come,[57] the greatest miracle of the Old. Three facts in

---

[55] Comp. W. BEYSCHLAG, on the Conversion of St. Paul, in *St. u. K.* (1864), ii.; G. WARNECK, *Pauli Bekehrung, eine Apologie des Christenthums*, in the *Beweis des Glaubens* (1872), p. 394, *sqq.*

[56] John v. 39; Acts xvii. 2, 3.

[57] John iv. 22.

particular remain absolutely inconceivable to us, if belief in special revelation is here utterly forbidden: we mean, Monotheism in Israel, the Theocracy over Israel, and the continued existence and fate of the people of Israel, considered in the light of ancient prophecy, and their later rejection of Christ.[58] The Jewish nation, regarded as a whole, is an aye-enduring proof for the truth of Christianity; an Ahasuerus who can hope for no departure like Simeon's, before he has found the Christ—*inimica testis fidei nostræ* (Augustine). If this is established in principle, then even in this domain the miraculous contains no insuperable difficulty, though separate narratives of miracles may demand further investigation. Israel is only to be explained as a "people of revelation," and the past, the present, and the future of that people remains a mystery, if no special revelation has been given in Christ and Christianity.

Compare on this subject a treatise of L. SURINGAR in *De Werken v. h. Haagsch. Gen.* (1809); I. DA COSTA, *Voorll. over de Vier Evang.* (1840), i. bl. 20, *sqq.*; C. H. KALKAR, *over de Theocratie onder Israel, H. G.* (1842); C. A. AUBERLEN, *Divine Revelation, etc.*; H. SCHULTZ, *Alt.-Testamentl. Theol.*, ii. Th. (1869); and E. W. HENGSTENBERG, *Geschichte des Reiches Gottes unter dem Alt. Bunde* (3 parts, 1869-71); specially the introduction.

11. As the circle thus returned to its point of departure, it is evident that the full force of our historical plea is only then seen when we take care not only to consider facts separately in themselves, but still more to combine them. There certainly remain not a few difficulties, but they become almost unimportant, as compared with the still greater difficulties in which men are inevitably involved, so long as, in opposition to all these voices, they continue to deny the supranatural character of the Christian revelation. No science but has its mysteries; that of religion, from the nature of the case, most so. Where, however, such valid reasons exist, the Apologist adheres to his full right, when, at the entrance of the Christian temple, he repeats, not merely with a loud voice, but also with head on high, "Introite, et hic Dei sunt." "Hoc unum gestit (religio), ne ignorata damnetur." (Tertullian.)

II. What has been obtained as the result of External proof, is contradicted in not one respect by the *Internal*, but, on the contrary, in many respects strongly supported. Internal—the name already makes us acquainted in general with the nature of the proof. It is not derived from any external wonder or sign, but from the contents of revelation itself. The Lord pointed to this in John vii. 17,[59] and promised that he who was really inclined to do God's will,—in other words, the man who honestly loved the truth, and was striving after holiness,—should convince himself experimentally of the Divinity of His doctrine. But that which is thus decidedly true of His doctrine can, in a no less degree, be repeated of the whole revelation. The external proof of its Divine origin can be brought forward in more than one way. We, for our part, prefer to draw the attention to the *impression* and the *influence* which the Gospel produces in the truly *receptive* spirit.

---

[58] Deut. xxviii.; Rom. ix.—xi.
[59] Compare John viii. 47; xviii. 37; 1 John iv. 6.

1. Great already is the *Impression* which (*a*) the *plan* of Jesus produces, as revealed by Him by word and deed. Never has a sublimer thought, than the central thought of His life, sprung up in any human heart. A kingdom of God, entirely universal, spiritual, eternal; founded not by material, but by moral forces; a spiritual creation, in a word, which embraces heaven and earth. The very thought seems folly; as such it never sprang up—this is historically proved—in the heart of philosophers or poets, of lawgivers or kings. And yet, it was cherished by Jesus of Nazareth, uttered by Him, and realized to a degree never before known.[60] Even a Frederick the Great and a Napoleon the First have observed here the trace of something supranatural. Does this betoken little or nothing?

(*b*) No less impression is aroused in the truth-loving soul by the *self-witness* of Christ. To feel the force of this proof, it must specially be considered that He was lowly in heart, and sought not His own honour.[61] And yet this mouth declares of His person, that which no one has ever testified of himself. We have these testimonies about His suprahuman dignity, not only in St. John, but also in the first three Gospels, and they are abundant and unequivocal. Only wilfulness can call them all unauthentic; only an unnatural wresting explain the words by a natural method. Historical and psychological reasons forbid us to think here either of self-deception or of fanaticism. Therefore, the utterance of this self-consciousness must be true; and even if truth were here incomprehensible, the contrary would be utterly inconceivable.

(*c*) This, indeed, is seen by a glance at the impression made by the whole personality of the Lord. "The impossibility of inventing such a personality as that of Christ overcomes every doubt" (Lavater). Fulness and harmony, force and calm, holiness and love, majesty and humility, are here united, as nowhere else, without ever coming in conflict with one another. This fact, hereafter (§ 93) expressly to be established against all contradiction, guarantees, on one side, the trustworthiness of His self-testimony, on the other, the genuineness of His history. Sooner might a Madonna of Raphael or Murillo be drawn by a tyro, than this image of Christ have been invented by these Galileans. He stands before us the highest, the ideal Man, and neither reason nor experience allow us to see in Him the merely natural product of sinful humanity.

(*d*) Least of all do we feel the courage to say this, as we consider the impression which is ever again produced by the *Moral and Religious Contents of the Revelation*. In this respect the religion of Moses already makes an impression which is exceedingly favourable. Think, *e.g.*, among others, of the strong ethical nature of his conception of God, as contrasted with the sensual representations of Polytheism; of the real human, philanthropic, and religious character of his legislation, compared with that of the other nations of antiquity; think of the moral character of the most celebrated prophets, who are known to us, too lofty for any

---

[60] Comp. F. N. REINHARD, *Plan van den Stichter des Christendoms* (1806); J. J. VAN OOSTERZEE, *Leven van Jezus*, i. 2, § 12; PH. SCHAFF, *Jesus Christ, the Miracle of History.*

[61] Matt. xi. 29; John v. 43.

fiction, as well as for any illusion; of the irreconcilable struggle of the religion of the Israelites with the almost indestructible character of the people, which forbids us to see in that religion the natural result of this character; lastly, of the gradual development of the expectation of the Messiah, to a height and with a definiteness which remains inexplicable, if we do not here recognise any fruit of special revelation.—But specially does the subject-matter of the New Testament bear the stamp of Divinity. Its principal contents, the anticipating love of God, shown out of grace to a sinful world, has never before found its way into a human heart. Still less has the Christian conception of God in its purity and sublimity been equalled or excelled by any single philosopher of antiquity. Here, too, has Christian morality, whether we look at the sublimity of its precepts, the purity of its principles, the force of its arguments and means, an excellence which becomes more evident as it is compared with that of any philosopher. This, above all, must not be overlooked, that while every human religious system is more or less optimistic, the Christian religion exhibits a remarkable pessimistic character. It does not flatter man, but it breaks his pride by branding him as a sinner; it makes humility, according to the saying of St. Augustine, the first, the second, and the third virtue; and leads us even by these gloomy depths to the highest moral perfection which is conceivable.[62] Is it probable that a system of faith and morals, so well suited to man, and yet so little according to man's nature, should have sprung out of and from man?

2. Thus we come naturally to the *Influence* which the Gospel of the kingdom of God exercises on the soul which is capable of receiving it. We have already spoken (§ xxxii. 1, 4) of the working of Christianity in a wider circle, but as we cast our glance on the little world of the individual heart, we are led to the very same conclusion. Experience proves that Christianity possesses a power of enlightening, comforting, and sanctifying man, which cannot be over-estimated.[63] Never has any one come forth with higher promises than Christ,[64] and yet they have been thoroughly fulfilled. As the complete recovery of the sick man is the best evidence of the virtue of the medicine, so is the fruit of the Gospel the guarantee of the value and origin of the plant. He that hath the Son hath really life, and becomes, in His communion, what he has never before been. What a number of eminent and blessed persons, "of whom the world was not worthy," have been formed by the word and the Spirit of Christ! He who accepts Him, and follows Him, may make the words expressed in John iv. 42, vi. 68, and ix. 25, his own. But here we come to a point where the proof of experience blends with the testimony of the Holy Spirit: and to this last we shall afterwards recur.

It is true that even in our days objections, not a few in number, and

---

[62] Compare, as to this argument, the three essays of J. CLARISSE, MOELLER, and an anonymous writer, in the works of the Hague Society, 1803; and also, as to the next point, the beautiful ninth and tenth letters of C. H. STIRM, *Apologie des Christenth.* (1836), p. 310, *sqq.*

[63] Comp. F. V. REINHARD, *De Praestantiâ Rel. Chr. in Consolandis Miseris;* S. K. THODEN VAN VELZEN, *De Hominis cum Deo Similitudine*, part. ii. Gron., 1835-37.

[64] John vi. 35; viii. 12; xiv. 12.

among them some of weight, have been made against this part of the internal proof. It is ever again asserted by a party hostile to Christianity, that it takes away from nature its Divine character; that it derogates from the rights of actual life; preaches slothfulness; injures common society to benefit a heavenly kingdom; excites a mistaken desire for reward by directing our eyes too much towards the other world, etc. But these objections, already often confuted, flow in no small degree from dreadful ignorance and wretched misunderstanding, and can even, at least in the oft-chosen form, be hardly regarded as honourably and seriously raised.[65] We are as yet waiting always in vain, till men give us, in place of the derided Gospel, a better one; and on the grounds of history and experience we assert that the Christian religion—if that name be used in the supranatural sense of the word—is the very best teacher of true humanity,[66] —and it is just this its force which, in our estimation, is at the same time the highest guarantee of its Divinity.

3. We cannot be surprised that the internal proof has at all times been urged with zeal and predilection. To the names already mentioned, we may add those of Tertullian, Athenagoras, Clemens Alexandrinus, and Augustine. Luther, too, pointed to the "high spiritual miracles," before which the external have sunk into the shade, and the predilection of Pascal and the school of Vinet for "the internal and moral proof" is universally known. It deserves that estimation on account of its evidence, its popularity, and its eminently practical tendency. As we listen to historic testimony, a critical investigation is required, that again and again elicits the well-known complaint "que d'hommes entre Dieu et moi." Here, on the contrary, the same end is reached by a shorter and more simple way, and belief based on these grounds, cannot possibly remain a cool assent, but becomes at once life and force. Not incorrectly—as far at least as concerns the fact, but not the etymology of the word—has this proof been called "a demonstration of the spirit and of power."[67] Where the testimony of the Gospel thus finds an echo in the inmost soul, there the certainty of belief becomes ours; I could more easily doubt that I was alive, than that those things which I heard were true."[68] (Augustine.)

III. We could be more brief concerning the Internal than the External proof, because it has relatively been less disputed. Concerning the *combination* of the two, however, a few questions must not be left unanswered.

1. The reason why this combination always, but especially in our days, is necessary, can easily be guessed. First, in this union lies the true force of the maintenance of the Christian belief in Revelation. To whatever height the internal proof may be brought, and however it might succeed in recommending Christianity as excellent and most worthy of God, this conviction could never have justified itself according to its claims, if it had not

---

[65] Comp. L. J. VAN RHIJN, *De nieuwe Dageraad en de oude Heilzon* (1860).

[66] Comp. J. J. VAN OOSTERZEE, *Oratio. de Rel. Christ. optimâ veræ humanitatis Magistrâ.* Dutch Transl. in *Voor Kerk en Theol.* (1872) ii., p. 118, *sqq.;* Dr. J. CRAMER, *Christendom en Humaniteit* (1871).

[67] 1 Cor. ii. 4.

[68] Facilius dubitarem me vivere, quam vera esse, quæ audivi.

appealed at all to historic facts. With the truth of these last stands or falls the recognition of the reality of the Revelation. Yet, on the other hand, the external proofs, from the nature of the case, leave so many questions unanswered, that their completion and elucidation by the internal is very desirable, and even necessary. It is precisely by this combination that the intellect and the heart are at the same time satisfied; the light is accompanied by heat, and with objective proof will not be wanting the subjective certainty.

This is even more needed in these days, when so often, to the injury of the cause, a sharp distinction is made between historical and religious truth; and the latter, as the higher, is even opposed to the former. This separation between facts and ideas, specially carried on in this case since Lessing's time, and under his influence, is the πρῶτον ψεῦδος of the modern Theology, by which it misunderstands miserably the peculiar character of the Christian Revelation. "Accidental historic truths can never be the proof of necessary rational truths." In itself this perhaps is most true, but here it has absolutely no connexion; because the Gospel preaches something more "than necessary rational truths," and something different from "accidental historic truths." Are not fact and dogma united most indissolubly in its chief subject-matter?[69] Whence does it appear that in the Holy Scripture as the word of God there is merely pointed out "religious truth," apart from "historic facts"? (Scholten.) Perhaps from Exodus xx. 2, 3, or Acts iv. 31—33, or Acts x. 36—43? We thought that both there and elsewhere we read the very opposite. It is precisely the peculiarity of Christianity that its ideas and facts can be as little separated as body and soul in man. Christianity is religion, we grant, but an historically revealed religion, which must establish itself as such by historic methods. It points to the deeds of God, in which thoughts of salvation are seen; without such deed of salvation on His part being irrevocably concealed from the creature. But if both these are inseparably one, then the internal proof cannot possibly do without the support of the external, or the external give up that of the internal.

2. The question, To which of these two must the precedence be given? is still answered in different ways. Next to the more historical Apologetic method, the more psychological continues to claim respectable representatives; specially is the number of the friends of this last of importance. In reality, even for the believer himself, the internal proof has the highest import; and if men think that in a time of scepticism and denial of miracles they can make further progress by this means, than by another way, they would certainly act foolishly if they did not choose the shortest. The tower must be propped up on that side where it perceptibly begins to lean over. In general, however, and usually, it seems preferable to place the historic arguments in the foreground, and support the force of these by moral ones. This is in complete accord with the historical character of Christianity, and much more fitted, if not to convince, at least to silence, unbelief, than a continual or exclusive appeal to internal reasons, which can indeed be only estimated by a certain tendency

[69] John i. 14; iii. 16; 1 Tim. iii. 16.

of spirit and soul. Besides, "the same thing does not suit everybody;" but a too great estimation of the internal proof above the external, may very easily lead to one-sidedness, and hence to uncertainty.[70]

3. A last question, in what connection must the proof of this continued argument be considered to stand to the Christian belief in revelation, has already found its answer in the beginning of this investigation;[71] an answer now established by the course of the demonstration itself, as well as by the nature of the case, and by experience. Belief is in no degree the natural product of a sum of well-arranged proofs: the believer generally comes to this conviction, not by the way of a logical process of thought, but by that of a psychological process of life. It does not yet follow from this that the thoughtful belief could or would do without the so-called proofs. The proof is not the source of belief, but its support, and its justification, in so far as it points to its irrefragable ground. It is indeed an unfathomable Mysticism, when a man can only say, "I believe, because God enables me to believe." Reasonable belief must be able to give account, not merely of its subject-matter, but also of its reasons. If men will only call the belief thus maintained a "human faith," it must in every case be explained and legitimated before men can boldly justify for others the "faith divine."

IV. Or, can it be that the certainty, thus justified, is nothing more than mere self-deceit? For there is *not* wanting to the believer a higher confirmation (*comprobatio*) of that which stands henceforth immoveably fixed for his inmost consciousness. The *testimony of the Holy Spirit* attracts here at last our attention. It imprints a Divine seal on that which intellect and heart have recognised as Divine truth. What is understood by this testimony? Is there reason to believe in its existence? and what value must be granted to it, specially for Christian Apologetics?

1. When we speak of the testimony of the Holy Spirit, we think at once of that which is said on this subject in Article 5 of the Netherlands Confession: "All these books we receive as holy and canonical, in order to regulate our belief according to them, to found it upon them, and to confirm it by them. And we believe without doubt all that is contained in the same, and that not so much because the Church accepts and considers them as such, but *specially because the Holy Spirit gives us the testimony in our hearts that they are from God.*"[72] It is Calvin, in particular, who appeals to this testimony to prove the Divine authority of Holy Scripture, independently of Church and tradition. If he, when he broke with Rome, placed on one side the authority of this last, we must not therefore think that the son of the Reformation could produce no higher than merely human reasons for his certainty of belief. On the contrary, he places it very clearly and forcibly in the light in his *Inst. R.C. I.* cap. vii.

---

[70] Compare the important answer to the conductors of *Waarheid in Liefde*, by H. E. VINKE; J. J. VAN OOSTERZEE, *Jaarboek* (1847); J. J. DOEDES, *Brieven over Apologetiek Jbb.* (1850).

[71] Section xxxii. 4, 6.

[72] Compare Art. 4 of *Confess. Gall.*

"Let this, therefore, remain fixed, that those whom the Holy Spirit has taught internally, acquiesce firmly in Scripture, and that this Scripture which is indeed ἀυτόπιστον, and cannot lawfully be subjected either to demonstration or reason, yet deserves to obtain among us certainty by the testimony of the Spirit; . . . for Scripture does not of its own accord proffer a more obscure sense of its truth, than black and white things do of their colour; or sweet and bitter, of their taste." So then belief rests, in the last instance, on something else than a merely syllogistic proof. "They act preposterously, who contend that by disputing they are building up the solid faith in Scripture." Full certainty is however there where the Holy Spirit has made the truth inwardly known. This privilege is the lot of the believer; we speak here of a "peculiar revelation of Divine wisdom, which God only vouchsafes to His children." Conceived thus in the spirit of the doctrine of the Reformed Church, the testimony of the Holy Spirit is a supranatural testimony, which the Holy Spirit gives to the heart of the believer concerning the Divinity of Holy Scripture, and which takes away from him every doubt.

2. Specially has the Dogmatics of the Reformed Church in almost every age attached the highest value to this testimony: J. H. Alstedt, *e.g.* († 1638), called it "demonstratio demonstrationum maxima," and, indeed, as to the question whether we have ground for accepting the existence of such a testimony, Scripture and experience will only give an affirmative answer. The promise of the Spirit of truth is made by the Lord to all His followers, and the history of centuries proves that it has constantly been fulfilled.[73] St. Paul considers it desirable and possible that that belief should stand, not in human wisdom, but in the power of God,[74] and knows an internal testimony of the Holy Spirit, which agrees with the Christian's own consciousness.[75] We find no different opinion in St. John.[76] In the most celebrated witnesses to the faith in all ages we meet, then, with such a certainty of faith, that they would sooner have doubts as to their own existence, than as to the reality of eternal things. In Justin Martyr, Origen, Athanasius, and specially in Augustine, we find the most unquestionable statements respecting it. Thus the last appeals to a voice, "intus in domicilio cogitationis, nec hebræa, nec barbara,"[77] which, without the sound of audible utterances, gives an unconditional testimony to the Mosaic narrative of the creation. A Bernard of Clairvaux, and an Anselm, a Luther and a Zwingle spoke in the same spirit, and, what decides everything, no really believing Christian will hesitate to accept their utterances, and to agree that he possesses within himself a Divine certainty, *i.e.*, a certainty brought about by God, of the truth of salvation, which he suffers no one to contest or take away.

3. It is already evident that the Testimonium Spiritus Sancti is not quite the same as the so-called proof by experience of the Divinity of the Gospel, though it is closely allied to it, and often mistaken for it. In the latter we find ourselves always in the historico-empiric domain; here, on

[73] John vi. 45; vii. 37, 38; xvi. 12—15.
[74] 1 Cor. ii. 4, 5.
[75] Rom. viii. 16.
[76] 1 John v. 6—10.
[77] Conf. xi. 3.

the contrary, in the domain of metaphysics, and we speak no longer of proper proof, but of a Divine attestation of the faith, which is legitimated and justified by external and internal proofs. We enter thus into the inmost sanctuary of the spiritual life, with respect to which the words of Spener are most emphatically true: "Of this little can be spoken, since no one understands it but he who feels it. It is a new name, which nobody knows but he who receives it." It does not, however, follow from this that we appeal to a kind of inner light in the sense of the mystics and fanatics, against whose "fatal ravings" and "oracles sought from the clouds," Calvin had already raised a loud and earnest voice of warning. The fanatic appeals to an immediate magical operation of God, places this inner voice of God far above, often in opposition to, the letter of Scripture, and against all refutation veils himself in the mists of a dim feeling. We, on the contrary, do not in any degree think here of an entirely extraordinary immediate revelation from above, but of a testimony, which the Holy Spirit brings to the Christian in a psychological way, not in contradiction to, but in harmony with, the word of Scripture; of a certainty of belief, in other words, which, just as belief itself, is of a higher than earthly origin. He who in this sense continues to assert that he has never yet perceived such a testimony, would deserve no other answer but "tant pis pour vous."

4. Only in this respect the Church Dogmatics will need a closer and better definition and demonstration that—according to Christian experience itself—this testimony is to be considered in reference, not to the Holy Scripture *en bloc*, but to its religious and soteriological contents; in other words, to the revelation contained in it. "The inner testimony can never assure us that no sacred writer has made a *mistake in memory* in purely historical matters, that Judas Galilæus rose up after Theudas, etc.[78] It can only refer to that which belongs to the Christian consciousness, and is a matter of Christian life" (Twesten). We shall see later; Holy Scripture has, along with its Divine, a human side as well, and contains a number of elements, which, considered in themselves, are of no particular importance for the spiritual life. He who will now prove the Divine authority and truth of all this by an appeal to the testimony of the Holy Spirit, runs the risk of being reduced to an absurdity. If in the age of the Reformation the ideas of revelation and Holy Scripture were too much confused one with another (§ xxviii. 1), it is the vocation of a better theology to help to dispel the cloud by a more accurate distinction. The Holy Spirit living in the heart of the Christian gives testimony to the religious soteriological *contents* of Scripture; in other words, to the historical revelation which the Scripture makes known to us.—For these reasons it is better to treat of the Testimonium Spiritus Sancti in treating of Apocalyptics rather than of Bibliology.

This nearer definition, however, makes no change in the nature of the fact. *The testimony of the Holy Spirit is the Christian internal certainty, produced by God Himself, concerning the Divinity of the revelation in Christ, unfolded in Holy Scripture.* The witness here is thus, not a man, nor intellect, reason,

---

[78] Acts v. 36.

or conscience, still less the natural feeling in man, but the Holy Ghost. The testimony concerns the truth and divinity of the word of life, learnt from Holy Scripture. They, in and by whom this testimony is received, are exclusively believing Christians; these all, but also these only.

5. What has been said enables us to explain the later polemics against this doctrine, and to estimate the value of its peculiar presentment in the present time. In the track of the Arminians and Socinians it was warmly disputed by the Rationalists of the preceding century, whilst Supranaturalism has always identified it with the so-called internal proof. Michaelis (ob. 1791) declared that he, however sincerely convinced of the Divinity of Christianity, had never yet heard such a testimony, and Reimarus (ob. 1768) asserted that the Turk undoubtedly felt a similar testimony when he read the Koran. These polemics had notably their source in a naturalistic misunderstanding of the nature and work of the Holy Spirit, but found, at the same time, their force in the often faulty manner in which the doctrine of the Testimonium Spiritus Sancti was presented. This last was gradually despised and forgotten, until, specially under the influence of Schleiermacher, it entered on a new period of esteem and development. In Holland it was brought into favour, though in a very altered form, by the Groningen school,[79] and was particularly developed in a manner of his own by Professor Scholten.[80] He described it as "the testimony of reason and conscience, which, developed and purified by communion with Christ, independently of all external authority, recognised the religious contents of Scripture as truth," and in this sense he explained the testimony of the Holy Spirit as the ultimate ground of faith. Certainly not quite the same as the "testimonium unicum solis Christi Spiritu renatis proprium, et his solis cognitum" (Ursinus) of the Theology of the Reformation.[81] This is not the place to renew an old strife, nor to show the justice of the sentence which was then pronounced, that it is thus merely "man himself who testifies of man to man" (La Saussaye). Whatever the value of the testimony may be which is given by the reason and conscience of the duly developed man to the Gospel, the testimony of the Holy Spirit is something totally different and higher. It is the fruit of a *supranatural* operation, *i.e*, of one which is not of man, but of God, however much it may agree absolutely with the natural disposition and needs of man. Appealing to this testimony, the Reformed Church thus takes its stand in no degree upon a merely subjective, but upon an objective ground of faith. It does not appeal to that which the Holy Spirit testifies in Scripture, but to that which the (personal) Holy Spirit testifies in the believer with regard to Scripture and the revelation contained in it. By that appeal it seeks not to establish its belief in the truth of the written word, "in so far as this commends itself as true and Divine to the intellect and heart of every one"—for this, finally, would become a belief in one's own authority, or indeed a belief in oneself, instead of in the

---

[79] See its *Compend. Dogm. et Apol. Chr.*, 3 ed. (1848), p. 180.

[80] See his *Oratio* (1843) *de Rel. Chr. suæ ipsius divinitatis in mente humanâ vindice*, and *Leer der H. K.*, 4 ed. (1861), bl. 115—233.

[81] Comp. Van Toorenenbergen, *Bijdragen enz.*, bl. 94, *sqq*.

testimony of God above and beyond us—but to build the certainty of the Christian concerning the divinity of God's Word upon an immoveable rock. "The witness is not any man, nor our reason, nor sense, but the testimony of the Holy Spirit; we acquiesce, therefore, in the authority of God, because we are persuaded that Scripture is from God, and for this reason we believe, not because we ourselves see that those things which are found in Holy Scripture are true. We believe God, not ourselves." (Calvin.)

6. But now it cannot be difficult to define the value of this testimony, both generally, and also for the work of Apologetics. As to this last, if no other work is granted to it than that of defending Christianity against the definite contradiction of unbelief, then the natural evidential force of this testimony can only be relative; "then arguments must be produced, not revelations" (Burman). We can scarcely hope to bring others to belief by means of that which only possesses irrefragable certainty for him who is already a believer. The testimony of the Holy Spirit is thus no *argumentum comprobativum* for others, but a *sigillum veritatis* for ourselves. As such, however, it has for the Christian a value which surpasses every other argument. If the evidence of experience is, as it were, the proof of the sum, the testimony of the Holy Spirit is as an Amen of God to the certainty of belief already properly legitimated by external and internal proofs. By it the believer is so surely convinced of the truth of revelation, that to the question, "Whence knowest thou that?" he can with Luther answer, "Because I hear it in the Word and Sacraments, *and* because the Holy Spirit also testifies to it in my heart." It is not so much an accessory proof, even superior to all proofs, as the crown and seal upon them, "obsignatur Sp. S. testimonio" (Calvin). But even on this account is it the source and support of an evidence which can scarcely be explained, but can still less be doubted. To the question, whether the Christian has a supranatural security for his belief, we must, therefore, not hesitate to give an affirmative answer. Even more, "We shall never believe with a sound and faithful belief, if God does not incline our hearts, and we believe as soon as He inclines them. This David knew full well when he said, 'Incline my heart, O Lord, to Thy testimonies'" (Pascal).

7. Then only could the appeal to the testimony of the Holy Spirit be justly called "the Achilles heel of the Protestant system" (Strauss), if indeed no answer whatever could be given to the question as to the guarantee that that testimony is really Divine, not human or devilish. But the testimony we mean has a certainty in itself, which goes far beyond all description: "The Holy Spirit gives in such wise testimony to our spirit, that we at once know that it is given by Him and is Divine" (Kromayer). If a new testimony were still required to prove that this is Divine, the same demand could be made on this new testimony, and so on *ad infinitum*. As the sun is seen by its own light, so is the testimony of the Holy Spirit perceived in its own force by every one who is acquainted with the distinction between flesh and spirit, nature and grace. Besides, the fruits of the Spirit are there to show that the testimony and working of that Spirit in the heart is no mere idle fancy. It is sometimes difficult, but certainly not impossible, to recognise with the inner ear the voice

of God, as distinguished from that of flesh and blood; and he who hears it, knows it as well as a man, *e.g.*, can distinguish in his own heart the voice of love from that of natural selfishness. It is true this inner consciousness, not less than the truth of salvation itself, always in the last instance remains a matter of *belief;* but also, of that which the Christian in this domain can prove to no one else, he can nevertheless be convinced for himself on such firm grounds that he can safely speak of a "cognitio simpliciter certa" (Buddeus).—Lastly, if it be now said that men cannot possibly give this certainty of belief to themselves, we shall not absolutely contradict this, but merely remark that it usually is not gained at the beginning, but only when some progress has been made in the way of faith. The testimony of the Holy Spirit is not perceived *before*, but *after*, we believe; it is not the ground on which belief is built, but the last seal which is impressed on belief; and hence, we do not begin, but end, our maintenance of the reality of Revelation with the discussion of it. We usually attain to belief by a psychological, and not by a dialectical, way; the personal acceptance of the Gospel is a step—if you will, a leap —to which God calls and leads us, yet which we must make of ourselves, and willingly, for reasons which justify themselves fully to our consciousness. These reasons are not the cause of internal belief, but they justify it to ourselves and others; and upon the reasonable conviction, thus proved, the testimony of the Holy Spirit imprints a seal, which at last makes even the possibility of doubt to cease. "Talis est persuasio, quæ rationes non requirat; talis notitia, cui optima ratio constet; talis denique sensus, qui nisi ex coelesti revelatione nasci non queat" (Calvin).

Compare, as to the testimony of the Holy Spirit, besides the works already named, the essays of H. WITSIUS in his *Miscell. Sac.* ii., pp. 126—128; of S. WERENFELS, *Opuscc. Theoll.* i., pp. 157—162; also J. J. VAN OOSTERZEE. *Jaarbb.* 1845, 1846, 1847; a treatise of KLAIBER in the *Jahrbuch für Deutsche Theol.* (1857), i., pp. 1—54; one of GESZ, in the *Apologet. Beiträge*, published by him and Riggenbach (1863), pp. 57—88; ROTHE, *a. a. O.*, pp. 139—144. F. H. R. FRANK, *System der Chr. Gewissheit* (1870), 1. We meet, too, with noteworthy observations on the authority of Scripture in an essay by G. J. VINKE, in the *Proceedings of the Ev. Alli.* (1867), p. 261, *sqq.* Upon the whole subject treated in this section we may consult H. VON DER GOLTZ, *Gottes Offenbarung durch heilige Geschichte, u. s. w.*, ii. Th. (1868), and the best known Apologetic writings of later years, most of which have been already mentioned, but specially those of LUTHARDT, DELITZSCH, and CHRISTLIEB. For the history of Apologetics, see HAGENBACH, *Theol. Encycl.*, § 81, and the works there quoted; to which may be added G. H. VAN SENDEN, *Geschied. der verded. van Bybel en openb.* 2 *dd.* (1827—1840.)

POINTS FOR INQUIRY.

What does the history of Apologetics teach as to the best method of defending the Christian belief in revelation?—What end must the Apologist purpose to himself, specially in our time? and by what way can that end be reached?—The import and importance of St. John vii. 17.—Why cannot the existence and continuance of the Christian Church be explained on entirely natural grounds?—Is not the appeal to the rapid spread of Christianity weakened by that to the careful preparation for it, or *vice versâ?*—To what points must we give special heed in reference to the beneficent working of Christianity?—The relation of the proof from miracles to the historic proof in general.—How to decide upon the old distinction between *miracula naturæ et gratiæ.*—What must we think of the Christian narratives of miracles of later times?—What do the Biblical miracles prove? for whom, and on what conditions?—How can the stiffnecked "Miraculophobia" be explained, and how best combated?—The true essence of foretelling, in conjunction with the idea of prophesy.—The possibility, recognisability, reality, and demonstrative force of foretelling considered more closely.—Is the force of this proof fully equal to that of the proof from miracles?—Defence of the prophecies of Jesus Himself against the most known objections of our time, as well as that of the most notable miracles in the history of His life.—How to establish the reality of the Revelation in the Apostolic and pre-Christian records, and why these are now first spoken of.—What sides of the external proof are specially elucidated and strengthened by the internal?—Have we not sufficient in the last alone?—The one-sidedness in exalting one set of proof above and at the cost of the other.—Import of the doctrine of the testimony of the Holy Spirit in the history of the birth of Evangelical Protestantism.—Necessity for an exact distinction in this domain between historic and saving faith.—Further elucidation of the manner in which the doctrine of the *Testimonium Spiritus Sancti* has been conceived and employed by Professor Scholten.—Union and difference between it and the so-called proof by experience.—How far does the preference shown by many in our days for the appeal to this testimony deserve the name of a happy phenomenon?—Standpoint, weapons, and force of *Apologetica semper victrix*.

SECTION XXXIII.—ITS EXCELLENCE.

The great excellence of the Revelation in Christ, proved by a number of evidences, is raised beyond the reach of all contradiction or eulogy. This appears already from its relation to general revelation, which it both confirms and completes; still more from its contents and tendency, considered in connexion with the spiritual wants of man; most of all, perhaps, by a careful comparison with everything else, which, either correctly or incorrectly, is recognised as special revelation. The predicate of perfectibility can therefore only be granted to the individual or common opinion about its contents; but in no case to the revelation itself, which must rather be called, not only the *highest*, but also, in a certain sense, the *last* manifestation of God's counsel and will for the salvation of mankind.

1. The demonstration of the great Excellence of special revelation follows that of its Necessity, Possibility, and Reality. This, too, is here necessary, not only because it is so often disregarded, but also because it strengthens the already acquired conviction of the divinity of the revelation, and at the same time furnishes the opportunity of duly judging the question as to the perfectibility of Christianity.

2. The relation of special revelation to the general (§ 29) at once confirms its great excellence. If it was irreconcilably contradictory to this last, we could not possibly believe it. But the two form, like two books of different compass, but from the same maker, one complete work. On one side the

testimony of the general revelation is *confirmed* by the special. What it has taught concerning God's existence and majesty, is here proved by facts, which morally compel us to believe in a living and free God, and make us see his Power, Wisdom, and Goodness in greater splendour. The claim of God, felt by the conscience, sounds to our ears much louder still in the law of Moses, but, above all, in the Gospel of Christ. . Thus, special revelation seals and explains that which general revelation has already expressed. Besides, that on which this has been silent, the other proclaims, and thus the ordinary revelation has been satisfactorily *completed* by the extraordinary. The unsolved questions, which were there left (§ 30), are here sufficiently answered, and the hope, which the creation had excited, is turned into certainty by the Gospel. We understand the language of nature much better, since it has been elucidated by Jesus; the revelation of God in history is not broken, but explained and completed, by the founding of Christianity; and the revelation in mankind receives in the manifestation of Christ alike its crown and its key. Thus the special revelation is connected with the general, *without, however, losing itself in it, or being explicable by it alone.* The methodistical contrasting, as well as the rationalistic identification, of Nature and Revelation must therefore be resisted in principle.

3. Still more does the contents of Saving Revelation plead for its invaluable worth. The *cardinal point* which here concerns us, in no way consists in this, that it announces a more pure conception of God, prescribes a more excellent morality, or teaches us to build the hope of immortality on firmer grounds. The proper centre of gravity lies here, not in the universal religious, but in the special soteriological domain. It is the announcement of an unparalleled fact, which has made the Gospel[1] to be the Gospel, a Gospel not so much of the providence as of the grace of God. That fact is the manifestation of all the virtues of God, the highest glory of belief, and the basis of the purest morality. The contents of the Revelation cannot thus possibly be conceived *à priori*, while *à posteriori* it exhibits a character ever more worthy of God, the better it is conceived.[2]—Besides, these contents are imparted in an *historical form*. Scripture has not incorrectly been called "the history of God in humanity." This peculiarity of Revelation increases its clearness,[3] guarantees its certainty,[4] and promotes the power of its efficacy. Nothing, indeed, makes more impression than facts, far more than the most beautiful abstract ideas, as may be seen by a number of instances from the history of the Church and missions.—It at the same time deserves notice that the contents of the Revelation have *gradually* been brought to notice. Thus, too, it testifies of the same God who has willed that there should be no gap, but as little a leap, in nature. In the same manner the revelation of the Gospel did not all of a sudden appear; it had its preparation before it came forth, and was itself subject to the law of development. The Patriarchal, the Mosaic, and the Christian periods exhibit each its peculiar character. Each period receives as much light as it requires and can bear, and at the same time prepares the way for the

---

[1] 1 John iv. 10; John iii. 16.
[2] 1 Cor. ii. 9; Rom. xi. 33.
[3] 1 Cor. xiii. 11.
[4] 1 John i. 1—3.

succeeding one. The form and the course of revelation are always in harmony with the condition and capacity of those to whom it is vouchsafed. Voices from heaven, dreams, visions, which now are the cause of numberless questions, were undoubtedly, in the earliest times, better suited than any other means to be the bearers of the revelation. First comes the Holy Spirit *over* the Prophets, then visibly rests *on* Christ, henceforth to dwell constantly *in* those to whom He has been given by Christ. Thus the whole course of the dispensation of salvation may be called one continual accommodation of God to human needs and capacities.

4. With these contents accords in every respect the Tendency of the Revelation. It indeed aims at nothing less than the enlightening, comforting, and re-creating of every sinner with whom it comes in contact, and the union of all these in one boundless kingdom of God; and that end it is fully suited to attain. It addresses itself to the whole man, and gives satisfaction to the wants of intellect, heart, and conscience, which are always the same. The doctrine, commands, and rites of Christianity exhibit no exclusive local or national character, but are suited for every nation and age. The Christian religion bears the double stamp of Universality and Humanity, and is plainly marked out to be the religion of the world.

5. Especially will a Comparison with that which elsewhere has been reverenced as revelation, make that of Christianity stand out in all its sublimity. No other religion or philosophy has had such an exceedingly marked beneficial effect. In Christianity all distinction between esoteric and exoteric wholly vanishes, and all are called to be a royal and priestly people. Heathenism could by no means satisfy the highest aspirations of spirit and heart, as is seen from the self-confession which was made by Clemens Romanus in the first of his homilies, and from what Justin Martyr relates concerning his own prior restless seeking and striving. Even the severely Ethical character of Christianity, as contrasted with the preponderating æsthetic tendency of Hellenism, is in this respect of import. With the Romans, religion was at the best a state machine, but in no case was it a principle of life. Compare the much-lauded essay of Marcus Aurelius, Πρὸς ἑαυτόν, with the moral maxims of the Gospel, and we shall feel what is the difference between Divine and human. "The Gospel in itself is, in its morality, always true, always certain, always unique, always like itself" (Rousseau). Of Islamism we need not speak more here (comp. § xxv. 7); but even Mosaism, raised as it is far above Polytheism, yet always stands below Christianity. Truth it contains, but in shadow and image; holiness it requires, but cannot properly bring that about, where the highest revelation of love is still withheld, and thus the principle of responsive love is not yet really aroused. And why more? From the standpoint of Christian belief in revelation can the so-called religious (§ xxv. 9) indifferentism of Lessing and others hardly escape the reproach of great ingratitude. The English Deist, Bolingbroke, spoke with at least a larger spirit of appreciation, when he said, "If Christianity were a merely human discovery, it would certainly be the loveliest and most beneficent with which mankind has ever been deceived to its own real benefit."

6. For all these reasons, then, we cannot possibly ascribe to Christian Revelation the predicate of Perfectibility. We have already seen, in § 19,

in what sense and on what grounds this must be ascribed to Dogmatics. But it is quite another matter with Revelation, and Religion itself in the objective sense of the words. This always is remarkable, that its true confessors, as distinguished from so many others, do not expect another more perfect religion. The noblest heathen had shown the deepest need of higher light; Israel lived almost exclusively by means of its expectation of salvation; many a religion of the present day in the East shows a presage of its coming end. But the Christian, however much he may expect and desire endless progress, will notwithstanding hesitate to speak of an objective perfectibility of the Revelation of Salvation. No wonder! it is perfect, *i.e.*, not complete, but sufficient; and it diffuses so much light, that there is neither right nor ground for hoping for a higher revelation. The contrary appears, partly from the manner in which Christianity itself has appeared as God's highest and last revelation;[5] this is often asserted with utterances the more remarkable, because Christ Himself was lowly of heart, and has plainly foreseen the struggle of His Gospel:[6] partly, again, from the character of this revelation as grounded on facts, which are irrevocable, eternal in import, and besides, of such a nature, that we cannot possibly conceive of anything higher in this domain: partly, in conclusion, from history and experience, which show that every inclination to exalt itself above Christianity is destructive both to belief and morality. He who rejects the Son has soon lost the Father too, and he who returns to Deism sinks almost inevitably into the opened arms of Pantheism and Atheism. The miserable results of the attempts of Theophilanthropists, St. Simonians, Friends of Light, Mormons, etc., is an involuntary homage to the Christianity which they deny. Just as superficial and hopeless is the attempt to build up on the ruins of Christianity a so-called independent morality. We hear even the apostles of unbelief, as if in contradiction of themselves, uttering warm eulogies of Jesus, and granting that there is little chance of expecting a higher religion. "No grand and completely original religious creation will rise in our civilisation. . . . Religions, like the spider, require a point to which to fasten their web. This point will be wanting in all new attempts. Christianity alone, then, rests in the possession of a future." (Renan.)

7. True, many objections are brought against this perfection of Christian Revelation, as well from the speculative as from the empiric standpoint. On the first side it is thought impossible that in any, least of all in the highest, domain of life the Perfect should at once be attained. "The privilege of being a *non plus ultra* for all times must be refused to every historical personality without exception" (Strauss). And certainly, if Jesus Christ was nothing but man, confined within the borders of finite perfection, we must at least admit the possibility that a greater than He may appear in the domain of religion. The proposition that Christianity may truly and for all time be called the highest religion of humanity, cannot possibly be maintained from an anti-supranaturalistic standpoint. It is,

[5] Matt. xxi. 37; John xiv. 6; Gal. i. 8, 9; Heb. xiii. 8, 9.
[6] Matt. x. 34—36.
[7] 1 Cor. ii. 9; 1 John i. 1—3.

however, a different thing when we cling to the revealed character of Christianity, and there take at once into account the promises of the Lord Himself, concerning the final triumph of His cause. In the domain of science infinite progress may be conceivable: quite different is that of religion and morality, founded on a higher revelation. There is not a single reason for calling it *à priori* inconceivable that here the highest has been given once for all, and that this can only be approached, but never excelled. As little has Experience sufficient ground to contradict stubbornly the confession of the perfection of this revelation. It shows, indeed, that many separate themselves from Christianity, but certainly not that these gain a standpoint higher than the Christian. Christianity is not below the level of the time, but the time is much below the level of Christianity. Even this apostacy is prophesied, condemns itself, and traces out the often obscure, but always sure, way to new conquests of truth.

Comp. STIRM, *a. a. O.*, pp. 499—568; E. ZELLER, *Die Annahme einer Perfectibilität des Christenthums, u. s. w.*, in the *Theol. Jahrb.* i. (1842), pp. 1—54; LANGE, *Dogm.* i., § 64 ff; C. A. G. VON ZEZSCHWITZ, *Zur Apologie der Offenb.* (1865), pp. 113—172; E. BERSIER, *La Morale Indépendante*, in the *Proceedings of the Evan. Alliance* (1867); Dr. THOMAS, *The Genius of the Gospel.*

POINTS FOR INQUIRY.

Testimonies as to the excellence of Christian Revelation, even on the part of unbelievers.—What is properly new in this Revelation? and in that new what is great, beautiful, and efficient? How far then can we thus speak of the perfectibility of Christianity?—Can it, even from the Empiric standpoint, be proved that in Christ there has really been given God's highest and last Revelation?—Whence comes the violent opposition to Revelation, especially in our days?

SECTION XXXIV.—ITS RELATION TO REASON.

Human reason has towards the Revelation of Salvation its unmistakable rights, but at the same time its sacred duties. It is as unchristian to prescribe to it an unconditional silence in this domain, as it is unreasonable to give it the deciding voice in respect to questions which are wholly or partially beyond its view. As the Revelation of Salvation exhibits a supranatural character, so must the Christian belief in Revelation be rational, but for that very reason averse in principle to all Rationalism. Built upon well-established testimonies, this belief must raise itself as far as possible to an independent insight into its subject-matter; but where this cannot be done, or can be done only imperfectly, it must finally bow to the words of Revelation. Thus from the Christian dogmatic standpoint we can as little approve the separation as the confusion of belief and knowledge. The mutual penetration and conciliation of both must rather be the object to be unceasingly striven after, and this will be more successfully attained as the Revelation of Salvation is more regarded in the light of Holy Scripture.

1. Only one question still remains for us; that of the relation which revelation has in regard to reason;—and to answer this question it is not superfluous, first of all, to say what we undersand by the *supranatural character* of Revelation, and what by *Reason*. The different use, however, which is made of these words has in no slight degree increased the confusion of language, and while on one side we are told, as, *e.g.*, by Rénan, "Le surnaturel serait le surdivin,"[1] on the other side we hear the promising words, "If one first knows what Reason is, then all discord with Revelation will cease" (Hamann). Without entering into a criticism of other definitions, we therefore simply declare that we reject as Naturalistic the idea according to which *everything* which occurs must be explained as the necessary consequence of finite causes, without leaving room anywhere for the working of a higher Factor; and, in opposition to this, we assert of Revelation that it is not explicable by mankind itself, but must be considered as the fruit of the free act of a God, who, in the history of mankind, speaks and acts in an extraordinary way. Supranatural is thus not merely supra-*sensuous*, but supra-*creatural* in the proper sense of the word. Revelation is thus not from man, but comes from above to man, and this, too, in contact with him, and specially with his *reason*. By this last word we don't mean that so-called sound intellect, nor even the acute judgment, but that faculty of the human spirit by which it raises itself to the invisible, to the infinite, to the world of ideas. If men speak sometimes of reason in the objective sense, to point out that amount of ideas which man obtains by his own thoughts on Divine matters, we speak of it in the subjective sense of the word, to denote the organ by which man rises to the conception of the Absolute and the Infinite. A personal God cannot be conceived as aught else but the highest, the eternal Reason which is revealed and reflected in the human capacity of reason, as the sun in a single drop of water. But Divine and human reason, however allied, are notwithstanding separated by an infinite distance; and where thus a thought of salvation of the first is made known to the second, the question of itself occurs, what on this ground are the rights, and what the duties for this last?

2. In the investigation into the relation between Reason and Revelation, we may easily *à priori* determine on one side that a really Divine revelation cannot possibly conflict with reason, but also, on the other hand, that even as a revelation of *salvation* to the sinner, it can and must contain much which reason could not of itself discover, and even after it has been revealed only penetrates to a certain extent. The Revelation of Salvation may thus

---

[1] The supranatural would be the supradivine.

be supranatural, in many points inscrutable, even in conflict with the fleshly wisdom of the sinner's darkened intellect, without on that account being unreasonable. It lies, however, in the nature of the case that the question as to the relation of Revelation to Reason—in other words, that as to the connection between belief and knowledge—is at all times differently answered. Here, too, must we learn to know the wrong paths before we can point out the right track.

3. There have never been wanting some who deny reason all right of vote in this domain, and cry out to it, "Mulier taceat in Ecclesiâ." As well on the side of belief as of unbelief has the irrevocable separation of belief and philosophy been in this case proclaimed as the highest wisdom. "Quid Athenis cum Hierosolymis, quid Academiæ et Ecclesiæ,"[2] Tertullian has already cried out in a tone of scorn, "Nostra institutio de porticu Salomonis est; nobis curiositate non opus est post Jesum Christum, nec inquisitione post Evangelium." The conclusion was the famous "credibile, quia ineptum; certum, quia impossibile est." Even Luther may in some degree serve as a type of this tendency, at least in the places where he calls reason in the domain of spirit "eine Bestie," who must be strangled—although on the other hand we meet with sundry eulogies from his lips on the excellence of reason. Not a few of the strict orthodox fully agree with this polemic against reason. Not to mention other names, at the Tercentenary of the Reformation similar expressions were discoverable in some of the theses of Harms. On the opposite side also this same Radicalism was cherished; among others by Spinoza, when he asserted that Christian faith did not ask for "*true*," but for "*pious* dogmas;" by Bayle, when he wrote, "A choice must of necessity be made between philosophy and the Gospel;" by Hume, Reimarus, and, not to mention any others, by Strauss, when he concluded the Introduction to his Glaubenslehre (1840, i., S. 356): "Let thus the believer let the scientific man go his way, and the man of science the believer his. We will leave them their belief, if they will leave us our philosophy. And if the over-pious people should succeed in excluding us from their Church, we should consider this as a favour. Enough has been done with false attempts at mediation, only separation can lead us further." We need hardly call to mind how much the leaders of the modern Naturalism are penetrated by this spirit. Theological strategics, however, require that we should not be at all guided by hints or wishes from the enemy's side, and we shall do well to take good heed to this before we determine upon the proposed separation.

4. It is indeed impossible, as will soon appear on a nearer investigation, that Reason can say to Belief, or Belief to Reason, "I have no need of thee." Such a separation is in the highest degree unpsychological; as it partly presupposes, partly establishes, an inner dualism, which may be conceivable as a transition, but cannot possibly continue as the normal condition. That separation is alike irreligious and unchristian; God cannot be glorified by the rejection of one of His two most glorious gifts, Reason and Faith; and the Lord nowhere disavowed in His contemporaries either

[2] De præscrip. hæret. 7. De carne Chr. 5.

the right of reason or the voice of natural feeling. He constantly appealed to both, and His apostles followed His example.[3] Lastly, this separation of belief and knowledge is unprotestant and specially unreformed. The well-known declaration of Luther at Worms, that he would not yield his consent unless he were convinced by Holy Scripture or by "clear reasoning," is in this respect symbolical, and it is universally known how little hostile the supporters of a healthy orthodoxy during the best period of our Church have shown themselves to philosophy. Their motto was rather "True philosophy, though it may differ greatly from the doctrine of the Church, yet neither fights with it, nor is a lie, as are the false doctrines of other sects, but is truth, even a spark of God's own wisdom kindled in the creation in the human mind" (Ursinus, Opp., Tom. 1, p. 48).

5. As little tenable, however, is their standpoint who overlook the border-line between belief and knowledge, confound one with the other, and finally by this way come to declare the supremacy of reason in the domain of religion. A type of this tendency was found in the ancient Church in Gnosticism, and in some degree in the school of Alexandria; in the middle ages, in J. Scotus Erigena, and Abelard; in later times, in Socinianism, Rationalism, and many tendencies of speculative philosophy. This standpoint, notwithstanding the warmth with which it is often defended, is utterly arbitrary. Even though reason can raise itself to the idea of the infinite world, its right is not thereby established to speak the final word concerning things, of which it would know nothing at all if they had not been brought by special Revelation within the reach of its vision. The Reason which claims supremacy in the domain of revelation has never yet proved its competency for this claim. "Reason is indeed a precious thing, and, according to its right notion, faultless, if it were but already one's own possession. But here, alas, is the failing. To be reasonable is as yet for man an unattained aim: like real liberty, Man has Reason, *i.e.*, he can think, and therefore has he reason only in that degree in which he *can* think; and who can do that but in a relative degree?" (Rothe). With only one word do we recall here the palpable fact, that even this faculty of thought of ours is moreover under the influence of sin, and rather observe here that the tendency we speak of can certainly never be more unsuccessful than when it attempts to maintain its right by an appeal to Holy Scripture. The reasonable service (λογικὴ λατρεία, Rom. xii. 1) is a spiritual worship, in contrast with the ceremonies of the law. Acts xxvi. 25 only proves that St. Paul spoke in a most reasonable manner, a fact which no one will deny. 1 Thess. v. 21 was written to Christians, who had to test everything, not by their reason, but by the word and Spirit of the Lord; and while criticism on everything is permitted to the spiritual man,[4] it is not therefore allowed to every one's natural reasoning faculty. Least of all is the supremacy of this last confirmed by an appeal to the spirit of Protestantism, which indeed must be called something more than a purely

[3] See Matt. xxi. 24; 1 Cor. x. 15; and many other places. While in expressions like Matt. xi. 25, 26; Col. ii. 8; 2 Cor. x. 4, 5, only that wisdom is condemned which assumes a hostile attitude towards the Gospel.

[4] 1 John iv. 1; 1 Cor. ii. 15.

negative principle. The proposition that he is most truly Protestant who most decidedly rejects what goes beyond his finite view, will certainly least of all find contradiction—at Rome.

6. Contrasted with both these one-sided views, we find our safety in a third tendency, which properly distinguishes knowledge and faith,[5] but does not on that account contrast them and rather attempts to reconcile the two. "Two extremes must be avoided; the exclusion of reason and the admission of nothing but reason" (Pascal). The first is as absurd as if we were first to deprive of sight the astronomer who is to observe the heavens through his telescope. But just as foolishly as that astronomer would act if he *à priori* determined what phenomena his glass should discover in this planet or that, so absurd would it be to reject arbitrarily as absurd that which makes itself known as the revelation of a higher world. The Christian philosopher is through reason itself in a certain sense dead to reason,[6] and says with A. Monod, "I do not understand, but this I understand, that I cannot understand." The question would be much simplified if men did not ask so much as to the relation of Reason and Revelation in general, but as to the relation of the reason of the sensuous, sinful man to this, *i.e.*, the Revelation of Salvation in its historical form. How can the reason ever determine what thoughts of salvation could rise in the mind of God, and what deeds were necessary to their realization? Facts belong to the domain of history, not to that of reasoning; and that which is above relative reason is not therefore yet at variance with absolute reason. The question with regard to any fact is not, Is it reasonable, but first of all, Is it sufficiently established? And if, according to the testimony of Scripture and experience, the entire man must be redeemed, then his faculty of thought too must be enlightened and released before he can recognise and judge the full truth.

7. If we ask what rights and duties must be conceded to Reason in its relation to the Revelation of Salvation, the answer is already determined in principle by what has been said. Reason may and must submit the grounds for the reality of this revelation to a close and accurate test; compare its contents with that which general revelation proclaims, and reject what appears to be in irreconcilable conflict therewith; it must seek to distinguish the unchangeable essence of this revelation from the temporary form in which it is now given, and try to penetrate more deeply into its internal coherence, its value, and Divine dignity; and attempt by its light to raise itself to the height of a really Christian notion of the world—believing, but also reasonable in the very highest sense of the word. In some degree—it is a comparison drawn from Liebnitz—in some degree Revelation, as contrasted with Reason, fulfils the task of an Extraordinary Royal Commissioner before a lawful assembly, to which he first of all delivers his credentials; but when these credentials have once been properly examined and approved, he now takes the place of President, communicating his decrees and commands, which were unknown before, and by the right of these rules all further deliberation (§ xvi. 8).

8. With this notion of our subject, we gain now the right way to give a

[5] Compare § 3.

[6] Gal. ii. 19.

satisfactory answer to the much-discussed question, whether, and in how far, we must then believe *on authority*. Lessing has already truly said, "A certain bias of Reason under the obedience of Faith rests upon the actual conception of Revelation; or rather, Reason yields itself captive as soon as it is assured of the reality of the Revelation." We must only take care to mark out the meaning, the grounds, and the limits of this claim. We acknowledge any one's *authority* in the Christian religious domain when we concede to him the *right to be believed on his word, even when we do not yet understand, or only imperfectly, the word itself*. In the absolute sense such an authority can only be ascribed to God, but it can also attain to very high proportions in men, of whom it is clearly seen that they speak and act in the name of God. In this case we accept their testimony already, because they really are *that* which they say they are, and their personality commands our respect and confidence. Thus belief on authority always, in a certain sense, differs from conviction obtained by means of an independent insight into that which is revealed; and the systematic opposition of some to such belief, even when put forth with the highest pretensions of science, is, in fact, nothing but superficiality itself.

As in every other domain, so most of all in the suprasensuous, is a certain degree of belief on authority natural, indispensable, and therefore thoroughly legitimate. Sever its main artery, then neither society, nor household life, nor mercantile transactions would be possible. Where it concerns a revelation of God's designs for salvation, of which we only obtain our knowledge by the way of well-established testimony, it is the greatest folly to say, "He who believes on authority does not *himself* believe; another believes in his place." Our Lord Jesus Christ Himself demands unconditional belief in His words, places this higher than belief on the ground of a sensible sign; and, notwithstanding all which in it seems inconceivable, has condemned the unbelieving rejection of His word as inexcusable sin.[7] It was indeed, in the nature of His utterances, specially in the metaphysical and prophetical character of many of His words, that these must either be rejected, or, if need be, accepted only on His dictum. Nor is it at all different with many assertions of the Apostles, to which they demand an unconditional assent.[8] We could only speak here of "*blind* faith," if this were claimed *without reason;* but not where it is demanded, after it has been fully shown why and for whom the demand is made. So little irrational is such a belief, that, on the contrary, we can hardly justify the opposition to it. Experience teaches, indeed, that man may yield to different authorities alternately, but never can raise himself above all authority. Many a one, who seemed to do this, has never rested until he has become an authority for himself or for others. Belief on authority is certainly not the highest, much less is it the only belief; he who has begun with it cannot rest until he has raised himself as much as is possible to an independent insight into the contents and grounds of his belief, and sanctified reflection cannot remain one step below the highest to which Christian Reason is able to rise by the light of Revelation. Dulness of spirit in this respect,

---

[7] Matt. v. 22; vii. 28, 29; John viii. 51; xii. 48.
[8] *E.g.*, 1 Thess. iv. 15; 1 Cor. xv. 51, 52; Rom. xi. 25, 26.

under the cloak of humility, is no sign of life, but a sign of disease, and the *credo quia absurdum* cannot in any case be the last words of our justification. But the *credo, quanquam absurdum videtur*, in this domain has still in some cases a higher right than the *intelligo ut credam*, which in its ultimate ground is unchristian and therefore also untheological. Where no further independent insight is possible, there Christian belief, even in its highest development, still remains always a belief on authority. In many cases, to the question, why the believer holds something as truth, we can give only as an answer the *αὐτος ἔφα* of the Master, and in this case this word must be quite sufficient for us. This remains, notwithstanding various continuing difficulties, "the end of all controversy," because it is (externally) historically proved, and is (internally) confirmed by the testimony of the Holy Spirit. In this sense, authority, but authority Divine and legitimated, appears at once the last ground of belief, and we thus believe, in the last resort, not *in ourselves, but in the living God, if need be, ourselves notwithstanding*. "Ratio auctoritatem non deserit, cum consideratur cui sit credendum" (Augustine). A *perfect* conciliation of belief and knowledge is not conceivable on this side of the grave,[9] and, going on from belief to knowledge, we constantly return again to childlike belief,[10] and walk in that belief, but by the light of *Holy Scripture.*

Comp. Dr. S. R. J. VAN SCHEVICHAVEN as to the import and value of belief on authority (1864); H. CREMER, *Vernunft, Gewissen, und Offenbarung*, in the *Neun Apologet. Vorträge* (1869), pp. 51—99; TH. CHRISTLIEB, *a. a. O.* (1870), pp. 78—147; E. DE PRESSENSÉ, *L'Autorité en Matière Religieuse*, in the *Rev. Chrétienne* of 1871.

POINTS FOR INQUIRY.

The idea of the Supranatural further elucidated.—The limits of reason in this domain recognised and defined.—Does the Revelation of Salvation announce absolutely nothing which conflicts with human reason?—How far is the right of Reason with regard to Revelation recognised by our Lord and His first witnesses?—Rationalism not rational. —Cannot the Christian belief in Revelation do entirely without the principle of authority?—Must men then, throughout their whole lives, adhere to the standpoint of authority?—Does there exist any prospect of a reconciliation of faith and knowledge? and what help can Dogmatics give in order to hasten the fulfilment of that prospect?

---

[9] 1 Cor. xiii. 9—12. [10] 1 John v. 13.

CHAPTER III.

HOLY SCRIPTURE.

SECTION XXXV.—ITS ESSENTIAL CONTENTS.

THE knowledge of the Revelation of Salvation is drawn from Holy Scripture, which thus must be well distinguished from the Revelation itself. The Holy Scriptures of the Old and the New Testament form together the authentic, and, as such, indispensable, documentary record of that which God has done, is doing, and will do, to establish His kingdom upon earth. By this its peculiar character is determined, on the one hand, the unity of the Bible, and on the other the very diverse value of its different parts.

1. The connection between this and the preceding chapter is self-evident. For the Revelation, of which we have thus far spoken, is made known to us above all by the Bible; the science of Apocalyptics thus prepares the way for that of Bibliology. Only it must be premised that we are here speaking of the Bible exclusively in relation to the Saving Revelation; of the Word of God therein contained, regarded as a means of grace, we shall speak under the head of Ecclesiology. Moreover the importance of the subject now to be treated of will be at once acknowledged. The question, "What think ye of Holy Scripture?" is, in a certain sense, of not less importance than the question, "What think ye of Christ?" It is least of all one of minor importance for the Reformed Theologian, and in the present day. The whole bearing of our Dogmatics is determined by the relation in which it stands to Scripture.

2. Only general hints, conveyed in few words, can here be given in regard to Holy Scripture. The name *Biblia*—in use since the fifth century, and owing its origin, as it would seem, to Chrysostom—indicates a collection of books *par excellence*. The distinction between the Old and the

New *Testament* points to the different *relationship* between God and man, before and after the coming of Christ, of which these books make mention. The original word whereby this relationship is expressed, Διαθήκη, בְּרִית is less happily rendered by the Latin fathers *testamentum* (in which sense it is, however, used in Heb. ix. 16), and must here be taken in the signification of *foedus*. As early as 1 Maccab. i. 57, mention is made of a book of the Covenant, as indicating the Mosaic Law; and in 2 Cor. iii. 14, the whole of the first and greater part of the Bible is characterised as the Old Covenant. Now in these Scriptures of the Old Covenant, a new and better covenant was spoken of, which God promised to make,[1] and which Jesus declared was confirmed in His shed blood.[2] Thus it was natural to confer this name of "Books of the New *Covenant*" upon the earliest records of the New Dispensation. The oldest division of the Scriptures of the Old Testament is found in Luke xxiv. 44, where the Psalms are mentioned as the beginning of the Hagiographa; while we very early see the Scriptures of the New Testament divided into *the Gospel* and *the Apostles*. Further particulars, in regard to the one and the other, in any general Introduction to the Scriptures of the Old and the New Testament.

3. If the extent of the Bible can be thus easily reviewed, the question "What *is* the Bible?" is less speedily answered. From the Bible itself, at least, the answer cannot possibly be derived. We cannot possibly apply texts like Ps. xix. 7—11; cxix. 105; John xvii. 17*b*; 2 Pet. i. 19, without nearer limitation, to the Bible *en bloc;* and it shows pretty much a want of reflection to explain of the Bible as a whole the concluding words of the book of Revelation, xxii. 18, 19, which were never written in relation thereto. Just as little satisfactory is the indefinite statement: the Bible *is* God's Word. The Bible itself, at least, never takes this appellation; for surely Rom. iii. 2*b* cannot imply that Bibles were committed to the Jews. From the very first we must distinguish between the *Bible* and the *Wor of God:* the Word of God is literally that which God utters and reveals concerning Himself, and that Word is found *in* the Bible.

4. The distinction already made before (§ xxviii. 1) between the Bible and revelation remains thus, here also, imperatively necessary. Yea, even at the first glance it is clear that the Bible contains not a little which cannot possibly, in the proper sense of the word, be termed Revelation. For instance, so many genealogical registers, geographical or statistical data, etc. Or even if it were thought that these also are to be regarded as a fruit of inspiration—about which we shall speak hereafter—even then Inspiration and Revelation are by no means the same thing. The confusion of Bible and Revelation rests upon a want of distinguishing between the *continens* and the *contentum*, the container and the contained, and is possible only as a result of an exceedingly imperfect conception of the nature of the Theopneustia. Already, in the Standards of our Church, the ideas of Holy Scripture and Word or Revelation of God are more or less distinguished the one from the other;[3] and it was therefore wholly in the

[1] Jer. xxxi. 31—34.
[2] Matt. xxvi. 28.
[3] *Netherlands Confession*, Artt. iii., vii., xxix.

spirit of our Confession of Faith that it was asserted: "Not all that is found in the Bible is Divine Revelation; but all Divine Revelation which is necessary for our salvation is found in the Bible. It would not, therefore, necessarily follow that if we should have to be without some single portion of the Bible, we should have on that account lost some part of God's Word."[4] Holy Scripture is not the Revelation itself, but the source of our knowledge of it,—the record, the memorial, the bearer thereof.

5. Thus appears clear—along with the manifest difference—also the inseparable connection between Revelation and Holy Scripture. We have already seen that the Revelation of Salvation is a fact, or rather that it takes place in a series of facts which make us acquainted with the Divine plan of salvation, and of words in which these facts are explained. But how are we to come to the precise knowledge, as well of these facts as of the sense in which they are to be apprehended? Here Holy Scripture comes to our help: this is the *documentary record* of what God has done, is doing, and will do to establish His kingdom on earth. It publicly proclaims that kingdom; makes us acquainted with its existence, its history, its laws, and its promises of salvation. It is true that the accuracy of this definition, too, cannot be proved by an appeal to particular texts; for the Bible was gradually formed, and no single book contains a passage which teaches us how the whole—which was not yet in existence then—is to be regarded. But the justice of this description appears from the impression which the Bible in its totality makes upon every attentive mind. For the idea of the Kingdom of God is the golden thread which runs through all: and of this kingdom the Bible is the document (*documentum*), because it not only bears witness to the founding thereof, but also explains it, and itself belongs to it—just as a gift of the Crown is only then acknowledged as an actual right when an official warrant thereof, a formal deed of gift, has been prepared. "The Word of God is the testimony of His kingdom, in the form of a history and doctrine explained and continued by personal organs." (Nitzsch.)

6. With full confidence we speak of this document as *authentic* and *indispensable*. *Authentic* not yet, as having regard to every single part of the Bible—of which the origin and genuineness must be proved as a result of historic-critical investigation—but in this sense, that without the Bible in its totality we should possess either no knowledge of the revelation, or at least no sufficient knowledge thereof; in other words, that all our knowledge on this point must be derived from Holy Scripture as the most original source. And *indispensable*, because, without such Scripture record, Revelation could not possibly have been preserved and handed down for all time in its purity. If He who revealed Himself desired this as a permanent condition, He must, at the same time, will that the history and import of His revelation should be recorded in durable characters. Hence we find He Himself constantly gives the command to write, where something of great importance for posterity is communicated.[5] Man thinks, speaks, and

[4] L. EGELING, *Weg der Zaligh.*, ii. p. 577; compare J. I. DOEDES, *Leer der Zaligh.*, p. 5, *sqq.*

[5] Compare Exod. xxxiv. 1; Deut. xxxi. 19; 1 Sam. x. 25; Isa. viii. 1; Jer. xxxvi. 2; Rev. i. 19.

preserves the word of his lips in writing. It is not otherwise with God; He has thoughts of redemption, utters them, and now also provides for their being preserved in writing. The before-mentioned places were formerly appealed to, without reason, to prove that God had commanded the writing of the whole Bible: the deduction from some parts in relation to the whole is not unconditionally allowed. Yet in general it may be asserted that He who willed the end must also have willed the means thereto. But while the revelation itself, indeed, is possible without the vehicle of Scripture, its communication and preservation in a trustworthy form through a prolonged course of time is impossible. "Revelation is not designed as a meteor to flash for a moment through the world, but to be set in the firmament for humanity as a bright sun which gradually brings in, over the whole extent of our earth, the clear, full day. This it can do only when the account thereof is fixed by writing, and that while it is yet in the process of formation—*i.e.*, attested by means of documents—consequently only when it is authenticated by documentary evidence" (Rothe).

7. What has been said confirms the inner *Unity* of the Bible. It cannot be overlooked that the first impression which it makes is that of a very great diversity of writers, age, language, etc. But in the midst of all this, the higher harmony of its central thought and tendency, which is contained in the idea of the *Kingdom of God*, cannot be denied. The Bible is like a body consisting of many members, some more honourable, others less so, but animated by one breath of life. It is as a Gothic temple, in which even the apparent caprices of architecture and ornamentation constitute, in connection with the whole, one beauty the more, and the form of the cross is everywhere to be traced; but at the same time the *value* of the different parts is determined by the relation of each one to the central thought of the whole. For no sound Christian consciousness has each part of the Scripture wholly the same value. In regard also to the light here shed, the saying of the Apostle (1 Cor. xv. 41) may be applied. What we have to do in this case is simply to preserve our estimate of the value of Scripture free from caprice and one-sidedness; and this will be done where the following rule is observed: A part of Scripture has so much the higher value in proportion as it is of greater importance for our knowledge of the Kingdom of God.

Compare, on this chapter in general, the Articles, Bible, Canon, etc., in the *Bijb. Woordenb.* (Dictionary of the Bible) and in Herzog's *R. E.;* the principal Introductions to the Scriptures of the Old and New Testaments; the general Introduction to the Holy Scriptures, prefixed by LANGE, in his *Bibel-Werk*, to his Commentary on Matthew, etc. Touching this section, D. J. KOEPPEN, *Die Bibel, ein Werk der Göttlichen Weisheit* (translated into Dutch, 1794); J. H. SCHOLTEN, *Hervormde Kerk*, i., p. 97, *seq.*; J. J. VAN TOORENENBERGEN, *Bijdragen*, etc., p. 9, *seq.*; H. EWALD, *Die Lehre vom Worte Gottes* (1871).

POINTS FOR INQUIRY.

Connexion with the preceding chapter.—Scripture and the Christ.—Explanation of the Scripture places referred to.—In what sense and on what grounds may we say that Holy Scripture was willed by God Himself?—The necessity for preserving the Revelation in writing, illustrated from the nature of the case and from the history of Religion.—Whence is it that the unity of the Bible has been alternately over-estimated and ignored?

SECTION XXXVI.—ITS ORIGIN.

Just as the essential contents of Holy Scripture are emphatically Divine, so does the history of the formation of the Sacred Scriptures give us the right to speak—after the Divine—of a human side of the Bible, which has never been ignored without serious loss to the cause of truth. The Holy Scriptures were written *by* men, *for* men, and in a truly human manner; and only after a long time were they united into a compact whole. Science cannot possibly allow the right and duty of free criticism of the Canon of the Scriptures of the Old and New Testament in the domain of Protestant Christian Theology to be disputed; but faith recognises, at the same time, in the whole history of the formation and preservation of the sacred collection, the traces of God's special care for the highest interests of humanity.

1. The question as to the *Origin* of the Bible is almost the first which presents itself in the domain of Bibliology, and is of decisive importance for its further treatment. If the Scripture is purely a Divine book, all criticism is out of place in regard to it; if it is merely human, it must be regarded, and judged of, not differently from any other writing. In order to find the true answer, it is necessary that we look at the Bible itself in an unprejudiced manner, and see in what light it presents itself. If we do this, it is plain that it displays as well a Divine, as a human, side. Divine, as we saw, (Chap. II.,) as to its essential contents—the Saving Revelation; human as to the form in which this treasure is contained. A striking parallel may be drawn in this respect between Holy Scripture and Him of whom it testifies. As we discover in the *person* of the Lord a Divine and a human side, united in the one life of a God-man; so in the sacred Scriptures of the Old and New Testament, Divine Revelation, Law, Promise, on the one side, human apprehension, conception, representation, on the other, co-operate to present a Divine-human whole of inestimable value. At every step the impartial reader must exclaim, "*How Divine*," and again, "*How human!*"

2. No wonder that the question, What is properly speaking the origin of the Bible? has been so differently answered. Bibliology also has at all times had its Docetæ on the one hand, its Socinians on the other. Alternately was the Divine here exalted at the cost of the human, or the converse. The first was especially the case in the seventeenth century, under the influence of Scholasticism. After the Reformation had restored the Scriptures to their former place of honour, they very soon came to be regarded in their totality as a sort of Nomo-canon, and were reverenced in an extravagant

manner. Men regarded the Scriptures as, so to speak, a book suddenly fallen from heaven, of which God was the *Auctor primarius*, while for the rest it was a matter of subordinate importance what persons served Him as *Auctores secundarii*. "*Solus Deus, si accurate loqui velimus, S. S. auctor dicendus est. Prophetæ autem et Apostoli auctores dici non possunt, nisi per* κατάχρησιν, *utpote qui potius Dei calami essent*" (Quenstadt, † 1688). If they were in any degree active, they were so, it was thought, in a purely mechanical way, and it was after all a matter of indifference whether or not they themselves understood the things of which they spoke. Not indeed that they might understand, but that they might record, were these things communicated to them from above, and their only task was, with the greatest accuracy possible, to set down what they heard. According to this view, everything in the Bible was inspired, *i.e.*, dictated; not merely the facts, but the words too; not merely the consonants, but even the vowels; not merely the religious and moral contents of the Scripture, but even its geography and history. On this account, even the language and style of the Bible must be wholly faultless; for every blemish therein observed would detract from the honour of the heavenly writer. The language, therefore, of the New Testament must not be judged of according to the ordinary laws of grammar; but, if need be, the latter must be modified with an eye to the former. Even the diversity of style and language was explained by the fact, that the invisible Author graciously modified His communication according to the individuality of His different organs. It was denied in so many words, (see, *e.g.*, Voetius, in his treatise, "*Quousque se extendat S.S. auctoritas*,") that any examination or reflection was necessary on the part of the inspired writer in regard to that which was written, since it was given him immediately, and in an extraordinary manner. The historical and human side of Holy Scripture, in a word, receded not only into the background, but was even as little as possible touched upon. Nay, "*Quæstio an SS. SS. Dei sint Verbum, homini Christiano indigna est*" (Wolleb).

3. That this view is, as a matter of abstract logic, unexceptionable, yea, admirably conclusive, can hardly be denied. But equally certain is it that the Bible itself neither teaches nor justifies it; but, on the contrary, in more than one way manifests its inaccuracy. To what absurdity it leads is seen, for example, by a glance at 1 Cor. i. 14—16, where, in the case supposed, the Holy Ghost dictated to the Apostle, first, an inaccuracy, then a correction, and finally a declaration of ignorance. The whole of this mechanical theory was evidently the fruit of a dogmatic prepossession. It was not asked what the Bible really is, but what it ought to be, in order to maintain its character as a perfectly infallible rule of faith and life; and each satisfied demand called forth another and yet more stringent one. It is now pretty generally acknowledged that this position may be regarded as untenable, since the last attempt at its partial defence, however well conceived in itself, was altogether unsuccessful. (See L. Gaussen, *Theopneustie*, 1842, [also in an English translation], and *Le Canon des S. Ecritures*, 2 vols., 1860.) It might, perhaps, even appear unnecessary to waste a single word upon it, were it not that this mechanical theory of inspiration still lives in the consciousness of some, at least in Holland and England, while the not yet for

gotten history of Edmond Scherer[1] and others shows what fatal reaction may be called forth by an intellectual exaggeration of the Scripture principle, combined with an ignoring of the human side of the Bible. Even in our own day the hint given by Herder to the young theologian is by no means unnecessary: "The best way of reading the Divine book is as a human book."[2]

4. "The more human (in the best sense of the word) the meaning you put upon the Word of God, so much the more nearly do you attain to the object of its Author" (Herder). Pity only that so often—especially since these words were written—men have rushed into the very opposite extreme. In an increasing degree has the human element of the Bible been acknowledged, whilst the Divine has been wholly, or in part, denied. This has been the case, in great measure, as the consequence of reaction, on the part of Deism, Rationalism, and the modern Naturalism. Regarded from this point of view, the Scripture of the Old Testament is nothing but the remaining literature of the nation of Israel; and that of the New Testament, of the Apostolic age. The writers in both cases treat, no doubt, of things more sacred than do many, but in no other respect had they any advantage over any other. They were, and remained, short-sighted men like all others; and every one has the right to know better than they. From the undeniable fact that the mechanical *theory of inspiration* has, as such, broken down, there is drawn from this standpoint the conclusion that there can be no such thing as *inspiration itself*. What scorn, in every way, lavished upon the Bible, our age especially has witnessed, after the Bibliolatry of an earlier period, can here only be hinted at in passing. But what must be brought especially into the foreground, is that this one-sidedness is also in manifest conflict, not only with express utterances of Holy Scripture,—*e.g.*, 2 Tim. iii. 16; 2 Pet. i. 21; comp. John xvi. 13,—but also, and above all, with the impression always produced by the Bible upon every honest and receptive mind. Even from the most violent assailants of the Bible, in our own and a previous age, have escaped, as it were in spite of their authors, eulogies of the Book of books, which were exaggeration itself, if the Bible is and claims to be absolutely nothing more than a mere work of men. Taught by such experiences, and above all taking our stand upon the nature and contents of the Holy Scriptures themselves, we may safely lay down the proposition, *Every conception of Holy Scripture is one-sided, and on that account untrue, in which its human side recedes into the background as compared with the Divine; or the converse.* Called thus to have regard to both, we believe we shall be acting most in accordance with the nature of the case, and with the special need of our time, if we begin with the human side, in order thence to proceed to the higher.

5. Only in its broad outline can Christian Dogmatics point out the history of the gradual rise of the sacred collection. As concerns the books of the Old Testament, they themselves contain sundry statements as to the preservation of the sacred literary deposit of which the *Thora* formed the basis, and which was gradually augmented by important additions.

---

[1] *La Critique et la Foi, deux Lettres*, 1850.
[2] *Briefe, das Stud. d. Theol. betr.* s. 1.

(Compare Deut. xxxi. 24—26; Josh. xxiv. 26; 1 Sam. x. 25, and other places.) Although the history of the sacred books, especially up to the time of the Babylonian Captivity, is in many respects lost in obscurity, it is nevertheless certain that, even before this time, various copies of the Law and the Prophets existed, so that, at the time of the restoration of Israel, the work of gathering again the sacred treasure could be attempted with the desired result. According to the Jewish tradition, this task was accomplished by no other than Ezra and the so-called Great Synagogue; a tradition of which the later fabulous embellishment has concealed indeed, but by no means destroyed, the original kernel of truth. Certain is it, at least, that, according to Josephus (*contra Apionem*, I. 8), the sacred Scriptures, from the time of Moses to that of Artaxerxes I., during whose reign the last of the Prophets died, formed a collection with which nothing written after this time could bear comparison in point of value; so that later books, such as that of Jesus Sirach, notwithstanding their relative importance, were clearly distinguished therefrom. That book, composed about two centuries before our era, mentions, among other things, the division of the Old Testament into Law, Prophets, and other books (Luke xxiv. 44), while the writer of the prologue makes mention of its existence in the Greek version.

As concerns the Scriptures of the New Testament, even at an early period the Apostolic Epistles were communicated by one assembly to another (Col. iv. 16). Thus there naturally arose greater or lesser collections (2 Pet. iii. 16), and their number would be augmented in proportion as reverence for the writings left by the Apostles increased. The appearance of spurious writings in their name (2 Thess. ii. 2, iii. 17) very soon rendered a critical sifting necessary, and the rise of a copious Apocryphal literature could not but lead to a sharp distinction between this and the genuine Apostolic literature. In the middle of the second century we hear Justin Martyr several times speak of the Memorials of the Apostles (*memorabilia*, ἀπομνημονεύματα) in a manner which justifies the supposition that by this word he designates our four Gospels; and we know that even Marcion recognised a collection of ten Pauline Epistles. The ancient Syriac version of the New Testament (Peshito), belonging to the end of the second century, contained, in addition to the four Gospels and the Acts, thirteen Epistles of Paul, together with the Epistle to the Hebrews, the Epistle of James, and the first Epistles of Peter and John; whilst the well-known fragment of Muratori, probably of a date between 170 and 180, mentions much the same writings, together with the Epistle of Jude, and the Apocalypse. With slight exception, we find all the writings of the New Testament acknowledged as authentic by Origen in the beginning of the third century; and in the beginning of the fourth we hear these divided by Eusebius (*Hist. Eccl.*, iii., 25) into ὁμολογούμενα (the four Gospels, Acts of the Apostles, thirteen Epistles of Paul, 1 Peter, 1 John, and (while leaving it open to any one to reject it) the Apocalypse), ἀντιλεγόμενα or νόθα (the Epistles of James and Jude, 2nd of Peter, 2nd and 3rd of John), and παντελῶς νόθα, or ἄτοπα καὶ δυσσεβῆ (forged writings of heretics). It is remarkable that he altogether passes over the Epistle to the Hebrews in silence. The Canon of the New Testament, as we possess it, was, on the ground of these and other testimonies, definitely fixed by the Council of Laodicea (360-364), still with the exception of the Apocalypse, which was accepted as an integral part of it by the Council of Hippo (393), and that of Carthage (397).

6. When we give to this collection of the books of the Old and the New Testament the name of *Canonical* writings, we mean those whose contents are acknowledged by the Christian Church as a rule of faith and life. [Compare the Sixth Article of the Church of England]. Entirely in conflict with ecclesiastical usage is the opinion of Semler and others—pretty generally held a while ago—that the word Κανών signifies *a list*, so that by Canonical books are to be understood those which, in contradistinction from the Apocrypha, were publicly read. Nothing else is signified by it but a fixed rule (Gal. vi. 16; Phil. iii. 16), as this was found at first in genuine tradition, and afterwards in the Apostolic writings. Just as little does history justify our understanding *Canonical writings* at once in the definitive sense of *inspired writings.* The dogmatic and the historic use of the word must—in the interest of perspicuity—be clearly distinguished, although it may hereafter become apparent, in the treatment of the doctrine of Inspiration, to what extent this attribute must be claimed definitely for the Canonical books of the Old and New Testament, above all other writings. We thus ascribe Canonicity to a book in the Bible, which has a right to a place in the sacred collection; and this right again depends—more than on anything else—upon the question whether this writing really proceeded from the person to whom it has been ascribed by Jewish or Christian antiquity.

7. Highly important, though difficult, is the question what judgment we must form as to the formation of the Canon; in other words, whether we may consider that the Christian Church—to speak only of the New Testament in the reception of these particular writings into its sacred collection, to the exclusion of others, has made a wise, yea, the only right choice. The answer is easy from the standpoint of the Romish Church, which in this act also recognises the fruit of an infallible wisdom, and confesses with Augustine: "*Scripturæ non crederem, nisi ne commoveret Ecclesiæ auctoritas.*" Easy also from the standpoint of the Reformed Confession, which (Confession of the Netherlands, Art. 5) appeals for the Canonical authority of the whole of Holy Scripture to the testimony of the Holy Ghost. But, as we have seen (§ 32), the Holy Ghost gives indeed testimony to the believer as to the Saving Revelation contained in it, yet not on this account necessarily to every single part, *and just as little* to the Bible *en bloc.* For us, therefore, the question as to the value to be attached to the collection contained in the Canon is and remains a purely historical question; the Church, through the medium of which we received it, exists for us not as an infallible authority, but as a venerable witness for the truth. But so much the more do we rejoice that to the question, even as thus presented, the answer upon nearer examination can prove only satisfactory.

8. This judgment it is not difficult to support. For it is evident, upon a careful comparison, that, as to contents and tendency, the collection of the New Testament writings, taken all together, stands far higher than do those which have been excluded. Let any one compare

the Canonical with the Apocryphal Gospels and Acts; the Apostolic Epistles with those of the Apostolic Fathers and their successors, and he will become aware of a difference very clearly appreciable. The very doubt which for a time prevailed regarding some of the Antilegomena, is a sign that the Church has in this by no means proceeded in so uncritical a manner as has sometimes been supposed, and did not rest satisfied so soon as something edifying had been received into the sacred collection. A high value must be attached by every impartial critic to the patristic testimony concerning the origin of the Gospels and Apostolic Epistles, when he regards, first, its antiquity; then its independence; then, finally, the assent to, and approbation of, this testimony on the part of Christian antiquity; frequently also on the part of the earliest heretics: while even in the present day an impartial examination of the contents of the sacred Scriptures entirely confirms the perfect justice thereof. It is asserted, it is true, that much was wanting in point of maturity in the knowledge and judgment of many (Papias, *e.g.*), and that their criticism generally, displayed more of a dogmatic than of a purely historic character. But this last accusation at least—mostly repeated by those whose own criticism of the writings of the New Testament is ruled by Naturalistic prejudice—is not so easily proved as asserted. The oldest witnesses speak not merely in their own name, but in that of their contemporaries and companions in the faith, and the high importance of the subject, too, must, in this case more than ever, lead them to exercise great circumspection. Even though at first one or two Apocryphal writings were held in almost equal honour with those of the Apostles, the spirit of impartial love of truth quickly recognised the incongruity, and separated the one from the other. Where it appeared that in some cases, even with good intention, spurious writings were circulated under the name of the Apostles, this was expressly opposed, and, so soon as made manifest, was condemned (Tertull., *De Baptismo*, cap. 17). It is possible indeed that one or another ancient Christian writing has been left out of the Canon, which merited a place in it, at least as much as some of the Antilegomena. Not in respect of every single part of the New Testament can this its particular choice, in preference to others, be equally satisfactorily defended. But in any case it cannot be shown that anything really indispensable has been left out of the sacred Collection, or that anything entirely superfluous has found a place in it. Without hesitation therefore do we regard the Canonical books of the New Testament as an authentic and precious collection of the writings left by the earliest witnesses of the Lord. Not a single writing lies before us, for the Canonicity of which credentials of a more or less conclusive nature cannot be adduced. The evidences for the genuineness of the principal books of the New Testament are much more manifold and powerful than those which can be adduced for the authenticity even of the most eminent productions of profane antiquity.

9. As concerns the Canon of the *Old* Testament Scriptures, the Christian Church has received it from the Jews, yet not without critical investigation. Melito of Sardis (about the year 172), and Origen († 254), made accurate investigations amongst the Palestinean Jews as to what writings belonged to the Canon, although along with these a certain value was still

attached to the Apocryphas of the Old Testament. To the question whether generally speaking it was wise to rely on Jewish tradition, an affirmative answer seems justified. For this tradition itself was the fruit of a critical examination, made at the time of the close of the Old Testament Canon, and assuredly not without earnestness and conscientiousness. The sharply defined distinction made both then and later, between Canonical and Apocryphal writings—*e.g.*, in those bearing the name of Daniel and of Ezra—can have had its ground only in a discriminating choice, the motives for which are no longer known to us, but whose results, so long as their inaccuracy is not demonstrated, are deserving of confidence. Other proofs also of an independent and liberal spirit are not wanting in connection with this history. "The collectors who could receive into the Canon the book of the Gentile woman Ruth, the writing concerning the extra-Israelite Emir Job, the song which celebrates the glory of conjugal love, the book of the denunciations of the prophet Jonah in the heathen city of Nineveh, can certainly be well distinguished from a forum of Pharisaic Synedrists; rising Pharisaism would hardly have received such books into its Canon as sacred" (Lange). In particular details, the accuracy of this critical judgment of antiquity is perhaps no longer to be defended against every possible objection; least of all has Christian Dogmatics to regard this defence as its proper task. But well may it, with grateful appreciation of the help of a thorough Isagogics, regard the Scriptures of the Old Testament as a whole as authentic sources of our knowledge of the Divine Revelation given by Moses and the Prophets.

10. The position which Christian Theologians, in the spirit of the Reformation, have to occupy in relation to the tradition which gave to the Church its Canon is already defined in principle by what has been said. It is not the attitude of a blind dogmatism, which at once begins to submit unreservedly to the authority of tradition; just as little that of a lofty criticism which attaches to the utterances of tradition no essential importance; but that of a truly independent, impartial, patiently conducted investigation. The Reformers received the whole Canon, as handed down from antiquity, and their age was certainly but little adapted to the vigorous prosecution of a critical examination as to the genuineness of each particular book. Yet it is well known that they, in the spirit of freedom, availed themselves of their right as Christian Theologians in this respect also. The judgment of Luther as to the Epistle of James, of Zwingli as to the Apocalypse, of Calvin as to the Epistle to the Hebrews, whether right or wrong in itself, is but the legitimate application of an inviolable principle. Yea, truly, "to know what one can give up, one must know what one possesses" (Tholuck). The history of the difference which has always been manifest in regard to some of the Antilegomena, proves that even the most orthodox Theologians had their own ideas as to the *Auctor secundarius* of the books of the Bible. It may be regretted that the right of criticism is so often abused as a cloak for caprice and license, yet it is just as little reasonable as desirable, to regard the investigation of the Canon in its whole or its parts as finally closed. Not merely the science of Criticism, but that also of Apologetics, has a preponderating interest in the further discussion of this question, especially as opposed to an atomistic criticism, which with

rude hand would tear out the leaves of the Bible to scatter them to all the winds of heaven.

11. All that is called for is, that the critical examination be conducted not merely without hindrance, but also, so far as possible, in an unprejudiced spirit, and according to fixed laws, after the maxim, "*Nec temere, nec timide,*" which has its just application in this case also. There is, with manifold knowledge, no less of caution also required in order to form, upon matters such as here present themselves, a really profound judgment, based upon an adequate acquaintance with the things themselves. Very easily may one be led away by appearances, very quickly also be induced by personal sympathies to accept the shadow instead of the reality. A striking example of blind prepossession is afforded, for instance, in latest times, in the uncritical treatment of the fourth Gospel, which—even though the crowd of witnesses were doubled—is *not allowed* to be genuine, because Modernism *must*, even at this price, continue to pass for truth. Even in regard to the subject of this investigation the principle should be held in honour, in opposition to all capricious treatment, that *only in God's light can we truly see light;* and Luther's rule is to be maintained, "That which has not Christ as its object is not Apostolic, even though St. Peter and St. Paul had taught it. On the other hand, to preach Christ is Apostolic, even though it were done by Judas, Annas, Pilate, or Herod." Christian science, moreover, has no sacred collection *to make up* out of a number of existing documents, but ever anew to apply the test to the collection already existing. If every individual is to regard the whole critical and isagogical work as *à refaire*, this will at least attain to something of the labour of Penelope; and it is still a question whether this mode of proceeding deserves the name of genuine theological criticism. We have, in this case also, not now to *produce* the reality, but, with interest and affection, to seek to understand our true position in regard to that already existing, and to separate the different elements with that discriminating and genuinely critical tact, which is a fruit of the Holy Ghost. A criticism of the Canon, to possess any value, must be something more than the expression of a merely subjective opinion, held perhaps but for the moment. True theological criticism will besides never forget that the sacred collection, though owing its formation to men, is yet something more than the fruit of human reflection and human wisdom alone.

12. Are we really justified in speaking of the *providential* origin of the Canon? However difficult it is here to define anything in detail, we do not hesitate to return an affirmative answer to the question as it thus stands. And that not simply in the general sense, that as everything, so also the formation of the Koran, the Bible, etc., took place under a higher guidance; but in the specific sense, that here is to be observed a fruit and manifestation of God's peculiar care for the highest interests of humanity. If God really willed the establishment of a Kingdom of God upon earth, and its propagation by means of the Scriptures (§ xxxv. 6), then the preservation and collection of writings destined to this end cannot have been effected without His especial guidance. Assuredly, not in the fixing of the Canon, any more than in any other act, was the Church infallible, but just as little was she forsaken by the Spirit of truth, and she was notably in

possession of a certain tact for discriminating between Apostolic and non-Apostolic writings, a tact which by practice and experience, by conflict and reaction, would attain to a rare degree of delicacy. Tact—one of the ancient *Charismata*—has in this case done its work in so happy a way, that we, for our part at least, and many others with us, would not feel justified in definitely contesting, in regard to any single book of the New Testament, its title to a place in the Canon. In this issue we may acknowledge with reverence the fruit of a higher influence, of which we hold fast to the ὅτι (the fact), even though we may not be able to define the πῶς (the manner). Before any one rejects this position as based on an *à priori* view, let him consider whether from a Christian standpoint its absolute denial is possible, and whether this does not lead in its consequences to far greater difficulties than its reverent acknowledgment. Certain is it, at least, that what may be considered *à priori* highly probable, is *à posteriori*, upon a careful consideration of the spirit, the contents, and the connected whole of the Bible, in a surprising manner confirmed. Nothing here can be strictly demonstrated, but to no small extent is it to be observed that, for any one who believes in a living God and a kingdom of God instituted by Him, the matter is raised above all reasonable doubt.

13. In itself the rise of such a national literature as that of the Old Testament, so early and so rapidly disseminated among a people like the Jews, in every other respect so much behindhand, is a wholly unique phenomenon in the history of the world, which of itself suggests a higher guidance. For the Old Testament manifests a dignity, a wealth of thought, a depth of contents, combined with a diversity and harmony of forms, of which we should in vain seek the counterpart elsewhere. "Se peut-il, qu'un livre à la fois si sublime et si simple soit l'œuvre d'un homme?" exclaimed Rousseau. Is it accidental that the Scriptures, precisely a short time before the appearance of Christianity in the world, should be translated into Greek? Accidental, that amongst the first witnesses of Christ there should be found writers of an ability like that of a Luke, a Paul, or a John? Accidental, that these writings should so speedily be scattered and multiplied, that to destroy them, or even to tamper with their contents, should thenceforth be impossible; that they were preserved throughout the Middle Ages; disinterred again at the Reformation from amongst the rubbish of the convents; that in our own day new proofs of the credibility of the Bible are continually coming to light, proofs drawn even from the ruins of Babylon, or the excavations of Nineveh? It is remarkable that none of the sacred writers thought of forming a Bible. Men of the most different natural constitution, manner of thought and life, of development and gifts, separated from each other by an interval of years or ages, labour in entire independence of each other, and yet there arises as a whole the Messianic Expectation of Israel, the Life of Jesus, the History of the Kingdom of God on earth. Cicero speaks of it as something inconceivable, that out of a number of letters promiscuously arranged the Annals of Ennius should arise. Equally absurd would be the supposition that out of a number of fragments of Jewish and early Christian literature a Bible should result. It is as has been said, "In the Latin literature there breathes almost audibly and palpably the spirit of valour; in

the Greek, that of Attic wisdom; and in the Hebrew, the Spirit of God," and with Augustine we repeat, "Mira profunditas, mi Deus, mira profunditas." Let any one read the same history—that of Joseph, for instance, which has called forth the admiration of Voltaire—first in the Bible and then in the Koran, and he will perceive what an entirely different spirit meets us in the former; and how this spirit, too lofty for human creation, everywhere from beginning to end, in the midst of the most perfect freedom, manifests the fairest harmony. At every step we must exclaim, The Bible is a truly human book, and yet, at the same time, something more than any other human book; and even in the history of the most violent assaults made upon it, the old proverb is but confirmed, "*The more they amuse themselves in smiting me, the more hammers they use up in doing it.*"[3] Result, "The secret of the equanimity of our modern theologians, even amidst the perils of critical operations, lies precisely in the clear recognition of the fact that faith in the inspiration of the Canon is not the essential condition —not even the first step necessary—in order to come to faith in Christ; that with *this* faith in the Scriptures, the Christian faith is not yet by any means given, or even its foundation laid; finally, that the moral, religious, actual —not merely intellectual—process of life, fails not, for any one who has uprightly and constantly yielded himself to its influence, to lead—as to life and full satisfaction in Christ, so also—to the recognition of the normative and Divine authority of the documents of Divine revelation" (Dorner.)

Compare the dissertation of D. F. VAN HEIJST on the Canon of Eusebius (Hague Soc., 1834); on the whole subject of Canon and Holy Scripture, that of NITZSCH, *Stud. u. Krit.* (1843), ii., and two articles of OEHLER and LANDERER, in Herzog, *R. E.* vii.; also, H. W. J. THIERSCH, *Versuch zur Herstellung des histor. Standp. für die Kritik des N. T.* (1845); a paper by H. EWALD, translated in *Waarh. in Liefde* (1850), iii., pp. 590—603; DORNER, *Jahrb. für deutsche Theol.* (1861), ii., p. 413, *sqq.*

POINTS FOR INQUIRY.

Historical review of the progress of the two opposite views with regard to the Bible.—Elucidation of some points, of particular importance for Christian Dogmatics, from the history of the Canon.—The right and duty of free criticism of the genuineness and textual integrity of the different books of the Bible.—Scientific and moral significance of the position held by modern criticism in relation to the utterances of Israelitish and Christian tradition.—Grounds and limits of the recognition of the providential Canon.—Total impression which we involuntarily receive from the Bible as a whole.—Canonical and Apocryphal.

SECTION XXXVII.—ITS EXTENT.

From the Canonical books of Holy Scripture the Apocryphal books of the Old and the New Testament must be well dis-

[3] Plus à me frapper on s'amuse,
Tant plus de marteaux on y use.

tinguished. Although, to a certain degree of undeniable importance, they are nevertheless, neither in an historical, nor a religious, nor a moral point of view, to be placed on a level with the forenamed; least of all in regard to that end for which Christian Dogmatics sees itself called upon to consult the Sacred Scriptures The position which the Protestant Church and Theology, as distinguished from the Roman Catholic, has always taken in regard to this Apocryphal literature, is justified as well by history as by the nature of the case, and ought on that account to be permanently maintained.

Already has the value of the Holy Scripture begun to unfold itself before our eyes: but how far does the domain of *Holy* Scripture, properly so called, extend? and is there sufficient reason for continuing to maintain the boundary line which divides the Canonical from the Apocryphal Scriptures? Before we enter farther upon the domain of Bibliology, this question must receive a reply.

1. By the Apocryphal (Deutero-Canonical) books of the Old Testament we understand those later writings of the Jews, which, though not originally belonging to the sacred collection, were added thereto in the Greek translation, and are enumerated (as well as in other Confessions) in the sixth article of the Dutch Reformed Church. The name points to writings of uncertain origin, which—not read in public—stood in more or less of opposition to the δεδημοσιευμένα, or *scripturæ publicæ*. In connection with some of the Grecian mysteries, also, were found such κρυπτά (*libri absconditi*), and in proportion also as the Gnostics of the earliest Christian centuries appealed to such-like writings, the word *Apocrypha* began to be employed in an increasingly unfavourable sense. Even at an early period the difference of opinions as to the proper value of the Apocryphas of the Old Testament comes into prominence. Origen had but little liking for them, and Cyril of Jerusalem recommended to his Catechumens, for their study, no other books of the Bible than the Canonical. Jerome even drew a sharp line of separation between these and the Apocrypha, and although he permitted its reading "*ad ædificationem*," he nevertheless expressly added, "*non ad auctoritatem dogmatum Ecclesiæ confirmandam.*" A tendency, however, set in in the West, under the influence of Augustine, more and more towards placing them on an equality with the Canonical writings. In proportion as the knowledge of Hebrew became rare, and the LXX. was held in a place of honour, with the less hesitation were both classes of books used interchangeably. Hence it was that the opinion of Augustine, at the Councils of Hippo (393) and Carthage (397), became the prevailing one, while that of Jerome counted ever fewer supporters. The conflict upon this point was allowed to slumber during the Middle Ages, but after the Reformation it arose again on different sides. Luther, following the example of the Greek Church, maintained anew the distinction between the Canonical and the Apocryphal writings, and Carlstadt even devoted a special work to its

defence (1520). The Council of Trent, on the other hand, placed the books of the second Canon, almost entirely on a level with those of the first, and in regard to this pronounced its anathema upon those who should think differently. The Church of Rome boldly appeals for the confirmation of her dogmas—the doctrine of Prayer on behalf of the Dead, of the Intercession of Saints, of Exorcism, etc.—to the testimony of the Apocryphal books of the Old Testament. The Reformed Church, on the contrary, has, in regard to this question, in opposition to the Church of Rome, placed itself in fact once more at the standpoint of Jerome, as distinguished from that of Augustine. Even to the second half of the present century the so-called Apocrypha-controversy was continued in Germany; and it is on this account of importance to devote further consideration to the grounds upon which the Confession of our Church, as of other Reformed Churches, has maintained this distinction.

2. On the one side the Confession of Faith [of the Church of the Netherlands] permits that "these writings may indeed be read, and instruction derived therefrom, in so far as they are in harmony with the Canonical books." A like spirit is breathed by Luther, expressed in the superscription upon this part of his translation of the Bible, and in his later declaration, that they may be read "*ad morum ædificationem et confirmationem fidelium*" (not "*fidei*"). And this with justice—for they certainly fill up the gap between the Old Testament and the New, afford striking proofs of God's care for His people, complete the history of the preparation for Christ's appearing, and contain excellent lessons of morality. But at the same time it is disputed that they have "the power and authority to confirm a single article of faith or of religion, much less to the diminution of the authority of the other sacred books." Consistently with this view, in the authorised translation of Holland, these books are not placed between those of the Old and those of the New Testament, but only after the latter, and with the addition of a word of caution. And this also will be seen to be not without justice. when we place both in the light of history.

3. For it is clear that the Palestinean Jews from the very first excluded the Apocryphal books from their Canon, and it is not probable that the Alexandrine Jews favoured in this respect a different view. One or two dubious traces of their use excepted, we find in the Scriptures of the New Testament no single appeal, or even reference, to this part of the literature. Our Lord cites the Canonical books of the Old Testament as a well-compacted whole,[1] but never alludes to the Apocrypha; and just as little do the Apostles, however frequently, for the rest, they employ the Greek translation. The opinion of the earliest Church also is not favourable to the Apocryphas; and the supposition of some Roman Catholic Theologians, that the Apostles gave to the newly founded Churches, along with the books of the Old Testament, these books, too, is at least unproved. Among the later Jews, finally, we discover a growing antipathy for the Deutero-canonical writings; doubtless in part from dislike to the profane language in which they are written, but at the same time from a sense of their less high value.

[1] Matt. xxiii. 35.

4. And then as to their contents: that a great part of these books cannot claim a purely historical character, is universally acknowledged. The third and fourth books of Maccabees were not even mentioned at Trent, and that of Judith had been already declared by Luther to be a fable. Regarded from a moral point of view, the book of Wisdom and that of Jesus Sirach (Ecclesiasticus) unquestionably contain much that is beautiful, but they owe it especially to the imitation of Solomon's wisdom, which, however, they scarcely equal, and certainly do not surpass. As concerns their religious character, they cannot by any means be regarded as the pure expression of the genuine Israelitish Theocratic spirit, but contain, on the contrary, not a few heterogeneous elements. The writers dwell in great part upon a glorious past, without furnishing an essentially new or entirely pure doctrine for the present or future. Especially are we struck with the almost entire absence of anything like a Christologic element, properly so called. One or two scattered allusions excepted, no single new link is added to the chain of the Messianic expectation. We hear only feeble echoes of ancient prophetic voices, but no new ones; the creative age of the national religious life has been superseded by the purely reproductive one. Finally, even as to their form, these writings stand far below the bulk of the Canonical writings; the animated language of original poetry is wanting, and the tone of inspiration has given place to that of calm reflection. If we add all this together, we find ourselves justified in speaking of a difference, not only in degree, but in kind, between the Canonical writings and the Apocrypha.

5. Much lower even than the last-named books stand the so-called Pseudepigrapha of the Old Testament, while upon the Apocryphal Gospels and Acts of the New Testament no more favourable judgment can be pronounced. It is true we cannot deny all value whatever to these last. They have, on the contrary, a significance partly historical, partly apologetical, and only from the Naturalistic standpoint could any one find the courage to speak here of a secondary myth-formation, after the first of the Canonical Gospels. He, however, who judges impartially will very soon discover that he is here moving in a wholly different circle of thought from that of the consecrated soil. Certainly the writers are under the influence, not merely of a boundless craving for the miraculous, but also of a strong desire to fill up all the gaps in the Evangelical history, and to exalt the mother of our Lord in an extravagant manner. What wonder that single honest doubters have been brought to a believing acknowledgment of the truth of the Apostolic Gospel, precisely by a comparison with it of these products of the ancient Christian imagination?

6. The distinction above maintained between the Canonical and the Apocryphal writings is dogmatically of great importance. On the one hand, because it justifies in the most natural way all that has been before said concerning the providential origin of the Canon; but also, on the other hand, because it demonstrates afresh the absolute necessity for a careful critical investigation according to a fixed principle. The Scripture is shown to be *Sacred* in proportion as, whether clearly or by implication, it testifies of, and points to, Christ; while the entire absence of the prophetic Christologic element in itself degrades an otherwise useful and important

writing to the class of the profane. Christ remains the touchstone of Biblical criticism (comp. § xxxvi 10), yet not merely the Pauline Christ—which was perhaps the one-sidedness of Luther—but Christ, as far as possible, contemplated on *all* sides, and in all His fulness. For such a criticism as has received the baptism of the Spirit the essential difference between Canonical and Apocryphal will, after a temporary obscuration, ever afresh come to the light.

Comp. GIESELER *Was heisst. Apocryphisch*, in the *Studien u. Kritiken.* (1829); KEIL, *Hist. Crit. Intr. to Apocryphas of O. T.* (1861); the article of OEHLER, *Canon of the O. T.*, in Herzog, *R. E.* vii., p. 260, *sqq.*, with the literature there adduced; C. TISCHENDORF, *De Evang. Apocr. origine et usu* (Society of the Hague, 1851); HOFMAN, in Herzog, *R. E.* xii.; J. J. VAN OOSTERZEE, *Life of Jesus*, i., § 15; *Christology*, i., p. 495, *sqq.*, ii., p. 486, *sqq.*

POINTS FOR INQUIRY.

Further illustration and explanation of the varying standpoint of the Christian Church of earlier and later times in regard to the Apocryphas of the Old Testament.—Comparison of the judgment in the Confessional Standards of the different Churches of the Reformation.—The present state of the question.—The historical, moral, and religious value of the Apocryphas of the Old Testament.—Which are the Pseudepigrapha of the Old Testament, and the Apocryphas of the New?—Is it possible, even from the Naturalistic standpoint, rightly to defend the distinction between the Canonical and Apocryphal writings?—What significance has this distinction for Bibliology and for the whole of Christian Dogmatics?

SECTION XXXVIII.—ITS CHARACTER.

As well regarded as a whole, as in its particular parts, the Holy Scriptures of the Old and New Testament display a preponderating *historic* character. The Revelation of Salvation comes to us in an historical form, of which the Bible is the depository, and Christ the centre. The credibility of the sacred history—*fides humana, Axiopistia*—is on this account a question of life and death for the Christian belief in revelation; and must be made apparent by means of an historico-critical investigation. In maintaining this credibility, it is of importance, especially in our time, to proceed from the well-authenticated contents of the New Testament, thence to look back upon the domain of the Old, and to judge of each part of the history, not only in itself, but above all in connexion with the great and glorious whole.

1. After the Essential Contents, Origin, and Extent of Holy Scripture,

we must now take into consideration its Character, properly so called. That character is no other than that of the Saving Revelation itself, of which it is the record. If we had to express in a single word what the Bible properly speaking is, we should be able to choose no better than this: *the Bible is, before and above all other things,* HISTORY. We naturally do not mean that the Bible has, as its contents, nothing else than the historical narratives: but that, regarded as a whole, it fully deserves the name of an historical memorial; for even the didactic, poetic, prophetic parts may be brought into natural connection with this historic whole. The Psalms, for example, belong to the history of the inner life of David and others; the Prophetic writings, to the history of the Theocracy under the reign of particular kings; the Pauline epistles, to the history of the Apostolic Church. Thus the historic character of the whole dominates the sum of the particular parts; and while the history of the Old Testament leads us as by the hand of God to Christ, that of the New leads us as by the hand of Christ to God. Yea, as Holy Scripture in the beginning speaks of life in an earthly Paradise, so it reveals to us at the end a heavenly Paradise in the faintly glimmering distance: the golden circle returns at its close to its point of departure. Between these two Paradises the history of the Kingdom of God develops itself in different phases, in ever more majestic proportions, and the end is only then when is heard the word: "It is *done!*"[1]

2. How admirably this its historic character renders the Bible adapted to become the vehicle of God's Revelation, is well-nigh self-evident. Let any one compare in this respect the Koran with the Scriptures of the Old and the New Testament. The Bible has been termed the great lesson-book of humanity; it can be so solely by virtue of this its peculiar character. Precisely because Holy Scripture contains such a number of highly remarkable facts, has it also become the fruitful mother of the highest ideas. It thereby reproduces the Saving Revelation, as it were, before the eye of every one, and gives us not only to hear of it, but also to contemplate it, to live it through once more, and *precisely in this way* to understand it better.

3. If—as surrounded by a circle of facts—we ask after the great and unchangeable centre, this can be no other than Christ, the historical Christ as—in contradistinction from the mere ideal one of Modern philosophy—we emphatically name Him. We call Him the centre of sacred history, not because each particular circumstance stands in immediate relation to Him, but because this history in its totality unceasingly points to Him, or then again proceeds immediately from Him. The Christ lies potentially in the history of Paradise, as the oak lies potentially in the acorn. To bring about His appearing, Israel is separated, guided, formed, chastened, redeemed. Ever more clear does the Messianic hope become in the course of the ages. Finally, He Himself comes; a host of heralds precedes Him, a cloud of witnesses follows Him. In one word, there is not a point in this circle, from which a line may not be drawn terminating at last in this centre. The Bible is a Christologic book, a biography of the Christ on an

---

[1] Γέγονε, Rev. xxi. 6, "Het is *geschied;*" with an allusion to the word "*Geschiedenis,*" *history*. This paranomasia is also preserved in the German.

immeasurable scale. Its testimony of salvation is as a symphony of the most varied tones, but of all of which He is the key-note. All truth is here concealed within the covering of a Fact, and the Fact of facts concentrates itself in an historical Person.

4. The high importance of the examination as to the credibility of the Biblical documents is from this standpoint self-evident. If it were established on good grounds that the Bible relates anything as a fact of Revelation, which had an existence only in the imagination of the narrator, we could no longer revere it as a trustworthy document of Divine revelation. Hence the powerful efforts which have been made by the Apologetes of earlier and later times to establish—next to the authenticity and integrity—especially the *Axiopistia* of the sacred Scriptures. No doubt, in this case also, that which is good has been now and then overdone, and the distinction, made wisely and according to truth by the older Theologians, between historical and saving faith, has been too much lost sight of. But this one-sidedness must not lead us to the opposite error, into which they fall who—we had almost said, "with a light heart"—assert that the Christian faith is absolutely independent of the results of historico-critical investigation. At least, if by the Christian faith is meant the believing acknowledgment of the Supernatural character of Christianity, and of the Divine dignity of Christ, this assertion is in our estimation altogether *untrue.* We can here only repeat and insist upon what we have before said (§ 32, iii. 1) against a sharp line of separation between ideas and facts. He who dissevers Christianity from its historic basis, fails therein in a most melancholy way to recognise its character as a Revelation, and with all his might plays into the hand of Naturalism. No doubt, "to love God and one's neighbour were true religion, even though not a single miracle had ever taken place;" but it remains a question, wherefore he who applies himself with all his power to accomplish this duty, yet claims for himself and those who are like-minded the name of *Christian;* and this question itself calls forth an historical examination as to the person of Christ and the origin of Christianity. But Christianity proclaims itself not only as the historical manifestation of true Religion in a more or less exalted person, it appears as the *Revelation* of a directly Divine plan of *Salvation,* a thought of Redemption embodied in a number of facts. "Not as tare and tret to nett weight is the Christian history related to the ideas, so that we must subtract the one to obtain the naked *facit;* but as body and soul, where to dissect and cut is to kill" (Tholuck). Or, we may say, fact and idea stand to each other as the alabaster lamp to the light which is therein placed and enkindled. Take the light away, and the beauty fades; break in pieces the vase, and the light is extinguished with the first gust of wind: combined, the lighted lamp presents to you the image of the history of Salvation. Distinction is necessary, but separation fatal; the so-called religion of Jesus, which forms the *residuum* after the above-named process, is, properly speaking, no other than that which already was written before His coming, though then less legibly, in every human heart, and which, without any special revealing *act* of God, has come forth most clearly in Jesus, so far, at least, as we can yet trace. We have already amply shown what becomes of all Christian faith, yea, of all Religion,

as soon as the facts in the history of Salvation are cast overboard as so much useless ballast. It is therefore a perverted mode of proceeding to look down upon the Apologetic defence of the historic credibility of the sacred writers, as the fruit of Arminian or Socinian one-sidedness; and equally unreasonable to raise loud tones of complaint about the tediousness and difficulty of an examination such as is indispensably requisite for the attaining of this end. "*Que d'hommes entre Dieu et moi!*" ("What a multitude of persons between God and myself!") Not a single one, if need be, is our answer, where the great vital question is at stake, but, naturally, not a few where the Theologian is called upon to justify his confession, "We have not followed cunningly devised fables." [2]

5. The required examination must be conducted in the way of objective as well as subjective criticism. (Comp. p. 131.) Before anything else, the question whether the sacred writers could really know the truth and wished to tell it must be answered. He who looks down upon this mode of proceeding as antiquated and unscientific, forgets that it is required by the nature of the case, and is withal eminently adapted to the end in view. But then, with the criticism of the witnesses, must that of the narrative go hand in hand, and the one as well as the other be conducted as impartially as possible. Absolutely impartial is no one in dealing with this matter; this is admitted with praiseworthy frankness by the Apostle of "*Voraus-setzungs-losigkeit*" (freedom from presupposition) himself.[3] But yet it can and may be demanded that one should proceed from no arbitrary presuppositions, but should as far as possible keep mind and spirit open to receive without prepossession impressions of truth. He who chooses as his starting-point the dogmatic hypothesis, that one Biblical narrative cannot possibly conflict with another, is equally as prejudiced as he who allows his historical examination to be guided by the philosophic premiss that miracles are impossible. In the former case, one will violently distort the history; in the latter, arbitrarily limit it; in either case one does not investigate a history, but manufacture it; one does not criticise, but construct. The result of the investigation is, then, naturally to confirm the given premises, but precisely on this account to excite and justify distrust. It is as with the Alchymists, who, after a complicated chemical process, actually had the good fortune to discover at the bottom of the cup gold, which *they themselves had before placed there.* "When the principle of the judgment is a prejudice, then the end can only be the full revealing of the beginning" (Marheinecke).

6. It seems more logical to begin our investigation with the history of the New Testament; not merely because this is for Christians of the greatest importance, but because in this way, at the same time, a firm standpoint is gained for the right estimation of the Old Testament. We have in this investigation, in the first place, to do with the personality of the sacred narrators, and to ask *who* and *what* they were. The answer to these questions is in a high degree satisfactory. Our four Canonical Gospels are

---

[2] Compare B. TER HAAR, *Oratio de Rel. Chr. indole historicâ, hodie nimie spretâ*, Traj. ad Rhen., 1859.

[3] D. F. STRAUSS, *Leben Jesu*, pop. edn. (1864), p. xiii.

no so-called private writings, which have suddenly made their appearance out of some book-collection or another, but composed by well-known persons, designed at once for public use, and openly read in circles of men who were familiar with the main contents of the Gospels as handed down by oral tradition. The writers were contemporaries and friends of the Lord; accurately acquainted, as is manifest from a number of minute traits, with the scene they describe, and the course of events; some of them eye- and ear-witnesses, others in possession of important documentary evidence, for the sifting of which they were fully competent and qualified.[4] We know what a storm of voices is raised against this statement, but we know also that not a little which is proclaimed, apparently without prepossession, in the name of *Criticism*, may rather be called the fruit of well-directed *Tactics*, the real object of which cannot be doubtful to any one. It is manifest that Dogmatics has no small interest in the investigation still proceeding as to the origin and relationship of the accounts given in the Gospels, and must accept on its side what in this domain is really *proved*. Judging, however, by the light of history, it would seem Christian Dogmatics may await the future with some degree of calmness, the more so since in the worst case it can afford to lose something, without being deprived of that which is indispensable for the maintenance of its essential contents. These would always be safely covered, even though only a single one of the Gospels should come forth unscathed out of the fiery ordeal through which they are passing.

If we inquire further *of what kind* these our reporters were, a glance at their intellect, their spirit, and life, suffices to strengthen our confidence. Their *intellect*—that of a Luke or a Paul for instance—was perfectly competent to distinguish truth from fiction, and yet their genius was not great enough to invent a fiction like this.[5] They themselves more than once declare that they did not understand the Lord,[6] but in this very way make manifest how objectively and faithfully they relate what they have seen and heard. Their *spirit*, as it reflects itself in their writings, was upright, truth-loving, and devout. So far are they removed from a craving after the miraculous, that they leave wholly unused many an opportunity for embellishment, which a romancer would unquestionably have seized, and frequently speak of miraculous deeds in passing, without describing them as we should have expected.[7] Frankly and without constraint they relate also facts and failures, which by no means redounded to the credit of themselves or of the circle to which they belonged. Clearly their heart is filled with a love to Jesus, whereby their spiritual vision is strengthened for the contemplation of His greatness, and His words and deeds are indelibly imprinted on their memories. Their *life*, finally, so far as we know it, produces a highly favourable moral impression. With the sacrifice of honour, advantage, and repose, it is consecrated wholly to the cause of truth, and is—in the case of not a few of them—sealed with the testimony of their blood. These proofs, we admit, are by no means new, but just as little is the gainsaying of unbelief; and what is ages

---

[4] Luke i. 1—4.
[5] Acts iv. 13.
[6] Mark ix. 10; John xii. 16.
[7] Matt. ix. 35; John ii. 23.

old, has not on that account become entirely antiquated. No one deserves the name of unreasoning or credulous who attaches importance to these proofs. So much the less so since the narratives of the Gospels themselves, when duly examined, both as regards *form* and *contents*, augment the confidence already awakened. For—

7. The *form* of the historic accounts of the New Testament is characterised frequently by a *simplicity*, which almost irresistibly reminds us of the maxim: "*simplex sigillum veri;*" by an *exactness*—ἀκρίβεια, comp. Luke i. 3—in the indicating of time, place, and circumstances, which can be explained only as springing from the consciousness of perfect good faith,[8] while for some instances of this kind no conceivable ulterior end can be assigned; by a *lifelike character*, finally, a *naïveté* and freshness of tone, which must *either* be the fruit of life, *or* must show the writers such consummate deceivers as to be less objects for criticism than for police surveillance. "There are no reflections on the history, but the facts themselves in full reality before us; it is the history itself; it speaks to us, and we are placed in the midst of this great history" (Luthardt).—And, as concerns the *contents*, it is true these differ not a little from other historic documents. On the other hand, however, we cannot but at once observe that we find ourselves here—as is manifest even from the indisputable moral impression which this history makes—upon very different ground from that of every-day life; upon that of *Sacred* history, the history of Salvation, which must be measured by a much higher standard than that of ordinary life. The effacing of the line of demarcation between Sacred and profane, between the ordinary and the Supernatural, with which Modern Theology is chargeable, inevitably renders the Gospel history not merely a fiction, but also an insoluble enigma. We would refer the reader to what has been before said on the question of miracles (§ 32, i. 6). He who occupies a Theistic standpoint, and in consequence admits the possibility of miracles, can hardly deny that *this* miraculous history breathes an *exalted spirit* which is found nowhere else, and at the same time is marked by a *harmony* between the whole and the parts, which bears the infallible stamp of inner truthfulness. Of one part, at least, which manifestly bears the character too of publicity, the fabrication so soon after the supposed inducement thereto, may be called, not only improbable, but utterly impossible. Take the case of the appearing to more than five hundred brethren at once, the repeated miracle of feeding the multitude, the day of Pentecost with its signs and results. Even the, in some sense varying, presentation of the circumstances of the same event—of the resurrection of the Lord, for instance—is an argument rather in favour of than against the veracity of these accounts, and can, even in the most unfavourable case, only render one or other of the circumstances doubtful, but not on that account render the whole entirely incredible.

8. Touching the *words* of the Lord as recorded in the Gospels, it must be observed that while it is true their credibility *as to the letter* cannot be raised above all doubt—since they were recorded in another language than that in which they were uttered by Him—yet, at the same time, there is

Compare, for example, Luke iii. 1, 2. [8] *E.g.*, John ii. 6; xxi. 11.

every ground to speak of an *essentially* faithful preservation of them as to contents and tendency. Not to speak again of the personality of the sacred writers, it must be borne in mind how, as well the contents as the form of these words united in itself everything that could permanently hold its place in the memory; how they were frequently most intimately associated with deeds or events of which the impression was never to be effaced; how, finally, the issue served not merely to explain and confirm them, but also to stamp them more deeply upon the soul. In proportion as the reverence of the Apostles for the Master was more deeply rooted, must they certainly have felt less freedom to place in His lips anything of their own; while in addition to this the constant repetition of the same testimony must the more easily impart to it a stereotyped character.[10]—However much that is enigmatical His *deeds* also may in many respects display, yet greater at the same time is the number of traces of truth and of genuineness about them. We hear how even His enemies render an undesigned testimony to His power of working miracles,[11] while His friends speak of it as of things generally acknowledged.[12] Now and then these acts present something strange—*e.g.*, the interview with the Syro-Phenician mother, and the blasting of the barren fig-tree—but this very feature renders the fabrication of such an account only the more improbable. Ever do we see the Lord, in relation to miracles also, consistent with Himself, even when He refuses to perform them, or shrouds them in the veil of secrecy.—And then, finally, as far as the *events* of His life are concerned, they are assuredly absolutely incredible, if we see in Him nothing more than simply a child of Adam. But precisely this compels us to look upon this history in the light of His own utterances, and to take into account the impression which His whole personality awakens.—Then again there falls sufficient light upon the history of the Apostolic age, regarded as the history of the revelation of the glorified Christ. (Comp. § 32, i. 9.) It is at least indisputable that the credibility of the accounts given in the Acts is supported by a number of valid grounds, and is apparent to every one who is not incurably smitten with Miraculophobia. The second book of Luke is by no means a work of special pleading (*Tendenz-schrift*), composed with the particular aim of reconciling, by means of a one-sided combination of accounts, in great part invented, the Paulinism with the Petrinism of the Early Church; but an historic document, drawn partly from trustworthy sources, partly from personal observation of the facts there related—which is confirmed on countless points by the Apostolic Epistles, and in manifold details affords the most surprising indications of strictest accuracy. As well the so-called Timothy-hypothesis, as the Silas-hypothesis, is already consigned to the region of history. The proof of Luke's identity, and of his presence in many of the scenes described, is continually manifest, especially in the second half of the book; and here again comparison with the Apocryphal Acts of the Apostles brings forward in a striking manner the value of the Canonical ones. Taken as a whole, the

---

[10] Compare, as far as John especially is concerned, our work, *The Gospel of John* [English translation].

[11] John xi. 47; Matt. xv. 1; xxvii. 42.

[12] Acts ii. 22; x. 38.

two writings of Luke agree as well together, as the historic testimony of the Synoptical Gospels is supported by the Gospel, the Epistles, and the Apocalypse of John.

9. For these reasons, which can here be only mentioned, we continue to maintain without hesitation the trustworthiness of the New Testament history generally, while— in regard to each particular account—so far as is needful and possible, a continued investigation must be made, how far, in that particular case, one may further build upon the basis laid down. It is true we do not deceive ourselves as to the importance to be attached to this mode of proof, by those who proceed from entirely opposite principles. Between mathematical and historical certainty the distance is sufficiently appreciable to leave open a pretty wide field for doubt. Even where it is supported by valid proofs for the merely natural intellect, the Extraordinary increases in improbability with every age that has passed since it intervened; because the number of the ordinary facts in contradiction with it has gone on steadily increasing, while, on the other hand, the extraordinary series of facts is evermore retiring into the background. This, so long as no new proofs are discovered, is but natural; but, on the other hand, we have need to be emphatically reminded that there exists a criticism against which no single historic account is secure. Is there *one* fact of the past which cannot be disputed with the appearance of reason, by one who once for all is resolved to doubt? Is not this polemic able to put on such a show of science, as to be in a position to calculate on the alliance of all who have a spiritual affinity?[13] Yea, is there, properly speaking, ever anything which cannot be contradicted with a so-called scientific earnestness? Have there been no astronomers who were Atheists? No philosophers who believed not in the sacredness of duty? And is the assertion too strong, that the attempt would be made even to deny axioms, if only some critics had a preponderating interest in doing so? The question, therefore, reduces itself to this: not whether anything is doubted in earnest, but whether it is justly doubted? and this, after all that has been said, must here be denied. *He who will successfully dispute the credibility of the Gospel history, must at least prove that the legitimate charges against it exceed, in importance and weight, the positive grounds in its favour. Until now this proof has not been given.*

10. Much more difficult than the defence of the historic credibility of the Scriptures of the New Testament, is that of the documents of the Old. Here also we can speak of the parts, only after the true standpoint has been gained for the contemplation of the whole. In the case of the documents of the kingdom of God, no less than of the book of nature, the words of Pliny find their application: "*Naturæ rerum vis atque majestas in omnibus momentis fide caret, si quis modo partes ejus ac non totum complectatur animo.*" For the truth and Divine character of the whole, the Christian faith has sufficient guarantees, (*a*) in the unequivocal and well-established testimony

---

[13] See "*The Great Fire of London, freely dealt with according to the principles of Modern Rationalism,*" a German article in PIPER'S *Beweis des Glaubens* (1869), p. 473 and following.

of Jesus and the Apostles;[14] (*b*) in the existence and rise of the Christian Church, which could spring up only out of the soil of Israelitism; (*c*) in the religion, the character, and the present condition of the people of Israel, who are comprehensible only as the chosen people to whom God specially revealed Himself; (*d*) in the testimony of profane history, which, taken along with the discoveries of later times, brings out in many respects the accuracy of the sacred narrative.[15]

Regarding a great many particulars, questions arise, even concerning the origin and collection of the Israelitish documents, in the treatment of which Dogmatics, as such, naturally can take no part. Upon good grounds, however, may it concede to Moses, as the earliest historian of his nation, a higher character for credibility than is allowed to him by the miracle-dreading criticism of the Anti-supranaturalistic school. That he was able, that he wished, yea, that he was constrained, to speak the truth in regard to those things which he had himself witnessed, is equally as certain as that it must be possible for him to draw from trustworthy sources the knowledge of what had before happened. Even for the credibility of the essential contents of the first eleven chapters of Genesis, arguments of no small force may be adduced from the domain of historical, physical, and philosophical science.[16] The later writers also are evidently well-instructed, devout, genuinely Theocratic men, so little given to partiality that they relate even that which does not in the least degree redound to the credit of the most illustrious names. Sometimes they refer the reader to the sources they have made use of,[17] and show thereby, at least, that they dread no inquiry or investigation. Not seldom here also is the one testimony confirmed and supported in the most surprising way by the other; as, for instance, the contents of the historical books by those of the poetical and prophetic books. Throughout, the form of the earliest narratives is characterised by a freshness, a simplicity, and a *naïveté* which gives one as it were to taste and touch the reality; the garb of the Chronicles is certainly just as little adapted, as the nomenclature of the Genealogy, to a romantic or legendary narrative. And, as concerns the contents, there are, above all, two peculiarities which, in our estimation, cast an important weight into the scale in favour of their credibility. On the one hand, the trenchant contrast between the whole spirit of this history, and the obdurate and almost incurable natural disposition of the people. In diametrical opposition to that which we elsewhere meet with, for instance among the Greeks and Romans, here the natural character is not flattered, but reproved, opposed, and corrected, in a way which can be explained only as arising from the overpowering influence of truth and of conscience. And then, besides, appears the wondrously beautiful unity of plan and controlling thought in this history—a unity which is apparent at every turn, and even in the minutest particulars, and which renders it, for us at least, impossible to see in its course anything else than a gradual

---

[14] Matt. xix. 4—6; xxiii. 35; 1 Cor. x. 1—11; Heb. xi; and many other places.

[15] Compare, for instance, J. J. VAN OOSTERZEE, *Nineveh en de H. Schrift*, Rott. (1855).

[16] Compare P. HOFSTEDE DE GROOT, *Voorl. over de opvoed. des Menschd.*, i. (1847), pp. 129, *sqq.*; AUBERLEN, *Divine Revelation*, i. (1862), pp. 174, *sqq.* [of the Dutch edition.]

[17] Josh. x. 13; 1 Kings xiv. 19.

realisation of a redemptive thought of God Himself. Yea, truly "at many a *particular* I am again and again perplexed; but these perplexities again are ever triumphantly overcome by the power of the *whole*. Israel alone is, through all the course of its history, *progressive*, and its history a continual act of God in word, calling, miracles" (Gunning).

11. He who has in this way gained an eye for the whole, is not on that account released from the obligation of justifying the dogmatic use of each part of this history against the manifold opposition which is heard ever more loud in its clamour against it. Even from the Supranaturalistic standpoint, difficulties will present themselves, derived *partly* from the domain of natural science, *partly* from that of profane history and chronology, *partly* from the philosophic mode of thinking, *partly*, finally, from Christian Theology, especially its Dogmatics and Ethics. Even the enumerating, much more the solution, of these difficulties lies far beyond the limits of our plan; therefore this little only by way of putting on a right track (*oriënteering*) on this fiercely contested ground. Where Natural Philosophy awakens doubts as to many parts of the Old Testament history, the Theologian has above all things to ask whether the difficulty is derived from that which is already universally *proved* to the conviction of all, or simply from a more or less probable hypothesis. In the latter case, to wait is the duty of prudent science; in the former, the peculiar standpoint of the sacred writer may at least, among other things, be taken into consideration, and the same freedom be allowed to his scientific views as faith allows to itself, not in opposition to, but side by side with, a well-established science. Only, it must never be forgotten that the Scripture of the Old Testament was never designed to answer questions which could be answered equally well, or better, by the investigations of science; but to enlighten us precisely upon those points upon which the latter must, and, if it is wise, certainly will, remain silent (comp. § xvi. 8).—Where Sacred and Profane History and Chronology contradict each other, an exact and impartial comparison of all the *data* will have to determine on which side the trut hlies, and then certainly in some cases many a one will defer as yet his final decision. More than one striking example of palpable errors being dished up as truth, in a tone of high authority, by assailants of the Sacred History, impels to a greater degree of cautiousness; though it cannot be denied, on the other hand, that sometimes on the side of its defenders, in regard to highly complicated points of controversy, the cry of victory has been raised too soon. Notably, Egyptology affords in our time a field of investigation, of which the issues, among other causes, on account of the very tendencies and results of its most renowned scholars, cannot even be approximately computed. In the meantime the study of ancient Egypt has already contributed not a little to the confirmation of the earliest history, so that a Bunsen could declare: "The account of Joseph leads us, even in minute particulars, to see in this tradition an historic character which surpasses all the expectations of believers in the Bible." Where, on many another point, the desired harmony is for the present wanting, one must for the time being rest content with the word of another Egyptologist, "that we have not to look in the Old Testament for any chronological revelations as to the outward details of human history; but only for the history of God's doings among

men, and His commandments, as they have been proclaimed, to the blessing of the nations, by the mouth of the Prophets and other holy men, in the mode of expression natural according to the knowledge of that time" (Lepsius).—How sometimes a chronological difficulty in the Old Testament, which has been a stone of stumbling, may be removed by the application of textual criticism, is apparent, for instance, from 2 Sam. xv. 7.

That a philosophic mode of thinking, even when it is not startled at the idea of a miracle, can still scarcely reconcile itself to some of the Old Testament accounts of miracles, need not above measure disturb us. The great question still remains, whether this mode of thinking protests against the grand fundamental conception from which the Scripture narrative proceeds, or merely against particular details. In the former case we can hardly come to an understanding with our opponents, since here there is a conflict of principles; in the latter, not seldom an accurate exegesis and thorough criticism will suffice to remove a stone of stumbling.[18] When the philosopher, on his side, is conscious of the rashness of a stout *à priori* negation, and the Theologian does not lose sight of the distinction between the demand of submission to God's Word and that of a slavish subjection to every letter of Scripture, then the two need not remain divided by any insuperable distance.—Christian Theology, finally, must never forget that while the Scriptures of the Old Testament are unquestionably the records of sacred history, they record a sacred history as yet by no means in its highest development. The better it is understood that here are preserved revelations, true indeed, but none the less provisional and imperfect, adapted to the childlike capacity of a long forgotten past, the less will Christian Dogmatics and Ethics rise against this part of the history with an inexorable protest on the lips. He who simply does not lose sight of the difference between the morning dawn and the noonday sun, who takes into consideration the difference between Eastern and Western ideas and customs, and who, above all, is mindful of the sound advice of Augustine: "*Distingue tempora, et concordabit Scriptura,*" will judge differently of many particulars in themselves strange, yea, will perhaps find in difficult places of the Old Testament so many more proofs of its hidden glory.[19]

12. The historic character of the Scriptures of the Old and the New Testament is for Christian Dogmatics satisfactorily maintained, when—in opposition to every renewed assault—it is clearly apparent that they are the sufficiently trustworthy documents of God's Saving Revelation in Christ, who forms their centre. Not belief in the Scriptures, however becoming this also is, but belief in the Christ, of whom the Scriptures testify, is still and always the only way of salvation. How high a value we with the greatest reason attach to this their testimony will be apparent from the investigation now to be instituted.

---

[18] Compare, for example, CHRISTLIEB, *l. c.* pp. 367—382, the chapter on *Some Scripture Miracles which have been especially assailed.*

[19] See the *Appendix* of LANGE in his Commentary on Genesis, "*On the so-called difficult places of the O. T.,*" etc.

Compare on the credibility of the Gospel history in general, besides the well-known writings of LARDNER, DA COSTA, and others, above all, A. THOLUCK, *Glaubwürdigk. der Ev. Gesch.* (1838); H. J. HOLTZMANN, *Die Synopt. Evang., ihr Ursprung und geschichtl. Charakter* (1863); A. EBRARD, *Wissenschaftl. Kritik der Evang. Geschichte* [English translation].—On that of the Acts of the Apostles, J. J. VAN OOSTERZEE'S prize treatise (Soc. of the Hague, 1840); LECHLER, *Das Apost. und nach-Ap. Zeitalter*, 2nd edn. (1857); E. DE PRESSENSÉ, *L'Ecole critique et les Apôtres*, against Rénan (1866); C. J. TRIP, *Paulus der Ap. des Herrn, nach der A. G.* (Soc. Hag., 1867).—On the Axiopistia of the O. T. history, KURTZ, *History of the Old Covenant* [English translation]; HENGSTENBERG, *Gesch. d. Reiches Gottes im A. B.*, i. (1869), pp. 30—58; P. HOFSTEDE DE GROOT, *De Godsd. van Israel*, etc., W. in L., 1870, p. 65 and following; F. GODET, *La Sainteté de l'Ancien Testament* (1869); TRAUTMANN, *Das Evangel. Schriftprincip, und die Bibelkritik*, in the *Beweis des Glaubens* (1872), p. 1, *sqq.*; L. FÜLLER, *Das A. T., der Zweifel und dem Anstoss gegenüber* (1870).

POINTS FOR INQUIRY.

In what sense, and to what extent, must a definite historic character be claimed for the Old Testament?—To what extent is the Christian faith dependent or not on the results of historical criticism?—Must the demonstration of the *fides humana* of Holy Scripture precede that of the *fides Divina*, or follow it?—Discussion of the principal objections raised by modern criticism against the credibility of the Gospel, in so far as these criticisms are of dogmatic importance.—Of those raised against the historic accounts in the Acts and Epistles.—Against those of the historical books of the Old Testament.—Inseparable connection between the maintenance of these last and of those of the New Testament.—What in this domain may be, if necessary, safely surrendered, without anything essential being lost?—What, on the other hand, must we defend and hold fast with all our might?

SECTION XXXIX.—ITS INSPIRATION.

The recognition of the trustworthiness of the historical testimony of Holy Scripture justifies at the same time the belief in its Divine origin, confessed by the Christian Church in all ages. The men of God, whose word is preserved to us in the books of the Old and the New Testament, were notably, each one in his measure, filled above others with the Holy Ghost, and their testimony in regard to the truths of salvation—those recorded in their writings, not less than their oral utterances—thus manifests the character of an infallible testimony of God. The Theopneustia of Scripture in its totality (*Γραφὴ Θεοπνευστος*, 2 Tim. iii. 16) is the natural consequence of this higher inspiration and guidance of the Writer; and must, while we reject every mechanical theory, be so conceived of, that full justice may be rendered as well to the unmistakably Divine as to the truly human character of the Bible, and that the two conceptions of *Holy Scripture* and *Word of God* must be on the one hand duly distinguished; on the other, presented in their higher unity and their proper connection.

The transition from the investigation as to the historical character of Holy Scripture to that as to its Divine origin, must not be made without a word of self-defence in regard to an objection frequently repeated and apparently well founded. Where, namely, we rest the doctrine of the Inspiration of Scripture upon that of its historic trustworthiness, we are accused of arguing in a vicious circle. "The Scripture utters the word of God, *because* it is inspired; and *that* it is inspired, you prove by an appeal to the Scripture." It is even so; and how could it possibly be otherwise? But when we appeal to the Scripture itself to bring into full light its Theopneustia, *we appeal to it exclusively as a trustworthy historic document.* We thus reason: if once its trustworthiness is established, then also the words, facts, etc., with which we shall further have to do, are indisputably true. If that is so, then we ask yet further: what is to be legitimately deduced therefrom in regard to the person and activity of those by whom the Saving Revelation was recorded for us in writing? Thus, without moving in a circle, we ascend gradually from the credibility of the Holy Scriptures to the investigation as to their Divine character. In other words, we put the questions: Is there indeed good reason for speaking, in regard to the sacred writers, of an especial enlightenment and guidance by the Holy Spirit? And if so, what conception have we in consequence to form to ourselves of the Doctrine of the Inspiration of Scripture? It is here consequently a question of well-established *historic testimony* and of accurate *dogmatic distinctions*, in order that not only the *that* (the fact) but also the *how* (the mode) of the inspiration may be brought into a clear light.

I. 1. If in reviewing the series of *Testimonies* which are with justice adduced in favour of the doctrine of Theopneustia, we begin with the Scriptures of the New Testament, then above all things *the testimony of the Lord concerning His first ambassadors* claims our attention. Thus much is at once apparent, that He not only places His Apostles on a level with, but even exalts them above, the Prophets of the Old Covenant.[1] Extraordinary assistance is promised them, not merely when they have to vindicate their cause, which is that of the truth,[2] but also, in general, when they arise as witnesses of the Lord.[3] Particularly in the parting discourses recorded by John, He gives them the most positive promises in this respect.[4] The Holy Ghost is promised them to lead them into all the truth,[5] and thus to raise them in their preaching above all danger of error. The past He shall bring again to their mind: in relation to the pre-

---

[1] Matt. v. 12; xi. 11; John xx. 21.
[2] Matt. x. 19, 20.
[3] Luke xxiv. 49; Acts i. 5.
[4] John xiv. 16, 17, 26; xv. 26; xvi. 7–15.
[5] εἰς τὴν ἀλήθειαν πᾶσαν, John xvi. 13.

sent, He shall teach them all things in the spiritual domain, and shall also enlighten them in regard to the future of the Kingdom of God. This promise, symbolically repeated after the Lord's resurrection,[6] and actually fulfilled upon the day of Pentecost, is at the same time apparent in its effects, from the great change in the outward and inner life of the Apostles, and consequently offers a trustworthy point of commencement for our investigation.

2. *The testimony of the Apostles concerning themselves and their writings* is not less noteworthy. We naturally include among these Paul, who—called later by Jesus Himself—was placed on an equality with the other witnesses, and enlightened by special revelation.[7] In consequence of this he terms the Gospel which he preaches the Word of God, and asks for the written word the same reverence which he claims for the spoken.[8] He pronounces an anathema upon any one who should proclaim *another* Gospel,[9] and not for a single moment does he doubt his right to enjoin that which is becoming.[10] He allows no freedom to differ from his precepts; but, on the other hand, expects that the spiritual man will recognise therein the will of God,[11] while he ever distinguishes his personal opinions from that which he has to say in the name of the Lord.[12] The other Apostles also are conscious—at least in the solemn actions belonging to their office—of writing under the guidance of the Holy Ghost.[13] Here and there, there would seem to be present, as early as in the Apostolic Epistles, traces of the ranking of the New Testament writings upon a level with those of the Old.[14]

3. Since it is not possible to reject these utterances of the Apostolic self-consciousness as the fruit either of fanaticism or of deception, of great importance must the meaning be which we are to attach to *the testimony of the Lord and His Apostles to the Scriptures of the Old Covenant.* With an appeal to that which is written, does Jesus Himself enter upon the great work of His life,[15] come forth at His first proclamation,[16] continually afterwards proceed, and tread the path leading to His sufferings and His glorification.[17] That the Scripture cannot be broken, is for Him irrevocably certain,[18] and not, "What thinkest thou?" but, "How readest thou?" is His great question to the lawyer.[19] A commandment of Moses is for Him a command of God;[20] ignorance of the Scripture, in His estimation, the source of the most fatal error;[21] yea, no means of deliverance is any longer possible for him who rejects its testimony.[22] Not only the spirit, but even the letter of Scripture, is for Him sacred,[23] and as well to it as a whole,[24] as to its different parts,[25] does He render unequivocal testimony.[26]—Nor is it, again,

---

[6] John xx. 22.
[7] 1 Cor. ix. 1; Gal. i. 16.
[8] 2 Thess. ii. 13—15.
[9] Gal. i. 7, 8.
[10] Philem. 8.
[11] 1 Cor. xiv. 37.
[12] 1 Cor. vii. 25, 40.
[13] Acts xv. 28.
[14] 1 Tim. v. 18; 2 Pet. iii. 16.
[15] Matt. iv. 4.
[16] Luke iv. 16—22.
[17] Matt. xxvi. 54; Luke xxii. 37; xxiv. 27.
[18] John x. 35.
[19] Luke x. 26.
[20] Matt. xv. 3, 4.
[21] Matt. xxii. 29.
[22] Luke xvi. 29—31.
[23] Luke xvi. 17.
[24] Matt. xxiii. 35.
[25] Luke xxiv. 44.
[26] Comp. MERLE D'AUBIGNE, *L'Autorité des Ecritures*, etc. (1850).

otherwise with the Apostles: the words of the Prophets are for them words of God,[27] and without any reserve they base their proclamation of salvation upon the Scriptures of the Old Testament, which they manifestly regard as the fountain and test of the highest truth. On this account Paul warns his converts against being wise above that which is written,[28] and pays in a single sentence the highest tribute both to Timothy and to Holy Scripture.[29] Not less distinctly does he, in the last-named place, give us to understand that the whole Scripture of the Old Testament, regarded in its totality, is a writing inspired by God, and precisely on this account of many-sided utility (θεόπν. = ὑπὸ θεοῦ πεπνυμένη, *divinitus inspirata*). If he here indicates this its character only by a single word, our conception of the nature of this inspiration is in some measure simplified by a hint given in the (in our opinion genuine) second Epistle of Peter.[30] He makes mention there of a powerful impulse of the Holy Ghost, in consequence of which the men of God speak; and it is not difficult to divine in what light he desires we should regard the word written by them.[31]

4. *The testimony of the Scriptures of the Old Testament regarding themselves* is in entire harmony with this view. The prophets, as extraordinary spokesmen of God, demand obedience to their words, since they think, speak, act, and also—where necessary—write, under higher direction. Frequently there was added a Divine command to do so,[32] and even where this is not said in so many words, we may safely assume that, in an age so little inclined to writing, they did not take up the office of writer, except in obedience to a higher impulse of the heart. The Spirit, who lived in them expressed Himself also in their writings, and their writings consequently have no less value than their words. Joshua manifests the highest reverence for the book of the law of Moses, and enjoins this also upon others.[33] David finds the task of his life indicated in "the volume of the book;"[34] and for all God-fearing kings, the written law remains the "magna charta" of the kingdom.[35] Often the prophets distinctly refer to each other's oracles as being Divine words; Daniel consults the prophecy of Jeremiah, in order to trace out when the end of the captivity should be.[36] So also, in the other historical and moral writings of the Old Testament, we discover the evident impress of the religious, moral, and Theocratic spirit of their age: and when, finally, the Canon was closed (§ 36), to the exclusion of other writings, however important in themselves, we hear its constituent parts spoken of by Josephus[37] as Divine writings, from which no one might take away, and

---

27 Acts ii. 17; iv. 25.
28 1 Cor. iv. 6.
29 2 Tim. iii. 15, 16.
30 2 Pet. i. 20, 21.
31 Comp. C. SEPP, *Onderzoek naar de leer des N. V. aang. de H. SS. des O. V.* (1849), pp. 168, *sqq.*
32 Compare Exod. xxxiv. 27; Deut. xxxi. 19; Isaiah viii. 1; xxx. 8; Jer. xxxvi. 2; Ezek. xxiv. 2.
33 Joshua i. 8; xxiv. 26.
34 Psalm xl. 7.
35 Comp. 2 Kings xxii. 8, 9.
36 Dan. ix. 2.
37 *Contra Ap.* 1. 8.

to which no one might add, and for which the Jew was ready, if need be, even to die. A mode of regarding them in the main similar to this, we have already found in the Lord and His Apostles.

5. If we inquire as to *the testimony of the Christian Church* in regard to the Holy Scriptures in their totality, it is apparent that it has ever ascribed to them a sacred character, and has recognised the main contents of the Bible as God's own Word. Justin Martyr[38] regarded it as inconceivable that the Sacred Writers should have penned so much that is great and glorious, unless the Holy Ghost had—as the plectrum from the lyre—drawn forth from them such sweet tones; and in a like spirit others also very soon expressed themselves. It cannot be denied that at first the Scriptures of the Old Testament were much more frequently cited than those of the New, so long as the Canon of the latter was yet in some measure unsettled, and the stream of tradition was copiously flowing. Yet there are not wanting proofs of the high value at once attached to the Gospels and Epistles of the New Testament, by the Apostolic Fathers and others, who appealed by preference to these authorities.[39] Theophilus[40] comprises the writers of the Old and of the New Testament, without any limitation, under the one name of Πνευματοφόροι. Gradually we now hear the dogma of their absolute infallibility more nearly defined by Irenæus, Eusebius, Augustine, and others; and the words of the last-named writer, "*Nullum eorum auctorum scribendo aliquid errâsse, firmissime credam*," may be regarded as the expression of the prevailing view. Later we meet alternately with a more rigid and a more elastic theory with regard to them; but by no one is the Inspiration itself denied or disputed. After the Reformation—consistently with the whole system of the Reformed Church—the defence of this doctrine was undertaken with the greatest zeal. While we find in Luther many an expression in which it is taught in more free terms, Calvin, especially, emphatically proclaimed that the whole of Holy Scripture had no less an author than God Himself, appealing for confirmation of his assertion to the testimony of the Holy Ghost.[41] As opposed to the more lax view of the Roman Catholic Church on the one hand, and of the Arminians and Socinians on the other, orthodox Dogmatics defended the doctrine of the Theopneustia as its most precious palladium. By the Scholasticism of the seventeenth century it was defined and maintained (§ xxxvi. 2) in a way which could not fail to call forth manifold opposition, although as late as our own day this view—especially in French Switzerland—has, at least to a certain extent, found able champions (Gaussen, De Gasparin, and others). It is now pretty generally acknowledged that the mechanical form, in which—under the influence of a one-sided doctrinalism—the doctrine has hitherto been commonly presented, stands in absolute need of revisal; but, just as much, that the treasure must not be rejected on account of the frailty of the earthen vessels, in

[38] *Cohort. ad Gr.*, cap. 8.

[39] See, *e.g.*, the Epistle of Clem. Rom., *ad Corinth.*, cap 47; and the Ep. of Barnab., cap. 4, in fine. Comp. TISCHENDORF, *When were our Gospels written?* [Eng. ed.]

[40] *Ad Autol.*, anno 170—180.

[41] *Instit. Rel. Chr.*, i. 7, 4.

which to this day it is borne. In the midst of much wavering and opposition, there have by no means been wanting, even in recent times, efforts to place in a more satisfactory light the Divine origin of the Scripture, in connection with the idea of Revelation, and these efforts cannot cease to be made. Yea, *the whole series of testimonies received is in a peculiar manner supported by the wholly unique impression produced by the Bible itself upon every susceptible spirit, an impression, from the influence of which even professed unbelievers have not always been able to withdraw themselves.* He who will acknowledge in Holy Scripture no higher than a purely human character, comes into collision, not only with the Lord's own word and that of His witnesses, but also with the Christian consciousness of all ages, and is thereby placed entirely out of a position to explain in a satisfactory manner the inimitable dignity and powerful influence of this book.[42] Here consequently it is more a question of accurate definition than of the broader upholding of a fact, which in itself—considered as an indefinite generality—could scarcely by any possibility be gainsaid.

II. In speaking of the *How*, in regard to Inspiration, there is naturally presupposed belief in a personal God, and in a special Revelation, of which the Holy Scriptures are the repository. Nevertheless, even where this belief is present, the matter yet retains its darker side. It is impossible, after the course which the investigation on this point has taken since the seventeenth century, to rest content with the little which the Church Confession has definitely expressed on this point,[43] however convenient this might otherwise appear. Only too frequently has even the science of faith contented itself either with presupposing or with stating the fact of Inspiration—(or Theopneustia)—instead of bringing the form in which this fact is to be conceived to the greatest possible degree of clearness and certainty. We venture upon the endeavour to give an account of our opinion in a few propositions.

1. *The Theopneustia which must be attributed to the Scriptures of the Old Covenant* (2 Tim. iii. 16), *and, by a legitimate deduction, also to those of the New, is the natural consequence of the Theopneustia of the writers; and not the converse.* The Holy Scriptures were of gradual formation, and have lived in the mind and heart of their several authors before they came into the hands of their contemporaries and of posterity. We must thus not descend from the Scripture to the writers, but ascend from the writers to the Scripture. Theopneustia—*i.e.*, guidance and animation by the Holy Ghost—is no attribute of a book in itself, but of men; and *solely in consequence of this*, also of their words *and writings.*

2. *This their Theopneustia must be conceived of, not as having an external-mechanical, but as having an inward-dynamical character.* He who, in connection with the word Theopneustia, at once thinks of a book, can scarcely conceive of the matter itself in any other light than that of a *dictamen* (lesson dictated). He who, on the other hand, comprehends that he has here to do with a working of God in and upon man, will at the same time

---

[42] Comp. G. F. N. SONNTAG, *Doctrina Inspir. ejusque ratio, historia, et usus pop.* Heidelb. (1810).

[43] Art. iii. of the Netherlands' Confession.

perceive that this working must be in harmony with the demands of personality. It is no blind impelling force, consequently, but a heavenly influence exerted upon the writers, whereby they are guided and strengthened for self-activity. This operation of God has its metaphysical ground in the personality and power of the Holy Spirit; its psychological ground in the receptivity and individuality of the men of God; its historic ground, finally, in the fact that it takes place amongst the people of Israel—a people destined to be, and who really became, a people of revelation in the special sense of the word; and in the Christian Church, which had its beginning in the Holy Ghost Himself. Take away this historic condition, and the arising of a succession of men, enlightened and animated by God, is entirely inexplicable (*unvermittelt*); let it have its due weight, and the starting-point is found for coming to the idea of Theopneustia. For indeed—

3. *Theopneustia and Revelation, although not identical, are nevertheless most intimately connected.* We may think of Revelation in the twofold sense of the word—*patefactio* and *revelatio*—without its being accompanied with an actual inspiration for speaking or writing; but we cannot possibly think of Inspiration, unless an objective as well as a subjective revelation has taken place. To the Revelation the Inspiration naturally attaches itself: it is the expression and consequence of that which, by way of Revelation, is made clear and certain to the innermost consciousness, and is now perpetuated in word and writing. To this extent the doctrine of the Theopneustia would perhaps be more suitably treated of in dealing with the subject of Apocalyptics, than in that of Bibliology. Nevertheless the distinction ever remains, that Revelation was the privilege of all true believers: Inspiration, that of those who were called by word and writing to give testimony concerning the truth.

4. *The Sacred Writers were in an especial manner—but at the same time in different degrees—organs of the Holy Spirit.* Without doubt, the Spirit wrought, as on the devout in Israel, so also in all the living members of the Church of the Lord. In this respect there was certainly no essential difference between them and the Lord's first witnesses.[44] But there is a diversity of gift and work; and to each one the Spirit is given for that which is profitable.[45] To the Apostolic *office* belonged naturally the Apostolic *gifts*: with the special call to write, was given also the special guidance and qualification for the work. Everything is a charisma in the spiritual domain, yet in this case there is found a difference—not specific indeed, but of degree—in the communications of grace. Hence, the churches, although themselves led by the Holy Spirit, nevertheless acknowledge the superiority of the Apostles' word, and continue so to do, even when they receive it in a written form.[46]

So the Sacred Writers have the Holy Ghost in an especial measure, but still *in a differing degree.* With the fullest justice have both Jewish and Christian Theologians spoken of different degrees of Inspiration, and made a

---

[44] John vii. 39; Acts xv. 8, 9; Ephes. iv. 4.
[45] πρὸς τὸ συμφέρον, 1 Cor. xii. 4, 7, 11.
[46] Acts xv. 30; xvi. 4; 2 Cor. xiii. 10.

distinction which has in later times been not without loss overlooked. This distinction is such as we might *à priori* expect to see made, from reasons derived from Divine Providence and human nature, and upon a careful examination its justice is apparent from almost every page of Scripture. Who, for instance, in the Scriptures of the New Testament, will ascribe the same fulness of the Spirit to Judas, the Lord's brother, as to John, His bosom friend? Who does not feel, in those of the Old, the distance in a spiritual sense between a Moses, a David, an Isaiah, on the one hand, and the writer of Ecclesiastes, or of the book of Esther, on the other? Here also, as everywhere in the domain of God's works, the words of 1 Cor. xv. 41 find their application. For—

5. *The Theopneustia of the Sacred Writers was not to the detriment, but to the benefit, of their individuality.* It is precisely through the overlooking of this great principle that misconception and aversion have arisen. Conceive of a psalm like the forty-second, a prophecy like that of Isaiah xl., or a glorying in the faith like that of Rom. viii., as merely *dictated*, or as having greater beauty than other places, simply because the Holy Ghost wished to show that He, when it pleased Him, could also sometimes be eloquent. Wherefore then, it might be asked, not more frequently, not everywhere, not always? The answer lies in the principle enunciated. The Holy Spirit nowhere, not even in this domain, fails to regard the rights of an individuality, which has its basis in the will of God; on the other hand, He fills up, develops, glorifies this individuality, as from step to step. Slumbering powers are called forth into activity under the light of the new sun of Revelation, since God makes of its interpreters, not instruments, but master-builders under Himself; and communicates to them His word and plan of salvation, for themselves and others, but makes this communication through the channel of their own human heart. Each one speaks his own language, not because the Holy Spirit adapts Himself to the man's style of language, but because the Spirit takes possession of him, and uses him as, according to the nature of his sanctified personality, he actually is.

6. *The Theopneustia of the sacred Writers must generally be conceived of, not as a momentary assistance, exclusively in or during the act of writing; but as a natural consequence of their being personally led by the Holy Ghost, who controlled all their thinking and working, and in this way also their writing.* This was especially the dark side of the old theory, even in its later supranaturalistic modification. The Sacred Writers were conceived of as having become wholly different beings as soon as a Divine "Write" sounded in their ears. The impulse itself was something entirely extraordinary; in an equally extraordinary way was the matter, no less than the words, supplied; in addition to this there was given occasionally, to mind and feelings, a "*directio ad mentem Sp. S. rite exprimendam.*" Where is there a trace of all this? Yea, to what end would it be called for, in the case of true men of God? A command like that of Rev. i. 19, was, so far as we know, not the rule; and what Christian psychologist can conceive of the Spirit acting merely externally and momentarily, at the time when the man must write, and departing when he was to cease? In undisguised opposition to this mechanical theory, we have to conceive of Inspiration, not otherwise than as the most intensive penetration of the whole personality by

the Holy Spirit; in consequence of which the writing, as well as speaking, of the men of God was, as an important part of their living and acting, Divinely controlled; "an operating upon them, not simply *with regard to* and *in the act of writing*, but, on the contrary, one extending in its effects *even to* [*usque ad*] their writing."

7. *As Theopneustia had different grades, so also had it its own limits.* This too has been forgotten, where the holy men have been conceived of as omniscient, at least as infallible in every respect. "*Il nous faut suffire qu'un chapitre ou une chose fasse partie des Écritures pour la croire divinement bonne; car Dieu a prononcé sur elle, comme sur la création: J'ai vu tout ce que j'ai fait, et voilà tout était bon*" (Gaussen). Few things perhaps have been more prejudicial to the existence of a rational belief in Scripture, than such an assertion, which conflicts with the most indisputable facts. In this hypothesis of an absolutely unlimited inspiration, the Sacred Writers at last cease to be men; and a number of contradictions, not merely apparent, but real, presenting themselves in Scripture, can only be removed by an almost desperate mode of harmonizing. It is an important step in advance, that even the most believing Scripture expositors of our age candidly confess they are not able to maintain the absolute infallibility of the Sacred Writers, *in every particular*. Augustine, indeed, declared long before, in regard to John: *Nec ipse dixit ut est, sed ut potuit, quia de Deo homo dixit; et quidem inspiratus a Deo, sed tamen homo.* "Nor did he speak of things as they are, but as he was able to express them, because as a man he spake of God; and that indeed as being inspired by God, but yet as a man." This is the only tenable theory of limited Inspiration: necessarily limited by the finite condition, and at the same time by the fallibility of man in regard to all which belonged not to the sphere of God's Saving Revelation. —Or, have all the expectations of the Prophets and Apostles received the fulfilment in the precise form in which they had conceived of them? Is it wise to ask what kind of Scripture would seem *to us* most useful and desirable, and not rather what kind we really have? Is it necessary to allow our ideas to be governed by the deductions of Scholasticism, in place of investigating the sense in which the Scripture itself declares and reveals its Inspiration? He who rejects a truly rational theory, *based on the teaching of Scripture itself*, renders thereby simply one service the more to—Rationalism.

8. *The Theopneustia proceeded gradually* (John xvi. 13). This also has formerly been only too often overlooked. It was as though the men of God must have an insight into all things at once, and rose straightway to the full height of their spiritual development. Yet the contrary is clearly evident on psychological and historic grounds, *e.g.*, from an attentive regard to the Petrine Christology, or the Pauline Eschatology. Inspiration consequently takes place only in harmony with the law of all development in spiritual life, and with that which we observe everywhere in the domain of general or of particular revelation.

9. *The Theopneustia extends not only to great things, but also to things of comparatively minor importance.* This follows as a simple consequence from the foregoing proposition. So long as one entertains the mechanical view, and at the same time strives after a reasonable conception, one will

necessarily shrink from extending this to the apparently insignificant details —salutations, for example—personal concerns, etc. Regarded from our standpoint, this difficulty vanishes, and the division, almost impossible to make, between the more and the less important, is unnecessary. If the Apostles were indeed, in all their thinking and acting—and thus also in their writing—under the guidance of the Holy Spirit, by whom they were daily more deeply penetrated, it may be asserted in a sense perfectly justifiable, that the Holy Spirit also inspired them in regard to those things which are comparatively small. The fulness of the Spirit of faith expresses itself in Paul, when he defends the resurrection from the dead, but also the tenderness of the Spirit of love, when he counsels his Timothy to add a little wine to his water.

10. *In like manner, the Theopneustia has reference, not only to the things taught, but also to the words, yea, to the whole style of speech, in Holy Scripture.* "To wish to maintain the inspiration of the subject-matter without that of the words, is a folly; for everywhere are thoughts and words inseparable" (Rothe). The reluctance of the earlier Supranaturalism to think of an Inspiration of the *words*, as well as that of the things taught, arose from the fact that the opinion of that day had not yet broken with the mechanical theory. Yet it is evident, upon a little reflection, that we must either accept or reject both alike, since form and contents cannot—least of all in this domain—be separated from each other. And we dare to *accept* both, without fearing the reproach of entertaining a view opposed to sound reason. If the Holy Spirit was the guiding principle in the Apostolic life, His influence must be manifest not only in the choice and presentation of the facts, but also in that of the words. If the true poetic spirit enables one to seize at once, and as by intuition, the exact and only suitable word for that which one desires to express, how much more shall the power of the Holy Spirit? Not even the Archaisms, Solecisms, or other peculiarities which may present themselves, need prevent our seeing in the language of Holy Scripture a creation of the Holy Spirit. The Holy. Spirit is no language-master in the vulgar sense of the word, any more than the exponent of His mind was an automaton or a flute. It is thus conceivable that the latter expressed himself in words which the Holy Ghost taught,[47] and yet that they none the less bore the traces of his human imperfection.[48] That nevertheless the language of Scripture is a language of Divine majesty, no one will deny who possesses a truly spiritual ear. Compared with profane literature, the sacred books display an equally peculiar physiognomy as the Revelation itself, compared with the ordinary course of the world's history.

11. *The Theopneustia of the writers of the Old Testament bears a character more or less different from that of the writers of the New.* This also has not at all times been taken into account,[49] and yet this position is justified by the authority of Holy Scripture itself. Clearly there was an immense difference between the operation of the Holy Spirit before the exaltation of Christ, and that afterwards,[50] and the least Apostle had a higher standing

---

[47] 1 Cor. ii. 13.
[48] 2 Cor. iv. 7; x. 10.
[49] See, for example, A. DE GASPARIN, *L'Ecole du doute*, etc. (1852), p. 220.
[50] John vii. 39.

than the greatest Prophet.[51] While the Holy Spirit came instantaneously, and often with irresistible power, upon the Prophets, He dwelt and wrought more regularly and constantly in the Apostles of the New Testament. The personality of the latter also is not less strongly manifest—especially in their writings—than that of the former, and the second half of the Bible displays a greater fulness of the Spirit (*plerophoria*), than the former. If there are among the writers of the Old Testament some who speak or write in a time of deep apostasy and spiritual barrenness, we cannot look in them for that which is found in the springtide of the religious life. It is true there breathes a genuinely Theocratic spirit in Israel's prophets and poets, but not without coming into manifold contact with their special human peculiarity. Much more loud and clear is the voice of the Spirit heard in one note of the Psalms than in the other.[52] Here the higher aspiration rises to its climax, there it is visibly on the decline.[53] In the Prophets the Spirit as a rule points forward, in the Apostles and their fellow-witnesses He as a rule points backward; although in both He speaks according to the requirements of the moment.

12. *The question as to the Canonicity of the books of Holy Scripture is to be clearly distinguished from that as to their Theopneustia.* While formerly both ideas were, as by tacit consent, regarded as almost identical, or as at least in all respects interchangeable, this at the present standpoint of the science can no longer be justified. We must and can allow it to be possible that a writing of an inspired person has been lost,[54] and regard it as equally conceivable that, on the other hand, a writing may have been received into the Canon which reveals but few or no signs of the inspiration of the writer.[55] Nothing can here be decided *à priori*: it may be that a careful historico-critical investigation will triumphantly vindicate the right of each book of the Bible to its place in the Canon; but the position that the ideas of Canonicity and Theopneustia mutually cover each other, may in no case be the starting-point for this investigation. Why not? The history of the Canon has already sufficiently answered this question.

13. With the observation of these main outlines we believe that a more accurate conception of the doctrine—nay, of the fact—of Inspiration is not unattainable, and consider we shall be gainers in every respect thereby. At least, *Holy Scripture does not present a single feature irreconcilably antagonistic to a conception thus formulated as to the Theopneustia of its Authors.* It has been said (*a*) that the sacred writers do not speak of their inspiration, and, on the other hand, now and then make reference to their authorities (Luke i. 1—4). Just as though to be silent were here the same thing as to deny, and such a guidance by the Holy Spirit as we have indicated forbade the use of trustworthy documents! As though the sacred writers do not *make manifest* their inspiration, and would not have called forth a well-merited distrust, had they testified of it in so many words! (John viii. 13.)

---

[51] Matt. xi. 11.
[52] Comp. *e.g.* Ps. xlii. 1, with Ps. cxxxvii. 8, 9.
[53] Comp. Jer. xxxi. 27—34, with chap. xx. 14, 15.
[54] 1 Cor. v. 9.
[55] Let any one think of Luther's judgment on the Epistle of James and the Apocalypse.

We are reminded (*b*) that the promise of the Holy Spirit was made and fulfilled, not exclusively to the Apostles, but to all believers, and at least was not personally addressed to the fellow-helpers of the Lord's first witnesses—Mark, Luke, and others. We shall not reply to this objection by a sharp distinction between ordinary and extraordinary gifts of the Holy Spirit, which is nowhere made in the Gospel itself; but we call attention to the fact that, from the nature of the case, the Spirit must work most abundantly in those who had stood closest to Jesus, and had in addition received the highest work to accomplish; at the same time, also, nothing forbids us to suppose, as among others Witsius did, a difference of degree in the inspiration of the different witnesses to the same Gospel. (*c*) We are pointed to the difference, *inter se*, of the various Prophetic and Apostolic doctrinal ideas (*Lehrbegriffe*); and this is a peculiarity we do not wish simply to ignore. It is an inseparable consequence of the difference of dispensation, of individuality, of circumstances; and is one proof the more that the Holy Spirit has guided them, not only with the highest freedom, but also with the highest wisdom. Only then would the difference cause us anxiety, if it could be shown that the one proclaimed to us what amounted to another Gospel from that proclaimed by the other. As it is, we owe precisely to this diversity the infinite fulness and the higher unity of the Scriptures. (*d*) Errors and inaccuracies, in matters of subordinate importance, are, as we have already seen, undoubtedly to be found in the Bible. A Luther, a Calvin, a Coccejus, among the older Theologians; a Tholuck, a Neander, a Lange, a Stier, among the more modern ones, have admitted this without hesitation. But this proves absolutely nothing against the truth and authority of the Word, where it is speaking of the Way of Salvation. If any one thinks himself at liberty, in this last respect also, to distrust the testimony of the Apostles, because, *e.g.*, they not obscurely reveal that they look for the return of the Lord within a very short time, let him not forget that with regard to the precise period nothing was revealed to them, and that the prospect itself does not vanish, although it be realised at another time and in another way than was at first expected. (Compare what we have written on this point in the *Jaarbb.* 1845, ii., pp. 90—99.) How the first organs of the Holy Spirit were led forward from light to light, is evident, for instance, from Acts x. 9, etc. (*e*) Certainly the history of the Apostles also speaks of differences among themselves, and of deplorable failures.[56] But of a variance which affects the distinct answering of the great question of life, there is not a word. The Apostles no more laid claim to perfect holiness than to omniscience, but every sin which we still discover in them manifested itself *notwithstanding* the Spirit under whose guidance they were; and where, moreover, their human imperfection remained, the Holy Spirit was able to preserve them from any error prejudicial to their right conception of the truth, and, as appears from the results, He has done so. All these scruples arise from not yet having the courage to recognise, along with the manifestly Divine character of Holy Scripture, also its truly human character.[57]

---

[56] Acts xv. 39; xxiii. 3; Gal. ii. 11—14.

[57] Compare, on the Divine-human character of Holy Scripture, the treatise of E. C. A. Riehm, *Stud. u. Krit.* (1859), ii.

14. *Just as little is the doctrine we have laid down in regard to Inspiration refuted by difficulties of another nature.*—It is perhaps spoken of as *without significance;* since profane Antiquity also regarded its greatest men as inspired, and we here consequently seem to ascribe to Prophets and Apostles nothing entirely extraordinary. And certainly Seneca, Cicero, and others have recognised in the great spirits of their age the influence of a higher inspiration. All inspiration in the extra-biblical domain we also would not willingly deny; more than this, we *could* not do so, if we truly believe in Him who, even before His incarnation, was the life and light of men (John i. 4). But we must here yet once more refer to the important place occupied by Israel as the people of Revelation, in whom, both before and after the coming of Christ, the Spirit of truth wrought and spake, as in no other sphere. We must direct attention to the difference between the Inspiration of the Prophets and Apostles and the soothsaying-faculty (μαντική) of the ancients.[58] We must ask, finally, to which of the profane speakers or writers has a testimony like that to the Prophets, a promise like that to the Apostles, been given and fulfilled by the King of truth? In no case can a guiding be regarded as unimportant, to which we owe a document, through which, as in no other writing, the Holy Spirit expresses Himself.

Just as little is it *insufficient,* because there is still left so much of obscurity and contradiction *in Holy Scripture,* and in addition to this, there is so great a diversity of readings, of translation, and of exposition. Or how shall we—because we do not possess everything that we could desire—despise so much that is good and great? Holy Scripture is constituted in precisely such a manner as to afford no cushions for our indolence, but always a stimulus to our continued investigation.[59] "We know well there are some scrupulous registrar-like souls, who, even if celestial spirits should appear to them, would not believe without viséd certificates from another world. We Christians, however, must learn to believe in testimonies of the Spirit, which stand higher than written certificates. If any one's faith in the Son of God is staggered because he knows not, for instance, whether in Acts xx. 28, 'The Church *of God,*' or '*of the Lord,*' is the true reading; because he is not sure whether he should believe with Matthew, that vinegar was offered to the Saviour, or with Mark, that it was sour wine; whether Christ healed the blind man on His entrance into Jericho, or His departure therefrom; what would a Paul have replied to the difficulties of such an one? 'Man,' he would have answered, '*thine hour is not yet come!*'"[60]

Impossible, finally, would the operation described by us be, only if *miracles* were impossible; but comp. § 32. He who truly believes in a living God, and in the spirit of man, must esteem an Inspiration of the sacred writers as the more probable, in proportion as with us he regards the Bible as the means designed and appointed of God, for testifying of His Kingdom and plan of Salvation (§ xxxvi. 12). Only in one case could this

---

58 Compare page 139.
59 Comp. DA COSTA, *Voorl. over het O. T.* (1848), ii. p. 395, etc.
60 THOLUCK, *Deutsche Zeitschr.* (1850), p. 344.

Inspiration have been considered unworthy of God, if it had degraded the witnesses of the truth into instruments, without will or consciousness. As it is now, however, it is one more admirable manifestation of Omnipotence and Liberty, of Wisdom and Love; and he who regards it as impossible must in principle also deny the possibility of all Conversion, since this—not less than Inspiration—is a Divine operation in the domain of the Spiritual Life.

15. *As Holy Scripture, on the one hand, contains the Word of God—i.e., the Divine Revelation—so may Scripture itself, in its totality, on the other, be termed the Word of God, as a consequence of the Theopneustia of its Writers.* At the end of this our investigation, this last statement can hardly stand in need of elucidation or proof. The fruitless controversy as to whether the Bible *is* God's Word, or whether it only *contains* it, is well known. Whereas formerly both propositions were identified, and sometimes confused, in later times an accurate distinction has been demanded with increasing emphasis. This demand, however frequently abused, is in principle a legitimate one, as opposed to the boundless misconception to which its non-recognition has but too frequently led. Only on both sides there is need for caution, lest the two sides of the same thing should be opposed to each other as in irreconcilable contrast. The statement, "the Bible *is* God's Word," brings into the foreground the higher unity of Holy Scripture; the counter-statement, "the Bible *contains* God's Word," brings into the foreground its manifest diversity. It *contains* the Word of God, because it is the record of that which God has spoken to man, as well in deeds as in words; it *is*, taken in its entirety, God's Word, because it is notably the work of one Spirit, which in different measure animated the inspired Writers, and which is the higher bond even between the most different parts.[61] But the formula, "the Bible *is* God's Word," must never be taken in such a way as to mean that every single word in the Bible is a word of God in the proper sense of this expression. Words of men, yea, of devils, as well as of God, are to be read in the Bible, although certainly written under Divine guidance. All in the Bible which is plainly seen to be a constituent part of Divine Revelation, is God's Word; and again, the Bible itself is God's Word, because—and in so far as—the Spirit of God here addresses us as nowhere else. Both statements are thus true, when they are allowed to stand side by side; but cease to be the pure and just expression of the truth, as soon as they are opposed to each other. *The proposition, "the Bible contains God's Word," is most in harmony with the Spirit of Holy Scripture, and also preferable on account of its greater perspicuity.*[62] The proposition, "the Bible *is* God's Word," points to the Divine origin of Holy Scripture regarded as a whole, but may—as applied to particular parts—very easily lead to misunderstanding. Here the accurate remark of Lange is in place, "Every single statement is susceptible of misconception: the Bible *in its totality* can, however, be misunderstood, and become a cause of offence, only in the case of a spirit more or less estranged from it. In this it may be compared to the Creation. The

---

[61] Compare the work on the *Continuity of Scripture*, by the present Lord Hatherley.
[62] Comp. DOEDES, *Leer der Zal.*, pp. 13—16.

one-sided observer of the single forms thereof may become a criticiser of the order of nature, or a Polytheist; but for him who allows the spirit of creation, as a whole, to speak to his spirit, the revelation of God in nature will disclose itself ever more clearly. So is it with the higher revelation of God in Holy Scripture. In its unity it is clear as sunlight—a sparkling crystal of the revelation and recognition of God." Let us add, precisely in this its at once Divine and human character is manifested the analogy between the Scripture and the Christ (comp. § xxviii. 1). But precisely therein lies also the reason why the origin and composition of the Scriptures has for us, no less than the person of the Lord—along with so much that is clear—also its mysterious side, and, like the latter, remains the object of continued research.

Compare, besides the works already mentioned, the article *Inspiration*, by THOLUCK, in Herzog, *R. E.* vi., p. 692, with the literature therein mentioned; and his treatise in the *Deutsche Zeitschrift* (1850), No. 16—18, 42—44; P. JALAGUYER, *L'Inspiration du N. T.* (1852); *Christel. Tijdvr. door een Jurist* (iv. Over Schrift-inspiratie, 1853); MEHRING, *Zur Revision des Inspir.-Begriffes*, in the *Zeitschrift für Luth. Theol.* (1862), i.; ROTHE, *Zur Dogmatik* (1863), p. 200, etc.; A. MONOD, *L'Inspiration prouvée par ses Œuvres* (1864); GUIZOT, *Meditations*, i. (1864), p. 150, etc.; E. VON MURALT, *Die göttliche Eingebung der H. S.*, Inaugural Discourse (1864); J. C. KNIGHT, *The Law, the Prophets, and the Psalms*, etc. (1866); a treatise of L. NESSELMAN, in the *Beweis des Glaubens*, (1868), p. 309, etc.; W. SCHMIDT, *Zur Inspirationsfrage* (1869); A. DIETZSCH, *Die Lehre von der Inspiration der Schrift*, in the *Studien u. Kritiken* (1869), iii., p. 428, etc.; J. J. VAN OOSTERZEE, Art. on *Bijbelbestrijding*, in *Voor Kerk en Theol.* i. (1871), pp. 345—375.

POINTS FOR INQUIRY.

The accusation of reasoning in a circle more nearly examined and criticised.—Agreement and difference between the promises of the Holy Spirit in the Synoptical Gospels and in John.—What is the sense of 2 Tim. iii. 16, as compared with 2 Pet. i. 20, 21?—Are there good grounds for asserting that the binding authority and inspiration of the Apostolic writings was at once acknowledged in the post-Apostolic age? (Credner, Stuffken, Vinke).—Further criticism of the theory of the inspiration of the letter, as it is presented by Gaussen and others.—Can the acknowledgment of errors and inacuracies in the Sacred Writings be brought into accord with the reverence due to the Bible?—In what way are we to conceive of the gradual progress in the Theopneustia of the Sacred Writers?—Can inspiration be ascribed also to the most illustrious witnesses for the faith in later times? and if so, to what extent?—Does the statement, that the Bible *contains* God's Word, open the door too wide to subjective speculation?—What value must thus be attached to Holy Scripture as a whole, and in its parts?

SECTION XL.—ITS VALUE.

As a sacred record of such exalted origin, Holy Scripture has an absolutely priceless value. While as a permanent condition it is *indispensable* for a clear knowledge of Divine revelation, it is to this end perfectly *sufficient.* And while sufficiently *clear* in itself, it is invested with irrefragable *Authority* in the domain of Religion and Christianity. Not every one of its parts has an equal claim to this high estimate; but in its totality, Holy Scripture, as the source of knowledge and the test of Saving Truth, has an importance which may not be ascribed either to Church tradition, or to any other word or writing of men. The defence of this its unique importance against the continued opposition of Roman Catholicism, Rationalism, and Mysticism, is for the Evangelical Protestant Church and Theology, a demand of preponderating obligation.

1. After establishing the Inspiration of Scripture, the examination as to its Value naturally takes the first place. More particularly must here the qualities (*Affectiones S. S.*) be treated, by which it is distinguished and commended as a fit document of the Saving Revelation. Especially since the Reformation have these attributes been treated of in Dogmatics, although not always defined and classified in the same manner. The Netherlands Confession speaks (Art. vii.) of the *Completeness* and *Authority* of the Holy Scriptures. In common with many others, we speak also of their *Indispensableness* and their *Perspicuity;* without considering it necessary, with some others, here to speak of their powerful operation (*Efficacia*), since this can be more properly treated of under the head of the *Means of Grace* (§ 136). The importance of this examination from the standpoint of Protestant Dogmatics—especially that of the Reformed Church—can hardly be disputed.

2. The *absolute* indispensableness (*necessitas*) of the Sacred Scriptures, especially those of the New Testament, has doubtless been sometimes defended in a way which has called forth legitimate opposition. It has not always been considered that the Church is older than the Bible, and that the first community primarily knew and followed no other rule of faith than the Word of the Lord and of His Apostles, orally transmitted to it.[1] Meanwhile Augustine had already observed with justice,[2] that there were Christians living in solitude, who were full of faith, hope, and love, without possessing any written books; and Lessing also, in his well-known controversy with Goeze, has pointed out the value of tradition in contradistinction from the indispensableness of the Bible. It must be acknowledged that the Church arose and was at first extended without Holy Writ, but no less must it be acknowledged that without the Scriptures a clear knowledge of the doctrine of Salvation is, *as a permanent condition*, impossible. "The Scripture belongs not to the Being, but to the Well-being of the Church" (Hase). Doubtless the word of the Apostles has laid the foundation of the Church, but after the last of the Apostles has ceased to speak, *either* the original source of knowledge is closed for all after ages, *or* it is preserved

[1] 2 Tim. ii. 2. [2] *De Doctrinâ Chr.*, c. 39.

pure and accessible to all in the word of Scripture. Christian festivals, ceremonies, and works of art, also, might be able to preserve for a while the remembrance of the facts of salvation; but not one of these accessory means would be able permanently to supply the place of Scripture. History shows that the time of the Church's prosperity has kept equal pace with the use or neglect of Scripture, and that she owes her Reformation to the renewed reading of the half-buried word of Scripture. The Bible itself contains utterances which convincingly prove that Protestantism has not overrated its value. Let any one compare the word of Paul with regard to the Old Testament;[3] which assuredly applies to the Scriptures of the New Testament with no less justice than do, *e.g.*, the words of Jesus, Matt. xxii. 29; John v. 39, and other places. Finally, experience teaches that at no stage of spiritual development can the salutary influence of Scripture be wholly dispensed with.[4] It serves not merely as a training book up to a state of maturity (*mondigheid*), which many Christians have attained to here below, but also as a guide to the highest degree of perfection, and an indispensable corrective against all error and sin in the domain of spiritual life; naturally under the condition that it is not employed and circulated as a dead letter, but is received as a living word, and is sanctified in truth to the heart by the Holy Spirit. With these qualifying explanations, however, we may accept the statement: "*Scriptura Ecclesiæ ita necessaria est, ut eâ non magis quam mundus sole, quin et ipso Deo carere possit*" (Heidegger, † 1698).

3. That which is in this sense indispensable, must also at the same time be recognised as *sufficient*. With the necessity for the Scripture, its sufficiency (*sufficientia*) is most closely connected. The limit of this sufficiency lies in the particular tendency of Scripture. Not seldom has it been put to the lower use of a textbook of Geography, Theology, Cosmogony; for this it is just as little designed as it is adapted. "Scripture is not given to make us acquainted with the course of heavenly bodies, but with the way to heaven itself" (Baronius). And that the knowledge of the way of salvation cannot possibly be dispensed with, even though its value is sometimes extolled in a one-sided manner, is just as certain as that the Holy Scriptures, although not all in an equal degree, are on this subject the source, *par excellence*, of our knowledge (comp. § 8). With less of precision has it formerly been sought to prove this its sufficiency from the repeated prohibition against taking anything from, or adding anything to, the Word of God;[5] since in none of the places referred to is the whole Bible spoken of. But taking into account only the subject-matter of Holy Scripture, its sufficiency can be deduced therefrom. We already hear the high value of the precepts and saving revelations of the Old Testament emphatically asserted;[6] and the value of the Gospel, even where it comes to us in a written form, is raised above all praise.[7] No wonder that in the Reformation Age we hear this property of Holy Scripture universally assented to without hesitation,

---

[3] 2 Tim. iii. 16.
[4] 2 Tim. iii. 16, 17.
[5] Deut. iv. 2; xii. 32; Prov. xxx. 5, 6; Rev. xxii. 18, 19.
[6] Ps. xix., cxix.; Luke xvi. 29—31; John v. 39.
[7] Rom. i. 16; Gal. i. 7, 8.

even by the Socinians. We maintain it, not only against the Romish Church, which, by the place it assigns to tradition, *ipso facto* declares Scripture to be insufficient, but also against every kind of Mysticism, which exalts the inner testimony above the written word.[8] The unceasing appeal, especially of this last, to 2 Cor. iii. 6, can only be regarded as the fruit of a mistaken exegesis.

4. With the two before-named properties of Holy Scripture is most intimately allied a third—its *perspicuity;* in consequence of which it is self-explanatory (*perspicuitas, et semet ipsam interpretandi facultas*). While we ascribe this to Holy Scripture in its totality, we naturally do not deny that many single parts thereof may be considered very obscure and mysterious. Even the ancient Psalmist thought the prayer for higher enlightenment necessary;[9] and we hear the Apostle Peter speak of some obscure things in the Epistles of Paul.[10] But although the subject is here and there too deep to be fathomed, the words are nevertheless sufficiently intelligible; and especially those utterances with which Dogmatics more particularly has to do (*dicta probantia*), are not seldom distinguished by a surprising degree of clearness. It is true the word of Scripture will not be for all equally clear; for some even, nearly unintelligible. "The *perspicuitas S.S.* presupposes certain definite subjective conditions, namely, religious wants and a desire for the knowledge of the truth" (J. Müller). Where, however, these prerequisites are not altogether wanting, there, as is manifest from history and experience, the Scripture, especially of the New Testament, is sufficiently intelligible, even if need be without any other means of help, to give a satisfactory answer to the great question of life. With good reason, therefore, do the sacred writers themselves boast of the clearness of the holy oracles, so far as they were given in their days.[11] This perspicuity of the Scripture is a consequence, partly, of its subject-matter, which is in great measure historic; partly, of its concrete, plastic form. It is in vain that this its clearness is assailed by the mention of so much misunderstanding and failure to understand, seeking to justify itself by an appeal to the "It is written" of Scripture. If every false doctrine can find its show of support (*heeft ieder ketter zijne letter*), each truth, on the other hand, has its self-evidencing clearness (*elke waarheid hare eigene klaarheid*); and upon much that was at first obscure, there later arises a satisfactory light. We need not say that intelligibleness is an attribute of the original, but not on this account of every translation, defective as many of them are; and that it does not exclude the use of suitable aids, but rather presuppose and call for them.

Such being the case there is no reason for maintaining with the Romish Church, the necessity for an official interpretation by the Church. What was obscure for the Ethiopian chamberlain (Acts viii. 31) was not the word of Scripture in itself, but the truth therein proclaimed; because he knew not yet the fact of its fulfilment. To take another instance, the sense of the words in which the Lord's Supper was instituted appears obscure,

---

[8] Calv. *Inst.*, i. 9, 1.
[9] Ps. cxix. 18.
[10] 2 Pet. iii. 16.
[11] Ps. cxix. 97—105; compare Rom. x. 5—10; 2 Pet. i. 19.

judged by the controversy still being waged in regard to their meaning; but the obscurity arises from the fact that the exegesis—here, perhaps, more than anywhere—is ruled by Dogmatic prepossession. It might rather be expected beforehand that the document of a revelation intended by God for all, would not be wanting in at least a certain measure of intelligibleness; and as a result of experience it is ever afresh apparent that the best preservative against a perverted interpretation of particular parts of Scripture is to be found in Scripture as a whole. And yet more, "*habet Scriptura suos haustus primos, habet secundos, habet tertios*" (Augustine). The Scripture, taken in separate parts, best explains itself; because with attentive comparison the light of one utterance communicates itself to another, while the knowledge of the whole assigns to each part its place in its just connection. This is also the higher truth of the requirement so frequently misunderstood, that the sound explanation of Scripture must be one in accordance with the analogy of faith. It implies that every passage must be understood in the light, not of the whole doctrinal system of the Church, but of the particular doctrinal conception of the speaker or writer, from whom it is taken. Where this method is observed in conjunction with the prayerful use of suitable aids, there usually the mists are dispersed; and with full right one may consequently maintain the intelligibleness of Holy Scripture against a cloudy Mysticism on the one hand, and an arrogant Ultramontanism on the other, which call the sunlight darkness, so long as it is not seen by the glare of their own smoking torch. What has been said of the infallibility of the sacred testimony has also its application in regard to the clearness thereof. "Not every portion of the Bible, not even every single doctrinal statement, is infallible, in the sense that it cannot be misunderstood, even by the honest and earnest inquirer; and yet it is *in its totality* infallible, and because in its totality, therefore also in its single parts. Since, namely, each single part stands in connection with the whole, it receives from this latter its light, and from it its exposition" (Schmid).

5. The Word of God, thus indispensable, sufficient, and perspicuous, is —in the domain of Christianity and Religion—endowed with a wholly unique ***Authority***. There is no principle, perhaps, which appeared with such vivifying power in the domain of Christian Dogmatics during the Reformation Age, as that of the exclusive and all-deciding authority of Holy Scripture. There was inscribed aloft on the banner of the Reformers the word of Augustine: "*Titubabit fides, si vacillet S. Scripturæ auctoritas*" (comp. § viii. 2). It would be superfluous to support by a number of citations, that which is by no one seriously doubted. In proportion as the Reformation powerfully protested against all human authority in the religious domain, did it unreservedly bow before that of the Holy Scriptures, which henceforth took the place of the infallible Church, as the highest court of appeal. If possible, yet more strongly than Luther, did Zwingli, Calvin, and those spiritually allied to them, express themselves on

---

[12] Rom. xii. 6.

this point.[13] Between the different Symbolical Writings, also, there prevails on this point a perfect unanimity. In proof, we adduce only the beginning of the *Confessio Helvetica Posterior:* "Credimus et confitemur, Scripturas Canonicas . . . . ipsum verum esse verbum Dei, et auctoritatem sufficientem ex semet ipsis, non ex hominibus habere. Nam Deus ipse locutus est Patribus, Prophetis et Apostolis, et loquitur adhuc per S. Scripturas." In a similar sense the Netherlands Confession expresses itself (Art. vii.), as also the Heidelberg Catechism (Answ. 25). In this sense also was the doctrine of the Scripture-authority developed by the Reformed Dogmatists. Holy Scripture in its totality was recognised not only as the highest standard for faith and walk, but also as the decisive arbiter in every religious difference.[14] It was called not only *Norma Correctionis*, but also *directionis*, a rule as well in the active as in the passive sense. This its authority it derived not from any ecclesiastical sanction; but possessed it—as God's own Word—in itself. By virtue of this its absolute authority, all that is actually taught in Scripture, or can be legitimately deduced therefrom, was held to be an unalterable doctrine of the Church; what was in conflict with the teaching of Scripture was to be unhesitatingly rejected; that which Scripture leaves undecided was looked upon as not actually necessary to salvation. It could not, therefore, possibly be admitted that the Scripture contradicts itself on any point; at most there could be only apparent contradictions, but the function of Harmonistic science is to resolve these; and where the latter had fulfilled its task, there a simple "It is written" became the decisive end of all controversy.

If it is asked whether this conception of the authority of Scripture can in the present day be in every respect endorsed by us, what has been before said (§§ 36—39) may suffice to answer this question. To a greater extent than was before thought possible or necessary, has the believing Theology of our time taught to distinguish between the Bible itself and the Word of God contained in the Bible, so that he who attaches any value to accuracy of expression, is under obligation henceforth to speak in every case of the *authority of the Word of God.* In doing so, it is further necessary to confine this last, to a greater extent than was frequently the case in former times, to the domain of Saving Truth, and consequently to seek in the Bible no solution of questions in regard to which it does not present itself as the highest arbiter. "So long as the majority of Theologians treat the Bible as a *book of oracles*, so long will the majority of educated laity regard it as a *book of fables*" (Beyschlag). All, finally, is to be banished from the notion of authority, which—in opposition to the Word of God itself—would lead to arbitrary limitation of one's own thinking and examination. Let every one freely examine as to the grounds on which a word, recorded in the Bible, claims to be regarded as the Word of God Himself. Nevertheless, where it is clearly manifest that He Himself has spoken by the mouth of perfectly qualified witnesses, we do not hesitate to ascribe to the word, in the sense before indicated (§ xxxiv. 8), the highest authority for doctrine and life. *The Word*

[13] See the places enumerated by Schweitzer, *Glaubenslehre*, etc., i., p. 198, *seq.*
[14] *Auctoritas normativa et judicialis.*

of God contained in the Holy Scriptures, especially of the New Testament, is and remains, not only the expression, but also the rule of our faith, and the test not only of the Christian character, but also and above all of the truth of our conviction.

Will it still be necessary to defend with many words this proposition to which we are naturally led by all that precedes? But even the nature of the case must, upon a little reflection, place it beyond doubt. If it is once apparent that God has spoken, then the word spoken is naturally also the rule and arbiter for human thinking; not the converse. Holy Scripture itself points out this standpoint to us as the only firm and tenable one, and shows the rejection thereof to be the climax of folly.[15] It is true the Lord and His Apostles repeatedly appeal to the sound reason, the natural feeling, or the living conscience of their hearers;[16] and they might well do so, since their teaching naturally and easily attached itself to all these. But from this it by no means follows, as a simple consequence, that they recognised in this natural insight of their hearers the final arbiter in the question as to truth unto life; on the contrary, they had not a little to say to them, of which the accuracy might be perceived to a certain extent, but of which the essential contents must either be accepted upon their word—even if this were not understood—or else unbelievingly rejected. Such a demand is indeed entirely in harmony with the earthly condition of childhood in which we live, and with the nature of that faith, which in its innermost kernel and essence is not merely confidence, but *obedience.*[17] Never will the character of the heroes of the faith mentioned in Hebrews xi. be duly appreciated, or awaken a kindred flame, so long as it is tacitly assumed in regard to their great deeds, that they thus acted or suffered *only after* they had of themselves perceived that God's word was, notwithstanding all, essential truth, and His requirement supremely good.

It is asserted, it is true, that Holy Scripture, which makes us acquainted with the word of God, is only a test for the *Christian* character of our conviction; but not on that account necessarily of its *truth.* We doubt, however, whether this opposition itself can in principle be called Christian: where Christ is recognised as the revealed truth, there that which is genuinely Christian is as such at the same time recognised as true. The whole of this opposition rests on the false separation between ideas and facts, religious and historic belief, to which reference has been before made (§ xxxviii. 3); in other words, on a lamentable failure to perceive the historic character of the Saving Revelation. He who holds firmly to this last will at the same time be conscious that though nine-tenths of the contents of this revelation had been mastered by human thought, yet for the last tenth, the unfathomable remainder, no other choice would be left us than unbelief, or—belief on authority. He who calls this standpoint Judaistic, is perhaps himself not very far removed from heathen Naturalism, and sees himself compelled to accept either Rationalism or Mysticism, with all its

---

[15] Isa. viii. 20; Jer. viii. 8, 9; John xvii. 17; Heb. iv. 12; 2 Pet. i. 19, and many other places.

[16] Luke x. 36; John vii. 24; 1 Cor. x. 15, and other places.

[17] 2 Cor. x. 4, 5; 2 Thess. i. 8.

inevitable consequences. Certainly he has in principle broken with the spirit of Protestantism, which has its basis and strength, not in the recognition of the individual autonomy, but, on the contrary, of the immovable Theonomy (comp. § x. 7).

The Word of God, as contained in the Scripture, remains consequently the infallible rule and highest arbiter in the domain of Christianity and of Religion.[18] To the question, "whether anything is true, because it is in the Bible; or whether it is in the Bible, because it is true," no better answer can be given than, "the one and the other." Because something is truth unto salvation, God has made it known to us by means of the Bible; and because that which the Bible declares to us of God's Saving Plan, manifests and proves itself on satisfactory grounds to be truth, we receive it as such with all gratitude, desiring now also as far as possible to comprehend it, but —if need be—even without comprehending it. To use a well-known figure, the truth is like a glorious sun, in the midst of which is a dark spot: he who gazes long upon this latter, gradually discovers therein a new sun, with a new dark spot; until he must at last turn away his dazzled eye, or rather adoringly close it. The Word of God, at first the "*asylum ignorantiæ nostræ*," becomes very soon the "*centrum scientiæ nostræ*," until the limited extent of our knowledge compels us so much the more to take refuge in this same "*asylum*."

6. No wonder, after what has been said, that the Dogmatics of the Reformed Church continues still to hold fast to the "*repudiamus traditiones humanas*" of the old Confessions of Faith. In uttering this word, we

---

[18] It will perhaps not be without interest to remark that the Netherlands Confession (Art. vi.) not indistinctly teaches that what is beyond the sphere of faith is not to be tried before the forum of God's word in Holy Scripture. Freedom of judgment in regard to other subjects, which stand in no direct relation to religion, was admitted, and for himself used by Calvin. (Compare his *Annotationes* on Gen. i. 15, 16.) In a similar sense has sound orthodoxy frequently expressed itself in both the main branches of the Protestant Church. The *Augsb. Conf.*, for instance, (c. 43) reads: Apostoli jusserunt abstinere a sanguine: quis nunc observat? Neque tamen peccant, qui non observant." J. A. Quenstadt († 1688), the Voetius of the Lutheran Church, observes (*Syst. Th.* i., p. 241) —"Licet fides, generaliter spectata, versetur circa omnia quæ in Dei verbo continentur, specialiter tamen versatur *circa dogmata fidei.* Quod observandum, ne quis in *Tanneri*, Jesuitæ, absurditatem incidat, qui omne, quod in Bibliis SS. occurrit, vim dogmatis obtinere . . . . ita asseruit, ut etiam ex incestu Judæ et cane Tobiæ caudam movente, novos Articulos fidei ridicule produceret. Sic etiam historia de caudis vulpecarum Samsonis, de asina Bileami, de annis Methusalem, de ædificatione turris Bab., articulis fidei annumeranda esset." In a similar sense also others, of an orthodoxy equally above suspicion. He who on this account, in stating the claim of obedience to the Word of God, in the name of consistency so far overstates it, that truly believing theologians must hold themselves obliged to assert, with the Berlin Preacher, G. Knak, on the ground of Josh. x. 12, 13, that the sun revolves round the earth, except when at a word of miracle it stands still, seems to demand that they should outstrip the orthodoxy of the sixteenth and seventeenth centuries, in order to tread in the footsteps of the Jesuit Tanner. On the whole controversy, compare the very sensible and moderate judgment of F. R. Fay (Lange's *Bible Work*, O. T. iv., p. 84 of the original), who justly charges Knak with a confusion of ideas, "arising from an entire want of scientific tact, from the injurious operation of which the true cause of faith has much to suffer." Must we then infer from [the Greek of] Acts xxvii. 27, "Some land was nearing them," that the land approaches us when we are sailing towards the shore? *Cave a consequentariis.*

approach the treatment of the great controversy on this subject, between the Protestant and the Romish Church.

By tradition (*traditio*, *παράδοσις*) the Romish Church understands the sum of those religious truths and duties, which were presented by the Lord and the Apostles only orally, and on that account are unwritten, yet by the Church, under the guidance of the Holy Spirit, have been transmitted uncorrupted and in unbroken order. This tradition, variously divided—historic, dogmatic, liturgical, etc.—has the design of complementing the Scripture, which does not absolutely embrace within itself all that is necessary for salvation. It is in great part contained in the writings of the Fathers, which consequently may be regarded as its witnesses; while only the authority of the Church (*consensus Patrum*) raises anything to the dignity of a universally acknowledged tradition. That which has been so stamped, has the same authority as Holy Scripture, and the Council of Trent decided: "*Si quis traditiones prædictas sciens et prudens contemserit, anathema sit.*" Indeed, being a fruit of the Holy Spirit, it is impossible that tradition should essentially contradict inspired Scripture. More definitely does Bellarmine yet further distinguish between a written and an unwritten word of God; and understands by this last, traditions, which he again divides into Divine, Apostolical, and Ecclesiastical. To uphold the value of the Ecclesiastical traditions, he appeals especially to the supposed fact that Scripture itself rests upon tradition, and also without the latter must remain obscure and unintelligible. In addition, he urges that Jesus and the greater part of the Apostles have left no writings behind them; and that notably Paul several times refers to tradition,[9] while moreover the Protestants themselves cannot give a good reason for Infant Baptism, the observance of the Sunday, etc., without an appeal to tradition. On similar grounds Bossuet also defended the Romish standpoint. Within the present century it has especially been defended in a talented manner by the renowned J. A. Möhler († 1838), in his *Symbolik*. He described tradition as "the Word living on in the hearts of the faithful"—the fruit of a peculiar Christian tact present in the Church, and which is handed down by means of the education given by the Church. On the Protestant side he has been especially controverted by Baur and Nitzsch, as was his spiritual kinsman Delbrück, by Lücke and Sack. How much, nevertheless, even at the present time, is covered and vindicated, on the part of the Romish Church, by an appeal to tradition, the history of the last few years suffices to show.

Now the Reformation of the sixteenth century, especially that in Switzerland, was an unequivocal protest against this over-valuing of Tradition. "*Domino suum regnum eripitur, quoties Ipse traditionum humanarum legibus colitur, quod gravissimum semper fuit crimen*" (Calvin). It was expressly declared by the Netherlands Confession (Art. vii.), that no other authority than that of the Word is to be acknowledged: other Confessions expressed themselves not less conclusively, and even the Arminians and Socinians held no other views on this point. It is true that later solitary voices even

---

[19] 1 Cor. xi. 2; 2 Thess. ii. 15; iii. 6; 2 Tim. i. 13; ii. 2; iii. 14.

within the Protestant Church have raised themselves in favour of tradition. G. Calixtus (1634) looked upon the tradition of the first five centuries as a subordinate source of our knowledge of the truth, and a basis for the unity of the Church. Lessing made the priority of tradition, in point of time, over Scripture his bulwark in the battle against Orthodoxy. In Denmark, Grundtvig made the attempt in our own time to unite the confessors of the Gospel around the banner of the Apostles' Creed, as the earliest and certain badge of their faith; and all the crypto-Catholic movements of our time seek openly or secretly to find, in tradition, a support for their authority. On the contrary, the Evangelical, and especially the Reformed Church, still continues to see a difference of principle between herself and Rome on this point; and the question presents itself, on which side we must take our place in this conflict.

We may readily admit that the Dogmatics of the seventeenth century, in its opposition to tradition, now and then exceeded the bounds, not only of the Reformers, but also of truth and soberness. The great value of tradition—especially in the first ages of the Church, when the Canon of the New Testament was not yet finally closed—however loudly proclaimed by an Irenæus, a Tertullian, an Augustine, and others, has not been always duly estimated on the part of ultra-Protestantism. It is of course undeniable that the stream of tradition, in the midst of so much mud and silt, may have brought down in its bed many grains of the pure gold of truth; and that it is the duty of the Protestant, also, to listen with devout and reverent attention to the testimony of the ages, where that testimony is unanimous and trustworthy. We may add, that from the standpoint of the so-called Modern Theology and mode of regarding Scripture, all right of polemic against Rome on the score of tradition is for ever annihilated. Between the fable of the assumption of Mary, and that of Christ, there is for Naturalism no essential difference.

Entirely different, however, is the position of modern Supranaturalism, which continues to build upon the recognition of God's Word as a sure foundation for its faith; and confesses with Cyprian, *Consuetudo sine veritate, vetustas erroris est.* It joins with a good conscience in the controversy which has been waged against Rome on this point also, now for nearly four centuries, and continues to confess that "neither great numbers, nor antiquity, nor the succession of times and persons, nor councils, decrees, and decisions," can bear any comparison with the truth of God according to the Holy Scriptures. Indeed, even admitting that Holy Scripture leaves unanswered questions on many points, yet that which is incomplete can in no case be filled up by that which is uncertain. A striking instance of the "*fama crescit eundo*," even in sacred things, has been preserved to us in John xxi. 23. An infallible tradition, supposing it were possible, the Church of Rome would be able to prove only by an appeal to the promise of oly Scripture, (John xvi. 13, for example,) which Scripture, however, she asserts she could not believe, unless impelled thereto by the authority of tradition. Moreover, the promise of the Lord belongs precisely to that Church which is built upon the foundation of the Apostles and Prophets; and with the utterances of these Apostles and Prophets the Church of Rome is, on numberless points, in direct conflict.

A miracle, such as they would here have us assume, is therefore neither promised nor to be expected.—*Exegetically*, the acknowledgment of tradition in the Romish sense can be equally little justified. While Paul exalts the Apostolic Paradosis (2 Thess. ii. 15; 2 Tim. ii. 2), yet precisely by adding a further written communication to that which had been formerly given by word of mouth, does he sufficiently show that he regards a supplementing and elucidation of the former as necessary. It is true all Scripture rests upon anterior tradition, but so soon as this has been fixed in writing, its oral transmission has become on that very account superfluous: the flowing stream is now as it were arrested.—*Historically*, moreover, it is sufficiently apparent that the Apostolic tradition, so far from being preserved in its purity, has become in an increasing measure polluted. Let any one think of the round of fables in the Apocryphal Gospels, of the absurd accounts of Papias concerning the death of Judas, of the foolish description of the millennium which Irenæus puts into the lips of the Lord, and let him draw for himself the conclusion with regard to later times. So many *bonorum lapsus*, *malorum imposturæ* (Chemnitz) are here manifest, that tradition must rather be corrected by Scripture, than the latter receive its complement from tradition.—In addition to this, the boasted *Consensus Patrum* exists nowhere else but in the imagination. Even the well-known *Sic et Non* of Abelard suffices to put an end for ever to all illusion on this point. Unceasingly do the earlier doctrine of the Church and the later tradition directly contradict each other. The irreconcilable contradiction with its own utterances in which the Church of Rome has been repeatedly involved in different ages, on the question, for instance, of the number of Sacraments, the immaculate conception of the Mother of the Lord, and the Papal infallibility, is no secret to any. Or, unless new historic sources have been discovered, has there been in regard to all this a new revelation of the Spirit? and if so, how has this established its claim to our confidence? and how came it to contradict in so direct a manner its own infallible utterances of former times?

It is evident therefore that, to say no more, the building upon the basis of tradition is, *in practice*, partly something not feasible, partly—so far as it does succeed—something hurtful. The rule "that all tradition is to be regarded as Apostolic, of which at the present time the origin cannot be positively proved from other sources" (Bossuet), must be pronounced as hazardous as it is arbitrary. Has then the Church remained entirely without any contact with the lying spirit of the world? Has tradition no need even of the least control? And where is this latter to be found, except in those very Scriptures which, in favour of tradition, are continually placed in the background? The matter is not mended if with Möhler we idealise tradition as "the Word still resounding and living on in the heart of the faithful," whether we think in connection with it of a voice like that of the *testimonium Sp. Sancti*, in the sense of Calvin; or of the Christian consciousness, as Schleiermacher conceives of it. For tradition is not the fruit of the Consensus of all upright believers, and of these alone; but of the Hierarchy, whose history we know. Yea, even the former itself remains always liable to error, and must find an unceasing corrective in the word of the Lord. "Our Lord called Himself, not custom, but the Truth," says an ancient Father.[20] And if it is still repeated that the Protestant, also, appeals for the authority of some ecclesiastical customs to tradition; we reply that the latter ought neither to be rejected nor neglected, provided only we never overlook the fact that this tradition is never in such a case to be *de jure divino*, but only *de jure humano*. Not as an infallible authority alongside of, or even above, the Scripture, but as the venerable witness of antiquity, there is given to it a qualified right of decision—not in the domain of ethical, but only of historical and ecclesiastical questions—subject always to the inalienable right and duty of testing all things by the utterance of God's Word in Holy Scripture. Without reserve therefore must we continue to reject the claim, that we should be in any way bound—in the interpretation of Scripture—by the exegesis of tradition. While this demand has nothing to legitimate it, it is one moreover which it is impossible to satisfy. The promise of the Romish priests, "I will never receive and interpret Holy Scripture, except according to the unanimous consent of the fathers," naturally calls forth the query, where in the world this "Consensus" is to be found; and a satisfactory answer to this question we still wait for. For all these reasons we take no other position in regard to the tradition of the Romish Church, than that which the Lord took in regard to the tradition of the Jews,[21] and apply in relation to it the Apostolic warning against the tradition of men.[22] Unquestionably the *quod ubique, semper, ab omnibus creditum est*, has something about it which awakens within us reverence and admiration, but only when it can endure the infallible test which is given us in the written Word of the God of truth. The Scripture of the Apostles, particularly that of the New Testament, has, as the *fons et norma veritatis*, not only the priority, but also the superiority, over every other voice; because the sacred stream, in the immediate vicinity of the Source, is necessarily much purer than where, farther on in its course, it has to a much greater extent received into itself impure elements.

The enduring importance of this question strikes us at once. It is true the difference with Rome is relatively small, as compared with the terrible conflict which the Belief in Revelation of all churches must wage against Naturalism and Materialism; but nevertheless important enough to be—above all in our day—contested with zeal. By nothing does one play more successfully into the hands of Rome, and all that leads to Rome or tends Romewards, than by rebellion against the authority of God's Word in Holy Scripture.—The same is the case with regard to Rationalism, which reveres the individual human authority—as Rome does the collective authority of men—as the highest arbiter in the domain of truth. It is impossible, doubtless, to reduce *this* assumption within becoming limits simply with an authoritative, "It is written." Not as a book of Law, but as a book of Life alone, can Scripture give the final verdict. "The nearer or more distant connection of the word of Scripture with Christ as the centre of our faith, affords a standard by which we can dis-

---

[20] Dominus noster se non consuetudinem, sed veritatem dixit.—TERTULLIAN.
[21] Mark vii. 8.
[22] Col. ii. 8.

tinguish what is more, and what is less, essential for the Christian consciousness" (Twesten). But ever more must the "hear Him" be repeated and responded to with renewed earnestness, if at last a decisive weight is to be cast into the trembling scale of uncertainty and doubt.—As opposed also to the sickly manifestations of a cloudy Mysticism, the "*ad Legem et Testimonium*" remains the only medicine which will permanently stand the test. The "*vertiginosi homines,*" to express ourselves with Calvin,[23] "*qui Spiritûs Magisterium fastuosissime obtendentes, lectionem omnem respuunt,*" must ride [as a ship] unceasingly over the gulfs of feeling and imagination, until they have learnt in this firm ground to cast their anchor. As opposed to the boundless negations of the Naturalism of the age, we may very soon expect to see an unbridled reaction towards an ignoble Mysticism, unless the heads and hearts of men are by a timely change led back to the obedience of faith in God's Word, as contained in Holy Scripture. But—how then, for the attainment of this end, are we *to make use of* Holy Scripture?

Compare K. H. SACK, *Vom Worte Gottes, eine Christl. Verständigung* (1825); P. JALAGUYER, *Le témoignage de Dieu, base de la foi Chrétienne* (1851); J. J. VAN TOORENENBERGEN, Treatise on the authority of Scripture, in *Ernst en Vrede* (1854), p. 19, *sqq.* On *Tradition,* the Treatise of J. H. STUFFKEN, in the works of Teyler's Theol. Society, pt. xxxiii. (1840); J. L. JACOBI, *Die kirchliche Lehre von der Trad. und H. S.,* i. (1847), not completed; the Art. *Tradition* by HOLTZMAN, in Herzog, *R. E.,* xvi.; and K. H. HASE, *Handbuch der Protest. Polemik gegen die Röm. Kath. Kirche* (1862), p. 73, *sqq.*

POINTS FOR INQUIRY.

What value is to be attached to the Holy Scriptures from the standpoint of the Roman Catholic, the Lutheran, and the Reformed Church?—The place of Scripture from the standpoint of the Modern Theology.—Nearer definition and defence of the *Affectiones S. S.*—The principle of Scripture authority frequently exaggerated or not recognised.—Historic development, ecclesiastical determining, Protestant contesting, Roman Catholic reconstruction of the doctrine of Tradition.—Whence so many crypto-Catholicising influences in the Church life of our day, and how best, with the desired result, to combat them?

SECTION XLI.—ITS USE.

The high value of Holy Scripture legitimates and defines its use, as well from the standpoint of the Church as of science. For every one who seeks after truth, and especially for a Christian of the Reformed Confession, the untrammelled investigation thereof is equally a right, a duty, and a blessing. In the domain of Christian doctrine the Scripture is rightly made use of, when it is duly tested, interpreted according to precise rules, employed in

---

[23] CALV., *Inst.* I. 9. 1.

explaining, purifying, and developing Church Confessions, and is consulted as a guide in individual Christian philosophic investigation of the truth. Only with such a use of the Bible, controlled and rendered fruitful by the Holy Spirit, is an efficient Apology of the Christian belief in Revelation to be expected, and the *Dogmatic Superstructure* rises upon the foundation thus laid and completed.

After the value of Scripture has been duly maintained, the question as to the ecclesiastical and scientific *Use* of the same is naturally in place. The former flows, as a matter of course, out of the polemic which we were just now obliged to wage; the latter is of supreme importance for the whole of the dogmatical investigation now following, and is precisely here in place where we have approached the boundaries which separate the Apologetic basis from the Dogmatic superstructure. In regard to the former, especially, it seems desirable to follow the pathway of history.

I. 1. The *general use of Scripture in the Church* we see at first *permitted* without any restriction. Together with the Scriptures of the Old Testament those of the New were openly read in the assemblies of the brethren,[1] were disseminated, translated, and so highly valued that they were prized even above life, while those who gave them up to the enemy received the name of *Traditores.*[2] The Emperor Julian reproached the Christians with allowing even women and children to read their sacred books. Augustine, Chrysostom, Gregory the First, expressly commend the reading of Scripture, and censure the neglect thereof. Even when the highest value was attached to tradition, the use of Scripture remained unrestrained. It is true, it was much too little placed in the hands of the newly converted peoples, but yet in the beginning, at least, of the Middle Ages, was still forbidden to none.

2. Gradually, however, we find the use of Scripture first neglected, and then *restricted* within narrower limits. The prevalence of ecclesiastical Latin in the public worship rendered the word of life accessible only to an ever smaller number. Gregory VII. saw a beneficent dispensation of Providence in the fact that the Scripture, by being partially involved in obscurity, was preserved from contempt and abuse. Voices like those of Anselm and Bonaventura, which still commended the reading of Scripture, became ever more rare. Especially did distrust and opposition increase on the part of the Church, when Scripture became the mighty weapon in the hand of the heretical sects. Innocent III. (1199), the Council of Toulouse (1229), and of Tarragona (1234), prohibited the reading of the Bible, and that of Oxford (1408), with an eye to Wycliffe, opposed its translation into the vernacular. When, however, after the discovery of the art of printing, the number of translations increased, and when an Erasmus recommended to laymen, also, the reading of the Bible,[3] and the Reforma-

---

[1] 1 Tim. iv. 13; Rev. i. 3.

[2] Compare the Article *Die Märtyrer der heil. Bücher*, in PIPER'S *Evang. Kal.* (1859), p. 107, *sqq.*

[3] Prol. to his *Paraphr. N. T.*

tion found its main support in the unrestrained use thereof, the Council of Trent (1545—1563) came forth with its emphatic *Veto.* The ten rules providing for the *Index librorum prohibitorum*, had also in part their application to this matter. The reading of heretical translations of the New Testament was forbidden to all; the use of the Bible in the vernacular was permitted to the laity only under the written sanction of the spiritual superior, and to the Vulgate with all its imperfections was accorded the right of final decision as to the Church's interpretation of the Scripture. Yet more strict became the prohibitive measures, after Jansenism in the person of Quesnel (1699) recommended the use of the Scripture, and thereby called forth the famous bull *Unigenitus* (1713). It is true that later, on the part of Pius VI. for example, milder views found expression; but the increased activity of the Bible Societies called forth a fresh reaction. Pius VII. (1816), Leo XII. (1824), Gregory XVI. (1832), renewed the ecclesiastical anathema; and very soon the freer spirit of many belonging to the first quarter of the present century—a Leander van Ess, Sailer, Schrant, and others — continued to live only in the memory. Although there are by no means wanting, in our day, traces of a zealous study of the Bible and ardent attachment thereto, on the part of learned laymen, even within the bosom of the Romish Church,[4] the spirit of the Council of Trent still remains, taken as a whole, there the prevailing one. The Greek Church also, at the Synod of Jerusalem (1672), prohibited to the laity the reading of the Bible; and, in point of practice, stands in regard to this matter even below the Romish. Is it strange if, in the presence of some episcopal mandamuses, (that of Malou at Bruges, for instance, in 1853,) the complaint is heard on the part of the Protestants, "*Ecclesia abhorret a Bibliis*"?

3. How the Reformation has *reconquered and recommended* the free use of the Bible is universally known. The grounds which are brought forward on the Protestant side for the unrestricted use of the Scripture, are derived *partly* from the peculiar character of Holy Scripture, as the trustworthy document of the Divine Revelation, designed for all, and indispensable for all; *partly* from the precept and example of the principal servants of God and believers of the Old Testament and the New;[5] and *partly* from history and experience, which gives the most striking testimony as to the blessing on a well-regulated investigation of Scripture. The objections brought against it, and drawn either from the obscurity of the Holy Scriptures, or from the sad divisions fostered by the different views of individual interpretation, or from the less chaste and moral language of some passages of the Bible, are partly exaggerated, partly only too well-founded; yet even in the latter case they simply show that the unlimited examination ought to be a highly cautious and at the same time well-regulated one. In any case the hurtful consequences of the ecclesiastical prohibition of the Bible are much greater than those of its unintelligent use. The charge of essential corruption of the

---

[4] See, for instance, the meritorious translation of the New Testament [into Dutch] by Dr. S. P. LIPMAN, second edition, 1861 and following years.

[5] Josh. i. 8; Ps. cxix. 9, 105; Isa. xxxiv. 16; Hos. viii. 12; Luke iv. 16; John v. 39; Acts xvii. 11; Col. iv. 16; 2 Tim. iii. 15, 16; 2 Pet. iii. 15.

Bible is one entirely wanting in proof, and the imperfections of the Vulgate—to which the erring mother-Church directs her sons—are, for all who are capable of judging on the question, fully proved. He who compares the difficulties placed by the Church in the way of reading the Bible, with its toleration and favouring of the rudest superstitions, can hardly explain the former in any other way than on the ground of an easily intelligible desire for self-preservation. No Biblicism, or idolatry of the letter, ever indulged in by P o estants, deserves so severe a reprimand as the hierarchical arbitrariness which renders applicable to Holy Scripture the words: "Thou shalt not eat of this tree, lest thou die" (Perrone). The prohibition of the Bible is the Achilles heel of Roman Catholicism; the free investigation of Scripture the bulwark of the Evangelical Church, as opposed to an antiquated Ultramontanism on the one hand, and to modern Naturalism on the other. As opposed to this last, also, it cannot be too strongly stated that Holy Scripture in its totality, and in its most essential parts, must ever retain its place in the religious life of Christendom, and that the Church which has in principle broken with the Gospel of the Scriptures, has thrown away its own future.

II. As far as the *Theological* use of Scripture is concerned—and more particularly in the service of Christian Dogmatics—the right of the Reformed Theologian needs here just as little to be maintained, as the solemn obligation under which he is to consult it needs to be formally recalled to mind. All depends, however, on the spirit and method in which he begins to consult the Sacred Scriptures. Let us distinguish for the sake of clearness—what for the rest will not be separated in our further treatment—the *Biblical*, *Ecclesiastical*, and *Critical* Dogmatics; and let us ask how Holy Scripture is to be used in connection with each of these three.

1. *Biblical* must Christian Dogmatics be, in this sense, that it concerns itself, above all things, to know the Lord's own teaching, and that of His witnesses; and strives to understand this in the true spirit, and to present it in its just connection. To this end, however, it is necessary that Holy Scripture, as the indispensable *principium cognoscendi*, should be duly *tested.* We must not, in Dogmatics either, think of limiting in any way the free examination of the Scriptures; but must, in the interest of the subject itself, insist so much the more that the criticism should be a legitimate and really unbiassed one, approaching the subject without any preformed opinion. As Christian Theologians, we must have cultivated such spirit—before Dogmatics can think of beginning its work—both in respect of the words and the facts in Holy Scripture, which must serve as stones in the building up of our edifice. Of how great importance, also, the words of Scripture may be regarded, is evident from a glance at such Scripture texts as Acts xv. 18; xx. 28; 1 Tim. iii. 16; 1 John v. 7, and the Articles of Doctrine not seldom based upon them. But also in regard to the facts, especially the most important and most fiercely assailed, it must be made apparent whether they really happened, and have been faithfully recorded. And not this alone. Out of such multiplicity of Religious ideas and utterances recorded in the Holy Scriptures, a cautious criticism will have to ascertain whether they virtually belong to the sphere of Revelation

properly so called, or whether they are rather personal opinions, to which in no case a Prophetic or Apostolic character can be ascribed. (Let any one think, for example, of the mistaken judgments of Job's friends, or of the philosophic doubts of the author of Ecclesiastes, in regard to life and death.) So also will it have duly to distinguish between the contents of the thoughts and exhortations here expressed, and the particular form in which they are given.[6] And not less between that which was prescribed to a definite circle of individuals, and that which remains of high significance for all in all time.[7] Universal rules for the one and the other of these cannot, of course, be given here; where we have exclusively to do with the establishing of the principle. While it remains ever true that each part of the Saving Revelation can only be comprehended in the light of the whole, it remains equally necessary to investigate the parts one by one, if we are to satisfy the requirement of a truly scientific examination.

That the Scripture must be accurately *explained* before Biblical Dogmatics can take into account the utterances thereof, is self-evident, and does not in the least conflict with what has been earlier said as to the perspicuity of Scripture (§ xl. 2). The most distinguished Biblical Theologians have been as a rule, at the same time, excellent Exegetes (Heringa, Vinke, and others). The rules for the grammatico-historic interpretation of Scripture, here presupposed as known, must thus form the fundamental law and basis of all exegetic-dogmatic examination. Only let no one suppose that that which is absolutely indispensable must also be, without anything further, in itself wholly sufficient. For a truly spiritual understanding of God's Word—and who has greater need of this than he who applies himself to dogmatic science?—a kind of knowledge is also required, different from that which is acquired as a result of linguistic and historic examination. The true exposition of the Scripture which brings forth for Dogmatics the most blessed fruits, must be above all a Theological, a truly Pneumatic one [under the influence of the Spirit of God], such as can be expected only of the man who has taken a deeper glance into the organic whole of the Saving Revelation; because the same Spirit which speaks to us in the Scriptures, dwells in him, and gives him to understand that which is of kindred origin, by the power of inner sympathy. The word spoken by the renowned Lücke, now more than fifty years ago (1817), has here its application; "that the Spirit who is of God is Himself the only true explainer of His words, the *Angelus interpres*, who discloses to us the meaning of the Scriptures." Naturally, by this demand for a purely spiritual apprehension of Holy Scripture, it is not by any means intended that Exegesis should for ever surrender itself into a state of bondage to Dogmatism, to inquire of the pillars of orthodoxy in what way one is allowed to apprehend the Scripture, and in what not. The Romish Church may forbid to explain Scripture in any other sense than that which she recognises as the only true one; not so the Protestant Theologian, who has to base his Dogmatics on independent Exegesis, never the Exegesis upon a perhaps very defective eccle-

---

[6] See, *e.g.*, Luke xi. 24—27; Ephes. vi. 12.

[7] Comp. Acts xv. 29; 1 Cor. xi. 10, *sqq.*, and other places.

siastical Dogmatics. But precisely this legitimately free Exegesis will penetrate the more deeply into the sacred documents, in proportion as it is the less exclusively occupied with the letter of each word, nor forgets the admonition of the Reformer; "*adferat mentem non profanam, non amantem sophistices, non furentem ambitione et studio; sed timentem Deum, amantem veritatis, quærentem veras consolationes in conversione, et volentem Deum recte invocare, dolentem etiam propter ecclesiæ vulnera, quæ magis magisque lacerantur; sæpe etiam lectioni miscentem gemitus, et petentem ut a Deo doceatur.*"[8] Only in this way is it possible to attain, not only to a pure, but also to a thoroughly Biblical Dogmatics—one which bears the distinct impress of the Spirit of the Lord, and of His Apostles.

2. Biblical Dogmatics necessarily passes over into the *Dogmatics of the Church*, because the Scripture is differently explained, while those who in the main interpret it in one sense soon agree together in one confession. The examination into the Dogmatics of a particular Church is naturally of an historico critical kind, but yet it is not possible that this element of the great whole of Christian Dogmatics should duly take the place it has a right to claim, unless as a consequence of the use of Scripture conducted in accordance with fixed laws.

Even for the *elucidation* of the Confession, Scripture affords an important aid. Not always does the latter express itself equally unambiguously and clearly; and the question as to the real meaning intended by those who drew it up is sometimes differently answered. But this at least may be taken for granted; the Confession itself is designed to be nothing else than the expression of a certain conviction as to the faith, based upon a certain conception of the Sacred Scriptures. In proportion as these last are thus better understood, we shall the better succeed in entering into the spirit and tendency of the Confession, since this is intended only to be the ecclesiastical official explanation of the word of truth, as this lives in the consciousness of a particular community. The Scripture is thus, as it were, the *torch* which must light us in our walking through the venerable, but sometimes dim, temple-hall of the Church's doctrine.—Yet more: for the *rectification* also of the Church's belief, the consulting of Scripture is absolutely necessary. A Church which truly holds fast to its Confession is bound—in conformity with this last, and with the spirit of Protestantism—to eliminate from its doctrine every element which is in positive contradiction with the well-established and well-explained utterance of God's Word in Holy Scripture. In what way this is to be done cannot here be so much as hinted at; but the principle itself was given utterance to thirty years before the framing of the Netherlands Confession, in the Confession of Basle (1534): "This our Confession we subject to the judgment of Holy Scripture, with the promise that if we are better informed out of the said Scripture, we will at all times be obedient to God and His Word." It must be carefully guarded against lest—as has been more than once the case of late years—the seventh Article of the Netherlands Confession should be used as a lever to overthrow the whole structure, and to justify

---

[8] Melancthon, *Proëm. ad Comm. in Ep. ad Rom.*

the renouncing of obedience to God's Word in Holy Scripture.[9] But just as much must we be also on our guard against retaining as an unalterable element of Confession or of doctrine, that of which the real ground cannot possibly be shown in God's Word. We must show ourselves in the first place *Christian*, in the second *Protestant*, and only in the third *Reformed* Theologians—not the converse. One may esteem it a personal happiness if one can with an honest Theological conscience stand on the ground of the Confession; but the honour of sound Orthodoxy, as measured by the standard of the Church is—regarded from a Christian standpoint—by no means the highest. It may well be that one feels himself, on the ground of Scripture itself, and by virtue of the Protestant principle, bound in conscience to differ on a certain point from the doctrine of the Church. Heterodoxy in such a case is not to be regarded at once as heresy. —The rectification of the traditional creed, which is in this way tested by the Word, may even lead to its further *development*, provided that it is tested only by means of Holy Scripture. *Precisely he truly holds to his Confession of Faith, in the Evangelical-Protestant sense of the term, who recognises in the Confession not the absolutely perfect form of his religious conviction, but that which may be constituted an ever more perfect form of it; and who seeks to attain to this higher perfection by an ever closer attachment, and an ever deeper subjection of himself, to God's Word in Holy Scripture.* There yet lie treasures in the gold mine, which await only the well-directed spade of the digger: of these Dogmatics must bring at least some part to light, and it will do so the better after each new and profound examination of the Bible, so long as the maxim is found to be true: "*Theologus in Scripturis nascitur.*"

3. Christian Dogmatics must, however, be not simply a reproduction of Bible teaching, and of the Church Confession. It must be, above all, an historico-critical investigation, a systematic presentation of the subject-matter and grounds of the faith. The science thus, in the last place, manifests a *critical* character, and it lies in the nature of the case, that Scripture can least of all be set aside just in this the most difficult part of the task of Dogmatics. On the contrary, what Cyprian was wont to say when he desired to consult the writings of Tertullian, "*Da mihi magistrum*," "Let us hear what the master says," the Christian theologian may repeat with yet greater justice in regard to his Bible. The word of God in Holy Scripture alone affords, not only a sure guide, but also the most trustworthy starting-point for Christian thought. Nothing can claim to be regarded as revealed truth, which cannot be traced back in some way to the Gospel of the Scriptures, or at least be justified therefrom; but every hint which God's Word in Scripture affords us concerning His plan of salvation, may at

---

[9] Confess. Belgica, Art. vii.—"Credimus autem sacram hanc Scripturam perfectissime omnem Dei voluntatem complecti, et in illa abunde ea omnia doceri, quaecunque ab hominibus credi necesse est, ut salutem consequantur. Itaque," *etc.* Compare the *Confessio Helvetica Secunda*:—"In Scriptura sancta habet universalis Christi Ecclesia plenissime exposita, quaecunque pertinent cum ad salvificam fidem, tum ad vitam Deo placentem. Non alium in causa fidei judicem, quam ipsum Deum per Scripturas sacras pronuntiantem, quid verum sit, quid falsum, quid sequendum sit, quidve fugiendum." Similarly does the *Confessio Gallicana* express itself. Compare also the sixth Art. of the Church of England, and the first chapter of the Westminster Confession.

the same time bring us on the trace of deeper reflection. "Dogmatic thinking must not merely be tested by Scripture, and not only not conflict with Scripture; but must be organically fructified, and rendered ever young again, out of the fulness of Scriptural teaching. As the typical [representative] work of the Spirit of Inspiration, the Scripture encloses within itself an infinity of germs, capable of a continued development; and while every dogmatic system grows old, the Bible remains eternally young, precisely because it gives to us, not a systematic presentation of truth, but the fulness of the truth, which offers the material for a multiplicity of systems" (Martensen).

It must, however, be not only a believing, but also a truly scientific use of Scripture, to which the dogmatist devotes himself. Dogmatics pursued in a critical spirit has not only to show that a statement is Scriptural, but also that it is intrinsically true. Its task is thus not completed when it has proved that a certain thing is in the Bible, or follows incontestably from its utterances; but only when it has made manifest that the proposition is wholly in harmony with the contents, spirit, and tendency of the Saving Revelation, and thus—according to the Word of Scripture—must be believed by us, so truly as we are men, are sinners, are Christians. For this purpose, it is evident that no reference to a single isolated text of Scripture is sufficient—in this way anything might be proved—but rather a use of Scripture on a greater and wider scale is necessary, like that to which Schleiermacher exhorted in his day;[10] although conducted in a wholly different manner from that of which he has given a precedent himself. By how much more the Christian philosophic thinking is in this sense made subject to the discipline of God's Word in Holy Scripture, by so much less does it run the risk of falling into error; while, on the other hand, in the champions of emancipation in this respect the word of Jeremiah viii. 8, 9, is fulfilled. In order, on the sea of speculation on invisible things, to suffer no shipwreck upon the otherwise inevitable rocks of Atheism on the one side, and Pantheism on the other, which deep under the water are linked together as by a mysterious root, there is only one successful precaution, the following of the compass of the Word, of which Scripture is the depository. Only where this guides us do we sail into a secure haven, and feel presently again under our feet the solid land. In the opposite case we never get further than to an ever-changing *Yea* and *Nay*, which—as has been justly said—is "no good theology."

Result: The true Dogmatist stands, in regard to the document of Saving Revelation, neither in the relation of slave nor of judge; but in a relation of self-conscious and voluntary dependence, in consequence of which he penetrates ever more deeply into the sense of God's written Word, and each time better understands it in the light of the Holy Spirit.

4. That a use of the Bible, such as has been recommended in the foregoing paragraphs, cannot but have a favourable effect upon the Apology of the Christian belief in Revelation—here, so far as our present object is con-

---

[10] *Christliche Glaubenslehre*, § xxvii. 3.

cerned, concluded by us—at the end of our argumentation scarcely needs any proof. The theology of the nineteenth century, in this respect entirely resembling that of the second, bears a peculiarly Apologetic character. There is scarcely any theologian of any eminence in our day, who has not within the last few years contributed more or less valuable materials to the upbuilding of the Apology of the Christian faith. To this Apology all the sciences of the whole theological encyclopædia must in the end render their contributions, and notably Dogmatics cannot possibly think of the raising of its doctrinal structure, without its apologetic basis being each time anew investigated, consolidated, and maintained. For this gigantic work itself, however, as well as for its basis, a careful and well-directed use of the Scripture remains, I do not say the only, but still ever the first requisite, since the truth of the words of Crusius is on each occasion strikingly confirmed by experience: "As the sun is seen by his own light, so the truth shows itself best by means of itself." The more truth is known in its whole extent, and *as a whole*, in the light of Scripture and of Scriptural experience, the more speedily will the unhappy prejudice against Christian Dogmatics and its study disappear—a prejudice which has the appearance of being so highly scientific, and yet is really as superficial as possible. Only let it never be forgotten that there is no Dogmatics worthy of the name without an ever-renewed Apologetics; no true Apologetics without a sound criticism—even though of criticism itself—but most of all of him who applies it. Only then does the path of the investigation lead through the depths to the heights; and thus only does Christian Dogmatics become, in the noblest sense of the word, a witness to the faith; and the clearer conception of the truth brings forth imperishable fruits in the life, because this conception itself is born out of the depths of a living experience.

Comp. LEANDER VAN ESS, *Auszüge über d. nothwend. u. nützliche Bibellesen, aus den Kirchenvätern und and. Kathol. Schriften* (1816); A. MONOD, *Lucile, ou la lecture de la Bible* (1845); the article of HERZOG, *R. E.*, ii., *Bibellesen der Laien;* the treatise of KIJLSTRA, *De Bijbel nog altijd onmisbaar*. W. in L. (1866), i. On the relation of Christian Dogmatics to Holy Scripture, C. A. AUBERLEN, *Das Verhältniss der gegenw. Theol. zu der H. S.*, Academic Inaugural Discourse (1851); a paper by A. T. REITSMA, *N. Jbb.* (1860), p. 91, *seq.;* V. D. GOLTZ, *Ueber die universelle Bedeutung der Bibel* (1865). On the task of Exegesis in relation to Dogmatics, J. I. DOEDES, *Hermeneutics of the Scriptures of the New Testament*, p. 33, *sqq.*, of the second edition of the original work (1869).

POINTS FOR INQUIRY.

Differences in principle as to the use to be made of the Bible.—Has the Romish Church always remained self-consistent in this respect?—What was the earlier, and what the later, judgment of Rationalism as to the unrestrained use of the Holy Scriptures?—On what grounds is this examination a duty, and under what conditions a blessing?—Further explanation of objections, especially those derived from modern Naturalism.—History of the use made of Scripture in relation to Dogmatics.—Scripture interpretation *ad analogiam fidei?*—Scripture and Church doctrine.—Scripture and the Christian philosophy of Religion.—Scripture and the Holy Spirit in their mutual and inseparable union in the domain of Apologetics and Dogmatics.—Conclusion and transition.

PART II.

THE DOGMATIC SUPERSTRUCTURE.

CHAPTER I.

ON GOD, OR THE SOVEREIGN OF THE KINGDOM OF HEAVEN.

(THEOLOGY.)

SECTION XLII.—INTRODUCTORY SURVEY.

THE Christian dogmatical examination of the mystery of the Kingdom of God ought, especially from the standpoint of the Evangelical Reformed Church and Theology, to begin with the doctrine concerning God. In this treatment regard must be had separately, first to the Nature, and then to the Works of God. The humble recognition of the incomprehensibleness of God for the finite understanding must serve, not as an obstacle, but as a stimulus and guide, in the way of this investigation.

Upon the *Apologetic Basis* already laid down, we now proceed to raise the *Dogmatic Superstructure;* from the outer court we now enter into the sanctuary itself. Ere we cross the threshold, however, a threefold question arises. . It has reference to the *Place*, the *Claim*, and the *Limit* of the investigation which awaits us in this chapter.

1. Must indeed the first *Place* in the Christian dogmatical investigation be conceded to the doctrine concerning God? (Theology) Not all have given or do now give an affirmative answer to this question; some have

chosen and recommended another starting-point. Melancthon, in his *Loci*, for instance, started from the point of man's free-will; the Heidelberg Catechism, with the doctrine of man's misery; in our own time the Groningen school, with Christ, etc. Yet we are and continue to be of opinion that to Theology, in the more restricted sense of the term, belongs the place of honour in the dogmatic investigation.

First of all, even the *nature of the case* favours this method above all others. If there is really a God, then He can be nothing less than the *Alpha* of all our science, especially in this special domain. Not in man, but only in God, is found the standard of highest truth. All other main points stand in relation to this as the planets to the sun: "*a Jove principium.*" The dictum of the Modern School, "*Dieu, qui est le fondement de tout, n'est l'explication de rien*" (Réville), inevitably abases Him whom it wishes to exalt to the throne. He who is the foundation of all hings, must also be the key to all, or He is not indeed the personal, the living God.

In the *second place*, the *word and spirit of the Holy Scriptures* indicate to us the same starting-point. Of those of the Old Testament, expressions like Psalm xxxvi. 9; Jer. ix. 23, 24; Job xxviii. 28, and others, here especially come under our attention. According to Jesus' own word, (John xvii. 3,) in the knowledge of God is eternal life; a life which is inseparably one with the highest truth. On this account Paul, also, begins with God in Acts xiv. 17; xvii. 26—28; Rom. i. 18, *sqq*. Dogmatics does well to follow this example. Symbolics indeed may select any characteristic ecclesiastical dogma as a starting-point: the doctrine of the Christian Faith has above all things to inquire after Him from whom the whole Revelation of Salvation has proceeded; and to make Him known as He has revealed Himself, above all, in and through Jesus Christ. When *God in Christ* is the light of our science, we shall best guard against the danger pointed out by Luther in the words: "*Plurimum periculi in eo est, si in eos* LABYRINTHOS *divinitatis te involvas.*"

In the *third place*, the choice of this starting-point is entirely in harmony with the peculiarity of the doctrine of the *Reformed Church*, in distinction from that of the Lutheran Church. The dogmatic standpoint of the latter is indicated in the saying of Melancthon: "*Mysteria divinitatis rectius adoraverimus, quam vestigaverimus;*" that of the former, on the other hand, in the order of thought observed in Calvin's *Institutio*, which in point of fact begins with God. The sovereign power of God, and man's absolute dependence upon Him in the work of salvation, is here presented in all its force in the foreground, with a concluding protest, directed not so much against a Jewish righteousness of works, as against an ethnical [heathenish] idolatry of the creature. Rightly therefore, from this standpoint, does the Dutch Confession of Faith begin with the recognition of God. Celebrated Theologians, moreover, of the Reformed Church—Schweitzer. Scholten, and others—have chosen this as their starting-point. Even single illustrious Lutheran Theologians—Martensen, for instance—have followed the same plan. It is indeed one excellency the more in the Dogmatics of the Reformed Church, that it takes that which is most indubitable as a basis for its further investigation.

This method is justified, *finally*, by the *phenomena and wants of the age.* At the time of the Reformation it might appear uncalled-for to begin with *Theology* properly so called, because in this domain there was hardly any controversy. Later Theological systems also betray here and there a certain *horror Dei*, an inclination rather to occupy themselves with Anthropological or Soteriological questions, than with Theological questions properly speaking; and certainly this is fully as easy. In our time, however, precisely that which is most difficult comes first in order; because all other controverted questions of Dogmatics are undoubtedly governed either entirely or in part by the conception we form of God. As preaching, so Dogmatics also, sees itself forced back upon the first principles of doctrine. Where Atheism, Pantheism, and Naturalism have more than ever become a terrible power, we have no choice left but to begin with the doctrine concerning God. The highest that the science of faith[1] declares—*e.g.*, concerning sin and

[1] In speaking of the *science of faith*, we mean not simply a science of which the truth revealed by faith is the object, but of which the life of faith forms the source and root, or if you will, the principle and starting-point. We indicate therefore by it, *that the true Christian can come—by the way of a living faith in Christ—to a knowledge and certainty of God and of Divine things, which is, in its nature, second to no other; and for this reason may with the most perfect right bear the name of science, provided only this word be understood in a sense somewhat wider than that in which it is ordinarily used by the Empiric philosophic school.* In maintaining this position we stand entirely on the ground of Holy Scripture; which opposes *believing* not to *knowing*, but always to *seeing* and to *doubting*, and affords us a number of most sublime utterances of an assurance of faith, of which the force must be indescribably weakened, if they are to be taken in the sense of "I suppose it indeed, but do not know it." In particular, we appeal to the utterances of Jesus Himself (Matt. xiii. 11; John viii. 32); of Paul (Ephes. iii. 4; 2 Tim. i. 12; Col. ii. 3, 8; compare 1 Cor. ii. 12; xii. 8; xiii. 2; Philipp. i. 9, 10, and many other places); of John (1 John ii. 20, 27; v. 13); of the Epistle to the Hebrews (Heb. xi. 3); yea, to the whole polemics of the Apostolic Epistles; which, however, is dominated throughout by the opposition—not between believing and knowing, but between a believing and an unbelieving science. Among the Fathers we see, *inter alios*, a Clemens Alexandrinus, Origen, Athanasius, Augustine, Chrysostom, and others, espouse the same view, afterwards so powerfully set forth by an Anselm in his well-known maxim, [*credo ut intelligam*,] which, rightly understood, is also ours. (See sections ii. iii. xvi. xxxiv.) The assertion that the personal Christian belief, to whatever degree raised, can never become a true knowledge, is, in our opinion, favoured no more by any of these testimonies than by the experience of the spiritual life of the Church of the Lord. The Christian faith *impels* indeed to the knowledge of things which are given to us of God in Christ; and *conducts* thereto, because it raises us to the most intimate *communion* with the Faithful One Himself, in this communion places us in a position for the spiritual *contemplation* (intuition) of the highest truth, and gives us by *experience* to feel its power, from which we draw conclusions with perfect justice as to the efficient cause. *If experience is in every other domain a source of knowledge, wherefore should it not be so here?* Because it is attained to by no one who has not begun with faith? Precisely on this account, therefore, do we speak of a science of *faith*, in distinction from the natural sciences and the remaining sciences of mind, and should in vain look for another name,—if, at least, we would continue to maintain the independent character of theological science,—whereby its peculiar nature, as distinguished from every other, is satisfactorily indicated. For surely, no one will wish to term it the science of *ignorance*, and still less to extol it as the science of *knowledge*. Or shall we henceforth speak of it only as the science of *religion*, and suppose that its superstructure can be more firmly raised upon an unstable anthropological foundation? For if all knowledge of God is altogether impossible, then all theology (λόγος περὶ τοῦ Θεοῦ) becomes an absurdity. If this consequence is to be rejected in principle, we for our part see no other course open to us, but—with Ulrici and others—to regard duly developed belief as "a knowing *in the wider sense of the term*," and to

grace—remains for the majority an absurdity, so long as Christian Theism has not been well determined. Only by means of a well-grounded *Theology* can—in the great Christological and Soteriological questions—the "Paul, thou art beside thyself," be for ever reduced to silence.

2. Where we, for this reason, give the first place in this investigation to the doctrine concerning God, we have to satisfy the *Claim* made upon us to fix our attention as well on the *Nature* as on the *Works* of God, the one as well as the other, of course, *ad majorem Dei gloriam.* The only question is, which of these two must stand first in order. It might perhaps appear optional whether we should speak first of God's Works, thence to rise to the contemplation of the Divine Nature. Thus Schleiermacher, for instance, treats of the doctrine of Creation and Preservation, even that of Angels and Devils, before he enters upon the question of the Divine perfections. But how shall we rightly understand and appreciate God's works, unless acquaintance with His nature holds forth the torch for us in this examination? Moreover, man himself ought certainly to be numbered first among the works of God, and thus the whole of Anthropology ought to be investigated before we could speak of Theology. If we do not desire to do this, we must—however closely connected Anthropology and Theology may be—adopt the opposite method. The sun glitters in every drop of dew; but if we will learn the sun's nature aright, we shall do well to turn the eye first to the heavens, and only afterwards to the dewdrop, and not the converse. God's nature is manifest in His works, but higher than the work stands the nature; from the higher must we consequently proceed, in order to find it reflected in the lower. That, in the contemplation of the one as of the other, the deepest reverence, together with the most sacred interest, should lead us, is a claim of which we here scarcely need to be reminded. Nothing indeed, it has been truly said, can exceed in interest the doctrine concerning God.

3. At all times, however, we have in this investigation to keep before

---

maintain that the most certain belief upon this point leads to the clearest knowledge. The standpoint taken, among others, by a Vinet, Naville, Twesten, Nitzsch, Dorner, J. Müller, Martensen, and others, is also ours, where we continue to speak of a science of faith. Not as in the Hegelian philosophy do we let the Christian faith as the lower form pass over into higher spheres of knowledge; but, on the contrary, we seek to raise it to a spiritual certainty and knowledge which never repudiates its origin and character, and presently—where it discovers its limits—leads to an ever firmer, but at the same time ever more reasonable, believing. In this way alone is, in our opinion, a truly scientific theology—yea, a philosophy of the Christian Revelation—to be spoken of. We do not therefore deny the distinction between this science and exact knowledge in a lower domain. But we doubt whether this distinction justifies us in rejecting the description we have given of Christian Dogmatics; and anticipate from the sharp opposition between believing and knowing much greater harm than is produced even by the confounding of the two. On this whole question, see F. FABRI, *Briefe gegen den Materialismus*, 2 Aufl. (1864), pp. 164—190; L. SCHOEBERLEIN, *Das Wesen und die Gewissheit des Glaubens*, in the *Beweis des Gl.* (1866), p. 177, *sqq.*; H. MARTENSEN, *Glauben und Wissen*, in the *Jahrb. für deutsche Theol.*, xiv. 3, p. 396, *sqq.*; J. MÜLLER, *Dogmatische Abhandl.* (1870), pp. 1—42; H. R. FRANCK, *System der Chr. Gewissheit* (1870); and the discourse of G. J. D. MARTENS, *Het Geloof aan Gods Openbaring, het levensbeg. der Godgeleerdh.* (1870). Compare, also, VAN OOSTERZEE's Treatise, "*Over de Christ. Theol., de Wetenschap des Geloofs*" in the *Tydschrift voor Kerk en Theol.* (1871), ii., p. 81, *sqq.* (Translated in the *Preacher's Lantern*, 1873, i., ii.)

us the *Limit* which is set to all our thinking and speaking on Divine things, by the fact that God is for man absolutely incomprehensible. "*Deus,*" in the words of Albertus Magnus, "*cognosci potest, comprehendi non potest.*" This incomprehensible character of the Deity, recognised and confessed by the most illustrious servants of God,[2] need nevertheless be no insuperable obstacle in the way of our investigation. On the contrary, it is natural, reasonable, yea, on more than one account beneficial; and, as it will very soon appear, by no means the same as being absolutely beyond the sphere of our knowledge. Rather may the conviction of this truth serve as a guide, yea, even as a stimulus, to us, on the way which opens before us. Mountain summits have unquestionably a tendency to make one dizzy, but at the same time they have something about them which attracts; and to *this* height we must not fail, if possible, to rise, in order that from thence a full view of the truth may be obtained. "*Hæc summa delicti,*" says Tertullian, "*nolle agnoscere, quem ignorare non possis.*" "This is the heaviest of offences, not to be willing to recognise Him, whom you cannot be ignorant of." Provided only we do not venture to decide what the Word of Revelation has wisely left undecided, and in many cases content ourselves with that "learned ignorance" which is in no one less to be disapproved of than in the Christian theologian. Before, therefore, we proceed a step further in the way of our investigation, the great truth proclaimed in 1 Cor. xiii. 9—12, must be emphatically recalled to mind; and that not in the interests of religion alone, but in those of science also, to which all illusions are sure in the end to prove fatal. It must become not merely reconciled to the incomprehensibleness of God, as to a misfortune which one *cannot* change, but as to something Divine, which one *would* not change. This is precisely the distinction between the sublime Mysteries, properly so called, into which the Christian faith will introduce us, and those of Heathen antiquity. To the adepts of the latter was promised that they should understand and fathom what they had never before so much as contemplated: we, on the contrary, are, even at the first step, reminded that there are limits which cannot be passed. Of comprehending, there can in this case be no thought; the question is simply whether it is possible to know anything of God; and, above all, whether there is solid ground for believing in God.

Compare the literature brought forward, part i., section xxi.; CALVIN, *Inst.*, i. 1; A. SCHWEITZER, *Christliche Glaubenslehre*, i., § viii.; EBRARD, *Ref. Dogm.*, i., § lxi.; MARTENSEN, *l. l.*, p. 91. On the supreme importance of the doctrine concerning God, J. I. DOEDES, *Inleid. tot de leer van God* (1870), i., p. 40, *sqq.*

POINTS FOR INQUIRY.

Is the question as to the starting-point for the Christian dogmatical investigation one of especial importance?—How can one proceed from the doctrine of God, until he has risen to the conception of God?—The characteristic differences of the Reformed and the Lutheran Dogmatics in this respect more nearly proved and explained.—Whence so great reluctance to begin the dogmatical examination with the doctrine concerning God?—The testimony of Scripture, the Church, and of constant Christian experience as to the incomprehensibleness of God?—Why cannot man possibly give up thinking about God, although he knows beforehand that he will come to a limit of thought?—Can the importance of the λόγος περὶ τοῦ Θεοῦ (Theology) ever be too highly rated?

---

[2] Job xxxvi. 26; Psalm cxxxix. 6; Rom. xi. 33.

FIRST DIVISION.

THE NATURE OF GOD.

SECTION XLIII.—THE KNOWLEDGE OF GOD.

FROM the incomprehensibleness of the Divine Essence, it by no means follows that He is absolutely beyond the sphere of our knowledge. The sanctuary of the knowledge of God is for man on earth just as little closed, as without limit accessible. Only here the distinction must be clearly made between a *complete* and a sufficiently *pure* knowledge of God; and never must it be forgotten that, as the sun by its own light, so God can be known and contemplated by the eye of faith, solely in the light of His own revelation.

1. In the inquiry as to the Nature of God, the question before all is: Is a true knowledge of God possible for man here on earth; and, if so, in what way is it attainable? As to so many other questions, so to this also, different answers have at all times been given. In the Middle Ages it even gave rise to a not unimportant controversy between the Thomists and the Scotists. To this day, opinions are far from being unanimous; and it is of importance to listen to these different voices, before we express our own opinion.

2. That God is incomprehensible, has been, in accordance with Holy Scripture, recognised and confessed by the Christian Church of all ages.[1] The more surprising therefore appears the assertion made in some quarters, that God even on this side the grave can be fully known. We hear it on the part of Eunomius in the Arian controversy;[2] while Aëtius asserted he could comprehend Him just as well as the stone or the wood which he held in his hand.[3] While they sought by such assertions to destroy the force of the constant appeal of their opponents to the unsearchableness of God, we later see Mysticism arrive by a totally different way at the same conviction. Through the life of love in God they asserted that they could contemplate Him immediately and clearly, in His own light. Thus J. Gerson († 1429) maintained the possibility of a knowledge of God, to which he gave the peculiar name of "*Theologia affectiva;*" and Tauler († 1361) taught that the soul, by wholly losing itself in God,

[1] See Justin Martyr, *Apol.* 2, 6; Minucius Felix, c. 18, and many other places.
[2] Epiph. *Haer.*, 76, 4.
[3] Socr. *Hist. Eccl.*, iv. 7.

became so Divine that, if it rightly expressed itself, it would regard itself as equal to God. Upon such heights of intuition and contemplation all clouds must, as it would seem, at last vanish. Since Mysticism was by no means free from a Pantheistic leaven, we cannot be surprised presently to hear Spinoza assert that he had an equally clear conception of God as of a triangle. It was consequently entirely in the spirit of this writer when, in the former half of the present century, speculative philosophy promised to lead up its disciples to the absolute knowledge of the Divine substance. It asserted, it is true, that God knew Himself, and arrived at self-consciousness, only in the consciousness of man. From this standpoint one could thus, as it is said, not only know God, but fathom, comprehend, genetically develop Him. "Men have formed for themselves a conception of the so-called Absolute, or—what is the same thing —an absolute conception, in which is included all that exists. Beside this Absolute, there can be nothing which does not belong to Him; our thinking is His thinking, our being His being. For the existence thereof there is no need of proof; for it is precisely existence itself, the be-all and the whole of being. The conception of the same proves and verifies itself, for in Him existence and thinking are identical; the conception thereof is His existence, consequently truth itself. The development and realisation of this conception is the self-development and self-realisation of God, and at the same time the origination and history of the world." (Ulrici.)

3. It is no more than natural that such wretched self-deception, combined with the most ridiculous self-idolatry, should not merely awaken undisguised contempt, but should also call forth the most powerful reaction. As well in the objective as the subjective sense of the word, the absolute unknowableness of God has been proclaimed by many in earlier and later times. In earlier times by those who asserted God did not even know Himself, and consequently could not be known by us. Thus, for instance, John Scotus Erigena:[4] "*Deus nescit se quid est, quia non est* QUID; *incomprehensibilis quippe in aliquo, et sibi Ipsi et omni intellectui.*" By banishing the notion of "*quidditas,*" definite properties, from the idea of God, they made of God merely abstract indefinable Being. The philosophers of later times also—Schelling and others—here claim our notice, who see in the Divine Being a sort of dark primary substance (Urgrund), not fathomed by Himself, nor indeed fathomable. It is, however, manifest that the supposition of such an *Urgrund* is in diametrical opposition to the idea of an absolute and perfect Being. This conception itself partakes more of a mythological heathen character, than of a sound speculative and ethical one. If God is really the infinitely perfect Spirit, and not simply a blind power, He can possess *no* sides which are for his own vision absolutely inscrutable; but must be, for Himself at least, perfectly transparent.

Nevertheless, God might be able perfectly to know Himself, without being in truth, on that account, knowable for us. Most positively is this latter supposition denied by the Scepticism which passes by the highest

---

[4] *De divis. Nat.*, ii. c. 28.

questions of life with a "*Que sais-je?*" of mockery or of melancholy on the lips. If by Scepticism is understood a systematic fostering of doubt where no reason for doubting exists; then certainly, after all that has been said (§§ ii., xxii., xxix.), a formal refutation of this mode of regarding things is least of all to be expected in this place. "*La discussion n'est pas le remède à cette maladie*" (Naville). But there are also not wanting others, whom no one can reckon among sceptics properly so called, and who yet assert that there can be absolutely no question of *science* in relation to God, but only of *faith*, by no means to be confused with science. And certainly, in the sense in which the Empirical school speaks of science, to denote an objectively certain knowledge arrived at by the way of observation and reasoning, we shall do better not to use the word here. But wherefore thus limit the idea of science, not without arbitrariness and to our own detriment? If only *that* is to adorn itself with this name which has been proved out for each one, and is on this account absolutely beyond doubt, the domain of science will certainly very soon appear of much less extent than is usually asserted. "If we strike out [from science] all which is in reality only a *scientific faith*, science is shrivelled up into a little residuum of propositions, whose contents are so scanty and insignificant as scarcely to repay the trouble of investigation" (Ulrici). For us the question is whether an accurate, well-founded, and well-ordered *knowledge* is possible, in whatever way attained to (Part I. § iii.); and if this question can be answered in the affirmative, it is in a certain sense indifferent whether this knowledge be stamped with the name of Science or not. To a negative answer, however, to the question as thus put, we are by no means disposed to come. What lies beyond the sphere of perception through the medium of the senses is not therefore to be excluded from the domain of spiritual experience and intellectual reasoning. Without preliminary faith there can here certainly be no possibility of *knowing*, just as reciprocally all believing is based upon an inner consciousness. But, according to the united testimony of Scripture and Experience, there is born in turn from living faith an equally clear as accurate knowledge, of no lower degree of certainty in its own sphere than that which is elsewhere arrived at by the way of observation or reasoning. What through faith we *understand*,[5] is by no means the fruit of a bare supposing, or highly probable conjecturing, a being almost certain: the believer knows not only *that*, but also truly *what*, and upon what ground, he believes. Here is knowledge just as certain as that which the astronomer has gleaned with his telescope from the depths of the heavens; since faith is as the telescope by means of which the Infinite is brought within the field of vision for our spirit's eye. Even if the absolute incapacity of the human reason for rising above a finite sphere had been in all ages victoriously demonstrated, there would not any the more follow necessarily from this the unknowableness of God, so long as the reality of an historical Revelation of Salvation remains an established fact.[6] "That faith is not the faith of the Gospel, which regards the object of religion—God in Christ—as unknowable" (Dorner). But even apart from this we

---

[5] Heb. xi. 3.

[6] John xiv. 8, 9.

continue, in accordance with Scripture and the Netherlands Confession of Faith, to maintain the reality and soundness of a knowledge of God by the light of nature; in accordance also, as opposed to the Socinian view, with the leading divines of the Dutch Church—Voëtius for example, who mentions even, among the more refined forms of Atheism, the phenomenon, *Si quis negat lumen naturæ ejusque certitudinem, quæ omnis cognitionis rerum, tam divinarum, quam humanarum, est principium.*[7] Where this is not acknowledged, there not only do the highest aspirations of the human mind and spirit remain in their profoundest depths unexplained, but there is proclaimed in principle an irreconcilable difference between believing and knowing, which in its consequences can lead only to the incalculable injury of both, yea, of the whole of Christian theology. "A living God, upholding and penetrating the life of nature and of spirit, *cannot* possibly have so realised His image in man, that for the latter a resolving of his consciousness into the opposition of believing and knowing were necessary" (Fabri).

4. Where, in opposition to the two extremes, we maintain the position that the knowledge of God is to a certain height possible for man, we must at the same time make due distinction between a perfect knowledge and a true one (*cognitio adæquata et vera*). The former is a knowledge which wholly comprehends its object; the latter a pure, although also a highly imperfect knowledge. The possibility of the former we deny: our theology is a "*theologia viatorum, non beatorum.*" Holding the possibility of the latter, we lay down the proposition that God may be truly known, not wholly, or as He is in Himself, but as and in so far as He reveals Himself. We see "as in a glass," but yet we see something—not the face of God, but yet the fringes of His kingly robe.[8]

5. For this possibility there exists a reason, partly of a philosophic, partly of an historic nature. The philosophic ground consists, on the one hand, in the nature of man as a reasonable and moral creature, and one related to God; and on the other, in that of God, conceived of as the absolutely perfect Being, who as such must both be desirous and able to reveal Himself; and, yet further, in the nature of the relation of the one to the other, which becomes a phantom, both objectively and subjectively, so soon as a genuine knowledge of God is admitted to be impossible. The latter in the fact that God *has* revealed Himself in an extraordinary manner, and since then has, better than ever before, become known to thousands.[9] He who will not admit that this revelation has taken place, must prove his denial, and—take the consequences for his own account.

"Thus, it is true God is knowable, but only so far as He gives Himself to be known, and so far as the power of active or passive receptivity in man extends" (Nitzsch). The highest guarantee for the infallible certainty of this knowledge consists precisely in this—that it comes from Himself. If He willed to keep Himself concealed, who could discover Him? But if He willed to reveal Himself, who shall dispute to man the possession of an eye wherewith to contemplate the beaming of His light? "*Qualiter*

[7] *De Atheismo*, p. 119. [8] Exod. xxxiii. 18—23.
[9] John xvii. 25; 1 John ii. 13; iv. 16.

cognovi Te? Cognovi te in te. Cognovi te, non sicuti Tibi es, sed sicuti mihi es, et non sine te, sed in te; quia tu es lux, qui illuminasti me. Sicut enim Tibi es, Tibi soli cognitus es; sicut mihi es, secundum gratiam tuam et mihi cognitus es. Cognovi, QUIA *Deus meus es* TU" (Augustine). So it is; God's original communication of life to man is the ground of the possibility of God and His truth being known to man.

6. Only it must never be forgotten that the knowledge of God, in this sense, remains exclusively the fruit of personal faith in God, and consequently becomes more extended and clear, in proportion as faith itself becomes more steadfast and devout. The eye of faith must, in every domain, observe, compare, combine, the facts of revelation; and thus must it rise, in the light of spiritual experience, in due order, from the contemplation of the known to the well-founded conception of the unknown. Faith is here, in the fullest sense, the root and principle of knowledge: according to the Apostle's word, "We have believed and known that Thou art the Holy One of God."[10] The opposition here also, by which the inner life of the man is dominated, is not between believing and knowing, but between believing and non-believing. But thus the question as to the nature and grounds of our *belief* in God becomes precisely for our science of the highest importance.

Compare the literature brought forward, § iii.; and besides this H. ULRICI, *l. l.*, p. 6; FABRI, *l. l.*, pp. 164—190; FABRI, *Das allgemeine Wahrheitsgefühl*, etc.; LANGE, *Positive Dogm.*, § xxxii.; and the art. *Gott*, by NITZSCH, in Herzog, *R. E.* v.

POINTS FOR INQUIRY.

The controversy between the Thomists and the Scotists.—How is it that the question as to the knowableness of God has, even with the light of Holy Scripture, been so differently answered in every age?—Value of the knowledge of God as presented by Mysticism and Speculative Philosophy.—The drawing of a sharp line between knowing and believing, in the sphere of Theology, favourable—contrary to the intention of its authors—to the cause of unbelief.—The standpoint occupied by us wholly in harmony with the doctrine of Holy Scripture, the principal Christian Fathers, and the confessional writings of the Reformed Church.

SECTION XLIV.—BELIEF IN GOD.

Belief in God is by no means the necessary product of abstract reasoning, but has its firm basis in the whole nature and being of man, who is originally and evidently constituted for this belief. Christian Dogmatics, therefore, is as little fitted as obliged to give a proof, properly so called, of the existence of the Godhead; it is

---

[10] John vi. 69 (according to all the best MSS.); 1 John v. 13.

simply called to affirm its confession of that belief, on grounds drawn by preference from its own domain. Without thus calling in question the relative value of other so-called proofs for the existence of God, it appeals, to this end, especially to the existence and effects of a special Revelation, which, once sufficiently established, of itself necessarily leads to the belief in a higher Causality.

1. In speaking of belief in God, we mean not simply an intellectual conviction that a higher Being really exists, but a confidence of the heart, which is not less firmly assured of the being of God than of its own existence. Such belief recognises God as existing, not merely in thought, but in reality; and adores Him as the *highest* Being, but undoubtedly, still more as the most really existing One (*Ens realissimum*). It holds itself convinced, not of the accuracy of its own conception of God; but ever the more of this, that the Being, to whom the conception has reference, is no creature of the imagination. The notion which is associated with the name of God varies infinitely, and is in its highest development imperfect and limited. Yet it has ever reference to a higher, invisible, and mighty Being, who must be served and glorified; and the belief that God IS, remains the basis of every religion.[1] The question is simply whether this belief can be satisfactorily maintained against doubt and opposition.

2. Belief in God is by no means the necessary product of demonstration. As old as humanity itself (§ xxii.), it was not produced at first by reasoning, but rather in its most primitive form preceded all reasoning. No one has ever begun to feel convinced of this truth, merely because it had been demonstrated to him in a strictly logical manner. Men would hardly, indeed, have given themselves the trouble to seek for proofs for this conviction, had it not with irresistible power forced itself, as it were, on their innermost consciousness. Everywhere do we discover this belief, even where no proof has ever yet been heard of; and it will last even where the weak sides of all known proofs are by no means ignored. Belief in God is consequently no result, but, on the contrary, a starting-point for human thinking on invisible things—a postulate of our whole rational and moral nature, but no result of a universally recognised syllogism.

3. The existence of God *cannot* even be proved in such a way that henceforth all doubt remains absolutely impossible. The startling character of this assertion disappears as soon as we form for ourselves a clear conception of what must be understood by the word *prove*. A proposition is proved so soon as it is incontestably apparent that it follows as an absolutely necessary consequence from another indisputable proposition. All proving therefore consists in an appeal to a higher truth, which forms the solid basis for that which must be established by this very appeal.

---

[1] Heb. xi. 6.

To prove the existence of God would thus, properly speaking, be to bring forward the ground for God's existence. But precisely because He is the most perfect, absolute Being, God has the ground of His existence not outside of or above Him, but in Himself alone; He is, because He is, and cannot possibly not be. The Infinite may indeed be dimly apprehended, may be revealed, adored, but cannot possibly be proved by demonstration. That only can be proved which falls within the sphere of the finite comprehension. From the infinitude and incomprehensibleness of God follows at the same time His absolute undemonstrableness. God is not demonstrated by us, but demonstrates Himself to us as the cause of all that exists. "A God who can be proved is no God; for the ground of proof is necessarily above the thing proved by it" (Jacobi). Assuredly the utterance of faith, *God exists*, must be capable of being justified by solid arguments, before we are at liberty to base anything upon the truth of this proposition. But the existence itself of the Infinite is and remains, nevertheless, a fact, which must be believed on good grounds; and which to a certain extent can be understood by faith, but cannot possibly as a scientific proposition be irrefutably proved to every one, without respect to the mind and disposition in which that question of all questions is discussed. He who here looks for a stringent proof, such as is to be found in the domain of exact science, and makes his assent dependent on the issue of this demonstration, entirely loses sight of the moral character of religious truth, and would—even supposing the experiment to be successful—precisely by this means degrade God to the category of finite things; and make his faith to rest upon something by which the nature and character of faith would be annihilated.

4. If consequently a proof for the existence of God, in the sense disputed, were possible, such a proof were to be looked for, not from Christian Dogmatics, but rather from the so-called Natural Theology. While this latter conducts its investigation in a general manner, and by the scientific method, as to the nature and ground of belief in God, the former has to do with a revealed doctrine of Salvation, and to draw its knowledge from sources in which the existence of God is presupposed and testified, but is so little demonstrated that the non-recognition of this fundamental truth is simply dismissed as folly.[2] The philosophic proofs for God's existence—this has been acknowledged, among others, by Schleiermacher and Twesten—do not consequently belong, properly speaking, to the sphere of Christian Dogmatics. The only thing to which this has to appeal is the existence and operation of the revelation of Saving Truth, which proves God in the same way in which the brightness of the sun proves the sun's existence, not by the method of philosophy, but in an historical and empirical manner.

5. Yet Christian Dogmatics ought not from its standpoint to overlook the importance of other so-called proofs for the existence of God; much less to make common cause with those who speak with a certain contempt thereof, as a fruit of defective reasoning and foolish imagination. On the contrary, it must and will deplore the levity with which the assertion—in

---

[2] Ps. xiv. 1.

itself true—that God's existence cannot be proved (demonstrated), is frequently repeated, understood, and applied in a way which as much as possible plays into the hands of unbelief and scepticism. "Modern Theology, which so readily gives up the proofs for the existence of God, abandons thereby not only its own position as a science; but also, in principle, annihilates faith, and the religion of which it is the Theology" (Ulrici). It is true, there is not a single proof against which objections more or less serious might not be, and have not been, adduced. All bear the unequivocal traces of the limitation of human thought, and each in its turn suggests to our mind the words of the poet:—

> Wer Gott nicht fühlt in sich und allen Lebenskreisen,
> Dem werdet ihr Ihn nicht beweisen mit Beweisen.[3]
>
> RUECKERT.

But yet they remain highly commendable, as more or less successful endeavours, not only to bring into satisfactory clearness the utterances of the innermost consciousness, but also to justify them to oneself and others as highly reasonable. In curious contrast with the superficial judgment, which "breaks the staff of condemnation" over the most gigantic efforts of the human mind, is the certainty with which we hear one of the greatest thinkers of our age express himself: "I hope to be able to make manifest how the existence of God follows as the result of the modern investigation of nature, with the same certainty, perhaps even with greater, than, *e.g.*, the existence of a universal power of attraction operating at a distance, of a material of light or heat (ether), of an electro-magnetic fluid, etc. For it will be seen that these assumptions of natural science equally belong only to the sphere of scientific faith" (Ulrici). A scientifically stringent demonstration such as is possible in a lower domain, and the kind of certainty which arises therefrom, is *here*, from the nature of the case, impossible. Yet, nevertheless, the proofs we speak of—properly conducted and suitably combined—are powerful enough to offer a scientific defence for faith in God, to overcome honest doubts, and to brand as inexcusable *sin*, as well as deplorable *folly*, the obdurate unbelief which—in the presence of so much light—retreats into its own darkness. And a proud ignoring of many a ray of light, which is shed in this way upon the sacred mystery of the cause of all things, conduces just as little to a sound Philosophy, as to a profound, believing Theology. That which effects nothing for him who is resolved to doubt, and accepts no other evidence than that of perception by the senses, is not on that account without value for one who, with receptive mind and unprejudiced spirit, surrenders himself to the powerful impression which the beauty of the Universe makes upon all who attentively contemplate it.

6. Even in this general estimate, however, of the value of the proofs or grounds—insensibly in this case the one idea flows into the other—of the central truth of all religion, Dogmatics cannot possibly for its purpose attach the same value to all of them. While it can leave to its proper place

---

[3] For him who feels not God in himself, and in all the spheres of life, you will not succeed in demonstrating God by proofs.

the argument *à tutiori*—"that scullery-maid among proofs" (Lange)—the ontological proof in its different forms, and even to a certain extent the purely cosmological argument, or, if you will, can resign them entirely to the criticism of a necessary sister science; the proofs which are for Dogmatics, above all others, important, are those drawn from Nature, from History, and from Humanity itself, because it recognises in these the mirror of a General Revelation, to which the Special attaches itself (comp. § xxix.). Especially does it value the physico-theological argument, in its simplest form employed by Jesus Himself, regarded with unfeigned esteem by philosophers like Kant; and by so many important contributions, even in the most recent times, brought to an evidence as strong as *faith* can wish. That which all these voices proclaim is for Dogmatics raised above all reasonable doubts, by the fact—contradicted indeed, but not deprived of its force—of the existence and working of the Saving Revelation.

7. But then it must never be forgotten that all proofs together can and ought only to serve to explain and confirm that which, before all proof, lived and expressed itself in every human heart. Man has by nature (§ xxii. 4) an original and deep-rooted sense of God's presence, which precedes all observation and reasoning, but by means of these is brought to its full distinctness. We do not hesitate to call this feeling a *Consciousness* of God (*Godsbewustzijn*); since we can explain it only by the fact that the Infinite One Himself, who is not merely above us, but *in* us,[4] thus immediately manifests His presence in the man who has been created after His image, and thereby placed in the closest relationship to Himself. Not of the finite world without him, but rather of the Infinite and All-present One, has man a primitive knowledge in himself; and it is a thought of the poet, equally true as it is beautiful, that the first name stammered forth by the first man on his first awakening, was no other than the name of "Father." It matters not whether the word *instinct* be employed in this connection or not; what is certain is, that no necessity makes itself felt more imperatively in man, than that which compels him to believe in God, the living God. Yea, truly, "I *am* not, claim not to be, if He is not. He that planted the ear, shall He not hear? He that formed the eye, shall He not see?" (Jacobi). Our whole personality is an enigma, which finds its solution only in belief in a Being who is Himself absolute Personality. Our intellect might perhaps be able to rest in the recognition of a perfectly independent something, a blind power of nature, an obscure basis of unity for all that exists. But our heart cries out for a Person, an absolutely perfect *I*, to whom it can unreservedly resign itself; and it is contrary to all analogy that an aspiration so old, so universal, and so powerful, should be able to exist without an object entirely adequate to it. "The fundamental presupposition of our personal existence, and personal self-consciousness, is the existence of the Divine Personality" (Chalybaeus). Atheism, which reduces to silence this inner voice, not only makes of the world a huge lunatic asylum, but makes despair itself to rank as wisdom. The proof, on the other hand, *e.g.*, from the realm of nature, which makes manifest that the

---

[4] Acts xvii. 27, 28; Ephes. iv. 6.

voice of creation is in harmony with this innermost consciousness, and confirms its utterance, has done all that we can reasonably expect from it. and gives, where it is successful, the right to say to the adversary, that he is without excuse.[5] But this calls forth in turn the question as to the *idea* of God, and leads us to the examination thereof.

Comp. H. ULRICI, *l. c.*, pp. 1—15; the treatise of W. F. GESS, *Natur oder Gott*, in the *Ten Lectures*, Basle, 1861; DÜSTERDIECK, *Apologet. Beitr.* (1867), ii., p. 19; CHRISTLIEB, *l. c.*, p. 78, *seq.;* and the writings mentioned by DOEDES, *l. c.*, p. 249.

POINTS FOR INQUIRY.

Origin and significance of the name *God* in ancient and modern languages.—One-sided over-estimate and ungrateful ignoring of the proofs of God's existence.—Whence is it that the same proofs are for some insufficient, and for others wholly superfluous?—Necessity for, and limits of, the examination as to God's existence, within the sphere of Christian Dogmatics.—The ultimate ground of the *Christian's* belief in God.

SECTION XLV.—THE IDEA OF GOD.

Belief in God seeks as far as possible to have a pure idea of God. The science of faith deduces it from the fact of Revelation itself, and the historical facts connected therewith. From a Christian standpoint God is recognised and confessed as the Being of Beings, the infinite Spirit, who, personally distinct from the creation, and exalted infinitely above it, nevertheless continually and directly stands to it in the closest relation. Notwithstanding all that is obscure, which inevitably cleaves to this supranaturalistic Theistic *idea of God*, its truth and value is raised above all reasonable questioning. For this reason must as well the Deistic as the Pantheistic idea of God, in its various forms, be utterly rejected, not merely in the name of Religion, but also of the Christian science of faith.

1. It may be considered superfluous to treat at large on the importance of an accurate idea of God. Sincere devoutness may be united even with an inaccurate and impure notion of God; but still religion will gain in light, warmth, and fruitfulness, in proportion as it rests upon a purer conception of the Supreme Being. For Christian theological thought such a conception is not merely desirable, but indispensable, and it is simply the question in what way it is to be attained to.

2. Reason alone—the history of philosophy renders this sufficiently plain—cannot possibly lead us up to a pure idea of God. It may conduct

---

[5] Rom. i. 20.

us to the idea of a Supreme Cause; but to the question how we are to conceive of this Cause, it cannot give a satisfactory solution. The best idea we can form of God must be derived from the highest thing we know, human nature; but in this way we obtain no other God than a supreme man. We have no data by which the idea of God can be fixed *à priori*, but must form it *à posteriori* by means of the light shed by Himself. It is even not sufficient to be guided by some separate utterances of Holy Scripture, which are frequently figurative ones, or which must receive their complement from others. Upon the great fact of the original Revelation of God we have above all to fix the mind—a revelation which, as we have already seen (§ xxvii.), must be accepted by us—and then upon the Facts, *i.e.*, the separate *acts*, of self-revelation on the part of God, of which sacred history speaks. Only where this, in its whole and in its parts, has been duly proved out and consulted, is firm ground attained for answering the question how we are to conceive of God. It is evident, however, that even with this, every answer will bear the unmistakable traces of human limitation. "Sicut summus ille spiritus, qui Deus est, a nullo intellectu valet proprie excogitari, nulla definitione potest proprie definiri aut determinari" (Augustine).

3. In the light of Divine Revelation the Christian Church in general, and the Reformed Church in particular,[1] has in all ages given the same answer to the question as to the Nature of God, in placing itself upon the basis of Supranaturalistic Theism. In speaking of God as a *Being*, we deny at once that He is a mere abstraction, the compendium of all the powers and laws of nature, which would thus necessarily vanish if these should disappear. We speak of Him, not simply as the totality of all being, but as the self-existent One, who unconditionally IS,[2] and would be, though all beyond Himself should be altogether non-existent. He is for us, consequently, not only All, but Lord over all; not a Something, but a Person; no *It*, but a *Thou*. We call Him the Being of *all Beings*, not only because He is above all others, but because He may be called the absolute ground of existence for them all; the highest reality, in a word, so that our thinking of Him, far indeed from surpassing the reality, on the contrary does not by a long way attain to it. The peculiar characteristic of the Being of God we describe by using here, with Jesus,[3] the name of *Spirit*. In doing so, we deny that in or about Him there is anything of corporeity, of however refined a nature, as has now and then been asserted by Gnosticism and Theosophy.[4] But at the same time we maintain that He possesses all that is inseparable from the life of the Spirit as such. For Spirit is not merely power, but above all self-consciousness; as Spirit, God must consequently be of necessity a thinking, self-determining being. We men *have* a spirit, which thinks and wills, in a limited, finite way; God *is* Spirit, yea, the Father of spirits;[5] not simply the spiritual principle in nature, but the cause of all

---

1 See the *Netherlands Confession*, Art. i.; *Heidelberg Catechism*, questions 26—28.
2 [Rev. i. 4a.]
3 John iv. 24.
4 Compare TERTULLIAN, *De Carne Chr.*, c. 11; *Adv. Prax.*, c. 7.
5 Heb. xii. 9.

nature, and of its spiritual principle at the same time. And as such we speak of Him as the *infinite* Spirit; not in the speculative sense, in which this word is often used, of the absolutely unlimited, so that beyond Himself nothing can be conceived of as existing—this would lead rather to Acosmism and Pantheism—but in the moral sense, of boundlessly perfect, and precisely on this account all-embracing, Spirit; so that nothing is to be found in God which does not bear the stamp of the highest perfection; and again, all perfection is in Him personally united. *Personally*, we repeat, in order thereby to express the fact, that in the absolute Being the highest self-consciousness is united with perfect freedom.

4. As such God is infinitely exalted above the world, and definitely distinguished therefrom. The powers of nature can and may then alone be called the powers of God, when we express thereby that His will—to be carefully distinguished from the law of nature appointed by Him—reveals itself by those powers, and thus actually operates in the world. Never must we regard a law or force of nature as a part of the Godhead Himself; and even when we speak of God's being in the world, or of the world's being in God, nothing more is indicated than a reciprocal *relationship* of that which originally was and *still remains* distinct. The original distinction between God and the world is not effaced, but simply more nearly defined, by such a mode of speech. We have just as little to think of the world without God, as of God without the world,[6] but so to conceive of God's infinite exaltedness above the world, as to lose in connection with it all conception of locality. Just as spirit is dynamically above matter, so the Father of spirits stands, self-conscious and free, alike above all spirit and all matter. Just as little as our spirit is imprisoned within the limits of our body, is God enclosed within the cosmos called into being by Him. And again, as the relation between spirit and body is most intimate and reciprocal, not other is that between God and the world. "Nature expresses by its types and its laws in the world of bodies and of spirits the eternal and Divine thought; it is the workman of God" (Caro). It is and remains a direct relation, even where God reveals Himself in the world, and works through the instrumentality of the means appointed by Him. The notion of God and of the world can therefore never become interchangeable, and the mutual relationship of both is best defined in the following manner: God is (as transcendent) personally above the world, but at the same time (as immanent) works unceasingly and independently *in* the world.

5. It is impossible to make even the most modest attempt at describing the Divine nature, without therein meeting with problems and questions too high for our human thinking. The matter seems comparatively easy if one confesses exclusively either the Transcendency of God above the world, or the Immanency of God in the world; but scarcely does one attempt to unite both ideas, when it becomes apparent that a perfectly satisfactory formula is still sought in vain. Unceasingly are we exposed to the danger, either of confounding God with the world, or of separating Him from the world. God transcendent, but then not truly immanent; or really immanent, but then no longer transcendent; it seems almost

---

[6] Acts xvii. 28.

impossible to the thinking mind to escape that inexorable alternative. Faith, however, understands that not only the notion of God, but what is more, God Himself, is lost to us, so soon as one of the two parts of this confession is sacrificed to the other; it will not suffer the denial of its right to maintain the truth of what cannot be comprehended, so long as it is manifest that preponderating reasons exist for doing so. Even where—with the Christian father—it calls God the great Anonymous, it cannot think of Him otherwise than as the infinite Personality; existing not merely above the parts of the world, but above the totality of the world, which is to be carefully distinguished from Himself. In other words, the Christian idea of God is that not of Monistic, but of Supranaturalistic Theism.

6. The greater accuracy of this idea of God, as compared with any other, is not doubtful.—Even the attentive contemplation of nature leads us up to such a conception of God. Everywhere do we meet with phenomena which are the manifestation of a thought that, to a certain extent, can be entered into, and thought out. Creation speaks not simply of an infinite Power, but of an all-embracing Spirit, and is explicable only as the work of a wise and holy Will.—Revelation, with which Holy Scripture makes us acquainted, everywhere favours the same conception. The very names of the Godhead which occur therein have, in this respect, great significance. That of *Elohím*, in the first place, indicates a royal dignity, which without self-consciousness and freedom would be inconceivable. The same may be said of *Adonai*, *El-Roëh* (God of Vision),[7] *El-Shaddai*, Lord of Hosts;[9] above all, of the name *Jehovah* or *Jahveh*, the covenant-name, by which the unchangeableness of God's nature is expressed.[10] Therefore He is emphatically called a God who IS,[11] the King of the ages,[12] who only hath immortality;[13] in all things the opposite of the idols, who hear not, neither do they see.[14] A great value must be attached, in this connection, above all, to the words of the Lord Himself, where He speaks of God as Spirit,[15] but at the same time recognises Him as the Father, the Lord of heaven and earth,[16] and to those of His first witnesses;[17] not to speak more particularly of so many an exalted prophetic utterance, especially in Isaiah.—Philosophic thinking has, through a number of ages, given testimony to the truth of this conception of God above every other; and the whole history of ancient and modern philosophy may be termed an endeavour to rise from a lower conception to this higher one. Let any one think of Anaxagoras and Plato among the earlier philosophers; of Descartes, Leibnitz, Kant, the younger Fichte, and others, among the later ones. One thing is clear: he who abandons Theism, exchanges a higher for a lower conception of God, and one from which the human spirit had not without difficulty freed itself. Only as regarded from this standpoint is God the absolutely perfect One, the LORD in the full force of the word. Personality is the highest form of existence, truly spiritual, and at the same time concrete; no mere force, or law, or life, is a being, and only a God who is truly a being, can be

---

[7] Gen. xvi. 13

[8] Gen. xvii. 1.

[9] James v. 4.

[10] Isaiah xli. 4.

[11] אֲנִי הוּא, Deut. xxxii. 39.

[12] 1 Tim. i. 17.

[13] 1 Tim. vi. 16.

[14] Psalm cxv. 3—8.

[15] John iv. 24.

[16] Matt. xi. 25.

[17] John i. 18; Rev. i. 8.

prayerfully approached.—Especial emphasis must here be laid upon this last particular: true religion (§ xxi.) is possible only in connection with a supranaturalistic Theistic conception of God. "We do not worship a law. however simple and fruitful it may be; we do not worship a force, if it is blind, however powerful, however universal it may be; nor an ideal, however pure, if it is an abstraction: we worship only a Being who is living perfection, perfection under the highest forms, Thought, Love" (Caro). With a God who is either separated from the world, or identical with it, no true, *i.e.* reciprocal, communion is possible. In the case of every other notion of God, God remains at least equally incomprehensible, while at the same time He is presented to us as less exalted and adorable.

7. The value of the conception of God thus maintained is quickly seen. It becomes manifest, partly as a fruit of reasoning, partly as a result of comparison with other representations of God, partly, and above all, as the product of one's own living experience. The supranaturalistic Theistic conception of God may be for a time abandoned; but ever again must it be returned to, unless one will finally give up all true religion, *i.e.*, God and one's self. Whatever problems and questions it leaves unsolved, it still remains always far preferable to that of Deism and Pantheism.

8. Deism is that school of thought which continues to maintain the Transcendency of God above the world; but sacrifices to this view His Immanency in it. In opposition to Atheism, it recognises God's existence; in opposition to Pantheism, His personality; but as distinguished from Theism, it entirely overlooks His continuous relation to the world created by Him. It thinks of the Cosmos as a clock or watch which runs on according to its own structure, while every act of intervention or interposition on the part of God in the course of things is regarded as opposed to His own perfection and the absolute faultlessness of His works. This notion of God, formerly entertained in part by the Monarchians, later by the Socinians and the older Rationalists, is now also favoured by the "Modern Tendency," which—while recognising the personal life of God—sees in all that happens only the natural consequence of finite causes, and admits of no free operation of God's will, above and beyond the rigid bond of causality. From a Christian-philosophic standpoint such a conception of God cannot possibly find acceptance. It is not only in irreconcilable contradiction with the word of Jesus Himself,[18] but also with the whole spirit of the Gospel; it is absolutely incapable of satisfying the deepest aspirations of the religious spirit; it explains absolutely nothing of the great enigma, while it necessarily makes of the world the engine of a *Perpetuum Mobile.* No wonder that many look down with especial contempt upon this "religion of the clockmakers," and rather look to a Pantheistic conception of God for that which they have without result sought in a Deistic conception.

9. Pantheism is that mode of thinking which emphatically recognises God's *Immanence* in the world, but denies His transcendency above it, There is no conception of God which reveals itself in the history of religion and philosophy in so many forms. The word is not yet two centuries old (1705), but the thing itself is found in the most diverse religious systems,

---

[18] See, for example, John v. 17.

both of those before and of those after Christ. It is well known that the Pantheistic systems have been variously divided, and it is unnecessary here to give the different divisions, or to test them at large; there is no single one, perhaps, which does not call forth more or less weighty objections. But in all its different forms Pantheism has this peculiarity, that it does not recognise the Personality of God, and maintains the absolute unity of God and the world against every dualistic division. Its conception of the world cannot therefore be any other than the Naturalistic one. Not only the history of Philosophy, but also that of Mysticism, both within and without the Christian Church, reveals to us at every step the most dissimilar examples of this mode of thinking; and it is not easy to judge with perfect equity of a conception of God, which serves as basis to so many different views. The complaint of Schleiermacher, that the name of Pantheist is frequently employed without reason as a "name of reproach and nickname," has just grounds. As opposed to a dry, mechanical Deism, Pantheism has a claim, relative indeed, but not the less indisputable. For the æsthetic feeling and the glowing imagination, the thought, God is the One and the All (τὸ ἓν καὶ τὸ πᾶν), has not only its dazzling side, but also its seductive power. And we cannot be surprised that He who can sacrifice everything else to the demand for strict unity in His mode of thinking, should repeat the words of Jacobi: "There is no philosophy, but the philosophy of Spinoza."

Yet this must not render us blind to the many and great difficulties which weigh against the Pantheistic conception of God, and render it wholly inadmissible. It must be rejected in the name of religious feeling, understanding, and conscience.—The *feeling* of need for personal communion with God remains unsatisfied, unless He truly exists, as another *Ego*, as distinguished from ourselves. Prayer becomes a folly, so soon as it is nothing more than a "plunging into the cooling depths of the one cause of all things" (Strauss). Love towards a blind power of nature, which rises to self-consciousness only in man, is equally impossible as obedience towards a being which can give effect to no will as contradistinguished from our own. Pantheism becomes auto-theism, and leads to self-adoration.—But the *understanding*, also, is unable to rest satisfied with the conception of a God who is supposed to have created the highest form of existence known to us, personality, without Himself being personal. Out of the mysterious originating material of all things (*Natura naturans*) can be explained just as little the harmonious beauty, as the order and fitness of all in the visible creation (*Natura naturata*). The genesis of all things; the development of the higher life out of inorganic matter; the whole course of the world's history, as the evident product of a thinking and willing power: these are all problems in regard to which Pantheism, with its unsuccessful attempts at solution, would compel us, in place of believing in a mystery, to believe in an absurdity.—The *conscience*, finally, protests against a doctrine which is in irreconcilable conflict with its own distinct utterance. It leaves just as little room for the ideas of sin and virtue, as for those of responsibility and retribution. Self-accusation becomes self-deception, where even the sin is a necessary part of that whole, which is essentially one with God. The great question, "Whence moral evil?" is entirely out of place in such connection; that which is so called is rather something natural, necessary, and is so far relatively good. The science of Ethics becomes from this standpoint simply psychological mechanics. Even the so highly praised effort to attain to the pure human ideal (*Humaniteit*) is in principle paralysed, so soon as the boundary-line between the merely natural life and the higher moral one is tacitly effaced. Either all conscience is an illusion, or Pantheism is false. If one has been led into it as the result of an intellectual process, he will best be delivered therefrom by means of this psychological-moral argument.

In vain does Pantheism seek countenance or support in Holy Scripture. Even the opening words of Genesis confirm the opposite view; and not less does all that is there taught concerning a constant speaking and self-revealing on the part of God, under whatever form this is conceived of. Places like Eccles. xii. 7; Isaiah xlv. 7; Acts xvii. 28; 1 Cor. xv. 28; 1 John iv. 16, testify in favour of this view, only so long as one clings unreflectingly to the mere ring of the words.—Still less is there ground for accusing of a crypto-Pantheistic tendency, as has sometimes been done, certain Reformers and Teachers of the Reformed Church, who held fast to the "cor ecclesiæ."—Least of all must the advocates of the Pantheistic view assert that they have attained to a higher standpoint in the domain of Theological thought, than is assumed by the representatives of Christian Theism. We are justified, on the contrary, in speaking of this last, not simply as the highest religious standpoint, but also as the highest philosophic one. The logical unity of thought to which the Spinozist rises, is simply attained at the cost of sacrificing part of the reality. Monism may perhaps be a postulate, but never a result, of a mode of thought which duly takes into account *all* the facts of the case. It is the fruit of an empty abstraction; while Theism alone can lay claim to be the accurate expression of that truth, of which Deism and Pantheism, each from its own standpoint, have had an inkling, and which both have alike overlooked. Only let it never be overlooked by the Theist that a very essential element of the Christian confession of God consists in the recognition of—His incomprehensibility.

Comp. CALVIN, *Instit.*, i., 5, 9; E. A. BORGER, *De Mysticismo* (1816); P. HOFSTEDE DE GROOT, *l. c.*, pp. 217—228; C. W. VAN DER POT, *Over de verhouding van der Evang. tot het metaphys. begrip der oneindigheid Gods* (W. in L., 1849, iii.); CARO, *L'Idée de Dieu* (1864); J. W. HANNE, *Die Idee der absoluten Persönlichkeit* (1865); a dissertation of THILO in the *Godg. Bijdr.* 1868, 9th part; ULRICI'S article, *Theism*, in Herzog's *R. E.*, with the literature there adduced; J. I. DOEDES, *l. c.*, pp. 68 and 280.

POINTS FOR INQUIRY.

Why must the religious belief necessarily rise to a definite conception of God?—Is it not possible to construct the conception of God *à priori*?—Has the Christian Church at all times had the same conception of God?—Nearer explanation and defence of the idea of the personality of God.—Difference between the Monistic and the Supernaturalistic Theism.—Criticism of the former.—Deism and Pantheism in relation to the principal points of Christian Dogmatics.—Does Pantheism in reality find not the slightest support in the Bible, or in the writings of the Reformers and their spiritual kinsmen?—Is it the case that, with the admission at the same time of the Immanence and Transcendency of God, all difficulty is at once removed?

SECTION XLVI.—THE UNITY OF GOD.

From the contents of the Christian conception of God the unity of the Divine Nature necessarily results. Lost sight of by Heathendom, maintained by Israel, yet more presupposed than taught in the Gospel, Monotheism is for intelligent belief simply a natural consequence of Theism, yet is none the less of most indisputable value for Religion and Morality.

1. The discussion of the conception of God leads naturally to that of the unity of God, with which it is most closely connected. In fixing the *idea* of this unity the older Dogmatics has rightly distinguished between unity of number and of kind (unitas *numerica* et *specifica*), and demanded the recognition of both in regard to the Divine Nature. We speak of it as one and indivisible, but also as unique and incomparable. This transcendental unity of nature is thus no property of God along with other attributes, such as holiness, wisdom, etc., but the absolute condition (*conditio sine quâ non*) of His whole existence. Genuine Theism cannot possibly present itself otherwise than as Monotheism.

2. The *proof* for this position is nowhere given in Holy Scripture, but its truth is everywhere presupposed, witnessed to, and where necessary, energetically maintained.[1] Against the absurdity of Polytheism is wielded the lash of satire.[2] Monotheism also in reality alone commends itself as truly religious and perfectly rational. Belief in the unity of God finds its support *partly* in the idea of absolute perfection itself, which can only be one and indivisible; *partly* in the harmony of the laws, forces, and phenomena in the kingdom of nature, and notably in the unity of the moral law; *partly*, in the last place, in history, which clearly shows that humanity, as it continues to develop itself, ever ascends from Polytheism to Monotheism, never the reverse. No wonder that the latter may be called the common basis of the Law, the Gospel, and of Islamism.

3. In presence of so much evidence the long-continued and manifold *ignoring* of this truth might well surprise us, were it not that this phenomenon must for other reasons be regarded as sufficiently easily explained. It cannot be disputed, that that which now appears to us so simple and natural, as scarcely to call for discussion, was clearly recognised and confessed only by a few sages of heathen antiquity; and even in these cases there is still a question whether the tradition of earlier revelation has not indirectly contributed to this result (comp. § xxv. 3). It is at least certain that the Gentile world wholly lost sight of the unity of God, to its

---

[1] See, in the Old Testament, Exod. xx. 3; Deut. iv. 35; vi. 4; Isaiah xlv. **22—25.** In the New Testament, John xvii. 3; 1 Cor. viii. 5, 6; 1 Tim. ii. 5.

[2] 1 Kings xviii. 27; Isaiah xl. 19; xliv. 10, and following.

own detriment;[3] that Israel could scarcely be cured, by means of severe discipline, of its tendency to idolatry; and that the youthful Christianity also had to withstand the temptation first to a heathen Dualism, and later even to Tritheism and Tetratheism. In every form, however, Polytheism is a fruit of sin. The darkened understanding could no longer raise itself to the clear conception of the one absolute perfection, because the imagination was at the same time captivated and deceived by the varying brightness of the creation. The sinful heart sought to express its admiration, love, or terror, in the superstitious adoration of the visible and finite. The impure will reached forth towards the enjoyment of the senses, so frequently associated with the Polytheistic form of worship (cultus), and the sullied conscience forgot the holiness of God, of which the recognition—so closely allied to that of His unity—was forbidden. Thus very soon was "the glory of the uncorruptible God changed into that of a corruptible creature."

4. As opposed to so much folly, the *defence* of the unity of God has not always been conducted with equal success. Rather strange, for instance, sounds the appeal of Cyprian,[4] to the analogy of the animal kingdom: "*Rex unus apibus, dux unus gregibus.*" With infinitely greater force is this truth upheld by each renewed manifestation of the Supreme Majesty of Him, who will not give His glory to another. The recognition thereof stands thus also in immediate connection with that of God's Sovereignty,[5] and is absolutely necessary, in order to the indispensable unity of the religious and moral life.[6] It binds together the whole of humanity, as being formed by one Creator, responsible to one Lawgiver, and called to conformity to one Ideal of the highest perfection.[7]

Comp. LACTANTIUS, *Div. Instt.*, i., c. 3—10; D. WYTTENBACH, *Disput. de Unitate Dei*, in his *Opuscula*, ii., pp. 373, *sqq.* On the question as to Cicero's mode of thinking on this point, an important *Monitum* in the *Chartæ Theol.* of H. BOUMAN, i., p. 172, *sqq.* (1853). On the origin of Monotheism, a treatise by P. HOFSTEDE DE GROOT, *W. in L.*, 1861, ii.

POINTS FOR INQUIRY.

Peculiarity of the belief in the unity of God, from an Israelitish, Islamitish, and Christian point of view.—Further elucidation of the testimonies of Holy Scripture.—History and criticism of the defence of the belief in God's unity put forth within the Christian Church.—Permanent religious and ethical importance of this dogma.

SECTION XLVII.—THE ATTRIBUTES OF GOD.

The eternally indivisible light of absolute perfection inevitably breaks out, for our finite vision, into different colours: in God's

---

[3] Rom. i. 18—32.
[4] *De idol. vanit.*, c. 5.
[5] Deut. xxxii. 39.
[6] Matt. vi. 24.
[7] Rom. iii. 29; Jas. iv. 12; Matt. v. 48.

attributes His nature reveals itself. It is on this account just as necessary on the one hand, accurately to distinguish in Christian Dogmatics the different attributes of God, as it is, on the other hand, impossible to deduce, divide, and combine these in a way which leaves no single difficulty remaining. Anthropomorphism and Anthropopathism can hardly be avoided in so doing, but neither on the other hand need it be entirely avoided.

1. The discussion of the idea of God and the unity of the Divine Nature leads now to the examination of the doctrine of His *Attributes*. The importance of this examination is at once manifest. The question what we are to understand by the Attributes or Perfections of God, is that which in this conn ction first demands an answer.

2. By properties (attributes) of a being we understand the qualities by which it, in distinction from others, is what it is. God's properties are thus the qualities of His Nature in consequence of the combined possession of which He is justly named the absolutely perfect One. They are called also the virtues of God (ἀρεταί),[1] attributes, predicates, *proprietates*. Earlier Dogmatists have occasionally distinguished between these different notions, but without the clearness of the conception gaining anything thereby. In any case there is here also this peculiar connection between Property and Nature, that the latter is known by means of the former. Now the existence of such properties in the Divine Nature flows of itself out of the notion of personality, and is accordingly—in harmony with the teaching of Scripture[2]—expressed in the Confession.[3] The recognition thereof detracts nothing from that of God s unity, for this reason that it is a living unity, not a mere sameness or uniformity—just as little does it this, as the observation of the law of the division of the light into colours is opposed to that of the harmony of the light. Only we must take care not to set God's Nature and His Attributes one against the other, or to regard these last as standing in a merely external relationship to the former, whereas they are in reality absolutely inseparable from His Nature. *Whatever is predicated of God, is not quality, but essence.*[4]

3. Is the distinction of different attributes simply the fruit of our limited capacity, and consequently something purely subjective; or has it, on the contrary, an objective *ground* in the nature of God Himself? It is imperatively necessary, before we go any farther, to take this question into consideration. For, suppose that the distinction referred to has no foundation whatever in the reality of things, then our whole investigation has lost much of its significance and worth. We have then simply to declare with Quenstadt that "God, if we wish to speak properly and accurately, has no properties,"[5] and then to pass at once to the doctrine of His works. Yet we

---

[1] 1 Pet. ii. 9.
[2] Psalms xix., civ.; Rom. i. 20.
[3] *Netherlands Confession*, Artt. i., ii.
[4] "Quidquid de Deo dicitur, non qualitas est, sed essentia."—AUGUSTINE.
[5] Deus, si proprie et accurate loqui velimus, nullas habet proprietates.

feel we cannot but reject this statement as one-sided and arbitrary. It is true that in God all perfection is *one;* but in the revelation of Himself this perfection becomes actually manifest in a varying light and in different ways. Nominalism, which merely attaches subjective significance to the whole distinction in this domain, leads thus inevitably to a wrong conception alike of the Christian idea of revelation, and of the Christian idea of God. The reason why Schleiermacher, Hegel, Strauss, and others, refuse to speak in this place of a real distinction, objectively founded in God Himself, lies in their more or less Pantheistical tendency of thought. No doubt, if God is simply another name for the Universum, it is in this case absurd to speak of an essential distinction in His spiritual attributes. If He is, on the other hand, true Personality, then the different qualities which He reveals must assuredly be something essential in Himself; since otherwise the revelation of Himself would be not the expression, but the denial of His innermost nature. We must thus, in regard to these properties, firmly maintain with Rothe, "They are not simply the product of our intellect in its reflecting upon God, but have existed in essential objectivity in God, before all activity of the distinguishing human intellect was called into existence." God's knowing cannot be wholly the same as His willing; His wrath must also be something in itself different from His long-suffering; He Himself must essentially stand in a different relation to the morally good, and to the morally bad; or else the eternal distinction between good and evil at last falls away. According to this view, He by no means becomes, as is objected by Schleiermacher, a composite Being; but precisely in this way becomes for us the truly personal and living God, who reveals Himself as He actually is. Opposition between the different attributes, it is true, is just as little conceivable as an even momentary separation of one attribute from another. But their essential difference, and at the same time capacity for being distinguished, must be recognised as existing not simply for our consciousness, but as immanent in the Divine Nature itself; if, at least, we are to retain a Theistic standpoint, and regard God's revelation of Himself not simply as a wholly inadequate accommodation to our needs, but as a faithful and sufficiently clear reflection of the highest reality. "The Divine attributes belong to God, not as though they made up His nature, as though His whole being consisted only of the combination of the same; but because they are the *forms* and *outward expressions* (*Richtungen*), in which His Being is revealed and becomes manifest" (Bruch).

4. In order to attain to a *knowledge*—as far as possible satisfactory—of the attributes of God, it is not sufficient to combine the principal utterances of Holy Scripture, as perfectly as we can, into one whole. In this way, indeed, we obtain Biblical Theology, but as yet no Christian Dogmatics, in the scientific sense of the word. That which is here incumbent upon us is to learn to recognise the attributes of God in their mutual relationships, and in their necessary connection with His Being. In what sense, and to what extent, we may speak of a knowledge of God, we have already seen (§ xliii.). It is now simply a question whether there exist means of so learning to know God from His works of creation, that His attributes also shall reveal themselves in sufficiently clear light before our eyes. To this

question an affirmative answer has been given by the Scholasticism of the Middle Ages,[6] an answer which has been supported by that of the seventeenth century. They even recommended three ways, by which to rise to a conception as pure as it is possible to attain to—the way of denial (*negationis*), the way of elevation (*eminentiæ*), and the way of causality (*causalitatis*). By the first of these was separated from the idea of God all that belongs to man's limited condition; by the second, all perfection of the creature was ascribed in an infinite degree to God; by the third were obtained as a logical result all the attributes which are contained in the idea of an infinite First Cause. Far be it from us to look with contempt upon this endeavour to justify as reasonable that which faith recognises as true. If it manifests the traces of the limitation of all human thought; yet where the supporting power of wings is wanting one must sometimes make shift with crutches. The Scripture itself, in a number of places, points now to the one, now to the other of these ways; and let him who rejects and cuts away all these, see that he has something more solid and better to offer to the intelligent belief. Yet it can scarcely be denied that this method, upon closer examination, promises far more than it really gives. In place of there being an essential distinction, the one way here passes over insensibly into the other. The first naturally loses itself in the second, both are resolved into the third, and the question finally arises, with what right we form, from our own idea of causality, conclusions as to the attributes of the Supreme Being. Even with the most favourable answer, we can hardly avoid thinking of the war of the Titans, who pile "Ossa upon Pelion, and again upon Ossa Olympus," without in reality making their way to heaven. Infinitely preferable to the method of an arid reasoning is a thoughtful observance of God's *revelation* of Himself, in His word, works, and ways, which rival each other in their unceasing manifestation of His attributes.

5. A nearer *division* of the attributes of God thus revealed appears desirable on account of the great mass of material at our disposal, and has also in reality been attempted in different ways in earlier and later times. It has been attempted—to name some examples—to divide them into proper and improper, positive and negative, absolute and relative, original and derived, natural and moral attributes, and so on. No single one of these divisions is there which does not call forth the old confession, "God is great, and we comprehend Him not;" no single one, also, against which no objections of more or less weight may not be adduced. No wonder that neither in Holy Scripture nor yet in the Church Confessions any attempt at such division is made. If, however, such division is thought desirable in the interest of a systematic treatment, we believe we shall encounter comparatively the fewest difficulties if in *the King of the Kingdom of God* we distinguish the *Majesty* which He has in *Himself*, and the *Glory* which He *outwardly* manifests; the inner brightness, consequently, and the outward radiance of the Light; the attributes which relate to *His own mode of existence*, and those which become known to us in *His mode of operation.*

6. Before we pass on to the treatment of both of these, yet a word on

[6] Dionysius the Areopagite, Durandus; to a certain extent also A. Hales.

the *Anthropomorphism* and *Anthropopathism* of which our mode of expression in this domain affords such abundant evidence. That both of the former, (the ascribing of human shapes and forms,) as of the latter, (the attributing of human emotions—such as anger, grief, joy, etc.—to God,) many traces are found, especially in the oldest writings of the Bible, is well known.[7] But also in the most scientific conceptions of the Supreme Being one meets constantly with modes of thinking, in which, even unconsciously, something of a finite human character is transferred to God. That it is the duty of the Christian Dogmatist, as far as possible to guard against this, will be doubted by no one. Holy Scripture itself seeks constantly to arm us against any confusion of the human and Divine.[8] There is an Anthropomorphism and Anthropopathism which is to be distinctly condemned, it is "where man compares God with himself, and reasons concerning God from his own limited point of view; like the snails and oysters from their own narrow shells, and the hedgehog out of his own self-contained Ego" (Clemens Alexandrinus). Nevertheless, also, on the other side, the avoiding of all anthropomorphic expressions is just as little necessary as it is possible. Of God man can speak only in a human manner; and, if our nature is truly related to that of God, how can we conceive of Him without the admixture of a single trait derived from ourselves? This is the deep significance of Jacobi's words: "In creating man God theomorphosised; therefore man necessarily anthropomorphosises." "God condescends to us, in order that we may rise to Him."[9] Anthropomorphism and Anthropopathism is therefore by no means the antipode, but rather the imperfect approximating expression of eternal truth; and in the interpretation, also, of Holy Scripture, our part is simply to trace out, as far as possible, the truth underlying such expressions. In doing so we must take care that we explain the anthropomorphic conceptions by the more purely spiritual ones, not the converse, and that we are guarded by a certain spiritual tact against "thinking after an earthly manner" (τὰ ἐπίγεια φρονεῖν) of the supreme majesty of God. Thus regarded and explained, even the anthropopathic expressions of Scripture become the means of a better knowledge of God; a sublime accommodation to human wants and weaknesses, sanctified for the eye of faith, since God's own Son has appeared as man on earth. Anthropomorphism belongs thus also to the necessary form of the revelations of God; and let him who takes offence at the husk see that he does not lose the kernel, to retain—a merely apathetic God.

Compare J. F. BRUCH, *Lehre von den göttl. Eigenschaften* (1842); C. B. MOLL, *De justo attributorum Dei discrimine* (1853), i. [JOHN HOWARD HINTON, *Lectures on Acquaintance with God* (London, 1856), Lecture vi.]

POINTS FOR INQUIRY.

The importance of the examination as to the doctrine of the attributes of God.—Is the

---

[7] See, *e.g.*, Gen. vi. 6; viii. 21; xi. 5, 6; and many other places.
[8] See, *e.g.*, Ps. l. 21; cxxi. 4; Isa. xl. 28; Hos. xi. 9.
[9] Condescendit nobis Deus, ut nos consurgamus.—AUGUSTINE.

recognition of many attributes in the Divine nature consistent with that of His unity?—Is it not sufficient simply to consult the Holy Scriptures, in order to arrive at an accurate deduction and classification of the Divine attributes?—Further review of the Scholastic method.—Résumé and criticism of the principal modes of dividing the Divine attributes.—The bright and the dark side of Anthropomorphism and Anthropopathism in the Theological domain.

SECTION XLVIII.—GOD'S MODE OF EXISTENCE.

The attributes which have relation to God's mode of existence are, properly, those which must be ascribed to His nature in itself, conceived of so far as possible without any relation to the creature. They have their basis in the fact that God, as Absolute Being, independent of all beyond Him, has life in Himself; so that He, existing entirely above the limits of time and space, and—as a perfectly spiritual nature—invisible and incomprehensible for the creature, is in Himself beyond description glorious and blessed.

At the beginning of our consideration of God's mode of existence, we are involuntarily reminded of the well-known account of Augustine and the lad sporting on the sea shore, and repeat the words of the Psalmist, "Such knowledge is too wonderful for me; it is high, I cannot attain unto it." The attributes of this first class are, from the nature of the case, the most difficult to define, and in their treatment call for the most careful and reverent consideration.

1. Starting from the conception of God we have settled, we cannot but further assert that God possesses—in the fullest sense of the word—life in Himself. This property (*Aseïtas*) can be ascribed to none but the Most High. Man also can have life in himself, but only in communion with the Son of God, yea, even to the Son Himself it is *given* by the Father.[2] The Father alone has it from no one; in Himself He has the cause, the source, the power of His life; He is *causa sui*, precisely because He is the absolute, infinite Being. For us it is impossible further to sound this depth; yet we clearly perceive that a non-recognition of this truth must lead to a destruction of the whole conception of God.

2. He who thus possesses life in Himself must be absolutely *independent* of all which exists beyond Himself. From this independence (*libertas metaphysica*) it follows as a direct consequence, that God needs not to receive anything of any one, in order to remain most glorious and blessed in Himself. Every creature needs other creatures, all stand in need of Him; but He is not served with men's hands, *as though He needed anything*.[3] This truth concerning the independence (αὐτάρκεια) of God, not recognised in

---

[1] John vi. 53. [2] John v. 26. [3] Acts xvii. 25.

Heathendom, we hear confessed in Israel,[4] and soon proclaimed by Jesus and His Apostles.[5] It is to a certain extent the test of the purity of our conception of God, whether it acknowledges this independence truly without any limitation; since the Mysticism of every age has limited or contested it. Yet from a Theistic standpoint it must be maintained, however difficult the thought may be to realise, that God needs no creation in order to be Himself, although, as the highest Love, He will not live without creatures of His own. Only we must take heed lest this absolute independence of God be conceived of as Stoical self-sufficiency, which would be mere selfishness. It must rather be conceived of as Love's inexhaustible fulness of life, which can give all, without needing to receive anything. This thought, far indeed from obscuring for our eyes the majesty of God, rather increases it; when it becomes apparent that He who needs not the greatest does not despise even the smallest.[6]

3. The absolutely independent Being cannot be thought of otherwise than as exalted also above that *time* in which all finite things exist,—in other words, as *eternal*. When we speak of God's eternity, we mean that He just as little knows a beginning to His existence as He will ever know an end. In an exalted and inimitable manner is this expressed in Holy Scripture (*e.g.*, Ps. xc. 2; cii. 26—28; 1 Tim. vi 16; 2 Peter iii. 8). Without beginning, He is Himself the Rock of eternal ages, in distinction also from the earliest object which has been called into existence by Him. If we finite creatures cannot possibly form to ourselves an adequate conception of eternity, yet it is very soon apparent that here we have not to think of an infinite succession of moments, but of an absolute superiority to all time; in consequence of which time also is through Him, while He, the King of eternity,[7] remains absolutely independent of time. His existence is not determined by time, it is an eternal To-day, without earlier or later, past or future, "a living eternity blooming forth in unfading youth" (Martensen). Here, however, every idea of rigid immobility is to be rejected; the Petra is no petrifaction. We cannot otherwise conceive of the case than that the Eternal regards things under the form of the time in which, according to His will, they arose; so that this eternity also by no means prevents Him from directly intervening by word and action in the course of events. But He looks upon the finite from the light of eternity, and from its standpoint, and time can be nothing for Him but the condition under which all that is not Himself successively appears and vanishes. He creates, orders, and changes time, without the latter having any influence upon Him; and must thus be thought of as independently co-existing with all things, past, present, and to come.

Most closely connected with this eternity of the Divine Being is the *Unchangeableness*, in virtue of which every idea of modification in His form of existence is utterly excluded,[8] since He *dwells* in eternity; so that His perfection just as little admits of increase as of diminution. In so far then it is less accurate to speak of God's *nature*, since this word, by virtue of its

---

[4] Job xxii. 2, 3; Ps. l. 10—12.
[5] Matt. xi. 25; Rom. xi. 34.
[6] Ps. cxiii. 5, 6; Isa. lvii. 15.
[7] 1 Tim. i. 17.
[8] Mal. iii. 6; James i. 17.

derivation—*natura*, from *nasci*—necessarily suggests the idea of growing or becoming. It is better to speak of the Being (*Wezenheid*) of God, as indicating that which in itself from eternity to eternity IS.[9] If proof were yet necessary that this conception of God in its pure sublimity is, as to its ultimate source, due to a higher revelation, this proof would be afforded us by the history of philosophy, which makes clearly manifest how frequently human thought has suffered shipwreck on this rock. Many a speculative Theology is, properly speaking, nothing but a Theogony; and yet sound Christian philosophic thought perceives that any denial or limitation of this Divine property must necessarily lead to absurdity. What strong consolation flows from a believing acknowledgment thereof, can here be only indicated. Compare the ninetieth Psalm.

4. He who is thus exalted above all time, cannot possibly be held captive by space. The acknowledgment of God's eternity must necessarily lead to that of His *Omnipresence*. If we men are, in regard to our body, bound by the laws of space, even while our spirit transports itself to distant regions, the Infinite One is exalted above all the bounds of space. Just as little as time sets limits to His being, does space impose them on His almighty will. When therefore, in harmony with Holy Scripture,[10] we speak of God as incommensurable and everywhere present, we have to understand this last expression, not in the extensive, but in the dynamical sense, and to be careful to keep ourselves free from all Pantheistic leaven. Not a substantial, but an operative presence of God in every point of His creation must be ascribed to Him. In creating He has not limited, but most gloriously revealed Himself. With His life-awakening power He is active in all things; but, nevertheless, is by no means imprisoned in His own work. He embraces, rules, penetrates it—not in the Pantheistic, but in the Theistic sense of the term—being neither excluded nor included by any extent of space. The manifestation of this Divine presence is differently modified according to the different domains of life. It is manifested under one form in the material, under another in the spiritual world; more directly was God's presence displayed in Israel than among the Gentile nations.[11] But this presence itself—here not acknowledged, there clearly acknowledged; here desired, there dreaded—is never and nowhere a dream. "The Omnipresence of God must not be conceived of as unfree, which is the root error of Pantheism, but as the presence of the free, self-determining God, who presents Himself under a different aspect in relation to the different creations" (Martensen).

With this omnipresence of God, the fact that Holy Scripture definitely represents *heaven* as the dwelling and throne of God is not in conflict. God, who is everywhere, manifests His glory more peculiarly and brightly in that region of His creation which we are accustomed to call heaven; just as the sun, which shines everywhere, yet especially displays its full splendour in the firmament. However frequently it is asserted that heaven is not to be thought of as a place, but merely as a condition, yet the idea of locality cannot be wholly banished from our conception. Nothing prevents our thinking, in connection with the word heaven, of that

---

[9] Exod. iii. 14. [10] Ps. cxxxix. 7—10; Jer. xxiii. 23, 24. [11] Ps. lxxvi. 1.

higher than earthly and material sphere of things to which Jesus points us when He speaks of "our Father in the heavens."[12] If this conception can only to a certain extent be reconciled with that of God's actual nearness,[13] this is in consequence of the limitation of our human mode of thinking. But this we feel, nevertheless, with full certainty, that He who in this sense is everywhere present, may also be called absolutely incommensurable. A measure can be applied only to that which is finite, enclosed within certain limits. Here, however, every standard fails us, because the object itself, to which this is to be applied, is absolutely boundless. To such an extent, the *incommensurableness* of God is most intimately connected with the spiritual simplicity of His being.

5. From what has been said, it follows with equal necessity that God, as a purely spiritual being, is *invisible* and *incomprehensible* for every creature. The invisibleness of God is the natural consequence of His incorporeity, and the metaphysical ground of the strict prohibition of idolatry.[14] It was nothing more than idle fancy when, in earlier and later times, a fine body of light of the most exceeding beauty has been ascribed to God. No one has ever seen God;[15] no one can see Him and live.[16] Even in the highest rapture of spirit, no seer of the Old Testament beholds and describes the face of Him who sits upon the throne of heaven; not even where His robe or His form is indicated.[17] Everywhere where He is thus said to have been seen, or to have appeared, this must be regarded as having taken place through the intervention, *e.g.*, of an angel's appearance, or some other form of revelation;[18] and even a promise like that of Matt. v. 8 can be taken only in a metaphorical sense. The popular belief that he who had seen God must die,[19] had as its foundation, not only an evil conscience, but also a very reasonable conviction. Even the cherubim veil their face before His glory (δ ξα), which is yet no more than the radiance of His adorable essence. That essence itself cannot, from the nature of the case, be anything other than incomprehensible for us.[20] To that which has been before said (§ xlii.) on this point, it is here necessary only to add that this incomprehensibleness is, least of all, the consequence of anything imperfect or self-contradictory in the Divine nature, but solely of our narrowness. "*Apprehendi aliquatenus potest: non comprehendi.*" This has been at all times acknowledged,[2] but in a tone rather of the most profound adoration than of melancholy complaint.

6. Nevertheless, whatever problems may remain unsolved, no conclusion can be more accurate than this, that He in whom all these properties are most perfectly united, must be in Himself, in the highest degree, *glorious* and *blessed*. As such He is accordingly also described by the Apostle;[22] and not otherwise than thus can reason, enlightened by faith, think of the highest Majesty. "Semper agens," says Augustine, "et semper quietus:

---

[12] Matt. vi. 9.
[13] Acts xvii. 27.
[14] Exod. xx. 4, 5.
[15] John i. 18.
[16] Exod. xxxiii. 18—23.
[17] Isaiah vi. 1; Dan. vii. 9.
[18] John xii. 41.
[19] Judges xiii. 22.
[20] Ps. cxlv. 3.
[21] Job xi. 7—9; Rom. xi. 33, 34.
[22] 1 Tim. vi. 15

colligens, et non egens ; quærens, cum nihil desit Tibi; nunquam inops, et gaudens lucri." Even so, here all the conditions of the highest glory and blessedness are present, and, on the other hand, no single obstacle thereto. The highest joy is tasted before His face,[8] and thus yet more by Himself. The conception of this idea is far beyond our power; but the idea itself is of undeniable importance, as the basis of the doctrine of the creation, that God needs not the Universe in order to be the absolutely Blessed One in Himself.

Comp. J. A. DORNER, *Ueber die richtige Fassung der Unveränderlichk. Gottes*, in the *Jahrb. für deutsche Theol.* (1856) ii., (1858) iii. ; C. J. TRIP, *Die Theophanien des A. B.* (Hague Society, 1856); F. FABRI, *Zeit und Ewigkeit* (1865).

POINTS FOR INQUIRY.

What becomes of God's independence, where the Theistic standpoint has been abandoned?—Further explanation of the idea of eternity.—The Omnipræsentia *substantialis* et *operativa*.—The Theophanies under the Old Covenant.—The Speculative and Theosophic conceptions of God's corporality.—The proper nature of the perfect blessedness of God.

SECTION XLIX.—GOD'S MODE OF WORKING.

The inner majesty of God's nature reveals itself in His method of working, bearing the most indisputable traces as well of a Divine *thought* as of a Divine *will*. To the former are ascribed with perfect justice the attributes of Omniscience and Supreme Wisdom ; to the latter, those of Omnipotence and Sovereignty, of Holiness and Righteousness, of Grace and Truth.

1. When we now pass over to those attributes of the Divine nature, which belong to God's mode of working, we feel deeply how difficult it is to avoid the rock of Anthropomorphism. The great mass of material calls for new distinctions, and that between the Divine thought and will naturally follows from the idea of personality. Still we must by no means suppose that with God—as so frequently with us—thinking and willing could ever be in opposition the one to the other. In Himself they are undoubtedly blended together; yet in the description of His perfection we must distinguish without separating them.

2. The first attribute which must be ascribed to the Divine thinking can be no other than that of *Omniscience*. This is that attribute of God by virtue of which He perfectly knows both Himself, and all that exists beyond

---

[23] Ps. xvi. 11.

Himself. The Pantheist has simply a God who is thought out; the Theist, a God who Himself thinks. But the perfectly thinking Spirit must of necessity be also the perfectly knowing Spirit. No wonder that we hear the highest knowledge ascribed to God, already by those heathen philosophers who had approached nearer than others to the recognition of His personality. Still more powerfully was this expressed by Israel's bards and prophets, and under the New Covenant by the Apostles of the Lord. Jesus Himself not only testified in the most emphatic manner to this Divine knowledge,[3] but also during His life on earth manifested it in Himself.[4] And indeed we must at once feel conscious that without it God could not possibly uphold, rule, and judge the world. No wonder that the sacred history contains most striking instances of this Divine knowledge.[5] Equally clear is it that the confession of this knowledge must fill us with profound reverence, but also with childlike confidence; and that it thus stands in direct connection with our consolation and sanctification. (Compare the hundred and thirty-ninth Psalm.)

The idea of absolute Omniscience has about it something by which we are involuntarily perplexed; hence the attempt made long since to master that overpowering idea, as far as possible, by some nearer distinction and definition. The Divine knowledge, then, is divided into a natural knowledge, which He has of Himself; and a so-called free knowledge, which He has of all that exists beyond Himself. And then again, from these two is further distinguished that conditional knowledge, *scientia media* or *hypothetica*, by virtue of which He is exactly acquainted, not only with all which will happen, but also with all which would or would not happen under certain non-existent conditions [6]—the so-called *futuribile*. That this last also is known to God, will certainly not be denied: it is simply an insignificant part of that great whole which lies naked and open before Him. The only question is whether there is reason for speaking of this as a special *kind* of knowledge; as was done in the sixteenth century by the Jesuits Fonseca and Molina, with the definite purpose of maintaining human freedom over against the Divine Foreknowledge. To this question we, in common with the Dominicans, and the majority of Reformed Theologians, must return a negative answer. A realm of abstract possibilities, which—independent of God's will and purpose—could form an essential object of Divine knowledge, is inconceivable; and the difficulty which it is thus sought to escape is not thereby removed. When, moreover, this conditional knowledge is regarded as a subordinate branch of the *free* knowledge, it must not be overlooked that this free knowledge itself, far indeed from being in any sense of the word arbitrary, is in God just as *natural* as the knowledge of His own perfections. Avoiding, therefore, all sophistical distinctions, let us rather simply confess that absolutely nothing is excluded from the Divine knowledge.

---

[1] See, for example, Ps. xxxiii. 13—15; Ezek. xi. 5; Isaiah xliv. 7; Dan. ii. 22. 2 Cor. xi. 11; Heb. iv. 13; 1 John iii. 20.

[3] Matt. vi. 8.

[4] John ii. 25; xxi. 15.

[5] See, *e.g.*, 1 Sam. ix. 15—17.

[6] See examples in 1 Sam. xxiii. 12 2 Kings xiii. 19.

Just as impracticable is the distinction between God's knowledge of the past, the present, and the future, as Remembrance, Intuition, and Foreknowledge. In fact, it leads us to forget that the highest perfection is also in this respect for ever exalted above time and its divisions. But least of all is there any reason for entirely excluding—as was done in earlier times by the Socinians, and in later times by the Groningen school—the Divine foreknowledge from the category of His Omniscience; because otherwise, it was supposed, human freedom would be an empty dream. In vain is it sought to find a warrant for such a view in Holy Scripture,[7] of which the letter and spirit rather express quite the contrary. According to this theory, God's knowledge would be constantly increasing, as the issue of our actions becomes apparent to Him; and, finally, He would Himself stand not above but below man, whose power to foresee, in a certain degree, things future, cannot be denied. He who thinks this view necessary in order to preserve moral freedom, forgets that God can indeed foresee the free actions of men as free actions, and that these actions take place not *because*, but only *after* they have been foreseen by Him. But we shall later treat of the connection between Divine foreknowledge and human freedom. —Finally, as regards the manner in which God knows all the creation—in distinction from our human knowledge, His must be spoken of as not derived, but original; not imperfect, but complete; not indefinite, but perfectly clear and certain; not admitting of increase, but infinitely perfect. God knows all things, always, of and by Himself, simultaneously, from eternity to eternity. For the Divine Intelligence, in a word, all things are transparent. He has not only eyes everywhere;[8] He Himself is the Eye which sees all things and everywhere. In the presence of this Divine knowledge we become conscious of our own limited capacity: "*Si alibi, hîc certe noctuarum instar cæcutimus*" (Heidegger).

3. If the Divine self-consciousness is thus at the same time an absolute consciousness of the world, this consciousness displays not simply a highly metaphysical, but also an exalted ethical character; from the Divine Omniscience, the Divine *Wisdom* must never be separated. The latter is in a certain sense the ethico-practical side of the former: "Wisdom is the virtue of knowledge" (Nitzsch). It is that perfection of God, by virtue of which He realises the highest designs by the use of the best means. The assertion of Spinoza and Strauss, that no design at all can be ascribed to God, is connected with the Pantheistic non-recognition of the idea of God's personality. Certainly there does not exist for the infinite understanding the opposition, not even the great disparity, between means and end, which so frequently is a hindrance to us; but he who will here exclude the whole idea of design, denies in other words that God is a Spirit who thinks and wills. As such He must not only be the All-wise, but also the Only Wise One, in comparison with whom all human wisdom is as nothing. In truth, Holy Scripture also presents Him to us in precisely this light[9]—a God who not only possesses in Himself wisdom in perfection,[10] but also communi-

---

[7] Gen. vi. 6; Isaiah v. 4; Matt. xxi. 37.
[8] Prov. xv. 3.
[9] 1 Tim. i. 17
[10] Prov. viii. 22.

cates it to others.[11] The Apostle even makes mention of a "manifold" wisdom, manifest for the eye of angels, although for that of man unsearchable.[12] Yet even here below it beams forth clearly enough to awaken within us deep reverence and filial confidence. We observe it in the kingdom of Nature, as well in that which is greatest as in that which is smallest;[13] in that of Providence, both in prosperity and adversity;[14] above all, in that of Grace, both in the person and in the work of the Lord, especially in the time of His coming,[15] the word of His cross,[16] and the ordering of His Church;[17] while one day it will shine forth unclouded in the kingdom of Glory.[18]

4. Forasmuch as the wisdom of God displays a definitely moral character, it forms at the same time the transition to those attributes in which the operation of God's *will* is more definitely manifested. At the head of these there meets us, first of all, His *Omnipotence*, that perfection by virtue of which God is able to do all that He pleases. With the exception of that which is contrary to His nature and character, there exists for Him nothing of which the realisation surpasses His power. He can do all, not indeed that is possible in the abstract, but that is possible for Him. "For God," says Tertullian, "to will is to be able, and not to will is not to be able." *Dei posse velle est, et non posse nolle.* The acknowledgment of this truth, both called forth and legitimated by the Christian conception of God, was already heard even from Gentile lips; but was more loudly proclaimed in Israel,[19] and constantly brought into prominence in the Scriptures of the New Testament.[20] Naturally so, where this omnipotence shines forth in so bright a succession of facts. Here must be particularly mentioned the Creation of all things out of nothing, and the whole domain of Miracles, especially also the appearing of Christ, and the spiritual creation wrought by Him. On the ground of the different ways in which this power manifests itself—now in a more ordinary, now in an entirely extraordinary manner—the distinction has often been made between a mediate and an immediate, an ordaining and ordained, an absolute and a relative activity of the Omnipotence of God—a distinction which, rightly understood, is allowable and useful, provided only it be never forgotten that this activity presents itself under a very different aspect from the human standpoint, than it does from the Divine.[21] Belief in this Omnipotence affords, on the one hand, occasion for deep adoration;[22] on the other, a firm support for quiet confidence.[23]

---

[11] James i. 5.
[12] Ephes. iii. 10, Rom. xi. 33.
[13] Ps. civ. 24.
[14] As exemplified in the lives of Job, Joseph, David, and others.
[15] Gal. iv. 4.
[16] ὁ λόγος ὁ τοῦ σταυροῦ, 1 Cor. i. 18.
[17] 1 Cor. xiv. 33.
[18] 1 Cor. xiii. 12.
[19] Ps. xxxiii. 9; Isa. xl. 12.
[20] John x. 29; Rom. iv. 17; Ephes. iii. 20.
[21] On the connection between the recognition of God's omnipotence and the admission of the idea of miracles, compare § xxxii., Pt. i., p. 128.
[22] Rev. iv. 9—11.
[23] Rom. viii. 31.

5. As the operation of God's will is thus an almighty one, so does it not less display the character of unlimited *Sovereignty*—an attribute again most closely connected with the foregoing. By nothing without Him is God ever hindered from doing what He pleases.[24] This, too, follows actually from the recognition of God as the infinitely perfect Being, and is frequently heard from the lips even of profane antiquity, and still more clearly from the sacred writers.[25] Even the Lord speaks of a good-pleasure of the Father, which is accomplished on earth;[26] and although to a certain extent this expression may display an anthropological character, it soon becomes apparent that it proclaims a truth equally incontestable as it is glorious. That truth is this, that God in reality does all that He wills, and only that which He wills. No doubt this truth is frequently exaggerated, and we would by no means dare to assert that God's absolute sovereignty is that particular side of the conception of God which is brought most distinctly into the foreground in the New Testament. It may even be deplored that the doctrine of God's Sovereignty has been frequently presented, especially by the hot-headed champions of Predestination, in so irrational a manner as to awaken more opposition than admiration. But, however much this exaggeration is to be condemned, still less is the complete disavowal of this truth to be justified in the form it has taken, earlier with the Socinians, and later with all those according to whose presentment God might equally well not have willed that which He willed, or have willed it in a manner precisely the opposite. According to this standpoint, that which God does would be based, not upon His nature, but only upon His will, as conceived of apart from that nature; and what is called freedom at last becomes only boundless caprice. No, for God freedom and necessity are not opposed to each other, but are rather resolved into perfect harmony. God does all that He will, because He—by virtue of His perfectly reasonable and moral nature—cannot but will precisely that which He does, and in that way in which He does it. The inner aversion of many to this truth —which, however, cannot be denied—ordinarily arises from the fact that God's sovereignty is too much separated from His other perfections, by which nevertheless it is wholly determined in its manifestation. God's sovereignty is not that of a capricious despot, but that of the Only Wise, Gracious, Righteous, Holy One. And thus regarded, this attribute is so pre-eminently worthy of God, that one does not comprehend how He could be God, if it could be seriously denied. The history of whole nations and of individuals presents not a little which, without the belief in this unlimited sovereignty, must be regarded as in principle inexplicable. Sometimes there even remains to us no other course than to correct the proud man who will find fault with God's free action, by an appeal to this sovereign right.[27] For faith, its humble acknowledgment presents no danger, provided we never overlook the boundary line which separates good-pleasure from caprice.

6. If it were still doubtful whether God's sovereignty may be spoken of as a moral attribute, this doubt vanishes so soon as we fix the eye more par-

---

[24] Ps. cxv. 3.
[25] Isaiah xlv. 7; Dan. iv. 35; Ephes. i. 11.
[26] Luke x. 21; xii. 32.
[27] Rom. ix. 20.

ticularly upon the *Holiness* of God. That this attribute also must be acknowledged as belonging to the Divine will, is in a general way certainly denied by no one. Yet it is far from easy properly to describe this holiness, as is already apparent from the great number and diversity of the dogmatic definitions thereof. The cause of this difficulty lies in the fact that we are not only finite, but sinful beings, whose eye can by no means endure the splendour of *this* light. "Where is the man who can tell me precisely what holiness is? let him come and call me to him," says Claus Harms. No one of the Divine attributes was accordingly less understood and prized in the heathen world. Under Monotheism—the fruit of a more perfect revelation—did a pure conception of holiness first become possible. The word by which it is indicated in Holy Scripture (קָדוֹשׁ, ἅγιος) denotes originally that which is separated, that which was designed to be used in the service of God, and was thereby consecrated to God. But this distinction itself, without anything further, serves already to show that the profane was conceived of also as unclean, and only that which has been separated therefrom is conceived of as freed from this defilement; first as in Mosaism the ideas of Levitical and moral purity constantly flow into one. In many places, however, the reference of these words is undoubtedly to moral purity,[28] as, from the nature of the case, the highest conceivable perfection can be nothing else than a purely moral and spiritual one. Holiness is that attribute of the Supreme Being, by virtue of which He, in separation from all moral imperfection, loves only that which is right and good, and cannot possibly have fellowship with that which is opposed thereto.[29] It is thus no mere negative idea, but a very positive one, with which we here have to do; an indication of an absolute perfection so great, that sinning is for God something absolutely impossible,[30] and equally so the toleration of sin with indifference.[31] Less accurately is this holiness described as God's perfect agreement with the law of morality (Kant). Nay, rather, the moral law itself does not exist outside of God, much less in contradistinction from Him, but has its basis in His own nature. God is Himself the highest law, and by virtue of His holiness there exists perfect harmony between the law and the lawgiver. As the Holy One, God cannot but love Himself above all, because even He knows nothing more perfect, and finds Himself separated as by a natural chasm from all that is impure and sinful. If, further, it follows from the nature of the case that this holiness especially occupied the foreground under the old dispensation, yet it is far from being true that the revelation thereof in the New Testament commonly recedes before the revelation of God's love. Jesus Himself calls the Father perfect,[32] alone good,[33] holy.[34] All His Apostles represent holiness as the will of God, and the final aim of redemption in Christ. By reason of this His perfection they

---

[28] Levit. xix. 2, compare 1 Pet. i. 15—17; Isaiah vi. 3, compare ver. 5.
[29] Hab. i. 12.
[30] ἀπείραστος κακῶν, James i. 13.
[31] Ps. v. 4, 5.
[32] Matt. v. 48.
[33] Matt. xix. 17.
[34] John xvii. 11.

speak of God as a consuming fire for the sinner;[35] a light wherein is no darkness at all.[36] Most illustriously do we see this attribute manifested and glorified in the faultlessly holy Christ.[37] Its recognition calls forth humility and good courage, since it presents to us in God the highest Ideal of our moral life.

7. Almost in the same breath with the Holiness of God do we usually speak of the *Righteousness* which necessarily flows therefrom. Difficult as this holiness is to conceive of, this righteousness may be described with comparative ease. A notion and sense of justice is peculiar to every man in a greater or less degree; according to the conception of the ancients, justice was at once the sum total of virtue, and righteousness the highest virtue in the Godhead. "*Justitia in se virtutem complectitur omnem.*" Yet all justice here below is only the faint reflection of that original, highest, eternal righteousness, which shines forth in the heavens. When we ascribe righteousness to God, we confess in other words that all injustice is in diametrical opposition to the perfect character of the Divine nature, so that with Him is found no respect of persons;[38] yea, all want of equity in His government of the world is something absolutely impossible. Of such a trait of character, which is found to a certain extent in every right-natured man, it can be least of all doubted that it belongs with other perfections to the nature o the Father of spirits. Both in the Scriptures of the Old Testament and in those of the New, it is everywhere emphatically proclaimed.[39] Not unsuitably is this righteousness divided into the Righteousness which God displays as Lawgiver, and that which He displays as Judge.—The former is manifested in the fact that He appoints no other laws than those which are equitable in themselves, and at the same time practicable for us; a fact which we could not but expect from Him, and which also has been confirmed by the spiritual experience of all ages.[40] That the Divine right to give laws, and precisely such laws, can be founded in nothing else than His nature and His wholly unique relation to the creature, scarcely needs to be recalled to the mind of the reader, after what has been said.—As Judge, God is the Righteous One, because He has most intimately connected obedience and happiness, disobedience and misery. From the nature of the case one must here speak of a retributive justice—as well in rewarding as in punishing—which is placed beyond all reasonable doubt, by a number of testimonies of Holy Scripture, of history, and of daily experience. Even where we must confess that the good is rewarded of grace,[41] it is not to be denied that the rewarding is a reality, and that on the other side the history of the world bears the character of an unceasing judgment of the world. Even the Heathen have been compelled to acknowledge the existence of an avenging Nemesis; and the Christian sees the righteous-

---

[35] Heb. xii. 29.
[36] 1 John i. 5.
[37] John viii. 46; xvii. 4.
[38] Rom. ii. 11.
[39] Gen. xviii. 25; Ps. xi. 7; John xvii. 25; Heb. vi. 10.
[40] Ps. xix. 7—10.
[41] *Heidelberg Catechism*, Ans. lxiii.

ness of God even in the revelation of His highest grace in Christ.[42] Only we have here especially to be on our guard against all Anthropopathism, and must understand that which Scripture speaks of God's holy wrath against the sin of the world in the sense that, precisely because He is God, He presents in word and deed the strongest possible negation to the evil which He cannot tolerate. Without such wrath the very love of God would lose its highest value: not without reason has this wrath been termed "the extreme burning point of the flame of love." What is the love which can never be angry? and what becomes of the Gospel if Christ has not redeemed us from that which we had otherwise to dread?[43] On the principle, the idea, and the aim of punishment, it will be more in place to speak hereafter, in connection with the doctrine of sin. Here only the additional remark that the frequently repeated assertion, to the effect that the righteousness of God is much more held in honour in the Scriptures of the Old Testament than in those of the New, is to say the least one-sided. The triumph of the Kingdom of God is, not simply that of the highest grace, but also that of the great judgment.[44] The difference is only this, that according to the ordinary conception of the Old Testament the retribution takes place more on this side the grave; according to the conception of the New Testament, more on the other side. The argument against the righteousness of God, derived under the former from the prosperity of the ungodly,[45] no longer exists, since under the latter life and immortality (incorruptibility) has been brought to light. The final answer, moreover, to each objection which so frequently renders belief in the righteousness of God difficult, will be received only beyond the grave; but even here the reverent acknowledgment of this righteousness must redound to His glory and to the work of our own perfection.[46]

8. The same revelation which testifies of God's righteousness, places also His *Kindness* in brighter lustre before our eye. In manifold ways this was also recognised by the heathen world; but only with the light of Saving Revelation was its full value understood, because He who displays it is the spotlessly Holy One. In harmony with Holy Scripture we speak of God as kind[47] (χρηστός, עֹשֶׂה חֶסֶד); because He wills the happiness of His creatures, and to this end confers upon them abundantly all things which they are capable of receiving, in themselves, or in connection with others. This Kindness bears different names, according as it displays itself towards different kinds of objects. As shown to the unfortunate and helpless it is called Mercy;[48] shown to guilty ones, whose punishment is still delayed, it is called Longsuffering;[49] glorified in transgressors, whose sentence is freely remitted, it is called Grace.[50] In all

---

42 Rom. iii. 25, 26.
43 1 Thess. i. 10.
44 Rev. xv. 3, 4.
45 Ps. xxxvii.; Mal. iii.
46 Ezek. xviii. 25; Micah vi. 8; Rom. ii. 6—11.
47 Ps. xxxvi. 5; Luke vi. 35.
48 ἔλεος, *misericordia*, Luke i. 78.
49 μακροθυμία, ἀνοχή, Luke xiii. 6—9.
50 χάρις, Ephes. i. 7.

three is manifested God's Compassion and Love towards Men, which Scripture extols with so great warmth.[51] Far, indeed, from this conflicting with God's righteousness as, following in the footsteps of the ancient Gnosticism, so many a one asserts, it on the contrary harmonises most gloriously therewith,[52] and together with this righteousness, shines forth in the same cross of reconciliation.[53] Although this attribute of God was already made known even under the old dispensation,[54] the Gospel of God's grace towards sinners merits to be called its highest revelation. Yet in the wider sense also there is no single kind of creatures to which God's kindness does not extend.[55] From the nature of the case the recognition thereof affords us renewed cause for glorifying Him,[56] a stimulus to repentance,[57] and an example for imitation.[58]

9. Have we, in what has been said, reviewed all the attributes of God revealed to us? Not so long as we have not learnt to know Him, finally, as the *True* and *Faithful* One. The one idea may thus be distinguished from the other, that we speak of God in Himself as true, and in all His words as faithful. In asserting the former, we deny that in Him there is any difference between appearance and reality; His power is true Omnipotence, His holiness essential Holiness. In expressing the latter, we maintain that not only His nature, but also the feeling He cherishes towards us, remains always absolutely self-consistent, so that we can unreservedly count upon all that He declares, promises, or threatens.[59] Every reason exists for doing so; because He is the Most High, the morally perfect One, for whom none of those reasons can exist, which so frequently lead *us* to fail in our promises or threatenings. He is accordingly also introduced as swearing by Himself,[60] and bears the name of a God who cannot lie.[61] If we read—in apparent contradiction with this—that He repents of anything,[62] this is not to be conceived of in any other sense than one worthy of God, as indicating the intensest grief of love;[63] while passages of Scripture like 1 Kings xxii. 20; 2 Thess. ii. 10—12, have reference to particular judgments, before announced, and thus least of all prove anything against God's truth and faithfulness. The whole history of Israel and of the Kingdom of God upon earth, as well as our daily experience, bears constant witness to this faithfulness.[64] Its recognition is the tacit condition of all belief in revelation, and at the same time an inexhaustible source of comfort and strength.[65]

10. It must yet be remarked, in regard to all these attributes of God, that they are inseparably connected in their operation and manifestation, and are limited the one by the other. God's omnipotence, for example, does not manifest itself otherwise than His wisdom allows; His kindness cannot cease to be holy and righteous. Nothing, therefore, must be

---

[51] Ps. cxvi. 5; Titus iii. 4.
[52] Matt. v. 45; Acts. x. 34, 35.
[53] Rom. iii. 24—26.
[54] Exod. xxxiv. 6, 7.
[55] Ps. cxlv. 9.
[56] Ps. xxxvi. 7.
[57] Rom. ii. 4.
[58] Luke vi. 36.
[59] Compare Num. xxiii. 19; Isa. xlvi. 10.
[60] Ezek. xxxiii. 11.
[61] Titus i. 2.
[62] Gen. vi. 6.
[63] 1 Sam. xv. 29.
[64] Ps. cxix. 89—91; Isa. liv. 10.
[65] 1 Cor. i. 9; 2 Tim. ii. 13.

expected of God on the ground of one attribute, which—being granted—would necessarily lead to the obscuring of some other of His perfections. All His perfections form one inseparable whole. "*Certe vita es, sapientia es, veritas es, bonitas es, æternitas es, et omne verum bonum es. . . . . Vita, et sapientia, et reliqua, non sunt partes Tui, sed omnia sunt unum, et unumquodque bonum est totum, quod est, et quod sunt reliqua omnia*" (Anselm). "Certainly Thou art life, art wisdom, truth, goodness, eternity, and every true good. . . . . Life, and wisdom, and the other perfections, are not parts of Thyself, but all are one, and each good is all that it is itself, and that all the others are."

[a] Compare, on the *scientia media*, G. VOETIUS, *Select. Disp.* i. (1648), pp. 254—257; DAEHNE, *De praesc. divinæ cum libert. hum. concordiâ.* (1830). On God's longsuffering, the treatise of PLUTARCH, *De serâ Numinis vindictâ.* On God's punitive righteousness, the treatise of v. d. WIJNPERSSE (Hague Soc., 1798), and LACTANTIUS, *De Irâ Dei;* as also a treatise of HERDER, (*Sämmtl. Werke zur. Litt. u. K.* xix). The treatise of DIESTEL, *On the holiness and righteousness of God,* in the *Jahrb. für deutsche Theol.* (1859) i., (1860) ii. On the signification of the word *Grace,* a paper by N. BEETS, *Jaarb. W. Th.* (1853), p. 742, *sqq.*

POINTS FOR INQUIRY.

Is it possible, in the doctrine of attributes, to separate from each other, by a sharp line of demarcation, the activity of God's *understanding* and of His *will?*—Explanation and defence of the idea of Foreknowledge.—Are the Divine Omnipotence and Sovereignty absolutely unlimited?—Explanation of Rom. ix. 14—23.—Whence is it, that the heathen world has not been able to rise to the conception of God's holiness?—The connection between God's righteousness and His compassion and grace.—Criticism of the principal objections, which have been brought from a different standpoint against the attributes here treated of.

SECTION L.—HARMONY. GOD IS LOVE.

The higher unity of all the different attributes of God is given in the idea of holy Love, which is first manifest in its full lustre in the Gospel. The saying of the Apostle, "God is Love,"[1] is therefore the best compendium of the Christian idea of God; and at the same time the appropriate basis on which, in the further development of this idea, carefully to raise up our superstructure.

1. If the contemplation of the particular attributes justly awakened admiration, so much the more natural becomes the question as to the proper *essence* of Him who unites them all in Himself. For that here a higher unity must exist, we should already tacitly assume, supposing that nothing of this kind had been made known to us; perfection without harmony is inconceivable. However gloriously the colours of the rainbow shine, they can only originate from the refraction of the one colourless light.

---

[1] 1 John iv. 8, 16.

Can we speak in regard to the Divine nature, as well as the human, of a "bond of perfectness"? The Gospel renders an affirmative answer to this question, by pointing to Love as the proper centre of God's nature.

2. "God is love." It must not be passed over unobserved, that this great saying is met with in the utterances of an Apostle who certainly penetrated more deeply than any other into the spirit of his Master. Even the form of the expression shows that it implies more than that God may be spoken of as loving and kind. Kindness and love are certainly not convertible terms, although the expressions are constantly interchanged. Kindness may be shown to irrational creatures—animals, for instance; love can be shown only to rational beings. "Kindness has reference to well-being in general love, on the other hand, has a higher aim, the development of the rational creature to its highest good. We may be kind even to the man whom we heartily despise—love to such an one is possible only in so far as we still recognise and respect human nature in him" (Bruch). In a word, kindness is one of God's attributes; but love is, properly speaking, the nature of Him who unites all these attributes in Himself; He is love Himself. All His properties must be regarded as the attributes of love, as adjectives of this peerless substantive. God's power is thus the power of love; God's knowledge the intelligence of love; God's righteousness the righteousness of love, and in its manifestation simply a means to attain to the exalted aim His love has in view. "God is Himself love, and His nature is nothing but pure love; so that if any one would paint and set forth God, he must draw such an image as should be pure love, representing the Divine nature as the furnace and burning point, of that love which fills heaven and earth" (Luther).

3. That such a view may be said to be wholly in the spirit of the Gospel, and moreover most worthy of God, is well-nigh self-evident. In the former the love of God, more than anything else, is brought into the foreground; and as the Lord ordinarily speaks of Him by preference as "the Father," so He calls Him even by the appellation "holy Father,"[2] and manifests thereby that in His conception of God the notions of love and holiness are by no means opposed. While the highest perfection of a personal being can be no other than a moral perfection, it is impossible we should conceive of a higher moral perfection, than that which manifests itself in love. No other than this can be the central point of the inner life of the Godhead: the highest in God is His heart; the life of that heart is love. Precisely on this account is He the absolutely perfect One, but at the same time also the indescribably blessed One.[3] *Ex suo amore*, says Augustine, *quisque vivit.*—The great proof that, even with God, it neither is nor can be otherwise, consists in the fact that in this love alone lies the right key to explain all that He has done and is doing. What can have moved Him to have called into existence anything outside Himself? to reveal Himself? to give His Son to sinners? The answer is ever again one and the same. Indeed, when giving this answer, we need not deny that many a fact, regarded in the light of God's love, appears inexplicable. But that is a consequence merely of our limited understanding, which

---

[2] John xvii. 11.

[3] Acts xx. 35.

can only in a very imperfect manner penetrate the connection between God's love and His righteousness. God is and remains holy love according to the united testimony of Nature, History, and Scripture, even where His path is for us veiled in darkness. The single word, "God first loved us," is at once the sum total of the doctrine of salvation, the basis of the doctrine of life, and the bond which unites the two.[4] No wonder that it has already called forth from countless hearts a tone of reverent adoration. *Prius dilexit nos Tantus, tantum gratis tantillos et tales.* "He first loved us, who was so great, loved us freely, when we were so little, and such as we were."[5] But no wonder, above all, that precisely this perfection of God is so emphatically presented to man—who is related to God—for imitation.[6]

4. The proper connection of the sacred utterances, "God is Spirit, God is Light, God is Love," can, after what has been said, be no longer obscure. To the question, *What* is God? the answer is, "God is Spirit;" His nature must be regarded as purely spiritual. But to the question, "*Who* is God? in regard to His inner being, the ideas of light and love have their application.[7] The infinite Spirit is equally the one and the other—spotless light, because He is holy love. This conception of God, already obscurely apprehended by illustrious Heathen, and indicated by some in Israel, was first expressed in its full majesty in the Gospel of the New Covenant. And naturally, the purest conception of God could only be a fruit of the contemplation of the highest revelation of God. Precisely in this conception of God lies, moreover, the secret of the enlightening, creating, redeeming power of Christianity. "If Satan could believe that, he would be saved." (Chrysostom.)

5. For Dogmatics the recognition of this truth is of preponderating importance, because it affords at the same time a satisfactory starting-point for further theological investigation. Yet other depths of God's nature are revealed to us in the Gospel than the attributes thus far under contemplation. It cannot but be that these depths should turn us dizzy, but at the same time they compel us to seek a light which dispels for our eyes at least a single cloud. Let us try how far it is possible, proceeding from God's love, to ascend gradually to the highest revealed mystery of the Divine nature.

Comp. J. H. SCHOLTEN, *Disq. de Dei amore*, etc. (1836); B. DOORENBOS, *De amore, omnem omnino Dei virtutem continente* (1838); M. A. JENTINK, *Brieven van Bato en Gruno over Gods heiligh. en liefde* (1841); L. SCHOEBERLEIN, *Die Grundlehre des Heils, entwickelt aus dem Princip. der Liebe* (1848); E. SARTORIUS, *Lehre von der heiligen Liebe* (1856); the dogmatic masterpieces of NITZSCH, THOMASIUS, LIEBNER; also the glorious discourse of ADOLPHE MONOD, *Dieu est Amour* (2nd Rec., 1857, p. 423.)

POINTS FOR INQUIRY.

To what extent is the doctrine of Love, as the highest characteristic of God, met with even outside of Christianity?—Further elucidation of 1 John iv. 8, 16, 19.—Is it possible for us, in the presentation of God's attributes, entirely to escape Dualism?—What significance has the knowledge of God's holy love for our theological conceptions and our spiritual life?—Transition to the Christian doctrine of the Trinity.

---

[4] 1 John iv. 19.
[5] Bernard of Clairvaux.
[6] Matt. v. 48; Ephes. v. 1.
[7] 1 John i. 5; iv. 8.

SECTION LI.—GOD AS FATHER.

As the highest Love, God is Creator and Father of all which exists outside Him, but at the same time through Him. This Fatherly relation of God must, from the nature of the case, be the more intimate, in proportion as its object has a greater capacity for receiving His favour and communion. No creature, however, nor even the whole creation, can be a perfect and wholly adequate object of the Divine love. The Father has this object, from eternity to eternity, in the Son of His good-pleasure.

1. When we speak of God first as *Love*, and then as *Father*, we do not by any means express the same idea. The former expresses the whole fulness of the Christian idea of God, so far as this is given to us men; the latter is as yet only the Alpha of new and profound mysteries, to which we must now be introduced. In accordance with the teaching of the Gospel, and in common with the whole Christian Church, the Reformed Church also confesses that God has revealed Himself as Father, Son, and Holy Ghost; and it is of this we must now speak. It is unnecessary to expatiate on the difficulty of this investigation; we approach a rock for our thought, rendered famous by countless shipwrecks. If, however, we select as our starting-point the incontestable fact: God, the holy Love, we shall not grope about in the dark. For the moment we occupy ourselves exclusively with the confession of the name of *Father*.

2. The name of Father, which faith gives to the Infinite One, bears in itself no exclusively Christian or Israelitish character. Amongst the Greeks and Romans also it was conferred upon the supreme God, and upon some others with Him. An instance of this we have in the Ζεῦ πάτερ of Homer, the *Father of gods and men*, *Diespiter*, *Liber Pater*, etc. Because the fatherly relationship was the highest with which men were acquainted, they ascribed this also to the Infinite in regard to His creatures. So also in the Old Testament Jahveh is termed the Father of Israel, because He had formed it by His miraculous power, and raised it to a nation. Here, however, not merely a natural relationship, but also a moral and spiritual one, is indicated thereby. As a Father, God loved Israel,[2] and is as such expressly invoked by particular saints.[3] In a number of places He is called the Father, as elsewhere the Husband, of His people. As such He pities them that fear Him,[4] most of all has compassion on the unfortunate and tried ones;[5] but demands in return strict obedience.[6] He then who charac-

---

[1] Deut. xxxii. 6; Mal. ii. 10.
[2] Hosea xi. 1.
[3] Isaiah lxiii. 16; lxiv. 8.
[4] Psalm ciii. 13.
[5] Ps. lxviii. 5; Deut. viii. 5; Prov. iii. 12.
[6] Mal. i. 6.

terises the presentation of God as *Father* as something entirely *new* in the Gospel of Jesus, has assuredly read the Scriptures of the Old Testament with very strange eyes.

3. Yet it cannot be overlooked that the character of God as Father is first presented in its full force in the New Testament. The expression so frequently repeated, "God the Father of all men," is never employed by Jesus in this indefinite sense; on the contrary, He says to the hostile Jews that they are of the father the Devil.[7] In the merely *natural* sense of Creator, the name of Father is not indeed employed by Jesus; He uses this name in regard to men exclusively in the *moral* sense, without making any distinction between Jews and Gentiles. The fatherly disposition of God towards the penitent sinner[8] is the basis of His whole Gospel; and the obligation, as His children, to bear the image of this Father, is incumbent upon all who will be in reality subjects of the kingdom of God.[9]

4. The significance of the name of Father is nevertheless far from being exhausted in that which has been just said. With manifest emphasis is this name repeated by Jesus, *partly* as indicating that which God was for Christ's own innermost consciousness, and *partly* as descriptive of the point of view from which He wished His disciples by preference to regard the Most High. Therefore He places the "Our Father," not upon the lips of the world, but of His disciples; yet shows at the same time that He makes an essential distinction between their relation to God and His own. It is always "my" or "your," never "our" Father, when He speaks of God to His disciples. On this account the Apostles also give to God the distinct title of the Father of our Lord Jesus Christ;[10] but at the same time mention as the most glorious privilege of believers that they, in His communion, are able to address the Invisible God as Father.[11]

5. So, by the light of Holy Scripture, the deep sense of the name of Father begins to reveal itself before our eyes. As Creator of all things, God stands in a *natural* relationship to every order of beings (πατριά) in heaven and on earth, which after Him is named; above all of man, who is created after His image.[12] This relation is differently modified, however, according to the differing nature and capacity of its countless objects. God is Father of the (heavenly) luminaries;[13] but also of spirits.[14] To the last-named alone is it, however, possible for Him to stand in a moral and spiritual relationship. The world of men is on this account, with all its sinfulness, the object of His infinite love;[15] and *they* participate therein, above all, who believe in and love the Son of His good-pleasure.[16] To this Son, as to no other being, God as Father stands in a *metaphysical* relation of nature; in other words, in Himself and of His own nature the absolute Personality distinguishes another I, whom He loves as Himself.

6. However surprising this last representation may seem—of which, without a special revelation, we should know nothing—we cannot hesitate

---

7 John viii. 44.
8 Luke xv. 17, *sqq.*
9 Matt. v. 9, 44—48.
10 Ephes. i. 17; 1 Cor. viii. 6; 1 Pet. i. 3.
11 Rom. viii. 15; 1 Pet. i. 17.
12 Ephes. iii. 15; Acts xvii. 28.
13 James i. 17.
14 Num. xvi. 22; Heb. xii. 9.
15 John iii. 16.
16 John xvi. 27.

to call it, in connection with the thought of God's Love (§ I.), in the highest sense reasonable and worthy of God. For, assuredly, love requires for its existence an object; and the adequate object of the highest love cannot but be perfect as this love itself, and thus must also be infinite. But the creation, existing outside God, especially such as it has now become under the influence of sin, is neither perfect nor infinite.[17] If we are not to assume the eternal existence of Matter, we must believe in a beginning of all things. But has then the Eternal had no adequate object for His love before the beginning of the creation, and thus from an inner necessity created the world to supply His own need, and afford Himself an object, which, after all, was not perfect and not eternal? If not, God must from all eternity—in order to be perfectly happy—have possessed that object in *something* higher than created nature. Nay, in *some one*, since the object worthy of the love of the absolute personal Spirit can, from the nature of the case, be only an eternal personal one. In other words, either an eternal and perfect Cosmos, or an eternal and truly Divine Logos; there is no alternative. If the human heart, even, cannot rest in the finite, how much less the Divine heart of love!

7. What has been already said leads to a preliminary criticism of the various Unitarian systems—a criticism which from the nature of the case can only lead to an unfavourable verdict. With all acknowledgment of the excellence which may be boasted of in certain illustrious Monarchians, Channing for example, it can hardly be ignored that the view of Unitarianism—apparently so simple—is in fact only superficial, and in principle even not purely Christian. The Christian idea of God is not Unitarian in the numerical sense of the word, but—let the expression be for a moment allowed—very essentially Trinitarian. The Gospel teaches here much more than the simple "There is but *one* God, the Father;" and that which it has more to teach, is what must presently occupy us. In the meanwhile, the reminder is by no means superfluous, "Equidem hîc, si quando aliis in S. S. mysteriis, sobrie multaque cum moderatione philosophandum puto, adhibita etiam multa cautione, ne aut cogitatio, aut lingua ultra procedat, quam V. D. fines se protendunt" (Calvin). "If in other mysteries of Holy Scripture, most certainly here, I think we ought to philosophise soberly and with great circumspection, lest either our thought or our tongue should proceed further than the limit of the Word of God extends."

Compare VAN O., *Biblical Theology of the New Testament*, i., § 12; W. F. GESS, *Die Lehre von der Person Christi.* (1856), § 35 [English translation]; MARTENSEN, *l. c.*, i., p. 122; the article *Anti-trinitarians*, in Herzog, *R. E.*, i., and the literature there adduced. For an introduction to the treatment of the whole idea of the Trinity, CHRISTLIEB, *l. c.*, p. 256, *sqq*.

POINTS FOR INQUIRY.

The proper distinction between the presentation of God as Father in the Scriptures of the Old Testament and those of the New.—Jesus' consciousness of God.—Must the highest Love necessarily possess an object?—And is it unable to find this beyond itself?—Monarchianism and Unitarianism in its historic career and its dogmatic significance.

---

[17] Ps. cii. 25—27; Rom. viii. 22.

SECTION LII.—THE SON OF GOD.

In the Divine Nature the Son of God is personally distinguished from the Father; but at the same time so intimately one with Him, that the two cannot even be conceived of as separately existing. The Father is the Cause, the Origin, and the Beginning of all things, visible and invisible; the Son is the Word, the Wisdom, and the Image of the Father, and thus the self-conscious sharer of the nature and majesty of God, which in and through Him most perfectly manifests itself.

1. God, as we have seen, bears the name of Father in relation, not merely to the creature, but also to His Son, our Lord Jesus Christ. Without an eternal and perfect object of His love, the Infinite could not possibly be the perfectly Blessed One; and this object He *has* in the Son of His good-pleasure. On this account—while we read that God loved the world (ἠγάπησεν)—it is written that He loves the Son (ἀγαπᾶ)[1] as in an endless present. When speaking here of the Son of God in His relation to the Father, we must have regard to an accurate division of the subject. We have now to look at it, not from the Christological, but from the Ontological side; in other words, we have not *here* to demonstrate that Jesus of Nazareth was actually the Son of God, but only in general to bring out, as clearly as possible, the *idea* of "the Son of God in His essential relationship to the Father."

2. The idea that God should have a Son has, at first sight, something strange about it. Is He not the perfect and infinite Spirit? But this Spirit is, at the same time, the highest Love, of which the inner life is known to us only by its own revelation; and what this revelation makes known to us concerning a personal distinction of nature in the supreme Godhead is mysterious indeed, but not absurd. Even in the Heathen Mythology we meet with a representation of sons of the Gods, demigods, heroes, etc., in which the consciousness, at least, seems to express itself, that the Godhead possesses a higher object of love than finite sinful man. In the Old Testament we find the name of son of God given to Israel;[2] to the theocratic king as such;[3] in the figurative language of the poets, even to the heavenly beings.[4] In the New Testament, also, the name occurs in different senses. It is bestowed upon the first man,[5] and likewise given by Jesus to men who in love manifest the image of the heavenly Father.[6] In regard to Himself, also—as we shall later show—the appellation is not always used in the same sense, and with the same design. But yet there is no doubt but in a number of utterances, both of the Lord and of His first

---

[1] John iii. 35.
[2] Exod. iv. 22.
[3] Ps. ii. 7.
[4] Job i. 6; xxxviii. 7.
[5] Luke iii. 38.
[6] Matt. v. 9, 45.

witnesses, a *metaphysical* relationship is thereby described, of which the natural connection between each father and each son on earth is only a faint reflection. That this relationship is, in its deepest essence, incomprehensible for the finite understanding, lies in the nature of the case, and is moreover recalled to our minds by Jesus Himself.[7] This, however, need restrain no one from gathering, with reverent spirit, the beams of light which the Gospel sheds on this depth of the Divine life.

3. In the description of this life of God, we expressly made use of the words of the Netherlands Confession (Art. viii.), because these, in their sacred sobriety, are in perfect accordance with the words of Holy Scripture. The Father here bears the name of God, κατ'ἐξοχήν, of Whom, and by Whom, and to Whom are all things,[8] in the adoration of Whom the glorification of the Son must ever end.[9] "By me to the Father," is the meet inscription on an excellent picture of Christ. It is unnecessary, moreover, to treat separately of the Godhead of the Father, which meets with no contradiction. The question, then, is what may be established with sufficient clearness and accuracy concerning the Godhead of the Son in relation to that of the Father.

4. The *Son* of God must, in the Divine nature, necessarily be *another* than the Father. It is true, God is unchangeably one; but this unity must by no means be conceived of as a merely numerical one. It is the unity of love, which bears in itself a fulness of life, and distinguishes from itself its other I. Undoubtedly, the word Person—of which more hereafter—has its peculiar difficulty. In any case, it must be understood in the sense, not of *individual*, but of *subject*. It simply indicates that the Father is not the same as the Son, but another (*alius*, non *aliud*). The fundamental propositions of Sabellianism and Samosatianism should, on this account, be rejected as absolutely unscriptural, and—however apparently intellectual—as in the highest degree unreasonable. The Father and the Son are, as the Netherlands Confession has it, "in truth and reality, distinct as to their incommunicable attributes."

5. The Son of God has as such *the ground of His existence* in the Father, as the Father has not in the Son. This also lies in the idea of Sonship, and is expressed, in John v. 26, in terms which cannot be applied interchangeably to the Father. The Father is therefore rightly spoken of in ecclesiastical usage as unbegotten (ἀγέννητος), the Son, on the other hand, in accordance with Scripture,[10] as the only begotten (μονογενής). For the same reason, He is called also, not *a* son of God, but *the* Son of God, God's Beloved, God's own Son.[11] The ecclesiastical doctrine of the *Generation* of the Son has, on this account, a scriptural basis—though not, however, as already perceived by Calvin, in the poetic expression of the second Psalm,[12] from which the term itself was borrowed—and it remains to the credit of Origen that he made a daring endeavour to sound the depths of this idea. That every anthropomorphistic view must here be as far as possible removed, scarcely needs reiteration; and certainly it is to be regretted that a conception, in itself as scriptural as it is highly worthy of God, should have become

---

7 Matt. xi. 27.
8 Rom. xi. 36; Ephes. iv. 6; 1 Cor. viii. 6.
9 Phil. ii. 11.
10 John iii. 16.
11 Matt. iii. 17; Rom. viii. 32.
12 Ps. ii. 7.

repeatedly a source of contention in the ecclesiastical world. Perhaps the misunderstanding would be in great measure avoided, if—with a reverent acknowledgment of the fact—the *word* "Generation" were wholly avoided or, to the entire exclusion of the idea of time, were employed rather of an eternal *being* begotten, than of an (already) *having been* begotten of the Son on the part of the Father. In this form, at least, the expression presents no insuperable difficulty, and simply indicates that the Son continually has the ground of His existence in the being and essence of God.

6. The Son of God is necessarily partaker of *the same nature* as the Father. Hence also the same attributes are ascribed to Him as to the Father; power, [13] knowledge, [14] wisdom, [15] and other properties. In consequence thereof we see that He performs the same works as the Father, such as forgiving sins,[16] quickening and judging men; [17] and moreover lays claim to no less honour than is rendered to the Father.[18] It is true that, as Son, He is subordinate to the Father,[19] and accordingly speaks of the Father as greater (μείζων) than Himself; [20] but this relation, inseparable from His Sonship, detracts nothing from that which belongs to His Godhead. "This is a subordinationism which metaphysically does not depart from the main line of the Church confession, but completes the same, and ethically, especially, fills it up; and therefore is not—as the historical, actual subordinationism — an obstacle to the dim (*ahnend*) apprehension of the mystery, but rather is a help thereto" (Plitt). He never calls Himself God—how could He do this, who, coming forth as the servant of the Father, sought not His own honour?—but He suffers, nevertheless, that this homage should be rendered to Him by a Thomas; [21] while the footprints of Thomas are presently followed by Paul [22] and John.[23] And with reason, since the fulness of the Godhead dwells in Him bodily, *i.e.*, essentially,[24] and the name of Lord (κύριος) under the Old Covenant given to Jahveh, is ascribed to Him without any limitation. If the word of Scripture is here to decide, such facts fully entitle us to speak not only of the God-likeness, but also of the Godhead of the Son, of θεότης, not simply θειότης [Divinity, in the more general sense], "the most full Godhead; not simply Divine properties (*virtutes*), but the Divine nature itself" (Bengel).

7. This, however, not in such wise as though the Son of God were another God, a sort of under-God. Between the Son and the Father there exists unceasingly the most intimate *community* of life and love. This lies in the nature of the case, and is besides constantly asserted by the Son Himself. The Father shows Him all that He Himself doeth,[25] honours the Son,[26] and has delivered all things unto Him.[27] The Son, on the other hand, does what He sees the Father do;[28] and is in heaven while He holds

---

[13] John v. 21.
[14] John xxi. 17.
[15] Luke xi. 49.
[16] Matt. ix. 2, *sqq.*
[17] John v. 24—29.
[18] John v. 23; xiv. 1; Matt. xxviii. 19.
[19] John v. 19.
[20] John xiv. 28.
[21] John xx. 28.
[22] Rom. ix. 5; Tit. ii. 13.
[23] John i. 1.
[24] Coloss. ii. 9.
[25] John v. 20.
[26] John viii. 54.
[27] Matt. xi. 27.
[28] John v. 19.

converse with men upon earth.[29] Without any limitation, therefore, He is able to speak of all that is the Father's as at the same time His;[30] and cannot possibly find a more forcible representation of the prayed-for oneness of His disciples than that which is borrowed from His own relation to the Father. This original (metaphysical) relationship is for Him as it were the archetype, of which the derived (moral and spiritual) oneness of His people must be the resembling copy. Thus He Himself justifies us in speaking of a true oneness of nature (ὁμοουσία) between Him and the Father. It is true this is not actually indicated in the great saying of John x. 30,[32] but it follows irresistibly from the oneness of power there alluded to. And far indeed from its being contradicted in those passages in which the Son speaks of Himself as subordinate to the Father,[33] precisely these last augment our right to confess Him who thus speaks as God Himself, since in the mouth even of the most eminent of the creatures they would sound absurd and blasphemous.

8. This relation between Father and Son had not a beginning, but existed from all *eternity*. Clearly enough is this assured to us by the Lord Himself,[34] and by His first witnesses.[35] For there is as little ground here for accepting a purely ideal pre-existence, as for speaking of a period of time before the Creation, at which the Son—previously not existing—was called into existence by the Father. Arianism, which asserts this last, is properly regarded exegetically absolutely unsupported. A sound exposition of Coloss. i. 15, 16, shows, not that the Son is here placed on a level with the creature as opposed to the Father, but on a level with the invisible God as opposed to the creature. It is at the same time logically untenable, since it gives us, in place of a revealed mystery, an evident absurdity. "The deep thought of Origen touching the eternal generation of the Logos remained incomprehensible for the commonplace intellect of Arius" (Neander). In depriving the Son of the predicate of eternity, he took from Him the crown of His Godhead, and admitted into his conception a very unphilosophic division of the Divine attributes into two parts. In its consequences this view must be regarded as even definitely unchristian, since it leads to the adoration of the creature, undermines the Christian idea of revelation, and detracts not only from the Godhead, but also from the humanity of the Lord, by disputing His possession of a human *soul* (ψυχή) properly so called. Even in its later and present forms, it remains open to similar objections; and has just as little chance as it has claim to become the Christology of the future.

9. As a legitimate consequence of all that has been said, it may be deduced that the Father gives the most perfect *revelation of Himself* in and through the Son. If the Father dwells in a light unapproachable, in the

---

[29] John iii. 13.
[30] John xvii. 10.
[31] John xvii. 21, 22.
[32] See Calvin, *in loco.*
[33] John v. 19.
[34] John viii. 58; xvii. 5, 24.
[35] John i. 1; Rev. xxii. 13; Coloss. i. 17, and many other places.

Son the Unseen has become visible.[36] In the Father we adore in like manner the Hidden One, in the Son we contemplate the God who reveals Himself.[37] "As the human figure reflects itself in the mirror, and all that is in the seal is found also in the impression thereof, so in Him, as the outbeaming of His invisible being, the Unseen has become visible. God finds Himself again, and reflects Himself in the Logos, as in His other I" (Tholuck). Thus is the Son one with the Father, in the communion of the Holy Ghost.

Compare, above all, the standard work of J. A. DORNER, *History of the Development of the Doctrine of the Person of Christ.* (English transl.); J. CRAMER, *Dissert. de Arianismo* (1856); S. HOFMEYR, *Diss. de loco Col.*, i., 15—20 (1856); H. J. E. VAN HOORN, *De Roëllii litibus* (1856); VAN OOSTERZEE, *Christologie*, especially the *second* and *third* parts (1857, 1861).

POINTS FOR INQUIRY.

What is the sense of Prov. xxx. 4, and Psalm ii. 7?—Sense and significance of Matt. xi. 27.—Difference and connection between the teaching concerning the Son of God in the Synoptical Gospels and that of John.—Critical review of the places in the New Testament in which the name of *God* is given to the Son of God.—Ideal or hypostatical pre-existence?—History and criticism of Arianism.—Nearer explanation of the idea of Subordination.—Close connection of the doctrine of the Son with the Christian idea of revelation.

SECTION LIII.—THE HOLY GHOST.

The Holy Ghost, no more to be separated from the Father and the Son, than to be identified with the one or the other, is the eternal power and virtue (*mogendheid*) of God, whereby the fulness of the Divine life, revealed in the Son, is communicated to the creature in its own measure.

1 If it was already difficult accurately to define the dogmatic conception of the Son of God, the difficulty is increased when we have to speak of the Holy Spirit. If God, as a purely spiritual being, lies wholly beyond the sphere of our conception, how shall we yet further succeed in thinking of a Holy Spirit within the Godhead, distinct from the Father and the Son? We must begin by reviewing, as far as possible, the doctrine of Holy Scripture on the subject, in order—in the light thereof—afterwards to inquire what notion we have to form, as well of the Holy Ghost conceived of in Himself, as in relation to the Father and the Son. Happily, not the sounding the depths of the Holy Spirit's nature, but the receiving and pos-

[36] John i. 18. [37] Heb. i. 3.

sessing of the Holy Spirit Himself, is for us, even as Christian theologians, the main point. Yet the necessity for the latter cannot set aside the right and obligation to essay the former.

2. The doctrine of the New Testament as to the Holy Ghost cannot be accurately comprehended so long as we do not know how this idea has been already developed in the Old Testament. As early as Genesis i. 2, the Spirit of God appears, hovering as a quickening power over the waters; for it is impossible here, without any qualifying addition, to think of a mighty wind.[1] This Spirit is conceived of in Genesis vi. 3, as standing in a definite relation to man; as striving with him, as being vexed on his account. Especially does He fill and animate noble, excellent men;[2] and where the language of prophecy is heard, it is through His powerful influence.[3] He comes with power upon the Judges in Israel, and they accomplish mighty deeds.[4] He transforms Saul into another man,[5] and renders David a prophet of later days.[6] Notably in the Psalms is He several times mentioned as the Author both of natural and spiritual life;[7] while in the Proverbs He is revered precisely as the Spirit of Wisdom.[8] In the Prophetic Scriptures, also, we learn to know the Holy Ghost as immanently present in the Godhead;[9] but at the same time as promised and communicated by God to men.[10] Determinately the genuine prophets are anointed by Him,[11] but His plenteous and universal distribution is reserved for later days.[12] Thus we see, in the days of the New Testament, a Zacharias, a Simeon, a John the Baptist and others, filled with the Holy Ghost.[13] Jesus is born of the operation of this Spirit,[14] filled without measure therewith;[15] and Himself declares that by the power of the Spirit He casts out devils. In turn He promises and gives the Spirit to His first messengers;[16] and by no means exclusively to them.[17] Everywhere in the Christian Church of the first age do we see this Spirit living and working, with the most diverse gifts.[18] Especially the Acts and Apostolic Epistles are rich in manifold utterances concerning His work and nature, of which a complete enumeration would here be scarcely possible, and is just as little necessary. What we have already said shows that the biblical conception is only by degrees developed and filled up. If at first the Word and the

---

1 Compare Job xxvi. 13; Ps. xxxiii. 6.
2 Gen. xli. 38; Exod. xxxi. 3; Deut. xxxiv. 9.
3 Num. xi. 25—30.
4 Judges xiv. 6.
5 1 Sam. x. 10.
6 2 Sam. xxiii. 2.
7 Ps. li. 12; civ. 30; cxliii. 10.
8 Prov. i. 23.
9 Isa. lix. 19.
10 Isa. xliv. 3.
11 Isa. lxi. 1.
12 Joel ii. 28, 29.
13 Luke, chaps. i., ii.
14 Luke i. 35.
15 Matt. iii. 16; John iii. 34; Matt. xii. 28.
16 Matt. x. 19, 20; John xiv. 16, 17; John xx. 22; Acts ii. 4.
17 John vii. 38
18 1 Cor. xii. 4.

Spirit of God are almost identified, later we see these distinguished the one from the other.[19] At the same time it is apparent that the Holy Ghost is ordinarily presented either in relation to God (objectively), or in relation to man, definitely to Christians (more subjectively). This last, the dynamical side of the subject, will not yet come under our attention; with the former, the metaphysical, we have here more especially to do.

3. We begin, then, with the observation that there has at all times existed yet greater diversity and confusion of ideas with regard to the Holy Ghost, whether conceived of in Himself, or in relation to the Son and the Father, than there has with regard to the Son. Gregory Nazianzen, in his day, declared, "Of the intelligent among us some regard the Holy Ghost as a power, others as a creature, others again as God Himself; yet others—out of reverence, as they say, for Holy Scripture—know not which part to choose, since Scripture teaches nothing definite in regard thereto." This wavering may be easily explained. The Son had, at all events, become man; the Spirit was known only from His gifts and operations. The controversies of the first four centuries had respect principally to the Son; and thus a considerable period elapsed before anything was determined in regard to the Holy Ghost. Not at Nicæa, A.D. 325, but only at Constantinople, A.D. 381, was He, for the refutation of rising error, confessed as *τὸ κύριον, τὸ ζωοποιὸν, τὸ ἐκ τοῦ Πατρὸς ἐκπορευόμενον, τὸ σὺν Πατρὶ καὶ Υἱῷ συμπροσκυνούμενον καὶ συνδοξαζόμενον* (the Lord and Giver of life, who proceedeth from the Father, who with the Father and the Son is together worshipped and glorified); while finally, not at an Œcumenical Council, but first at that of Toledo, A.D. 589, the words *filioque* (and the Son) were added: which addition afterwards became the sad occasion of the schism between the Eastern and the Western Church.

4. If, however, we seek—after what has been said—to attain to greater clearness, it is speedily evident that the Holy Ghost is *another* than either the Son or the Father. The ancient Church found this distinction already indicated in Matt. iii. 16, 17; hence the well-known words: *I ad Jordanem, et videbis Trinitatem*—"Repair to the Jordan, and thou shalt see the Trinity." For him who feels a difficulty in basing a dogmatic idea upon an account like this, the word of Jesus Himself, in the fourteenth of John, may at least be conclusive. The other Comforter, whom the Son desires of the Father, and sends,[20] cannot be wholly identified either with the Father or the Son. The Apostles, too, make this distinction with the necessary clearness and sharpness of outline.[21] Very distinctly does Paul ascribe to the Holy Ghost the attributes of personality, self-consciousness, and freedom.[22] A thing is said to have seemed good to him;[23] and believers are expressly warned, not simply against quenching, but also against grieving, the Holy Spirit[24]—a thing which appears conceivable only in regard to a thinking and feeling subject.

---

[19] Isa. lxiii. 9, 10, and John iii. 34, as compared with Ps. xxxiii. 6.
[20] John xiv. 16, 17; comp. xv. 26.
[21] 1 Cor. xii. 4—6; 1 Pet. i. 2; Rev. i. 4—6.
[22] 1 Cor. ii. 10; xii. 11.
[23] Acts xv. 28.
[24] Ephes. iv. 30.

5. The Holy Ghost must thus be thought of not as a blind and unconscious force, but as the personal "power and virtue of God."[25] Only in a constrained manner can this natural conclusion from distinct data be evaded. It is true, sustained personifications of an impersonal attribute—such as occur, for instance, in the eighth chapter of Proverbs and the thirteenth of First Corinthians—are cited in favour of the opposite view. But discourses like these, partly of a poetic, partly of an oratorical nature, in praise of Wisdom or of Love, afford no parallel to didactic utterances and prophetic assurances, such as those we have just referred to. Again and again does the idea of personality here become apparent, even where at first sight one would not expect it, *e.g.*, in the opposition between the Holy Ghost and Satan.[26] How indeed could that power which, with creative energy, in the act of regeneration calls forth in the sinner the highest personal life, be itself anything less than a personal power? If it is said that they to whom the "other Comforter" was first promised, yet received, after their Master's departure, no person, but simply gifts; it is forgotten that it is here the very question whether these gifts themselves are not due to a personal—although as being a spirit, invisible—Giver. For frequently the gift and the Giver are definitely distinguished from each other;[27] to make no mention of the fact that the Son of God also is, at the same time, Giver and gift.[28] It is true there is found in the New Testament no actual trace of precept for the adoration of the Holy Spirit. No wonder, since it is He Himself who prays in believers;[29] so that they come *to* the Father, *by* the Son, *in the communion* of the Holy Ghost. On the other side, however, Divine homage is rendered to Him in the Baptismal command,[30] and in the Apostolic benediction;[31] while moreover that which is nowhere definitely enjoined, is at least just as little forbidden by the letter or the Spirit of the Gospel of the Scriptures.

6. To this personal power of God must be ascribed, therefore, after all that has been said, nothing less than a truly Divine *nature*. This follows of itself from the nature of the case, and is moreover repeatedly indicated by Holy Scripture. Divine properties are therein ascribed to the Holy Spirit, as kno wledge,[32] sovereignty,[33] eternity;[34] Divine works, such as the creation,[35] the new birth,[36] inspiration of Holy Scripture;[37] Divine honour, so great that its non-recognition is placed on a parallel with the non-recognition of God Himself,[38] and the sin against Him is represented as absolutely unpardonable sin.[39] The Arian opinion that the Holy Ghost is the earliest of all the creatures who were brought into existence by the created Son, does not find in the Gospel anywhere even the appearance of countenance.

7. In seeking precisely to determine the *relation* of the Holy Spirit to

---

[25] *Netherlands Confession*, Art. viii.
[26] Matt. xii. 28; 1 Cor. vii. 5; comp. chap. vi. 19.
[27] 1 Cor. xii. 4.
[28] Comp. John iv. 10; 2 Cor. ix. 15.
[29] Rom. viii. 27; Gal. iv. 6.
[30] Matt. xxviii. 19.
[31] 2 Cor. xiii. 14.
[32] 1 Cor. ii. 11.
[33] 1 Cor. xii. 11.
[34] Heb. ix. 14.
[35] Ps. xxxiii. 6.
[36] John iii. 3, 8.
[37] 2 Tim. iii. 16.
[38] Acts v. 4; 1 Cor. iii. 16.
[39] Matt. xii. 31, 32.

the whole Divine Nature, the Apostolic word (1 Cor. ii. 10, 11) sheds light for us, and leads us naturally to the supposition that the Holy Ghost (immanently) stands in relation to the Godhead, as the spirit of man to the whole man. If no one knows that which is man's, save only his own spirit, just as little does any one know that which is God's, save the Spirit of God which is in Him. He knows God's properties, counsels, works, etc., because He explores precisely these depths (ἐρευνᾷ). That exploring is an activity which has for its object the depths of God, and must be definitely ascribed to the Spirit, as the subject. In God, who necessarily unites the highest self-consciousness with perfect knowledge, naturally nothing more can be indicated by this assertion than an infinitely progressive process of thought and life: "the actuosity of knowledge"—*die Actuosität der Erkenntniss.* As in man, so in God, the Holy Spirit is, according to this statement, the personal principle whereby He, and He exclusively, knows and penetrates Himself, as no one else can do. Naturally our reasoning must here be confined to the *tertium comparationis*, the point of analogy, and by no means must the idea be entertained of a transition from not knowing to knowing; but an eternally perfect penetrating and comprehending of His own nature is here to be thought of. God is wholly spirit, and nothing but spirit; but that in Him whereby He knows Himself in the most perfect manner is, according to Paul, the Holy Spirit.

8. By means of this Spirit is (transcendently) the fulness of the Divine life—manifested in the Son—communicated to the creatures. God manifests Himself in the Son, but communicates His life by the Holy Spirit. If we do not misunderstand the hints given by the New Testament, we are to conceive the Holy Spirit as a quickening energy incessantly proceeding from God, even as the breathing of man, as an utterance of his life, continually proceeds from him. This proceeding of the Spirit[40] from the Father must necessarily be something different from the eternal generation of the Son, but the difference between the two does not fall within the limits of our conception. The well-known question in dispute between the Greek Church and the Latin is perhaps best resolved in this sense, that the Holy Ghost proceeds from the Father by the Son, and thus, for this reason also, is called the Spirit of the Son.[41] The Son is one with the Father, in the communion of the Holy Ghost. To the Son God gives the Spirit without measure;[42] by the Son the Spirit is unceasingly communicated to His people.[43] To this extent the Holy Spirit is, according to the Scripture, dependent on the Son, as He again is on the Father; yet just as little as this last detracts anything from the truly Divine nature of the Son, just so little does the other detract from the true Deity of the Holy Ghost. On the contrary, precisely in the Holy Ghost does the circle of life and being in the Godhead return, so to speak, to its own starting-point. *Est Spiritus a Patre per Filium*, says Tertullian. "The Spirit is from the Father by the Son." With the Father and the Son He is a sharer of the nature and majesty of God. The Son is the self-revealing God; the Holy

---

[40] John xv. 26.
[41] Gal. iv. 6.
[42] John iii. 34.
[43] John i. 33.

Ghost, the self-communicating God. "He is the proper self of God, so surely as the spirit of man is his proper self; and yet not the whole God, as the spirit of man is not the whole man. The revelation of the Father closes in the Holy Spirit, in that through Him the Father and the Son make their abode in the believer; and precisely on this account the blasphemy of the Holy Ghost is (Mark iii. 29) a sin for which there is throughout eternity no forgiveness" (Beck).

9. The Holy Ghost was not shed forth,[44] and thus not yet revealed in His fulness, before Jesus was glorified. Thus the historic manifestation of the Holy Ghost was preceded by that of the Son, as this was by the preparatory activity of the Father. Is it perhaps to be attributed to this fact, as well as to the nature of the case itself, that the dogma of the Holy Spirit cannot be presented with the same degree of clearness as that of the Son and the Father, and still, with the future development of the spiritual life of the Church, awaits its own full development? In this case the wavering of the utterances especially in the earliest Fathers on this point can the less surprise us. Assuredly we have not, with the ancient followers of Macedonius, to regard Him as a creature and servant of God, to the ignoring of His Divine nature and dignity. Rather must we conclude with Athanasius—therewith to proceed to the recapitulation of all the preceding argument: *τριὰς ἅγια τέλεια ἐστίν*. [The Holy Trinity is also a perfect Trinity.]

Comp. D. DOEDES, *Onderzoek naar het personeel bestaan van den H. Geest* (1844); C. F. FRITZSCHE, *Nova Opusc. Academ.* (1846), *contin.* 4 *dispp. de Sp. S.*; C. F. A. KAHNIS, *Die Lehre vom Heiligen Geist*, i. (1847); VAN OOSTERZEE, *Christologie*, iii., pp. 47—53; and the article *Geistesgaben* in Herzog, *R. E.*, iv.

POINTS FOR INQUIRY.

Diversity and harmony between the doctrine of the Old Testament and that of the New concerning the Holy Spirit.—Review and criticism of the development of the dogma of the Church.—What is there in favour of the recognition of the personality of the Holy Spirit? and what against?—Is the Holy Spirit also termed *God* in the New Testament? —What is to be deduced from 1 Cor. ii. 10, 11, as to the relation of the Holy Spirit to the whole Divine Being?—The difference on this point between the Eastern and the Western Church.—Significance and force of the hint, John vii. 39b.

SECTION LIV.—THE FATHER, THE SON, AND THE HOLY GHOST.

If the Father, the Son, and the Holy Ghost are personally distinct from each other, but at the same time joint partakers of

---

[44] John vii. 39.

the same nature and majesty of God; then the Christian confession, that God has revealed Himself as a Trinity, is not merely based on the Gospel, but also logically necessary, and, with all that is obscure in its contents, and imperfect in its expression, decidedly preferable to anything that has been substituted for it in earlier or later times. Only in this threefold Name is disclosed all the fulness of the Christian idea of God, so far as this is possible; but at the same time the incomprehensible character of the Divine Essence. The pure confession of this, the greatest of all the revealed mysteries, is the bulwark of Christian Theism; and for Christians themselves the inexhaustible source of enlightenment, consolation, and sanctification.

1. After we have thus far treated separately of the Father, the Son, and the Holy Ghost, it will be less difficult to determine with dogmatic accuracy the *contents* of the Christian confession of God's thrice holy Name. Thus much is already apparent, that the Sabellian Modalism in its earlier and later forms, far from being the pure expression of the revealed truth, does not even afford us a superficial, much less a thorough, acquaintance with the facts of the case. The Christian idea of God is Monotheistic, but not Unitarian. *Deus solus est, sed non solitarius*, "God is one, but not solitary" (Peter Chrysologus). Faith recognises one God; but confesses as such, with the Father, also the Son and the Holy Ghost. Between these three there is just as little confusion as there is separation; the plan of salvation proceeds from the Father; but is executed by the Son, in the power of the Holy Ghost. The Son says not, "I am the Father," but, "I am *in* the Father;" and equally is the Holy Spirit distinguished from the Father—from whom He proceeds, and from the Son—by whom He is sent. There is, consequently, not simply a duplicity or triplicity of impersonal powers, but a triplicity of personal self-consciousness in the Divine Being, a triplicity which ever blends in higher unity. As well to the Son of God as to the Holy Spirit must be ascribed, on this account, together with the properties and operations which they have in common with the Father, a certain characteristic peculiarity—let the expression be allowed—of nature and operation, which belongs to Them separately. In Scripture we usually see more definitely ascribed to the Father the work of Creation; to the Son, the work of Redemption; and to the Holy Ghost, the work of Sanctification; without, however, the other two hypostases of the Divine Being being altogether excluded from the task of the one. The Father is God, but not without the Son and the Holy Ghost; the Son is Himself God (not God Himself), in communion with the Father and the Holy Ghost. The Holy Ghost is partaker with the Father and the Son of the same Divine life and nature; without there existing, on that account, a plurality of Gods. It is consequently inaccurate, and a tritheistic heresy under the badge of orthodoxy, if one baptizes, *e.g.*, into the name of God the

Father, God the Son, and God the Holy Ghost. The errors of John Ascusnages and John Philoponus may safely be allowed to rest in their graves.

2. The only question is whether this Trinity is to be conceived of simply as a Trinity of *manifestation*, or really a Trinity of *essence;* in other words, whether we here become acquainted with the Divine nature on its œconomical [dispensational], or its ontological side—τρόπος ἀποκαλύψεως alone, or also τρόπος ὑπάρξεως. The former can, from the Scriptural standpoint, scarcely be denied; but the latter is doubted by many, for this reason as well as others, that it is supposed the obscurity of the problem for Christian thought is considerably lessened by this limitation. Such, however, is so far from being the case, that, on the contrary, precisely the sharp opposition in the question just mentioned increases the difficulty in our estimation. For, if it is said that God reveals *Himself*, it is said in other words that He makes known to us His *Nature;* and with Him, the true and faithful One, nature and revelation cannot possibly stand opposed to each other. The Revelation must at least be the tempered reflection of the innermost Being, or it would, contrary to its design, sadly mislead us. To assume a Trinity of Revelation without a Trinity of Nature, appears thus an inconsistency and choice of half-measures. One may make the Trinity of Revelation a starting-point for his thinking, but will feel himself unsatisfied so long as he does not, from that starting-point, ascend to the trias of Being. For it will be found in the long run that God cannot really have revealed Himself other than as He actually is.

3. To the question as to the *ground* of this confession, the positive answer must be preceded by a negative. We confess the name of the Father, Son, and Spirit upon grounds by no means purely *philosophical.* It has been sought to confirm the reasonableness and necessity of this belief by an appeal to many a remarkable Trinitarian distinction, to be found not merely in the system of Christian revelation, but also in other religious or philosophical systems. Reference has been made, *e.g.*, to the Trimurti of the Hindoos; to a sort of Trinity between the Gods of the Edda; to Egyptian, Platonic, Cabbalistic and other *Triades.* But although, in our estimation also, such-like correspondences are remarkable, and possibly far from being accidental; yet, on the other hand, we must not overlook the fact that they frequently exist more in appearance than in reality, and that analogy in this domain does not amount to a sign of identity. In the most favourable case the maxim applies also here: *Comparaison n'est pas raison;* and although it is asserted that the belief in the Holy Trinity may to a certain extent be justified *à posteriori* as rational, this is still no proof that reason by its own light could either penetrate or divine this mystery. Even though from the Christian philosophic standpoint it is thought that the reflection of this dazzling light may be seen resplendent in many a domain of God's works; we can at best conclude therefrom, that at least we do not here find ourselves in the domain of absurdity. "It is sufficient to maintain that that which faith teaches is not impossible," says Thomas Aquinas: *sufficit defendere, non esse impossibile quod prædicat fides.* The engagement made in a former century to prove the plurality in the Divine nature, *mathematicorum methodo*, would—even if its fulfilment

were attempted and boasted of—in the more deeply thinking mind rather awaken distrust than confidence.

4. Just as little does there exist a chance of coming to a satisfactory degree of clearness and certainty by an appeal to the *Christian consciousness* alone. It sounds very beautiful, and is also relatively true, when we hear it said, as by Martensen, "For we know by faith that eternal Life streams down to us out of three personal fountains of Life: from God the Father, who has created us; from God the Son, who has redeemed us; and from God the Holy Ghost, who sanctifies us, and makes us the children of God: in this Trinity alone do we possess the whole of Love." Following the same course, men like Liebner, Thomasius, and others, have attempted the development and defence of this dogma in their own manner. But who does not see that the Christian consciousness would never have thought of expressing itself in this way, unless it had first been guided and influenced by the *data* of Holy Scripture? While it is true that the believer can speak from experience of the grace of the Son, the love of the Father, and the communion of the Holy Ghost; still the nature as well as the mutual relation of this Divine Three remains a purely ontological question, which lies wholly beyond the empirical domain, and on which the Christian consciousness, as such, can give no answer.

5. One cannot even declare, without nearer definition of the terms, that the doctrine of the Father, the Son, and the Holy Ghost can be maintained from *Holy Scripture.* Here, at least, we must carefully distinguish between the Scriptures of the Old Testament and those of the New; and the former, especially, must not be made use of without great circumspection. Who does not know how frequently—especially at an earlier period—this rule was overlooked; so that theosophy found a trace of this mystery even in the Hebrew word signifying *to create* (בָּרָא)? Now, better instructed by exegetical and historical study, no scientific theologian would any longer hesitate to return a negative answer to the question propounded—not without trembling—by Calixtus, two centuries ago: "Whether the doctrine of the Trinity can be proved from the Old Testament Scriptures alone?" (*num ex solo V. T. Trinitatis dogma probari queat*). There is not one of the so-called proof passages of the Old Testament which can stand the searching test. It was surely to be expected, from the nature of the case, that the deepest mystery of the Divine nature could not possibly be revealed and confessed before the fulness of the time. The Israelitish Monotheism would probably have suffered more loss than it would have derived benefit from an untimely disclosure of this truth. It is something very different, however, if it is asked whether now, *à posteriori*, with the light of the New Testament Scriptures shed upon us, we meet with no *traces*, or, if you will, no distinct indications, of this truth in the Scriptures of the Old Testament. To this question we, for our part, cannot refuse to return a positive answer. In so speaking, we have before us places in which the Deity is introduced as conversing with Himself; we think of the plural form of the name *Elohim;* of the Aaronitic blessing;[1] of the Trisagion heard by the prophet;[2] of the sanctity of the symbolical number

[1] Num. vi. 24—26. [2] Isa. vi. 3.

three; and other phenomena, which prove nothing in themselves, but, in a striking manner, shed light upon the truth already established on independent grounds. Least of all must the Angel of the Covenant—in a word of prophecy, such, for instance, as that of Isaiah lxiii. 9, 10—pass unobserved. We shall not say too much in asserting, with Christlieb, that "the impulse urging to the formation of this doctrine was already active throughout the whole of the Old Testament." Would not the doctrine of the Salomonic *Chokma* (Wisdom) also merit, in this connection, more attention than is sometimes bestowed upon it?

6. Where, however, it is a question of dogmatic proof, we see ourselves, on all sides, directed back to the *Gospel of the New Testament.*[3] Here again a necessary classification of texts must precede the adducing of proofs. Places like Acts xx. 28; 1 Tim. iii. 16; 1 John v. 7, may, for well-known critical reasons, be here quietly left out of the argument. Moreover, we must never overlook the fact that the Scriptures of the New Testament nowhere present us with a compact system of doctrines, but simply supply the stones with which the building can and must be put together. "The revelation consists, not in the communication of an astronomy to men, but in the unveiling of the starry heavens before their gaze, and for this gaze: they are to learn and reckon out therefrom an astronomy for themselves" (Rothe). It is, consequently, not the question whether the Church doctrine is proclaimed literally, and in this form, in the Scriptures of the New Testament; but whether it can legitimately be deduced—yea, necessarily must be deduced—from all the Scriptural *data.* And to *this* question an affirmative answer is warranted on an appeal to the utterances of the Lord and His Apostles, which have been already adduced (§§ lii., liii.) in connection with the doctrine of the Son and the Holy Spirit; especially to those which, in our opinion, admit of no other conception than that of the ontological unity of the whole Divine Nature. Notably we refer to the baptismal command,[4] of which the genuineness is here, on good grounds, presupposed; to the promise of John xiv. 16, 17; and to the apostolic teaching in general. When we consider that these strict Monotheists do not hesitate a moment to worship the Son of God, as Lord and God; that they constantly distinguish the utterances of the Holy Spirit from their own word and will;[5] that no other distinction in their conception of God occurs so frequently as precisely the Trinitarian one;[6] and that they constantly ascribe to the Son what is elsewhere attributed to the Father, or to the Spirit what is immediately before or after attributed to the Son or the Father, then we cannot possibly deny that only in this threefold name did they see indicated the whole living fulness of the Divine Essence. That also which has not yet been produced as a formula is already postulated by their teaching; and with all that the Church Confession has upon this point that is imperfect, it is not difficult to show that what has been substituted for it on essential points, in earlier and later times, is in more or less direct opposition to the letter and spirit of the sacred documents.

---

[3] Compare *Netherlands Confession,* Art. ix.

[4] Matt. xxviii. 19.

[5] Acts xv. 28; 1 Cor. vii.; Rom. viii. 16.

[6] 1 Cor. xii. 4—6; 2 Cor. xiii. 13; Ephes. iv. 4—6; 1 Pet. i. 2; Rev. i. 4—6.

7. The *objections* raised on many sides against this confession are considerable, but not of such a kind as to be able to destroy the firm basis of our faith. *Reason* unceasingly asserts that three can never be one, or the converse; but it forgets to substantiate its right to speak with supreme authority and *à priori* in this domain. That God is alike one Person, and, in the same sense, three Persons, is what Christianity has nowhere professed: the word *person* itself it uses only reluctantly. "*Tres personæ*," says Augustine somewhere, "*si ita dicendæ sunt, non enim rei ineffabilis eminentia hoc vocabulo explicari valet:*" "Three persons, *if they are to be so called*, for the unspeakable exaltedness of the object cannot be set forth by this term." He, however, who asserts that the unity necessarily sets aside the plurality sees himself refuted by every ray of light, to the nature of which it belongs to be refracted in seven-fold colours; nay, by the human personality itself, of which the unity is certainly not destroyed by the division into body, soul, and spirit.—If we are referred to utterances in *Holy Scripture* which seem to favour another view, it must not be overlooked that in this domain each separate part can receive light only from the whole—not the converse. That the whole of the writings of the New Testament advocates much more the Trinitarian than the Unitarian view, has been not seldom honourably acknowledged by opponents of the former view. He, further, who finds Subordinationism, in the evangelical sense, taught here, will seek in vain for an exegetical argument in favour of the Arian conception so frequently confused therewith.—To *experience*, also, an appeal is made in proof of the charge that our doctrine is frequently defended in an ill-judged manner, and repels thoughtful men from Christianity. For the latter of these we shall not be troubled above measure, if only that which is gainsaid is truth; and the former makes manifest only human ignorance, which is not found precisely among the *Professors* of the Gospel alone. When, for instance, the ingenious Jean Paul allows himself the antithesis, "that he who rather disputes about the divinity of the Lord, than does His will, is like a peasant who daily makes investigations as to his lord's patent of nobility, instead of showing him obedience and love," he affords us a striking instance of the caprice with which unbelief often treats us to alternatives which exist only in the imagination of its adepts.—And when, finally, *history* is adduced in proof that the doctrine of the Church—so far as its essential contents are concerned—is much more recent than the Apostolic Writings, the question is called forth and justified, whether this history has ever really been looked at with an unprejudiced eye.

8. The *history* of the doctrine—the contents and grounds of which we have examined—cannot here be sketched in all its details. Only those questions regarding the history of Christian doctrine are here in place, which are of paramount importance for Dogmatics itself. As far as the *earliest* history is concerned, nothing is more common than the decided assurance that at least the ecclesiastical fathers of the first three centuries were the spiritual kinsmen and forerunners of the later Antitrinitarians. Even though this were so, we must not forget that our faith, for its final authority, rests, not upon the testimony of the Church Fathers, but upon the Lord's own word, and that of His Apostles. But it is far from true

that the Confession of Nicæa at an earlier period met with more resistance than acceptance, and that the Church at first held the opinion of Apollinaris, which she herself later condemned.[7] It is true, the second century, as a whole, stands, in point of gnosis, not above, or on a level with, but below, the Apostolic age. Only by degrees, and after a long period, in its continual conflict with Judaism and Heathenism, did Christian thinking learn to make its own the fulness and depth of the Evangelical idea of God. Definitely, in regard to the Holy Spirit, the desired unity and clearness was long wanting. The period of the Martyrs and Apologists could not possibly be that of refined doctrinal distinctions. Yet closer research ever confirms the truth of Melancthon's words, in a letter to Calixtus: "*De multis magnis rebus vix suspicari possumus quid senserint Veteres. Causam vero de divinitate Filii video firmissimam esse, et sane gaudeo, me in promptu habere tam multa de re tanta testimonia.*" "Concerning many great questions, we can scarcely conjecture what the Ancients held. But the cause of the divinity of the Son of God I see to be most solidly supported, and, indeed, I rejoice to have at hand so many testimonies on so great a question." The Greek name τριάς, we meet with first in Theophilus,[8] while the Latin *Trinitas* is only coming into use in Tertullian.[9] But the confession itself, thereby indicated, belonged, beyond doubt, at a much earlier period, to the *regula fidei;*[10] among the Apostolic Fathers we find the threefold name constantly mentioned in union; and Justin Martyr does not hesitate a single moment to glory as in the Father, so also in the Son (ἐν δευτέρᾳ), and the Holy Spirit (ἐν τρίτῃ τάξει).[11]

9. The development of doctrine in the Church during and after the *fourth* century must be regarded as a well-meant, but, at the same time, only human—*i.e.*, imperfect—attempt to enclose the Divine as within a cadre of as finely spun formulas as possible, and thus to preserve it against being distorted by unhallowed hands. One must, in opposition to dangerous error, coin imperfect words, *non ut aliquid diceretur, sed ne taceretur*, says Augustine—"not in order to say something, but in order not to keep silence." Thus the terms *person*, *nature* (οὐσία), *Trinity*, *unity of nature* (ὁμοουσία), *begotten*, *proceeding*, etc., came into vogue, terms which but too often gave the adversaries an opportunity of concealing their antipathy to the doctrine under a comparatively reasonable polemic against the form. If a fair judgment is to be formed with regard to these terms, they must be regarded as technical terms; such as are permitted in every other domain, but in relation to the infinite and unfathomable are least satisfactory. "From their origin and design they do not claim to be regarded as religious-philosophical and perfect explanations as to the nature of the Trinity, but as ecclesiastical and social protests against definite and matured degenerate forms, mutilations, and caricatures of the doctrine of the Trinity, protests having their origin in historical circumstances" (Lange). The most orthodox fathers—Athanasius, for example—distinctly declared that they cared nothing for the words in themselves, provided only the fact was ac-

---

[7] Cf. *Comp. Dogm.*, Gron. 1848, p. 35.
[8] *Ad Autol.* ii. 15.
[9] *De Pud.* c. 21.
[10] Matt. xxviii. 19.
[11] *Apol.* i. 13.

knowledged. Certainly the expression *Drievuldigheid* (=threefold nature, Latin *Trinitas*) is preferable to the more usual *Drieëenheid* (=triune nature); *person* is to be taken not in the sense of *individual*, but of self-conscious existence. We may also readily admit that the *Homo-ousia* (oneness of nature), although a legitimate postulate from the data of Scripture teaching, is yet no actual enunciate of Jesus and the Apostles; and, above all, that the so-called Athanasian Creed does not everywhere keep within the limits of the desired sobriety and solemnity of language. There is here only too much playing in a dialectical manner upon the numbers one and three; and the whole symbol of faith reminds us involuntarily of an arithmetical sum, in which everlasting salvation is at last made the product of an accurate computation. Salvation's being thus, in a one-sided intellectual manner, made dependent upon an orthodox notion, must, regarded from a sound Christian standpoint, ever remain objectionable. Still we must here be on our guard against acting unreasonably, and casting away a precious pearl on account of its less valuable shell. "Such-like formulas have their edifying side," as is well said by Hagenbach, "in so far as they make manifest the struggling of the Christian spirit to find a satisfactory expression, for that which is full truth in the depth of the Christian consciousness."

10. A like judgment must be formed upon the *later* doctrinal definitions, as well of the Scholasticism of the Middle Ages, as of the rigid ecclesiastical orthodoxy of the seventeenth century. As far as the latter is concerned, it were to be desired that the theologians of that age had better profited by the example of wisdom and simplicity given them (in this respect also) by the Reformers. So circumspectly did Calvin at first express himself, that he was even accused of Arianism; and Melancthon hesitated not to declare, *Proinde non est, cur multum operæ ponamus in locis illis supremis de Deo, de unitate, de trinitate Dei.* "There is, then, no reason why we should greatly devote ourselves to those most lofty subjects, the doctrine of God, of the unity of God, of the Trinity of God." This practical bent of mind preserved for a time[12] from such speculation as was needless, and might easily become dangerous; but then the polemic against the Anti-Trinitarians called forth more subtle definitions. Very soon arose hair-splitting distinctions between the unity of the nature and the triality of the persons; between the attributes of these last, and their activity partly in common, partly separate; and the whole dogma thus laid down was argued as a logical proposition out of the whole sacred Codex, without any distinction worth mentioning between the Old Testament and the New. Thus the mathematical point of view was confused most sadly with the spiritual; and scarcely can one refrain, in listening to so many sophisms, from thinking of the questions of God out of the whirlwind, to which Job must listen, but which he was not able to answer. "Ecclesiastical Dogmatics," says Nitzsch, "has succeeded in preserving the treasure of the Truth, without having rendered its formulas intelligible for the reason and intellect."

11. By this weak side of the Church's development of doctrine is

---

[12] Witness, amongst others, the *Netherlands Confession*, Art. viii.; and the *Heidelberg Catechism*, Answ. xxv.

explained—although not entirely justified—the unceasing *opposition* which this dogma has met with in the course of the ages, not only on the side of Jews and Mahomedans, but also of Christians. The history of Anti-Trinitarianism is almost as old, and marked with as delicate shades of definitions, as that of the Trinitarian belief. The *course* of this opposition from the Apostolic age till the present time belongs to the history of doctrines. Its *value* is naturally entirely determined by the purity of its principle, the choice of its weapons, the greater or less earnestness of its endeavour. What a difference between a Paul of Samosata and a Schleiermacher,—between a Michael Servetus and a Channing! Moreover, the difference between the highly speculative and the popular and practical opposition must not here be overlooked. But the strife against this part of the truth has ever this *significance*, that it makes manifest on the one hand the strength of the rationalistic principle; and, on the other, the powerlessness of the effort so to fathom the depths of the Divine nature that it should cease to be a stumbling-block for Christian thought. One is almost tempted to repeat the words of the celebrated theologian (Alstedt), "The mystery of the Trinity cannot be comprehended by any creature, either by the light of nature, or by the light of grace, or by the light of glory"—*neque lumine naturæ, neque lumine gratiæ, neque lumine gloriæ potest comprehendi ab ulla creatura.*

12. Yet there have seldom been wanting attempts at the *maintenance* of this truth in the way of speculative construction and deduction of the dogma; and it is not easy to form a perfectly just judgment on these attempts. Augustine in his day sought, in starting from the idea of love, to render the subject more clear by distinguishing in God: the Father, as He who loves; the Son, as He who is loved; and the Holy Ghost, as the bond of love between the two—*Amans, amatus, et mutuus amor*. The Schoolmen referred in explanation to the analogy of the human psychical life—*intellect, feeling, will*—and to the logical difference between the first, second, and third person in every conversation, as an image of the difference and the relation between the Father, the Son, and the Holy Ghost. Melancthon also ventured in later times—following in the footsteps of Augustine—to tread the speculative path, and to give a presentation of this truth, which was forthwith saluted by the Orthodox as a "*somnium Philippi.*" That the earlier and later Mystics, too, would not remain behind on this point, will be believed by every one who comprehends anything of the peculiar tendency of Mysticism.[13] But, above all, the last century saw the number of these attempts increase, because it was thought that in opposition to the vulgar Rationalism—the despised dogma could thus be scientifically rehabilitated. Schelling, for instance, pronounced this conception of God folly, unless it was speculatively explained. Daub regards the Father as *Deus a quo;* the Son as *Deus in quo;* the Holy Ghost as *cui satis est Deus*. According to Hegel, this doctrine is the expression of the idea of the self-realisation of God, as the one who distinguishes Himself from Himself, and nevertheless is conscious of being unchangeably one with Himself; he even assigned to the dogma, as thus construed, a first place in his system

[13] Compare TWESTEN, *l.c.* ii., pp. 210—214.

of doctrine. Others, again, have called to their help the mutual relation of thesis, antithesis, and synthesis. Somewhat strange, in opposition to all this restless endeavour, sounds the bold assertion of Scholten, that "not the slightest speculative importance is to be attached to the doctrine of the Trinity." As though the highest truth did not necessarily furnish the most abundant material for the deepest speculation! Nevertheless, however laudable the endeavour may be to master the contents of our belief in the way of reflection, we must here especially be on our guard against accepting a creation of our own for the revealed truth. Already many a heresy under a speculative form has been applauded as the triumph of orthodoxy—until it has been put to a test, the result of which has called forth a cry of disdain, like that of Strauss against Weisse: "Where is the Symbolum *Quicunque?* (Athanasian Creed.) Give it me here; I will swear to it ten times over, rather than I will once call the propositions of our philosopher anything but nonsense." That more especially the recognition of the Divine love can shed light upon the mystery of the Son, we would not willingly deny; but the personal existence of the Holy Ghost has as yet been by no means explained in this way. It would be dangerous thus to find an immoveable *foundation* for our faith in speculation and reasoning, which—even in the most favourable case—would better serve as a meet *support.* For us, at least, the firm foundation is given in the Lord's own words, and in those of His witnesses, which we seek as far as possible to comprehend, but, if need be, even uncomprehended accept. That which remains a cross for our thinking is thus at the same time the crown of the Christian conception of God.

13. The *importance,* both in a theoretical and practical sense, of the confession thus explained, can hardly be estimated too highly. Not only does the doctrine of the Father, Son, and Holy Ghost afford us—more than any other—a deep glance into the full glory of the Divine Being, but also it merits, in the fullest sense of the word, to be called a bulwark for Christian Theism. It has been said with truth that many a one in his anxious avoiding of the so-called "three-God faith," has only too soon given up belief in the living God at all. An abstract Monotheism which shrinks back from this depth, easily falls away into an arid Deism, if not even into a dreary Pantheism. Only where the Trinitarian fulness of life and being in God is recognised as an adorable fact, is also the recognition of the Divine transcendency, together with God's immanency, actually assured. It is true the finite understanding is unable to fathom this depth; but from this very fact the dogma of which we are speaking assumes a higher degree of importance. It is at once the expression and the justification of belief in God's absolute incomprehensibleness, "a memorial," as Nitzsch expresses it, "of the impossibility of comprehending God, an impossibility not merely stated, but even understood and comprehended."

14. That which appears to be a gold mine for speculation, is at the same time a school for practical life. The confession of the threefold name points to a God who is not only exalted infinitely *above* us, but in Christ is *with* us, and in the Holy Spirit will dwell *in* us. It stands consequently in direct connection with our enlightenment, consolation, and sanctification. Only where the Son of God is in truth inseparably one

with the Father, is He for us God's highest, unspeakable *gift*, in whom is given us at once the last revelation and the most perfect redemption. Only where God Himself comes to dwell by the Holy Spirit in the heart of the sinner, is the new life awakened, the Church of the Lord built up, the regeneration of humanity completed. That which makes Christianity a religion for the world, and the Gospel glad tidings in all the force of the word, is in almost every point closely connected with this our confession. In its popular practical treatment for the Church of the Lord, all must be avoided which would rather confuse the head than warm the heart and sanctify the life. Not the intellectual assent to an obscure article of doctrine, but the living belief in God, who has revealed Himself as Father, Son, and Holy Ghost, is absolutely indispensable to salvation. But for the science of faith there lies here a treasure, which it may just as little surrender as overlook. "The intellect will never penetrate this mystery in its *quomodo* (mode of existence), but the *quid* and *quare*, the essential contents and the inner necessity, our thinking can well comprehend" (Plitt). It becomes apparent, also, with regard to this truth, that the knowledge even of the profoundest seers is but in part; depths like these are the more calculated to call forth the hope for that higher light which will rise in a better world. A Dante enjoyed for his feeling the highest blessedness, where he heard sung in Paradise the praise of the threefold name; and a Melancthon dwelt upon the prospect, "there we shall see the Holy Trinity"—"*ibi sanctam Trinitatem videbimus*." He who with the latter expects that that which is here in part shall one day be done away, goes his way, in this investigation also, consoled by a higher light, ever "in the name of the Father, and of the Son, and of the Holy Ghost."

Compare F. C. BAUR, *Die Lehre von der Dreieinigkeit und Menschwerdung Gottes, u. s. w.* (1841—1843); MEIER, *Die Lehre von der Trin. in hist. Entw.* (1844); J. H. SCHOLTEN, *De Chr. leer des V., Z. en H. G.*, in the *Jaarbb. voor W. Th.* (1845); J. J. VAN TOORENENBERGEN, *l. c.*, pp. 48—80; the article of NEUDECKER, *Trinität*, in Herzog, *R. E.* xvi., and the literature there referred to; our *Christologie*, iii., p. 53. Further, the principal handbooks of the History of Doctrine. On the present state of the question, C. BECK, *Chr. Dogm. Gesch.* (1864), p. 264, *sqq.* On its scientific treatment and practical significance, CHRISTLIEB, *l. c.*, p. 297, *sqq.* For a model of homiletical treatment, A. MONOD, *La Doctrine Chrét.* (1869), pp. 57—107.

POINTS FOR INQUIRY.

The Church's doctrine of the Trinity as opposed to Sabellianism.—Sense and significance of the distinction between Trinity of essence and Trinity of revelation.—Review and criticism of the proofs from the Old Testament, especially as formerly cited for this doctrine.—Is the doctrine to be proved κατὰ διάνοιαν, or also κατὰ ῥητόν, from the Scriptures of the New Testament?—The polemic against the Church doctrine of the Trinity in its different phases.—The Antitrinitarians of the first three centuries compared with those of the age of the Reformation.—The position of Rationalism and of Mysticism, in relation to the doctrine of the Father, Son, and Holy Ghost.—The doctrine of the Trinity in the newer speculative systems.—Necessity, possibility, and importance of continued investigation.—Christian art in presence of this revealed mystery.—What may be safely surrendered in the treatment of this mystery publicly to edification, and what must be preserved at any price?

SECTION LV.—GOD'S PLAN OF THE WORLD.

The developed idea of God leads necessarily to the idea of a Divine plan with regard to the world; which—eternal and independent as God Himself—develops itself in the course of time, but to which the fitting key is found only in the records of the Christian Revelation of Salvation. That plan of the world has in view nothing less than the founding of a kingdom of God, immeasurable in extent, under one Head, the God-man; through whom all the members stand in the closest relation to each other and to Him. The gradual realisation of this thought, fraught with blessing, to the glorifying of His Name, is the final aim of all God's *works*.

1. The *connection* between the discussion of the idea of God and that of the Divine plan of the world is not difficult to discover. Thus far we were learning to know God as the self-conscious and freely-working Spirit, who possesses in Himself an infinite fulness of life, which, as He is the highest Love, He cannot cease to reveal and to communicate to others. That He actually has done and is doing this, will become very soon apparent to us upon a glance at God's works. But these works are simply the expression and realisation of an eternal thought of God; and in order properly to comprehend them, the knowledge of the Divine plan of the world is thus necessary beforehand. Of this plan *in general*—to be carefully distinguished as yet from the decree of redemption and from the doctrine of election—we have now to treat, in order thus to preface the way for the doctrine of Creation and Restoration.

2. The *idea* of a Divine plan in regard to the world calls for further elucidation, that it may not lead to a wrong conception. Rightly are we here warned against every anthropomorphistic view. Man also forms for himself a plan, but time separates between his projecting and the execution of his design, and not seldom is the latter delayed or prevented by wholly unexpected circumstances. All such thoughts must, as is self-evident, be as far as possible got rid of in connection with the Infinitely Perfect One, and nothing must be admitted into the idea of the world-plan, which would lead us to ascribe to the Eternal anything absurd. No lapse of time between plan and execution; no wavering in the determination either of end or means; no more or less arbitrary choice out of various abstract possibilities. Speaking in our imperfect language of a Divine plan of the world, we mean that which God definitely *wills*, and thus, consequently, presents to Himself as the *final aim* of all His works, in contradistinction from that which He either does not will, or does not thus

will. No Divine world of ideas, in the Platonic sense, herein stands before our mind ; but a holy, Divine decree; for which that which at God's behest became gradually realised, already existed beforehand in thought.

3. God thus wills something, and He knows what He wills, and wherefore He wills it. The *existence* of a plan of the world in this sense cannot be disputed, where the personality of God is acknowledged. Here, it is not something purely human which is arbitrarily transferred to God ; but, on the contrary, something Divine, of which the trace also is to be discovered in man created after His image. If God is eternal and omniscient, He must also have foreseen what happens in time,—have foreseen, yea, even have determined and ordained, or the whole world would not be unconditionally dependent upon Him. If He is wise and holy, He must have had also a perfect aim before His Spirit, and must will the attaining of this end by means worthy of Himself. If He is supreme and sovereign, He must be absolute Disposer of all that exists ; and if nothing of an arbitrary kind is to be ascribed to this Sovereign, He must have a plan in regard to the world. The existence of such a world-plan is a postulate of the thinking mind, but, at the same time, of the religious feeling, which cannot possibly rest satisfied with the conception of an inactive God. Certainly the question what God was doing before the creation of the world, has often been put in an unbecoming manner, and in that case has deservingly been discountenanced. But this question cannot always be answered by authoritative utterances, and the Dogmatics of the Church has acknowledged its relative right in treating the doctrine of God's decrees before that of His Works. It felt the necessity to make for itself a representation of God as from all eternity thinking, willing, determining, preparing, that which should take place in the course of time. As well earlier as later philosophers—in so far as they have approached to the recognition of the personality of God—have admitted this element in their notion of God, and the earlier ecclesiastical conception of a "Counsel of Peace" also originated in this necessity. Nothing is easier than contemptuously to mock at all Teleology; but if this be wholly denied, there results a Naturalistic view, which only too easily slides into practical Atheism. If we are not to assume that the universe has no higher ground and aim than that which is to be found in itself, then the purely æsthetical view of the world must alternate with an ethical-teleological one,—*i.e.*, we must seek to comprehend creation as the work of a Being who from all eternity had conceived it in His mind. Naturally this will and counsel of God is not to be separated from His essential being, which, on the contrary, is therein shadowed forth and expressed. But although (in point of fact) one therewith, this counsel and will must be able to a certain extent to disclose itself to the eye of thoughtful believers. It is, as it were, the *inner* work of God which precedes His activity *without*.

4. If thus reason already compels us to assume the existence of a Divine plan of the world, the *contents* of that plan can be known to us only in the light of its own revelation. Here also the history of religion and philosophy confirms to us the uncertainty of all human conjecture ; at every turn the thread which we thought we had secured escapes us again. Great is our debt of thankfulness to God that He has given a more satis-

factory answer to these ever-recurring questionings, in the word of prophet and apostle—above all, in that of Christ. Even the Scriptures of the Old Testament unequivocally testify that all things take place according to the counsel and the foreknowledge of God.[1] The Lord Himself also refers to an exalted Divine good-pleasure ;[2] and in harmony therewith, to the spiritual oneness of His people, in Him, with each other, and with God, as the final aim to be realised with regard to them in the future.[3] Especially is it the highly enlightened and deeply philosophic Paul who makes known to us the mystery of God's good-pleasure, as aiming at nothing less than the founding of an all-embracing kingdom of God under His Son, as the at once Divine and human Head.[4] In consequence of a higher revelation,[5] he here gives expression to a thought already in principle implied in the Gospel of the Kingdom, which was proclaimed by Jesus Himself. Thus he places before us an ideal, which derives its surest guarantee from its own contents, because nothing can be conceived of in comparison which may be regarded as more godlike, glorious, and blessed.

5. The exaltedness of this plan already appears when we consider it in itself, but still more when we compare it with other presentations which have been in earlier or later times commended instead of it. It is wholly *unlimited*, and comprehends all that exists. Consciously or unconsciously, all must subserve and work together to one adorable end. It is moreover purely *moral*, such as is only to be expected of a holy God: the founding of one spiritual kingdom of truth and love, of holiness and blessedness. The solution of the highest life-questions for the individual man and for humanity lies thus, not in the physical, not even in the purely intellectual, but in the religious and ethical domain. This Divine plan of the world is moreover *independent* and *eternal*.[6] It was not first formed with a view to counteract the effects of sin; but was originated independently thereof. Neither reason nor Holy Scripture affords ground for the opinion that the free will of sinful man has set aside God's original design. On the contrary, God's plan with regard to the world dates from before the times of the ages; and even the abuse of freedom made by man was taken up by God as a link in the chain of its development. It has its ground, not in the creature, but in God's own sovereign, immutable good-pleasure; and has as its centre Him in whom, as its spiritual Head, the whole of humanity is represented before God, the Chosen One, in whom the good-pleasure of the Father is fulfilled to an ever greater extent.

No philosophic notion of God's plan in regard to the world, whether of earlier or later times, can bear comparison, in point of inner sublimity, with that of the Gospel. The *absolutistic* theory of Leibnitz and others, who see the final aim of all things exclusively in the glorifying of God—especially of His sovereignty—runs the risk of bringing this sovereignty of God into opposition with His wisdom and love, and while insisting merely on that which is in itself true, "creavit *sibi*" (He created for Himself), to overlook the equally true assertion, "creavit *nobis*" (He created for us); while, in its conse-

[1] Ps. xxxiii. 11; Isa. xlvi. 10.
[2] Matt. xi. 25, 26.
[3] John xvii. 20, 21.
[4] Ephes. i. 10; compare Coloss. i. 19, 20.
[5] Compare Ephes. iii. 4—6.
[6] Ephes. i. 4, 5; Rom. xi. 34, 35.

quences, it leads to Fatalism and Quietism.—The *eudæmonistic* view, as advocated by Steinbart and those of his school, avoids this rock, it is true, in making the happiness of the creature, particularly that of man, the final aim in the creation. But, on the other hand, this view awakens and cherishes a spirit of pride, which is ever again contradicted and humbled by every glance at the universe; and it is moreover absolutely unable to give even a tolerable explanation in regard to a countless number of facts.—The *moralistic* theory, finally, as represented by Kant and his school, which regards the final aim in creation to be the promotion of a higher order of things—an order which cannot but be a moral one—no doubt takes a higher rank than the two preceding ones, yea, is even in a certain respect "not far from the kingdom of God." But that which it proclaims of truth is expressed much more clearly and powerfully in the Gospel of the kingdom; and that order of the world which the philosopher sets before himself as the highest ideal is, according to the testimony alike of the Gospel, and of experience, brought about only by God in Christ. Far above every airy abstraction stands thus the revealed mystery of the kingdom of God. The higher truth of Absolutism, Eudæmonism and Moralism has already been comprehended ages ago, in the great word of Paul, Ephes. i. 10. It is quite true "God has created all things . . . . to serve their Creator;"[7] but this final aim cannot be separated even in thought from the well-being of His creatures, notably of man, because God wills to be glorified precisely therein and thereby. And that happiness again is most effectually advanced where the moral order of things, nay, where the kingdom of truth and love, of light and life, is founded. "As love," says Martensen, "is the impelling cause of the creation, so is the kingdom of love its final aim—*causa finalis creationis.* In the kingdom of love, however, God and the creation are mutually related as means and end."

6. A *modification* of this Divine plan of the world is evidently, after what has been said, just as inconceivable as a change of God's own nature. It is not even Scriptural, and just as little is it rational, to speak of Divine *decrees* in the plural. There is simply *one* Divine decree, which we have already learnt to recognise in a general way, and which we shall later speak of to a greater extent. Since, however, this plan of the world is realised in Christ, the question arises of itself, whether the Son of God would still have become incarnate, even though sin had not entered into the world. More than formerly has the question begun to occupy theologians in our day; and presumptuous as it would be to decide the question in an offhand manner, just as superficial would it be straightway to pass by it with an indifferent shrug of the shoulders. It is closely connected with another, whether, namely, humanity, even in an uninterrupted normal development, could have attained to its destination without contemplating the highest *Revelation* of the Godhead; and if not, whether this could have been conferred out of Him who was Himself the image of God, after which man was made, and who consequently already stood in an *original* relationship to God's rational creatures. However this question may be answered, in no case can it be spoken of as an alteration, or essential modification, of God's plan in

[7] *Netherlands Confession*, Art. xii.

regard to the world, that He, who as the highest revelation of God, and the most exalted ideal of humanity, was originally destined to be the *Head* of the kingdom of God, did after the fall appear in human flesh as the *Redeemer* of sinners.

7. The *realisation* of the world-plan of God takes place in time, *i.e.*, by degrees and after a long interval. In order to be able to watch the progress of its fulfilment, we must set before our eyes the *works* of God. This plural also is not irreprehensible; properly speaking, God accomplishes only *one* work, the execution of His eternal counsel; but the extent of His sphere of working, combined with our limited capacity, renders necessary a further division. The works of *Creation*, *Providence*, and *Redemption* afford us thus a threefold material for contemplation. Since, however, we can speak of Redemption only after we have treated of Anthropology and Hamartology, we have in this part of our inquiry to confine ourselves only to the two first-named.

Compare on this whole subject, F. HOSSEUS, *De notionibus providentiæ et prædestinationis in ipsa S. S. exhibitis* (1868); on the question raised in the *sixth* paragraph, my *Christologie*, part iii., pp. 85—90; to which may now he added the new edition of the there-mentioned treatise of J. MÜLLER, in his *Dogm. Abhandl.* (1870), pp. 66—126.

POINTS FOR INQUIRY.

The rights and the limits of Teleology in the sphere of Christian philosophy.—Sense and significance of Ephes. i. 10.—Further criticism of the different philosophical presentations of the Divine world-plan.—Is the proper reason for the incarnation of the Son of God to be found in the presence of sin?—The light shed, by the knowledge of this plan, upon the history of the world and of humanity.—Adoration the last word, as well as the first, in the doctrine concerning God.

SECOND DIVISION.

GOD'S WORKS.

SECTION LVI.—THE UNIVERSE.

THE Christian confession of God, as the Creator of the Universe, is the expression of the belief that all which exists outside of God, has the ground of its existence only in His almighty will. This belief demands that God should be thought of as the free-working Cause, not only of the present form, but also of the original material of all things. It confesses that He called all things, both visible and invisible, into existence by the word of His power. It rejects the idea of an eternal creation as self-contradictory; and further rejects, in this domain, every presentation which would detract, even in the slightest degree, whether in principle or in fact, from the recognition of the living God as the self-conscious and independent cause and fountain of life to all things.

1. "I believe in God the Father Almighty, *Maker* of heaven and earth." This first article of belief[1] affords us at the same time a suitable point of transition from the former chapter, and inexhaustible material for further examination. That examination has its recommendation in itself and in the history of all ages, which shows that no thinking mind can dispense with the question as to the first origin of that which exists. "I ever return," wrote d'Alembert once to Voltaire, "to the question of the ancient Indian king, 'Wherefore, after all, does anything exist?' since this is in reality the most astonishing thing of all." And Voltaire himself, the sage of Ferney, as his contemporaries called him, was not ashamed to make the confession :—

> "Le monde m'embarrasse, et je ne puis songer
> Qu'un horloge si beau soit sans horlogier."

It is indeed so; every glance we take at the glorious universe compels us to inquire as to its origin, and the idea of causation—which we all have in common—urges us to ascend to the conception of a Supreme Cause.

---

[1] Comp. *Neth. Confess.*, Art. xii.

Already convinced of His existence, we are now prepared studiously to observe the revelation of His character as seen in His *works*—in the work of *Creation* first of all, the proper consideration of which may be regarded at the same time as the touchstone of the purity of our whole conception of God.

2. Where we speak of God as the *Creator* of all that lives and exists, we make use of a word with which it is far from easy for us, finite beings as we are, to associate the right meaning. The idea is expressed by various terms in the Scriptures of the Old and the New Testament;[2] but they always indicate that working of Divine Omnipotence to which the universe owes not only its existence (*bestaan*), but its first origin (*ontstaan*). In the form of *Kal*, in which the first word is used (Gen. i. 1), it is employed only of a Divine operation. And, however little the fact itself comes within the sphere of our imagination, it is clear that here a beginning of all things is meant, which takes place through Him who originally was; so that the world is not *causa sui*,—not of, from, and by itself, but of, from, and by the Almighty. And this, not in the sense that it is simply an emanation from being, an *accidens* of the Divine life-substance, a genesis or transformation of God, a blind, passive, pathological evolution of His nature; but in such wise that it is the product of His life-awakening power; not God Himself, or a second God, but His work; not a passivity of God, but an act; not His self-realisation, but His self-revelation. The beginning of the world must thus be conceived of as a transition, not from one form of being to another, but from non-being to being; as a rising into a continued existence, in consequence of an absolute causality.

3. To the question, *wherefore* God thus created, an answer can only be returned by a reference to God's wise and holy *will*.[3] Moved by nothing and no one, except Himself, it pleased Him to call forth without Him, that life which He has in Himself, and to diffuse it in the widest circle. Not that He did this to meet a want experienced in Himself, by the filling up of a nameless void. The perfectly Blessed One had need of no Cosmos, since he possessed in the Logos the perfect and eternal object of His love. Not as the fruit of an irresistible impulse of nature in His being, but of the highest freedom on the part of God, is the work of creation to be regarded and comprehended. Yet this freedom has nothing arbitrary about it; but is one with the highest wisdom and love, and in so far itself a moral necessity. God creates just as little out of caprice, as out of necessity; nor does He create in order to add thereby something to His own perfection, or, as has been said, to be more fully God, than He would otherwise have been; but to reveal, to communicate, to glorify Himself in the work of His hands. To this extent the old Dogmatists were right, in representing God's communicating goodness (*bonitas communicativa*), as the motive for the act of creation. That this goodness, however, manifests itself in *this* special form, has its ground merely in the wholly free moral self-determination of His holy counsel.[4]

---

[2] בָּרָא, עָשָׂה, *κτίζειν, καταρτίζειν, ἑτοιμάζειν*, etc.
[3] Rev. iv. 11.
[4] Ephes. i. 11.

4. *Out of what* God has created all things, is a question which cannot be entered upon without a lively sense of the limited character of human thought. The answer, "out of nothing," now heard even from the lips of childhood, is in vain sought amongst the most renowned sages of antiquity. Where they exalt God as the author of the world, they mean thereby nothing else but that He gave to all that exists its present form. Even Plato could not entirely free himself from the idea of an eternal matter, and Aristotle started from what he took for an axiom, that "out of nothing, nothing can arise." Christian Gnosticism also placed in the foreground the eternity of matter; Hermogenes, towards the end of the second century, called forth by this his view a formal refutation on the part of Tertullian;[5] and when, later, Socinianism made its appearance, it held—in opposition to the doctrine of the Church—no creation out of nothing, but one out of an already existing matter. The difficulty arose from the fact that one could not otherwise think of God, than after the analogy of a human artist, who certainly also can form and reform all things *ad infinitum*, but can bring forth absolutely nothing out of that which does not exist. We say accordingly, without hesitation, that we here find ourselves wholly in the domain of *faith;* but at the same time, that the non-recognition of this truth revealed to faith, leads inevitably to absurdity. However perplexing the thought of a properly so called creation from nothing may be, yet it follows with absolute necessity from belief in an absolutely almighty Creator. Nay, matter without any form cannot be conceived of; an eternal matter must also be an independent matter, another God; of which it would be hard to explain why it ought or should need to yield to the will of a mighty Fashioner. In the Old Testament, moreover, the conception of a creation out of nothing is here and there already clearly apparent;[6] and in its Apocryphas[7] we hear the heroic mother of seven sons cry to her dying child, "Consider that God made all things of things that were not" (ἐξ οὐκ ὄντων; Vulg., *ex nihilo*). An echo of this tone we find in the Scriptures of the New Testament;[8] and the Christian Church stands thus with its confession upon Scriptural, but at the same time upon truly philosophic ground. By this *Nihil* is naturally intended no formless matter, such as even the Platonic philosophy places side by side with the Godhead, a ὕλη ἄμορφος; but thereby is precisely indicated the absence of *all* matter, independent of the creative power, by which alone it could originate. We have here to do with the truth that God is the independent cause, not simply of the present form, but also of the first material of the world, conceived of in its most original form of existence. To such an extent we may distinguish between a first or immediate creative act of God, and a second or mediate one; and in the former think of the material, in the latter of the after-form of that which was earlier created. In the application of the well-known proverb, "Out of nothing, nothing comes," we must at least carefully distinguish between a limited material cause of things, and an absolute spiritual one; between a *growing*

---

[5] TERTULL., *Advers. Hermog.*

[6] Ps. xxxiii. 6; Neh. ix. 6.

[7] 2 Macc. vii. 28.

[8] Rom. iv. 17; Heb. xi. 3.

and a *creating;* and must ever afresh bring into the foreground the belief in an Omnipotence, which "calleth those things which be not, as though they were." Far indeed from our seeing in all this only an idle speculation, this confession is one of great practical importance, since neither our confidence in God nor our obedience to Him could be unlimited, if He Himself were even in the slightest degree dependent on any material without Himself.

5. *By what means* or by whom did God create all things? To this question Holy Scripture returns answer, by directing us to the Word of God's power. We understand by this expression not simply the impersonal word of power, or command,[9] but think of the Logos, the word and wisdom of the Father. It is an essential element in the *Christian* belief in creation, that He whom we confess as Redeemer was in His higher nature the mediate cause of the creation. In some measure this is already disclosed in the word of the Lord in John v. 17, 19, 20; yet more distinctly is it declared by the Evangelist himself, John i. 3, 4; by Paul, 1 Cor. viii. 6; Coloss. i. 16, 17;[10] and in the Epistle to the Hebrews, i. 2. We at least think that these expressions can be taken in no secondary sense, and feel ourselves just as little at liberty to regard them as a purely subjective philosopheme. Indeed, they are wholly in harmony with that which the Gospel proclaims concerning the nature of the Logos, and so much the better do they explain to us wherefore no other than the Christ is the centre of God's plan of the world (§ lv.), and the Redeemer of a race to which He originally stood in the closest relation. That which many a philosopher dimly conjectured, namely, that God did not produce the world in an absolutely immediate manner, but, some way or other, mediately, here presents itself to us as invested with the lustre of revelation, and exalts so much the more the claim of the Son of God to our deep and reverential homage.

6. While it has ever been seen, that the apparently most simple questions are at the same time the most profound, this is certainly the case with regard to that which now arises: *when* did the Universe come into existence? Assuredly, that which God willed from eternity, He has called into being in a certain moment of time, but nothing perhaps is more difficult than to conceive of a period in which the All arose out of the Nothing. The doctrine of a so-called eternal creation has therefore been defended in different ways during all ages. Not to speak of the Manichæans, we see this idea vigorously defended in the Alexandrine School, and above all by Origen. Without regarding matter—which he considered to be the seat of the Evil One—as an independent power, he assumed an eternal creation of countless ideal worlds;[11] partly as having taken place before this of ours, partly as to be looked for after this, since he could not conceive of an inactive God. Although rejected by the orthodox Church, this idea continued to live on in various forms, especially where the influence of the

---

[9] Ps. xxxiii. 6; cxlvii. 15.

[10] Not Ephes. iii. 9; where, as is apparent from the connection, a spiritual creation is exclusively referred to.

[11] *De Princ.*, iv. 16.

Platonic philosophy made itself felt. Erigena (Duns Scotus) defended it, and the Pantheistic Mysticism of the Middle Ages regarded the whole of creaturedom as a sort of decadence from God. While the Reformation confessed with fresh alacrity the creating of the universe in time, and a later Scholasticism sought even to determine the day and the hour of creation, the newer Theology and Philosophy, on the other hand, under the influence of Spinoza, has declared itself ever more distinctly in favour of an eternal creation. Kant regarded the whole alternative as a cosmological antinomy, the solution of which surpassed the power of theoretical reason. And even among believing Theologians of our own day we observe here and there a hesitation on this point, which certainly pleads for their modesty, but no less really shows the difficulty of this question.

Yet, as far as we can see, the idea of an eternal creation is not less self-contradictory than that of a square circle; for to create, in the proper sense of the word, is nothing else than to bring into existence that which hitherto had no existence. "No creature can exist," as has been well said by Quenstadt, "*unless after previously not existing.*" "*Nulla creatura esse potest, nisi post non esse.*" By the theory of an eternal creation—Strauss, also, has acknowledged this—the idea of creation is thus, in fact, destroyed; and he who favours this view would do better, for the avoiding of misunderstanding, no longer to speak of a creation at all. Moreover, the above-mentioned theory is in irreconcilable conflict as well with the Christian idea of God as with the nature of the Cosmos. It may be defended, indeed, from the dualistic or pantheistic standpoint, but never from the supranaturalistic theistic one. The Universe presents itself to our vision as something which is not absolute, but relative, contingent, exposed to all kinds of variation; in a word, not as existing from eternity, but as having at one time begun to be. That with the opposite mode of view, the doctrine of a creation out of nothing also disappears, has scarcely need of proof: the *Nihilum* in this case exists nowhere else than in the imagination alone. No wonder, accordingly, that profound thinkers—a Nitzsch, for example—maintain the idea of a Beginning, however difficult to comprehend, as absolutely necessary. The pure idea of History is sacrificed, so soon as its starting-point must be relegated to the list of fictions. Every teleological view of the world at once loses its support, since the final aim (τέλος, terminus *ad quem*) presupposes a beginning (ἀρχή, terminus *à quo*). If the world is without a beginning, it will also continue to exist without end; and what is thus in itself eternal and independent, needs for its infinite revolutions no longer a centre in the personal and living God.

On the ground of all this it must be maintained that God was, indeed, from eternity, God, but not from eternity the Creator of the world. If it is said that in this case a change must have taken place in the Infinite, the fact is overlooked that a change in the working of God by no means compels us to speak of a variation in His nature. Or must God then—to speak after a human manner—never be able to create anything new, lest thereby the unchangeableness of His being should be brought to an end? Assuredly we cannot possibly conceive of an inactive God; but we need not do this, if we again revert to the doctrine of the Divine plan of the world, as seen in section lv. Or does any one stumble at the difficulty of not being able to conceive of a point in eternity at which time has begun? Augustine has already expressed this difficulty in the well-known words, "Nor could the ages revolve before Thou hadst made the ages"—*nec præterire potuerunt tempora, antequam faceres tempora*;—but he afforded at the same time the only tolerable solution, when he reminds us that the world was called into being not *in* but *with* time—*non in sed cum tempore*—or,[12] to speak more exactly, time *with* the world. Time, indeed, is the succession of moments for finite things; so long thus as these latter did not yet exist, there could be no room to speak of the former. A time before the creation did not exist: then it was only eternity. Or yet better with Augustine—"If before heaven and earth there was no time, why is it asked, 'What wast Thou then doing?' For there was no *then*, when there was no time. And Thou dost not in time precede the ages; but Thou art raised above all the past by the height of Thine ever-present majesty."[13]

To bring the matter into greater clearness we must carefully distinguish between the two senses of the word Creation. It signifies, namely, as well the proper creative *act* of God as the whole of *created objects* themselves which are called forth by this act. In the former case we can say that the creation is an *eternal* act; because the Creator Himself is, in His living and working, exalted above all time. In the latter case we must assume that that which is created, *at some time*—when, is for us now a matter of indifference—received a *beginning;* since it could not otherwise be spoken of as *created*. The world *began to be* so soon as this was willed by God, who placed it in time, and for it—at its birth (*wording*)—gave to time a beginning. On this account time has existed precisely as long as the world, and the world precisely as long as time. And time? This is God's secret; but enough—natural science proclaims it, as well as Holy Scripture—the realm of Creation at some time received a beginning, precisely because it is essentially distinguished from the eternal Creator. He who refuses to accept this position, would do better to read simply *Cosmos* in place of the word *Logos*, in John i. 1; and breaks in principle both with the Christian idea of God and the Christian belief in revelation.

7. From the standpoint of Christian belief in creation, must thus be definitely rejected, as being in irreconcilable conflict with its utterance:—

(*a.*) *Materialism*, which recognises the existence of nothing but matter, and explains all things as far as possible from the law of material changes. From this point of view the whole problem of creation does not, properly speaking, exist, since matter is regarded as eternal; but therewith is also the hope of a solution of the world-problem for ever lost. For the power which dominates matter cannot possibly be explained from the existence of matter alone; and, with this power, life itself remains an absolutely unfathomable mystery. Above all, since the science of our age has, by the labours of a

---

[12] *De Civ. Dei*, xi. 6.

[13] *Si ante cœlum et terras nullum erat tempus, cur quæritur, quid tunc faciebas? Non enim erat* TUNC, *ubi non erat tempus. Nec Tu tempore tempora præcedis, sed præcedis omnia præterita celsitudine semper præsentis majestatis.*

Pasteur and others, admirably demonstrated the untenableness of the theory of the *generatio æquivoca*, while the absolute impossibility of explaining organic life as brought forth by inorganic matter is ever more distinctly recognised, it is rendered apparent that Materialism gives us, in place of the despised mystery, simply an absurdity.—Not less is this the case with

(*b.*) *Hylozoism*, which certainly acknowledges a formative principle of the world, but a principle to be sought exclusively in matter itself. God, so far as He can here be spoken of, is only the universal life, the world-soul, which pervades the Cosmos, as our soul the body. As well the history of ancient as of modern philosophy affords distinguished exponents of this view; and certainly from this standpoint one need trouble himself just as little about a creation from nothing as about a beginning of things, properly so called. But this seeming advantage, how dearly is it purchased, and how little gain does it bring with it! The entire result of this tendency is to make of God a vain name, and of the world nothing but a riddle; whilst itself, when it does not end in Pantheism, must inevitably run into Atheism. If you conceive, for a moment, the absence of matter, God Himself has then disappeared in vapour and mist! If the soul of the world is an unconscious one, how is the order and design in creation to be explained? If it is a conscious one, wherefore not, at the same time, a free agent?—and if a free agent, how does it become and remain so inseparably bound to its gigantic material raiment?

(*c.*) The *Emanation*-theory certainly does not suffer from the same difficulties, but on its side calls forth wholly different ones. According to this theory, Creation has flowed forth from God, as a stream from a fountain, a ray of light from the sun's disc; and to such an extent accordingly finds its ultimate cause of life in Him. Only, unfortunately, such a creation is to be regarded as anything but the free *act* of the highest love! Far, indeed, from being here in the highest degree active, the Godhead thus becomes purely passive, and the Cosmos, in the end, a part of the totality of God's own life. How can the Eternal Being be subject to such an outflowing, without His nature admitting of diminution or exhaustion? Has not the part the same properties as the whole? And is God then also material, mutable, imperfect, as the visible world? What room is there yet left, in the case of an unconscious emanation, to speak of a proper *design* in creation? And what explanation is to be given of the methodical order, the gradual rise in the scale of being, the infinite diversity, which we discover in the work of creation? For the third time—no answer.

(*d.*) But also the *Evolution* or *Transmutation* theory of Darwin and his school, however great the applause with which it has been received in our days, can scarcely expect to hold its ground against the Christian belief as to the creation. For assuredly the great question is not here sufficiently answered, but only pushed infinitely far back. However many million years we may allow its advocates to explain the beginning and the orderly course of the great process of development, the earliest material of the universe remains equally incomprehensible, as the power which gave it the first impulse to an everlasting movement. The gulf between the animate and the inanimate, between the irrational and the rational, continues to yawn, in spite of every attempt which the Development-hypothesis has made to fill it up. Under the watchword of progress it leads us back—as far as concerns the great principle—to the standpoint of the earliest natural philosophy, long before Socrates and Plato. Even with the most comprehensive scientific knowledge, the attempt to solve the enigma—though it should so happen that *every* key was tried, *except the only fitting one*—must inevitably lead to absurdity. "In his account of creation, Moses *is in advance of* all the efforts of ancient and modern philosophy" (Lange).

8. Duly maintained, the Christian belief in God as the Almighty Creator of all things is of an undeniable *theoretical and practical importance*, which cannot be overlooked. Even though we should leave unnoticed all which has relation to the creation of this earth in particular, its high degree of significance is apparent upon a moment's reflection.—*The perfection of God* is raised above all doubt, where it appears that He is not only the Fashioner of an eternal matter, but Creator of the material of the world itself: Lord, therefore, in the most absolute sense of the word. *The claim of Religion* can no longer be disputed, so soon as it must be acknowledged that there exists an Almighty Creator, upon whom everything is absolutely dependent, and to the glorification of whom every creature is under obligation, as "*par droit divin.*" If it appears, on the other hand, that creation is simply the result of a blind process of nature, Religion has some value as an aspiration, but an aspiration to which there is nothing real beyond the nature of man himself to correspond. *The existence of a revelation* must also be admitted by him who truly confesses God as the Almighty Creator. In point of fact He has already revealed Himself in the work of His hands; and to Him who did this, neither the right nor the power can be disputed of making Himself yet further known by more particular acts of revelation. Yea, *the possibility of miracles* is established, so soon as the Christian Theistic belief in creation is confirmed on solid grounds. Whatever particular account of miracles may appear critically untenable, thus much is certain, that the beginning of all things remains absolutely inexplicable without an actual miracle of creative Omnipotence. "*Le miracle existe, il est à la première page de la Bible*" (Poulain). If a miracle has once taken place, with what right shall one speak of a miracle as henceforth impossible, so long at least as we believe in a living God, an almighty Creator? Thus the dogma of the creation is one of the foundation-stones upon which the edifice of the whole Christian doctrine of faith is built up; and we cannot wonder that the maintenance of that faith against the furious attacks of Naturalism is in our time attempted on different sides with increased zeal. Provided, however—with the clear recognition of the fact that here, if anywhere, we find ourselves in the domain of *faith*—it never be overlooked that we have to do with no truth of speculation alone, but one above all of practice. If, according to Scripture, all created things are *to* God,[14] notably must then also the treatment of the doctrine of creation be conducted with a view to His glory. This will be the better effected, in proportion as the science of faith the more humbly acknowledges the limits which have been imposed upon it once for all in this mysterious

[14] Rom. xi. 36.

clear our vision of the glory of God and His Kingdom. In this respect the sacred Angelology has not merely an æsthetic, but also a deeply religious significance; and justly maintains its place in the Christian system of thought, although it must be acknowledged that, as regards many particulars, the number of unanswered questions far surpasses that of the rightly answered ones.

1. From the Universe, considered in all its extent as the work of God, our eye now turns to its different parts, this visible world and the invisible one; the latter first, because—its existence once presupposed—it unquestionably stands higher than the earth which we inhabit, and of which the origin will later occupy us. Different views have always been entertained as to the place which Angelology ought to take in the Christian system of doctrine. For us its treatment is more appropriate, not in connection with the doctrine of Providence, but as early as that of Creation; with the understanding, however, that we here speak of Angels in general, without yet entering on the obscure domain of Satanology and Dæmonology, which must be treated of hereafter, in the investigation as to Hamartology.

2. That in reality Holy Scripture partly presupposes, partly distinctly teaches, the existence of angels—*i.e.*, of spiritual beings higher than men—no impartial reader will deny. The time is past when it was sought by all kinds of exegetical and critical artifices to clear the sacred soil of these enigmatical beings; either by making of them purely human ambassadors, informers, fair youths, etc., or by seeing in them nothing but symbols of some unknown power. The sacred writers manifestly thought of something else, when they made repeated mention of angels.[1] Not to speak here of Cherubim and Seraphim—as it would seem distinct from the spirits just named—nor of the Angel of (God's) presence, in whom was the name of Jahveh,[2] we see repeatedly, in earlier and later periods of the history of Revelation, ministering spirits from heaven appearing for the guidance, protection, or consolation of the pious, or for the punishment of the ungodly. They are represented as composing a sort of heavenly court, unceasingly active in glorifying God's name and accomplishing His will. Although not of spotless purity in the sight of the Holy One,[3] they are, however, regarded as far superior to man in moral excellency, as well as in wisdom and power. Especially in and after the Babylonian captivity we find the Angelology in many respects developed. Guardian angels, mentioned by name, appear in Daniel and Zechariah on behalf of different lands and persons; and soon after, in the Apocrypha of the Old Testament, (in the book of Tobit for instance,) they are even more fully described. In the days of the New Testament we see their existence generally acknowledged by the Jewish people, and particularly by the Pharisees; denied by the Sadducees;[4]

---

1 מַלְאָכִי, בְּנֵי אֱלֹהִים, ἄγγελοι, πνεύματα λειτουργικά, etc.

2 Exod. xxiii. 21.

3 Job xv. 15.

4 Acts xxiii. 8.

maintained and brought constantly into the foreground by the Lord and His Apostles, without distinction. Appearances of angels we find related in the history of the birth of John and of Jesus, in the desert of the Temptation and in Gethsemane, in connection with the Resurrection and Ascension of Christ, and at remarkable moments in the life of His Apostles.[5] Especially do we see the Lord frequently, and with manifest satisfaction, dwelling on the subject of these friendly and radiant forms, and directing His disciples thereto. Angels are, according to His teaching, personal, immaterial, sinless, immortal beings,[6] countless in number;[7] and placed in the closest relation, not simply to the individual man,[8] but also to that whole kingdom, at the future revelation and triumph of which they are called to fulfil a highly important task.[9] Paul also has not a little that is remarkable to say of them;[10] and while Peter also speaks of them as subjects of the glorified Christ,[11] they appear again repeatedly in the Apocalypse before the eye of the ecstatic John. Only a very few books of the Bible—such as Nehemiah, Esther, the Epistles of John and James—are entirely silent with regard to the angels; but, although for the rest this idea is much more strongly coloured and developed in some than in others, it cannot be proved that the various writers differ from each other in principle on this question, so far as the main underlying thought is concerned.

3. The question, what value is to be attached to this Biblical Angelology? has been always differently answered. As opposed to the scriptural doctrine—which is also acknowledged and held in esteem by the Christian Church in general, and the Reformed Church in particular[12]—many a one in earlier and later times has placed himself at the standpoint of a whole or half *rationalistic denial*. Especially in and after the seventeenth century, have Deism, Naturalism, and Pantheism assailed the Biblical Angelology with great force of weapons; and the older Supranaturalism defended the same out of reverence for the Bible, but within the most modest proportions, and without—as it would seem—properly knowing what to do with these mysterious beings. Schleiermacher named the whole subject problematical and indifferent; the Groningen school admitted the existence of angels, while, with but little consistency on this point, denying that of devils; for the *Modern* conception, both the one and the other have become an offence and foolishness. Here, if anywhere, one moves in what is, according to the opinion of many, the region of conscious or unconscious fiction. Angelology is from this standpoint nothing more than the fruit of a thoroughly antiquated Cosmology, equivalent to the mythology of religion.

Against this opposition, however, it may be now—setting aside particular points—in general remarked that the belief in a world of spirits is in itself *by no means unreasonable;* but even without taking the Bible into

---

[5] Acts v. 19; viii. 26; x. 3; xii. 7; xxvii. 23.
[6] Matt. xxii. 30, and similar places.
[7] Matt. xxvi. 53.
[8] Matt. xviii. 10; Luke xv. 10; xvi. 22.
[9] Matt. xiii. 39; xxv. 31.
[10] See, for instance, 1 Cor. vi. 3; xi. 10; Gal. iii. 19; Ephes. iii. 10.
[11] 1 Pet. iii. 22.
[12] *Netherlands Confession*, Art. xii.

account, is rather to be assumed. The amazing extent of the Universe leads us involuntarily to the supposition that it contains an infinite diversity, as of irrational, so also of rational inhabitants. The gradual ascent which we discover in the order and rank of being, renders it probable that there exist, not only beneath, but also above man, different links in this chain. The naturalness of this supposition is apparent from this fact—as well as others—that we meet with ideas amongst the most different nations and forms of religion, which point to a belief in a world of spirits, in an order of heroes and demigods (such for instance as the Genii among the Greeks and Romans, the Elves in the Edda, the Dews of Parseeism, etc.); so that systematic denial on this point says more perhaps for the acuteness than for the profoundness of its numerous advocates. He who knows not how to make room for any Angelology in his doctrine of faith, at least passes beyond the bounds of his competency, when with lofty tone he utters the words *absurd* and *impossible*. It were pride itself to assert that God could create nothing higher in the domain of spirits than—man. In the whole work of creation we see a manifest aspiration towards Personality, that free and self-conscious life which sets the crown upon the wonders of creation. The mineral, vegetable, and animal kingdom finds repose, as it were, and culminates in Man, the representative of God here below. But with what right shall this latter look up to heaven, and say, "Between Thee and me can no higher being exist"?

Besides, this radical denial is in conflict with well-supported and important facts. In whatever way many an Old Testament account of Angelophany may be judged of, it cannot be denied that Jesus Himself believed in the existence of angels, and brought that existence into direct connection with the main contents of His Gospel. There is no single reason for here speaking of an accommodation to that which was in His judgment a blameworthy error: not only to the Pharisees, but also to the Sadducees,[13] does He speak of them; not merely in the parable, but also in its explanation;[14] and even with death immediately before Him, He sees their legions invisibly drawn up for His help.[15] Who can here think either of an illusion or of an immoral accommodation of Himself to a narrow popular belief? Equally impossible is it to explain from this latter the accounts of the appearing of angels in the history of the Lord and His first witnesses. Belonging to a purely historic period, they can just as little be conceived of as taking place in a merely natural way, as they can be explained by the acceptance of a mythical theory; and they are, moreover, at least now and then—Acts xii. 7, for example—of such a nature that, if miracle is here to be given up, we can only see therein a deliberate and calculated act of deception. But this latter is in conflict with the moral impression which these accounts produce, and is for other reasons least of all necessary.

Unquestionably, *in the last place*, the objections brought from the negative standpoint against the doctrine of Angels, are by no means to be regarded as absolutely insuperable. The impossibility of their existence or appearing is no doubt asserted, but as yet absolutely unproved. Here,

---

[13] Matt. xxii. 29, 30. [14] Matt. xiii. 39. [15] Matt. xxvi. 53.

if anywhere, the familiar words of the poet have their application: "There are more things in heaven and earth than are dreamt of in our philosophy." The *empirical* difficulty derived from the fact that no Angel-appearances ever take place now, is—even if we unreservedly admit the truth of this assertion—only then of preponderating force, when the right has been established to judge of the experience of earlier ages exclusively by the standard of the experience of the present day. There is at least just as little reason for entirely denying to man any organ for the reception of such revelation, as for declaring this belief mere superstition, because it has, undoubtedly, often and often served to foster a miserable superstition. —The *historic* objection, that the whole of this belief, originating from the earliest period of the human race, is only a surviving remnant of Polytheism, is just as much wanting in every semblance of proof as the opposite one, that we owe it to the influence of foreign ideas upon those of the later Jews. The later more developed form of Jewish Angelology may perhaps in part be explained thereby; but long before the Babylonian captivity the substance of this doctrine lived in the consciousness of the wisest and most devout in Israel, and continued to live even when in after ages this form of revelation became more and more rare.—Finally, as far as the *inner* value of this belief itself is concerned, it is by no means of such subordinate importance as a superficial criticism would wish to assert. Precisely the barren Deistic view, which separates God and His angels from the world, has called forth the loud and oft-repeated complaint of a "God-denuded Nature" (*die entgötterte Natur*). That God *needs* no Angels in order to execute His counsel, must assuredly be admitted: but from this it does not yet absolutely follow that, to the accomplishment of this end, He cannot and may not—in addition to other means—also make use of Angels.—The great difficulty, it must be confessed, lies in the Modern view of the world, in which literally no place is left open for these friendly celestial spirits. "Since," says Strauss, "the starry heavens are no longer a layer spread above and around the earth, and forming the boundary between the physical and metaphysical world; there has been taken from us, by the Copernican system, the place where Jewish and Christian antiquity imagined the throne of God surrounded by Angels." In opposition to this assertion, it must be observed that there are many dwellings in the great Father's house, and that a more cautious judgment becomes us, in proportion as the telescope has disclosed to us more of the boundless extent of the heavens. If it be said, that the presumable inhabitants of higher worlds are still not the Angels of the Bible, this is relatively true; but at the same time it is forgotten that here the question is not so much as to the dwelling-place, as it is as to the existence and service, of the Angels. Angelology attaches itself to the doctrine of the Kingdom of God, as Dæmonology to that of Sin; but with natural science neither the one nor the other has directly to do. Astronomy, as such, knows absolutely nothing of the spiritual life in the Universe, to give to it the right of confirming or denying on this point. He who combats the doctrine of Angels on grounds derived from Astronomy, must also—in order to be consistent—say farewell to all thought of a heaven, a personal God, a particular Revelation. The systematic combating of

Angelology is usually determined by a Deistic or Pantheistic tendency, and easily leads to an entire denial of all spirit in nature and humanity, in other words, to absolute Materialism.

4. Notwithstanding all this, however, we need scarcely say, the *fantastic embellishment* of this doctrine, of which, on the other hand, the history of the Christian Church—above all, of the Romish Church—affords us so many examples, is yet far from being justified. There is no part of Christian doctrine, after that of Eschatology, on which the glowing imagination has so early and so eagerly seized, as on this. What a wide difference between the Biblical sobriety of representation, and the wild creations of Gnosticism, in this mysterious domain! When the doctrine of emanations and of æons regards the Angels as ethereal creatures, orthodoxy soon lays increased stress upon their corporeity; of guardian Angels, too, much more is heard[16] than in the Apostolic age. On the authority of Ambrose and others, the veneration of Angels is recommended; from the time of Constantine, churches are dedicated to them by emperors and bishops; and Pseudo-Dionysius, in the beginning of the sixth century, is able to give us the account of a whole heavenly hierarchy, divided into three classes and nine orders. The day of their creation, the freedom of their will, the possibility of their fall, the peculiarity of their knowledge even—in distinction from that of men, of a purely *à priori* nature—is all described by the Scholastics with hair-splitting exactness. It is true that in this domain, also, the Reformers set themselves against error and superstition; and Calvin gave up the idea of guardian angels, which had been still retained by Luther. But very soon Scholasticism again began to make itself felt with fresh vigour; the Swiss Theologian, J. H. Heidegger († 1698), was still able to fill twenty folio pages with a catalogue (*breviarium*) of Angels. In what a revolutionary manner the fancy of Swedenborg († 1772) constructed a world of spirits, and what strange ideas the newer Theosophy has given birth to, in this respect also, cannot here be analysed. In presence of these eccentricities, the Romish Church merits comparative praise, in that it has at least retained the standpoint of earlier ages. Pity, however, that its absolutely unscriptural interpretation and embellishment of many particular points has not merely contributed to the growth of superstition, but in great part called forth and given colour to that rationalistic and naturalistic reaction which we have before characterised, and of which—so far as appears at present—the end cannot be anticipated.

5. The *literal-biblical* conception has unquestionably, as opposed to the two extremes, essential right on its side; but yet the watchword: *ad biblicam simplicitatem*, by no means raises us above all difficulties. Even with the most unreserved admission of the credibility of the narratives in the sacred history, one must admit that the appearances of Angels present a too fleeting, sporadic, mysterious character, for us to build definite theories upon them. In many a word of Scripture, also, the poetic character is not to be denied;[17] others, which afford a hint concerning

---

[16] Hermes, for example; Clemens Alexandrinus; Origen.

[17] *E.g.*, Ps. xxxiv. 7.

Angels, are clothed in the transparent raiment of a parable.[18] Then again we hear the voice of the popular belief,[19] and it becomes the question what value we are to attach thereto? The same is the case with some traditions,[20] not to speak of passages of Scripture which—like Gen. vi. 2; 1 Cor. vi. 3; xi. 10—are the known *cruces interpretum.* In general it surely will not be the same thing, whether we receive an utterance of our Lord, or, *e.g.*, of one of the friends of Job, touching the world of spirits. What is apprehended in regard thereto in a visionary condition, differs in the case of one and another; and it is not possible to blend together the aggregate of that which appears in Holy Scripture concerning Angels, into one well-compacted whole. In any case, sifting (κρίσις) is necessary, before one step farther can be taken here.

6. Thus, in this case also, the *believing-critical* conception is the only one which can lead to wished-for results. Believing, inasmuch as here also it allows that weight and authority to the word of revelation in Christ, which it must have in the investigation of Christian science; and critical, in this respect, that as regards particulars it judges of the utterances of Holy Scripture according to their value, carefully explains, mutually compares, and duly distinguishes between the accidental form and the eternal contents of the doctrine of the Bible. In order here to find firm ground under our feet, it is unquestionably best to take counsel with the Lord's own words, and to make them our starting-point. Where He is acknowledged as the Truth in the spiritual domain of life, and as King of the creation, certainly such expressions as, *e.g.*, Matt. xviii. 10; xxv. 31; xxvi. 53; Luke xv. 10, will be regarded as something more than a poetic figure of speech. If He is held, on the ground of His own witness of Himself, to be God's own Son, one will find it on the other hand conceivable, and something that commends itself to our judgment, that His appearing in the flesh should receive lustre from revelations of the world of spirits. If we take this appearing as the centre of the history of the Kingdom of God in the world, that of Israel becomes its preparation, that of the Apostolic age its after-operation; and in this light not a little in this domain also is comprehensible, which otherwise, regarded in itself, would legitimately call forth astonishment: and if we now in general agree as respects this sphere of thought, the judgment on particular appearances of Angels will naturally depend upon further exegetical and critical investigation, which, however—from the Christian-theistic standpoint—may in no case be dominated by the preconceived opinion that miracles are impossible. We must not import our own conceptions and denials in regard to the world of spirits—conceptions and denials derived we know not whence—in order thereby to test the Bible; but, on the contrary, must regulate our ideas on a subject, of which by our own light we can know nothing, by the well-pondered word of Revelation. In this way it is possible even here to arrive at a certain degree of clearness and certainty, although sufficient data are wanting to answer many a question in a decisive manner.

7. Following in this way, there is not a little concerning the world of

[18] *E.g.*, Luke xvi. 22. [19] *E.g.*, Acts xii. 15. [20] Jude 8, 9.

spirits which we may *accept* as sufficiently certain. It may then be regarded as certain that Angels exist, that they are not simply impersonal powers (Potenzen), which are represented in Holy Scripture as messengers of God; but higher spirits, who know, and serve, and praise Him better than man, and, just as man, were created by the word of God's power. "If," says Plitt, "we once place ourselves distinctly and definitely at the essentially Theistic standpoint of Scripture, and have from that standpoint recognised the unique and absolute value of the idea of real free personality, in a metaphysical and ethical point of view; we have no longer even the inclination to doubt that which the Scripture of the Old and the New Testament tells us about the creatures of God in the invisible world, the Angels." We may also, on reasonable grounds, believe that they were originally created good, and yet have a capacity for continual development.[21] That in this domain also an infinite fulness and diversity exists, we should probably suppose, even though Scripture had given us no suggestive hints in regard thereto.[22] The same is true with respect to that which is here taught as to their constant interest in the wellbeing and salvation of men and sinners, and the continual intercourse between heaven and earth, in regard to which the service of Angels also is by no means excluded, although the How and the How-far thereof is not to be further defined. We thus reject "the error of the Sadducees, who say that there are no spirits or Angels."[23] God, who has need of no one, makes use of Angels, as well as men, to accomplish His counsel and will. Perhaps we may assume that their service and activity comes yet more definitively into the foreground at great turning-points in the history of the world and of the Kingdom of God; such as the founding of the Old and the New Covenant, the humiliation and exaltation of Christ, the judgment of the world. From this, at the same time, may be explained the long-enduring absence of all Angelophanies at other periods, without proving anything against the existence and work of Angels in itself.

8. As opposed to these, there are other conceptions, which—with an eye to the word of the Lord, and wholly in the spirit of the Saving Revelation—may in our opinion be decidedly *denied*. To this number belongs the belief in guardian angels, at least in the form in which this is confessed by Rome. In Matt. xviii. 10, it is indeed taught in general that "the little ones" have their Angels; but from this it still does not follow that a personal and particular Angelic guardian is assigned to every man. Acts xii. 15 is the expression of a popular belief, of which the value is not more nearly defined.—Just as much to be rejected appears the assertion that the Angels are the advocates and mediators of men before the throne of God. Poetical prophetic utterances of the Old Testament on this subject—*e.g.*, Job xxxiii. 23; Zech. i. 12; Dan. ix. 21-23—supported by no single word of the Lord, afford no sufficiently firm ground to build upon them alone an article of Christian doctrine (comp. § viii. 5, 6); the less so, since the Gospel knows only of One Advocate and Mediator.—Least of all is the religious veneration of Angels to be permitted; since this is condemned by the Scriptures of the New Testament with the strongest

[21] Ephes. iii. 10; 1 Pet. i. 12. [22] Luke i. 19; Ephes. i. 21. [23] *Neth. Conf.* Art. xii.

emphasis,[24] and has been censured and prohibited by the Synod of Laodicæa, towards the middle of the fourth century, and later by Augustine and Gregory the First. The invocation of Angels has no meaning, so long as it is not manifest that we must regard them as almighty and omnipresent. And the boundary line which Rome draws between δουλεία, which may be rendered to the Angels also, and λατρεία, which must be rendered to God alone, appears in practice much too superficial to oppose with the desired result a superstitious deification of the creature.

9. Wholly *uncertain*, finally, remain questions like these. Touching the nature of angels: whether they were created before man, rather than after him; created free from all corporeity, or simply from our more gross one; absolutely raised above all temptation, or in some sense still susceptible thereof; in all or only in some respects more excellent than men. Touching their place or abode: where they are properly to be sought, and to what extent we are to suppose that they are constantly, although invisibly, near to us on earth. Touching their activity: wherein it consists, how far it yet extends to this part of creation, in what way it is recognised and experienced, etc. To such-like questions the answer still remains, "We know in part." Still this by no means justifies us in wholly rejecting the doctrine. On the contrary, in the words of Melancthon: *non propterea abjicienda est doctrina certa et utilis vitæ, de multis rebus etiamsi multa ignoramus. Præparemus nos ad æternam illam Academiam, in qua integram Physicam discemus, cum Ideam mundi nobis Architectus ipse monstrabit.*

10. Without justice has it been asserted, by Schleiermacher, Scholten, and others, that Angelology has no religious and theological *significance.* It is true we have here to do with no fundamental article of doctrine, in the sense in which, for instance, the Incarnation of the Son of God and the Resurrection of our Lord are thus named; but yet it is a question here of something more than that which is a matter of absolute indifference, whether for the doctrine of Salvation or the doctrine of Life. Belief in the existence of Angels, built up upon trustworthy utterances and facts of revelation, renders more clear our conception of the all-surpassing majesty of God, of the Divine greatness of the Lord, and the glory of His yet future last appearing. Certainly it may be abused, as is apparent from history, to the ends of superstition, indolence, ascetic rigorism towards oneself.[25] But restricted within the above-defined limits, the recognition of this truth also has an exceedingly practical bearing. It raises man, by reminding him of his exalted rank[26] and his high destiny.[27] It shames the sinner by asserting to him the possibility of a normal development of spiritual beings, but at the same time by showing to him their interest in the work of his conversion. It directs the Christian to a lofty source of consolation,[28] an excellent example,[29] and a heart-cheering perspective.[30] The life of the Church and of the heart would certainly be in no worse position if the suggestive hint of

---

[24] Col. ii. 18; Rev. xix. 10; xxii. 8, 9.
[25] Col. ii. 23.
[26] Ps. viii. 5.
[27] Matt. xxii. 30.
[28] Ps. xci. 11, 12.
[29] Matt. vi. 10.
[30] Heb. xii. 22.

Calvin were taken to heart: *In omni conventu sacro sentimus nos in conspectu Dei et Angelorum.*

Compare three Sermons by LUTHER on *Good and Bad Angels* (1533), Walch x.; J. HERINGA, *Verhandeling over de Engelen*, Soc. of the Hague (1811); the article of BOEHMER, in Herzog, *R. E.*, iv.; A. ROHLING, *Ueber den Jeh.-Engel des A. B.* (1866).

POINTS FOR INQUIRY.

The gradual progress and development of the Angelology of the Bible.—Further discussion of single *cruces interpretum* in this domain.—What value is to be attached to the older and more modern polemic against the doctrine of Angels?—The *Hierarchia cœlestis* of the Romish Church more nearly examined.—Significance of belief in this truth also, especially for the Christian Theologian and the Preacher of the Gospel.

SECTION LVIII.—THE CREATION OF THE WORLD.

As the creation of the Universe, and particularly of the World of Spirits, so is also that of our Earth, the work of an Almighty Will, whereby it once began to be out of nothing, and was brought into its present condition. The Christian religious belief in God as the Creator of the World does not necessarily stand or fall with one particular interpretation of the Mosaic Document; but still the unbiassed study of this last—compared with the cosmogonies of other nations, and the discoveries of natural science—will strengthen the conviction that its essential contents contain undeniable truth, and ultimately rest upon Divine revelation. In this light, the world in its genesis presents the scene on which the Omnipotence, Wisdom, and Goodness of God is displayed; originally good, and perfectly adapted to its destination.

1. After we have spoken in general of the Universe and the World of Spirits, we have now to investigate what the science of faith proclaims concerning the creation of this our world. It is scarcely necessary to show that this investigation is for us of yet greater importance than the former; but, at the same time, that it was already thereby prepared for, and may therefore now be abbreviated. For what is true of the totality of things which exist distinct from God, is also true of this part—that it was originally created by God, in the beginning, out of nothing. This is also in reality understood or expressed in Scripture places like Neh. ix. 6; Ps. viii., xix., civ., cxlvi. 6; Isa. xl. 12; Acts iv. 24. But now it becomes the question, whether anything yet more definite than these general facts is known to us concern-

ing the origin of this our earth. All other utterances of Holy Scripture direct us back to the Mosaic document of Gen. i. 1—ii. 3. The examination as to the *essential contents*, the *character*, and the abiding *significance* of this document, must consequently now more particularly occupy us.

2. The literal interpretation of the Mosaic document of creation does not properly belong to the domain of Christian doctrine, least of all within the limits here marked out to us. We have to do only with the knowledge of the *essential contents*, so far as these continue to be of actual significance for a clear and well-grounded conception of the creation. It may contribute to the attainment of this to observe at once, that while the solemn beginning (ver. 1) evidently has reference to the genesis of all things, to which thus also this earth belongs; the second verse, on the other hand, begins the fuller description of the mode in which afterwards the earth—originally like a waste, unformed chaos—was by Omnipotence formed and adapted to be the dwelling-place of men and animals. More is read "between the lines" than is therein really communicated, when in the "without form and void" a total desolation is thought to be indicated, in consequence of a presumed insurrection of the world of spirits, which at an earlier period are supposed to have inhabited this globe, but are now banished therefrom. Not upon a moral, but upon a natural domain, does the Writer conduct us, as he describes the yet unformed world, wholly covered with water; but over which the Spirit of Life, like the brooding dove, already hovers with outspread wings.[1] How that life arose is sketched forth to us in a series of six pictures, evidently divided into two parallel groups; so that the fourth day of creation points back to the first, the fifth to the second, and the sixth to the third. The whole of the six days' creative work—the Hexaëmeron—is crowned by a seventh day, of which no evening is mentioned; it is the day of the Sabbath rest of God, which is still continued, and in which the work of upholding, governing, and bringing to completion all things, succeeds the proper work of creation. So the creation proceeds by degrees and after long intervals, in such wise that Omnipotence ascends in an orderly manner from the lower to the higher, and begins with the creation of light—the first condition of all life—to conclude with man, as the ultimate object and crown of all its works. As concerns the *days* of creation, of which the beginning is reckoned, according to the Israelitish division of time, from the evening: to the question whether the sacred narrator here meant ordinary days, or greater periods of perhaps overwhelming extent, the answer of an unbiassed exegesis cannot be doubtful. It is clear that he thought of ordinary days, as is manifest, for example, from the mentioning of the seventh in connection with the weekly Sabbath rest; although, on the other hand, it must be admitted that at least for the first three days—when as yet the heavenly luminaries were placed in no ordered relation to our earth—we cannot think of any precisely marked-out period of time. Since, as is well known, this narrative describes the things of heaven, also, *from the standpoint of the earth*, that which we read concerning the fourth creative day must be understood as implying that the heavenly luminaries, created by God, now began

[1] Compare Deut. xxxii. 11.

henceforth, in their regular succession, to render their service to the earth by day and by night. With the light of the sun the great work is now carried nearer to its completion, and that in such a way that the higher ranks of creatures do not of themselves proceed from the lower in the way of merely natural development, but in consequence of an ever renewed creative power of God, appear successively after and side by side with each other. God gives not simply the first impulse to the gigantic physiological process of development, whereby the Chaos becomes a Cosmos, but at every new act in this matchless drama He Himself is present, and directly operative by His quickening power. The vegetable kingdom prepares the way for the animal; and not *out of* but *after* this last, man appears on the scene, as the beginning of a new kind of creatures, who now stands at the head of the completed Creation, and—after so many ages, still only imperfectly interprets it.

3. As to the beauty and sublimity of a document in which, from beginning to end, a stately psalm-tone resounds, there can be but *one* opinion. As regards the definite *character*, however, which must be ascribed to it, opinions have at all times differed. Not a few, as Eichhorn, Gabler, Bauer, and others, have found here a so-called *philosophical myth*, wherein a highly cultivated Israelite has given us the fruit of his reflections as to the origin of all things, clothed in the form of history. That, however, neither the contents, nor the tone, nor the place of the narrative of creation speaks in favour of this construction, is at once apparent to every one. By all later men of God, as also by Jesus and the Apostles, the contents thereof are manifestly regarded as history.[2] The form in which the genesis of all things is here clothed can be just as little explained from the mythical standpoint, as can the particular object contemplated by the anonymous thinker in giving it precisely *this* form. The origination of such a sublime poem at a time when, in other respects, religion and philosophy were in an extremely undeveloped condition, remains incomprehensible; and not less so the remarkable agreement between its contents and the cosmogonies of other nations, which rather warrants the conjecture that all proceeded from a common source. By what fatal accident came the thinker on the genesis of the world, who stood so much higher than the most renowned philosophers, to remain unknown to posterity? Assuredly "the historical account which is given there, bears in itself a fulness of speculative thoughts and poetic glory; but is itself free from the influences of human philosophemes: the whole narrative is sober, definite, clear, concrete."[3]

4. Not much more favourable can our judgment be as to the so-called *allegorical* conception, formerly advocated in various ways by some of the ecclesiastical Fathers, as Theophilus, Basil, Clemens Alexandrinus, Origen, Augustine, and others,[4] developed in more than one way by the Schoolmen of the Middle Ages, and still defended with much ability by Herder, in the second half of the past century. The account of the crea-

---

[2] Matt. xix. 4; Acts iv. 24.

[3] DELITZSCH; comp. PAREAU, *De myth. S. S. interpretat.* 2nd edition (1824), p. 86, *sqq.*

[4] See the places in STRAUSS, *Chr. Glaube*, i., p. 618, and following.

tion was, according to this last, an optical representation of the beginning of all things, derived from that which is still seen to take place every morning at sunrise. "The Divine commentary on the first chapter of Genesis breathes in the morning air. We have here a hieroglyph of creation."[5] Yet it may be doubted whether this hieroglyph has found in Herder its Champollion. The account itself at least gives no single hint that it is thus to be understood; and the conception, however ingenious, is not natural enough to be really in the spirit of the ancient world. Although the poetic mind sees now, in the awakening of Creation at the rising of the morning sun, a remarkable image of the first arising of all things, this does not prove that it was so intended by Moses, still less that an angelic being, from the height of a mountain top, should have instructed in this form the first man about the origin of the world.—Yet more baseless is the assertion of Schenkel, that the Hexaëmeron was to be simply an emblem (N.B.) of the holiness of the week.

5. Undoubtedly higher than the mythical and allegorical conceptions stands the *visionary* one, advocated by Kurtz, Keerl, and others. According to their view, the great process of the world's beginning was made known in a series of retrospective visions, either to Moses, or to another whose written evidence Moses made use of. As in other cases the future is unveiled before the eye of the Seer, so on this occasion the past is unveiled, in such wise that the objective truth of the revelation blends with the subjective conception of the man of God. Yet even this key seems not entirely to fit into this oldest of all enigmas. The account itself contains just as little to favour its being taken as a vision, as does that which is later communicated concerning Paradise or the fall. No second instance of such a retrospective prophetic vision is known to us in the history of revelation. In conjunction with this view it becomes to us incomprehensible even, how in Exod. xx. 8—11, the Sabbath commandment could be brought into connection with the six days' work of creation; a precept of the law may well rest upon a known fact, but not upon a visionary representation. Neither is the first page of the Bible understood by any Prophet or Apostle otherwise than as a purely historic account of Divine deeds in the morning of creation.

6. Thus everything conspires to lead us back to the *historic* interpretation, which needs only to be more fully described and defended, in order to find its commendation in itself. We believe we are really reading here the history of the world's genesis, naturally not in the every-day sense of that word, but in the higher religious and theocratical sense thereof; an historic account, resting on tradition, coming down from the first man, preserved ages long in oral tradition, later in a written form, brought within the knowledge of Moses, placed at the head of the Thora, and now, after so many centuries, better adapted than anything else to afford us satisfactory guidance as to the origin of all things. That opinion, advocated *inter alios* by Delitzsch, Keil, and others, has not a little by which it commends itself.—Even *à priori* it is probable, that a traditional belief on this point would have pre-

[5] Compare P. Hofst. d. Groot, *Opvoed. d. Menschd.*, i., p. 37; D. N. in the *Bijb. Woordenb.*, iii., p. 286.

vailed amongst the oldest inhabitants of the earth, just as all popular and religious history of antiquity took its start in tradition. To this must be added the undeniable fact that Holy Scripture—as has been already observed by Vitringa, and after him by d'Astruc—contains two different documents referring to the creation, that of the Elohist and that of the Jahvist;[6] agreeing with each other, it is true, in the leading features, but yet differing from each other as regards particulars, and simply placed beside each other, as it were, as a sign that the earliest tradition was preserved, not in slavish subjection to the letter, but in a free form.—Moreover this opinion is confirmed by a glance at the prevailing spirit of the East, even in later, but much more in earlier, times. The history of Islam shows how many words and deeds of "the Prophet" were passed down from mouth to mouth, in doing which every one must give the name of his authority, as he in turn must name that of his predecessor; while only later, mention could be made of systematic historiography. Even in the present day many an Arab knows the genealogy of his horse, without one link being wanting in the long chain of its descent. Something similar do we find in the genealogy of Gen. v., the earliest which exists on earth. In no other way can the old narrative of the world's creation have been preserved and communicated in the original language of the world; and he who first wrote it was already removed by a multitude of ages from the cradle of humanity. There is, in this scarcely to be disputed view, nothing which could call forth suspicion or doubt. That the art of writing was practised at—yea, before—the time of Moses in Egypt, we may safely regard as established. Equally clear is it, that Moses, in his youth, had abundant opportunity, and certainly an equally great desire, to become acquainted with the traditions of the patriarchal age, and those of an earlier period. It would thus be wrong to take the word tradition forthwith in an unfavourable meaning, as though Tradition (*Sage*) and fiction were tacitly to be understood as words of the same significance. Here rather should the rule find its application: "the older, the more certainly trustworthy." If, as we believe, the account of Gen. v., concerning the long duration of life in the earliest generations, is to be accepted, then the treasure of sacred tradition needed to pass through but few hands. Noah probably was acquainted with Seth, the son of Adam.—If we now *finally* add, that also the very surprising agreement between the Mosaic and other cosmogonies is certainly thus best explained—indeed, "the same undertones are heard everywhere, from the Nile to the Ganges"—and that this conception is at the same time wholly in harmony with the letter and spirit of the New Testament Scriptures, we shall confidently repeat the words of Luther: "Moses is writing a history, and recording things which really happened."

7. Everything depends solely on the inner value which must be attributed to this historical tradition; and this value is at once apparent if the conviction is confirmed that we here find ourselves in no lower terrein than that of God's own special *Revelation*. For him who believes in a living God and the possibility of a special revelation, not a few reasons may be advanced

[6] Gen. ii. 4—25.

which render worthy of our acceptance the thought that the first fruit of this revelation lies before us on the first page of the Bible.

Even *à priori* we may safely assert, that if there is really a God, who willed to be known and worshipped by men, He *must* begin by revealing Himself, and affording them so much light as to the creation of the world as was called for by their capacity and need. For he who wills the end must also will the means; and this law has its application even to the Supreme wisdom. Knowledge touching the origin of things was—as the foundation of all religion—indispensable; and this could not be attained to unless it were furnished by Him. In what way this may have taken place is a question which certainly will never be answered, and also is, in a certain respect, of comparatively small importance. Here we are concerned with the great principle, and that principle can be rejected only where one no longer reserves in his thinking a place for a personal God, and a direct communion between Him and the humanity allied to Him. Not a little combines to lead us to conjecture that in the first age, before the fall, this communion was much more intimate than in after ages; and the religious faith in a higher education of humanity leads naturally to the conviction that the highest Educator has in this respect least of all "left Himself without witness."

Then the inner excellence of this narrative must be taken into account, an excellence so striking that an origin in a purely natural manner, in such extreme antiquity, may be regarded as inconceivable. The high inner value of the Mosaic Geogony, compared with the cosmogonical traditions of other nations—already frequently brought into prominence—can here be only indicated. Enough that the latter, without exception, display either a hylozoistic or a pantheistic-emanatistic character; while not a single one out of them all rises to the pure idea of a properly so called *Creation* of the world. The boundary line which separates the sublime from the ridiculous, is there unceasingly overlooked; by Moses, never. In its whole and in its parts, his document proclaims a fundamental character not simply strongly Monotheistic, but also purely moral. This phenomenon is inexplicable, except on a supposition, to which literally everything impels us, and to which nothing is opposed, except—a Naturalistic prejudice.

Natural science, finally, in its turn places an important weight in the scale, in favour of this utterance of faith. This science not only confirms in every way the necessity of fixing a point of Commencement, properly so called, a Beginning of all things; but even postulates, for the satisfactory explanation of its problems, an *act* of creative omnipotence, whereby the first life was awakened, and—so to speak—all was first set in movement. In addition to this, the indisputable phenomenon is to be taken into account, that, according to the testimony also of renowned naturalists, the accuracy of the Mosaic representation has been confirmed in a number of details by scientific investigation, and often in the most surprising manner. "*Elevé dans toute la science des Egyptiens, mais supérieur à son siècle,*" says Cuvier, "*Moïse nous laisse une Cosmogonie, dont l'exactitude se vérifie chaque jour d'une manière admirable.*" Similar testimonies have since been repeated by men like an Ampère, Marcel de Serres, Buckland, Wagner, Burmeister, Hugh Miller, Fabri, and many others with them. They abundantly counterbalance the undeserved contempt, with which this venerable memorial of antiquity has been met on the other side; but at the same time legitimate our right confidently to express the judgment, that he who here with determination rejects all idea of revelation, finds himself in difficulties infinitely more numerous and infinitely greater, than he who finds in this idea the only satisfactory answer to a number of questions. Here also, if anywhere, belief in God is the light of all our science.

8. The fierce and important controversy, which is now being waged with varying success, between Natural Science and Biblical Theology, need not—after what has been said—terrify us above measure. This is not the place to venture on even a single attempt at its decision; but only to become in some way acquainted with what is going on in the contested field. But then our *first* remark must be, that an essential injustice is done to Scripture, and an incalculable injury inflicted on faith, so soon as here the *Cuique suum* is not carefully regarded, and the boundary line between Natural Science and Theology is in the least overlooked. The Scripture is the trustworthy document of the Divine Saving Revelation, no handbook of astronomy or geology; and it is thus just as much out of place to wish to bind or conduct these last by an appeal to Holy Scripture, as to seek in Holy Scripture that which it neither promises nor designs to furnish. The maxim "quietly, peacefully" (*schiedlich, friedlich*), in this case is a rule not simply of prudence, but also of genuine impartiality. A conflict arises only where this law is forgotten. Natural Science will, if it is genuine, *i.e.*, modest, be obliged to admit that it knows nothing of the *first* origin of things; Theology can, without losing anything, acknowledge that the *revelation* of this first cause is here given in an exceedingly childlike form. Calvin has already declared: *Moses, vulgi ruditati se accommodans, scripsit;*[7] and elsewhere: *nos potius consideravit sidera, quam prouti theologum decebat.*

In the second place it is to be observed with thankfulness, that already the "testimony of the rocks" has spoken on more than one point with desirable result, to the honour of the Mosaic document, and that many an objection formerly raised against it has found a satisfactory answer. The creative days of the Bible have been found again, to a surprising degree of accuracy, according to the testimony of many of its most illustrious students, in the gigantic periods of the earth's formation, of which Geology has to speak. That our earth, before the rise of any life upon it, was overspread with water, seems indubitable. Only ignorance can any longer sport with the idea that light was created so soon as the first day, while the sun only on the fourth day shone upon the earth. Here the word of an American Theologian has its application: "This stumbling-block is the corner-stone of creation." That the first life was born in the depth of the sea; that a gigantic world of plants arose, still without the influence of the sun's rays, which only afterwards began to shine; that the creation of animals preceded that of man, and that he was really the last and highest work of Omnipotence, is acknowledged even by those who cannot be suspected of any special prepossession for the word of Scripture.

---

[7] CALVIN, *l. l.* i. 14, 3

Then it must be taken into consideration, *in the third place*, that the value of many a loudly praised scientific result, frequently urged with lofty tone against the word of Scripture, is by no means raised above reasonable doubts. We do not determine whether Lichtenberg, for instance, said too much when he wrote that nine-tenths of the theories touching the origin of the world belong more to the domain of the history of *mind*, than of the history of the *earth*, in other words, are to be regarded as more or less happy imaginings. But already the nature of the case confirms the observation that, as the oldest history of nations is lost in tradition and *Sagas* (legendary lore), so that of the earth, for the greater part, must move in the region of hypothesis. The greatest authorities in the domain of science, on this account, preach modesty both by word and example. "True Geognosy," says Alexander von Humboldt, "makes us acquainted with the outer crust of the earth, as it is now. On the other hand, all that has reference to the former condition of our planet is . . . . just as uncertain as the manner in which the atmosphere of the planets was formed." Burmeister also spoke of his theory of the earth's formation simply as an hypothesis. The alternation of the most opposite theories in the geogonic domain has long become a proverb, and even yet the moment does not appear to be come, when the science can speak of a result as absolutely proved, so as to command universal assent. More than one oracle, on the contrary, which once made itself loudly heard, has afterwards—not without shame—recalled its words.

This being so, it is *finally* clear that neither on the one side, nor on the other, has the last word yet been spoken; so that in many respects the tone of jubilation over a complete reconcilement may be regarded as being as precipitate as the complaint about irreconcilable conflict. The only safe way thus appears for the moment to be this, that as well the science of faith as the study of nature, each in its own sphere, should be prosecuted with caution, and the result to which this leads be awaited; yet, with the addition of the full conviction that the latter can, in our opinion, by no means be a gainer if it refuses to listen to the ultimate answer to its questions given by the word of Revelation. For from *this* point of view, indifferent as to the rest in what form this revelation may be, we continue to regard the first page of the Bible. We cannot possibly believe that among a people less learned than the Egyptians, less philosophic than the Greeks, and in an age when natural science could be scarcely said to have an existence, a Cosmogony like this could have arisen in a merely natural way, *i.e.*, as a result of purely human thought.

9. The *value* of the account of creation, regarded from this point of view, now becomes at once apparent. It possesses this even in itself, as a memorial of the highest antiquity, rich in unsurpassed beauty, sublimity, truth, and power. Besides, we have here the authentic basis of all religion, especially of the Israelitish, and notably also of Israel's Sabbath-commandment; the epitome of that universal revelation, to which the particular was subsequently joined. No wonder that Holy Scripture afterwards constantly proceeds from this great fact of creation, and continually refers thereto. Even after so many ages the light here kindled has lost nothing of its brilliancy. And for our time too an instruction is here given which

protests with all its force against the nature-idolatry of the modern Ethnicism. It is true the answer which is here given to the great question may be despised, and the complaint may be raised, that it calls forth a number of new interrogations. But then as the upshot nothing remains but to grope in utter darkness; boasting of a science which, if it will proclaim no absurdities, must end with a confession of absolute ignorance.

10. In the light of Holy Scripture the creation of this earth may be considered as a glorious revelation of God's infinite Majesty. His Omnipotence appears where, as Luther says, "creating is for Him no more than for us the mere naming of things." His wisdom beams forth in the gradual progress, the infinite diversity, and the beautiful harmony of the works of Creation, all concurrent to one adorable end. His goodness strikes us ever again, where we see each creature endowed, not only with what is necessary, but also with what is superabundant; and all so arranged, that everything that lives can rejoice in its existence, and glorify its Maker. Certainly there is good reason for speaking, as in the second Article of the Netherlands Confession, of "a beautiful book, in which all creatures, great and small, are as it were so many letters which give us to behold the invisible things of God." The exact sciences, in all this, direct us to powers, phenomena, laws; the science of faith overlooks nothing of these, but seeks and reads behind these things the one Name, which alone is *le dernier mot* of all that is finite. Only it must not forget that, in the words of Fr. von Baader, "it must be said, in regard to the Creation, that the intelligent creature can never know and comprehend the way and manner in which God produces and upholds it; so that a theory of Creation *in this sense* is nothing but a presumptuous expression."

11. Yet whatever may remain doubtful, this at least can by no means be contradicted, that there exist solid grounds for speaking of the world as originally *good*, and perfectly adapted to its destination.[8] Belief in the wisdom and goodness of God leads of itself to this position, and daily experience confirms it. The question whether this world is really the best of all possible conceivable worlds, a question so frequently discussed by philosophy, and with such varying results, rests at least in part upon a misconception. We cannot possibly think of the Infinite One as resembling a human artist, who, out of a number of objects, chooses at last that one which appears to him best adapted to his purpose. The absolute Optimisim of Leibnitz and others has—in the presence of so much misery—inevitably called forth opposition.[9] And it must by no means be forgotten that sin has disturbed the harmony of God's glorious Creation. Yet there is no reason for doubting whether the world objectively, *as it came forth from the hand of its Maker*, was in reality "very good;" and this, well considered, covers more than the question whether it may still in our estimation be regarded as unconditionally the best. The doctrine of the Creation can lead to no other conclusion; and that of Providence will confirm the soundness of

---

Gen. i. 31.

[9] Take, for example, amongst others, VOLTAIRE'S *Candide*, and KANT'S *Kritik der Urtheilskraft*. Berlin, 1790.

this conclusion. *Mundus fini, quam per creationem Deus intendit, maxime convenit et accommodatus est.*[10]

Compare, on the Mosaic account of Creation, the *Commentaries on Genesis* of DELITZSCH, BAUMGARTEN, KEIL, LANGE, and others, not forgetting those of LUTHER and CALVIN ; as also KURTZ, *History of the Old Covenant*, i. On the Creation itself, in addition to the literature already adduced in § lvi., that also which is furnished by LANGE, *Bibel Werk, A. T.*, i., p. 22, *sqq.* On its glory, KÖSTLIN, *God in de Nat.*, 3 parts (1856) ; C. FLAMMARION, *Dieu dans la Nature* (1867). On the Cosmogony of the Gentile nations, as compared with that of Moses, the Prize Essay of A. WUTTKE (Hag. Soc., 1849) ; H. LUEKEN, *Die Traditionen des Menschengeschl., oder die Uroffenb. G. unter d. Heid.* (1856), a highly interesting book. On the Credibility of the first chapter of Genesis, C. A. AUBERLEN, *The Divine Revelation ;* compare P. HOFSTEDE DE GROOT, *Opvoed. d. M.* (1847), i., p. 127, *sqq.* On the harmony of the account of Creation with the results of the study of Nature, F. W. SCHULTZ, *Die Schöpf.-Gesch. nach Naturwissensch. und Bibel. Zur Verständigung* (1865) ; and above all, the Prize Essay of TH. ZOLLMANN, *Bibel und Natur in der Harmonie ihrer Offenb.* (2nd ed., 1869) ; O. ZOECKLER, *Die Urgesch. der Erde und d. M.*, in the *Beweis des Glaubens* (1868), pp. 498—614 ; F. H. REUSCH, *Bibel und Natur* (3rd ed., 1870), where at the same time is found a full review of the most recent literature of the question. Add to these, A. F. FUEHRER, *Naturwiss. u. H. Schr.* in W. HOFFMANN'S *Deutschland*, i. (1870), ii. (1871), iv., and J. H. KURTZ, *Bibel und Astron.* (5th ed., 1870).

POINTS FOR INQUIRY.

In what relation do the two accounts of Creation in Genesis stand to each other?—The Theosophic interpretation of Gen. i. 2.—The different ways of understanding the narrative of Creation more nearly examined.—A glance at the principal Cosmogonies of antiquity.—The most important objections adduced against the historic character and credibility of the most ancient document.—The conflict between Theology and Natural Science under the alternate dominion of Orthodoxy and Freethinking.— History and criticism of Optimism, in connection with the doctrine of Creation.

SECTION LIX.—THE PROVIDENCE OF GOD.

That which God has once created remains the object of His continual care, which most rightly is called *Providence* (*fore-seeing*). The existence of this Providence is indubitable, its domain unlimited, its manifestation manifold, and its mode of operation in many respects raised above human comprehension ; but its final aim, the realisation of the Divine plan with regard to the world, and the believing recognition thereof, is of the highest significance, alike for the Theological mode of thinking, and the spiritual life.

---

[10] The world in the highest degree corresponds, and is adapted, to the end which God aims at in creation (Leibnitz).

In treating of this subject, attention must be given separately to the Upholding and the Government of all things by God; without, however, its being needful, in addition to these, to consider under a separate head the Divine Co-operation (*concursus*).

1. With the doctrine of Creation that of Providence is most intimately connected. It is as it were the continuation of the line, of which the first point is afforded in the beginning of all things. The idea implied thereby is already indicated with sufficient clearness by the word itself. In speaking of Providence, we do not think of the foreknowledge of God properly so called; but of His constant care for all that exists, outside of Himself, but still through Him. The word Providence—*πρόνοια*, *providentia*—derived from Gen. xxii. 8, 14, is never used in the New Testament of God, but (twice) of man.[1] The idea, however, is expressed in manifold ways by the poets and prophets of Israel,[2] and is proclaimed with the greatest emphasis in the Scriptures of the New Testament.[3] In accordance therewith we find indeed this belief confessed by the Christian Church of all ages, and even more frequently presupposed than distinctly expressed. Thus in the confession which bears the name of the Apostles' Creed, mention is made of the Creation, but not of Providence; in principle, the confession of the latter is already contained in that of the former. In the Symbolical Writings of the Lutheran Church it is only briefly mentioned, but is treated of more at large in those of the Reformed Church,[4] for this reason amongst others, that it was most intimately connected with the "*cor ecclesiæ;*" but was treated specially from its practical side.

2. The *existence* of the Providence of God is absolutely indisputable. Belief in this truth flows at once from the Supranaturalistic Theistic idea of God. We have here not even to do with a special Christian idea, but with an idea of religion in general, an idea which, rightly regarded, is absolutely inseparable from true religion. For religion presupposes not merely an original, but also a continued and reciprocal relation between God and man. The word Providence moreover—like Supreme Being, Godhead, and other words—is employed even by those who in other respects do not choose to start from Christian conceptions. The recognition of the fact was, and still is, found among enlightened Heathen; and its denial was warmly contested, amongst others, by a Cicero and a Seneca.[5] The noblest of the Greeks, even in their day, were raised above the doctrine of a blind inexorable necessity; and the earliest of the Apologetes—a Lactantius and a Clemens Alexandrinus, for instance,—did not hesitate to rank the opponents of the belief in Providence with the Atheists. Even in times of the boldest unbelief this dogma has held its ground longer than most others;

---

[1] Acts xxiv. 2; Rom. xiii. 14.

[2] Ps. xxxiii. 13—15; Isa. xlv. 7.

[3] Matt. x. 30; John v. 17; Acts xvii. 26, 27.

[4] *Neth. Confess.*, Art. xiii.; *Heid. Cat.*, Answ. 27, 28.

[5] Cic. *De Nat. Deor.*, i. 20, ii. 22. Seneca, *De Providentiâ*. Compare Homer's Διὸς δ'ἐτελείετο βουλή· θεοῦ ἐν γούνασι κεῖται.

it has even found its panegyrists among the assailants of Christianity itself. It was perceived that a God who was indeed a Creator, but cared not for that which was created by Him, would not deserve the name of the highest, the absolutely perfect Being; and—in opposition to every conception of a deistical or pantheistical tendency—all the attributes which are ascribed to His nature were applied also to the work of His Providence.—No wonder, indeed, that the *history*, sacred and profane, of whole nations and particular persons, in the greater and smaller features of their lives, adds confirmation to the same confession. However frequently the leading thread may escape our observation in particular details, in its totality history everywhere displays connection and order, guidance and aim. Not everything in the domain of history can be explained as a merely natural consequence of purely finite causes; phenomena present themselves, in which every one who believes in a living God, feels himself compelled to recognise the power of a higher hand and will. Think, for instance, of so many little unexpected circumstances, out of which an entirely new condition of things has sprung; of the arising of great geniuses in the history of nations, in the domain of science or of the kingdom of God, precisely at those junctures when all was ripe for their mighty influence; of dates—now to speak only of those within the past century—like 1795, 1812, 1848, 1870; above all, think of the fulness of the time (Gal. iv. 4) in connection with the appearing of Christ. Will it be said that chance willed all this just in this order? But chance, as such, *wills* and orders nothing, because it does not think and does not act.—So much the less can this be the last word of our creed, since with the voice of history that of every-day *experience* constantly unites in placing the word Providence in our heart and on our lips.

3. Of this Providence the *domain* is absolutely unlimited. Sometimes, it is true, the small and unimportant has been excluded from the sphere of its action;[6] but without reason. Indeed, the whole antithesis between great and small is but relative, and exists not for the Infinite One. He could not possibly control the great, if the small—so intimately connected therewith—escaped His watchful regard. Yea, precisely herein is the glory of God manifested, that He bows down to that which is least, and is *Maximus in minimo.*[7] Doubt on this point, of which we here and there meet with traces among the ancient Sages, yea, even among Christian "Fathers,"[8] is connected with an anthropomorphistic narrowness; and mockery of this belief—such as is heard, for instance, on the part of a Voltaire, a Bayle, etc.—is simply an irreverent blasphemy of that which is not even understood. The history of Revelation contains the most surprising proofs of the Divine ruling, even in regard to that which is minute and apparently accidental;[9] and the Lord's own word[10] presents to us this wondrous truth in a most consolatory light.

4. The *manifestation* of the Providence of God is manifold, according to

---

[6] Even Cicero, *De Nat. Deor.*, c. lxvi., declared, "The gods care for great things, and are careless about the small:" *Magna Dii curant, parva negligunt.*

[7] Ps. cxiii. 5, 6.

[8] See, *e.g.*, Jerome, *in Habac.* i.

[9] See, for example, 1 Kings xxii. 34; Esther vi. 1; Matt. xxvii. 19; Acts xxiii. 16.

[10] Luke xii. 6, 7.

the nature of its different objects. God's care embraces all things; but not all in the same way, and in like measure. This is the ground for, and the relative justification of, the whole distinction between the general, the particular, and the entirely special Providence of God; of which the first has relation to the whole creation, the second to man, and the last to God's faithful servants and the whole of the Kingdom of God. This distinction may be justified from Holy Scripture,[11] and reason also comprehends that the Living and Holy God must stand in another relation towards rational and moral beings, from that in which He stands towards irrational and non-moral ones. We find thus no reason for regarding, with some, this whole distinction as something purely subjective, or for limiting it merely to the conception that, although God's care is the same for all His creatures, the receptivity for experiencing this care differs on their side. God Himself stood, not only in conception, but also in reality, in a wholly different relation towards Israel, from that which He occupied towards other nations, and manifested His care for the former in an entirely peculiar way.[12]

5. In whatever domain, however, the manifestation of God's Providence takes place, *the manner of its operation* in many respects surpasses human comprehension. We may certainly presuppose in general with regard to it, that it is equally perfect and irreprehensible as God Himself. We may also add, on the authority of the Gospel, that, as God created all things by the Son, so also the Son bears them, *i.e.*, maintains them in existence, by the word of His power.[13] Yet if we now wish to point out in detail *how* God maintains and governs all things, we at once feel the limitation of human thought. Starting from the idea of the Divine Transcendency, three theories have been in turn presented, yet their advocates have been by these very theories involved in serious difficulties. *Occasionalism*—(*systema causarum occasionalium*)—advocated by Des Cartes, Malebranche, Bayle, etc., asserted that God was the immediate and only cause of all that happens; so that the so-called mediate causes simply afforded Him occasions (*occasiones*) of action. *Mechanism*, on the other hand, saw in all that happens the simple consequence of an original force implanted by God in that which is created, which no doubt is also maintained by Him, but through which He operates exclusively, consequently in a purely mediate way, and never immediately. This theory, represented by the Deists, threatens just as much the Divine freedom, as the former in point of fact, in the name of philosophy, annihilates that of man. A middle path between the two was sought and found, especially on the side of Orthodoxy, in the doctrine of the Divine *Co-operation* (*concursus generalis*). This assumes a common activity (*co-operatio*) on the part of God with the mediate causes, whereby, however, the result of these last is made subservient by God to the attainment of His purposes. But this whole conception, even though it admitted of being reduced to perfect clearness, leads of itself away from the idea of a constant help and joint-operation on the part of God, thus conferred upon the creature from without, to a Deistic mode of regarding the relation between God and the world. The difficulties are not diminished, if—attaching the

[11] Matt. vi. 25—32; Ps. xci. 11, 12. [12] Ps. cxlvii. 19, 20; compare Acts xiv. 16, 17.
[13] Heb. i. 3; Col. i. 16, 17.

full weight to the Immanency of God in the world—we seek to realise in our contemplation the manner of God's providential activity. Scarcely have we escaped the rock of Deism, when we see ourselves threatened by that of Pantheism; and necessary as it is duly to distinguish between the law of nature and the will that manifests itself in that law, it is equally impossible to find the exact formula for indicating the intimate connection between the two. If it is thought necessary to separate between the activity of God Himself and the operation of the creature, in order to assure the independence of this latter, we then attain no farther than to the old confession, as expressed by Morus: "*Limites non definiuntur, quousque operetur sol, agricola, et ubi incipiat Deus.*" But even this separate *incipiat* is, upon a full recognition of the Immanency of God, found not to be raised above serious objections.

6. Thus much, however, is fully established, that the *final aim* in the work of Providence can be no other than that in the Creation (§ lv.), so that it is and continues to be God who, according to the profound words of Plato, out of all things "brings forth the better." As opposed to the Empirico-realistic view of the world taken by Naturalism, which in its consequences necessarily leads to the hopelessness of Fatalism, the teleologic-ideal view thus appears in its full lustre, as the ripened fruit of the Christian belief in an ever-living and ever-working Providence of God.—Just as clearly is it apparent that this belief is of the highest *importance*, on account of its close connection with the *doctrine* of Creation, of Prayer, and of Redemption; and with the *life* of gratitude, of patience, and of well-grounded hope for the future, of which the possibility and the power would be wholly lost, if we must abandon the belief in the "almighty and omnipresent power of God, by which He still upholds and governs, as with His own hand, heaven and earth, together with all creatures."

7. Before we more fully discuss this Government, yet a single word as to the doctrine of the Divine *Concursus*, by some again more or less distinguished from that of the Upholding and Government of all things. We understand thereby the co-operation of God with the natural causes of things, by virtue of which these accomplish what according to His counsel and will they must accomplish; especially His influence upon the free acts of men. This notion, already indicated by Clemens Alexandrinus and Thomas Aquinas, was applied and developed especially by the Lutheran and Reformed theologians of the seventeenth century; and even in our own day, De Wette, Twesten, and Ebrard, amongst others, have dwelt particularly thereon in their treatment of the doctrine of Providence. The distinction arose from the desire to recognise a certain independence as belonging to the so-called second causes, and at the same time to guard against the danger of God's being regarded as the author of sin. On this account a distinction was made between the Co-operation in the material and the formal character of the act, and the latter only was admitted where moral evil is committed. But to this praiseworthy end the means do not appear to be happily chosen. For if a certain general influence of God upon all that happens is here thought of, the Co-operation is, properly speaking, already included in the idea of Upholding. Or if it is wished simply to indicate that God has indeed a guiding influence on our actions,

but that it is ever we ourselves who carry them out, we here touch the question as to the connection between God's government and moral freedom, which is better treated of when we discuss the doctrine of the Government of all things. The Co-operation thus belongs to both, and is in a certain sense the higher unity of the two. We have nothing against the thing implied, but a great deal against the method of discussing the subject as a particular subdivision of the doctrine of Providence. As such it has been—not wholly without justice—named by Strauss, "the abortion of a barbarous metaphysics."

Compare LANGE's Art. *Vorsehung* in Herzog, *R. E.*, and the literature there presented. On the word Πρόνοια, SUICER, *Thesaurus*, in voce. On the subject, E. A. BORGER, *De historiæ doctore, providentiæ divinæ administro* (1817); and, among the Dogmatists, especially TWESTEN, *l. l.* ii. 1, p. 98, *sqq.*

POINTS FOR INQUIRY.

Wherein consists the "detestable error of the Epicureans"?—What becomes of the idea of Providence from the standpoint of Deism and of Pantheism?—Is the Israelitish and the Christian idea of Providence in every respect the same?—Is the history of the world also not sufficiently explicable without this idea?—History and criticism of the doctrine of the *Concursus.*

SECTION LX.—THE UPHOLDING OF ALL THINGS.

The Upholding (*Conservatio*) of all things is that operation of God's will, by which He maintains in existence and order the whole organism of the creation, and its particular parts, so long as it pleases Him. The certainty of this continued care is guaranteed by the Christian idea of God itself; its necessity is founded in the nature of finite things, and the manner in which it displays itself proclaims a majesty of God, which redounds to His glorification.

1. Creation and Upholding, however closely connected, are nevertheless distinct from each other. To the former the Universe owes its origin: to the latter its continued existence. The Creation is the original operation of God's omnipotence: the Upholding, the continued act of God's faithfulness. The latter has been termed a *continuous* creation, and with justice, in so far as there is thereby indicated that the Universe continues to exist only by means of the same power which called all things into being. But behind this continuous act there remains the *original* creating as something distinct, and we must carefully see to it that the one idea is not sacrificed to the other. From the Deistic standpoint

Creation and Upholding are arbitrarily separated the one from the other: God creates the world, but it upholds itself by its own inherent power. From the Pantheistic standpoint, on the other hand, Creation and Upholding are confused the one with the other; that which exists continues in existence, but one cannot speak of creating, properly so called. From the Theistic standpoint alone, as well the difference as the close connection between the two, receives its due recognition.

2. By the Upholding we understand something distinct from the Government of the world. The notion of the latter is more extensive; but it is not therefore useless (as Scholten supposes) to devote attention separately to the former. In the sight of God undoubtedly the one includes the other; but for our power of thought the distinction is necessary. "The Upholding as such," as Lange justly observes, "secures the natural existence and order of the world: the Government secures the ideality of its progress [correspondence to the Divine ideal]." By the former we mean, not only that God *allows* the world to continue in existence—that He does not put an end to its existence—but more, that He *causes* it to continue in existence; in other words, that He aims at and effects by His almighty will its continued existence. This activity has regard, from the nature of the case, as well to the whole organism of Creation (*nexus cosmicus*), as to each particular part. What would be the use of the maintenance of the whole, without that of the parts, and *vice versâ ?* The one and the other remains in existence and order, *so long as it pleases Him*, *i.e.*, so long as it corresponds to its destination. "So long," in the words of Rothe, "as the result of the existence of the creature is the glory of God, His good-pleasure can rest upon it; and if this truly rests upon it, it is preserved." The partial, or even the entire, disappearance of some orders of creatures can prove absolutely nothing against the doctrine which we are here discussing.

3. The *certainty* of this upholding of all things by God is, according to the utterances of Holy Scripture, firmly established.[1] Even where mention is made of second causes only, He is usually exalted as the Master-builder of all that takes place in the creation. He not only stands transcendentally above the world, but is immanent in the world, with His all-pervading power. No power of nature, however formidable, could come into operation, except it were every moment determined in its course by His almighty will. Because God is the Living One, He cannot be anything less than the fountain of life for all His creatures.[2] This by no means contradicts that which we read of the eternal sabbath-rest of God;[3] of which already Isaiah testified[4] that this was to be understood in a sense worthy of God. Even for the properly developed mind of man, rest and inactivity are by no means words of the same import; and He who was called God's highest image on earth, worked so long as it was day for Him.[5] The resting of God only says that He now ceased to create entirely new sorts of beings, since He placed in those already created the

---

[1] Ps. civ. 29, 30; cxix. 90; Matt. vi. 26—30.
[2] Ps. xxxvi. 9; John v. 17.
[3] Gen. ii. 3; Heb. iv. 9—11.
[4] Isa. xl. 28.
[5] John ix. 4.

power of continuing, and continually preserves them. To what extent the creative activity of God is manifesting itself perhaps at this very moment in some other sphere, is absolutely unknown to us. But here He continues to uphold all things by the word of His power, and all that lives continues to live, solely in Him.

4. The absolute *necessity* for this Upholding is based on the nature of finite things. The Universe is no mechanical work of art; but a living organism, which continues to exist only in unceasing communion with the Ever-living One. The Egyptian Pyramid, once raised by man, can defy the course of the ages, without being constantly supported by the hand of the founder; but the branch torn from the parent trunk, and cast on the earth, droops and withers: not the former, but the latter, is the meet image for representing the created world. Think of this dependence of the Cosmos as not being, and conceive to yourself that it continues to exist by its own strength, like a colony which, dissevered from the mother-country, continues to develop itself: this colony might rival in glory the mother-state, the world might assert its claims as against God; in other words, Deism necessarily leads to Dualism. The objection, "whether the world is then so imperfect as to call for a continual care from above, in order that it may continue to exist," would have some significance, only if it should appear that the world was originally intended to stand wholly by itself, but was afterwards seen to be incapable of doing so. The question here is not what world would seem to us, regarded altogether in the abstract, to be the most perfect; but what world the reality presents to our view, when we look to it in the light of faith.

5. To the question, *how* and in what manner God upholds all things, no perfectly satisfactory answer can be given. God's word in Holy Scripture gives no positive hints with regard thereto; nor has enlightened reason any power here to say anything really decisive. Neither is it necessary, in order to continue to believe on good grounds that God maintains all things in existence, that we should be able wholly to review and point out the ways and means employed by Him. That God here works by the word of His will, and without its costing Him any trouble or effort, scarcely needs to be suggested to the mind of the reader.[6] It is also manifest to us, upon an attentive observation, accompanied with sustained reflection, that God upholds things in a manner differing according to their different nature. Lifeless objects accordingly without their co-operation; living, but irrational, beings with their co-operation, but without their consciousness; rational and moral beings under the condition of voluntary co-operation on their part. Of some—plants, animals, men,—God maintains the species; of others—the luminaries of our planetary system,—the number once created. As a rule, He does so—so far as we can see—by means; man, for instance, by strengthening his vital forces; these forces, by food supplied by plants; the plants, by dew and rain; this rain, by the sun—and here we stop: shall we on this account at once pronounce the word, *im*mediately? We can do so only as indicating the undeniable fact that here no *known* means are applied, though we presuppose, not without reason, that the mediate way is followed

[6] Ps. cxlv. 15, 16.

in this case too. In order, however, to lay down the principle that God *cannot* immediately sustain any creature, one must first limit in an arbitrary manner His omnipotence and sovereignty; and at least openly contradict the testimony of Holy Scripture, in its account, for instance, of the sustenance of the widow and her son.[7] The causal connection is often spoken of in our day in a tone which would lead one to suppose that only during the last few years it had been discovered that a countless series of causes and consequences connects finite things; and assuredly the language of Holy Scripture differs not a little from that of the modern view in this respect. While the former proceeds from, and ends in God, the other goes no farther than nearer or more remote causes, and pursues their series until it comes to a stand at an unknown *x*. Yet even this difference involves no irreconcilable conflict, so long as we simply continue to remember that, as Wolleb has it, "*providentia causas secundas non tollit, sed ponit.*" The Scripture does not fail to recognise the existence of second causes; and reason cannot possibly explain all things from these alone. Thus, even in the Upholding of all things, God respects the causal connection appointed by Himself; but has in no case unconditionally bound Himself thereto. Further, the whole work of upholding testifies—for him who traces it a little in detail, even though it be only in a single domain—of a wisdom, solicitude, and tender-hearted fidelity, which unceasingly calls forth and justifies the Psalmist's exalted strain of praise.[8] Especially when we place the Upholding of a sinful world in the light of God's holiness, does it become the fruit and manifestation of a grace surpassing all praise.

6. The doctrine of the Upholding of all things is of essential importance for the Religious and Christian life. It is especially a powerful counteractive against any merely mechanical way of regarding the world, and not less against that proud sense of self-sufficiency which is fatal to a life in true communion with God. Only a God who continues to stand in actual relationship to the world can we love and trust; the Creator we can adore, but only the Upholder can we every moment thank, and from Him look for that which is wanting in ourselves. For, as Luther truly says, "He is not like an architect who, when he has built a house, or ship, or other work, straightway takes his departure and asks no more about it; but He abides with His work. He loves the creatures, and animates, moves, and sustains them each one after its own fashion." "He who feeds His birds, shall He ever forget His children?" There is danger of this doctrine being abused, only when it is forgotten that the care of God is regularly connected with the use of the means appointed by Him. Properly used, it implants a holy freedom from care, a deep feeling of dependence, but also a living sense of obligation to devote every gift and power to the glorifying of Him by whom it is conferred and preserved.

Comp. P. HOFSTEDE DE GROOT, *Theol. Nat.*, ed. 4a (1861), pp. 154—177, and the literature there given; J. I. DOEDES, *Oud en Nieuw* (1865), pp. 44—48; our *Leerrede* on the *Heidelberg Catechism*, 10th and 50th Sundays, (2nd ed., 1872); CALVIN, *l. l.*, i. 16.

---

[7] 1 Kings xvii. 8–16.

[8] Ps. xxxvi. 5.

POINTS FOR INQUIRY.

Is the definition of the Upholding as a *creatio continuata* an absolutely pure one?—Explanation of Acts xvii. 25—28.—Is there still room for miracles, in connection with a thoughtful belief in the Upholding of all things by God?—What attributes of God's nature are especially manifested in the Divine work of Upholding all things?

SECTION LXI.—THE DIVINE GOVERNMENT.

The Government of all things is that operation of God's will, whereby—as Lord over His own works—He sovereignly and freely controls at once the whole organism of Creation and its particular parts; and in such wise makes it minister to the accomplishment of His exalted aims, that the final event is nothing else than the fulfilment of His eternal counsel. In the domain of this Divine Government an inexorable Fate is just as little to be thought of as is Chance, or mere Will and Pleasure; all, on the contrary, is the revelation of the highest freedom, resulting in the maintenance of an eternal order. In the recognition of such an independent Divine Government, faith finds—through the consequent possibility of Miracles, and of the Hearing of Prayer—on the one hand its immovable foundation, and on the other its natural limit.

1. That which God upholds, He at the same time controls and governs, and so much is this latter here the main idea, that it frequently even bears exclusively the name of Providence. The government of God embraces as well Creation in general, as Man—his experiences and his actions—in particular. In this place we confine ourselves exclusively to the former, and ask, what is *meant*, what is *denied*, and what is *asserted* by the confession that God *rules*.

2. In speaking of God's Government, we say, in other words, that God is and remains Lord in His own creation; so that not the least thing happens therein upon which He did not count. That the whole of Scripture really teaches such a Divine Government needs not to be proved. The very thought, "The Lord will not do good, neither will He do evil," is there repelled as blasphemous, and the opposite thereof proclaimed in every way.[1] He even, who does not believe in this government, cannot deny that it is taught in the Scriptures of the Old and New Testament. Equally clear is it that the government of God there revealed embraces not simply the great whole, but also every one of its parts; so that by the final issue of

---

[1] Ps. xciii., xcvii.; Isa. xlv. 7, *sqq.*

things, God's counsel is in no case made void, but, on the contrary, gloriously fulfilled.[2] While this may indeed in many respects appear to us incomprehensible, we feel at once that the opposite would be absurdity itself. But what here must be least of all overlooked is, that in the government of the world is revealed not only the operation of God's power, but also—and above all—of God's holy *will*. The former is recognised even from the Naturalistic standpoint, and the confession that God rules signifies on this side nothing else than that, although there be temporary interruption, the eternal order of nature continues to determine the course of events; for God is here nothing but the sum of the powers of nature. From the Christian-theistic standpoint we confess, on the other hand, that God works all things after the counsel of His own will;[3] in other words, that He is not dissolved into, but rules over, the work of His own hands. Modern Naturalism knows only a God who is, in the words of Heine, "bound hand and foot," and who "troubles Himself about nothing." Belief in Revelation renders homage to one who is Sovereign, alike over every part of the Cosmos, and over the whole, who can do and does what pleases Him, after the counsel of His own wisdom and love.

3. If it is asked whether we can triumphantly prove the reality of such Divine Government, to the satisfaction of absolutely every one, we have to give a negative answer. It is with the Government as with the Upholding of all things; it cannot be *proved*, but simply *indicated*, and this even only under certain conditions, above all of a psychological nature. One may mention a thousand surprising facts, and quivering with admiration, point out in them the finger of God; yet he who does not proceed from a tacit admission of the Supranaturalistic Theistic idea of God will nevertheless either take his stand at natural causes, or end with the confession of his ignorance, but in either case refuse to proceed one step further. In reality the inference, "Here God has intervened," is in any case a transition, a bound into another sphere, which one will avoid, so long as he is decidedly disinclined to it. But thus much can be proved, that everything impels us to take this bound, that this alone bears us to solid ground, and that he who refuses to take it gropes in far denser mist than we. Certainly he who does not acknowledge the Government of God in the sense indicated, is forced to believe that all things in the long run govern themselves, and that thus the most wonderful order is the natural consequence of—what? We esteem it not only more consolatory, but also more intelligent, still to believe with sacred antiquity that there is even "no evil in a city" which has not been sent by the Lord;[4] in other words, that the course of events not only *has been* set in order by Him once for all, but *is being* constantly guided and governed by Him.

4. From this standpoint is naturally denied the doctrine of an inexorable *Fate*—"the interwoven succession of causes"[5]—and the Fatalism based thereupon; according to which everything takes place by virtue of a blind but inevitable necessity of nature, which is superior alike to gods and men. Fatalism manifested itself, in the ancient world, now as Astrology, among

---

[2] Isa. xlvi. 10.
[3] Ephes. i. 11.
[4] Lam. iii. 38; Amos iii. 6.
[5] "*Series implexa causarum*" (Seneca).

the Chaldæans ; now as Philosophy, among the Greeks ; later as Religion and Theology, among the Islamites. Ever again the old Stoical dilemma of which already Cicero speaks : "If thou art destined to recover from this sickness, thou wilt recover, whether thou sendest for the physician or not."[6] This Fatalism is the natural consequence of the denial of Supranaturalistic Theism, and is usually associated with the Pantheism of the present day. From this standpoint the government of the world is "not the determination of the world's course by an intellect beyond the world ; but by the reason immanent in the powers and relations of the world itself" (Strauss). How any intelligible sense is to be attached to the word "reason" in this connection, we leave others to make out; but it is certain that those who thus conceive of the world would do infinitely better no longer to speak of Providence and the Government of the world. As with Materialism, so modern Naturalism can only by means of a happy inconsistency escape from the power of Fatalism with its theoretical and practical consequences. On the other hand, it is a sign of the truth and genuineness of our Theism, that it rises to the honest recognition of the Divine freedom.

5. Neither can we regard as successful the endeavours which have been made—while acknowledging an all-embracing government of the world on the part of God—to retain beside this an independent place for *Chance* (*fortuna*) properly so called. The attempt has been made, *e.g.*, by Ebrard, to point out a region of objective contingency, for instance, in the domain of meteorology or of botany; and certainly we cannot here speak of caprice, or the relative freedom of living creatures, such as is to be observed, for example, in the animal world. It is easy to mention a number of events which take place, and which one supposes could as well not have taken place, or have taken place in an entirely different manner. But it very soon becomes apparent that this multitude of so-called casual and accidental events and conditions is to be observed, not only in the lower spheres, but also in the higher; and that a realm of actual contingencies, be it larger or smaller, would destroy the unity of creation, perhaps even render impossible the development and execution of God's counsel. Holy Scripture, moreover, most distinctly denies the existence of such a series of absolutely contingent events,[7] and to be consistent one must assert that either all or nothing is accidental. The whole idea of chance has a simply subjective significance, and must be regarded exclusively as the fruit of the narrowness of the human range of vision. It is true, so-called accidents are frequently of such overwhelming influence, that the well-known expression, "Accident rules the world," may appear wholly justified. But in reality there is no other contingency than in the sense in which the whole world must be called contingent (*contingens*) ; nothing is isolated,—all stands and serves in its own place. Unbelief speaks of blind Fortune, faith confesses "Nothing by accident, and nothing without an aim."

6. And thus also no mere *Will and Pleasure*. In maintaining the doc-

---

[6] Si fatum tibi est, ex hoc morbo convalescere, sive Medicum adhibueris, sive non, convalesces (Cicero, *De Fato*).

[7] Prov. xvi. 33 ; Matt. x. 29.

trine of the Government of the world, we maintain also the freedom of God, as the infinite capacity for Himself determining His actions in such a way as is demanded by, and is in harmony with, His morally-perfect nature. How far, at the same time, this freedom is removed from that which is usually termed caprice, we have already pointed out (§ xlix. 5). Here we would only remind the reader that the last-named idea, instead of exalting God, degrades Him as deeply as possible. For all caprice is the play of humour, without one's taking counsel of anything but this, and reveals a being who does not govern his own will, but allows himself to be governed by his will. If—to bring the question actually into connection with this point—no other view of the world were possible than that which rests upon the presupposition of arbitrary will, we ourselves should be the first to reject that view as absurd.

7. In point of fact, however, we see belief in Miracles and in the Hearing of Prayer legitimated precisely by the acknowledgment of God's government of the world. It can be no matter of surprise to us that the twofold question here raised—although upon a superficial view belonging to another province—is by many treated of in immediate connection with the Providence of God; in reality it forms only a subordinate part of this vast whole. As far as miracle is concerned, we have already learnt to recognise it as an extraordinary and direct—but not on that account by any means arbitrary—operation and intervention of God in the course of finite things (§ xxxii. i. 5). And now of two things one: Either the law of nature and the will of God is absolutely the same thing, and then let us be consistent Pantheists; or the two are distinct, and then at least the possibility of miracles is assured. He who in his heart says to the Infinite One, "Thou canst not upon any single point of Creation suspend the law of gravity ordained by Thee; Thou canst not direct a single ray of light otherwise than is prescribed in Thine own laws; Thou canst not avert from me any disaster which must befal me in the ordinary course of things,"—this man believes not in a Personal God. It is thus not enough that one should be willing to admit the possibility of miracles; no, it must be joyfully assented to, not as questionable fact, but as a matter on account of which to glorify God. He who regards a miracle as inconceivable, maintains, not the unchangeableness of God, but His rigid immobility; and forbids Him, in the name of his logic, even the slightest manifestation of *grace*. "The action of the laws of nature is ruled by God; they are in His power, and are so elastic that He can by means of them take away at any moment the existence of every being in the world" (Rothe).—If this is the case, there is thus also no reason for doubting the possibility of the answering of prayer in the proper sense of the word; *i.e.*, not simply of a psychological effect of prayer, but also a metaphysical one (§ xxvii. 5), in consequence of which God grants, in accordance with and through prayer, in particular circumstances, particular issues willed by Him. The mystery of the answering of prayer is, in other words, that of freedom in the presence of an order which is eternal, but not on that account a rigid order. Just as man's own actions (§ lxii.), so must his prayers, be regarded as a factor in the hand of God's government of the world. Whether God will and ought to hear a particular prayer, and for what reason so frequently the very opposite

takes place, is a question which may here safely remain unanswered. It is enough if the possibility is assented to, that God, if He pleases, can do, also in answer to prayer, beyond not only our asking, but even our thinking. That the Scripture everywhere presupposes, not only the possibility, but also the absolute certainty of His doing so, is evident as well from other places as, more particularly, from those in which it so frequently enjoins the duty of intercession *for others*, of which there can be no serious thought from a Naturalistic point of view. From that standpoint all the force in the well-known maxim, "*Ora et labora*," falls more and more upon the last member alone.

8. On the other hand, belief in miracles and the answering of prayer finds here its ineffaceable *limit*. God can do all that He wills, but He cannot will all that is possible. Miracles are conceivable which cannot take place; prayers, which cannot be answered, because—although possible in the abstract—they are morally impossible. The causal connection is not indeed the chain by which God has bound Himself, but it *is* the systematic order in which He wills that things should present themselves. Departure therefrom is conceivable only in the interests of the moral order of the world, because this is the higher. The concr e possibility of miracles thus exists solely where it is possible that a holy and gracious God can will this. The same must be said of the granting of particular wishes and prayers; on this account also the petition, "Thy will be done," remains in every case the final and deepest utterance of the devout spirit. Where, however, the moral conditions of being heard are present, the possibility thereof in particular cases cannot seriously be doubted, or one will very soon learn no longer to pray in time of distress, and when it is over will be ready indeed to congratulate himself, but will no longer give thanks from the heart; for who thanks a blind course of nature? Order is something glorious and sacred; but only where *in*, and *beside*, and if necessary *above* Order, is recognised the Freedom of God, can one continue to speak of an adorable Government of God.

Compare, besides the literature referred to, page 135, and § lix., A. T. REITSMA, *Voor en tegen de moderne Theologie* (1861); E. GUEDER, *Ueber das Wunder* (1868); O. FLUEGEL, *Das Wunder und die Erkennbarkeit Gottes* (1870); ROTHE, *Dogm.* (1870), i., § xlvii.

POINTS FOR INQUIRY.

Is there sufficient ground for actually distinguishing the Government of all things from the Upholding of all things?—The opposition between the Supranaturalistic and the Naturalistic conception of Government of the world.—Fatalism in its different forms.—The conception of the fortuitous more nearly criticised.—To what extent may the objections to the doctrine of a particular answer to prayer be satisfactorily solved?

SECTION LXII.—THE DIVINE GOVERNMENT.

(*Continuation.*)

As the Divine Government extends to the whole Creation, so does it most definitely extend to the life, the experiences, and deeds of men; which are either willed or permitted by God, but in either case are to be regarded as links in the chain of His adorable plan of the world. Thus the history of Mankind becomes alike the work and the ministry of God's Providence; without, however, the freedom of the individual man being thereby annihilated. The decree of God, on the contrary, provides for the free action of man as a rational and moral being; and the science of faith justly rejects every mode of conception whereby one of the two factors of the world's history is degraded to a purely imaginary power, and the utterance, either of the religious or of the moral feeling, is denied.

1. What has hitherto been taught as to God's government in general, has naturally its more particular application to the world of men, as the theatre and workplace of the Providence of God. Yet as well the importance as the difficulty of the subject demands that we should devote some time to the special study thereof.

2. That the government of God, while extending to all things, especially extends to man and humanity, is beyond all doubt. Even the unique place which man occupies in creation, leads us to suppose that he is the special object of Divine providence.[1] Moreover, the peculiar constitution of man, as a rational and moral being, renders especial guidance necessary. The material world is the domain of necessity, regulated by eternal laws; the moral, that of freedom, conferred by God Himself, but precisely on that account also to be guided by God Himself. History and experience moreover constantly afford us the most striking proofs that "the way of man is not in himself."[2] It is sufficient here to mention the names of a Joseph, a Moses, a David. No one's career is seen in the long run to be entirely his own work; and the sense of unlimited dependence, confessed by the most illustrious men,[3] is not simply the utterance of pious feeling, but the fruit of an attentive observance of life.

3. The limits of this domain of Providence necessarily extend as well to the fate, as to the acts of men. Birthplace and sphere of labour,[4] good and evil in our lot,[5] length of life, and manner of death,[6] all is determined by

---

[1] Matt. vi. 25—32.
[2] Jer. x. 23.
[3] Ps. cxxvii. 1; Heb. vi. 3; James iv. 15.
[4] Acts xvii. 26.
[5] Job ii. 10.
[6] Dan. v. 23; Acts xiii. 36.

higher wisdom. [In the Standards also of the Netherlands Reformed Church the same thing is expressed.[7]] In like manner, according to the constant teaching of Holy Scripture, have we to recognise the hand of God as well in the good as in the evil that is wrought by men.[8]

4. Yet it will soon become apparent, upon a little reflection, that God's government does not stand entirely *in the same* relation to the acts, as to the experience of men. Where man experiences anything, be it pleasant or unpleasant, he is usually passive; where, on the other hand, he effects something, he shows himself acting just as he himself chooses; and the great question with which we have here to do, thus becomes the question as to the connection between the guidance of Providence and the so-called free activity of men: a question indeed of the first importance in regard to the whole domain of religion and morality, but at the same time—from the nature of the case—so intricate, that here, least of all, will it be out of place to remind the inquirer that we must be content, "if we are disciples of Christ, to learn that alone which He points out to us in His Word, without overstepping these limits" (Netherlands Confession). If even in this way no absolutely complete solution is to be expected, yet we need not wholly grope in the dark, provided only we regard the great problem from a Christian Theistic standpoint, in the combined light of Holy Scripture and of the experience of a spiritual life.

5. As well natural evil, that of suffering, as spiritual evil, that of sin, takes place under the control of Providence. Nevertheless, as we have already begun to observe, this government stands in by no means the same relation to the one as to the other. God may in His wisdom *will* (*i.e.*, approve) that I should endure the severest sufferings; but He can never will (approve) that I should commit the smallest sin; since He, the All-wise, is also the Holy and Righteous One. God is not only the highest causality, but at the same time the highest possible moral perfection. The evil apprehended by the senses, however painful, may be a relative good; moral evil, however specious, remains unconditionally evil, and the two cannot possibly proceed in the same sense from the Infinite One.

6. Moral evil, moreover, cannot possibly be willed of God, in the same sense as moral good. He unconditionally wills the latter, and where, in this way anything good is performed, from Him is the opportunity, the desire, the power, and the blessing. But who can have the courage seriously to repeat all this of that which is morally evil? Only he who forgets to regard evil in the light in which it must above all be regarded, in the infallible light of conscience. Loudly does the conscience proclaim that sin renders us guilty and deserving of punishment; but also that God cannot therefore possibly will that which He Himself condemns and punishes. Notwithstanding all the difficulties which present themselves for our thought in connection with a sharp line of distinction between the *permitting*, and the *will* of God, this distinction must be emphatically maintained in the study of the present question, and that in the interest,

---

[7] *Confessio Belgica*, Art. xiii.; *Heidelb. Catech.*, answer 27.

[8] Phil. ii. 13; Acts iv. 27, 28.

alike of a pure Christian conception of God, and of the positive demand of the conscience. On this account, as early as the time of Augustine, it was declared, "nothing takes place without the Almighty One willing it, either by suffering it to be done, or by Himself doing it."[9] God allows the evil to take place, but He does not on that account will (approve) that which in long-suffering He endures. In no case can He have willed moral evil in itself, not even as a means of bringing about the morally good—unless we should dare to apply to Him the word of the Apostle in Rom. iii. 8—but He can only, where it has already arisen and continues to exist, take it up as a link in the chain of His plan of the world.[10] To the question: Whence, nevertheless, moral evil? no answer can be given, except that *what God absolutely wills not, but, on the contrary, hates and punishes, He could not wholly have prevented, without annihilating that human freedom, willed and conferred by Himself.* When He has once—we shall return to this subject presently—when He has once conferred upon man the perilous privilege of comparatively free self-determination, Omnipotence itself cannot arrest the consequences of this gift, without at the same time destroying its own work. God wills the good unconditionally; but only the good voluntarily wrought, because without that, it does not deserve the name of moral good. Where now freedom of choice is given, the possibility of resistance is also granted. We may, for this reason, speak in a very sound sense of God's self-limitation by the creation of rational and moral beings, provided we never forget that this self-limitation is a relative and voluntary one, and in the end conducive to a higher self-manifestation. God can do all that He will, but does not on that account will all that in the abstract He can do. Voltaire's word of unbelief and mockery, "We are the puppets of Providence,"[11] is equally dishonouring to Him as to man. He did not desire Automata, because He wished to found a moral kingdom; but this freedom conceded to a finite being, brings in of itself the possibility of an abuse of freedom, which He at most can only endure, but never enjoin.

7. Moral evil, just as little willed by God as by irresistible force prevented, was by Him foreseen, permitted, and in various ways limited. Here especially it is of importance not to lose sight of the important distinction between the Foreknowledge and the Decree of God. However closely connected, even in the language of the New Testament, they are yet by no means the same. All that is an object of God's decree is naturally an object also of His foreknowledge; but we cannot on that account say that God has thus unconditionally willed all that He has foreseen. It is easy to speak of this whole distinction as baseless and arbitrary, but one must surely know that he who without any restriction rejects it, makes God the author of sin, yea, the sinner, κατ' ἐξοχήν. At such a price, we confess, the logical unity of our reasoning in this domain seems to us too dearly bought, since the entire destruction of morality would thus become inevitable. He who has once discovered this secret of Intellectualism,

[9] "Non fit aliquid, nisi Omnipotens velit, vel sinendò ut fiat, vel ipse faciendo" (Aug.) Compare Ps. lxxxi. 11, 12; Rom. i. 24—28.
[10] James i. 13.
[11] "Nous sommes les marionettes de la Providence."

that the whole notion of sin has for God no objective significance, would be folly incarnate if he should be concerned for a single moment about a single sin; his so-called repentance becomes an ungrateful and unbelieving failure to recognise the inevitable ordination of God with regard to the world, to which it would be far better to resign oneself without contradiction. He who shrinks from this immoral conclusion must admit that God may have foreseen a fact or action, without having on this account determined or ordained it. The act does not in this case take place because it is foreseen, but it is foreseen because as a free action it will take place. It is permitted without hindrance; but permission and fore-ordination are two different things. As soon as this is overlooked, the idea of causality necessarily gives place to that of fatality; and one passes over the bridge of Monism into the open arms of Pantheism.

Scripture also everywhere presupposes and proclaims that that which is evil, not only *ought* to have been different, but also *could* have been so. For him who denies this, places like Ps. lxxxi. 13; Matt. xi. 20-24; xxiii. 37; Luke xix. 41, 42, are absolutely inexplicable. The most orthodox Theologians of the Reformed Church also, both in earlier and later times, have admitted the relative justice of the idea of permission; while others, spite of themselves, have been compelled very soon to call to their help again that which they had at first rejected. Hence the dogmatic distinction between *voluntas efficiens* and *permittens;* the conception of the *permissio* in the sense of *non impeditio*, not *actio* but *abstinentia ab actione.* Well known indeed and generally assented to are the words of Calvin: "*Cadit Adam, moderante divinâ Providentiâ, sed suo vitio cadit.*"[12] Even Augustine declared with regard to the Divine will: "*Non sic tamen ut iis (=hominibus) adimat liberum arbitrium, quo vel bene vel male utentes, justissime judicentur.*"[13] From these citations it becomes apparent with what slight show of justice Determinism is placed by many in the present day without reserve upon a level with the doctrine of Predestination as held by the Reformed Church. According to the doctrine alike of Scripture and of the Church, man must be held responsible, not indeed for his destiny, but certainly for his own acts. How far indeed God is from willing evil as such, is evident from the undeniable fact, that, on the contrary, He—as is proved by a number of witnesses in the sacred history[14]—in various ways restrains it; and to this fact the conscience of every one bears testimony.

8. The evil which God in His prescience foresees, and—where He does not restrain it—in His long-suffering endures, is by His righteousness punished, and by His wisdom and love made to work together for good. To such an extent it may be said that God wills the sin, in so far as, where it already exists, He employs it as a means of punishment and discipline,[15] and constantly so directs its course as that it shall ultimately subserve the cause of that which is good. The experience of Joseph, with regard to his

---

[12] "Adam's fall was under the control of Divine Providence, but nevertheless he fell *by his own fault.*"

[13] "Not, however, in such a way as to deprive them, *i.e.*, mankind, of free-will, in regard to which—as they use it well or badly—they will be most righteously judged."

[14] Gen. xx. 6; xxxi. 24; xxxvii. 22; 1 Sam. xxv. 32—34.

Rom. i. 24—28

brethren, is constantly repeated in a variety of forms.[16] Naturally the immoral character of the action itself is not thereby changed. For the merit of an action is never determined by the result, which usually lies beyond our control, but by its principle and its motive alone. *Peccatum per se, sc. naturâ suâ, Deum afficit contumeliâ, gloriæ autem Dei inservit per accidens*"[17] (Ursinus). The rejection of Christ remains in itself the most terrible sin: but nevertheless there is brought in precisely thereby the highest blessing, salvation for a lost world.

9. In no case is there cause to fear that, where thus relative freedom is left to man, it will ultimately be in his power to frustrate God's plan of the world. For the evil bears in its own bosom the seeds of disunion and dissolution,[18] and finds to this extent alike its curb and its corrective in itself. The good, on the other hand, has in itself a principle of life and incorruptibility, and comes to the desired development through its very conflict with evil. But, the case being so, there can also be no doubt but the result of the world's history will—under the guidance of the spotlessly Holy One—be the triumph, not of the evil, but of the morally good. Although the possibility of an everlasting resistance against God cannot be denied,[19] yet the dominion of evil as a hostile power in the Kingdom of God will be ultimately annihilated; while, so long as it yet continues, it is compelled to become subservient to the cause of the good, even where for a time it is hurtful to it. The evil has its time; the good, time and eternity before it; since God and the good is one. To such an extent—but also to such an extent only—can the believing Christian, in looking back upon former wanderings, reckon these also among the things which God has made to work together for good,[20] and even the "*O felix culpa*"[21] of the Christian Father has its deep significance; although a deed, concerning which faith acknowledges that it has been unexpectedly overruled for good, is nevertheless constantly condemned by the conscience as something evil, upon which conscience looks back not without the deepest shame. An example of this is Paul, where shortly before his death he looks back upon his blindness and his conversion.[22]

10. This triumph, however, of the good over the bad is wrought by God, without His degrading man to the level of a mere instrument, and in this special feature is revealed the glory of His government of the world. It is true the freedom of man is on all sides limited by God; the freedom of choice is subject to manifold influences, of which not one is exerted without a higher guidance; and even where the act of choice is free, the freedom of action is frequently limited by circumstances of which the number and the bearing lies wholly beyond the domain of human calculation. But limited

---

[16] Gen. l. 20; comp. Acts iv. 27, 28; viii. 1—4; Phil. i. 12—14.

[17] "Sin of itself, *i.e.*, by its own nature, dishonours God; it is only by that which is non-essential to it that it brings glory to Him."

[18] Matt. xii. 25.

[19] Matt. xii. 32.

[20] Rom. viii. 28.

[21] Augustine's exclamation in reference to the fall: "O happy transgression, which called forth so great a Redeemer!"

[22] 1 Tim. i. 13—16.

freedom is after all by no means unfreedom and compulsion, and man has in reality the perilous privilege of being able to will or do that which God wills not, but forbids. Yet precisely in this fact is apparent the sovereignty, and at the same time the wisdom and compassion, of God, that even out of the snares of evil, into which the sinner falls, He weaves together the threads into the texture of His government of the world. God does not, as it were, annihilate sin at a blow, but allows it to annihilate itself after it has fulfilled its bond-service in the kingdom of freedom. "Inasmuch as God has willed freedom, He has willed also the possibility of sin; but this only because the impossibility of sin, which exists in Himself, must also be developed in the free agents whom He has called to His kingdom of love, by a free determination of choice made in His strength and grace" (Lange). For the determinist we feel that there can be, properly speaking, no question of a revelation of God's glory. For from this standpoint God is no longer the Supreme Will, at every moment directing all things, but the Supreme Power, from eternity deciding, or rather having decided, all things, which carries out its own decree, or, more properly speaking, has nothing to direct, because all is already fixed. The consequence in the sphere of morals is self-evident, and cannot be escaped, so long as one is not delivered from the bondage of an abstract logical Intellectualism. Even where this tendency presents itself as an Ethical determinism, we can only regard the matter as essentially the same. Ethical determinism is, properly regarded, just as inconceivable as wooden iron, or a square circle. He who truly takes his start from an Ethical principle must recognise the right of a relatively free self-determination; but at the same time maintain that God realises His plan with regard to the world, notwithstanding, or rather by means of, the unfettered actions of men, and herein brings about the triumph of that manifold wisdom spoken of in Ephesians iii. 10.

11. We must, after what has been said, conclude that the precise formula for the defining of the connection between Divine causality and human freedom has not yet been discovered. Nothing is easier than, proceeding from the Theological principle, to deny the freedom of man; or, choosing Anthropology as a starting-point, to limit the sovereignty of God: but the exact boundary-line between the one domain and the other can be drawn only in thought. For we have here to take into account, as well that which we believe in regard to God, as that which we discover in ourselves; and it has been said, not without reason, even the liberty of man is not less entirely an object of belief than Providence itself. In thought we can continue indefinitely the two lines—human and Divine—without their meeting; it is only in actual life that we meet with points at which they ever again touch; and while perfect harmony assuredly exists for the *knowledge* of God, it exists only for the *faith* of man. Yet it must be by no means overlooked that autonomy in the domain of thought does not present an insoluble difficulty in the domain of spiritual experience. The more man lives in communion with God, the more the opposition between Liberty and Necessity is resolved into a higher harmony. In the Son of man we see liberty manifest itself in the form of voluntary dependence; and the more one is led by His spirit, the less will he speak of

freedom beyond and as distinguished from God, or regard dependence upon Him as incompatible in principle with a rightly defined liberty. The assertion therefore has perhaps been too strong, when it has been said that the higher unity of the two factors is absolutely undiscoverable. That it has, however, up to the present time been sought in vain, is apparent from the ever-varying conflict waged on this domain—a conflict which only temporarily ceases, and which, with any knowledge of the extent and depth of the difference, cannot in the least surprise us.

Compare the Articles *Freiheit, Vorsehung, Zulassung*, in Herzog's *R. E.;* J. H. A. EBRAR, *Das Verhältniss der Reform. Dogm. zum Determinismus* (1849); J. H. SCHOLTEN, *De vrije wil*, Krit. Onderz. (1859); N. C. KIST, *De mensch, een redelijk en zedelijk vrijwerkend wezen* (1859); D. KOORDERS, *Het Determinisme der Leidsche School* (1859); ROORDA, *De vrijh. van den mensch;* Dr. Ph. J. HOEDEMAKER, *Het Probleem der vrijheid en het Theistisch Godsbegrip* (1867); J. CRAMER, *Het berouw en het ethisch determinisme* (1868); S. HOEKSTRA, *Vrijheid, in verb. met zelfbew. zedelijkh. en zonde* (1858).

POINTS FOR INQUIRY.

Nearer distinction between the Divine government, with regard to the experiences and to the acts of men.—Has the notion of natural and moral *evil* merely a subjective, or also objective, significance?—Nearer determining and defence of the doctrine of Divine permission.—Difference and connection between foreknowledge and fore-ordination. —The distinction between freedom of will and freedom of action.—The theory of the modern psychological and ethical Determinism, as compared with that of Calvinism.—Is one not absolutely compelled, from a Biblical standpoint, to be unreservedly a determinist? —Sense and force of Rom. viii. 28, and such-like passages.—Does the government of God stand entirely in the same relation to the free actions of *all* men?

SECTION LXIII.—THE THEODICÉE.

With all its sublimity, the government of Providence displays enigmatical sides enough to call forth ever new attempts for its justification, in opposition to so many forms of objection raised against it. This Theodicée, attempted at all times with various results, can be crowned with a comparative and satisfactory degree of success only where it is undertaken from the standpoint of belief in the Christian revelation. Even from this standpoint, however, a complete Theodicée is not attainable, and at the same time is not actually necessary. The problem of the world will first be fully solved when the accomplishment of the plan of the world—which we look for on sure grounds—is at length seen.

1. We found it was not possible to direct our glance to the Upholding and Government of all things by the Providence of God, without our eyes becoming dazzled by the brightness of this sun. Problems even arose which seemed to justify us in speaking of *spots* in the sun. In all ages they have called forth more or less successful attempts at their solution, and we must not close our present argument without also for a moment directing our attention thereto.

2. The *notion* of the Theodicée is already indicated in the word, which is in all probability derived from Leibnitz.[1] We give this name to every formal attempt to justify the government of God against the objections which are brought against it from different standpoints. The Theodicée seeks, as far as possible, to prove that, notwithstanding all the sin and misery in the world, God may be regarded as the highest Wisdom and Goodness. The legitimacy and appropriateness of such an attempt cannot be seriously disputed. It is necessary, not only on God's account, but often more on account of ourselves and others; and so has been undertaken from the standpoint of every religious system in the least degree developed. As an example of a Theodicée among the writings of the Old Testament may be mentioned the Jobeide and Psalms xxxvii., lxxiii., and lxxvii.; and among those of the New, Rom. ix.—xi. From the writings also of the oldest Apologetes and Ecclesiastical Fathers, remarkable instances may be adduced, notably from those of Lactantius, Basil the Great, and Augustine; while among the Schoolmen, the names of Anselm and Thomas Aquinas suggest themselves.[2] The Reformers, too, have just as little left themselves without testimony in this domain, as have the most renowned Theologians of the Romish Church; and the footsteps of a more philosophic mode of defence have been and are followed even in our day, with more or less of success, by practical thinkers; although Kant did not hesitate for a moment to speak of the attempts of this kind—those at least which had been made up to his time—as entire failures.[3]

3. The value of the Theodicée of course depends entirely upon the *standpoint* from which it is attempted. From that of Reason and Experience alone, a satisfactory solution cannot possibly be expected; and we cannot be in the least surprised that a Bayle, for instance,[4] should regard the objections which he adduces against the doctrine of a Divine government as absolutely insuperable. It remains a difficulty to us, "until we go into the sanctuary of God."[5] Without that, one discovers here and there, indeed, light in the darkness; but not the higher law in accordance with which their relationship to each other is determined, and just as little the pledge that the light shall at last triumph over the darkness. Even the Revelation of the Old Testament, in itself, is insufficient to raise us above the region of dark and perturbing clouds. The problem, for instance,

---

[1] Compare his *Essais de Théod. sur la bonté de Dieu, la liberté de l'homme, et l'origine du mal*, Amst., 1710, frequently reprinted, and followed by other similar writings.

[2] Compare Hagenbach, *History of Doctrines*, [Eng. translation], pp. 303 and 408 of Dutch translation.

[3] See his *Vermischte Schriften*, iii., part 7.

[4] See his art. *Manichéens*.

[5] Ps. lxxiii. 16, 17.

of the prosperity of the wicked, as contrasted with the adversity of the pious,[6] remained in part unsolved, so long as the eye rested exclusively on the world on this side the grave. Only belief in the revelation of God's highest grace in Christ sets us in a position to review with calmness the enigmas of the Divine government.

4. The *contents* of a Theodicée which is thus undertaken are naturally determined by the number and importance of the problems necessarily presenting themselves to the observant reflection. It is impossible here to do more than sketch the merest outline of that which must be brought into special prominence in the upholding of God's glory against opposition of such various kinds.

(*a.*) The co-existence of God and of *moral evil* remains, after all that has been just said, assuredly the most difficult of all problems. Yet one is not on that account in any case justified in asserting that the Christian idea of God and the Christian idea of sin are in irreconcilable conflict. Not with the Christian idea of God, but with the Monistic-deterministic idea, is the acknowledgment of the existence of moral evil absolutely incompatible. This latter retains the character of rebellion and guilt (comp. § lxxv.); not willed by God, but punished by Him. But each responsible deed is, at the same time, a fact by which the execution of God's counsel is subserved in a manner which could not be calculated beforehand. Herod and Pontius Pilate do that which God's hand and counsel had before determined (προώρισε)—should *be done* (ποιεῖσθαι)? no, but should *take place* (γενέσθαι.[7]) *That* evil is accomplished, is the work of freedom; but how it shall be accomplished, and to what it shall be subservient, is at the disposal of God's Providence. "Evil is a thing the course of which can be determined"—*malum ordinabile est*—in the words of Hugo de St. Victor. The very allowance of evil becomes its own sentence; and in answer to the question, whether it would not have been better to avoid it at any price, the word of the philosopher has still its force: "*Le meilleur parti n'est pas toujours celui qui tend à éviter le mal, parce qu'il se peut que le mal soit accompagné par un plus grand bien.*"[8]

(*b.*) The Divine government and *natural evil* displays to a certain extent something less *incomprehensible*, because all natural evil is at any rate a powerful corrective to absolute, *i.e.*, moral, evil. But it is at the same time a fruit of this latter, the extirpation of which—so long as the root has not been taken away—would without a miracle be impossible. And *this* miracle could not be even regarded as desirable; because a sinful world would, without pain and suffering, become assuredly not better, but rather worse than it now is. Not a little of this suffering, moreover, is imaginary, relative, and in such wise bound up with the well-being of life, that with the vanishing of the shadow the light itself also would be extinguished. The essentially evil is not only equalled in measure and degree by that which is good, but commonly far surpassed by it.[9] It lasts no longer than is

---

[6] Mal. iii. 13—18.

[7] Acts iv. 28.

[8] The better course is not always that which tends to avoid evil, because it may so happen that the evil is accompanied by a greater good (Leibnitz).

[9] Ps. xxx. 5.

necessary,[10] and contributes in God's time to the realisation of the noblest purposes.[11] Bacon well speaks of prosperity as being "the blessing of the Old Testament, adversity that of the New;" because in the latter the light of eternity rises upon this earthly "vale of tears." Such passages as Rom. viii. 18—39; Heb. xii. 4—11; James i. 2—4; Rev. vii. 9—17, contain precious material for composing a Theodicée upon this point—a Theodicée which now and then insensibly rises to a Doxology. Even heathen antiquity has expressed by the mouth of one of its noblest representatives, Seneca, the dim perception of many a consolatory truth in this domain; *e.g.*, "*Patrium habet Deus adversus bonos homines animum, et illos fortiter amat, et operibus, inquit, doloribus et damnis exagitentur, ut rerum colligant robur*" —that God cherishes a fatherly spirit towards good men, and loves them with a love too great to be indulgent towards them, and tries them with labours, with griefs, and losses, that they may learn to draw out the strength of all things (*De Prov.* ii. 3). Only modern Ethnicism (*heathenism*, as distinguished from heathendom) proclaims here, from its fatalistic standpoint, a Gospel of despair, which in the long run calls forth the shriek of a comfortless pessimism, "What, this world the work of a God? nay, rather of a Devil," words actually uttered by Schopenhauer. From the Christian standpoint, on the other hand, we are equally armed against Stoical insensibility as against a sentimental repining (*weltschmerz*), in the conflict of life. It is, however, of the greatest importance, above all, early to direct the youthful mind to such an apprehension of this problem as shall preserve it against abandoning belief in God.[12]

(*c.*) The Divine government and *human experience in regard to life and death*, looked at in a more general way, without doubt gives rise to extremely painful questions; but here also, least of all, need there be wanting to thoughtful belief a relatively satisfactory answer. The great dissimilarity, for example, between the outward lot of individuals is imperatively necessary for the continued existence and well-being of the great whole.[13] It is moreover only relative, in many respects beneficial, even in the most unfavourable case only temporary, and always beyond the reach of censure; since prosperity and good fortune are not, indeed, words of *one* meaning, and since, moreover, the holy God is under no obligation to grant to a single sinful man any particular blessing.—As concerns the time of death, for the ungodly often so long delayed, while the pious one is early cut off, even antiquity has said, not without reason, that he whom God loves dies young: "*quem Deus diligit, adolescens moritur;*" and while in the Old Testament a long life is regarded as an especially desirable reward of proved fidelity to God,[14] and for this reason the opposite is an object of deprecatory prayer,[15] for the Christian the opposition between life and death

---

[10] 1 Pet. i. 6.
[11] Ps. cxix. 67.
[12] The earthquake at Lisbon in 1755 called forth doubts within the mind of the youthful Goethe, against which his mother—a woman of genius rather than of piety—had not a single antidote.
[13] 1 Cor. xii. 12—26.
[14] Gen. xv. 15; Prov. x. 27.
[15] Ps. cii. 24.

is solved in a higher harmony.[16]—The question which here naturally presents itself, to what extent the shortening or prolonging of life lies within the power of man, is, in other words, simply a special form of the general question as to the connection between the Divine government and human freedom of action, and is on that account an unprofitable one.[17] No one dies before his time, *i.e.*, the time assigned to him by God ;[18] but one may die before the (ordinary) time, in consequence of his own misconduct or that of others, and in such case we must say that such dying is not willed but permitted of God. The prolonging of life in answer to prayer[19] is no modification, but rather a manifestation and carrying into execution, of God's counsel ; the shortening of life, on the other hand, by manslaughter or suicide for instance, takes place not according to the will of God, but according to His foreknowledge, and under the universal rule of God's providence.

(*d.*) The government of God and *man's own obligation to activity* are so little opposed to each other, that, on the other hand, in the government of the former the subordinate activity of the latter has been taken into account. We know not what God has determined with regard to us, but we may assume on good grounds that sluggish inactivity on our part must run counter to God's ordination for our true well-being. The narrative of the twenty-seventh chapter of Acts is at once a proof and illustration of the co-operation of the two factors in the bringing about of an assured result. As concerns *intercessory prayer*, more particularly, regarded as the free act of man (comp. § lxi. 7, 8), it is only from the standpoint of Determinism and Naturalism, but never from that of Christian Theism, that its actual hearing can be regarded as inconceivable. If the connection between asking and receiving ever remains, from the nature of the case, mysterious, nothing prevents our supposing that the foreknown act of prayer also, as a consequence of a certain pre-established harmony, "*harmonia præstabilita*," is included by God in His eternal counsel as a means to, and condition of, the attainment of His purpose. "We must add to this that true prayer is not *merely* human, but sustained and carried on by the Divine Spirit as the Spirit of prayer, and that it has to such an extent a prophetic character, in which the Providence of God is one with the presentiment of man. Hence the sealing of prayer by the Amen. . . . . Prayer comes forth from the eternal freedom of the child, and goes back to the eternal freedom of the Father" (Lange). To the living freely acting God there must at least be allowed the liberty which one man has in regard to the supplication of another, the liberty to hear and help. All independent activity may be equally well combated with the same objections which are brought against the effectiveness of prayer, as powerless in presence of the eternal order of the world, since against the former also precisely the same objections lie.

(*e.*) The Divine government and *the moral perfection of humanity* offers to many an occasion of complaint and doubt. If humanity is really on the advance, and if God actually rules, must not this progress be more rapid and manifest? Sometimes periods arrive when this question is renewed

---

[16] Rom. xiv. 8.

[17] Compare Beverovicius, *Quæstt. Epistt. de termino vitæ fatali*, 1634.

[18] Acts xiii. 36.

[19] Isa. xxxviii. 5.

with increased emphasis, and faith has to sustain a severe conflict because human folly and wickedness, in unbridled rage, hurl back the world, as it were, from the comparative height attained to with the utmost effort. Luther, Melancthon, Arndt, and many others, for this reason asserted that humanity became ever worse; while not a few even in the present day believe only in material and intellectual progress, but not in that of a moral and spiritual kind. In opposition to these we cannot, however hopeless things may sometimes look, abandon belief in this last also, as being based upon the nature of God and of man, and confirmed by history and experience in a number of instances. Only we must seek to extend our vision beyond the immediate future and our nearest surroundings; and must never forget that the evil makes far more noise than the good, which usually operates but slowly and unseen. "*Patiens quia æternus.*" God's way with our race is not the shortest, but the best; the safe but frequently wearisome circuit by which Israel was led forward.[20]

(*f.*) Finally, as concerns the Divine government *and the mysteries of Providence in general*, the demand that the latter should not exist at all, so that the wisdom and goodness of God should be at once evident to absolutely every one, merits the name of arbitrariness itself. For the question is not whether a thing is doubted, but whether it is with reason doubted; not whether mysteries present themselves, but whether they are of such a nature as to compel us to abandon belief in the wisdom and goodness of God. A government of Providence without a single cloud would assuredly not be Divine;[21] and upon the darkest ways we see at every turn such bright footsteps that we very soon no longer need to ask whether the heavenly Traveller has passed here too.

5. After what has been said it is scarcely necessary to point out that even the best Theodicée here upon earth sees a limit imposed to it, which it is neither possible nor desirable to pass beyond. What has already been said earlier, in general, concerning the incomprehensibleness of God (§ xlii. 3), finds also its application in this particular domain. A complete Theodicée is not possible on account of the wide distance between God's exaltedness and our insignificance, God's wisdom and our shortsightedness, God's infiniteness and our transitoriness. At best we can observe something of the *quid* (the *what*), much less of the *quomodo* (the *how*), and least of all of the *quare* (the *wherefore*) of the Divine activity. Nor is this necessary, either for the honour of God or for the edification of our neighbour, or for our own essential well-being. The mysterious element in the Divine government on its part curbs the pride of man, calls forth faith with its precious fruits, and justifies the hope which it awakens in the promised revelation of the future.[22] If we cannot here below either supply or expect a complete Theodicée, based upon solid grounds, we may, nevertheless, form a tolerably accurate and satisfactory one. "The *true* Theodicée must be undertaken from the standpoint of Christianity, but the *complete* Theodicée can only be given with the completed history of the world" (Martensen). This is to be looked for from no single man, nor from all men together, but only from God Himself.

---

[20] Exod. xiii. 17. [21] Isa. xlv.; Ps. xcvii. [22] John xiii. 7.

6. The *accomplishment* of the Divine world-plan, which will be at the same time its glorious vindication, notwithstanding all conflict and opposition, may be predicted upon the most solid grounds. This belief is the natural fruit of the Christian idea of God itself. From the Naturalistic standpoint one can at best but hope that order, so far as it may now be said to exist, will continue to exist; but one has no ground for supposing that eventually it will, in the moral domain, completely triumph over all opposition. Then all must ever remain as it was, since God, according to this doctrine, has no power to produce anything that is new by His own Supranatural means. If, on the other hand, we firmly hold to faith in a God who is not simply the absolute causality, but also the highest moral power, the Father of spirits, which He has created unto life and freedom, but without the possibility of their withdrawing themselves for a moment from His hand, the satisfactory catastrophe of the world-drama is raised above all question. "Providence is in no respect abstract *Power;* but in all, the most living, tender, immediate *sway* and *government*" (Lange).—In addition to this, the most positive promises of God in His word give us to look forward with confidence to this issue.[23]—Finally, the history of the world and of the Kingdom of God gives us to see an approximation, slow indeed, and frequently interrupted, but yet constant, towards this glorious end. The world's history is the world's judgment, but that judgment at the same time a continual world-restoration, which ceases not until the closing word of Creation's history (Gen. i. 31) shall have become also that of the annals of the Divine government. Nothing is more hopeless than to oppose this work of God, nothing more blessed than willingly to advance it.[24] When finally it shall be manifestly completed—and in principle it is so already for the eye of faith—the "*nil mirari*" (to wonder at nothing) will be no longer possible, and wonder (τὸ θαυμάζειν) more than ever be recognised not simply as τῆς φιλοσοφίας, but also as τῆς προσκυνησέως ἀρχή—the beginning not only of philosophy, but also of adoration. In the words of the great Dutch poet, Da Costa:—

At the confines of the ages, sees my eye the spirit of evil
Vanquished and disarmed, for rebellion no more able.
When the Lord God in all things and in all is all,
Will it light be, ever light be, light of light and darkness born.

Compare ULRICI'S article, *Theodicée,* in Herzog's *R. E.*, xv., pp. 707—713, and the literature there adduced; to which may be added *Theodicée, Etudes sur Dieu, la Creation, et la Providence,* par AM. DE MARGERIE, Prof. à Nancy (1865), a spiritualistic Theistic polemic against Naturalism; E. DE PRESSENSÉ, *The Mystery of Suffering* [Eng. trans.]; J. H. GUNNING, Junr., *Blikken in de Offenb.*, ii. (1868), p. 265, *sqq.;* CREMER, *Beiträge zu einer Christl. Weltanschauung,* in the *Beweis des Glaubens* (1869), p. 40, *sqq.*

POINTS FOR INQUIRY.

What demands may legitimately be made upon a satisfactory Theodicée?—Whence is it that so many a Theodicée has partially or wholly failed?—Discussion and elucidation of the most essential points in a Theodicée.—The history of the kingdom of God a Theodicée ever receiving fresh contributions.

---

[23] See, for example, Isa. xlvi. 10; Matt. xvi. 18; xxviii. 20; 1 Cor. xv. 24—28, and many other places.
[24] 1 Cor. iii. 9.

SECTION LXIV.—CONCLUSION.—HARMONY BETWEEN GOD'S NATURE AND WORKS.

The harmony between God's nature and works is so manifest, that, though for belief in God the answer to many a question must still remain wanting, unbelief in regard to His existence and government of the world, undeniably condemns itself. The constantly repeated observation of this harmony is for the science of faith an urgent duty, and for the life of faith an inestimable blessing.

1. At the end of this examination we look back yet once more. Starting from the well-founded belief in God, we have sought to formulate the Christian conception of God, and to consider the majesty of the Infinite as this is revealed in His various Attributes. As the central point of all, we learnt to recognise *Love*, which at once afforded us a starting-point for the discussion of the doctrine of the Father, the Son, and the Holy Ghost. As proceeding from the Divine Being, the plan of the world unfolded itself before our eyes, as it is realised, partly in the creation of the universe, of the world of spirits, of this earth especially; partly in the sustaining and governing of all things, especially of man and humanity. (Comp. §§ xlii.—lxiii.) Without any blank, or abrupt transition, we continued our research, and find that, whatever questions have remained unsolved, that which has been said concerning God's nature has been confirmed by the contemplation of His works, and, conversely, that which has been said concerning God's works, by the contemplation of His nature. As two beams, fitting into each other, uphold the same arched roof, so we see the two parts of the Christian doctrine concerning God mutually support and cover each other.

2. Notwithstanding all the imperfection which, from the nature of the case, inseparably attaches to such demonstration, the absurdity of its non-acknowledgment now stands in a clearer light before our eye. Without belief in God, as the Creator and Governor of the world, that which is most certain becomes at once uncertain and incomprehensible. This belief has been termed an "hypothesis:" be it so, provided only it be added that this alone explains—at least to a certain extent—the mystery of the world, and even thereby is manifested to be something infinitely more than mere hypothesis. For the theologian, as for the simplest child, the great question of conscience and of life ultimately becomes: "Believest thou truly in a living God?" and he who can answer it only in the negative, and can speak only of an eternal "order of the world" in the Naturalistic sense, should at least—with his so-called science—possess sufficient conscience to prevent his forcing himself into the sacred service of a Church, which is built up exclusively upon the foundation of faith in the

God of Revelation. Only he who can call this belief his own, is in his place and at home in the theological and ecclesiastical world; but then also on this account the more called upon to watch over this treasure, to increase it, and to defend it against every hostile attack. Nevertheless here also life in God remains the best way to a knowledge which—nourished by experience and adoration—disposes the mind to an ever higher glorifying of God.[1]

[1] Rom. xi. 33—36; 1 Tim. i. 17.

CHAPTER II.

ON MAN; OR, THE SUBJECT OF THE KINGDOM OF GOD.

(ANTHROPOLOGY.)

SECTION LXV.—TRANSITION AND GENERAL SURVEY.

WITH the doctrine concerning God (Theology), that concerning man (Anthropology) is most closely connected, and, from the nature of the case, of no less preponderating importance for Christian Dogmatics. Equally with the knowledge of Theology is that of Anthropology—better than from any other source—drawn from the sacred documents. In the treatment of this subject, the consideration of man's original nature and constitution must precede that of his present moral condition.

1. The high *importance* of the study of Christian Anthropology needs no formal demonstration. In itself it is of the highest significance for the man, the Christian, the Theologian. "The proper study of mankind is man." If to the question, "What is man?" the number of wise and foolish answers has been legion, this very number shows that no thoughtful mind can be indifferent to this inquiry. No wonder: "l'homme n'est qu'un roseau, le plus faible de la nature, mais c'est un roseau pensant."[1] Notably for Christian Dogmatics a profound contemplation of man, his aspirations, wants, condition, destination, etc., is not only desirable, but indispensable. The more thorough the Anthropology, the more solid the Soteriology. Especially in our days is a continued study of this topic required · because, as Theology is more than ever threatened by Scepticism, so is Anthropology by Materialism. So much hostility, indifference, and misunderstanding in regard to the truth proceeds simply from the fact that men know not *man, i.e.*, themselves.

2. The *connection* between Anthropology and Theology in the narrower

[1] "Man is but a reed, the feeblest thing in nature; but he is one endowed with thought." —PASCAL.

sense of the term is close, and obviously reciprocal too. On the one hand God is known through man, the most excellent of all those creatures in which is made manifest His eternal power and Godhead;[2] but on the other hand it may be said that the pure knowledge of man is derived from that of God. Here also the words, "*In Thy light shall we see light*," have their application. How would it be possible to solve the enigma of humanity, if we did not find the key thereto in Him who is the first and the last word, the Alpha and the Omega of all things? The stream is best explained by the fountain, the tree by the soil from which it has sprung. As has been already well remarked by Calvin, "Each one by a knowledge of himself is not only urged to seek God, but also as it were guided by the hand to find Him."[3]

3. The *source* from which this knowledge of man is derived has been already indicated. It is true we possess numerous aids to assist us in arriving at a deeper knowledge of man and of humanity, even without Holy Scripture. The observations of others may shed for us not a little light upon this mysterious domain, reflection thereon yet more, and careful self-examination and long-continued experience may throw even very much light thereupon. Yet the final answer to the important questions which here arise, lies beyond the speculative as well as beyond the merely empirical sphere. Physiology and Psychology may dissect the man, but cannot fully explain him; and precisely the most distinguished students of these sciences will be the first to join in the confession: "Into the heart of nature penetrates no created spirit." These depths also are disclosed only when not merely the eye of the spirit is opened, but light is shed from above. We therefore speak of Holy Scripture, which is the original documentary evidence of the Saving Revelation, as at the same time *the best source* whence we may also become acquainted with man. It is true, not all questions which awaken our interest are here decided or receive a complete answer. Holy Scripture is no textbook of Anthropology, any more than of Astronomy or Geology. More than this, the light which is here shed upon man is by no means equal to that which arises for us in relation to God. God reveals Himself to us: man is made manifest to us and to himself by the torch of Holy Scripture. Scripture itself awakens a sense of the incomprehensible nature of man, even for his fellow-men.[4] Hence the demand for self-examination,[5] in place of the higher demand of self-knowledge—a qualification not easily attainable upon earth. Here also the distinction between a pure and a complete knowledge must for this reason be observed from the first. But, with this limitation, we do not hesitate a single moment to speak of Holy Scripture as the best guide upon the path of a true knowledge of man and of ourselves. To the twofold question continually suggested to humanity in its wanderings, "Whence comest thou, and whither goest thou?"[6] Scripture alone returns

---

[2] Rom. i. 19, 20.
[3] "Unusquisque non tantum agnitione sui instigatur ad quærendum Deum, sed etiam reperiendum quasi manu ducitur" (Calv. *Inst.*, i. 1).
[4] Jer. xvii. 9; 1 Cor. ii. 11.
[5] 2 Cor. xiii. 5.
[6] Gen. xvi. 8.

an answer at all satisfactory. In the first place, because it gives us to contemplate God in the clearest light, does it dispel many a cloud which had concealed from our eye the image of humanity. Moreover, it affords us trustworthy information as to the origin and nature of sin, and without a thorough Hamartology there is no satisfactory Anthropology. Above all, Holy Scripture displays to us the image of Him in whom, as even unbelief admits, the ideal of humanity was most fully realised, and from whom consequently we can best learn "what is implied in being man." In Him we behold at the same time what we must be, and what we are not. From Him we constantly hear words which testify to the deepest acquaintance with mankind, and which are equivalent to so many revelations in this domain. Thus light falls from this centre of Saving Revelation upon the whole circumference of human living and dying. Holy Scripture does not merely tell us who man is, but presents him in his light and shadowy side; and merits as no other source of knowledge does—on this account also—the name not only of a truly Divine, but also of a truly human book. Such as we are here depicted, are we in reality; the highest revelation of the Godhead is at the same time the clearest mirror of humanity. From its sanctuary sounds forth in manifold tones, not only the "*Introite, et hîc Dei sunt*" [Enter, for here also God is present], but also the "*Ecce homo!*"

4. The *value* of the Biblical Christian Anthropology becomes apparent, above all, when it is observed how, in placing ourselves at this standpoint, we are ever most preserved from the two opposite rocks, each of which is to be shunned with equal solicitude—that of a foolish *worship* of humanity on the one hand, and of a profound *contempt* for humanity on the other. All the history of philosophy, as well as all experience, goes to show how man left to himself has ever oscillated between these extremes. Holy Scripture alone preserves, in this respect, the just mean; or rather, it raises us above either onesidedness, by proclaiming to him who deifies humanity, not only the insignificance, but also the unworthiness and deep misery of the race; and conversely, by reminding him who extravagantly degrades humanity, that we are God's offspring, and were created after His image. Nowhere is man more degraded than from the standpoint of unbelief; nowhere, on the other hand, is pride so deeply humbled, but at the same time the humbled one so highly exalted, as from the standpoint of Holy Scripture. In proof we take only the seventh chapter of Romans, the *Confessions* of Augustine, and the glorious *Pensées* of Pascal. While the questions arise in every thoughtful mind, "If man's nature is so excellent, whence his deeply wretched condition?" and again, "If man is so mean and worthless a being, whence is it that he is never reconciled to this condition?" Holy Scripture alone explains to us the enigma, by teaching us sharply to distinguish between the original *nature* and the present *condition* of man, and thus to come to the conclusion that he is helplessly and yet not hopelessly lost.

5. The *division* of this chapter, in the manner above indicated, has its reason in the nature of the subject, and is justified by what we have just said. At the very outset it at the same time bears witness against the opinion of those who regard sin not as a degeneration, but rather as a

development. The second half of our examination must, from the standpoint we have here taken, occupy us not merely as a separate subject, but also even more in detail than the first, and above all must serve as a basis for that opposition between *Sin* and *Grace* which dominates all dogmatic thinking which is in the spirit of the Gospel and of the Reformation. On the threshold of neither of these can the ancient prayer of the Psalmist be dispensed with: "Send out Thy light and Thy truth: let them lead me!"

Compare for the whole of this chapter, and especially for the first division, G. H. VON SCHUBERT, *Geschichte der Seele*, 3rd edn. (1839); I. H. FICHTE, *Anthropologie* (1856); and the principal handbooks of Psychology of the present day; notably H. ULRICI, *Leib und Seele;* compare also the art. *Mensch*, in Herzog's *R. E.;* C. RUDLOFF, *Die Lehre vom Menschen, begründet aus der göttl. Offenb.* (1858); LUTHARDT, *Apologetical Lectures on the Saving Truths of Christianity* (Eng. trans.); and a paper by STEMLER, *Het Chr. leerbegrip over den Mensch*, in the *Godg. Bijdr.* (1869), i.

POINTS FOR INQUIRY.

Reason why man is so differently viewed from the standpoint of Heathenism, Judaism, and Christianity respectively.—Can Holy Scripture be regarded as the *fons primarius* in the domain of Anthropology, in the same sense in which it is, *e.g.*, in the domain of Theology or Christology?—Has philosophy without the Bible really unceasingly been guilty of the worship of humanity or contempt for humanity, and whence this common phenomenon?—What is the best method of studying Christian Anthropology, so as to gain the desired result?

FIRST DIVISION.

MAN'S ORIGINAL NATURE.

SECTION LXVI.—HIS ORIGIN.

MAN, the most excellent being upon earth, owes his origin to a definite creative act of God, in consequence of which he may in no sense be called the merely natural product of a lower order of creatures, but rather a separate link in the chain of animated beings. The doctrine of the original unity of the human race, announced in the Bible, and maintained by later science against continual contradiction, has not only a moral, but a definitively religious importance, and ought on this account, also in Christian Dogmatics, to receive due recognition.

1. We place our assertion that "man is the most excellent being on earth," at once in the forefront, not only because nothing meets us earlier than this, but also because Materialism most sadly disavows this truth, by forgetting the real distinction between man and beast. And yet this distinction appears again and again, whether we cast our eyes on the corporeal or on the spiritual side of our nature. Though man is surpassed in length of life, in strength of body, in rapidity of movement, or in other qualities, by many a beast; yet is his superiority seen from his upright form, from the finer mechanism of some of his limbs, *e.g.*, the hand or the eye; from the beauteous harmony of the normally developed human body (as is shown in the Apollo Belvedere); from his adaptability to live in all kinds of climates; from his power of disarming, dominating, or domesticating the animal world; specially, however, from his power of speech, so infinitely raised above the uttering or the imitation of sounds of beasts; and, finally, only explicable as the fruit of a Divine operation.

It is, however, the psychical and spiritual side of our being which still more confirms the truth of the words of the poet in Ps. viii. 4—6, compared with Ps. cxxxix. 14. Man alone upon earth deserves the name of a rational, moral, religious being. Though the lower powers of the soul are operative in the beasts, the highest power, that of ideas, by which the sense is directed to the ideal, is sought even in the most developed beast in vain. The very remarkable imitative faculty of some beasts is nothing more than an admirable instinct; but the element of constant progress, by which human endeavour is marked, is missed in that of the animal world. *There* is a propensity by which the creature is led, *here* only a working of the free and active will, which leads even to the most unfortunate abuse of freedom of choice. The animal is a type of his class; man an individuality in a highly privileged race. In an animal, therefore, it is absurd to speak of moral good and evil, or of a responsibility, which attaches to it; prosecutions of witches were cruel, but prosecutions of animals merely ridiculous. Above all, man alone is fitted for personal communion with God. The animal cannot pray, even when it is taught to assume the attitude of prayer. Here, if anywhere, the saying is true, "Ist alles nur Dressur, und von ein' Geist vernehm ich keine Spur" (Goethe). The Psalm of the Panting Hart and that of the Good Shepherd could only spring from the heart of *man.*

2. Whence then this man? It is not enough to say that he, as everything else, has his origin from God; the question is whether any more accurate definition concerning the proper origin of the human race can be attained. Without reason this question is put on one side, as not belonging to the domain of Theology, but to that of physical science. "There are fundamental principles in our contemplation of nature which have an immediate religious import" (Kurtz). So he who wishes to see the question as to the origin of mankind relegated from the Theological to the zoological sphere, expresses thereby, though silently, a proposition and at the same time a denial, of which the rights at any rate must be first proved. If natural philosophy after so many centuries has not yet been able to uplift the last veil, we may not refuse to the science of faith the modest attempts which it on its part ventures to essay. And yet she may by no means call this investigation a matter of indifference, as far as concerns the interests which affect her most supremely. Supposing it were made really evident that man is nothing more than the Naturalism of these days asserts, then would everything, which according to the Gospel has been done by God for the salvation of this man, become, if not absolutely absurd, at least most improbable. The more reason that Dogmatics should not exclude this question from the sphere of its investigations, even when continuing to observe those of natural philosophy with undiminished interest. Or would it be absolutely impossible for her to throw any light upon this darkness? Undoubtedly, if it were at the outset evident that nothing which Holy Scripture teaches on this point deserves the slightest confidence. But, when once we stand at the Christian Theistic standpoint, we find no sufficient reasons for such a decision, and the question must be seriously discussed, whether or not a light has been kindled for Belief, which we in this domain look for in vain from the side of Experience or Speculation.

3. If we consult the Bible, we learn from the Lord Jesus that it is God who has "made them male and female" (Matt. xix. 4). St. Paul speaks in a like sense in 1 Cor. xi. 8—12; 1 Tim. ii. 13; and his words are only the echo of the testimony of the Old Testament.[1] All these voices refer us to the record of Moses, which in Gen. i. 26, compared with Gen.

[1] See Exod. iv. 11; Job xxxv. 10; Ps. xciv. 9; Mal. ii. 10; and many more passages.

ii. 7, relates the creation of man, in a manner completely different from that of any other of the kinds of creatures, and in that respect indubitably deserves complete confidence. Moreover, that which has before been observed in § lviii., respecting this record as a whole, is applicable to this particular section. The words of Jesus and the Apostles have stamped upon its utterance a seal of high import for every Christian. A comparison with other Eastern Anthropogonies gives a result most favourable to the Mosaic, and the discrepancy which is seen between the two narratives of Genesis is by no means insuperable. Even if it were thought that some particulars of the hoary narrative, *e.g.*, that relating to the formation of woman, must be regarded as a dream or a vision, there is still no doubt that here, too, the chief idea predominates; viz., man by no means a mere product of nature, but a distinct and direct work of God's hand.

4. With this teaching of Scripture, the doctrine of the Christian Church, and specially that of the Dutch Reformed, agrees.[2] In order to prevent any misconception, Calvin added that "man is non substantiâ, sed qualitate Dei progenies,"[3] and others laid particular stress on the fact that he was made "e nihilo," by an operation of God's almighty will. This truth had already been dimly presaged, and nobly expressed by some heathen poets and philosophers,[4] in opposition to the foolish arrogance of those who considered themselves as sprung from the ground on which they lived.[5] In reality, too, the self-consciousness of man, that he, however closely allied to the beast, is yet in his inmost being something different, cannot be better explained, than by assuming that we really are God's workmanship in the proper sense of the word.

5. Naturalism, however, contests this position, and has done so for ages. Already did Lactantius twit the Stoics with their ignorance in regard to the creation of man by God, combined with the foolish fancy that the first rational dwellers on the earth had appeared as a kind of mushroom out of the ground, "putant homines in omnibus terris et agris tanquam fungos esse generatos" (Instt. Divv. vii. 4). Never, however, has the attempt to regard man as a merely natural result of a lower kind of creature, been so general as in the present century. Physicists lend a helping hand to the modern theologians in proving our descent from a closely allied kind of animal; it is merely a question whether the Gorilla, or the Chimpanzee, or the Sapajou is to be our forefather. Even in Genesis is the proof found[6] that the first men as shameless beings peered down from between the branches of the forest on the watch for other beasts, and have only by slow gradations developed into discipline and order. Not incredible certainly, if nature, as Strauss thinks,[7] like a woman in the bloom of youth, had formerly a power of fertility which she has now lost, in consequence of which there sprang from inorganic matter, the lower organic

---

[2] Compare Neth. Conf. Art. xiv.; H. C., Ans. 6.
[3] Calv. *Inst.*, i. 15, 5.
[4] See, *e.g.*, Acts xvii. 28.
[5] αὐτόχθονες.
[6] Réville, *Manuel d'Inst. Rel.*, p. 186.
[7] *Christ. Glaubensl.*, i., p. 686.

beings, and from these again at last, after an infinite variety of links, man himself. It is hardly necessary to declare again that the renowned transmutation-theory of Darwin cannot lead to any other results. Enough! If all these voices speak the truth, then may the psalmn-note, "God made man in His own image," be changed into the song, "Great is the Goddess of Nature."

6. Faith, however, against all this opposition, has no reason as yet to feel ashamed of its confession that, notwithstanding the close union which exists everywhere in the whole Creation, and thus joins man himself to the lower links, a *new*, a *separate* word has here been spoken by the almighty Creator. The Naturalistic presentment of the origin of man is an hypothesis very far from being sufficiently legitimated, nay, on the contrary, weighed down by great and insuperable difficulties. However often it may be asserted, it still remains entirely undemonstrated, that organic beings could spring from inorganic matter; still more that man could originate from the beasts. The so-called "generatio æquivoca" is so little proved, that the opposite assertion, "omne vivum ex ovo," has even within the latest years gained important ground. But Naturalism, which seemed to have determined that a miracle could by no means be allowed at the beginning of our race, has advanced over mountains of difficulties, as if they were mole hills; and even a von Humboldt found himself compelled to express his dissatisfaction at the levity with which Strauss represented our first parents as sprung from "the Chaldaic primeval slime." The descent of men from apes cannot be demonstrated, either from history, since nowhere is there a record that during thousands of years one beast has developed itself into a man; or from natural science, since it cannot show the indispensable links by means of which the transition from beast to man is explicable; or from the peculiar constitution of man, who is as manifestly born to walk erect, as a fish is to swim, or a worm to creep, and who, if originally a four-footed being, would be alike the most unfortunate and most ridiculous of all beasts. The immense difference between man and beast can never be explained by the opposite system, and equally inexplicable is from this point of view the origin of speech and language. But enough has been already said for our purpose, of a theory, which, if it does not entirely contest the existence of the living God, at least utterly disregards His creative working in its highest domain, and so must not only lead to the undermining of religion and morality, but—and deservedly—at the same time to the abasement of mankind itself, which is from the same side often extravagantly exalted. "The man separated from God becomes a Brute, and even that kind of Brute, to which we are accustomed to give the name Beast" (Zollmann). The result of this view on the revealed mystery of the incarnation of the Logos, can only be thought of with shuddering.

Compare BLUMENBACH, *Ein Wort zur Beruhigung in einer allgemeinen Familienangelegenheit* (1806); F. DE ROUGEMONT, *De Mensch en de aap, of het Materialisme onzer dagen.* (Dutch transl.), 1863; GUIZOT, *Meditations*, i. (1864), p. 21, *sqq.;* LUTHARDT, *Apol. Vorles.* (1864), p. 238, *sqq.;* FABRI, *Briefe gegen den Materialismus* (1864), p. 195, *sqq.;* J. GRIMM, *Ueber den Ursprung der Sprache*, 6th ed. (1866); N. POULAIN, *Un Christianisme sans dogmes, etc.* (1864), p. 121, *sqq.;* specially TH. ZOLLMANN, *a. a. O.* (cf. p. 326), §§ 148—160; and THOLUCK'S article in Herzog, i.

7. To the question as to the *antiquity* of the human race, Biblical Chronology replies that it has not yet reached its sixtieth century. The sacred chronology, however, here and there presents difficulties, which may make us hesitate to regard the chronological question as a dogmatic one. On the other hand, it is evident that the directly contrary assertions—even 300,000 years have been mentioned—are not free from great exaggeration, and have arisen from an evident attempt to construct the history of mankind in a form wherein every supranatural element is pushed aside, and a romantic embellishment takes the place of history. That man came last of all the dwellers upon earth out of the hands of the Creator, is a truth which even natural science has strongly vindicated, and is after all the most important truth.

8. The original *unity* of the human race, already announced on the first page of the Bible, is also expressly confirmed by Jesus (Matt. xix. 4), and by the Apostle Paul.[8] There is not, however, the slightest reason for assuming, that the word Adam in a collective sense[9] should serve to denote the human race, and thus should leave room for the hypothesis of the contemporaneous creation of several human pairs.[10] The Biblical statement that "God hath made of one blood all nations of men," finds its support in the principle of economy which the Creator always pursues, and in the observation that man displays God's image, even in the fact that all have sprung from one. As yet natural science has not discovered any races of men so completely different, that it is really impossible to regard them as branches of one tree. Perhaps we may assume, with Kant, that already in the first pair there were present in preformation the germs of different races, which developed under the influence of climate, mode of life, etc., into such a variety of forms. From influences such as these can the undeniable difference be to a remarkable degree explained, and the continued study of the history of religious civilisation, languages, etc., constantly points back to a unity, which was the trunk from which every variety sprang. No wonder then, that not only orthodox theologians, but even distinguished natural philosophers, (Buffon, Linnæus, Blumenbach, Wagner, von Schubert, Al. von Humboldt, De Quatrefages, Owen Prichard, and many others,) place themselves in this matter on the side of the Mosaic narrative. No careful investigator of nature will at least reject the possibility of the original unity of the human race, which the theologian accepts on the testimony of a record in all respects trustworthy.

Along with the hypothesis of Co-Adamites, we may reject that of Præ-Adamites, which, propounded in 1655 by J. la Peyrère (in an *Exercit. Exeg. in Rom.* v. 12), was afterwards withdrawn. His assumption that Adam was only the ancestor of the people of Israel, has as little exegetical foundation as dogmatic or historic value. The theory of Autocthones (Aborigines), *i.e.*, of men who sprang out of and from the ground which they inhabited, as for instance, the Athenians believed of

---

[8] Compare Acts xvii. 26; Rom. v. 12; 1 Cor. xv. 21, 47—49.

[9] אָדָם.

[10] Compare in favour of and against this explanation the articles in the *Godgel. Bijdrag.* (1870), Nos. 6, 11, and 12.

themselves, whereon they were refuted by St. Paul in Acts xvii. 26, may be described as in absolute opposition to Holy Scripture. Least of all does Scripture in its sober and holy simplicity favour the theosophic representation that in the original man the sexual distinction was as yet entirely wanting, and only appeared in later time. Whatever explanation may be given to the narrative of the creation of Eve, it must always be regarded as the filling up of a certain void, and to such extent as an increase of the happiness of Paradise; not as a transition from a higher to a lower sensual condition in the first man.

9. The doctrine of the original unity of the human race is by no means a matter of indifference for religious and moral life. By it the high nobility of mankind is proved,[11] by it the original equality and duty of brotherly love is shown,[12] by it the origin and complete universality of sin is declared,[13] by it the harmony between the domain of Creation and Redemption is announced,[14] and by it is secured the truth that the Kingdom of God will come to all, since the Gospel without distinction must be brought to every human being.[15]

10. At the close of this investigation there can be no doubt where man obtains the greatest dignity—in the Holy Scripture which represents him as a born King's son, or in the school of Naturalism, where we hear the echo of the "eritis sicut Deus," but where, nevertheless, is secretly whispered in our ears that the oldest man has probably "first sucked at the teats of an ape." Above the ape-garden, with its abundant varieties, Paradise still continues to attract us through the transparent cloud which surrounds it on every side.

Compare, as to the original unity of the human race, an important treatise by SCHROEDER V. D. KOLK, in *Waarheid in Liefde* (1845), i.; A. DE QUATREFAGE, *L'unité de l'espèce humaine*, *Revue des deux Mondes* (1860); ZÖCKLER, *Die einheitl Abstammung des Menschengeschlechts* in the *Deutsche Jahrbuch für Theol.* (1862), i.; C. DE TOULOUSE, *Sur l'origine et l'anc. de l'Homme*, in the *Revue Chret.* (1864), p. 572, *sqq.*; G. MOORE, *The First Man and his place in Creation* (1866); P. JANET, *De eenheid van het menschdom op zedelijk gebied* (1869).

POINTS FOR INQUIRY.

Further definition of the faculties which distinguish man from every other beast upon earth.—Explanation and comparison of the two oldest Biblical accounts of the origin of man.—How did the first man learn to speak?—Was the first man a kind of hermaphrodite?—The creation of woman.

---

[11] Acts xvii. 28.
[12] Matt. vii. 12; Luke x. 30—37.
[13] Rom. v. 12.
[14] 1 Cor. xv. 21, 22.
[15] Eph. i. 10; Matt. xxviii. 19.

SECTION LXVII.—HIS NATURE.

Man is both a sensuous and a spiritual being, allied by his body to the dust of the earth, by his spirit to God, the Father of Spirits; a personality, according to its whole organisation, in all its parts, activities, and forces, definitely suited for a life in communion with God. On this ground, Christian Anthropology, developed by the light of Holy Scripture and spiritual experience, cannot but reject, as well a one-sided Spiritualism as a spiritless Materialism.

1. In the investigation into the nature of man, closely allied as it is to that into his origin, our glance is of itself first turned to his corporeity. If natural science makes us acquainted with the different elements of which it is composed, Holy Scripture teaches us that the body was taken from the dust of the earth, in consequence of a special creative act of God,[1] and thus in this way testifies both to the greatness and littleness of man. Nowhere, however, in it is the representation made, or justified, that the body was to be the prison of the soul, a hindrance to moral development. On the contrary, the corporeity obtains here its right and dignity, as not merely the bearer, but an indispensable *element* of the whole personality of man. Only from the scriptural standpoint must we, in a more accurate manner than has hitherto often been done, distinguish between *body* (σῶμα) as a material organism, composed of different parts, and *flesh* (σάρξ), animal substance through which the blood flows. This distinction, in itself already just, is of great importance, especially in the domain of Hamartology and Eschatology.

2. The spiritual side of our being is, however, definitely distinguished from the material, and according to the sacred narrative is of an essentially higher origin.[2] God is the God of the spirits of all flesh,[3] and that spirit returns at the hour of death to Him, even where the body returns to the earth.[4] The Biblical Anthropological standpoint is thus not monistic, but thoroughly dualistic; in this sense, however, that the higher and the lower are not merely outwardly connected, but combined into a living unity. The body is evidently adapted to serve the spirit; the spirit to rule over the body. It is unnecessary here to collect and decide upon all the signs which the sacred writers give as to the Physiological and Psychological side of our personality. For Christian Dogmatics in particular it is an important question whether by the light of Holy Scripture we must regard that personality as dichotomistic or trichotomistic; in other words, whether we must again distinguish man's soul from his spirit, or must consider them

[1] Gen. ii. 7.
[2] Gen. ii. 7.
[3] Heb. xii. 9; compare Num. xvi. 22.
[4] Eccles. xii. 7.

identical. If we accept the teaching of St. Paul, there seems no doubt but that the question must be answered in the former sense.[5] Even where it appears that there are other passages in Scripture which seem to favour a more dualistic presentment, yet the trichotomistic seems to us preferable, on internal psychological grounds; and we cannot be surprised that, already shadowed forth by the Platonic and Cabbalistic Philosophy, it has also found support and defence by the Fathers, as Irenæus, Justin Martyr, Tatian, Melito, Origen, and others. It would probably have met with still more general support, had not the dread of Apollinarianism, which also appealed to this distinction, made the Orthodox Church afterwards averse to it. If we accept it, we must then understand by soul the lower principle of life in the body, specially in the blood, which man has in common with the beasts; by spirit, the higher rational and moral principle, which is only found in man. "Man *is* soul,[6] and *has* spirit," says von Schubert. We must only take care not to consider *spirit* in this sense exclusively as an element in the personality of the Christian, but of every man, in whom the originally human element is by sin corrupted, but not maimed or diminished; a view moreover in which St. Paul precedes us, as he also extends to the spirit the demand for transformation of the mind.[7]

3. Concerning the origin of each human spirit, and the manner in which it unites itself to the body, Holy Scripture has remained silent, and the theories have at all times been very various. We find that of the more cultivated heathen put forth, among others, by Cicero in the Tusculan Disputations i. 9, 10, who comes to this conclusion: "harum sententiarum quæ vera sit, Deus aliquis viderit; quæ verosimillima, magna quæstio est." In the Christian Church three theories have gradually been formed. (1.) That of *Præ-existence, i.e.*, the doctrine that the souls, already in foretime created by God, unite themselves with the body at the birth; this, originally held by Plato and Philo, was accepted by Justin Martyr Theodoret, Origen, etc., but was condemned at Constantinople in the 6th century, as a heresy of the last named; in our days it has been emphatically defended by J. Müller in his *Lehre v. d. Sünde*, ii. § 92, *sqq.*, following in the steps of Kant and Schelling. (2.) That of *Creation, i.e.*, the doctrine that ever afresh at the formation of new bodies new souls were created by God; this was held by Aristotle, Jerome, Pelagius, most Romish and Reformed Theologians, Calixtus and the orthodox Reformed Church of the 17th century. (3.) That of *Traduction, i.e.*, the theory that along with the bodies the souls of the fathers were transferred to the children "per traducem, vel per propaginem;" Tertullian propounded this theory in his treatise *de Animâ*, c. 19, and it has been supported in earlier and later times by many, specially in the interests of the dogma of original sin; not, however, by Augustine, who often showed his hesitation to determine anything in this domain. In reality, the whole of this question lies on the very border, if not beyond the limits, of human investigation; and where an appeal has been made from both sides

---

[5] Compare 1 Thess. v. 23, with Heb. iv. 12, 1 Cor. xv. 45, and the entire contrast between the ἀνθρ. ψυχικός and πνευματικός, 1 Cor. ii. 14, and similar passages, as well as Jude 19.

[6] 1 Cor. xv. 45.

[7] Rom. xii. 2; Eph. iv. 23; 2 Cor. vii. 1.

to different words of Holy Scripture in favour of any of these propositions, we must not overlook the fact that such problems do not belong to the domain in which the word of Revelation speaks with decisive authority.

4. Enough, if we can present to ourselves the being of man as a *personality*, just thereby definitely distinguished from all other living beings on the earth. In the brute world we may here and there discover an evident striving after individuality, in man first we see the properly so called individuality developed, and indeed we too often find individualism predominating. That personality is revealed in the fact, that man has understanding and will; two sides of his being, whose proper centre, according to the representation of Holy Scripture, is found in the heart (לֵב, καρδία). Here lies the well-spring of life,[8] the secret laboratory, where as well the thought of the understanding, as the inclination of the will, is born. In that heart *conscience*[9] holds her fixed seat; she was in no way first roused in the sinner after the fall; but must be conceived as *conscientia sui et legis*, an original and indefeasible element of our being, the source of all our knowledge of God and of ourselves as moral creatures, and by a normal development the arbiter of all our will and action. There can be no doubt that, according to the united utterance of Scripture and self-consciousness, we must grant to man the power of the will, or that of free self-determination. If through the dominion of sin freedom in the higher sense of the word has been lost,[10] the freedom of choice (the formal as distinguished from the moral)—in other words, the power to will what our heart desires, without the existence of any power external to ourselves to compel us in the contrary direction—is still more presupposed than announced in so many words in Holy Scripture.[11] With this consciousness of having in many cases not only been called, but of having been able, to act in a different way, the working of the conscience stands in such direct connection, that, if this consciousness be denied, it immediately becomes a chimera. Upon the exclusively intellectual line this freedom of choice may easily be denied, but from the deeper psychological and spiritual empiric standpoint it will ever be recognised again. "Conscience cuts the knot, which the intellect is unable to untie, and without troubling itself with proving *how* man is free, it establishes the fact of that freedom by an instinctive revelation and inward feeling. We feel that we are free, just as we feel that we exist" (A. Monod).

5. That which strikes us most, when considering the being of man, is, that he is entirely fitted for life in personal communion with God.[12] All the lines, which are drawn from the periphery of his being, meet in God as their common centre.[13] The understanding cannot rest in an endless chain of mediate causes, until it has climbed to the highest cause of all. The feeling of the beautiful, the true, the good, remains unsatisfied until He is found, in whom the highest beauty and truth and goodness are united. The will first gains real freedom, when it willingly submits itself to Him, on whom man is indefinitely dependent; whilst on the contrary sin,

---

[8] Prov. iv. 23; xxiii. 26.

[9] συνειδησις, Heb. x. 22; compare § x. 8.

[10] John viii. 34—36.

[11] See Josh. xxiv. 15; Isa. lv. 6, *sqq.*

[12] Compare § xxii. 3.

[13] Ps. lxxiii. 25, 26.

as a foreign power, leads him to that which he in his innermost nature wills not.[14] Thus is being man, on the one side, an actuality; on the other, only a design for a voluntary life in God; and where this design is not realised, that peculiarity which distinguishes man from stone, plant, or beast, is gradually destroyed. At the same time it is seen here, "Man would not be the most excellent upon earth, if he were not too excellent for it" (Goethe).

6. From the purely Christian-anthropological standpoint must be maintained, against every spiritualistic and materialistic partiality, the right of each of the two sides in the inseparable human being. Against the first-named, which had already shown itself in the Apostolic age,[15] and which appeared afterward in different forms in the Ascetics, Anchorites, Spiritualists and Puritans, Holy Scripture teaches the right and duty of a becoming enjoyment of life,[16] accompanied by a scrupulous care and preservation of the body.[17] Against the selfish emancipation of the flesh, already condemned by St. Paul,[18] but exalted as the highest wisdom by the Materialism of earlier times, as well as of the present day, the spiritual is everywhere represented here as the highest, on behalf of which the lower must necessarily be denied and sacrificed.[19] The truth, which lies at the root both of Spiritualism and Materialism, is recognised by the Bible, but its one-sided conception and perverted application is combated by the light of a higher truth, and the nature of man is unriddled by pointing him to his highest destination.

Comp. T. J. VAN GRIETHUYZEN, *Diss. de notion. vocab. σῶμα et σάρξ* (1846). Upon the entire physiological portion of Biblical Anthropology, S. HOEKSTRA, in the *Jaarb. v. W. Th.*, vii. As to the Trichotomy, F. C. VAN DEN HAM, in the same periodical, V., p. 3, *sqq.* Further, in addition to the literature in § x., J. T. BECK, *Umriss der Bibl. Seelenlehre*, 2 Aufl. (1862); F. DELITZSCH, *System der Christl. Psychologie*, 2 Aufl. (1862); CH. SECRETAN, *Philosophie de la Liberté* (2nd ed., 1866); J. B. HEARD, *The Tripartite Nature of Man* (2nd ed.).

POINTS FOR INQUIRY.

Extent, reasons for, and importance of the distinction between *σῶμα* and *σαρξ* in the language of the Bible.—Is the trichotomy of man taught by other sacred writers than St. Paul?—Further elucidation of the Biblical representation of heart, understanding, conscience, etc.—Is there then reason to regard the *πνεῦμα* as an integral element of the personality, not only of the Christian, but of every man?—In what sense, in accordance with the teaching of Holy Scripture, must we ascribe freedom to the human will?—What value must generally be attributed to the Biblical presentment of man's being?

---

[14] Rom. vii. 18—24.
[15] Col. ii. 21—23; compare 1 Tim. iv. 8.
[16] Eccles. ix. 9; 1 Tim. iv. 4.
[17] 1 Cor. vi. 14, *sqq.*
[18] 1 Cor. xv. 32.
[19] Matt. x. 39; Gal. v. 24.

SECTION LXVIII.—HIS DESTINATION.

Man is destined to realise the design of his nature, that is, as citizen of a spiritual Kingdom, in conjunction with others, to seek God to glorify Him, and to become continually more conformed to Him. In this his endless destination lies the surest warrant of his personal duration, even after the death of the body. This hope of immortality cannot be proved syllogistically, any more than the existence of God; but, from the Christian Theistic standpoint, it can still less be doubted. It is the natural fruit of belief in the living God, and of the consciousness of a spiritual relation to Him, over which death has no power.

1. It has been already seen, from the consideration of the nature of man, that his proper destination lies in the moral-religious domain. Holy Scripture,[1] as well as our own self-consciousness, gives testimony to this destination. Man is then first really man, when he has become a man of God. We must not, however, here overlook the fact that this destiny,[2] though in the highest degree personal, is not separated from, but is first attained in communion with, our fellow-men. A religious, but also a social being, man is designed and intended for the Kingdom of God, which on this account must be the proper object of his endeavours.[3] The question is only, whether this destiny can be realised even on this side of the grave, and if not, whether there is reason to expect that it will be attained in another and higher life. In other words, it is the question as to the *immortality* of man.

2. The *idea* of immortality, with which we are here concerned, from the nature of the case cannot easily be determined. We do not use this word in the pantheistic sense of a return to and a resolution into God, by which the entire personality is destroyed; but we think in connection with it of the self-conscious continuance of the individual after the death of the body. Every other use of the word, in the sense maintained by Spinoza and Hegel, is a lamentable play upon words. Immortality is not merely the continuance of life, but also of the sense of life.

3. The *belief* in immortality in this sense, as a continuance of life, is almost as old as humanity, and not less universal than belief in God; so old and universal, that some have even spoken here of an instinctive feeling (Fichte), while others again (J. Müller) have lately appealed to an original revelation, in order to explain it. Amidst the most uncivilised

---

[1] Amos v. 6; Matt. v. 48; John xvii. 3. [2] 1 Tim. vi. 11.
[3] Luke xii. 33; compare Matt. xiii. 44—46.

tribes we meet with traces of it; and philosophy, too, has before the time of Christ, specially by Plato in his Phædo, most emphatically pleaded for it. With Israel the hope of immortality forms no part of the Mosaic revelation of God: it is not the contrast between the present and the future life, but that between the people of the Lord and the Gentiles: it is not the individual but the national life which there is everywhere made most prominent. And yet expressions such as "was gathered unto his people,"[4] and customs such as the forbidding of exorcism of the dead, sufficiently testify that this life was by no means regarded by every one as the end of existence, and thus the hope of the most exalted saints was at least raised higher than the gates of death.[5] In a special degree just before and pre-eminently after the Babylonian exile did this hope, though often hidden under very sensuous forms,[6] become the common property of the nation, being only disputed by the Sadducees.[7] Everywhere, where Christianity penetrated, the belief in immortality became at once more universal, more firm, and more clear, than it had ever before been.[8] In opposition to the gloomy idea (specially to be observed in Buddhism), "Death is better than Life," was here the fixed certainty, that life is revealed and secured; and the obligation which even in this respect the world owes to the Gospel of the Cross, is one which cannot be overrated. "Just as Christianity first made man and the human race worthy of and suited to true spiritual immortality; so has it first proclaimed the right belief in it, and this it could and must do, since thereby man first gained the power of living in this eternal world of the spirit, and becoming happy through it. The promise and the fulfilment here coincide" (Fichte).

4. The *proof* of this hope cannot, however, be drawn out in a strictly scientific form. We are not here in the domain of exact science, but in that of pious faith, and we cannot be surprised that this faith has in every age been as strongly disputed as defended. The history of philosophy proves that no one has ever yet succeeded in producing a proof which has rendered all contradiction absolutely impossible; and also, that where this last gave way for a moment, it again reappeared with fresh force.[9] Nor is this surprising; *nature* may furnish us with her symbols of revival after death (spring after winter, etc.); she may arouse a presentiment of new life, and confirm the hopes already aroused; but she cannot give any real certainty. We are here concerned with the continued life of an identical personality, and the shooting forth of ever new leaves on the same tree cannot possibly prove this.—Of the *soul* we know too little to find, by an appeal to its constitution, sufficient ground for our demonstration; we cannot even represent to ourselves this soul, or its independent continuance separated from the bodily life; and the uncertain can hardly be proved by the unknown.—If we appeal to the *disharmony* between virtue

[4] Gen. xlix. 33.
[5] Job. xix 25; Ps. xvi. 10, 11; xvii. 15, etc.
[6] Luke xiv. 15.
[7] Acts xxiii. 6—8.
[8] 2 Tim. i. 10.
[9] Compare the account of Cicero's experience with respect to the Phædo of Plato, *Tusc. Quæstt.* i. 11.

and happiness, we involuntarily confuse this last with prosperity, and overlook the fact that the truly pious man has an internal peace, which counterbalances, for himself at least, all the luxury of the sinner.—If we speak of the beneficent *force* of this hope, this, even where it is fully recognised, does not yet prove its certainty. The immortality of the hope might be full well explained, even where the hope of immortality has perished.

5. The *foundation* of this hope can only be shown where it is most closely united with a living belief in a personal God. When separated from this, it falters, or assumes an irreligious egoistical character. Man would at last cease to seek after God, if he were only able to save himself. But in opposition to such a hope of eternity, utterly untrue and immoral, there is a pious belief in immortality, which is then most powerful where man is assured of God, and of His personal revelation of salvation. We cannot therefore be surprised that, from the standpoint of Naturalism, the hope of which we are treating is either disputed as something uncertain, or put aside as a matter of indifference. It is only in consequence of a happy inconsistency which does more credit to the heart than to the head of its supporters, that a portion of the "modern" theologians still cling to it. It first gains its highest justification from the Christian Theistic standpoint, as indeed might well be expected beforehand.

6. The *possibility* of an eternal destination is grounded in the nature and essence of the human spirit, as distinguished from its material body. The materialistic theory, that what we call spirit is merely a function of the bodily organism, is not proven, but is rather encumbered with insuperable difficulties. From none of the chemical elements of the body can anything be discovered which in the least degree resembles the life of the soul. The spirit is indeed in many respects dependent on the body, and *vice versâ;* but even that dependence testifies of original difference, just as this difference tells of mutual independence. The spirit is a simple, not a compound being; but that only which is compounded can resolve itself or be dissolved. However much of obscurity there may be here, even when we do not lose sight of the distinction between soul and spirit, this is clear, that there is nothing in what we know of the spirit-life of mankind which forbids, and much which compels, us to think of an eternal destination.

7. This belief also becomes in the highest degree *probable* on moral-religious grounds. The recognition of God's *supremacy* excludes the representation that man might by a voluntary deed entirely annihilate himself, and thus after the greatest misdeeds withdraw himself from the hands of the supreme Judge.—God's *justice* demands that the balance between virtue and happiness should not only be preserved and restored in secret, but should be revealed and maintained in the sight of all; this certainly is not done, or is only imperfectly effected, on this side of the grave. However much it may be the judgment of the world, the history of the world cannot be the final judgment.—The *holiness* of God requires that we should choose the good unconditionally, even before life itself; this requirement would be unreasonable, and self-denial would be alike a

crime and a folly, if it led to complete self-annihilation.[10]—The *wisdom* of God would not have provided man with a pre-eminent moral disposition, if the term of his existence had been limited to this life. It is the most highly developed minds which find themselves here least satisfied; and who, at their highest attainment, would desire to be able to begin, not only once again, but even in an infinitely better way. Life is an indispensable condition for the attainment of the very highest, the moral ideal, and death is only beneficial, in so far as it is a change. Can then God's most excellent creature be condemned to the fate of a Prometheus or a Tantalus? No proper teleological view of life can limit itself to this side of the grave.—The *goodness* of God, finally, would not have implanted so deeply in our hearts this desire for continuance, if that desire must continue unsatisfied for ever. The fear of death makes man much more unhappy than the beast, if there be no immortality. The desire for life, even in cases where we cannot any longer speak of a physical enjoyment of life, proves that death in the absolute sense of the word must be called something contrary to nature. The satiety of life, which is observable in some people, does not prove the contrary, since it is just the opposite of real satisfaction. Men are satiated with this form of life, because they have not found *life* in it; they are satiated with the *esse*, not with the *vivere*, which is the highest aspiration of the soul. Here, if anywhere, the aspiration proves the reality of the object of desire. What a striking revelation of the infinite is already given in the longing feeling of "Heimweh" for a better life! If now in addition to all this we add the proof *è contrario*, in other words, if we ask what men must accept when they reject this view, and what is lost where this hope is buried, men will certainly think long before they place an expectation like this on the list of vain follies, and will confess that the "non omnis moriar" of Christian faith has no slight basis for its immovable expectation.

8. Still this only thus becomes infallibly *certain* when the believer is conscious of his life in personal communion with God. Hence belief in immortality is always shaken at a time, and in a community, which has lost the profound perception of a living and holy God; whilst, on the contrary, Christian belief has assured itself that "death cannot separate it from the love of God."[11] We see already in the Scriptures of the Old Testament the one most closely joined to the other,[12] and Jesus Himself, in His well-known discourse with the Sadducees[13] has specially placed this proof in the foreground, when He calls God not the God of the dead, but the God of the living. Where God once enters into personal communion of life with man, there He makes him also a partaker of His own life. A personal being, who is the object of God's love, cannot be designed for annihilation. That is the guidepost, as even Lessing, among others, has allowed, which the observant eye can discover in the words, "the God of Abraham, of Isaac, and of Jacob." Hence, too, we do not meet with

---

[10] See Matt. x. 39; compare Cic., *Tusc. Quæstt.* i. 15.
[11] Rom. viii. 38, 39.
[12] Gen. xlix. 18; Ps. lxxiii. 25, 26.
[13] Matt. xxii. 23—32.

the slightest trace of doubt upon this point in Him, who always lived in communion with the Father.[14] And they who believe in Him are by Him *assured*, not only of God, but of their own eternal life. All that God has done in Christ to bring about a personal relation between Himself and the sinner, by the way of revelation and reconciliation, seems a mere folly, if man is not designed for an infinite life in the fullest sense of the word. Even the way in which God upholds, preserves, and perfects that *relation*, by all the leadings of His grace, becomes both arbitrary and aimless, if "in this life only we have hope in Christ." If it be said that a certainty founded on such grounds is after all subjective; we know not what else it could be or need be, as long as it may, notwithstanding, become the property of all. If further it be alleged in opposition, that in this view immortality is nothing but a sentiment, which is only realised where one begins personally to live in God; this is perfectly true as regards the happiness of the future,[15] but we must then remember, that the creation of man in the image of God,[16] when duly established, is at the same time a warrant for his personal eternity, so long as the image is not destroyed.

9. The *importance* of a clear and well-founded belief in an eternal destination can scarcely be overrated. It elevates, comforts, and sanctifies man with a peculiar power, whilst the resistance of it ordinarily brings about the most unfortunate results for religion and morality, as well as for the cause of true humanity. Happily for us, that the words of Kant seem applicable to much of the polemics of the Materialism of these days: "The drum attracts attention because it is—empty."

Comp. D. WYTTENBACH, *De doctrinâ vet. Philosophorum de immortal. animi*, Teyler's Godg., Gen. iv.; C. J. VAN ASSEN, *Over Leven, Geluk, en Dood, naar de begrippen der Ouden* (1850); J. MEYER, *De vi, quam habuit institutum Mosaicum in Hebræorum de rebus p. m. fut. opiniones* (1835); J. L. C. SCHROEDER V. D. KOLK, *Het verschil tusschen doode natuurkrachten, levenskrachten, en ziel* (1835); J. MÜLLER, *Unsterblichkeitsglaube und Auferstehungshoffnung* (1855); M. S. POLAK, *Die Unsterblichkeitsfrage* (1857); E. NAVILLE, *La vie éternelle* (1861); BAGENAULT DE PUCHESSE, *L'immortalité, la mort, et la vie* (1864); C. R. PFAFF, *Ideen eines Arztés über die Unsterbl. der menschl. Seele* (1864); H. RITTER, *Unsterblichkeit* (1866); J. H. FITCHE, *Die Seelenfortdauer und die Weltstellung des Menschen* (1867); S. HOEKSTRA, Bz., *De hoop der onsterflijkheid* (1867). Also the two important articles of ULRICI and OEHLER, in Herzog's *Real. Enc.*, xxv., and the literature there referred to. For the entire ancient history of the question, see specially MENZEL, *Die Vorchristl. Unsterblichkeitslehre*, 2 vol. (1870).

POINTS FOR INQUIRY.

Can the destiny of man be proved with sufficient accuracy, even without the light of Christian faith in Revelation?—Does the question as to immortality belong to the religious, or more to the philosophico-anthropological domain?—Further elucidation and determination of the belief in immortality among the Heathen, Jews, and Christians.—The views of the ancient Church compared with the utterances of ancient philosophy.—Cannot man be directly certain of his immortality?—Is not the desire for immortality in a great degree pride and egoism?—Further exposition of the chief grounds, accompanied with a reply to the chief objections.—The cause of the increasing doubt upon this point in our time, and the best method of combating this doubt in ourselves and others.

---

[14] Matt. x. 28; Luke xxiii. 46. [15] Compare Luke xx. 35a. [16] § lxix.

SECTION LXIX.—THE IMAGE OF GOD.

The peculiar excellence of man, as a rational and moral being, is expressed with the most striking sententiousness in the Biblical expression, used only of him, that he is made in the image and likeness of God. There is as little ground for supposing that this image did not originally belong to man's peculiar nature and essence, as for asserting that it was once for all completely destroyed and annihilated in him through sin. In contrast with these one-sided views, the properly understood Biblical representation, maintained in principle by the Reformation, is to be preferred to every other, on account of its sublimity, truth, and force.

1. The consideration of man's origin, nature, and destination has already prepared us for that of man as bearing the image of God. "God made m n in His image, after His likeness,"[1] says the sacred record with remarkable emphasis. "The narrative is here unusually strong in its joyful exultation, as if the thought could not be expressed with sufficient vivacity" (Ewald). What then is the import of the *word*, and what idea must we form for ourself of the *thing* itself? The question is of preponderating import, not merely for Anthropology, but also for Christology and Soteriology, and in the course of centuries has been answered in the most diverse ways. It is unnecessary to give here all the different replies, but not superfluous to examine more closely at least some of the most important.

2. Where God says, "Let us make man in our *image*, after our *likeness*,"[2] it is at once plain that by these words a special privilege is implied, which man, as such, shares with no other creature on earth. Equally so that the likeness here meant to God, who is a spirit, cannot be found exclusively, or even principally, in anything corporeal. Finally, that the second word merely serves to explain the first, which is evident from other places in Holy Scripture, where the subject is spoken of. Though some of the Greek Fathers have distinguished between *image* and *likeness* in this way, that the first denotes the nature of man itself, and the second points out the gifts and powers bestowed upon him; this distinction cannot be maintained, and has probably only arisen from the *καὶ*, which in the Greek translation has been arbitrarily inserted between the two nouns. Both words plainly convey the same meaning, though some have desired to distinguish them in this way, that by the first is declared the more abstract properties, while the second denotes the more concrete properties which flow from it. And according to that striking image God created man *as such*,

[1] Gen. i. 26, 27.

[2] בְּצַלְמֵנוּ כִּדְמוּתֵנוּ,

i.e., not merely *the first man*, but the whole race, which began in and with this first individual, and of which all the members are in the New Testament[3] said to be made after the likeness of God.

3. There is no foundation for the opinion of the Socinians, which was afterwards followed by some Remonstrants and Rationalists, that the image of God consisted in that sovereignty over the whole creation, which is immediately afterwards announced.[4] Then this latter verse would only be a weak repetition of verse 26. This is already in itself improbable, especially since the two ideas are not brought in any other place in the Bible into direct connection. That man has rule over all the works of God's hands, may be the consequence, or rather perhaps the revelation, of the fact that he bears the image of his Maker; that image itself must undoubtedly be looked for in something different and higher.

4. There is, however, just as little reason to understand the sententious expression with the Church Dogmatics exclusively of the original righteousness and holiness in which the first man was created, and which he lost through the fall. This expression seemingly finds sufficient support in the Pauline statements,[5] where knowledge and holiness are declared to be elements of God's image, which the new man must exhibit. The conclusion seemed self-evident, that the original image, which Adam bore, was to be seen in these two features. This, however, is incorrect, since nowhere in the Gospel is the Salvation in the second Adam represented as a simple reconstruction of that which was lost through and in the first. Still less does it appear that St. Paul, in the passages quoted above, intends to give an explanation of the expression in Moses. Evidently the Adam of Church Dogmatics is represented much more in the light of the New Testament than in that of the Old. An innate knowledge and righteousness such as there assumed, are at once in themselves scarcely conceivable, and render, in proportion as they are more developed, the origin of sin ever less intelligible. But besides, Holy Scripture nowhere teaches that the first man alone was made after God's image, and that this image was at once lost by him and his descendants; indeed, it rather teaches the contrary.[6] The ideal of renewal is in no way offered to us in the first Adam, while it is definitely seen in the Second,[7] who Himself exhibits in undimmed splendour the image of the Father, into which we are to be transformed.[8] When we take all this into consideration, it cannot be denied that upon this point the Church Confession needs some revision, in order to be the exact expression of the contents of the sacred revelation. The distinction, however, made by some theologians between the image of God in the narrower and wider sense of the words seems rather arbitrary and the result of misunderstanding.

5. The difficulty, which rises here when the image of God is without sufficient ground brought in too exclusive connection with the first man, and his condition before the fall, will disappear when we aim at a more general meaning for this expression, and discover (with Calvin) the excel-

[3] James iii. 9.
[4] Gen. i. 28.
[5] Eph. iv. 23, 24; Col. iii. 9, 10.
[6] See Gen. v. 1, 3a; ix. 6; James iii. 9; 1 Cor. xi. 7.
[7] Comp. 1 Cor. xv. 49; 2 Cor. iii. 18.
[8] Comp. Rom. viii. 29; Col. i. 15.

lency of human nature in its entirety to be thus denoted. "Imago Dei est integra naturæ humanæ præstantia" (Calv. *Inst.* i. 15, 4). Man bears the likeness of God, because he, as distinguished from all other dwellers on the earth, is a rational and moral personality, directly allied to God, and formed for fellowship with Him.[9] His likeness to God consists thus in the possession of self-consciousness and freedom, and fixes itself in the spiritual domain, while it reflects itself again in the material world, as well in his corporeity as in the sovereignty (under God) granted to him over all creation. This was so in all its force in the first man, especially before his fall, but it continues to be so with all men; since sin, though it has changed our present condition, has not altered our original nature. This truth lies at the foundation of the churchly, as well as of the Socinian conception, though neither, without some further exposition, can avail as the pure expression of the full truth. We must also admit that the fundamental character of the image of God is in our conception entirely moral. Hence the spiritual renewal after that image must necessarily be revealed in knowledge and holiness; but that which from the nature of the case in the first man could only be present in principle,[10] is developed in a much higher degree by the redeemed through his fellowship with Christ.

6. If this explication be the true one, we have no ground for complaining with some of the fathers (Gregory Nazianzen, Theodoret, etc.), that we cannot now define in what the image of God originally consisted; still less have we reason, with the Audiani, as Irenæus in earlier times, to conceive of something purely corporeal, or, with the Encratites and Severiani, to limit this privilege only to man, to the exclusion of woman. Least of all, however, should we, with the Romish Church, assume that the image of God in the first man was something merely additional (*accedens*), bestowed upon him in consequence of a supernatural communication; but not belonging to the essence of his nature. "Originalis justitiæ donum admirabile addidit, ac deinde cæteris animantibus præesse voluit" (*Catech. Rom.* i. 2, 19). Man created "in puris naturalibus," must then by this extraordinary gift have primordially known and glorified his Maker; but he has lost it through sin, and thus falls short of God's glory. The Reformers most justly assert, in opposition to this mechanical view, that "justitia originalis" was an original and actual element of our nature, as it came forth from the hand of the Creator. This was Luther's Commentary on Gen. iii., "Justitiam originalem non fuisse quoddam donum, quod ad extra accederet, sed fuisse vere naturalem, ita ut natura Adæ esset diligere Deum, credere Deo, cognoscere Deum." To a superficial observer the whole of this question may seem of subordinate importance; but when more closely examined, it is of preponderating theological and anthropological value. For it is, in other words the question as to the existence and right of a natural knowledge of God;[11] or even if this be put aside, it is at once apparent that, from the standpoint of the Romish Church, the fall only becomes more enigmatical, and in no case can be regarded as a properly so-called declension of human nature itself. Besides, the whole conception of such a "donum superadditum" is foreign to Holy Scrip-

[9] Compare Luke iii. 38; Acts xvii. 28. [10] Section lxx. [11] Compare § iii. 9.

ture, and originates in the unbiblical conception that the first man alone bore the image of God, and—lost it through sin.

7. The image of God is "man's title of royalty" "des Menschen könig's diploma." The enigma of man's origin, nature, and destiny,[12] is only then in a certain degree explicable, when this statement is accepted without any limitation, on scriptural grounds. In the first man mankind is created after the image of God; and while we must regard this image as natural and capable of propagation, *naturalis et propagabilis*, (cf. Gen. v. 3,) we must deny that it is, as something accidental, even in the least degree capable of being lost, *accidentalis et amissibilis*. It was not merely an ideal, after which man was to strive, but actually a treasure which he was to keep, and hand over to posterity unimpaired. "The image of God in man cannot be destroyed. Even in hell it can burn, but cannot be consumed: it may be tormented, but cannot be extirpated" (Bernard of Clairvaux). Certainly, for it forms an original element of our human nature; and if we were wholly despoiled of it, we should then be as little men, as the bird when deprived of the means of flying can bear the name of bird. It is therefore perfectly accurate, when we assert that the splendour of God's image is dimmed and injured by sin, but inaccurate, when we deny that the sinner too is formed after the image of God. Very justly does Calvin say (i. 15, 4) "Etsi demus non prorsus exinanitam ac deletam in eo fuisse Dei imaginem, sic tamen corrupta fuit, ut quidquid superest, horrenda est deformitas." In a like spirit does the Netherlands Confession speak of "slender vestiges" (petites traces) which are sufficient to take away from man all innocence.

8. The sacred representation of man's original relationship to God excels in sublimity, truth, and force. Contrast it once again with that given by Naturalism, and we shall see on what side man is most exalted and most deeply abased. Ancient philosophers have already felt and in some degree expressed this truth;[13] but Revelation has been the first to give to that feeling its just expression and its highest meaning. It teaches us to think humbly of ourselves, but loftily of mankind, and tunes the heart to the note which is so grandly touched in the eighth Psalm.

Comp. S. K. THODEN VAN VELZEN, *De hominis cum Deo similitudine*, i., ii. (1835); J. MÜLLER, *Die Christl. Lehre v. d. Sunde*, 2nd ed. (1844), ii., pp. 472—480; SCHOEBERLEIN's Article in Herzog, *R. E.*, iii.; PH. F. KEERL, *Der Mensch das Ebenbild Gottes*, i., ii. (1861, 1866); J. H. GUNNING, Jr., *Blikken*, iii., p. 1, *sqq.*; ENGELHARDT, *Die Gottesbildlichkeit des Menschen*, in the *Jahrb. für deutsche Theol.* (1870), i.

POINTS FOR INQUIRY.

What is the reason that such different views concerning the image of God in man have at all times prevailed?—Difficulty and importance of the question.—Further elucidation of the passages of Scripture which touch upon it.—Criticism of the doctrine of the Church. —History of the origin of the Roman view, and limitation of its worth.—Is there sufficient ground for a dogmatic distinction between the image of God in the natural sense, which remained, and in the moral sense, which was lost?—The image of God in man, and the Logos.

---

[12] Sections lxvi.—lxviii.

[13] Compare the words of Aratus, Acts xvii. 28, and the θεοείκελος, θεοειδής, etc., in Homer.

SECTION LXX.—THE ORIGINAL CONDITION.

Of man, formed after the image of God, nought else could be expected but that he, so long as he displayed that image in untarnished splendour, should know God, and obey Him, and in His communion enjoy the purest happiness, without being subject to death. The little information which Holy Scripture gives us concerning the first man, fully confirms this expectation, and presents him to us in a condition which contained both the possibility of a normal, as well as the necessity for a continued, development. Notwithstanding all its mysteriousness, this Biblical representation of a so-called state of uprightness has a firm ground and a high import; which makes it not only desirable, but also possible, to sustain it continually against opposition, from whatever side it may arise.

1. From man in general we come now to the first man, and thus to the question, as natural as it is important, What conclusion must we form as to his original condition? Even if we had here no further light than that of the knowledge that the personal living God formed man after His own image, the answer could, at least in general, not be doubtful. From such a God, and such a man, it would be impossible to look for aught else, but that the latter would have begun his existence, not in a condition of complete helplessness, but of sufficient maturity, not of sin, but of sinlessness, not of misery, but of happiness, such as was suited to his capacity. It must have been a state of original sinlessness and purity; for God, who by man's conscience forbids him to commit sin, could not by any possibility begin by Himself originating evil.[1]

2. To such a presentment as this, in itself quite acceptable, the Bible leads us, rendering at the same time sufficiently clear what it declares concerning the so-called state of uprightness. It would be an error if, misled by the sound of the words, we referred here to what is said in Eccles. vii. 29. But we may safely make use of everything which Scripture teaches us concerning the spotless holiness of God, when combined with the certain testimony that everything which He had created, and specially man, was in His eyes "very good." As to the trustworthiness of the Mosaic narrative in this respect, we may refer to what has been already said in § lviii. Here we only observe that nothing can be called for God (objectively) "very good," save that which is in harmony with itself, and with the destiny which God has willed for it. Wherein this "very good" as regards the first man consisted, may be difficult to determine, on account of the brevity and obscurity of the sacred narratives; on the other hand, these awaken a confidence which we should scarcely be willing to grant to more lengthy and definite records of such early date.

---

[1] Heb. i. 13; James i. 13.

3. Thus much is at once evident; the first man must have possessed *knowledge* of God, in consequence of his being allied to God, and of God's revealing Himself in him and to him. This knowledge may have been incomplete, of course; it was without doubt pure, since it was derived from the fountain-head itself, and the eye of the spirit was not yet dimmed by sin. He not only hears the voice of his Creator, but understands it also, and in consequence he knows his duty.[2] So there is thus no ground for supposing in him a condition of childish simplicity, "like sheep in a meadow," as Strauss says; and it certainly sounds strange when men will deduce from the Mosaic narrative, which is contradicted by them on all other points, that these first men were like wild beasts, in an animal condition, and without any feeling of shame.[3] There is, however, a holy innocence and simplicity, which holds a much higher place than the development which is obtained by an experimental knowledge of the distinction between good and evil, and this "sancta simplicitas" is that of which we must now speak.

4. We may the more safely attribute to the first man such knowledge of God, because he was united to Him by the bond of the purest *love.* If this love is the essential character of God, it must also be the proper vital force, and the guiding principle in him who bears His image. "Quo nisi Deo plenus est, qui plenus est dilectione?" (Augustine). *That* love was the principle of the purest knowledge, for indeed we understand nothing better than that which we love: "ubi caritas est, claritas est" (Hugo de S. Victor). But at the same time it was the regulating power of the whole inner and outer life; for again it is here that we live as we love. Where love reigns, is the "ordo amoris," there is the harmony of the man with himself, and with Him whom he loves. Of course, in the case to which we refer, there can be no question of a holiness, which is only to be obtained as the result of an inner development; but if no other perfection than this were conceivable, it could not be ascribed even to God Himself. Enough! the absolute moral perfection of the Creator must have been relatively in the creature, and as it attains its culmination in love, man must also through that love have been able to know God's will, and to fulfil it faithfully. From its nature it was at the same time the capacity to discriminate, as it were instinctively, and successively to resist, all that was ungodly, or opposed to God. What a love to God would that be, which, while in all its first power, did not place man in the position of a "posse non peccare"!

5. It is self-evident that such a condition, from the nature of the case, could not be aught else but the *happiest* possible. It does not fall within the sphere of Dogmatics to discuss the many questions which may be put concerning Paradise. The doubt, which has now and then been expressed, *e.g.*, by John Scotus Erigena, etc., as to such an abode of happiness ever having existed, is quite arbitrary, and only partially explicable from the repugnance which was excited by the too plastic representation of the happiness of Paradise by Augustine and other fathers. The history of civilisation, too, offers proofs that the cradle of our race was in the East, and more definitely in Central Asia, and we cannot possibly conceive

---

[2] Gen. iii. 3. [3] Réville.

of it, but as placed by the highest Love in a most blessed spot. The three sources of our misery—recollection, restlessness, fear, had no need to flow there for the still sinless man; while all the external and internal conditions of happiness existed there undoubtedly in the highest degree.

6. That happiness was enjoyed by the first man, without as yet being subject to *death*. The threat in Genesis ii. 17, that he should surely die if he broke the law—for this is the original sense—would be quite devoid of meaning if death had in any case been the absolutely inevitable destiny of man. As to his body, he was undoubtedly taken out of the dust of the earth,[4] and in that fact was contained the possibility of death, but the absolute necessity thereof was in no way declared. On the contrary, our deepest self-feeling declares that death in the true and the highest sense of the word must be termed something contrary to nature; "rien n'est plus absurde que la mort" (Renan). If natural science teaches us that in the animal world death and destruction had already ruled, long before the first man trod the earth; as a separate link in the chain of beings, he was sufficiently raised above them for the fundamental law of their kingdom not necessarily and without limitation to apply to him. In the fulness of love to God there was also present the possibility (the *potentia*) of being able to continue alive, since love and life are one. Whether this possibility would have been actually (*actu*) realised (in other words, whether the *posse non mori* would rise to a *non posse mori*), this depended on his obedience to the test command. If in Gen. iii. 22, we see the tree of life placed over against the tree of temptation, the supposition seems legitimate that the latter must have been either a symbol of, or a means towards, the prolongation of life by a continuance in obedience, which was on this account denied immediately after the first trangression. We need not therefore assume that the sinless man would have continued to live always upon earth in the body: he might even without death have been brought over into a higher sphere of life.[5] Enough, however, if by continuing steadfast in love he could have escaped that death, which is the penalty of sin, with its sharp string and its terrible consequences. In love to God, and in fellowship with Him, the possibility of an endless life had a psychological and ethical ground.

7. Much, too, was done by God for *augmenting* the happiness of this state. Nothing less was already *à priori* to be expected than that the Creator should also be the Educator of the most highly privileged race, and that this education must begin even in Paradise. The form which it took may remain quite undefined; a too plastic and fantastic description of it only elicits needless contradiction. The fact can by no means be disputed, because the first man, without such a higher training and guidance, could not possibly have attained to the destiny which God designed for him. We may even assume that in the infancy of creation, when sin had not yet made any separation, the communion between heaven and earth was much closer than it has since been. Thus we can by no means reject what the Mosaic record states concerning God's special

---

[4] χοϊκός, 1 Cor. xv. 47; compare Gen. ii. 7.
[5] Compare Gen. v. 24; 2 Kings ii. 11; 2 Cor. v. 4.

care for the first pair, even when we can only understand it partially. His placing of them in Paradise already testifies to this care. Before the still undimmed glance the creation must, as it were, have been transparent, and have revealed God in a much greater degree than it now conceals Him from our eyes. Along with the dressing of the garden,[6] the *keeping* of it against a still unknown, but even then present and threatening hostile power must have elevated the life of the spirit. Reflection was strengthened even by the giving names to the creatures, while the power of speech was exercised and the feeling of solitude aroused, soon after satisfied in so surprising a way. Even God Himself communicates with and speaks to man.[7] Whatever conception we may form of this, God Himself became the Teacher of men (Delitzsch). It is possible that the ordinance of the observance of the Sabbath[8] dates from the first pair; Exod. xx. 8, when compared with Exod. xvi. 23—25, seems at any rate to point to a pre-Mosaic institution. Certainly the trial-command[9] was the most excellent way of leading man one step forward on the road of his destination.

8. The *prohibiting* of man's eating from one tree, or one kind of tree, is entirely misunderstood, when it is supposed that this eating could have been either morally wrong in itself, or destructive to health or life. The former is inconceivable, and in the latter case the physical and moral injury (Schleiermacher) could have been prevented by a seasonably applied medicine. It must be simply regarded as a trial-command, that is, as a demand in a moral sense and in itself indifferent, but one from which man's feeling towards God and goodness would show itself. This trial was necessary, for what is virtue without conflict? It might have been temporary, and have been afterwards succeeded by other trials, of a heavier or lighter character. It was not too heavy; for the command was plain, the privation unimportant, the threat definite; and in addition to all this, love must have been strong enough to preserve man from the power of temptation. Only where such temptation was withstood, could virtue and holiness arise. *Arbor bona, sed obedientia melior.* There is not, however, the slightest ground for conceiving here of a properly so-called *covenant* made by God with all mankind in Adam, in which eternal life, as the reward of the work of obedience, was the promise, and the tree of life was the sign and seal (Coccejus). The exegetical grounds for this view in Hosea vi. 7 are absolutely insufficient, and its dogmatic value has not the slightest importance. Scripture does not teach that God has made a contract with man, but only that He designs to lead him, plainly by a moral road, to greater happiness.

9. In consequence of these different statements, we see in the first man a being, to whom continuous *development* was possible, and even absolutely necessary. He was in principle perfect, but he was as yet standing at the starting-point of his career, and that which was to be acquired by conflict could not originally exist for him in all its completeness. We must here think of a condition of natural and moral health, but one which had not yet gone through a single shock. Potentially Adam was everything which he must primarily have been, but actually he had still to become all of which the germs had been implanted in him. To this end the trial-command was

[6] Gen. ii. 15. [7] Gen. iii. 8. [8] Gen. ii. 3. [9] Gen. ii. 17.

given, by which God designed perhaps both to strengthen and to arm him against the might and craft of darkness. If there is here something of mystery, thus much is at least plain, that we cannot conceive of virtue without freedom, nor of freedom without the possibility of, and the opportunity for, sinning. There can be no talk of any moral development, so long as we have not learned to know the good as well as the evil closely; no continuous enjoyment of the tree of life, without a continuous avoidance of the tree of temptation. Man would then, when he had first overcome temptation, be able to maintain himself upon the high position which was assigned to him as the head of the earthly creation.

10. That continuous development might, however, have been *normal*, without the necessity of the first man falling into sin. We have certainly not to conceive of a purely negative innocence, in which the lust already present was as yet only slumbering, at a certain point of development to lead inevitably to evil. This view makes God indirectly the cause of sin, and does not find the very slightest shadow of proof in the sacred record. The will could without doubt incline to one side, as well as to the other, but it did not therefore any the more stand in the presence of God in a merely neutral relation. Not only was an excellent disposition given, but a beginning full of much promise was made; there was not merely innocence (*innocentia*), but a moral rectitude (*integritas*), which was to become holiness. Thus was Adam "able with his will to agree in everything with the will of God."[10] It is incorrect to assert that the command in itself must have been fatal to this normal development, since it excited the very desire toward that which was forbidden. With us, in whom the evil desire is already slumbering, this may often be the case, and the experience of St. Paul will often repeat itself;[11] it is different in the still uncorrupted nature. A prohibition indeed presupposes that the highest moral perfection has not yet been attained, but it need not become a trap to the foot, which wishes to tread the right path; if this were so, every lawgiver would also be an author of sin. Love to God, originally proper to man as a moral being, as we have already said, was the principle of life, in which was contained the possibility of continuance in that which was good (the *posse non peccare*). "The likeness to God is not imprinted as a cultivated faculty, nor immediately as developed Holiness, Righteousness, and Wisdom, just as this, too, is not effected in the New Birth; but man in the possession of a Divine capacity for life, furnished with God's royal law of Love, and provided with the light of the Spirit, and the desire to recognise truth, possesses the living capacity for, and destination to, holiness and righteousness as the fruit of a clear recognition of truth, and of wisdom" (Beck).

11. But with regard to the question, how this normal development would have proceeded, only conjectures are possible. If we reflect, however, how the image of God, which really was exhibited in man, is originally present in the Logos,[12] then are we naturally led to the thought that in the Son of God was presented the highest ideal of the development of the first Adam, and that it would have been attained by the contemplation—in some way or other—of God's highest revelation in Him. The question on which we

---

[10] Neth. Conf., Art. xiv. [11] Rom. vii. 9—11. [12] Col. i. 15.

have already touched in § lv. 6, whether the Logos would have become flesh, if sin had not already been in the world, would thus, from this point of view, require an affirmative answer. Here, however, there is the less need to discuss it, since this normal development, which we might in this way conceive to be possible, has, alas! never been at all realised.

12. Meanwhile, though much that is mysterious may still remain, the doctrine of an original sinless normal condition of the first man remains much more acceptable than any which has been advanced against it, and on this account deserves to be still maintained against Theosophic exaggeration on the one hand, and Naturalistic negation and weakness on the other. We find traces of the first even in Augustine, when he asserts that Adam's reason before the fall was, as compared to ours, as the bird is to the tortoise; that, with a continued state of rectitude, the propagation of the race would have taken place without the least concupiscence; and that the newly-born child would very speedily, through the special working of Omnipotence, have attained a perfect state: in Albertus Magnus, when he declares that the first man would have felt no pain, though he had been stoned with heavy stones: in J. Scotus Erigena, when he states, that in the human creature, as yet without sin, the male and female element originally existed together undistinguished; and that if he had continued in this state, his descendants would have proceeded from him as the angels from their Creator: and in J. Böhme, when he conjectures that the intestinal canal, and everything connected with it, was the consequence of the fall; while we need not speak of the views of later times, and even of the present day.[13] Whatever value these fictions may possess as plays of imagination, and instances of an unlimited belief in that which some consider the doctrine of the Bible, or the natural consequences of such doctrine, a rational science must with all seriousness protest against eccentricities of this kind, *partly*, because they meet with no support in the words of Scripture, but are even sometimes loudly contradicted in it; *partly*, because they make the first man a man only in appearance, and render the fall from such a height merely more inconceivable; *partly*, in the last place, because such an over-excited fancy only too quickly leads the way to an increased contradiction from the side of a more sober philosophy.

13. It can at any rate hardly be disputed that the Naturalistic denial and undermining of the Scriptural doctrine has but too frequently found in these very variegated representations both a pretext and a support. This was specially the case, in opposition to the bold conjectures of Augustine, with Pelagius in the fifth century, and in contrast to the highly wrought representation of a "justitia concreata" by the Reformers, with the Socinians in the sixteenth century, taken up immediately by some of the Remonstrants, and afterwards by the Deists and Rationalists. With unimportant variation their ideas always came back to this, that the first man, created in a state of childish innocence, was naturally subject to death, and much more in capacity than in reality the bearer of the image of the Creator. Schleiermacher considered it inexpedient to come to any dogmatical definition as to the original condition of mankind, and the older Supranaturalism

[13] Compare the references in Strauss, *Chr. Glaubensl.*, i. 691.

always contented itself with an undefined recognition of man's excellent capacity. We have already seen (§ lxvi.) what the modern Naturalism declares or rather denies, concerning the first men, and no one can be entirely unacquainted with the superciliousness with which the spirit of unbelief, even in its less trained disciples (tirones), looks down upon the view of the orthodox.

14. This latter view, however, if it be suitably retained within Biblical limits, we continue not only to accept as our own, but also to support as the most rational and intrinsically acceptable. The idea of an earlier and better condition is so far from being unreasonable, that, on the contrary, we meet with it in varied forms among the most diverse nations of antiquity. This has been perforce confessed even by the unbeliever, "La chute de l'homme dégénéré est le fondement de la théologie de presque toutes les anciennes nations" (Voltaire). The antiquity, the relative universality, and the similarity of these representations cannot, it seems, be explained in a better mode than as the fruit of an original tradition, whose purest form is found in Holy Scripture. The statement that we meet here with nothing but an ingenious allegory and a philosophic myth, has not yet been duly proved. The Mosaic narratives bear separately the stamp of truth, agree in the main, and are supported by the teaching of the New Testament.[14] Philosophic objections have any real value only when, forsaking the Christian Theistic standpoint, we make the history of mankind begin not from above, but from below; on the other hand, even nobler heathen, such as Plato, have believed in an original purity of the soul before its present restricted state, and have thus in principle granted a representation similar to the Mosaic. If it has its peculiar difficulty, the Naturalistic assertion that all organic beings ultimately proceed from inorganic matter, passes by mountains of difficulties, and deserves, in consequence of the audacity of not a few of its teachers, to be rejected with the words of Scripture in Job xxxviii. 4. If we once grant a place to a special miracle of creation in the formation of man, there is nothing to prevent us from accepting satisfactory evidence that his original condition was in many respects different from that which is now most usual and natural. Only let us avoid the temptation to depict this condition too vividly, instead of reflecting on those words of wisdom, "Oh that we might learn to stop at the right place!" (Stier.) As it is with the doctrine of Eschatology, so it is with that of the creation, even of man; both require great care, since they come finally beyond the reach, not only of our thought, but also of our imagination. And yet, ultimately, a deficient representation is better than none at all, and ours adheres to this as its conclusion: the first man began his existence as a rational and moral being, not yet tainted with evil, and thus was man in the fullest sense of the word, to whose original nature sin does not in any way belong.

15. The result thus obtained is of great value, not merely because it contains the truth, which now on its own account asks for recognition and support, but specially because this latter stands in direct connection with the right knowledge of God, of man, and of man's deliverance by God.

---

[14] Rom. v. 12; 2 Cor. xi. 3; 1 Tim. ii. 14.

We see now for the first time, in its full splendour, the truth of the words of Hab. i. 13; James i. 13. If man had at the beginning been a sinner what would become of God's holiness in the forbidding, of God's wisdom in permitting, of God's justice in punishing sin?—The enigma, too, of man and of mankind is then first solved, when we assume that an original better condition has preceded the present sinful one; while the honour of our race is also concerned that the head of the race should be regarded rather as a dethroned king than as a properly developed animal. Finally, we see the possibility of deliverance when we regard the original constitution of the first man; the necessity, when we recognise our sinful condition as something contrary to nature; and above all its glory, when we observe that by it the original dignity of our race is not only restored, but enhanced. Thus the dogma we have been discussing is an indispensable corner-stone of the buildings of Theology and Theodicée; and with the great Reformer we declare, "Non possumus clarius perspicere, quid habeamus in Christo, quam ubi nobis demonstratum fuerit, quid perdiderimus in Adamo" (Calv. ad. Rom. v. 12).

Compare as to man's original state, in addition to the literature named in § lxix., SARTORIUS, *Die Lehre von der heiligen Liebe* (1840), i., p. 32, *sqq.*; H. LÜKEN, *Die Traditionen des Menschengeschlechtes* (1856), p. 49, *sqq.*; the article *Adam und seine Söhne* in Herzog's *R. E.* i.; and the elaborate article on Paradise in the same work, vol. xx.

POINTS FOR INQUIRY.

Whence springs the difficulty of accurately defining the original condition of man?—Do the different Bible accounts agree, and are they sufficiently trustworthy?—What does the trial command, Gen. ii. 16, 17, pre-suppose, import, and aim at?—What is the meaning of Eccles. vii. 29?—How far can we predicate an education properly so called of the first men by God?—History and criticism of the exaggeration and misconception of that doctrine.—Comparison of the sacred and profane representations of the golden age before mankind.—How can we account for the determined opposition to this doctrine?

SECTION LXXI.—THE POSSIBILITY OF FALLING.

The possibility that the first man, placed in such a lofty state, could, notwithstanding, fall, had its ground, anthropologically, in the liberty of choice given to him by the possession of a sensuous nature, and, theologically, in the fact that God wishes for moral goodness only by means of voluntary obedience. That this possibility must necessarily have been realised is, however, a proposition which, while finding no justification, is rejected because it conflicts with the religious and moral consciousness. Sin is as little called into being by a Divine causality, as it is originally teleologically willed and ordained by God.

1. If the first man stood so relatively high, how comes it to pass that he did not continue in that happy state? The answer to this question will cause us to speak of Christian Hamartology; but, before we consider this sad reality more closely, rational faith feels already the necessity of searching into the reason for the possibility of so great a fall. The investigation of the physical and metaphysical possibility of the entrance of sin forms a natural passage to the succeeding section.

2. Anthropologically the possibility of falling is grounded on the liberty of choice,[1] which God has given to man, by means of which all moral compulsion is entirely excluded. That, however, this freedom of choice, presupposed even in the trial-command, is yet not moral freedom in the highest sense of the word, is self-evident; the latter is then first reached, when the former is used in giving of its own accord the preference to moral goodness. With the first man, however, it had not yet come to this; in opposition to the power of not sinning (the *posse non peccare*) stood the possibility of breaking the law, and that possibility was by no means imaginary. Man certainly was not only a spiritual, but also a sensuous being, and his sensuous nature, though in no way the cause of sin, nevertheless gave an opportunity for temptation. There was a natural difference between flesh and spirit, intended without doubt to be resolved into the most beautiful agreement; but which also contained the possibility of the contrary, though it must not in any case be conceived of as the beginning or germ of sin. It was in consequence of this that the will was, as Calvin says, "flexibilis in utramque partem;" the possibility, but not the absolute necessity, of continuance in good was indeed the privilege of man. He did not yet stand at the end, but, like Hercules once at the cross roads, only at the *beginning* of his course, the end must be willed and attained by *himself*. Not that he thus stood in a state of unconscious enmity against his Maker; on the contrary, the love of God was in him and dwelt with him, but it was his duty voluntarily to follow its impulse, if the possibility of the opposite course was not to be realised in him. His first step would thus at the same time be the first revelation of his freedom of choice, hitherto undetermined. We speak here of course only of a *mere* possibility, which by no means of necessity bears in itself the germ of reality. Without such a possibility man would not have been the bearer of God's image, but merely an automaton. A personality, which does not possess in itself the foundation of life, may, by means of the freedom granted to it, turn away from God, just because it is a creature and not a Creator. This possibility was thus inevitable and actual, but at the same time intended to be merely temporary, and to lead to that higher state in which the *posse non peccare* would rise into the *non posse peccare*.

3. From a *theological* point of view, the possibility of fall can, it must be confessed, be comprehended only to a certain degree, but this at least can be demonstrated, and it will be quite sufficient for our purpose, that it is as little opposed by God's omnipotence and prescience, as by His holiness, wisdom, and love. The *omnipotence* of God, as we have already said, must not be conceived as an irresistible, blind natural force, but as the almightiness of

[1] Section lxvii. 4.

a holy will, restricted by nothing but by the perfection of its own being. When He thus grants to a creature which exists without, but by Him, a freedom which he can at any moment limit for a sufficient reason, He does not then in any degree give up His own omnipotence. If the Almighty gives a command to reasonable and moral beings, He creates at the same time the possibility, that it may not be obeyed, without thereby ceasing to be omnipotent. The freedom of the creature is a plant whose branches the Creator trains, but whose roots He does not tear up. Or is the possibility of sin in conflict with God's *prescience?*[2] But not everything which God has foreseen, is on that account willed by God; man does not sin *because* God has thus determined, but as God has foreseen. Man need just as little sin because God foresaw it, as the child need stumble because the mother warns it.—But for this very reason the recognition of the possibility of sin does not even in the least degree affect the spotless *holiness* of God. Indeed, the leave to sin was in no way a permission, but simply a *laisser faire*, or leaving it to itself; no moral permission, but a mere abstaining from active interference. God has not willed that there should be sin, but only that man should be really free, even to sin. If His holiness did not forbid Him to create such free agents, the natural consequences of their deeds could only be diverted by a constant interposition of miracles, such as were least of all to be expected from the highest *wisdom* and *love.* Or could this unceasingly do away with what it had itself willed and ordained? Could man by any other road than that of trial have risen to a higher perfection? Would obedience have possessed the slightest value without liberty? and does not grace now attain a higher lustre since it leads our race through the depth of sin to the height of deliverance? It is evident that the possibility of sin has both an anthropological and a theological basis, without thereby in the very least failing to render justice either to the original integrity of man, or to the absolute perfection of God.

4. This, however, must never be overlooked; it is *only* the possibility of sin, and not its reality, which must be regarded as a fruit of God's ordinance. If He permitted sin, it was not because He *could* not prevent it, since man *must* necessarily sin, but because He willed not to prevent it. What He, however, has originally willed, and aimed at, was a world not with, but without sin. Sin is not an inevitable element of the perfected world, but is for that very reason opposed by God, in order that the world should become perfect. Sin is originally found, not in the Kingdom of God, but in that of darkness; not in the world itself, but in God's government of the world it has its proper and permitted place. This follows necessarily from the Christian conception of God,[3] and reason itself bears witness to the truth, "peccati ultor non potest esse peccati auctor." Our conscience says the same when it humbly recognises the imputability of sin, and for that very reason welcomes the Gospel of non-imputation[4] as a message of glad tidings. Certainly, though we must declare that sin is absolutely inexplicable, if it has not in God its ultimate reason, even this proposition would claim the preference above the blasphemy against God

[2] Compare § lxii. 6. [3] James i. 13; Rom. iii. 8. [4] 2 Cor. v. 19.

which says "that God has done evil that good might come." When first it is granted unconditionally, "the possibility of sin only from God, but not its reality," is His honour properly maintained, and the sinner alike humbled, comforted, and sanctified.[5]

Comp. C. I. NITZSCH, *a. a. O.*, § 102; K. H. SACK, *Psychol. Moralische Bemerkungen in Bezug auf Geschichte und Lehre vom Sündenfall* in *Studien und Kritiken* (1869), § ii., 336, *sqq.*; J. MÜLLER, *a. a. O.*, ii., 7—300.

POINTS FOR INQUIRY.

Is not the question as to the necessity of sin superfluous? and if not, does it admit of an answer?—Is there conceded in any case with freedom itself the possibility of evil?—Elucidation and defence of the idea of *permissio.*—Are there any passages of Scripture where God is represented as the cause of sin? (Prov. xvi. 4; Isa. xlv. 7; Rom. ix. 22; 1 Pet. ii. 8, etc.)—How far is it possible, from the standpoint of the Church, to escape entirely the conclusion that God is *auctor peccati?*—Importance and use of the result obtained.

---

[5] Compare Rom. iii. 4—19.

www.ingramcontent.com/pod-product-compliance
Lightning Source LLC
LaVergne TN
LVHW020059110826
845151LV00001B/21

9781425544959